Thaddeus Mason Harris, William Biglow

The Massachusetts magazine

Monthly museum of knowledge and rational entertainment

Thaddeus Mason Harris, William Biglow

The Massachusetts magazine
Monthly museum of knowledge and rational entertainment

ISBN/EAN: 9783337257996

Printed in Europe, USA, Canada, Australia, Japan

Cover: Foto ©Andreas Hilbeck / pixelio.de

More available books at **www.hansebooks.com**

THE

██████ETTS M█████NE:

OR,

██████HLY MUS████M

OF

KNOWLEDGE and RATIONAL ENTERTAINMENT.

No. VII.]   FOR   JULY,   1794.   [Vol. VI.

CONTAINING,

WITH TWO HANDSOME ENGRAVINGS.

PRINTED AT *BOSTON*, FOR THE PROPRIETORS,
By EZRA W. WELD AND WILLIAM GREENOUGH,
No. 49, STATE STREET.
Sold at JOHN WEST's Bookftore, No. 75, *Cornhill*, BOSTON ; and by the feveral
GENTLEMEN who receive Subfcriptions for this WORK.
MDCCXCIV.

ACKNOWLEDGMENTS to CORRESPONDENTS.

We tender our thanks to our Harvard friends for their communications, particularly the author of the elegant Oration. Similar favours are requefted from Yale and Dartmouth Univerfities.

The Memorialift is refpectfully thanked for his offer. We gratefully accept it.

Anti-Neceffarian.—We meddle not with polemic divinity.

View of Parnaffus. We recommend to the author the waters of Lethe.

Clariffa no Prude—the writer no wit.

The Inveftigator, No. I, is received; a page fhall be referved for it next month.

PRICES of PUBLIC SECURITIES, BANK STOCK, &c.

July.	Six per Cents.	Three per Cents.	Defer'd Stock.	Maffachuf. State Notes.	U.S.B. Shares ab. par.	Maffachuf. Bank Shares.	Union Bank Shares ab. pr.	Final & L. Of. Cert.inter.fr. Jan. 1788.	Reg. Dt. with int.fr. March 4, 1789.	Indents. Int. on Loan Off.	Cer.&Reg.Dt. New Emiffion Money.	O. Emif. Mo.
	s. d.	s. d.	s. d.	s. d.	per ct.	dols.	per ct.	s. d.	s. d.	s. d.	s. d.	s.
1	18 2	10 0	11 0	14 0	121-2	None	4	16 6	15 6	9 0	8 0	40
2	18 4	10 2	11 2	14 0	121-2	at	5	16 6	15 6	9 0	8 0	40
3	18 4	10 2	11 2	14 0	121-2	mkt.	5	16 6	15 6	9 0	8 0	40
4	18 4	10 2	11 2	14 0	121-2		5 1-2	16 6	15 6	9 0	8 0	40
5	18 4	10 2	11 2	14 0	121-2		6	16 6	15 6	9 0	8 0	40
7	18 4	10 2	11 2	14 0	121-2		6	16 6	15 6	9 0	8 0	40
8	18 4	10 2	11 2	14 0	121-2		6	16 6	15 6	9 0	8 0	40
9	18 4	10 2	11 2	14 0	121-2		6	16 6	15 6	9 0	8 0	40
10	18 4	10 2	11 2	14 0	121-2		6	16 6	15 6	9 0	8 0	40
11	18 4	10 2	11 2	14 2	121-2		6	16 6	15 6	9 0	8 0	40
12	18 4	10 2	11 2	14 2	121-2		6	16 6	15 6	9 0	8 0	40
14	18 6	10 4	11 4	14 2	121-2		6	16 6	15 6	9 0	8 0	40
15	18 6	10 4	11 4	14 2	121-2		6	16 6	15 6	9 0	8 0	40
16	18 6	10 4	11 4	14 3	121-2		6	16 6	15 6	9 0	8 0	40
17	18 6	10 4	11 4	14 3	14		6	16 6	15 6	9 0	8 0	40
18	18 6	10 4	11 4	14 3	14		6	16 6	15 6	9 0	8 0	40
19	18 6	10 4	11 4	14 3	14		6	16 6	15 6	9 0	8 0	40
21	18 6	10 4	11 4	14 3	14		6	16 6	15 6	9 0	8 0	40
22	18 6	10 4	11 4	14 3	14		6	16 6	15 6	9 0	8 0	40
23	18 8	10 6	11 6	14 6	16		6	16 6	15 6	9 0	8 0	40
24	18 8	10 6	11 6	14 6	16		6	16 6	15 6	9 0	8 0	40
25	18 9	10 8	11 8	14 6	16		6	16 6	15 6	9 0	8 0	40
26	18 10	10 9	11 9	14 9	17		6	16 6	15 6	9 0	8 0	40
28	18 10	10 9	11 9	14 9	17		6	16 6	15 6	9 0	8 0	40
29	18 10	10 9	11 9	14 9	17		6	16 6	15 6	9 0	8 0	40
30	18 10	10 9	11 9	14 9	17		6	16 6	15 6	9 0	8 0	40
31	18 10	10 9	11 9	14 9	17		6	16 6	15 6	9 0	8 0	40

JOHN MARSTON, Stock Broker.

THE

MASSACHUSETTS MAGAZINE.

FOR *JULY*, 1794.

FOR THE MASSACHUSETTS MAGAZINE.

DESCRIPTION of the PLATE.
SUMMER.

THE Plate is an emblematical representation of Summer. The *contemplative* mind ;—the mind, whofe faculties are engaged in the fublime employment of tracing the exiftence of a Deity thro' the mazy fabric of creation, can dwell upon no theme more calculated for its purpofe, than the regular and harmonious fucceffion of the feafons.—The *vernal* charms of recufcitated nature ;—her vigorous vegetation in *fummer* ;—her bounteous flow of bleffings in *autumn,* and her fublime horrors when ice-crowned *winter* " clofes the fcene," are objects, which muft equally excite the wonder, the praife, and the gratitude of man. The general fucceffion of the feafons, is mirably analogous to the natural gradations which divide and fify the variegated checkerment of human life.—Infancy is the fpring ;. youth, the fummer ; maturity, the autumn ; and old age, the winter, of man's fublunary exiftence.

Morality here finds a fubject,

upon which fhe dwells with melancholy fondnefs. The immutable laws of our nature, demand our willing fubmiffion. To die, is the lot of all below. *Mutation* is the deftiny of *matter.* There is a dreary winter, which ends the year ;—there is a relentlefs death, that heaps the mould of the grave upon " human prefumption."

The feafon of Summer is calculated to infpire us with the moft pleafing and the moft awful fenfations.—Hark !—In the diftant weft, the muttering thunder proclaims the approach of creation's GOD !—advancing in gloomy majefty, the fable cloud lowers under the canopy of the fky ! winged with energy refiftlefs, acrofs the fable welkin darts the vivid lightning—hoarfe crafhing, peal on peal redoubling ; the artilleries of heaven fhake our fyftem to its centre ;—in mighty torrents down rufh the burfting clouds !—all is terror, doubt, fufpenfe and confufion.

How changed the fcene !—The
cloud

cloud has paffed over. Far in the eaft, a fire electric flafhes, and the dying founds of exhaufted thunders, remind us of the danger that is paft. Exulting . œbus breaks from the clouds which had fhrouded his fplendor, and pours upon a rejoicing world the effulgence of day.—From the fields, the meadows, the mountains, and the dales, arife fragrant fcents and wholefome perfumes. Now, through the glittering foliage of the trees, fports the zephyr of fummer, fcattering from his downy pinions, the odours of fpring. All nature rejoices. The orifons of devotion rife to the throne of God, borne amid the incenfe of gratitude.—The mind, expanded and ennobled by the frefh and repeated inftances of divine " and preferving love," acknowledges the power of that Deity, who can deftroy the univerfe with his omnipotent fiat, and adores that goodnefs, which deigns to protect his creature, *man*, when the elements are mingled in confufion and in war.

But why do I enlarge on the fubject ?—Let the moralizing, the infpired Thomfon, explain the annexed plate, and charm with the dignity of reafon, and the melody of fong.

"ALL-CONQU'RING Heat, oh intermit thy wrath !
And on my throbbing temples potent thus
Beam not fo fierce! Inceffant ftill you flow,
And ftill another fervent flood fucceeds,
Pour'd on the head profufe. In vain I figh,

And reftlefs turn, and look around for Night;
Night is far off; and hotter hours approach.

"Welcome, ye fhades ! ye bow'ry thickets, hail !
Ye lofty pines ! Ye venerable oaks !
Ye afhes wild, refounding o'er the fteep !
Delicious is your fhelter to the foul,
As to the hunted hart the fallying fpring,
Or ftream full flowing, that his fwelling fides
Laves, as he floats along the herbag'd brink.
Cool, thro' the nerves, your pleafing comfort glides ;
The heart beats glad ; the frefh expanded eye
And ear refume their watch ; the finews knit ;
And life fhoots fwift thro' all the lighten'd limbs.

" Around th' adjoining brook, that purls along
The vocal grove, now fretting o'er a rock,
Now fcarcely moving through a reedy pool,
Now ftarting to a fudden ftream, and now
Gently diffus'd into a limpid plain.
A various group the herds and flocks compofe,
Rural confufion ! On the graffy bank
Some ruminating lie ; while others ftand
Half in the flood, and often bending, fip.
The circling furface. In the middle droops
The ftrong laborious ox, of honeft front,
Which incompos'd he fhakes ; and from his fides
The troublous infects lafhes with his tail,
Returning ftill. Amid his fubjects fafe,
Slumbers the monarch fwain, his carelefs arm
Thrown round his head, on downy mofs fuftain'd :
Here laid his fcrip, with wholefome viands fill'd ;
There, lift'ning ev'ry noife, his watchful dog."

The DRUNKARD: An ANECDODE.

A DEVOTEE to the fhrine of the *Semelian deity* returning home, late at night, after a high campaign, took his rout through a wood. He had fcarcely entered it when he faw an object, which, as he fancied, had the appearance of a man. As he approached it he was better fatisfied. Impudence and audacity, the concomitants of inebriation,

inebriation, were by no means quiescent in our bacchanalian. The sense of his own superiority to a fellow worm was such as totally superseded the propriety, much more the expediency, of his going out of the path for the other. He paused, and demanded the road. His words were disregarded. He repeated them under the commination of a blow. Sill the object of his insult stood firm in the middle of the path, and did not deign to answer a word. Get out of the way in a moment, said the bacchanalian, or I will strike you to the ground. Immediately, going a little nearer for that purpose, the man, regardless of his threats, seized him about the waist, and held him locked fast in his arms. The bacchanalian was at length obliged to beg for freedom ; but his begging was in vain. He then swore that, if the fellow did not let him go directly, he would stab him. Accordingly, he took a knife from his pocket and plunged it into his vitals ! Then, being liberated from the dire gripe of his antagonist, went his way.

Before the close of the next day, reason had assumed her empire, and the rash man was smitten with such remorse of conscience, as extorted a voluntary confession of the horrid crime he had perpetrated in the hour of intoxication ! The village was alarmed ! A number was forthwith dispatched to take care of the *murdered*, while the humble and self convicted *murderer* was conducted to prison.

The astonishment and joy can be conceived better than described, when, instead of a *murdered man*, a huge *murdered bear* was found sprawled on the spot ! Q.

For the MASSACHUSETTS MAGAZINE.

The MAN of GENIUS.

A MAN, endued with great natural and acquired abilities, who constantly pursues the course, which reason, aided by revelation, has marked out, is a blessing of inestimable worth to his friends, his country, and the world. Like some vast river, which pours along its wonted channel with unremitting regularity, he diffuses life and happiness to all around. A man, however, who devotes his superior talents to sordid carnality and vice, is a monster more terrible than hydras, gorgons, and harpies. Like a mighty torrent, which has burst its mound, he spreads terror and devastation far and wide.

MODENA.

ANECDOTE.

MR. * was not remarkable for his punctual attendance on public worship. A friend once asked him why he was so frequently culpable in that respect? His reply we think a little singular. He said that *neighbour such a one, who sat near his pew, snored so intolerably that he could not sleep !*

Q.

Dr.

Dr. JOHNSON's MARRIAGE.

DR. JOHNSON gave the following curious account of his journey to church on the nuptial morn. The church at which we chofe the ceremony fhould be performed lay in a diftant parifh, and we fet out on horfe back. *It was a love match on both fides,* but the bride had read the old romances and had got into her head the fantaftical notion that a woman of fpirit fhould ufe her lover like a dog. So, Sir, at firft fhe told me that I rode too faft, and fhe could not keep up with me; and when I rode a little flower, fhe paffed me, and complained that I lagged behind. I was not to be made the flave of caprice; and I refolved to begin as I could end. I therefore pufhed on brifkly till I was fairly out of her fight. The road lay between two hedges, fo I was fure fhe could not mifs it; and I contrived that fhe fhould foon come up with me. When fhe did, I obferved her to be in tears.

For the MASSACHUSETTS MAGAZINE.

A SHORT ACCOUNT of the TOWN of CONCORD, illuftrative of the annexed PLATE.

THE names of places, and of the various divifions of our globe, gain celebrity, as often from being theatres of great actions and brilliant exploits, as from the extent of their territory, their population or their wealth. The birth of a bard, of a hero, of a philofopher; contingencies the moft accidental, and events the moft unexpected, have ftamped immortality upon the local defignations of hamlets and villages, which muft, otherwife, have been configned to perpetual obfcurity, and loft in the lapfe of ages. The valour of *Leonidas* has tranfmitted Thermopylæ ftraits with brilliant honour to an admiring pofterity. While we admire the hero, we are led to venerate the ground upon which he reaped his laurels. The diminutive town of UTICA is confecrated to eternal memory, on the fame hiftoric page, which records the grandeur of IMPERIAL ROME. The one was miftrefs of a fubjugated world; the other was dignified by the fenate of CATO; of that CATO whom Cæfar could not conquer.

Previous to our attempt of a defcription of the town of Concord, we muft acknowledge our being indebted to Mr. William Jones, at prefent a ftudent at law in that place, for all the particulars of the following account. As we had not room to infert his *topographical defcription* of *Concord,* which was prefented by him to the *Hiftorical Society,* entire, we have taken liberty to avail ourfelves of his ingenious performance for the acquifition of *facts* conducive to the completion of our defign, and in fome places have ufed his ftyle and expreffions, verbatim.

CONCORD, in the Commonwealth of Maffachufetts, is fituated in the County of Middlefex, and is about 19 miles from the metropolis of the State. Its foil, confifting of rocky, fandy, and moift land, is happily calculated for the various kinds of agricultural improvement. Grain, hay, rye, and Indian corn, are raifed in fuch abundance, as is fufficient, not only for the inhabitants,

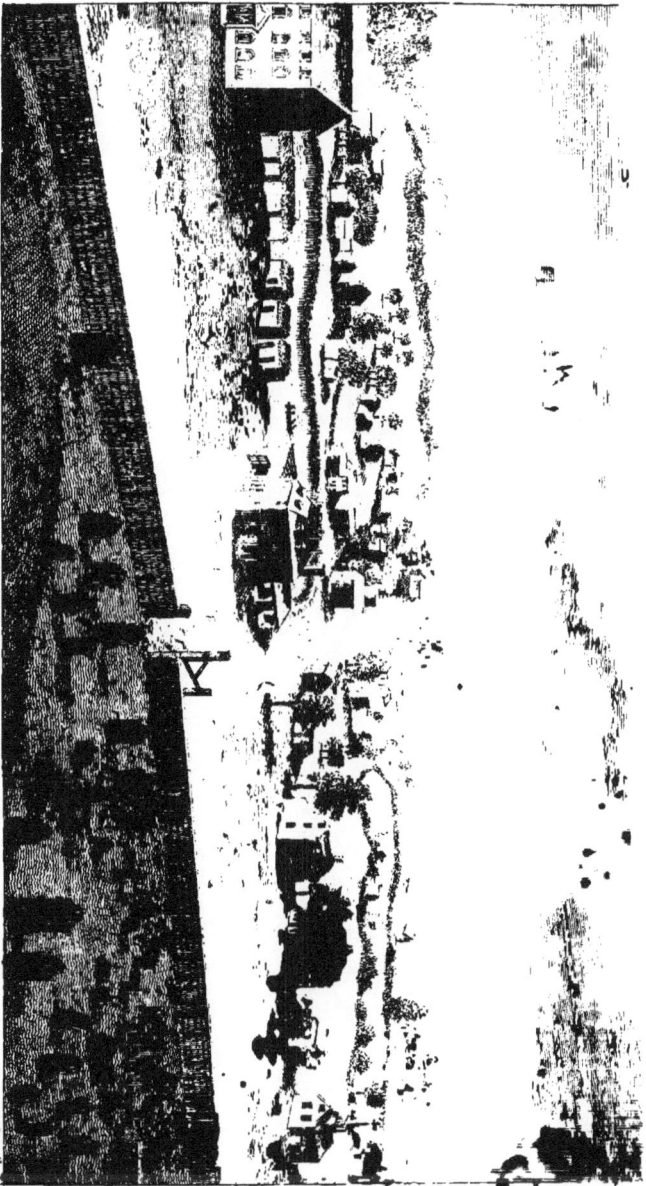

A View of CONCORD, taken in 1776.

S. Hill.

ants, but a valuable part of their produce is sent to market.

There are no hills of any consequence, except one, at the northwest part of the town. A fine river, and three ponds, adorn and fertilize that pleasant village. These ponds and the river, afford plenty of fish, supplying the inhabitants, especially the poorer class of them, with many a wholesome and delicious repast.

The public edifices in Concord, are the meeting house, the court house, and the prison. The first is pleasantly situated on the east side of the mill pond, and is an elegant building, worthy of the design for which it was erected, and of the excellent clergyman, who in it dispenses the word of God. A new court house is now erecting upon an eminence, which will form a convenient and elegant temple for the administration of justice. A desire to ornament their town, and to add to the welfare of the State, distinguishes the enterprizing inhabitants of this place. Happy in the possession of a fertile glebe, and of the means to increase their property by industry, their patriotic wishes are with facility carried into effect and execution. The county of Middlesex, demands our applause for the expense which it has been at, in erecting the prison in Concord, and which is the best in the Commonwealth. The style of architecture in which it is built is the *Tuscan*. The apartments of it are numerous, neat, and convenient. A fine stream of water runs under it, by which it is cleansed; conducing much to the health and comfort of its hapless tenants. The philanthropic Howard would have viewed this unwished for and unwelcome *retreat* of the unfortunate and the vicious; this mansion, erected by sad *necessity*, and peopled

by justice, with a mixture of joy and approbation. The lot of misery is here alleviated as much as the nature of the case can possibly admit; and the chains of the criminal, are deprived of half their irksomeness by the mild influence of pitying humanity.

The roads, from the upper part of Middlesex to Boston, lead thro' Concord, and are kept in good repair. At a small distance from the centre of the town, a very handsome bridge has been lately completed, at the expense of a few spirited and patriotic individuals, for the service of the public. Not many roods below this bridge, stands the famous NORTH BRIDGE, where the Americans first engaged the British troops, several of whom lie buried upon the banks of the river. It was at this place that British insolence received a most vigorous chastisement from a small party of the Massachusetts yeomanry. This event shall adorn one of the most interesting pages of our country's history, as it has given birth to a brilliant era in the annals of time.

Most of the inhabitants of Concord are *farmers*; however, near its centre, there are a number of professional men and traders, who transact business to considerable advantage. There is a library, consisting of well chosen books in the various branches of literature, belonging to a company, and purchased by subscription. The town, upon the whole, is in a prosperous situation; the people are industrious, enterprising, patriotic, and hospitable.

CONCORD was incorporated September 3, 1635, and was the first settlement at so great a distance from the sea shore in New-England. The inhabitants never had any contests with the Indians. This quietness of the *aborigines* is imputed " to the full satisfaction they receiv-

ed

ed at the time of purchafe. The General Court has frequently fet in this town, and enacted laws conducive to the fafety and to the happinefs of our Commonwealth. The *Provincial Congrefs* was held at Concord in 1774. Of late years three fifths of the courts of juftice in the county have met in this flourifhing place, alternately dividing the county bufinefs between Concord and Cambridge.

We know not how to conclude this account better, than by extracting from the aforementioned performance of Mr. Jones, the following interefting fentences.

" A large quantity of provifions and military ftores being depofited here, induced General Gage, who commanded the Britifh troops at Bofton, on the memorable 19th of April, 1775, to fend a detachment to deftroy them. Who, after they had thrown a confiderable quantity of flour and ammunition into the mill pond, knocked of the trunnions and burnt the carriages of feveral field pieces, and committed other outrages, were oppofed at the North Bridge by the militia of this and the neighbouring towns; and after a fhort engagement, in which feveral on both fides were flain, they were forced to retreat with great precipitation.

" While the troops were in town, they fired the court houfe, in the garret of which there was a great quantity of powder. This fire, by the interceffion of one Mrs. Moulton, a woman of above eighty years of age, the troops extinguifhed; otherwife, the houfes adjoining, would have been deftroyed by the explofion of the powder. Indeed, in every part of the conduct of the inhabitants, there appeared to be a furprifing prefence of mind, which protected them from the infults of the foldiery, and, in a great meafure, defeated the defign of the expedition. A tavern keeper, whofe houfe they came to plunder, declared in a fpirited manner, that they fhould not take the leaft article without paying for it. A gentleman who is now in town, and had at that time the fuperintendence of a confiderable quantity of the public ftores, preferved the fame by an innocent evafion, which few in his fituation would have dared to attempt. When the troops came to his door, he appeared to be very complaifant, invited them in, told them he was glad to fee them, afked them to fit and eat fome bread and cheefe and drink fome cider, which they did. After this, they went out of doors, and were about to break open his corn houfe. He called them to ftop, and not to trouble themfelves to fplit the door; if they would wait a minute, he would fetch the keys and open it himfelf, which he did. There being a large quantity of flour in the corn houfe, belonging to the public, he fays, " Gentlemen, I am a miller, I improve thofe mills yonder, by which I get my living, and every gill of this flour," at the fame time putting his hand upon a bag of flour, that was *really* his own, " I raifed and manufactured on my own farm, and it is all my own; this is my ftore houfe; I keep my flour here, until fuch time as I can make a market for it." Upon this, the commanding officer fays, " Well, I believe you are a pretty honeft old chap; you don't look as if you could do any body much hurt, and we won't meddle with you." Then he ordered his men to march. By this, and feveral other fuch inftances of policy and refolution, but few of the public ftores were deftroyed."

The

The SPECULATOR. No. IV.

> There would he dream of graves, and corfes pale ;
> And ghofts, that to the charnel dungeon throng,
> And drag a length of clanking chain, and wail,
> Till filenc'd by the owl's terrific fong,
> Or blaft that fhrieks by fits the fhuddering ifles along.
>
> BEATTIE.

OF the various kinds of fuperftition which have in any age influenced the human mind, none appear to have operated with fo much effect as what has been termed the Gothic. Even in the prefent polifhed period of fociety, there are thoufands who are yet alive to all the horrors of witchcraft, to all the folemn and terrible graces of the appalling fpectre. The moft enlightened mind, the mind free from all taint of fuperftition involuntarily acknowledges the power of Gothic agency ; and the late favourable reception which two or three publications in this ftyle have met with, is a convincing proof of the affertion. The enchanted foreft of Taffo, the fpectre of Camoens, and the apparitions of Shakfpeare, are to this day highly pleafing, ftriking, and fublime features in thefe delightful compofitions.

And although this kind of fuperftition be able to arreft every faculty of the human mind, and to fhake as it were, all nature with horror, yet does it alfo delight in the moft fportive and elegant imagery. The traditionary tales of elves and fairies ftill convey to a warm imagination an inexhaufted fource of invention, fupplying all thofe wild, romantic, and varied ideas with which a wayward fancy loves to fport. The Provencal bards, and the neglected Chaucer and Spencer, are the originals from whence this exquifite mythology has been drawn, improved, and applied with fo much

inventive elegance by Shakfpeare. The flower and the leaf of Chaucer is replete with the moft luxuriant defcription of thefe præternatural beings.

Next to the Gothic in point of fublimity and imagination comes the Celtic, which, if the fuperftition of the Lowlands be efteemed a part of it, may, with equal propriety be divided into the terrible and the fportive ; the former, as difplayed in the poems of Offian ; the latter, in the fongs and ballads of the Low Country. Offian has opened a new field for invention, he has coloured a fet of beings unknown to Gothic fiction ; his ghofts are not the ghofts of Shakfpeare, yet are they equally folemn and ftriking. The abrupt and rapid fervor of imagination, the vived touches of enthufiafm, mark his compofition, and his fpectres rufh upon the eye with all the ftupendous vigour of wild and momentary creation. So deep and uniform a melancholy pervades the poetry of this author, that, whether from natural difpofition, or the preffure of misfortune, from the face of the country which he inhabited, or the infulated ftate of fociety, he feems ever to have avoided imagery of a light and airy kind ; otherwife, from the originality of his genius, much in this way might have been expected. As to the fuperftition of the Lowlands, it differs fo little from the lighter Gothic, that I know not whether I am warranted in drawing any dif- tinction

tinction between them. It is not, however, peculiar to this district of Scotland, the Highlanders in many parts, especially in their beautiful little vales, being still enthusiastic in their belief of it.

These are then the two species of superstition which seem most capable of invigorating the powers of imagination ; how feeble, cold, and insipid are the mythological fables of the classic bard, compared to the bold and daring fictions of the Gothic Muse.

It has been, however, too much the fashion among critical writers, to condemn the introduction of this kind of imagery, as puerile and absurd ; but, whilst it is thus formed to influence mankind, to surprize, elevate, and delight, with a willing admiration, every faculty of the human mind, how shall criticism with impunity dare to expunge it ? Genius has ever had a predilection for it, and it has ever been the favourite superstition of the poets. I may venture, I think, to predict, that if at any time this species of fabling be totally laid aside, our national poetry will degenerate into mere morality, criticism, and satire ; and that the sublime, the terrible, and the fanciful in poetry, will no longer exist. The recent publication of Mr. Hole's Arthur, or the Northern Enchantment, will again call the attention of the public to these fertile sources of invention ; for it is

In scenes like these, which daring to depart
    From sober truth, are still to nature true,
And call forth fresh delight to Fancy's view,
    Th' heroic muse employ'd her Tasso's art !
How have I sat, when pip'd the pensive wind,

To hear his harp, by British Fairfax strung,
Prevailing poet, whose undoubting mind
    Believ'd the magic wonders which he sung;
Hence at each found imagination glows;
Hence his warm lay with softest sweetness flows ;
Melting, it flows, pure, num'rous, strong and clear,
And fills th' impassion'd heart, and wins th' harmonious ear.
                    COLLINS.

The poet from whose works the above quotation has been taken, possessed all that fervor of enthusiasm, all that warmth of imagination characteristic of true genius ; and although ignorance and bad taste have not unfrequently classed him with a Tickell and a Hammond, yet with the discerning few will he ever hold an exalted rank in the regions of pathos and invention.

By fairy hands his knell is rung ;
By forms unseen his dirge is sung :
Oft " Fancy" comes " at twilight" gray,
To bless the turf that wraps his clay ;
And " Pity" shall a while repair
To dwell a weeping " Votress" there.

But to return to our subject.—Although so great a disparity evidently obtains between the two species of Gothic superstition, the terrible and the sportive ; yet no author, that I am acquainted with, has availed himself of this circumstance, and thrown them into immediate contrast. In a fragment lately published by Mrs. Barbauld, under the title of Sir Bertrand, the transition is immediately from the deep Gothic to the Arabic or Saracenic superstition ; which, although calculated to surprize, would have given more pleasure, and would have rendered the preceding scenes of horror more striking, had it been of a light and contrasted

trasted kind. Struck, therefore, with the propriety of the attempt, and the exquisite beauty that would probably result from such an opposition of imagery, I have determined to devote a few Papers to this design, and to give exemplifications in an Ode and Tale ; and, as I have often abserved this kind of superstition to take great hold of the reader's ᵎcuriosity, I doubt not they will meet with a favourable reception,

N.

―――――――

ALEXIS : Or, The COTTAGE in the WOODS.

[FROM THE FRENCH.]

(Continued from the 368th page.)

PART SECOND.

ALEXIS passes a twelvemonth in the Cottage.—He is forced to leave it.

CHAPTER I.

A NIGHT SCENE IN THE COTTAGE.

THE narrative of our hero's misfortune operated, in a singular manner, upon Candor, Germain, and Clara. Candor, above all, could not be tired on looking at him for the whole time the supper lasted. He had placed Alexis next to him, and from time to time would exclaim, " What, my son !—So young, and such a knowledge of mankind !—How, you know them well !—Your philosophy,your courage, all in thee interest me to a point !—O my Alexis, I depend upon your steadiness with the most consolatory expectations.—I will disclose them some day, you shall help me. But stay, I will try you still for a twelvemonth. Be my son, you have no father ; let me supply his place ! Alexis, promise me as much submission and docility, as you would have for a father !"—" Yes, father, I promise every thing. "Upon your honour ?" " Heaven be my witness."—" Give me thy hand, and remember one day, the sacred engagement you have entered into with Candor."—" Your favours will never make me forget it."—" I

was happy and powerful in the world, my closest bosom friends have thrown me into the abyss of ills ; Germain, alone, stood by me: Germain, my good and honest friend, love him as I do ! what a treasure is a trusty, faithful servant! Behold Clara ; my only daughter, my every thing—be her tutor ! teach her all the sciences, all the accomplishments you are master of : May she profit by your lessons, and above all, may she take your sage advice, that prudence, that mistrust in mankind, qualities so requisite for a being destined to live, some day, in the bosom of society. For I am old and hoary my good children, I cannot always be with you, and when I am once gone, perhaps you may have the most ardent desire of living in towns, of launching into the whirlpool."—"Ah ! never, never, answered Alexis and Clara in conjunction with each other."

Alexis was transported with joy: Clara squeezed his hand, embraced her father and Germain, and enraptured with the happy prospect that glowed in her beauteous eyes, she could not conceal her satisfaction.

They soon rose from their frugal repast, and Candor would have Alexis to take an exact view of the hermitage.

hermitage, and in which the old man thought he would remain for life.

Clara laid hold immediately of the youth's arm, Candor supported himfelf upon Germain's fhoulder, and all four went to vifit the feveral parts of this retreat. Let us follow their traces, and get acquainted with an abode where we fhall, for fome time dwell with them.

They firft entered a yard, ninety feet in fquare, its centre is occupied by the cottage. The lateral extent of the edifice is thirty, and the height fifty feet.

They afcend four fteps, enter a fmall veftibule ; where Alexis perceives at the bottom of the ftairs, two doors, the one on the right and the other on the left. The firft conducts to the kitchen, and the fecond to a hall fifteen feet high, furnifhed with a chimney, a table, chairs, and a confiderable library.

He leaves the hall, and goes up fome winding ftairs to the firft floor; on this fide is Candor's bed chamber. A bed, a large cheft of drawers, two portraits, half a dozen of fowling pieces, and fome chairs are the only furniture he fees in it.

Clara's chamber is not better decorated, excepting a fine harpficord which takes up the greateft part of the room.

In the fecond ftory he enters two little rooms, without a chimney, but very fnug and decent.

Above them is a large garret, which fupplies the place of a hay-loft, and granary.

Every ceiling is vaulted, and built of ftone : Every window of the apartments is grated with iron bars, and does not exceed fix feet in height. Below ftairs is a door leading to a cellar, to which nobody but Candor and Germain, had accefs. This cave or cellar, con-

tains neither wine nor liquors, (our hermits had long fince left off to make ufe of them) there is nothing pent in it but—This is a myftery we fhall certainly difcover hereafter, but now, it muft remain concealed. Let us therefore follow our hero to the garden.

It is an inclofure of about one acre and a half, the third part planted with peas, beans, potatoes, oats, &c. &c. and the remainder a meadow yielding hay for the horfe. There were alfo feveral fruit trees, and at the garden's end, a very lofty poplar, which appeared to have been left fince the ground was firft cleared to build the cottage and its premifes. At the foot of the poplar, a limpid rivulet fpringing from a remote part of the woods, ftreams over a layer of pebbles, and eafes itfelf in a frightful precipice, at the diftance of two leagues from the cottage.

This rivulet, croffing the little garden, is hemmed in its career by a dike of fhell work, which it furmounts, and forms a cafcade, whofe waters fall into a bafon near the meadow, hewn, as it were, by the hand of nature, in the heart of a rock.

A little bridge leading to a grove, the work of Candor, invites the philofopher to tafte the fweets of the evening, and reft from the toils of day : The whole of this rural and tranquil refidence breathes calm thought and folitude.

Alexis, furveying with admiration thofe wonders of art and nature, lifted up his hand to heaven, to return thanks to the fublime Author, for having brought him to this delightful abode, where he can at leaft enjoy repofe in the arms of the only beings, in whofe hearts he had found generofity, fympathy, and virtue.

Clara, who was leading him before her father, eager to shew him all the beauties of her garden, did not fail to expatiate upon its charms. " Do you see," said she, " yonder, that field? I alone have cultivated it; but now, as you are my partner, my labour will be changed into mere pleasure: It is in this rivulet we will quench our thirst; you will offer me this limped water, and I will receive it at your hands: Here you will smile; there, we shall seek shelter from the heat of the day: I will press one of those fruits upon your burning lips, and its nectar will refresh your blood. Oh! how often shall we at the decline of day, go to take rest in this grove. It is there, unknown to all the world, far from the bustling and noise of cities, we shall bless and endear our being. The sun goes down, the moon plays, here and there, her silver beams through the foliage of the thicket. The bosom of the earth opens and exhales a thousand perfumes. We sit by one another; the gentle purling of this rivulet, which glides beneath our feet, throws us into the sweets of thought; you press my hand to your heart, it beats, we give up all thinking; yet we gaze, and enjoy! O Alexis, Alexis, believe thy Clara, it is here thou wilt find happiness."

In vain Alexis endeavoured to reply, his feelings would not suffer him to express his thoughts; he contented himself with squeezing Clara's hand, and beholding her with that expression of sentiment which is more obvious to the pencil than to the eloquence. " Oh, yes" said he, with a low voice, " yes, I am already as happy as mortal can be."

Candor and Germain who came soon after, found the young couple in that extacy of delight. Germain shook his head, Candor smiled, and his children were put to the blush.

By this time the night began to lower upon nature. The birds, perched in the wood, waited silently the retreat of the sun, to suspend their warbling, and to rest upon the hospitable branch. The nightingale alone enchanted the woods with her sweet melodies, and the moping owls, in deference to her, forebore their funeral howlings. All invited our anchorets to return to the cottage, to enjoy a repose, claimed by the emotions which they felt that day, and the fatigue the preceding night.

They had no convenience to substitute artificial light to that of day; the sun shut their eyes, and Aurora reopened them. Thus they retired to their respective apartments, not to meet till day-break.

Alexis having received the tender embrace of the three hosts went up stairs to his room situated on the second floor; he was determined to reject the parots of sleep, to reflect freely upon his present situation, and upon what conduct he should observe towards his new friends, so as to convince them of his gratitude and tenderness. He had already forgot his misanthrophy and mistrust, when a very particular event revived them, bolted in his mind, and perplexed his senses.

He had hardly commenced his meditations, than he heard a noise at the door: He listens, hears the rattling of keys, one is put into the lock of his door, he asks who is there? no answer, in a moment the door is locked, and the goaler disappears! What means this unexpected precaution? why will they shut him up? what do they want of him? O heaven! should it be treachery?

ery ? the houſe where he was received with open arms, ſhould it be a den of ruffians ? what, Candor, Germain, Clara, Clara! it is impoſſible. Perfidiouſneſs cannot conceal itſelf ſo well under the veil of virtue : A look, a geſture, the leaſt motions detect it. They are not traitors, but why is he locked up ? They have not appriſed him of this detention ; nor even did his goaler give him an anſwer. Ah! they ſurely will undo him ; he has been too confident, to indiſcreet: He ſhould not have expoſed himſelf : In a word, people that inhabit a fortified retreat, in a foreſt, notorious for its robbers and banditti. All becomes ſuſpicion to him ; he recollects the converſation of the day, an expreſſion of Candor's chills him with terror : *O my Alexis! I depend upon your ſteadineſs with the moſt conſolatory expectation. I will diſcloſe them ſome day ; you ſhall help me.* Great God! will they conſtrain a virtuous and well principled youth to become a robber! after all, what do they mean by this ? ſhould not the cellar, which they would not let him ſee, conceal the murdered victims and their ſpoil ? Surely this diſcourſe, and myſterious cellar conceal crimes. Alexis doubts no longer ; his head becomes light, his imagination works, ghaſtly ſpectres appear to him, horrid phantoms, from all ſides croſs his chamber, his hair ſtands at an end, his tongue becomes heavy, he remains motionleſs, and reſolves upon ſome violent meaſure.

The window of his room was on the garden ſide, he runs to it, he will elope from the fatal houſe where the moſt dreadful omens trouble his reaſon. But an unforeſeen obſtacle is in his way, and ſanctions his ſuſpicions by certainty. Large iron bars oppoſe his deſign : It is all over, he is impriſoned, betrayed, undone.

As the timid bird who falls into the net, and is afterwards put in a cage, beats the hoſtile wire with its wings, and paſſing his bill acroſs, pants for the tree, which he perceives, and on which he was perched a little before ; thus our hero applies his mouth to the fatal bars, beholding acroſs the garden, and the vaſt extent of the foreſt, whoſe gloomy abode appears to him preferable to the odious priſon, where he preſumes he will be obliged to remain all his life time.

In ſpite of all this, his ſenſible ſoul was ſtill to undergo another ſhock. Will he have ſtrength ſufficient to bear the frightful ſpectacle that will preſent itſelf to his ſight ? At firſt he hears ſomebody ſhut the door of the cellar, that object of his terror, with a terrible noiſe, ſoon after Candor and Germain come forth, carrying each a lighted flambeaux in their hand. A kind of a coffin covered with a pall is ſeen on their ſhoulders : They ſilently croſs the garden, and advance to the foot of the poplar tree, near the borders of the limpid rivulet : Here they take off their burden, and the diſtance alone hinders Alexis from hearing or ſeeing what they do.

Meanwhile Candor appears to open the coffin : He lays down upon it, he riſes again, a fire is kindled, the flame blazes, riſes, and on a ſudden becomes extinct ; the tree is glanced, the leaves tremble, and the birds ſitting on its branches flee with diſmal ſhrieks : the flambeaux are diſtinguiſhed, all vaniſhes.

Is it an illuſion ? is it a phantom ? the moon rendered obſcure by the pale light of the torches ſpread alone her myſtic beams ; the birds return to their wonted tree, Candor and Germain appear again, they

they crofs the garden, return to fet by the coffin in the fecret cave, the door is fhut, the rattling of keys, and the hollow found of bolts are heard again.

Let now the reader place himfelf in the fituation of my Alexis. He knows his fearful, fufpicious, and miftrufting temper ! Let him have an idea of his embarraffment, his apprehenfions, his fhuddering ! How agitated his mind ! That coffin, that flame ! what can have been that ceremony he could not diftinguifh : It is perhaps the body of fome ftrayed traveller, which they burnt, after having ftript it. He doubts no more : To-morrow the fame fate awaits him : But where are his riches ? why fhould they kill him ? his fpoil is not brilliant enough : No matter, he has all to fear. Perhaps Candor, deceived by the world, has fworn to facrifice all fuch as will fall in his hands, to gratify his ven-geance. Alexis is perhaps to aug-ment the number of his victims : All confirm him in that idea. Alas ! what has he done, that fate fhould have brought him to this deteftable den ? He regrets not life, it is a burden to him ! but to fall by fo bafe a treachery, after having trufted to the good faith and hu-manity of his butchers. This, this alone, caufes his defpair, and makes him wifh for the approach of day, in order to take a refolution : He will not fuffer himfelf to be flaugh-tered thus patiently ; he will fell his life as dear as he can. Tremble, affaffins, you fhall not give him the mortal blow without having ftood moft vigorous in his own defence againft Candor, Germain, and— Clara ! what, is Clara guilty too ?

(To be continued.)

The STORY of SARAH PHILLIPS. *A Novel.*

[By M. de Saint Lambert.]

(Concluded from page 352.)

WHEN my uncle had taken his leave, I retired to a thick wood, where I walked about a confiderable time in great agita-tion, fometimes fuddenly ftopping when I found it difficult to invent means to remove certain obftacles, or obviate certain objections. I at length fat down, or rather fell, up-on the grafs, where I remained, in a profound reverie, till the arrival of Mr. Phillips, who had been look-ing for me. I never before expe-rienced fo great a pleafure at the fight of him, nor ever felt fo forci-bly that I could not bear to part from him. I communicated to him my uncle's defigns, and my fin-cere regret to difpleafe my family, by refufing to accept fuch reafona-ble propofals.

I certainly dwelt too long on the fubject, for I fhall forever reproach myfelf with the cruel pain to which I put my beloved Phillips. I faw him turn pale, his whole frame was feized with a trembling, he looked wild, and could fcarcely articulate a fyllable. It muft be fo—faid he —Yes it muft be fo—he is a worthy young man—Your relations—Your rank—It muft—It muft be fo.

I faw he was ready to burft into tears, as he looked fteadfaftly upon me ; at length he dropped on his knees before me.

I could

I could now conceal my emotions no longer, I rufhed forward to fupport the object of my affections ; I threw my arms around him, crying out, my dear hufband ! At this tender and vehement exclamation he returned no anfwer, but raifing himfelf, by little and little, with his eyes bathed in tears, looked at me with inexpreffible tendernefs while I continued ftill to repeat the words, My hufband ! my hufband ! As foon as he was able to fpeak, he attempted to perfuade me from my refolution ; but I ftopped him, and intreated him, in the name of our mutual love, at leaft, to hear me. He feated himfelf near me ; his heart was all love, but a thoufand contending ideas and principles ftill marked his countenance with a thoufand fears.— This moment, on which depended the happinefs of my life, is ftill fo prefent to my imagination that I have not forgotten the flighteft circumftance of what paffed.

I am well aware, faid I, of all you can fay, and am prepared to anfwer. My paffion is not blind and unreafonable. I know you well ; I am perfuaded you are the man for whom nature defigned me. It is on the amiable qualities I difcover in you that the happinefs of marriage depends ; the neceffity of an equality of rank is only prefcribed by human conventions. You and I are well convinced that the truly wife refpect thefe conventions fince they maintain order in fociety. The rank in which we are born ought not to be difgraced by any alliance which the prejudices, it may be, of the reft of the world would condemn. This is a fault which cannot fail to be punifhed with contempt ; a contempt which though unjuft, I fhould be unable to bear. But ought the law of nature to yield to the interefts of fociety ? Perhaps it ought. Yet we have it in our power to obey the impulfe of our hearts, and at the fame time fhow refpect to the prejudices of the world. The death of my parents has put me in poffeffion of two thoufand pounds per annum, and three thoufand in ready money ; I will refign my eftate, only preferving the latter fum, to live with you.

Here Mr. Phillips attempted to interrupt me. He propofed we fhould live fingle. No faid I, that would be to offend againft the law of nature which requires us to increafe and multiply. But why fhould we not marry ? To preferve my poffeffions ? They cannot make me rich in my prefent rank ; but, if I defcend to your fituation in life, even the fortune I mean to retain will be fufficient. If I marry my coufin, we fhall be but moderately rich for our condition ; but I can render you very opulent for a farmer. I will prefently fet out for London and have a report fpread that I am dead. The law will difpofe of my eftate to the family of my coufin, and we will return to Scotland, with what I have referved for myfelf, and obtain your father's permiffion to marry.

Mr. Phillips kneeled at my feet, conjured me to defer the execution of fuch a plan, and carefully to examine whether I fhould not regret what I was about to throw away.

No, replied I, I have maturely weighed every confequence. What can I regret ? What pleafure can riches give which nature will not fupply in the way of life I have chofen ? Will not the real landfcape delight as much as the imitation of it by the painter's art ? or can filk and diamonds be neceffary to happinefs ? We fhall enjoy every convenience which nature can require,

quire, and superfluity is only neceſſary for idleneſs.

As to the loſs of preſent connexions, how can I regret them when I ſhall become the daughter of your father, and the mother of your children?

Mr. Phillips loved and eſteemed me too much to doubt, any longer, that I ſhould be happy in this new condition of life, which I was ſo deſirous to embrace. I ſhall not attempt to deſcribe either his joy and gratitude, or my own delight, when I had prevailed on him to accept my offer. Never did any one feel ſuch pleaſure in the ſudden acquiſition of a great fortune, as I did in renouncing mine.

After having taken the neceſſary meaſures, we ſat out for London, where I cauſed a report to be circulated that I was dead. It will not be neceſſary to relate all the artifices employed to render it probable and gain it credit.

At length we returned to Scotland. It is now ſeven years ſince I firſt entered this beloved retirement, and embraced, for the firſt time, that excellent old man whom you ſee ſitting on that ſtone, enjoying the early rays of the ſun, and endeavouring to recal ſome portion of his former vigour, by the reviving influences of the morning and the ſpring. Receive, ſaid I, your daughter, who comes to render your old age cheery, and devote herſelf to promote the happineſs of your ſon. You, my huſband, ſhall inſtruct me in every part of my new occupation, and I have no doubt but you will find me a frugal manager, and that thoſe who depend on me, and thoſe on whom I have the pleaſure to depend, will be equally contented.

The old man was tranſported with joy, and this reverſe in his fortune, may perhaps, have prolonged his life. He now bought the farm which he had before only rented; our marriage was concluded, and, from the moment I aſſumed the name and condition of the man I love, no hour has paſſed in which I have not bleſſed my good fortune. We are happy, and may reaſonably flatter ourſelves that we ſhall continue ſo, for as long a term as nature uſually permits.

Mr. Phillips and myſelf endeavour only to employ our knowledge, and love for literature, to give new ſtrength to our enjoyments. We are attentive to procure every pleaſure which our ſituation affords, and to haſten its reliſh. One of the moſt uſual ſources of diſcontent, among mankind, is that they are continually endeavouring to obtain pleaſures not intended for them, for want of being able to conform their ideas and deſires to their condition and character. Into this error we have not fallen. We never loſe our time in vain reſearches, or uſeleſs wiſhes; nor do we ever forget to enjoy the happineſs within our reach. The teſtimony of a good conſcience, and our mutual affection, inſure our felicity. We cultivate that philoſophy which inſpires us with the love of virtue; and, though we ſhould be miſtaken, we conſider thoſe illuſions which are capable of exalting and purifying the ſoul as a benefit to mankind. We reſolutely and wholly reject that ſpecies of philoſophy which degrades human nature, and extinguiſhes in the heart the enthuſiaſm of humanity and virtue; we wiſh to preſerve, in all their force and all their charms, the rapturous feelings of love and friendſhip.

There is, no doubt, always a ſpecies of illuſion in theſe ſenſations,

if

if carried to excefs ; we do not believe ourfelves perfect, but we endeavour to become fo. We heighten the enjoyment of the good we poffefs, by the hope of what is better. We are contented with the prefent, and tranfported with the profpect of futurity. The better to preferve this internal love for virtue, we frequently perufe the novels of Richardfon. We, likewife, often read the poets ; among whom we prefer thofe who treat of the country, in which we live ; and the beauties of nature, which we love.

Rural poetry is particularly pleafing, when we have the objects it defcribes before our eyes. The enthufiafm of the poet always increafes the enthufiafm of the fpectator, and prevents its being extinguifhed by too great a familiarity with the objects by which it is excited. Poetry infpires us with refpect and love for the ancient and venerable arts of agriculture, for our occupation, and the fcenes amid which we refide.

We frequently fay to ourfelves, here would Homer and Virgil have been delighted. Here would Tibullus have fung the beauties of his Delia, and celebrated the charms of that infpiring wood, and this delicious valley. It was in the country that Haller and Gefner compofed their exquifite poems. Thofe great men preferred our way of life to every other. Poets, and all writers, who defcribe with warmth, and abound in feeling and imagery, give new force to the charms of fenfibility ; and, while we profecute thefe ftudies, our reafon and our fenfes combine to make us happy.

This appears to me to be making a proper ufe of philofophy, which has degenerated into fubtlety and affection. It has too often rendered man ridiculous, inftead of

proving his confolation, and directing him to the happinefs fuitable to each ftation of life. Such was the philofophy of my father, and fuch is ours. We educate our children in thefe principles ; they enjoy the delights accordant to infancy and youth, and we participate their pleafures.

I had frequently defired to interrupt Mrs. Phillips to make myfelf known to her, but fhe fpoke with fo much energy and rapidity I had no opportunity. No fooner did fhe paufe than, yielding to the effufions of the heart, and feizing one of her hands, I exclaimed, Oh, happy Mifs Thornton ! and doubly happy Mrs. Phillips !

Immediately, as I pronounced her maiden name, fhe haftily rofe— Heavens ! exclaimed fhe, What can this mean ? You fee before you, anfwered I, that very relation who loved you from your infancy, and who has long mourned your lofs. Blufh not that you have avowed fo tender a paffion for a virtuous hufband. You have left me your fortune, which I am ready to reftore. Let me conjure you to accept it. But whatever refolution you form, be certain of inviolable fecrecy.

I found no fmall difficulty in appleafing Mrs. Phillips, who could not forgive herfelf for having placed fo much confidence in me ; but fhe would by no means confent to receive back her eftate, and her hufband, who came in a moment afterwards, being informed of all that had paffed, coincided with her in opinion.

Survey, faid fhe, our houfe and grounds, and fay if any thing feems wanting which may conduce to our happinefs. Is not our furniture commodious and our table plentiful ? If we poffeffed greater riches we fhould no longer purfue our prefent

-ant occupations with the fame delight ; we fhould find lefs pleafure in our labours ; amufement would take place of ufeful employment, and what amufed us one hour would difguft us the next. Should we ceafe to cultivate our fields and tend our flocks, we fhould no longer know the pleafing expectation of plentiful harvefts and rich fleeces. We fhould look on the country, then become lefs valuable to us, with indifference. And who knows but a fofter enthufiafm which is the delight of our hearts, would be extinguifhed together with that which Nature infpires ? Our fentiments, perfectly fuited to and connected with our condition, are the fource of our happinefs. That happinefs may depend on an arrangement and combination of circumftances, which the leaft change might deftroy.

All my endeavours to perfuade my virtuous relations to fuffer me to reftore them their poffeffions,

were without effect ; but they promifed me their friendfhip, and that I fhould frequently hear from them, and might pafs every year, fome days with them at the farm. At length I took my leave, not without tears, of this amiable and intelligent pair.

I was now convinced that reafon and happinefs, were yet to be found in the world. May I profit from this conviction to become rational and happy ! However the eftate I poffefs, near that moft pleafant fpot, has acquired a double value, in my efteem, for its vicinity to this excellent family ; I fhall rebuild the houfe, and frequently refide there. As to the poffeffions which are the right of Mrs. Phillips, I fhall not apply them to my own ufe ; the rents they produce fhall be diftributed among our poorer relations, and the eftate one day return to the children of this happy and amiable pair.

For the MASSACHUSETTS MAGAZINE.
The GENERAL OBSERVER. No. XLVI.

" Slander, that worft of poifons, ever finds
" An eafy entrance to ignoble minds."

IT is a univerfal complaint, and it is a complaint of long exiftence ; a complaint which has been heard from ages immemorial, and is ftill echoed from generations paft, to the generation prefent, that mankind are generally unfriendly to each other's reputation. All complain of the ungenerous ufage ; for almoft all in their turns are forced to receive it ; and yet, all, at times, are too willing to practife it. And well may the injured complain ; for the mortifications and vexation, which they feel from the poifoned arrows of the defamer ; from fly

infinuations ; from dirty and undeferved afperfions ; and from bold, though groundlefs charges, are very great diminutions of their happinefs ; the pain of a wounded fame, being equal to the pain of a broken bone.

Many will inflict this pain merely from a malignity of difpofition ; and becaufe they feel a diabolical pleafure in depreffing others, and making them unhappy. Some will flander their neighbours, becaufe their neighbours are in better circumftances, or in better efteem, than themfelves. Some will black-
en

en the characters of others, becaufe their own characters are black. Some will deal in fcandal by way of retaliation. Some, through mere talkativenefs. And fome, becaufe they think they cannot choofe a more agreeable topic, with which to entertain their company. The tea-table, be fure, according to the repeated farcafm of the wits, is feldom deftitute of this poifonous infufion.

That this ignoble vice infefts the country, more than the city, I am not fo invidious as to affirm. If the ignorant and low bred are addicted to it, the inftructed and well bred cannot always be exculpated from it. I wifh I could affirm with truth, that cities, in addition to their other exemptions, are exempt from the crime of detraction; and that polite circles, from a feeling of delicacy and propriety, never condefcended to lend an ear to the tale of flander; much lefs to utter it. In the country, though the air in general, be pure and wholefome; yet it is fometimes infected with thofe fogs which obfcure, and with thofe poifonous blafts which taint, a fair and promifing character. In the city, together with other founds which grate upon the air, we too often hear, efpecially from a noify prefs, thofe mutterings, growlings and bellowings, againft men and meafures, which have been compared to, but which are but faintly reprefented by, the croaking of ravens, the hooting of owls, and the barking of dogs. In elegant rooms where ladies affemble as well as in clubs at dirty taverns, and among crowds in the ftreets, if we are not fuffocated with other offenfive fcents, we are almoft fure of being offended with the breath of fcandal. Hints are given, and whifpers are breathed out, that fuch an enter-

prizing genius has defeated his own purpofes by fome ftrange imprudence; that fuch an active man in trade, owes more than he is worth; that the owner of fuch an elegant carriage, has not yet paid for it; that the father of that lady fo richly dreffed, muft foon fail; that a certain gentleman the other night, loft a gold watch at a houfe of ill fame; that fuch a beauty has been foiled by the arts of feduction; and that a certain fea captain's wife, is now determined, by her fecret amours, to be, at leaft, even with her hufband.

That a difpofition to afperfe and diminifh the reputation of others, is a fign of bafenefs and depravity, needs no laboured arguments to prove. The vulgar cannot but fee, as I may vulgarly exprefs it, that the practice of fcandal is a fcandalous practice. It takes its rife from fome bafe paffion; perhaps principally from envy. It is made ufe of to anfwer fome bafe defigns. The pleafure which is enjoyed, either by thofe who propagate it, or thofe who liften to it, is an unworthy pleafure. They who afpire after any thing that is excellent and noble; after greatnefs, or fairnefs, of character, fhould not act fo inconfiftently as to blow the trumpet of ill fame themfelves, or eagerly drink in the found when it is blown by others.

The deteftation in which the wife Romans held the crime of defamation, and the feverity with which they punifhed it, has been quoted by moralifts, to fhow its malignant nature, and to deter others from the practice of it. In fome periods of their government, the murderer of characters, as well as the murderer of men, was punifhed with death. And though modern States are not fo fevere; yet perfons of fenfibility and

and elevation of foul, have felt the wounds of infamy to be mortal, and the poifon and pain of it to be worfe than death.

"It is to me amazing," fays a humane moralift, "that ever any man, bred up in the knowledge of virtue and humanity, fhould fo far caft off all fhame and tendernefs, as to ftand up in the face of thoufands, and utter fuch contumelies as I have read and heard of. Let fuch a one know that he is making fools merry, and wife men fick; and that, in the eye of confidering perfons, he hath lefs compunction than the common hangman, and lefs fhame than a proftitute."

Erratum.—In p. 291. 2d. c. l. 17. for *Sally* read *valley.*

On the CONDUCT of a Young LADY during COURTSHIP.

(Continued from page 302.)

IF by *love* is meant that romantic folly which urges your fex to the moft unaccountable and unjuftifiable connexions, I am fure it is not a neceffary ingredient in the matrimonial cup. Love, as I have already hinted, is founded o:. the juft bafis of efteem and confidence; but it is fomething more. Between amiable people, of different fexes, it acquires an animating warmth which raifes it above friendfhip; it acquires an interefting attraction fuperior to efteem. This warmth, and this attraction, often fubfift feparate from what ought to be their foundation; but it is invariably found, that while they are "bafelefs as the fabric of a vifion," they are equally unftable alfo. They leave only unavailing remorfe, and an ufelefs, but lafting repentance. In that rational attachment, where efteem is not only the foundation but the diftinguifhing feature; where the romantic raptures are obfcure and indiftinct, there is, at leaft, a fubftance durable and permanent—it is not the morning cloud, or the early dew, which the fun or the wind may diffipate: It is interwoven in our natures; it is a part of our conftitution; and its duration is equally ftable. Suppofing that every feeling which can

characterize the warmeft love, fhould happen to be joined to this efteem, you will then foon diftinguifh their different natures. The impetuous paffion will, by degrees, foften down to tendernefs; the animated warmth will become more temperate, and the whole fabric will difappear, leaving only the fteady foundation, which time cannot diffolve. This, Nancy, is not theory only—look into the world, and each moment will fhow you a ftriking example of both particulars.

How many has the fecond pofition deceived? yet it will continue to deceive more; for there is fcarcely a girl who thinks that it is poffible to love a fecond time. If it were worth while to contend with this phantom, for be affured, my dear girl, it is one, I need only again direct you to the dictates of experience: and if love *can* be characterized, it has certainly been found *more* than *once* in the fame perfon. The refuge from the force of thefe examples is trifling and contemptible. A ftrenuous antagonift tells you, that ONE of thefe paffions is the only true love; another that it is not two, but a continuation of the fame feeling; the perfon only is changed. I will allow both thefe anfwers, ridiculous

as

as they are ; for they will teach you, Nancy, another useful leſſon ; though you have loved once, you may yet be happy. If I do not allow them, the leſſon is equally eſtabliſhed by what is my firm opinion, that love, *ſo far as it is connected with happineſs*, may be felt more than once for objects very different. The feelings may, in one inſtance, be more vivid than in another ; and conſequently the moſt active flame will be alone recognized as the favourite paſſion.

With your eyes opened to the ſource of theſe different errors, your determination will be more correct ; and the conſequences more probably fortunate.

If you accept of your preſent offer, from the moſt deliberate examination, I ſhall next offer you ſome advice on your conduct. In love affairs there is an eſtabliſhed language, but it is a mere ſyſtem of words, and you ſhould conſider it in no other light, " honour and favour, coldneſs and cruelty, raptures and deſpair," all mean the ſame, that is, in fact, neither of them mean any thing. If a man addreſſes you in a ſtyle ſo trifling, it is an affront to your underſtanding ; if in another, in a more aſſured and licentious manner, it is an affront to your delicacy. A man of ſenſe will addreſs himſelf to your mind ; yet, in ſuch a ſituation, there is ſo great a difficulty, the ſubject itſelf is ſo important, and the ſucceſs, in general, ſo precarious, that it ſtaggers the firmeſt reſolutions, and diſconcerts the moſt deliberate determinations. It is ſaid, and with juſtice, that, at this time, every man behaves like a fool ; but, perhaps, there is not a more ſtrong mark of folly, than a careleſs confident aſſurance, in a ſtep on which future happineſs ſo much depends.

Do not, therefore, think the worſe of any man who delays his declaration, and, after frequent opportunities, loſes every chance by a ſeemingly unreaſonable diffidence. The anſwer of every woman, in ſimilar circumſtances, is not very different. If ſhe is not aware of the declaration, ſhe muſt neceſſarily be aſtoniſhed, and unable to reply ; if ſhe is, her anſwer wears the ſame air of doubt, of heſitation, and ſeemingly of coldneſs. The whole ſex reſemble Milton's picture of Eve, who would not " *unſought*, be won." I do not mean to blame this conduct, it is proper in almoſt every view. Some deviations from it I have known ; and, in ſuch circumſtances, admired the candor and ſincerity of the female heart. In this ſituation, I ſuppoſe that the perſon who aſks is not indifferent to the lady, for on this part of the ſubject we are now talking. If ſhe has determined to reject her lover, nothing can excuſe the folly, the injuſtice, of not making an explicit declaration in the ſofteſt, but moſt determined language. The delicacy, the *real* delicacy, which for a period of time ſeems to ſhrink from a requeſt of this kind, though ſometimes affected, is frequently ſincere. The ſoftneſs of the female mind is not always equal to an inſtant deciſion ; and its timidity is terrified by the proſpect of the important change. But remember, Nancy, every virtue has its kindred vice. This proper, this juſtifiable delicacy may, when indulged too far, degenerate unto the moſt trifling procraſtination. It is not eaſy to fix its limits, becauſe they muſt vary with the circumſtances of each individual ; but I think a woman may know her own opinion, and that of her friends, in two, or at fartheſt three weeks. If the lover, in that time,

is

is not absolutely rejected, the woman's character will certainly suffer in his mind, and in the opinion of the world, if without any unforeseen circumstance, he be not at last accepted. In this case delay gives encouragement, and silence, in the common language, gives consent.

The struggle, I imagine, my dear Nancy, is now over. Your whole appearance wears an air of calmness and ease, which are never the characteristics of doubt, or of uncertainty. As your resolution seems to be formed on the most solid basis, it will, I hope, produce the sincerest happiness. You have no doubt of the affection of your lover: His is not a momentary passion; for it has been matured by reflection: It does not arise from the fancied lustre of general admiration; for it has not been your lot frequently to shine in the gay world. But regret not this imaginary happiness: If your humbler state has put you beyond its brilliancies, it has also secured you from its uneasinesses; if it has deprived you of its pleasures, it has saved you from its triflings and disgusts. You are not wholly unacquainted with it; but, if the general appearance of, and the occurrences in polished life, do not exhibit to your eyes, one of the most ridiculous insipid farces that ever was performed on a stage, either you must be deficient in understanding and feeling, or you must be dazzled by its show. To return, as you are now secure of the affection of the person who solicits your distinction, it must be your business not to lose it by a trifling, or to *fritter it away* by a capricious behaviour. It is an awkward phrase, but there is no other equally expressive. If your humour is variable as the accidents of life; if every trifle influences your disposi-

tion; and your lover must feel the effects of it in your behaviour, it is very probable that, with the usual facility, he will yield to the little blasts, rather than contend with them: He will sue for pardon, for imaginary faults; he will endeavour to restore the smile to your clouded brow, that smile in which the Loves and the Graces play; and, when he cannot remove the cause, he will obviate the effect. This is the scene of your sexes triumph; but remember, that, in every such pettish quarrel, you must lose a portion of his love; some atom of his esteem. The effects may not soon appear; and, like drops of water on a stone, a frequent succession may probably make no visible impression; yet, in both instances, a constant repetition will produce considerable effects. It is a principle deeply implanted, that we fly to what gives us pleasure, and avoid what produces different impressions. For a time, perhaps, these little frowardnesses may be endured; for a short period, they may even be admired; but you must soon expect very different effects. If love is not destroyed by these follies, it is much impaired; and the husband most commonly revenges the sufferings of the lover. But, at all events, remember that you sacrifice some portion of his regard; that you risk the polish of the diamond by your wanton experiments on its hardness; that you undermine the foundation, by examining its depth.

It is not uncommon, even after a fixed resolution, for young ladies, in your situation, to treat their lovers with an unreasonable coldness: This, Nancy, was what I meant by losing his affection by a trifling behaviour. That coldness is to stand for virtue; that reserve for a rigid delicacy;

delicacy ; and, by thus imitating the exterior of thefe valuable qualities, by carrying them to an unjuftifiable excefs, many of your fex vainly endeavour to affume the merit which their real prefence would confer juft with the fame fuccefs that the Roman poets hoped to rival Horace, by attempting to look as pale as he did. True virtue and true delicacy, my dear girl, conduct themfelves very differently. I do not fufpect your poffeffing them in their utmoft purity ; but I fear your being led away by unjuft, though delufive maxims ; by deceitful, though plaufible examples. Is it inconfiftent with the trueft delicacy to return the love of a worthy man, who folicits it in the moft honourable manner ; who wifhes to fhare with you, riches and poverty, honours and misfortunes ? Is it inconfiftent with the moft unfpotted virtue, to connect yourfelf with him by thofe ties which religion and your country's laws have appointed ? The queftions you fay are trifling ; I allow it, but fuch conduct is more fo. It is a greater difgrace to connect yourfelf with any man, without feeling that rational efteem which can make your duty pleafing, without that preference which can enable you to look at even poverty and misfortune with a fteady eye, when united with him : This, I fay, is a greater indelicacy, than owning either an efteem or a warmer paffion. If you admit his vifits, you either fubject yourfelf to the imputation of deceit, or a want of candour, when you endeavour to keep him ignorant of what, if he poffefs the leaft penetration, you are unable to conceal. I am no advocate for forward and indelicate confeffions : The modeft blufh, the irrefolute breaks in converfation, convey much more than " all the forms of ftudied eloquence," a word and a look will tell the interefting fecret ; and if he defires to know more, he does not deferve it.

Let your whole conduct then be rational, candid and difcreet ; treat him with a generous opennefs, conceal no part of your own fentiments, and attend to his with care ; attend to them, Nancy, for they muft be yours. If you cannot combat his prejudices, comply with them ; if you cannot correct his errors, refpect them, when they lead to no improper conduct, when they affect neither the principles of religion nor morality. From the firft moment that *you* fufpect either, from *that moment* defpife and reject him. The man who cannot be juft to his Creator, will not be fo to you ; he who can defpife the laws of either God or man, can be bound by no ties to you. It would be pollution, for a moment, to harbour his image in your bofom ; and every rational profpect of happinefs is at an end. You have then but one ftep, take it decidedly and refolutely, and never again meet or fpeak to him whatever temptation may be thrown in your way, however glittering the bait. There is another part of a man's character, which, though not defenfible, yet is not treated with equal harfhnefs ; I mean an acquaintance with the abandoned part of your own fex. I would guard you againft fuch a one, if it were not to condemn you to celibacy, for *very* few, I fear, are fo chafte as a delicate woman would require. We cannot now ftop to inquire into the fource of this depravity ; but I fear fome part of the blame would fall upon your own fex. I do not mean from the temptations which they difplay, or from the frailty, which weakens refiftance ; but from the

the inattention with which thefe vices are treated by modeft women, and from the facility with which thefe errors are forgiven. Do, not, however, run into the oppofite extreme. A woman, *outrageoufly* virtuous, is always fufpected ; and fhe who *rails* with acrimony againft the too eafy compliance of the yielding fair ones, endangers the reputation, if not of her own virtue, at leaft of her prudence. But though in the prefent ftate of fociety you muft unavoidably affociate with thofe whofe conduct is highly reprehenfible, and good manners may require you to treat them with attention, yet encourage no man as a lover, of whofe virtue you are not well affured. But this is from the fubject ; I was unwillingly drawn into it ; and though I would not feek, yet I need not avoid it.

While your fentiments are free and unreftrained, for I do not think that one of your's requires reftraint, while you attend to him with that refpect and deference which his fuperior advantages, and perhaps abilities, fhould command, yet you muft carefully watch both his actions and your own. I need not warn you againft indelicate liberties, for, if it were not for political motives, yet I have much reafon to believe that your delicacy would fhrink from improper attempts, and that your fenfibility, " tremblingly alive," would feel the wound, before you were actually hurt. But innocent liberties are a mark of confidence in her who admits them ; and what fo flattering as a well founded confidence ? But where, Nancy, fhall we draw the line ?

Alas ! the bounds between right and wrong are fo narrow, that this confidence has led to ruin, and has deftroyed, what it ought, what it fondly wifhed, to have cherifhed. Remember, that it may eafily go too far, and will lull every fentiment, but that of love, afleep : If this paffion is not a fubject, it will foon be a tyrant. Think then that you walk on a precipice, and, though you may be really fafe, within a foot of the " extreme verge," yet that a cafual flip, a momentary inattention, at that diftance, may be fatal. To be *fecure* you fhould be within the *poffibility* of danger. The conduct of your lover will depend much on his former life. To a man of loofe manners, a woman of virtue is above humanity ; fhe is an angel, which he adores at a diftance. Unufed to her delicate purity, he almoft forgets her fex in his admiration ; but from the moment fhe, by inadvertence, betrays it, from that moment, in *his* mind, fhe mingles with the common herd : He addreffes her with little apprehenfion, and treats her with little ceremony. On the contrary, a man of a more fober caft, who is anxious for a whole life of happinefs, neither rifes fo high in his veneration, nor finks into equal familiarity. In all circumftances he treats his miftrefs with attention and refpect, nor will he rifk for a momentary pleafure the calm ferenity of his future days. Such a man, my dear, fhould be your object, and fuch a one I hope you will obtain. It will then be your own fault if you are not happy.

ANECDOTE.

A Britifh Nobleman, who had not the character of being very courageous, one day afked a mifer, what pleafure he experienced in hoarding

hoarding up fo many guineas, and not making any ufe of them? " I find as many charms in them," replied the mifer," as you in carrying a fword."

For the MASSACHUSETTS MAGAZINE.

On the DOUBLE USE of INTERROGATIVE POINTS.

THE ufe of interrogative points, both at the beginning and end of interrogative fentences, appears to be countenanced by fome of our moft eminent typographers; and is even recommended in a fyftem of punctuation, lately publifhed in Bofton. As a friend to the cultivation of the ufeful arts, I cannot but regret that a practice, which ferves no other purpofe than to deform the page, fhould be countenanced under a falfe idea of its utility. I am fenfible that, in combatting this doctrine, I combat the opinion of the juftly celebrated Dr. Franklin; and, fuch is my veneration for his knowledge of the lefs as well as the greater branches of the arts and fciences, I fhould perhaps have blindly acquiefced in his opinion, had he not condefcended to favour us with his reafoning on the fubject. He tells us, in a letter to N. W. Efq. that, by placing the interrogative point at the end of the interrogative fentence, the reader is not apprized of the nature of the fentence, fo as to modulate his voice in a proper manner, till he comes to the clofe of the fentence, and is then, finding his miftake, under the neceffity of beginning the fentence again. This, if true, would indeed convince us of the propriety of placing the point at the beginning of the fentence rather than at the end; but it certainly does not prove the neceffity of the *double* ufe. But, upon examination, the advantage in either cafe will be found to be little more than imaginary.

The conftruction of interrogative fentences, with very few exceptions, is fuch as to inform the reader or hearer of their nature, without any particular marks or points; and this, almoft univerfally, by the arrangement of the very firft words in the fentence. For inftance: Has the man any friends? Is it true? Who was the informer? What elfe can be expected? Did you believe the report? Here either the verb or auxiliary is placed, contrary to the arrangement in affirmative fentences, *before* the noun or pronoun; or the words who and what ftand at the beginning of the fentences, either of which circumftances is fufficient to apprize the reader of the nature of the fentence.

But, granting that we depend altogether upon the point for our knowledge of the nature of the interrogative fentence, the point itfelf is fo prominent, as to be eafily difcovered at the diftance of three, four, or even ten lines on a common page. A proficient therefore in the art of reading rarely requires this additional affiftance; and an ordinary reader will never avail himfelf of it fo far, as to deviate from his habitual monotony.

In fhort, I cannot perceive any the leaft advantage, which can be derived from this practice. If, as is commonly the cafe, the interrogative fentence is fhort, the reader cannot but perceive the point, although

though placed at the end of the sentence, and may modulate his voice accordingly. If the sentence is long, still the point will be discovered, when the reader comes to the close, where, if at any part of the sentence, a different modulation is required. It is said, I am sensible, that interrogative sentences require, at the close, an elevation of the voice; and, from this supposition, I presume, the advantage which is to be derived from the information of the point at the beginning of the sentence, is predicated. But this is a rule, which furnishes more exceptions than examples. When the interrogative sentence begins with a word, which has itself an interrogative signification, the voice ought to fall in the same manner as at a period. For example : " Who hath wo ?" " Where was't thou, when I laid the foundations of the earth ?" " What shall a man give in exchange for his soul ?" " How many loaves have ye ?" " Which of the prophets have not your fathers persecuted ?" In these and such like instances, which undoubtedly compose by far the greater part of interrogative sentences, no good reader makes at the close, an ele-

vation of his voice. Indeed, the points, which are used in writing and printing, are not intended to direct the modulation of the voice. The infinite variety of modulation, which different sentences and the same sentences, in different connexions, require, renders the use of points, for this purpose, impracticable. The points mark the grammatical construction of sentences, and designate their nature, so far as to communicate to the reader the sense of their author, which, when gained, will naturally regulate the modulation of the voice.

The above observations equally apply to the double use of the notes of admiration, which, I hope, will likewise be discontinued. The frequent use of the Italic letter and the small capital, serves no other purpose, than to deform the page, and to destroy that effect, which, if sparingly used, they might occasionally produce. The fair Roman letter, without the diminutive Italic, and the deformity of points of interrogation and admiration, yoked together by an insignificant dash, exhibits, on a fine paper, a very inviting appearance to a reader of taste.

THE MEDDLER.

For the MASSACHUSETTS MAGAZINE.

The GLEANER. No. XXVI.

The deed of worth is register'd on high,
Own'd and approv'd in worlds beyond the sky—
Nor only so—we feel an answering glow,
Which but the virtuous action can bestow :
Nor these alone—an earnest oft is given,
Immediate good—the award of righteous Heaven.

THE author who leaves nothing to the imagination of his readers, is frequently accused of blameable arrogance, and it is often asserted that, puffed up by an overweening self conceit, he vainly supposes,

poſes, that the germe of fancy can flouriſh no where but in the ſoil of his own wonderful pericranium.—— Now, as the fact is, that I am anxiouſly ſolicitous to avoid every occaſion of offence, I ſhall, taking into conſideration the feelings of ſenſibility, and properly influenced, by an idea of the ingenuity which is its accompaniment, wave the deſcription of thoſe delightful ſenſations, which, in rapturous ſucceſſion, were the natural appendages of the introduction, of the father of Margaretta. The extatic fondneſs with which he hung upon the accents of his daughter ; the mingling pleaſures and regrets ; the big emotions which ſurpriſed his ſoul, as he traced each lovely feature ; thoſe well known features, which exhibited to his view, a beauteous tranſcript of thoſe that he had early learned to admire in the face of her departed mother. Mr. *Melworth* wore in his boſom a miniature of his lady ; it might have paſſed for an exact copy of Mrs. Hamilton. The exquiſite ſenſations with which he traced the kindred lineaments ; the glowing expreſſions of paternal tenderneſs, with which he folded the little William to his boſom ; the marked approbation, unequivocally demonſtrated toward every movement of the huſband of his Margaretta ; the manly and complacent regards that he beſtowed upon Miſs Clifford ; the ſweet incenſe of expanſive, and immeaſurable praiſe, that he addreſſed to me, ſtyling me the ſaviour, the benefactor, the genuine father of his poor orphan girl ; the elevated regards, ſhort only of adoration, which he devoted to my dear Mary ; thoſe charming effuſions, conſiſting in expreſſive looks, broken words, and unambiguous geſtures ; effuſions which were the ſpontane-

ous growth of uncommon felicity ; the reciprocity of exquiſite ſatisfaction which we abundantly inhaled ; all this, and whatever elſe the ſoul of ſenſibility can conceive, gladly do I refer to the glowing mind of the feeling ſentimentaliſt. Imagination, in its utmoſt latitude, I hereby inveſt with full ſcope. It is impoſſible to paint too high. Language is indeed inſufficient, and fancy, with its moſt vivid tints, can alone portray.

Nay, gentle reader, I take upon me to aſſert, that however elaborately thou mayſt finiſh thy picture, after thou haſt beſtowed upon it thy laſt touches, it may, after all, fall vaſtly ſhort of the original, and, right ſorry am I, that my powers are ſo circumſcribed, as to render it impoſſible for me to place it in its genuine luſtre before thee. But, finite efforts, being doomed to ſubmit to a neceſſity, the effects of which, it muſt ever be unavailing to lament ; we will, without further preamble, proceed in our narration. I would not have thee conceive, that I am ſo unreaſonable as to condemn thee to the drudgery of accounting for the ſudden appearance of Mr. Melworth ; nor can I conſent, that ſetting me down as a deſcendant of Merlin, thou ſhouldſt place in my hand the magic wand ; inveſt me with the powers of incantation, the gift of working miracles, or, of ſummoning " *ſpirits from the vaſtly deep.*" No, believe me, I am no conjurer, and the better to baniſh every idea of a ſupernatural interpoſition, I haſten to bring forward the promiſed facts. Imagine then, that the tumultuous and perturbed ſenſations of ungovernable tranſport, which were conſequent upon the late development, have ſubſided into that bland and pleaſing calm,

which

which is the refult of high complacency in the prefent, and the
moft agreeable anticipations of the
future ; or into that ftate of tranquillity, which muft always be confidered as a defirable fubftitute for
the hurricane of the paffions, whatever may be the magnitude of the
event which produced it. The
extreme of joy and forrow, originating commotions as deftructive
to the order of the mental fyftem,
as the uprooting ftorm to the apparent harmony of the natural
world. The mild and equal difpofition cannot but regard as a relief, the regular fucceffion of events.
Imagine that our happy circle is
retired to the little apartment facred to fentimental pleafures ; to
that apartment, upon which the
ftep of inconfiderate levity, or indifference, obtrudeth not. Margaretta is feated between her enraptured father, and that hufband,
who for her exemplary worth, experiences with every rifing hour,
augmenting admiration and new
efteem.—Mary, Serafina and myfelf, complete the group. Mr. Melworth, preffing the hand of Mrs.
Hamilton, thus commences his interefting communications.—" I obferved, my dear, the fweet blufh
that tinged thy lovely cheek, upon
my mentioning in terms of repre-
henfion, the name of Mrs. Arbuthnot ; but you muft allow for the
feelings of a defolated father. But
for her unforgiving and obdurate
fpirit, the probability is, that your
angelic mother would, at this delightful moment, have partook, and
doubled all thofe exquifitely charming fenfations, which fwell a parent's bofom, and which prefent fuch
an ample compenfation for every
evil. From the hour which bleffed
me with the hand of my Margaretta, fhe continued feduloufly intent

upon procuring a reconciliation
with her fifter, and the utter improb-
ability of obtaining her wifhes in
this refpect, embittered our moft
pleafurable moments. She continued to figh for the companion of
her youth, and her intenfe, and unavailing folicitude, vifibly impaired
her health. I flattered myfelf that
the period which gave thee, my
love, to her arms, would fupply
that void in her bofom, which, however ardent the attachment of your
fex to the man of their choice may
be, fuch is the delicacy of the female mind, a tender and refpectable *female friend* can alone fill.
Your mother, my dear, was early
left an orphan. Her fifter had for
a long period reigned fupreme in
her bofom. Fate prefented her
not a Mrs. Vigellius ; goodnefs fo
unexampled is not the growth of
every clime ; neither was a Serafina Clifford contained in the circle
of her connexions. Yet, as I had
hoped, the birth of her daughter
opened a refource of new, and exhauftlefs pleafure ; and when fhe
clafped her lovely infant to her
bofom, for a moment fhe forgot her
fifter. Yet memory, too faithful
to its office, officioufly prefented
the mirror.—" Dear implacable
Henrietta !" fhe exclaimed, " why
wilt thou ftand aloof ? why wilt
thou refufe to heighten the tranfports of this delicious moment ?
Thy prefence, thy fanction would,
indeed, add a completion to my
felicity which would mark me the
moft bleffed of women. The novelty, however, the foft endearments,
the thoufand namelefs perturba-
tions, and tender intereft of the
maternal character, were powerful
alleviations, and the tranquillity
of the mother was in a meafure reftored. Eighteen halcyon
months revolved, when fate, as if
envious

envious of our felicity, presented me with a prospect of obtaining great emolument, by engaging on board a ship bound for the East-Indies. I was flattered by the idea of obtaining for my Margaretta and her infant, an elegant independence, and that resolution which became the superstructure of a basis so proper and so deeply laid, could not be easily shaken. Margaretta, while she acknowledged the eligibility of my plan, shrunk from its execution. Her tenderly apprehensive bosom foreboded a thousand evils.—Yet the heroism of her character can never be too much admired. " Go, my Charles"—with emotions of tender and unutterable agony, she exclaimed—" since it must be so—go !—and may the upholding hand of heaven be in every event thy never failing support !—Repeatedly she sobbed out the convulsed, and agonizing adieu, while ingenious in inventions to retard my departure, she pressed me to her throbbing heart. Oh ! my love, in broken accents she whispered, if we meet again we shall then be happy. But alas ! alas ! she could not add. Yet still her clasped hands, and streaming eyes, continued to supplicate the protection of that God, on whom her firm reliance was invariably placed. I was inexpressibly moved. My soul was little less tempested ; yet the splendor of my prospects, my previous arrangements, my pledged honour, all urged me on ; and by one violent effort I tore myself from the most beloved of women. Our mutual sufferings, may be regarded as a prediction of the fatal event. It was decreed that we never more should meet ! Propitious gales attended the first part of our voyage, and I had began to anticipate the rich harvest that a

few painful seasons would enable me to lay at the feet of my heart's best treasure. We had already doubled the southern extremity of the great continent of Africa, commonly called the Cape of Good Hope, and shaping our course North East to the continent of India, we were proceeding with all dispatch. When, lo ! on a sudden, the scowling atmosphere gathered darkness ; dreadfully portentous the winds of heaven arose. Waves beat on waves frightfully tempested. The tumultuous ocean seemed to lash the contending skies. Louder and louder the destructive whirlwinds bellowed round. Hoarse thunders roared terrific peals succeeding peals. The heavens poured forth a deluge of rain, and the forked lightnings were all abroad. Surrounded on every side by the tremendous world of waters, assistance was impossible, no asylum presented. The seaman's art was in vain, and death, in its most shocking form, appeared inevitable. But to describe the horrors of our situation is beyond the reach of language. In the latitude in which we then were, there is a large ridge of rocks, they are pointed out in most of our sea charts ; but if our pilot was aware of them it was not in his power to avoid them, for accelerating that fate which, imagining that the ship might live many hours, I had not so speedily expected bilging instantly, upon one of those rocks ; a second stroke severed her in twain. The shrieks of the mariners were beyond expression shocking. How long they survived, or what efforts they made, I am not able to say, for seizing a part of a shattered raft, I committed myself to the care of that God, whose protection I had never ceased to invoke.—Floating

at

at the mercy of the winds and waves, I momently expected diffolution ; but what circumftances are beyond the reach of Omnipotence ? Suddenly the winds were hufhed, and I was driven upon a fmall uninhabited Ifland. My firft fenfations, it will not be doubted, fpontaneoufly iffued in the moft grateful orifons to the God of my life, who had thus gracioufly interpofed for my prefervation. But foon the image of my Margaretta, clothed in the habiliments of immeafurable wo, harrowed up my foul ; her forlorn and helplefs fituation—her unprotected infant !— My God ! madnefs was in the thought.—I was on the point of again plunging into that ocean from which I had fo recently efcaped, but the good hand of upholding Deity ftill prevented me, and was ftill my fhield. Gradually the heavens refumed a ferene afpect, my mind became aftonifhingly calm, and drying the only veftments which now remained to me upon a fun beat rock, whofe craggy fides, received the moft intenfe rays of that luminary, beneath the foliage of a fheltering tree I ftretched my weary limbs. Sleep foon fpread over me its downy mantle, and I obtained a temporary oblivion of thofe lacerating reflections, with which fucceeding hours, in dreadful order appalled my finking fpirit. Neceffity compelled me to fearch out the good, if any remained, which was yet within my grafp. At the falutary ftream I flacked my thirft, and the nutritious berry, zefted by hunger, afforded me a delicious repaft. By one foothing hope I was ftill buoyed up. I traced unequivocal veftiges of the human ftep. Ships I was pofitive had recently touched there. I might yet recognize my fellow man. I might

yet be borne to my native Ifle. Defpair, however, two often gained the afcendancy, and at fuch intervals, inexpreffible anguifh overwhelmed my foul. But it is impoffible to paint the unequalled calamities of his fituation, who is thus circumftanced. Even the glowing imagination of a Thomfon could only fketch them.—Yet, not a revolving hour but heard me, to the liftening echo repeat—

" Unhappy he ! who from the firft of joys,
" Society cut off, is left alone   [day
" Amid this world of death. Day after
" Sad on the jutting iminence he fits,
" And views the main that ever toils below ;
" Ships, dim difcover'd, dropping from the clouds ;
" At evening to the fetting fun he turns,
" A mournful eye, and down his *dying heart*
" Sinks hopelefs ; while the *wonted roar* is up
" And hifs continual through the tedious night.

But forever bleffed be the benignant Difpofer of events ! The term of my fufferings was cut fhort. It was the employment of my firft rational moment, after I had been thrown upon the ifland, to make, with a part of my clothing, a fignal of diftrefs. Upon a prominent angle, afcended a fmall acclivity, on the fummit of which ftood the tall trunk of a tree, that contending ftorms had ftripped of its branches. To this difrobed trunk, I contrived to faften the beacon of my diftrefs, and I confecrated it with many fupplications to him who was alone able to fave.

The morning of the fifth day after I had fo providentially efcaped the waves, broke divinely ferene. An amazing continuity was outftretched before me. With folded arms, and an aching heart, I contemplated

templated the extensive main. The frightful solitude, the awful stillness to which I was condemned, arose dreadfully terrific to my soul. I threw abroad my anxiously inquiring gaze ; a cloud seemed to gather at a distance. It is not a cloud. What can it be ? Swiftly it approaches. Great God ! is it possible !—Saviour of sinners, it is, indeed, the white sails of a heaven directed bark !—It is bending toward me !—Ah ! it recedes, and my bounding spirit dies within me !

Again, however, its altered course bore rapidly down upon my desolate abode. The insignia of calamity, reared not in vain its petitioning head. The necessary arrangements were made. The boat was manned. My heart leaped exulting ; it was too big for its prison. My tongue refused utterance, while, with that commiserating cordiality, which seamen know so well to practise, and which is a characteristic trait of their order, I was received on board the ship. To complete my joy, the captain and crew were English. The captain was a humane and venerable man ; more than threescore years he had numbered. A shower of tears relieved my bursting heart. I told my tale of wo, and he regarded me with even paternal goodness. Few know how to respect the unfortunate ; inestimable are the soothings of benevolence, to the children of adversity.

A tedious voyage was now to be performed, and although a proper sense of the divine interposition in my favour, forbid every murmur, yet a recurrence to those pangs which I well knew would lacerate the gentle bosom of her my soul held most dear, could not fail of pointing the keenest arrows of af-

fliction ! Ten long months, dating from the time of my departure, performed their tedious round, ere the white cliffs of Albion again met my longing gaze. With what extacy did I leap upon the strand. Lowly to the parent soil I bent my head ; with filial lips I kissed the kindred turf, and my bounding spirit, struggling with its mingling sensations, poured forth the rapt orisons of a shipwrecked, exiled, rescued, and restored man ! On the wings of speed I hasted to my native village ; to that village, which, I supposed contained my only treasure. But what became of me, when posting to the apartments of Margaretta, I found them occupied by strangers !—Yet, hope still whispered she had removed to some other abode. I hasted to the dwelling of a friend, from whom I learned the sum of my misfortunes. You are, my friends, acquainted with the feelings of the heart. Every feature in your expressive countenances, are vouchers of your sensibility—Why should I aim at delineation !

" When to the height of hopeless sorrow
   " wrought !
" The fainting spirit feels a pang of thought,
   " Which never painted in the hues of
      " speech,
" Lives at the soul, and mocks expression's
      " reach."

I drop the curtain over a train of succeeding ills ; sickness, loss of reason, comfortless calamities !

Mrs. Arbuthnot, when she accompanied her husband to Ireland, bore my child with her. My aged, widowed mother, gently remonstrated. My supposed death, and the demise of Margaretta, had centered her every remaining with in the little prattler. Mrs. Arbuthnot plead the dying injunctions, and
                              bequest

bequeſt of her ſiſter. This was de-
ciſive. The regulations ſuggeſted
by the everlaſtingly abſent, ſhould
be deemed inviolably ſacred, and
my mother with floods of unavailing tears ſubmitted. A few painful weeks devoted to heartfelt regret, had ſucceeded a ſeparation
judged unavoidable, when my unfortunate mother received a line
from Mrs. Arbuthnot, acquainting
her that the little Margaretta was
nu more. This proved a finiſhing
ſtroke. So many calamities, in ſuch
ſwift ſucceſſion, treading upon the
heels of each other, brought down
the gray hairs of my aged parent with ſorrow to the grave.
Could ſhe have been ſpared to have
witneſſed the returning footſteps of
the ſon of her youth, a gleam of
joy would have diffuſed its genial
and ſolacing influence over her parting ſpirit. But Heaven thought
not beſt, and ſhe cloſed a life, the
ſorrows of which had accumulated
with every added moment. What
could induce Mrs. Arbuthnot to
pen a miſrepreſentation, calculated
to pierce with ſo keen a ſhaft, the
boſom of an aged and ſorrow worn
ſufferer, I can only conjecture.
Probably ſhe might be influenced
by her plan of paſſing the child for
her own ; or, ſhe might imagine
that my mother, being inveſted with
the rights of a parent, would again
demand the child, ſhould the contingencies, peculiar to a ſoldier's life,
remove Capt. Arbuthnot, whom it
was well known ſhe determined to
follow, to a remote or foreign deftination ; and it may be preſumed
that ſhe made up the matter in her
own mind, by a conſideration that
if ſhe returned her neice to our village, the extreme age of my mother, would ſoon leave her deſtitute
of every natural guide. For me,
after a long and debilitating fever,

Vol. VI. E

obtaining a ſtate of convaleſcence ;
youth, and a conſtitution uncommonly good, ſoon completed my
reſtoration. The ſame intereſt which
had before placed me on board an
Eaſt India ſhip, procured me a ſecond employment. I made ſeveral
ſucceſsful voyages. I accumulated
riches, and, I at length ſaw myſelf
poſſeſſed of affluence. But alas !
tranquillity was not in the gift of
affluence. In the variety by which
I was ſurrounded my heart took
no intereſt, and it refuſed to acknowledge a ſecond attachment.
Yet I determined to regulate my
feelings by the dictates of fortitude,
and to bend my wayward ſpirit, to
a ſtate of acquieſcence, in the deſig-
nation of that God who ruleth in
the heavens. I became a citizen
of the world. I conſidered myſelf
born for the univerſal family, and,
for the emolument of my fellow
men, I induſtriouſly made the moſt
of every acquiſition. Under the
influence of this ſentiment I proceeded in the career of life, and if
my path produced not thoſe high
ſcented perfumes, of which the exquiſite ſucceſſion of domeſtic enjoyments is ſuſceptible, I was, notwithſtanding, ſo far favoured, as to
obtain a degree of compoſure.
Thus rolled on ſucceeding years,
until upon an uncommon fine night,
three months ſince, feeling no dif-
poſition to retire to my chamber,
I felt conſtrained to devote an
hour to a contemplative walk. After having ſtrolled ſome moments
upon the road ſide, I bent my ſteps
towards St. George's fields, and
when there, with folded arms, and
raiſed eyes, I paſſed and repaſſed,
experiencing an unuſual kind of perturbation. Methought that the ſhade
of my Margaretta accompanied my
ſteps. The ample heavens, the ſtarry luminaries, the full orbed moon,
the

the blue expanfe ; thefe all combined to image the beauteous form of her, on whom fond remembrance ftill regretting dwelt.

An affociation of ideas gave birth to a wifh, to pafs fome moments befide a fketch of thofe waters, on which, bidding an eternal adieu to the injured fufferer, I had heretofore cruelly embarked. With rapid movements toward Weftminfter bridge, I took my way, which, having reached, I defcended the fteps of the landing place, with an expedition for which I could not account. But no fooner had I put my foot upon the third ftair, than an unufual dafh of the waters of the Thames, for which the ftillnefs of the night rendered it impoffible to affign a reafon, ftill further accelerated my progrefs. I hafted forward, and was only in time to feize by his garments, an unfortunate man, who had plunged into the ftream, with the unwarrantable purpofe of putting a period to his exiftence. I remonftrated againft the atrocious audacity of the deed, that he had well near perpetrated, in terms expreffive of the horror which it infpired. For a time he preferved an indignant kind of filence, and when he deigned to utter himfelf, he breathed only expreffions of refentment, for what he termed my officious interpofition. It was manifeft that his reafon was difordered, and pity grew in my foul. I addreffed him in the language of commiferation, and he gradually became foftened and communicative. " Generous ftranger," he exclaimed, " I give thee no mark of confidence in the brief recital, which as an apology for my fuppofed rafhnefs, your apparent commiferation demands. To him, who is refolved on death, the difclofure of fecrets which effect only

himfelf, can be of little importance. Know then, that born to affluence, I was bred a gentleman. Know alfo, that purfuing my pleafures in a neighbouring kingdom, I faw and loved a beauteous woman. I wooed and won her. Her parents were no more ; but her brethren, her fifters, a numerous family, her fortune, her country, her religion, all thefe fhe forfook, and fled with me to our Albion coaft. Indifcretion and misfortunes have robbed me of every penny which I poffeffed. I have no means of obtaining the common neceffaries of life ; the few articles of which I have not yet difpofed, will not difcharge the debts already contracted. Thofe flatterers who bafked in the funfhine of my fortune, have now utterly forfaken me. My wife, my beloved wife, and her helplefs children, are reduced to the laft extremity. I have left no means unaffayed, by which I could prefume upon relief ; but every effort hath proved ineffectual, and I have now quitted my Almira, with an expreffed hope, for which, alas ! there is no foundation. She will expect me with the returning fun ; but fhe will no more behold me. I can no longer exift a witnefs of thofe ills, of which I have been the wretched caufe !" Need I add, that I was eager to fpeak, to this fon of forrow, the words of confolation ? Confidering myfelf as the banker of the unfortunate, his draught upon me was indifputable ; and the rays of night's fair emprefs, lent a light fufficiently ftrong, to evince the authenticity of its characters. I accompanied my new claimant, now incredulous, and now frantic with joy, to his dwelling. I had determined to keep guard the remainder of the night. We entered foftly. His little family had retired

tired to reſt. I inſiſted that he ſhould inſtantly ſpeak peace to his beloved. I inſiſted that he ſhould not reviſit the parlour, until the riſing ſun ſhould enable me to commence my propoſed arrangements. I will repoſe, ſaid I, in this eaſy chair; or here are books, with which I may amuſe myſelf. Awed by that tone of authority which I had aſſumed, with looks of aſtoniſhment, and the moſt profound obeiſance, he left me; and ſleep being beyond my graſp, I endeavoured to obtain ſufficient compoſure to amuſe myſelf by reading. I turned over the books; it would not do. A new and painful kind of agitation hurried my ſpirits; at length a parcel of magazines ſeized my attention. I glanced confuſedly upon the bundle. The Maſſachuſetts Magazine caught my eye, an American produćtion; curioſity was enliſted; I opened one and another; an irreſiſtible impulſe ſtill urged me on; the firſt page of the Magazine for March, 1792, arreſted my eye—" Bleſs me, cried Margaretta," you will recollećt, Sir, that you thus commenced the enchanting narrative. The appellation Margaretta vibrated intereſtingly upon my ear; it was the ſweet taliſman of a thouſand mingling ſenſations; no power on earth could have prevented my reading on. I accompanied you in your journey to South-Carolina, and I entered with you the city of Charleſton. The little Margaretta's tap at the door poſſeſſed a faſcinating power; the introdućtion of the pretty cherub penetrated my very ſoul; I waited impatiently for the iſſue; I attended at the bed of death; but, great and good God! what were my ſenſations when I learned from the lips of Mrs. Arbuthnot, the well known ſtory of my Margaretta's

ſufferings; when I learned that the dear pledge of our ſacred loves was yet alive! when I recognized her in the perſon of the little petitioner; when I became aſſured that ſhe had been received by ſuch protećtors! I ſhrieked aloud, wrung my hands, wept, laughed, proſtrated myſelf in adoration of a preſerving God; traverſed up and down the apartment, until at length impelled by perturbed anxiety, I was conſtrained to trace my daughter's wonderous fortune, through the various Magazines, which, until the cloſe of the month of November laſt, preſented themſelves in order before me. How did my full ſoul bleſs her godlike benefaćtors! During the connexion with Courtland, the moſt tumultuous agitations tempeſted my boſom; but the cataſtrophe, I conceived, gave her honoured guardians a title to almoſt divine honors. Again I became a prey to all thoſe agonizing fears, which can lacerate a father's heart. Even of Miſs Clifford I muſt confeſs that I was not a little ſuſpicious; my feelings againſt thee, my ſon, were replete with indignation, and I beſtowed upon thy ſuppoſed inconſtancy a parent's maledićtion. But November preſented the extatic ecclairciſſement. I ſaw that nothing was wanting, but what I poſſeſſed abundant ability to ſupply; and, in broken, and almoſt frantic ejaculations, I ſobbed out my gratitude. The dawn at length broke; memorable, ever memorable night! Never, may I never, be forgetful of the events which thou produced!

An early hour preſented the now not deſpairing Altamont. He led his Almira by the hand. I had cautioned him not to ſhock the delicacy of her feelings, by a recital of the extremity to which he had been precipitated, and he had been diſcrete

crete enough to follow my advice. He had simply informed her that heaven had sent him a friend, and this information had proved sufficient to excite the most lively emotions. Altamont began a speech, expressive of his gratitude, but I cut him short, by decisively pronouncing, that fate had ordained me eternally his debtor. My disordered countenance, and the energy of my manner, alarmed him, and he in his turn became doubtful of *my* reason. I gave him, however, a simple relation of facts. I held up the divine pages; had I not met thee; had I not consented to deliver to thee that dividend of our common father's interest, with which he has entrusted me for thy behoof, I had not met these blessed records; I had not received intelligence, which hath communicated to my soul immeasurable felicity. *Thus amply hath our God rewarded me for designing an act of common justice.*

Grateful tears of rapture, it will not be doubted that we mingled. Every thing was speedily adjusted, to the complete satisfaction of Altamont, and his Almira. With the first ship, I embarked for America. The name of Colonel Worthington, of Newhaven, was my clew; and I bore with me the heaven inspired Magazines. From Colonel Worthington I learned every necessary particular. I was told, my son, of your intended voyage, of the consequent anguish of my daughter's

soul. I bless God that I am in time to prevent its prosecution. Every individual shall receive his dues; that good young man, your *forbearing friend*, the benignant Seymour—Every one shall be happy!

Unwilling to leave the curiosity of the reader ungratified, during the tardy revolution of another month, I have felt myself necessitated to curtail the narrative of Mr. Melworth; many useful observations are omitted. The frequent interruption, breaks, and pauses, occasioned by the susceptibility of Mrs. Hamilton, and the agitation of her father; the unbounded and venerating gratitude of Edward; the combining admiration, and rapt felicity of our whole party; all this was in course, and to every thing of this sort, I must repeat, that the silently expressive touches of that vivid pencil, which is found in the glowing hand of fancy, can alone do justice.

Already our young people have resumed their elegant family seat. Miss Clifford is still the companion of Margaretta. Amelia Worthington is now a congratulating visitor at Hamilton place. Mr. Melworth is for the present a resident in that sweetly romantic mansion, and this very morning, the second day of July, one thousand seven hundred and ninety-four, witnessing the birth of a daughter to Margaretta, hath seemed to complete our family felicity.

ERRATA.—In p. 354, 1st col. 11th l. fr. b. after *amicable* insert *compromise* (omission in copy)—In p. 361, 2d c, l. 3d fr. t. for *qualify*, read *gratify*.

A N E C D O T E.

DR. JOHNSON, Dr. Goldsmith and others, were supping at a tavern in London. Dr. Ogilvie chose for the topick of his conversation, the praises of his native country. Among other things, he observed that Scotland had a great many noble wild prospects.

Dr.

Dr. Johnson replied—"I believe, Sir, you have a great many. Norway, too, has noble wild prospects; and Lapland is remarkable for prodigious noble wild prospects: But, Sir, let me tell you, the noblest prospect, which a Scotchman ever sees, is the high road that leads him to England."

To the EDITORS of the MASSACHUSETTS MAGAZINE.

GENTLEMEN,

The celebrity of Voltaire, whose writings unite morality with an exhaustless fund of genuine humour, will be a sufficient recommendation for the insertion of the following extract from his Philosophical Dictionary, in your entertaining Museum. A.

GLORY.

BEN-AL-BETIF, that worthy superior of the Dervises, one day said to them, Brethren, it is very fit that you should often use that sacred form of our Koran; *in the name of the most merciful God;* for God sheweth mercy, and you learn to practise it by the frequent repetition of the words, recommending a virtue without which there would be few people remaining on earth; but, brethren, far be it from you to imitate the presumption of those who are continually boasting that what they do is to the Glory of God. When a raw scholar maintains a thesis on the categories before some furred ignoramus of a president, he is sure to write in large characters at the head of his thesis, *Ek aliha abron dox, Ad majorem Dei gloriam:* So a devout Mussulman, having caused his faloon to be white washed, must have the like folly over his door; a Saka likewise carries water to promote God's glory.—This is a devout practice of a profane custom.

What would you say of a pitiful Chiaoux, who, when emptying our Sultan's close stool, should bawl out, To the greater glory of our invincible monarch? Now certainly the difference is greater between the Sultan and God, than between the pitiful Chiaoux and the sublime Sultan.

Ye poor earth worms, called *men,* what have you in common with the Glory of the Infinite Essence? Can he desire Glory? Can he receive any from you? Can he enjoy it? How long, ye two legged featherless animals, will you make God in your likeness? being yourselves vain and fond of glory, God must needs be so too! Were there several Gods, each of them would be desirous of the applause of his equals, and in that would consist the glory of a God. If infinite grandeur might be brought into a comparison with the extremity of meanness, such a God would be like king Alexander or Scander, who would enter the lists against kings only: But you, poor creatures, what glory can you give to God? Forbear any longer to profane his sacred name.

An Emperor, named Octavius Augustus, ordered no panegyrics to be made on him in the schools of Rome, that his name might not be debased. But you can neither debase nor exalt the Supreme Being—Prostrate yourselves and worship in silence.

Thus spoke Ben-al-betif, and the Dervises shouted, "Glory to God! well has Ben-al-betif spoken."

The

For the MASSACHUSETTS MAGAZINE.

The SENTIMENTALIST. No. II.

HENRY HARWOOD ! alas, with what mingled emotions of pity, pleafure, forrow, anxiety and hope, do I hear thy name mentioned ! What pleafing and what painful fcenes are recalled to my memory by the magic of the found ! I have feen thee bafking in the noon tide rays of magnificent profperity ; I have feen thee ftruggling to fhake off the wearifome load of life in the murkieft gloom of mifery's vale. I have feen the hand of thy munificence, of thy liberality, pouring forth the exuberance of bounty to cheer and comfort thy afflicted fellow mortals ; I have feen thee poor and diftreffed—wet and cold, in the fhattered cottage of penury, furrounded by wretches, eagerly waiting thy laft groan as the fignal to ftrip thy pallid corfe of its tattered clothing. I remember thy charity, " which covereth a multitude of fins," and the remembrance is pleafing to my heart ; I remember the agonies in which thou didft expire, and my foul is melted with pity for thy forrows, and thy pains.

I have feen thee bleffed by heaven with *an abundance of the good things of this* life. But thy company was chofen from among the gay and unthinking. Thy affociates were vicious, and they hurried thee into fcenes of diffipation, which debafed the natural dignity of thy mind and enfeebled the energy of thy virtues. Though much of thy eftate was given to make glad the widow's heart, to comfort the orphan and feed the poor with bread ; yet, how much, alas ! was wafted in unneceffary profufion, and fcattered abroad with criminal extravagance. *I think on thefe things, and am forrowful.*

I have feen thee fpending thy precious time in fcenes of riot and debauchery ; attending to the pampering of thy appetites and revelling in the luxuries of life. Sedulous to decorate thy body with coftly raiment, but inattentive to the improvement of thy mind or of thy heart. To drown the voice of confcience in the clamors of noify pleafure ; to eat and drink luxurioufly, and outvie thy companions in their fafhionable vices and follies, was to thee, *the thing needful. I think on thefe things*, and am anxious, Henry, concerning thy happinefs in that world where no impurity can enter.

Yet, *I hope.* Thou hadft much charity, and the bleffings of the poor are thine. For thee fhall ceafelefs oraifons arife to the throne of that God, whofe darling attributes are MERCY and LOVE. Thy faults were the faults of youth—they proceeded rather from an unthinking head than a depraved heart. Thy liberality was as unbounded as thy wifhes were benevolent, and thefe embraced in their regards the whole world of man. I think on thefe things, my friend, and hope comforts my foul.

I have thus anatomized Henry Harwood's character, for the good of the youth of the prefent day. It, upon infpection, will be found, neither an unnatural nor an uncommon one. View in it, all the principal traits, which diftinguifh the man of the world. Thoughtlefs, gay, extravagant and luxurious. But mark ! View in it features, which feldom adorn the *mere man of pleafure.* Benevolent and kind ; he waited not for the fight of an object in diftrefs to remind him of
his

his duty, but he fought out mifery in her moft fequeftered haunts, and converted the hovel of poverty into the cottage of contentment. Copy his virtue ! Shun his errors ! The one reduced him to wo and diftrefs, the other entitles him to a crown of glory. Think not I mean to jufti-fy the admiffion of foibles and faults into the heart, becaufe, in the fame bofom, a virtue has chofen to refide. No. Nor think 1 ef-teem it neceffary to eradicate eyery weed of vice from human nature, ere the rofe of virtue can bloom luxuriant. To be liable to err, is the lot of humanity, and who will prefume to feek for an immaculate character below ? L.

[*The following Oration, delivered on the day of PUBLIC COMMENCE-MENT, at Harvard Univerfity, we are happy to infert in our Magazine. The applaufe with which its delivery was received ; the intrinfic excel-lence of the performance, and a wifh to make our* Monthly Mufeum, *in reality, a repofitory of knowledge and ufeful entertainment, unite in an inducement to prefent it entire, to the patrons of our publication. Happy in this opportunity of affording a delicious mental repaft, to the patriotic litera-ry epicure, we have, to indulge his laudable appetite, deferred the exhibition of fome difhes of leffer flavour and importance, until our board requires them to fill up vacancies at fome future attic feftival.*]

For the MASSACHUSETTS MAGAZINE.

AN ORATION on ELOQUENCE,

Pronounced at the Anniverfary Commencement of Harvard Univerfity, in Cambridge, July 16th, 1794. By JOSEPH PERKINS, A.B.

THE excellence, utility, and importance of eloquence ; its origin, progrefs, and prefent ftate ; and its fuperior claim to the partic-ular attention of Columbia's free born fons, will exercife for a few moments the already exhaufted pa-tience of this learned, polite, and refpected affembly. Senfible, as the fpeaker is, that while he at-tempts to recommend a fubject, worthy the nobleft efforts of the ableft pens, his own defects will more ftrikingly evince the impor-tance of his theme, than any argu-ments which he can adduce ; though the well known difcernment of his hearers precludes the moft diftant hope of praife, yet their oft experi-enced liberality enfures a fafe re-treat from the terrors of unfeeling, cenforious criticifm.

Speech and reafon are the char-acteriftics, the glory, and the happi-nefs of man. Thefe are the pillars which fupport the fair fabric of el-oquence ; the foundation, upon which is erected the moft magnifi-cent edifice, that genius could de-fign or art conftruct. To cultivate eloquence, then, is to improve the nobleft faculties of our nature, the richeft talents, with which we are intrufted. A more convincing proof of the dignity and importance of our fubject need not, cannot be ad-vanced.

The benevolent defign and the beneficial effects of eloquence, e-vince its great fuperiority over ev-ery other art, which ever exercifed the ingenuity of man. To inftruct, to perfuade, to pleafe ; thefe are its objects. To fcatter the clouds of of ignorance and error from the atmosphere of reason; to remove the film of prejudice from the mental eye; and thus to irradiate the benighted mind with the cheering beams of truth, is at once the business and the glory of eloquence. To promote the innocent and refined pleasures of the fancy and intellect; to strip the monster vice of all his borrowed charms, and expose to view his native deformity; to display the resistless attractions of virtue; and, in one word, to rouse to action all the latent energies of man in the proper and ardent pursuit of the great end of his existence, is the orator's pleasing, benevolent, sublime employment.

Nor let it be objected, that eloquence sometimes impedes the course of justice, and screens the guilty from the punishment due to their crimes. Is there any thing, which is not obnoxious to abuse? Even the peaceful religion of the Prince of Peace has been made the unwilling instrument of the greatest calamities ever experienced by man. The greater the benefits which naturally result from any thing, the more pernicious are its effects, when diverted from its proper course. This objection to eloquence is therefore its highest eulogium. The orator does not succeed, as some would insinuate, by dazzling the eye of reason with the illusive glare of his rhetorical art, nor, by silencing her still small voice in the thunder of his declamation; for to her impartial tribunal he refers the truth and propriety of whatever he asserts or proposes. After fairly convincing the understanding, he may, without the imputation of disingenuousness, proceed to address the fancy and passions. In this way he will more effectually transfuse into his hearers his own sentiments, and make every spring in the human machine co-operate in the production of the desired effect.

The astonishing powers of eloquence are well known, at least to those who are conversant in ancient history. Like a resistless torrent it bears down every obstacle, and turns even the current of opposing ignorance and prejudice into the desired channel of active and zealous compliance. It is indisputably the most potent art within the compass of human acquirement. An Alexander and a Cesar could conquer a world; but to overcome the passions, to subdue the wills, and to command at pleasure the inclinations of men, can be effected only by the all powerful charm of enrapturing eloquence.

Having just hinted at the excellence, utility and importance of eloquence, we are next to endeavour to mark its origin, and briefly trace its progress thence to the present period.

In the earliest ages of the world the language of men, like that of other animals, was just sufficient to enable them to warn each other of danger and to make known their mutual wants. By gradual improvements in knowledge, and by the invention and cultivation of arts, both useful and ornamental, the powers of the human mind became better known, and language, the great vehicle of thought, and the soul of society, began to be esteemed an object deserving attention. The art of writing was invented, the stock of words enlarged, language reduced to rules, and found possessed of powers before unknown. Though it be more than probable, that oratory was known and cultivated in some degree in those eastern nations, where science firft began to dawn upon the world, yet it was not till Greece became civilized and formed into diftinct governments, that it made its appearance in its native, peerlefs majefty. Here we may fix the era of eloquence ; here was its morn, here its meridian too, for here it fhone with fplendor never fince furpaffed.

It is a common and a juft remark, that eloquence can flourifh only in the foil of liberty. Athens was a republic, where the affairs of ftate were tranfacted in the affembly of the whole people. This afforded to eloquence a field too fertile to remain long uncultivated by the ingenious Athenians. Orators foon made their appearance, who did honour to language, to Greece, to humanity. But though the names of many have been tranfmitted to us, whofe genius and eloquence demand our veneration and applaufe ; yet, like ftars, when the fun appears, they are loft in the fuperior blaze of the divine Demofthenes. His ftory is well known. Though endowed with an excellent genius, he encountered almoft infuperable obftacles in his way to eloquence from fome natural defects in his perfon and delivery. He perfevered till he had conquered them all, animated by an invincible ambition to fhine an orator. Never, perhaps, were difplayed fuch indefatigable induftry, fuch obftinate perfeverance, fuch unremitting attention to the grand object of purfuit. His efforts were crowned with that fuccefs, which is the neceffary confequence of fo much application and care. Though the beginning of his career was peculiarly unpromifing, for he was even hiffed from the ftage on his firft public appearance, he afterwards became fo powerful an orator, that

he ruled even the fickle Athenians almoft as he pleafed. His example affords the greateft encouragement to ftudents in eloquence, as it proves, that by art, almoft in defiance of nature, a man may attain fuch excellence in oratory, as fhall ftamp his name with the feal of immortality. Demofthenes and the liberty of Greece together expired; and from this period we hear very little more of Grecian eloquence.

Let us now direct our attention to that other garden of eloquence, the Roman commonwealth. Here, as in Greece, a free government opened the lifts to fuch, as wifhed to difpute the palm in oratory. Numbers advance, and contend manfully for the prize. But their glory is foon to fade, for Tully appears ; Tully, another name for eloquence itfelf. It is needlefs to enlarge on his character as an orator. Suffice it to fay, that if we ranfack the hiftories of the world to find a rival for Demofthenes, Cicero alone can be found capable of fupporting a claim to that diftinguifhed honor. The freedom of Rome and the life of Cicero together fell a facrifice to cruelty and lawlefs ambition. Eloquence, as if unwilling to furvive her favourite fon, feems with him to have taken her flight from this guilty world. For though France may boaft her orators, and England ftill dwell with rapture on the name of Pitt, and even America put in her claim for a fcrap of praife, the eloquence of Demofthenes and Cicero, like the furprifing fire of Callinicus, feems to be one of thofe arts, which were once known, but which are now forever loft to mankind.

The caufe of the great inferiority of modern eloquence deferves a ferious inquiry. Can we plead the imperfections of the living languages ?

guages ? The noblest productions of Greece and Rome do not perhaps surpass some, which our native tongue can boast. Shall we urge our want of genius ? Scarcely a branch of curious, useful or ornamental learning can be named, in which the moderns do not at least equal these supposed matchless ancients. Is our situation unfavourable ? When did Greece or Rome present a fairer field for eloquence, than that which now invites the culture of the enlightened citizens of Columbia ? We live in a republic, the orator's natal soil ; we enjoy as much liberty, as is consistent with the nature of man ; we possess as a nation all the advantages, which climate, soil and situation can bestow ; and nothing but *real merit* is here required as a qualification for the most dignified offices of state. Never had eloquence more ample scope. Why then does it not flourish ? We blush to assign the cause. It is shameful neglect, it is a want of ambition alone, which suffers this fertile field to lie uncultivated. And shall we rest satisfied with only admiring, or at most with following at an awful distance the most illustrious orators of Greece and Rome, while our mechanics, our warriors, our patriots, our statesmen and our philosophers, put all antiquity to the blush ? Shall every other useful and ornamental art speed swiftly towards perfection, while oratory, that most sublime of all arts, that art, which could render one man more dreadful to a tyrant, than hostile fleets and armies, is almost forgotton ? It must not, cannot be. That refinement of taste, that laudable ambition to excel in every thing that does honour, to humanity, which distinguishes the Americans, and their free and popular government, are so many

springs, which, though not instantaneous in their operation, cannot fail in time to raise Columbian eloquence "above all Greek, above all Roman fame."

With pleasure we descry the dawning of that bright day of eloquence, which we have anticipated. The grand council of our nation has already evinced, that in this respect, as in all others, our republic acknowledges no existing superior. And we trust, that, as our sacred teachers make it their constant endeavour to imitate the great learning, the exemplary virtue, the exalted piety, and the extensive usefulness, of the great apostle of the gentiles ; they will not fail to resemble him in that commanding, that heavenly eloquence, which made an avaricious, an unbelieving Felix tremble.

Too little has this most important branch of public education been hitherto regarded. But we hope, that ere long our alma mater and our rising country will realize in their largest extent the long anticipated benefits of a *Boylston's* munificence. May eloquence be fostered in this nursery of literature and extend its benign influence to every department of society, till time and Harvard shall together expire. May Columbia always afford more than one Demosthenes, to support the sacred cause of freedom, and to thunder terror in the ears of every transatlantic Philip. May more than Ciceronian eloquence be ever ready, to plead for injured innocence and suffering virtue, and to carry confusion and despair to the heart of every infamous aspiring Anthony, of every restless Catilinarian demagogue. Rich as our country is of her own fund, and now adorned with the brightest gem in the literary cabinet of the
old

old world by the welcome arrival of a *Priestley* upon our shores from the ignorance, the bigotry, the barbarity, the slavery, and the slaughters of Europe ; we doubt not, that she will ere long be as much superior to all the nations of the earth in every useful art and science, in virtue and in happiness, as she now is in her constitution of government, the equity of her laws, the wisdom of her rulers, and the good sense of her citizens. Warned by the fate of her predecessors, may she escape those quick sands of vice, which have ever proved the bane of empire. May her glory and her felicity increase with each revolving year, till the last trumph shall announce the catastrophe of nature, and time shall immerge in the ocean of eternity.

On this auspicious anniversary, when we are assembled to celebrate the birth day of our university, those benevolent and illustrious characters, who first planted the tree of science on this western shore, and who have since added new vigour to its root by copious irrigations from the fountain of their liberality, demand that tribute of respect and applause, which the warmest gratitude can inspire. While the name of *Harvard* is already known almost as far as his benevolence extended, his memory, like his bounty, shall blossom and bear fruit to the remotest period of time. When with a melancholy pleasure we recognise the spot, which once supported the princely munificence of a *Stoughton*, we are induced to indulge a hope, that a new and much wanted edifice will soon be graced with his revered name. *Hollis*, whose philanthropy, not confined to the isle which gave him birth, crossed the wide Atlantic and showered its

many blessings on our alma mater, shall live in the mouths and in the hearts of every future age. The name of *Hancock* is doubly dear to every grateful American. Can that name perish, which has been twice stamped on all those united virtues, which fall to the share of imperfect humanity ? The liberality of an *Alford*, a *Boylston*, a *Hearsey*, a *Hubbard*, an *Erving*, and a *Cumings*, will rank those illustrious characters among the great benefactors of mankind. While freedom, science, literature, and virtue, drop a tear on the urn of their votary, their ornament, and their support, every future generation " shall rise up and call a *Bowdoin* blessed."

From the gentler sex we behold a *Derby* and a *Holden* rising superior to those illiberal prejudices, which for a long time had almost excluded the fairest part of nature's works from the means of mental improvement, and with a dignity peculiar to great minds, overcoming evil with good by generous donations to our University. While their liberality reflects the highest honor on themselves and claims our warmest gratitude, it at the same time conveys a severe reproof to our too selfish sex. Was female education so long neglected because it was supposed unnecessary ? It ought however to be remembered, that the richest diamond cannot be perfect without the assisting polish of art. Was the fair sex imagined incapable of improvement ? What female genius can achieve, let a *Philenia*, and a *Warren* to remotest time declare.

May the worthy example of those, whose names have been mentioned, and of others, whom we cannot now particularize, prove an effectual stimulus to all, whose situation

uation and ability render it their duty and their privilege, " *to go and do likewise.*"

This learned and brilliant affembly will be pleafed to accept thofe grateful acknowledgments, which their condefcending goodnefs demands. In the exuberance of their humanity they have extended not only their indulgence but even their applaufe to thofe efforts of youthful inexperience, which advance no other claim to their approbation, than the moft ardent wifhes to deferve it. And while the lovely daughters of Columbia deign to grace with their prefence this annual folemnity, and to confer even on imperfections the richeft rewards of genius, *their approving fmiles,* fain would we raife our feeble voice to lifp their praife. But we will not, we dare not profane their facred merits by attempting the impoffible tafk of doing juftice to their worth. We can only add with equal fimplicity and confidence, that while nature, virtue, wit, and beauty, retain a charm, the matchlefs fair of this our weftern world will command the admiration of every eye, the love and homage of every heart.

While gratitude to our literary fathers would prompt an effort to exprefs to them our prefent fenfations, delicacy and inability forbid the prefumptuous attempt. We muft therefore leave to more expreffive filence to paint in proper colours thofe feelings of our hearts, which the moft perfect language could at beft but faintly adumbrate. We would only offer one fervent wifh, that their ufefulnefs may be commenfurate with their erudition, and their happinefs coextenfive with their benevolence, till heaven fhall claim its own, and crown their virtues with immortal felicity.

My affectionate Claffmates,

The parting moment has arrived. This day diffolves our claffic connexion. We now ftand on the margin of life's boifterous ocean, ready to launch forth and explore the untried deep. What a flood of diftracting ideas rufhes at once on the mind ! The memory adds poignancy to our otherwife too painful fenfations, by recalling all thofe pleafing fcenes, which we have together witneffed, and which, alas ! are now no more. On the other hand, new objects are opening to our view, which employ at once our hopes and our fears.

" The wide, the unbounded profpect lies before us ;

" But fhadows, clouds, and darknefs, reft upon it."

How fleet are the pinions of time ! Four years, which in anticipation feemed almoft an age, have imperceptibly wafted us to the verge of our collegiate exiftence, and we are now called to pronounce a fad, and perhaps a laft, ADIEU !

Let us, ere we part, devote one moment to the calls of bleeding friendfhip ; let us give vent to one fincere though unavailing figh for the untimely fate of a worthy claffmate. *Jacobs,* our once efteemed *Jacobs,* like a fair expanding flower, cropt by the ruthlefs hand of death, now fleeps in the filent manfion of the tomb ! While we love, while we revere his memory and drop a tear on his urn, let us emulate his many virtues, and like him we fhall be able to meet the grim meffenger, in our turn, with a fmile, which will diveft him of all his terrors, and to hail him as our welcome convoy to the realms of uninterrupted and unending blifs.

May our mutual friendfhip, which has been generated by four

years

years familiar converse, and which some trifling jars and momentary misunderstandings have but the more strongly cemented, notwithstanding our necessary separation, remain forever firm and inviolate. May your success in all your future employments be ever equal to your superior merits ; may your lives be useful to the world, happy and honourable to yourselves; may your exit be peaceful and glorious ; may your memory live, till time itself shall die ; and may your felicity hereafter be boundless as immensity and endless as eternity.

CLAUDINE: *A Swiss Tale.*

[From the French of M. de FLORIAN.]

HAPPENING in the month of July, 1788, to be at Ferney, which ever since the death of Voltaire, has resembled one of those deserted castles which were formerly inhabited by genii, I resolved to pay a visit to the famous glaciers of Savoy. A friend, an inhabitant of Geneva, had the goodness to accompany me. In order to suit the present taste, it would be necessary that I should adopt that style, exalted, sublime, unintelligible to the profane, which a sentimental traveller, after he has advanced two leagues on his journey, cannot possibly do without : I must speak of nothing but my feeling, my susceptibilities, and my extatic sensations ; but I must confess that those phrases, although now so common, still found strange to my ears. I have seen Mont Blanc, the Frozen sea, and the Source of the Averon. I long contemplated in silence those dreadful rocks, covered with hoar frost ; those points of ice which pierce the clouds ; that large river which is called a sea, arrested in the midst of its course, whose solid billows appear as if still in agitation ; that immense vault formed by the accumulated snows of so many ages, from whence there issues a foaming torrent, forcing in its course huge blocks of ice over the rocky precipices. The whole scene impressed on my mind a mingled sensation of terror and melancholy : Methought I beheld the horrid scene of Nature, without a sun, abandoned to the fury of the god of tempests.

Oh my good friend Gesner, you sang the shady woods, the verdant fields, the limpid streams ; but shepherds and rural swains were never wanting to inculcate lessons of love, of piety, or of beneficence. Reading you, the pleased eye runs over the landscape which you have described ; and the mind, still more delighted, is ameliorated by useful precepts, and enjoys a delicious calm.

Such were the ideas that employed my mind while descending from Montanverd on my return from the frozen sea. After two hours of a painful journey, I arrived at the fountain where I had rested in the morning. There I again wished to repose myself ; for though I am no admirer of torrents, I am very fond of fountains ; besides I was extremely fatigued. I entreated my brave and honest guide, Francis Paccard, to sit down by me, and we began an excellent conversation concerning the manners, the character, and the mode of living of the inhabitants of Chamouny. I was pleased with the good Paccard's account of those simple manners about which it is so pleasing to converse, were it only to regret them, when a beautiful girl came and offered me a basket of cherries. I took them, and paid her for them. As soon as she was gone, Paccard said to me, laughing, " About ten years ago, in this very spot where we now are, it cost one of our young peasants very dear for coming to offer a basket of fruit to a traveller." I begged of Paccard to relate the story. " It is somewhat long," said he ; " I have learned the most minute circumstances of it from the curate of Salenches, who himself bore a considerable part in it." I pressed Paccard to relate to me what he had heard from the curate of Salenches ; and being both seated on the ground, leaning our backs against two ash trees, and eating our cherries, Paccard thus began his tale :

THE TALE.

" YOU must know, Sir, that our valley of Chamouny, ten years ago, was not so celebrated as it is now a days. Travellers did not then come to give us their gold for the sake of looking at frozen snow, and picking up our pebbles. We were poor, ignorant of evil, and our wives and daughters, employed in the cares of the family, were still more ignorant than ourselves. I mention this that you may have some charity for the fault of Claudine. The poor child was so simple, that it was an easy matter to deceive her.

" Claudine was the daughter of old Simon, a labourer at Pricure *. This Simon, whom I knew well, for he has only been dead two years, was the Syndic of our parish. All the country respected him for his probity, but his character was naturally severe ; he pardoned nothing to himself, and very little to others ; he was equally esteemed and feared. If any of our neighbours had quarrelled with his wife, or drank a glass too much on a holiday, he would not have dared to speak to Simon the whole week. When he passed, even the children stopped their noise ; they took off their hats, and never returned to their amusements till M. Simon was at a distance.

" Simon had remained a widower since the death of Madelene his wife, who had left him two daughters. Nanette, the eldest, was well enough ; but Claudine, the youngest, was an angel of beauty. Her handsome round countenance—her black eyes, full of animation—her thick eye brows—her little mouth, the very picture of that cherry—her appearance of innocence and gaiety, made all the young men of our village, her admirers ; and when on a Sunday she joined the dance, with a vest of blue cloth closely fitted to her fine shape, her straw hat ornamented with ribbons, and her little cap, which could hardly contain her beautiful hair, it was who should have the honour to dance with Claudine.

" Claudine was only fourteen ; her sister Nanette, was nineteen, and commonly remained at home to look after the affairs of the family. Claudine, as being the youngest, took care of the flock which grazed on Montanverd. She carried with her her dinner and her distaff, and passed the day in singing, in spinning or chatting with the other shepherdesses. In the evening she came home to Simon, who read some portion of the Bible to his daughters, gave them his blessing,

* The principal village of the valley of Chamouny.

FOR J U L Y, 1794.

blessing, and then all the family went to bed.

" About that time strangers began to visit our glaciers. A young Englishman of the name of Belton, the son of a rich merchant of London, in passing through Geneva to go to Italy, had the curiosity to make the tour of Chamouny. He stopped at Madame de Couteran's,* and the next day, at four o'clock in the morning, he ascended Montanverd to see the frozen sea, conducted by my brother Michael, who is now deacon of the guides. He returned about eleven, and rested himself, as we do, by the side of this fountain, when Claudine, who tended her sheep just by, came to offer the fruit and milk she had for her dinner. The Englishman thanked her, looked at her very attentively, and offered her five or six guineas, which Claudine refused ; but poor Claudine did not refuse to take Mr. Belton to see her flock, which she had left among these lofty trees. He desired the guide to wait for him, and departed with Claudine. He was absent for two long hours. As to the sequel of their conversation, I cannot indeed repeat it to you, as nobody heard it. It is sufficient to know that Mr. Belton set out the same evening, and that Claudine on her return home to her father, appeared pensive and melancholy, and had on her finger a beautiful emerald which the Englishman had given her. Her sister asked her where she got that ring : Claudine answered she had found it. Simon, with a discontented air, took the ring, and carried it to Madame de Couteran, in order to discover the person who had lost it. No traveller ever claimed it. Mr. Belton was already far off, and Claudine, to

whom the emerald was restored, became every day more melancholy.

" Five or six months thus passed away. Claudine, who every evening returned with reddened eyes, at length resolved to confide in her sister Nanette. She confessed that the day she met Mr. Belton on Montanverd, Mr. Belton had told her that he was in love with her—that he meant to settle at Chamouny, never more to leave it, and to marry her. " I believed it," added Claudine, " for he swore it to me more than a hundred times. He said, that business obliged him to return to Geneva ; but that in a fortnight he would again be here— that he would buy a house, and that our marriage should take place immediately. He sat down beside me, called me his wife, and gave me this beautiful ring as a token of our marriage. I dare not tell you any more, my sister, but I have many fears ; I am very ill ; I weep all day ; in vain do I fix my eyes on the road to Geneva, there is no appearance of Mr. Belton !"

" Nanette, who was just married, pressed poor Claudine with questions ; at length, after many tears, she learned that the Englishman had basely betrayed this simple and unhappy girl, and that Claudine was with child.

" What was to be done ! How was it possible to announce this misfortune to the terrible M. Simon ? To conceal it from him was impossible. The good Nanette did not augment the despair of her sister by useless reproaches : She even endeavoured to console her by expressing hopes of a pardon which she knew would not be obtained. After long consideration, Nanette, with her consent, went to find our good curate, and confided to him the whole
secret—

* The well known name of the mistress of the most ancient inn at Chamouny.

secret—begged him to mention it to her father—to endeavour to appease his wrath, and try to save the honour, or at least the life, of the unhappy victim of deceit. Our curate was much hurt at the news; he however, undertook the task, and repaired to the house of Simon at the time he was sure Claudine would be upon Montanverd.

"Simon was as usual reading the Old Testament. Our good curate sat down by him, and began to talk of the beautiful stories which are contained in that divine book; he dwelt particularly on that of Joseph when he pardons his brethren—on that of the great king David when he pardons his son Absalom, and many others I do not know, but are well known to the curate. Simon was of the same opinion. The curate said, that God had given us those examples of mercy, that we in like manner, being compassionate to others, might at the last day, expect to find mercy from the Father of all. All this was said in a much better manner than I can tell it to you; but you may easily perceive that our curate endeavoured to prepare the old man for the reception of his bad news. He was long of comprehending him—at last he did, and starting up, pale, and trembling with rage, he seized the musket with which he used to hunt the chamois, and was rushing forth to kill his daughter. The curate threw himself upon him, and disarmed him; and by rousing his attention to the duties of a Christian, by lamenting his misfortunes, and sharing in his grief, he at length prevailed so far, that old Simon, whose eyes had been hitherto dry, his lips pale, and his whole frame convulsed, sunk back into his chair, covered his face with his two hands, and burst into tears.

"The curate allowed him to weep for some time without saying a word; at length he wished to consult with him relative to the measures it was necessary to take, in order to save the honour of Claudine;—but Simon interrupted him; "Master curate," said he, "it is impossible to save that which is lost—every means we could take would render us more culpable, by obliging us to tell lies. The unhappy wretch must no longer remain here; she would be the scandal of us all, and the punishment of her father! let her be gone, master curate; let her live, since infamy can live, but let me die far distant from her: Let her depart this very day—she must leave this country, and never let her again present herself before my gray hairs, which she has dishonoured."

"The curate tried to soften Simon, but his efforts were in vain. Simon repeated the positive order for the departure of Claudine. Our good old curate was going away in sadness, when the old man ran after him, brought him back into his apartment, and shut the door; then putting into his hand an old purse of leather, containing fifty crowns, "Master curate," said he, "this wretch will be in want of every thing.—Give her these fifty crowns, not as from me, but as a charity from yourself—tell her that it is the goods of the poor, which compassion induces you to bestow on vice; and if you could write to any one in her favour, or give her a letter of recommendation—I know your goodness, and I neither wish to hear, or to speak any more about her."

"The curate answered him by a squeeze of the hand, then ran to meet Nanette, who was waiting for him in the street, more dead than alive.

alive. " Go inftantly," faid he, " and pack up all your fifter's clothes, and bring them to my houfe." She obeyed with tears in her eyes, being but too fure of what had happened, and put into Claudine's bundle the little money fhe was miftrefs of. She then returned to the curate, who related to her the converfation he had with Simon, and gave her a long letter for the curate of Salenches, and faid to her, " My dear child, you muft this very day conduct your fifter to Salenches ; give her this purfe, and this letter to my good brother. Accompany her to the village and then return to your father, who has occafion for your wifdom and virtue to leffen the chagrin produced by the conduct of your fifter." Nanette, fighing, went in queft of her fifter on Montanverd. She found Claudine ftretched weeping on the ground ;—but when fhe heard that her departure muft be immediate, fhe fcreamed, and tore her hair, repeating continually, " I am banifhed with my father's curfe ! Kill me ! my fifter, kill me ! or I will throw myfelf over this precipice." Gradually fhe became more calm, by promifing that things might ftill be made up. At length Claudine refolved to fet out, and at nightfall they took the road to Salenches, avoiding our village, where, notwithftanding the darknefs, poor Claudine would have thought that every one faw her crime painted in her face.

" It was a melancholy journey, as you may eafily imagine, nor did they arrive till break of day. Nanette took her leave of Claudine before they entered the village, and, after preffing her a long while to her bofom, left her, being nearly as miferable as her unhappy fifter.

" As foon as Claudine found herfelf alone, all her courage deferted her ; fhe hid herfelf in the mountain, and paffed the whole day without taking any nourifhment ; but when the night drew on, her fears forced her towards the village, where fhe inquired for the houfe of the curate, and knocked foftly at the door, which was opened by an old houfekeeper.

" Claudine faid fhe came from M. the curate of Prieure. The houfekeeper led her directly to her mafter, who was then alone, eating his fupper by the corner of his fire. Without uttering a word, or lifting her eyes, Claudine, with a trembling hand delivered the letter, and whilft the curate drew near the light in order to read it, the poor girl covered her face with her hands, and dropped on her knees near the door. The curate of Salenches is a good and a worthy man, and is refpected as a parent by his whole parifh. When he had finifhed the letter, and turning his head faw this young girl on her knees, and bathed with tears, he alfo wept. He raifed her, praifed the fincerity of her repentance, gave her hopes of a pardon for a fault that had coft her fo many tears, and obliged her to eat in fpite of her refufal, and calling his governefs, defired her to prepare a bed for Claudine.

(To be continued.)

The R E P O S I T O R Y. No. XXII.

October, 1775.

IT is moft true—woes do indeed clufter woes. While the tear is yet wet upon my cheek for a beauteous fifter, I am called to mourn the

the exit of a friend, whose meliorated worth, was of many years the rich and luxuriant growth. Yes, she too is gone—death hath closed the scene, and from my tearful view, my dear Elmira, hath forever fled! How long did I indulge hope; how listen to the flattering deluder! Of the investitures of this phantom, even the fatal predictions of the physicians could not despoil me, and my ardent and trembling soul exclaimed, she must, she will be restored to the fervid wishes of her supplicating friends. But these pleasing illusions are now dissipated; imagination can no more embody them. Her anointed spirit hath indeed escaped, and the palm of victory is already her's. Yes, it is too true: Never again shall these eyes behold thee, my almost faultless friend. How steady was thy soul, how affectionate thy bosom, and how warm thy regards!—By every tie of tender friendship thou wert mine, and the same blood which flowed in our veins, was distinguished but as the sanction for our fond attachment. In thy bosom, with unbroken confidence, I could repose my every thought, the inmost wishes

of my soul. Retired with thee, in the saloon of amity, my heart was disrobed before thee. Dear, sacred haunts, may my feet no more revisit them, since their beloved mistress hath taken her flight from those once peaceful abodes; from those scenes of past pleasure, let me still continue forever estranged. Sweet and delicately susceptible sufferer, few were the white hours of thy life;—but thou art now at rest in the bosom of thy God. How serene were her parting moments, how perfect the resignation of her soul, and how strong her affiance in the Redeemer! Anxiously I watched around her bed of death, industriously turning my eyes from every fatal symptom; but the agonies of dissolving nature commenced; they were terrible to view; the severing angel cut the thread of mortality; her guardian spirit received my friend, while with despairing ken I in vain endeavoured to explore her trackless way. Alas! alas! what a despoiler this October, 1775! How hath it broken in upon, and rifled my hoard of joys!

CONSTANTIA.

For the MASSACHUSETTS MAGAZINE.
The MEMORIALIST. No. III.

"KNOWLEDGE, says an ingenious author, is as pleasant to the understanding as light to the eyes." The excellency of this observation is confirmed by the testimony of ages. Nothing is of more advantage to the mind than to keep it in a continual state of action. But the daily employments of life, by fixing the attention steadily on one point, would exhaust the spirits and impair the constitution. This arises from the

formation of man. The divine Author of our existence has made us capable of receiving a variety of information through the inlets of the senses. How different are the pleasures of the eye and the ear! The organs of perception being so various, the soul must abhor uniformity. How delightful is it then to retire occasionally from the world, and to rest on the pleasing speculations of knowledge! Besides, the mind has a natural inclination

...ation for fomething vaſt and infinite. Lord Bacon, who muſt be allowed to be a genius of the firſt magnitude, uſes this as an argument to prove the capacioufneſs of the mind. Do we not then do injuſtice to our natures when we confine our refearches and deny ourfelves the acquiſition of fuch exalted enjoyments ? But are the elegant arts and fciences conducive to no other good purpoſe than mere amuſements ? Their influence on the moral character is extenſive. By them a delicacy of ſentiment is created which ſhrinks like the fenſitive plant from every fordid conception.—An admirable connoiſſeur in painting or poetry will be found to uſe the fame delicacy in the choice of his friends or companions, as he would in the ſelection of a beautiful picture or poetical performance. The ſcientific foul feels a magnanimous contempt for the misfortunes of life. A man poſſeſſed of this taliſman can look from the eminence of his mind and behold the world groveling beneath him. Such high principles preſerve to the ſtate many invaluable citizens. Otherwife genius might be proſtituted to the baſeſt purpoſes, and cringe like a flatterer before the throne of a monarch. But the fame proud ſpirit which ſpurns the fordid purſuits of felf intereſt will forever deſpiſe the low defigns of ambition.

But before I proceed I will take notice of a favourite creed of fome writers, which is in fact a rank abfurdity, though varnished with a plauſible pretext. It is aſſerted, that when our knowledge diſcovers to us the weakneſs or imperfection of our natures, ignorance is infinitely preferable. This is building on an unfubſtantial baſis. Every rational being muſt conclude, that

the happineſs of mankind depends not on a feclufion from misfortune, but from poſitive fruition. A familiar intercourfe with human calamities may make us more fenſible of the misfortunes of life, but by exerciſing the focial affections it will encreafe our felicity in the fame ratio. It is abfurd to ſuppoſe man capable of no greater degree of happineſs than the brutiſh creation. A bare unacquaintance with mifery is all the pleafure they poſſeſs, which is very remote from poſitive enjoyment. But while we contemplate the fuperior worth and excellency of a literary genius to the reſt of mankind, let us not confound him with the literary coxcomb. Florio gives us a pedantic difplay of all his knowledge on all occaſions. He remarks with much gravity, that happineſs is the purſuit of all men, and proves it by a long quotation from Cicero. He obſerves that wine is pleaſant to the taſte, and ſupports his aſſertion by the authority of Horace. Or if he ſtumbles on morality, he obſerves that Vice is deteſtable, and that Virtue, as the divine Plato expreſſes it, if ſhe ſhould appear in her natural dreſs, would make all mankind enraptured with her beauties. The moſt trifling and commonplace obfervations muſt be proved by fome pompous quotation.

Shall I be thought to refine too much, if I aſſert that the happineſs of man, both in proſperity and adverſity, is heightened by a relish for the arts and ſciences ? In adverſity the man of ſcience may derive confolation from reflecting that the greateſt and beſt of men in all ages, have undergone fimilar viciſſitudes. Surely, the very thought of ſharing the fame fate which Socrates once ſhared, muſt kindle in the mind a fovereign contempt for its horrors,

" That

"That faint, with a countenance of triumph, entered the walls of his prison and banished ignominy from the place ; for how could that asylum be called ignominious while the glory of Athens was there ?" Yet even these are not the only sources of consolation which will suggest themselves to a reflecting mind. As mankind are composed of one great community, there must be as great a variety of opposite interests. From whence the literary man may fairly infer, that, even by his own misfortunes, the great designs of nature are promoted. In a reverse of circumstances in the golden hour of prosperity this same reflection will guard him from a proud and ostentatious disposition. When he reflects that his own fortune may be built on the misfortunes of his fellow men, his heart will be humanized. his mind touched with pity, and his munificence extended to objects of distress. Finally, in whatever situation Providence may place him, he will feel himself contented and happy. He will behold the same sun hung in the centre of the system ; the same moon and stars will sparkle in the concave of heaven—He will find the same great principles of nature flowing through the same channels, but varied according to the infinite modifications of civil society. But does not the humble peasant enjoy these advantages in as much perfection as the greatest philosopher ? No, he may be conversant with the same objects but is debarred from the faculty of enjoying them. Science must refine the soul before it can receive the impression.

Indeed, in whatever light we view literature, it seems to have been highly favoured by the patronage of heaven. Who could have believed when the Goths and the Vandals swarmed from the North and invaded Europe, when every principle of learning was lost in the general devastation, that the tapers of knowledge would ever have been reluminated ? But after the lapse of a few centuries, the dark monkish ages of superstition disappeared ; the absurd tenets of Popish infallibility, and all the rant and rhapsody of designing enthusiasts, those foes to learning, were exposed to public indignation. A numerous concatenation of events, the most surprising of any recorded in history, rapidly succeeded, and finally ushered in the resurrection of literature. In the present enlightened age, our country calls for the exertions of her noblest citizens. Offices of state are opened indiscriminately to all who may claim a part by the preeminence of virtue. A crown, that glittering bauble, ceases to delude—no longer do the people pay homage to the star or the garter. Such vain and empty delusions are lost in the majesty of genius and merit. If the youth of this country would but nobly exert themselves in the acquisition of science, America would justly be considered in literature, as she is in politics, the glory of the WORLD.

ANECDOTE.

DURING the siege of Valenciennes, a gentleman asked a Colonel of a British Regiment of Militia—" How the besiegers managed to destroy the men in the *Zigzags* ?" The reply from the intelligent warrior was, "By having *crooked* artillery to be sure."

CABINET

CABINET of APOLLO.

A POEM,

Commemorative of GOFFE, WHALEY, *and* DIXWELL.

(Concluded from page 376.)

WHALEY and GOFFE to Maſſachu-
　　ſetts ſteer ;
The young applauding ſtate would fain
　　ſecure :
E'en then *a liberal will exiſted* here,
　And *equal rights* were *deſtin'd* to endure.

Edicts condemn the exil'd regicides ;
　They learn their ſentence with unal-
　　ter'd mien ;
Diverſe emotion different minds divides—
　Alarm would immolate and pity ſcreen.

Prevail'd upon by ſuch as ſought their
　　weal,
　Long lurk'd the world's great citizens
　　unſeen,
Oblig'd their haunts continual to conceal,
　And e'er forego the beſt delights of
　　men.

Itinerant next, the weſtern wilds they
　　trac'd,
　Till reach'd Connecticut's extended
　　ſtrand,　　　　　　　　　[waſte,
Where freeborn ſpirits had explor'd the
　And Providence decreed that Yale
　　ſhould ſtand.

With zealous promptitude, the enamour'd
　　town　　　　　　　　　[love,
　Conſole their hearts in ſympathetic
Until to foes, at length, the aſylum known,
　Their counſellors conſent to their re-
　　move.

Awhile the reverend DAVENPORT ſecretes ;
　Now JONES provides a ſubterraneous
　　grot,
With generous gladneſs charitably treats,
　And oft admits them to his humble cot.

Conſtrain'd e'en hence and where com-
　　pell'd purſu'd,
　Nor knew they where to reſt, nor
　　where to roam ;

Now ſearch'd a ſhelter in a trackleſs
　　wood,
　Now made a truſty peaſant's hut their
　　home.

Thus ſuffer'd they what JESSE's righteous
　　ſon
　From SAUL receiv'd, (the meed of
　　ISRAEL ſav'd ;)
While frauds ‖ in friends, like watchful
　　Jonathan,
　Accompliſh'd for them whatſoe'er they
　　crav'd.

Though hunted ſtill, ſubmiſſive to endure
　What heav'n's high will ordain'd of
　　future griefs ;
To HADLEY laſt they take their nightly
　　tour,　　　　　　　　　[chiefs.
　And reverend RUSSEL entertains the

Rare man ! diſintereſted, benevolent !
　(Bleſt as was Rahab by the Hebrew
　　ſpies ;)
Thy hoſpitable houſe with aliment,
　With ſolace thy condolent heart ſup-
　　plies.

DIXWELL explores the far remov'd re-
　　treat,
　Once join'd in league and now alli'd
　　in loſs ;
Recogniz'd mutually with joy they meet ;
　Here live recluſe from other intercourſe.
　　　　　　　　　　　　　　　　But

‖ *When Governor Endicot, to avoid incurring the charge of diſobedience, was apparently
trying to have them diſcovered, he endeavoured it
ſhould be thought they had quitted the country, and
wrote home, that he believed they had gone to the
Dutch at Manhadoes, and thence to Holland.
Randolph, ſent over afterwards to obtain knowledge of them, was informed by Bradſtreet, then
Governor, they had not been heard of ſince leaving
New Heaven. While concealed there, likewiſe,
reports were intentionally propagated, that they
had left the place and paſſed Northward ; in conſequence of which Kirk and Kellond continued
their rout in that direction.*

But Dixwell felt the force of human
   ties—
  Him to Quinnipiak * led the social
   flame ;
A borrow'd appellation gave difguife ;
He rear'd a family and rofe to fame.

The pair colleagu'd remain fequefter'd
   ftill,
  Nor fee of Adam's race nor e'er are
   feen,
Save when they fuccour the affaulted
   vill, †
Or, with familiars clos'd, for prayer
   convene.

Russel, with thee, long years thy guefts
   fojourn,
  Thy pious hands are ftretch'd to feal
   their eyes ;
Thy tears devotional their exit mourn,
Thy lips perform their fecret obfequies

So when high-favour'd Pifgah's top fuf-
   tain'd
  The humble hoar-grown fervant of the
   Lord ;
The feer, (furvey'd the promis'd land-
   fcape) gain'd
An unknown tomb, by hands divine
   interr'd.

Nor lefs the chiefs (that ftrong in faith
   they liv'd
  Let ftill their lines epiftolar ‡ atteft ;)
In profpect, plain from prophecy, per-
   ceiv'd
A future age fuperlatively bleft.

---

* *The original Indian name of New Haven.*

† *The following anecdote is traditional at Hadley : The fettlement there, being attacked by Indians, in 1675, during public worfhip, were put in confternation and entirely routed. Immediately a venerable old perfonage appeared, reconnoitered the people, and lead them on to victory. Their angelic preferver, as fuddenly, difappeared, and the feemingly fupernatural phænomenon could never be explained.*

‡ *Among their papers, which, after their death, were collected and lodged in a library in Bofton, are extant many copies and originals of letters to and from their friends remaining in England. Thefe breathe warmly the fpirit of piety, but are tinctured a little with the fuperftition of the times. They were firmly perfuaded that the execution of the judges was the flaying of the witneffes, and, from calculations upon the prophecies, had formed great expectations of the year 1666, and when it was paft without any extraordinary revolution, they believed the Chriftian æra to be erroneous.* Hutchins. hiftory.

Perhaps, their mortal warfare near an end,
  With death alone the combat left to
   wage ;
A fweeter antepaft the Omnifcient deign'd,
  In vifions, Gabriel gives the fure pre-
   fage :

" Champions of earth, and candidates for
   heav'n !
" Life's dark defcending vale ye tread
   fubmifs ;
" For you a gofpel-lighted path is giv'n
"To bright domains of everlafting blifs.

"Enough to injur'd Britain has been paid ;
" Her longer fubjugation is decreed ;
" Might it have been annull'd by human
   aid,
" E'en by thine aid Britannia had been
   freed.

" In vain thy arm effay'd the Herculean
   toil,   [fence ;
" In vain thy counfels ftrove in her de-
  The foil you prefs is freedom's natal foil,
" And her redemption muft redound
   from hence.

" Her king, a century more revolv'd, fhall
   aim
" To crufh this land, the foot-ftool of
   his throne ;
" A race felf govern'd fhall refent the
   claim,   [own.
" Its proper lords fhall vindicate their

' Their generous warmth fhall Gallia's
   fons infpire ;
" The fparks diffus'd extenfively illume ;
" While heads imperial plod to pen the
   fire,
" Their diadems the glowing flames
   confume.

" The nation'd empire, ancient feuds forgot,   [prize ;
" Excites the Englifh realm to like em-
" By her enfranchis'd, other ftates are
   taught
" Themfelves and fifter ftates to en-
   franchife.

" Stanislaus, fole of Europe's crown'd
   compeers,   [throng ;
" Would raife to citizens the plebeian
" As bafe alike, his arduous fpirit fears,
" Or to be forc'd to right, or forc'd to
   wrong :

" And though the emprefs of the Mufco-
   vies,   [deftroy, §
" In zenith pride, would fain the grant
     " While

---

§ *So greatly was the kingdom abridged by the extraordinary partition of its moft valuable territories*

" While lasts thy memory, matchless Pole,
    the prize
" Thy *manumitted* millions shall enjoy.
" Still wider spreads the genial glorious
    blaze,
" And repercussive brightens as it runs,
" Till shines religion's reason's *general*
    rays   [sons.
" On each of India's, each of Afric's
" The *triple* crown forsakes the pontiff's
    brows,
" The Inquisition's rage no more en-
    dures;
" A conscienc'd clergy tolerance shall es-
    pouse,
" Estrang'd from sceptres and from
    sinecures.||
" Opinions heterodox revert to right——
" Scripture alone shall sway the intel-
    lect;
" No party persecutes its opposite,
" And zealots cease to constitute a sect.
" Nor bigots bind, nor potentates oppress,
" But light, and love, and liberty a-
    bounds,   [climes possess,
" From where mankind the Arctic *
" To where the Antarctic * zone the
    world surrounds.

---

*tories between the Russian, Germanic and Prussi-
an powers, who unitedly invaded it in 1772,
that when his present Polish majesty was lately
relinquishing his own influence to effect a constitution from principles of equality, such absolute control had the Czarina Catherine, that she compelled him to resume his superiority, to exist, however, only as her titled vassal. But thus much
his subjects have already gained by his exertions—
they are no longer transferable, like common
property, and, beginning to know, they begin to appreciate the inviolable enjoyments and privileges
of MAN.*

|| *The establishment of benefices and dignitaries
in the church, and its unnatural connexion with
secular authority, have produced the swarm of
worldly and imperious ecclesiastics, that has
converted religion, originally benign, into an instrument of fraud, persecution and cruelty.*

*Let but its ministers be divested of magistra-
cy, and let their perquisites be moderate and equa-
ble—duty then induces them to the sacred office;
their precepts are incorrupt, their example eminent.——Such a church establishment irradi-
ates America.*

* * *All the habitable parts of the globe are
contained between the Arctic and Antarctic circles.*

" Now Abraham's proselyted seed return,
    " The recollected tribes adore the
    LAMB——
" One sacrifice the union'd earth shall
    burn,
    " And, hush'd in concord, hymn JEHO-
    VAH's name."

For the MASSACHUSETTS MAGAZINE.

COMELAH : A FRAGMENT.

*Quem virum, aut heroa, lyrâ vel acri
Tibiâ sumes celebrare, Clio ?
Quem Deum ?*——

                          HORACE. ODE XII.

O'ER heaven's bright azure roll'd the
      deep'ning clouds,
And misty darkness spread her sombre
    veil.
The sun retir'd and hid his golden rays;
The sun retir'd and blush'd upon the
    earth.
In horrid gloom all nature was involv'd;
And pallid terror shook the thinking
    world.
The turtle mourn'd, and screech owl's
    hidious voice
Reecho'd horror 'midst the rustling grove.
When Com'lah's ghost approach'd Ico-
    nah's cell ;
From the blue hills he bore his 'erial way,
As blazing stars, that cleave the frowning
    air,
And 'wake to thought each gazing, tor-
    pid soul.
His eyes gleam'd meteors thro' the dark
    expanse,
His shield beam'd glory, and his spear
    wav'd light.
A robe celestial o'er his shoulders flow'd,
And curling, hung in tresses on the breeze.
[He trod like waters rolling to their shore;
Like horse rushing to the sound of war.]
At his approach the rivers ceas'd their
    noise,
The wind was calm, and silence reign'd
    around.
Up from their sacred tombs arose the
    forms
Of saints departed and of heroes dead.
They rose to hear the counsels of the
    brave ;
The words of Com'lah, their beloved
    chief.
*   *   *   *   *   *   *   *   *   *
Resting upon Iconah's mossy cave,
The much rever'd Comelah thus began.

Hear, saints, and mighty heroes of the
    field ;
For Banionis with his warlike band

                                          In

In fullen anger leave their peaceful domes,
And down the hill impetuous bear their
way,   [deer.
As leaps the hound towards the trembling
Ther.fore Iconah blow thy hollow fhell ;
And ftrike on Fingal's fhield the found of
war.
Collect thy ftrength within Caduthor's
vale,   [bow
And range the nervous. children of the
Upon the fteep, that over looks the field.
Speak to thy warriors of their fathers'
fame,
Paint out the glory of our younger days,
And make their youthful fouls exult with
joy,
Till their eyes beam with luftre like the fun,
And their hearts leap rejoicing to the fight.

ALCADOUR.

For the MASSACHUSETTS MAGAZNE.

INDEPENDENCE : An ODE.

Progeniem LIBERTATIS canemus.

By the Same.

ONCE more an *anniverfal* day
Invites the rural poet's lay ;
Invokes an *independent fong.*
Columbia's children join the found ;
Each freeman's heart with joy rebound,
And halelujahs burft along.

From fhore to fhore, from port to port ;
From hill to dale, from vill to court ;
From north to fouth, from eaft to weft ;
From Miffifippi's curling tide,
And old Miammi's waving pride,
Afcend the found that marks us bleft.

Beneath the olive branch of peace,
Which, God prolong and man increafe,
Our country grows and fame extends ;
May fifter France ne'er be bereft
Of this celeftial, facred gift,
Which with it blifs unceafing blends.

May fhe an *independence* fee,
And be forever bleft and free :
Our noble and our great ally,
Who, with us rear'd Columbia's fame,
And gave her an immortal name,
A name which ne'er till time fhall die.

Who 'midft the depth of our diftrefs,
When threaten'd from the wildernefs,
And butcher'd by an impious band,
That o'er the ocean fpread their fleet,
Aud cut us from our laft retreat ;
Stretch'd out her ever gen'rous hand.

Sent her brave leaders o'er the main,
Rang'd her battalions on our plain,
And with us fwept the menial hoft.

She now contends with freedom's foes ;
Amidft them hurls her deadly blows,
And bids their tyrants ceafe to boaft.

Columbia's children lift your voice ;
Lift high and bid the world rejoice
That we enjoy the charms of peace ;
While old Britannia feels the rod,
Inflicted by the hand of God ;
Inflicted till her crimes fhall ceafe.

And now with one united found,
That fhall be heard by all around—
Thank, thank the Lord, fupremely great,
That *Wafbington*, the hero, fage,
Lives and adorns our infant age ;
Lives and preferves our peaceful ftate.

W—n, July 4, 1794.

For the MASSACHUSETTS MAGAZINE.

From the French of M. De Fenelon.

By Dr. M'K——

HARD by a fountain's graffy fide,
The love fick EDWIN fate,
And thus, in broken numbers, figh'd,
And thus bewail'd his fate.

" Why rears yon hill its verdant head ?
" Why flow'rets deck yon plain ?
" Such beauties round my Emma fpread !
" Such, Emma's graceful mien.

" The rifing morn, on yonder fkies,
" Unfolds its crimfon hue !
" Its fplendor, EMMA, blooms and dies—
" Its glow refides with you !

" The fetting fun's departing rays
" Illume yon weftern peak ;
" More fix'd, more permanent than thefe
" The blufh on EMMA's cheek.

" But, ah ! yon tranfient waters roll,
" Yon zephyr fleets away ;—
" Thus emblems of my EMMA's foul—
" Inconftant, fleet as they."

Worcefter, June 30, 1794.

FRIENDSHIP : An ODE.

By Dr. JOHNSON.

FRIENDSHIP, peculiar boon of heav'n,
The noble mind's delight and pride,
To men and angels only giv'n,
To all the lower world deny'd.

While love, unknown among the bleft,
Parent of thoufand wild defires,
The favage and the human breaft
Torments alike with raging fires.

With bright, but oft deftructive gleam,
Alike o'er all his lightnings fly ;

Thy

Thy lambent glories only beam
Around the fav'rites of the sky.

Thy gentle flows of guiltless joys
On fools and villians ne'er descend;
In vain for thee the tyrant sighs,
And hugs a flatterer for a friend.

Directress of the brave and just,
O guide us thro' life's darksome way!
And let the tortures of mistrust
On selfish bosoms only prey.

Nor shall thine ardours cease to glow,
When souls to blissful climes remove;
What rais'd our virtue here below
Shall aid our happiness above.

For the MASSACHUSETTS MAGAZINE.

LINES,

*Written by a Parent to his Son, previous to
the embarkation of the latter for a distant
port.*

GOD's presence gives sincere delight
 To those, who fear his name;
It dissipates the gloom of night—
Affords relief from pain.

Air, sea, and land may intervene,
 And place our friends remote;
But to his praise, a joyful theme,
 Our songs we will devote.

Incircled by the friendly arm
 Of his almighty power,
We shall be ever safe from harm,
 Ev'n in death's gloomy hour.

His presence let us call to mind,
 When gloomy thoughts arise,
He's ever merciful and kind,
 And every want supplies.
        Y.

To the Editors *of the* Massachusetts *Magazine.*

GENTLEMEN,

*Please to insert the following Lines (if you deem
them worthy) in your next Magazine.*

HOW smoothly flows this limpid stream,
 Kiss'd by morning's sportive beam;
While the softly whispering breeze
Breathes among yon trembling trees.
Oh! how soon these charms shall die!—
Lowering tempests wrap the sky,
Morning's balmy sweets are flown,
And the rosy joys are gone.—
So in the fair morn of life
Pleasures bloom—till storms of strife
Blast each promis'd bud of peace,
And the opening blossoms cease.
        ANNA.

To the Editors *of the* Massachusetts Magazine.

GENTLEMEN,

*I send you for publication the following POEM,
which I found inserted in the New England
Weekly Journal, a paper published in Boston,
June 28, 1731. If it wants the elegance of
our modern poesy, I think that is amply com-
pensated by the beautiful description and venerable simplicity which characterize the piece.
It must be highly gratifying to the curiosity of
those votaries of pleasure, who frequent that
distinguished resort of company at this season of
the year, (viz. Fresh Pond in Cambridge) to
perceive that the praises of their favourite seat
of pleasure have been sung by a bard more than
sixty years ago : and that it has ever since
been the principal resort of all those who wish
to exchange the noise and smoke of the Town
for the salubrious breezes of the country.*

*Hic sunt gelidi fontes, hic mollia prata Lycori;
Hic nemus, hic tecum toto consumerer aro.*
        VIRGIL.

OF ancient streams presume no more
    to tell,
The fam'd Castalian or Pierian well.
Fresh Pond superior must those rills con-
   fess,   [or Greece.
As much as Cambridge yields to Rome
More limpid water can no fountain show,
A fairer bottom, or a smoother brow;
A painted world its peaceful gleam con-
  tains,
The heav'nly arch, the bord'ring groves
  and plains
Here in mock silver Cynthia seems to roll,
And trusty pointers watch the frozen pole.
Here sages might observe the wand'ring
  stars,
And rudest swains commence astrologers :
Along the brim the lonely plougher stalks,
And to his visionary fellow talks;
Amid the wave the vagrant black bird sees,
And tries to perch upon the imag'd trees;
On flying clouds the simple bullocks gaze,
And vainly reach to crop the shady grass;
From neighbouring hills the stately horse
  espies,
Himself a feeding and himself envies.
Thither pursu'd by opening hounds, the
  hare
Blesses himself to see a forest near;
The waving shrubs he takes for real wood,
And boldly plunges in the yielding flood.
On this side willows hem the bason round,
There graceful trees the promontory
  crown;
Those mingled tufts and outspread arms
  compose

           A

A fhade delightful for the laurell'd brows.
Here mofly couches tempt to pleafing
   dreams
The love-fiek foul, and eafe the weary
   limbs.
No noxious fnake difperfes poifon here,
Nor fcreams of night-bird rend the
   twilight air ;   [ftill,
Excepting him, who when the groves are
Sings am'rous tunes, and whiftles whip-
   poor-will ;
To hear whofe carol elves in circles trip,
And lovers' hearts within their bofoms
   leap ;
Whofe favage notes the troubled mind
   amufe,
Banifh defpair, and hold the falling dews.
No ghaftly horrors conjure thoughts of woe,
Or difmal profpects to the fancy fhow.
If to the weft your ravifh'd eyes you turn,
Behold the glitt'ring fpire of Watertown ;
Thence fhaggy hills prop up the bending
   fkies,
And fmoky fpires from lowly cots arife.
Towards the northweft the diftant ⎫
   mountains wear   ⎬
In fpring a green, in fall a whit'ning ear; ⎭
Or all alive with woolly flocks appear.
Beneath their feet a wide extended plain,
Or rich in cyder or in fwelling grain,
Does to the margin of the water ftretch,
Bounded by meadows and a rufhy beach.
The reft a motley mixture hill and dale,
There open fields, here mingled woods
   prevail.
Here lafting oaks, the hopes of navies
   ftand,
There beauteous poplars hide th' un-
   fightly ftrand ;
In autumn there the full ripe clufters blufh,
Around the walnut or the hawthorn bufh.
Here fruitful orchards bend their aged
   boughs,   [mows.
Here fweats the reaper, there the peafant
Each fmiling month diverfifies the view,
E'en hoary winter teems with fomething
   new ;
A milk-white fleece does then the lawns
   o'erfpread,
The pond becomes a looking-glafs indeed.
A polifh'd furface fpreads acrofs the deep,
O'er which the youth with rapid vigor
   flip.
But now the groves the gayeft liv'ries
   wear,
How pleas'd could it be fpring through-
   out the year !
And in thefe walks eternity be fpent,
Atheifts would then to immortality con-
   fent.

The grateful fhifting of the colour'd fcene,
The rich embroid'ry of the level green.
The trees and ruftling of the branches
   there,
The filent whifpers of the paffing air,
The fweet harmony of the winged choir,
Awake the fancy and the poet's fire.
Here rural Maro might attend his fheep,
And the Mæonian with advantage fleep.
Hither ye bards for infpiration come,
Let every other fount but this be dumb.
Which way foe'er your airy genius leads,
Receive your model from thefe vocal
   fhades.
Would you in homely paftoral excel,
Take pattern from the merry-piping
   quail ;
Obferve the bluebird for a roundelay,
The chatt'ring pye or ever babbling jay.
The plaintive dove the foft love verfe
   can teach,
And mimic thrufh to imitators preach.
In Pindar's ftrain the lark falutes the
   dawn,
The lyric robin chirps the evening on.
For poignant fatire mind the movis well,
And hear the fparrow for a madrigal.
For every verfe a pattern hear you have,
From ftrains heroic down to humble ftave.
Not Phœbus' felf, altho' the god of verfe,
Cou'd hit fuch fine and entertaining airs;
Nor the fair maids that round the foun-
   tain fat,
Such artlefs heav'nly mufic modulate.
Each thicket feems a paradife renew'd,
The foft vibrations fire the moving blood.
Each fenfe its part of fweet delufion
   fhares,   [ears.
The fcenes bewitch the eye, the fong the
Pregnant with fcent each wind regales the
   fmell,
Like cooling fheets th' enwrapping breez-
   es fwell.
During the dark, if poets' eyes we truft,
Thefe lawns are haunted by fome fwarthy
   ghoft.   [joys,
Some Indian Prince who fond of former
With bow and quiver through the fhadow
   plies ;
He can't in death his native groves forget,
But leaves Elyfium for his ancient feat.
O happy pond, hadft thou in Grecia flow'd
The bounteous blefling of fome wat'ry
   god,
Or had fome Ovid fung this liquid rife,
Diftill'd perhaps from flighted Virgil's
   eyes.
Well is thy worth in Indian ftory known,
Thy living lymph, and fertile borders
   fhown ;

                      Thy

Thy various flocks the cover'd fhore can
   fhun,
Drove by the fowler and the fatal gun.
Thy fhining roach and yellow brifly
   bream,
And pick'rel, rav'nous monarch of the
   ftream.
The perch, whofe back a ring of colours
   fhows,
And horned pout that courts the flimy
   ooze ;
The eel ferpentine, fome of dubious race,
The tortoife with his golden fpotted cafe;
Thy hairy mufk-rat, whofe perfume defies
The balmy odours of Arabian fpice.
The throng of Harvard know thy pleaf-
   ures well,
Joys too extravagant perhaps to tell.
Hither oftimes the learned tribe repair,
When Sol returning warms the growing
   year.
Some take the fifh with a delufive bait,
Or for the fowl beneath the arbors wait ;
And arm'd with fire, endanger ev'ry fhade,
Teaching e'en unfledg'd innocence a dread;
To gratify a nice luxurious tafte,
How many pretty fongfers breathe their
   laft. [down,
Spite of his voice, they fire the linnet
And make the widow'd dove renew his
   moan.
But fome more humane feek the fhady
   gloom,
Tafte nature's bounty, and admire her
   bloom : [toil,
In penfive thought revolve long vanifh'd
Or in foft fong the pleafing hours beguile.
What Eden was by ev'ry profpect told,
Strive to regain the temper of that age of
   gold.
No artful harms for fimple hutes contrive,
And fcorn to take a life they cannot give.
To leafy woods refort for health and eafe,
Not to difturb their melody and peace.

For the MASSACHUSETTS MAGAZINE,

L I N E S,

*Occafioned by a Mifs' fhedding Tears on the Com-
miffion of a Fault.*

THE liquid *globules* that fhine
   In Seraphina's eye,
Dim the bright luftre of the MINE.
   And lave the crimfon dye.

The figh that from that bofom ftole,
   The heart of VIRTUE'D win ;
Would purify the blemifh'd foul,
   And SANCTIFY a fin.
       THE COUNTRY BOY

Worcefter, July, 6, 1794.

VERSES to the WIND.

GO, gentle zephyr, foftly blow,
   And fan my Stella's face,
Paint on her cheek health's vermil glow,
   And heighten every grace.

And if fhe afk who fondly now,
   Breathes on her dimpling cheek :
Ah ! then in fofter ftrains do thou
   Her tendereft care befpeak :

Oh ! fay it is a figh from me,
   That flutters in her ear ;
That I, fweet gale, commiffion'd thee
   My fofteft vows to bear.

And if my Stella fondly kind,
   Attends thy amorous lay,
And pours to thee her glowing mind,
   Do then her wifh obey.

So when thy trembling airy gale,
   Breathes o'er my cot again ;
O ! fay thy whifpering did prevail,
   Nor haft thou figh'd in vain.
          [*Lady's Mag.*

To the Editors *of the* Maffachufetts Magazine.

GENTLEMEN,

*Perhaps the following Ode, faid to have been
compofed and fet to Mufic by Dr. Willard of
Stafford, may afford Entertainment to fome of
your Readers.*

ODE for INDEPENDENCE,
1793.

BEHOLD ! the glorious day appears !
   A blifsful found falutes our ears—
This happy morn gave Independence
   birth !
Columbia, rouze ! with joy fupreme
Dwell on the bleft delightful theme :
Proclaim your joy to all the wond'ring
   Earth.

All hail ! thou highly favour'd land !
See Freedom's bleffings wide expand—
See fmiling Plenty crown thy fertile fields :
   For thee fhall blow the gentle gales—
   For thee fhall fwell the whitening fails,
For thee old Ocean his rich treafure yields,

As arteries and veins convey
The purple tide of life, and ftray
In num'rous windings thro' the human
   frame :
So thy fair rivers prove the fource
Of joyous plenty thro' their courfe,
And are the life-blood of thy wealth and
   fame.

Lo ! meek-ey'd Peace, with lenient
   hand,
Waves o'er thy plains her olive wand,
              And

And mildly bids war's rude commotion
  ceafe :
While Europe's guilt-ftain'd barb'rous
  realms
A mighty fea of blood o'erwhelms,
And Death's vaft empire finds a fwift increafe.

May gratitude to heav'n infpire
Each heart with pure devotion's fire,
While Independence rites to the view :
Columbia, venerate that power
Which cheer'd thee in thy darkeft
  hour,
And with thy joy thy fongs of praife re-
  new.

Behold ! the glorious day appears—
The birth-day of revolving years—
The day that gave to Independence birth :
Columbians, rouze ; with joy fupreme
Think o'er the bleft enchanting theme,
And fhout your tranfports through the
  lift'ning earth.

For the MASSACHUSETTS MAGAZINE.

ACROSTIC.

By CHAPMAN WHITCOMB.

BLESS'D with thofe talents men of
  fenfe admire,
Endow'd with art their friendfhip to ac-
  quire.
Neat is his perfon, and genteel his air,
Juftice his aim, his character is fair.
Although he's wealthy, fighs not to be
  great ;
Made to be honour'd and carefs'd in
  ftate.
Intent on virtue, and to peace inclin'd,
Noble his feelings, generous his mind.
Knowledge of bufinefs, qualifies him well,
In public fphere to act, and to excel :
Modeft in his pretentions, don't endeavour
By fly intrigues, to gain the public fav-
  our.
And happy, in himfelf ferenely great ;
Looks with indifference on a throne of
  ftate :
Lov'd and efteem, for real good behaviour.

LINES written over a SUN DIAL.

OLD Time, with your fcythe and your
  fnake, and your glafs,
Have a care of you-felf, there's a fnake
  in the gra's—
A fnake like the ferpent in Mofes's hand,
That will wallow your fnake at word of
  command.

To the VILLAGE of FANCY.

By a Lady.

DEAR, wild illufions of creative mind !
  Whofe varying hues arife to Fan-
  cy's art,
And by her magic force are fwift com-
  bin'd
In forms that pleafe, and fcenes that
  touch the heart :
Oh ! whether at her voice ye foft affume
  The penfive grace of forrow drooping
  low ;
Or rife fublime on terror's foftly plume,
  And fhake the foul with widly thrilling
  woe ;
Or, fweetly bright, your gayer tints ye
  fpread,
  Bid fcenes of pleafure fteal upon my
  view,
Love was his purple pinions o'er my head,
  And wake the tender thought to paf-
  fion true ;
O ! ftill—ye fhadowy forms ! attend my
  lonely hours,
Still chafe my real cares with your illu-
  five powers !

SONG.

LIFE'S a varied, bright illufion,
  Joy and forrow—light and fhade ;
Turn from forrow's dark fuffufion,
  Catch the pleafures ere they fade.
Fancy paints with hues unreal,
  Smile of blifs, and forrow's mood ;
If they both are but ideal,
  Why reject the feeming good ?
Hence ! no more ! 'tis Wifdom calls ye,
  Bids ye court Time's prefent aid ;
The future truft not—hope enthrals ye,
  " Catch the pleafures ere they fade."

EPITAPH,

*Taken from a grave ftone in the common bury-
ing place in Bofton. The dates of the age
and death of the perfon to whofe memory thefe
lines are confecrated could not be difcover'd, as
the heavy hand of time had preffed the ftone,
on which they were infcribed, very deep into
the ground.*

HERE lyes Rebecca in duft,
  Until the fecond life ;—
Who, was 62 months juft,
  Joyliffe Price's wife.

Curious EPITAPH from a Grave Stone in England.

HERE lies a wife, who never vex't one ;
  We can't fay that of her at th' next
  ftone.

MONTHLY GAZETTE.

Summary of Foreign Intelligence.

GERMANY.
VIENNA.

LETTERS from Poland announce that the Ruſſians, to the number of eighteen thouſand men, attacked between the 11th and 12th inſt. General Koſciuſko; that the latter loſt a great number of men, but ſtill kept his ground; finally that Koſciuſko attacked the Ruſſians in his turn on the 14th, routed them entirely, and took 20 pieces of cannon.

PRUSSIA.
THORN.

We learn that a ſtrong army of Pruſſians is put in motion to advance againſt the ſeditious Poles. A liſt of all the Pruſſian regiments, who received marching orders, is now to be ſeen The whole of this corps is ſaid to amount to 40.000 men. His Pruſſian Majeſty is expected in South Pruſſia, in the middle of May, to put himſelf at the head of that army.

POLAND.
APRIL 22.

The patriots on the 17th inſt. after having rendered themſelves maſters of the grand arſenal at Warſaw, obliged the Ruſſian garriſon, conſiſting of 3000 troops, to evacuate the town. Baron Igelſtrohm, the Ruſſian ambaſſador, was obliged to take refuge with the Pruſſian army under General Wolky, encamped a league's diſtance from that capital. His majeſty, the king of Poland, is retained as an hoſtage, by the patriots. Some reports ſtate that his majeſty eſcaped into a convent, under eſcort of 500 Ruſſians. The ambaſſador of a neigbouring power, (probably the Ruſſian) has alſo been retained as a hoſtage. The inſurgents have eſtabliſhed a revolutionary tribunal, and ſeveral perſons are ſaid already to have ſuffered death. Lithuania, according to the lateſt accounts, is likewiſe in a ſtate of inſurrection. Gen. Koſciuſko is very active in fortifying the town of Cracow; he ordered a declaration to be publiſhed, by which thoſe citizens who do not wiſh to remain in the town, in caſe of a ſiege, are permitted to quit within eight days time, in conſe-

quence of which declaration, a great number of rich merchants, with their goods, together with a great number of women and children, have paſſed the bridge over the Viſtula, in order to ſettle in the village of Podgorze, belonging to Gallicia. We likewiſe learn that Gen. Koſciuſko has ordered the bridge to be broken down, and a number of boats which were on this ſide the Viſtula, to be rowed into a place of ſecurity. The three complete Poliſh regiments, Lubomirſky, Czapſky, and Ozarowſky, have joined his ſtandard.

APRIL 24.

The 17th of this month proved a dreadful day to Warſaw; General Igelſtrohm, a few days before, had given orders to the whole of the Ruſſian cavalry, in garriſon there, to march from Warſaw, to join the troops which had been previouſly detached, in order to act againſt the army under Gen. Koſciuſko. When the inſurrection took place on the 17th in the morning, Gen. Igelſtrohm ordered the only three battalions of Ruſſian infantry who remained in the garriſon, to take up arms; at the ſame time, he ſent a meſſage to the King, informing his majeſty of the event. The King ſent him word, that he had already been informed of what had happened; that his majeſty had only to add a requeſt of the General to ſend all his troops out of the capital, in order to prevent bloodſhed, until the mind of the people ſhould, in ſome meaſure be pacified.

General Igelſtrohm, in the mean time, had ſent General Bauer, at the head of a detachment to protect the arſenal, but this was too late. The patriots had already rendered themſelves maſters of all the artillery contained in that building; and the latter General with his detachment, on their arrival, were forced to lay down their arms and to ſurrender priſoners of war. The patriots afterwards, provided with arms from the arſenal, formed themſelves in order of battle, and marched againſt a battalion of the Ruſſian infantry, whom they drove out of the town. Gen. Igelſtrohm however, placed himſelf at the head of the two other battalions,

and

and took poft in Catherine fleeet, where he was determined to defend himfelf; thefe battalions were fired upon with great violence from every window, and after an engagement which lafted 33 hours, without intermiffion, the Ruffians retreated from Warfaw, with the lofs of half their number, almoft all killed. Their Generals Igelftrohm, Aphraxin and Subow, at the head of the remaining Ruffian infantry, joined the Pruffian corps under Gen. Wolky, ftationed in the neighbourhood of that capital.

The people of Warfaw were obliged to fet feveral houfes on fire, where the Ruffian foldiers had pofted themfelves during the engagement. The houfes and palaces which had been inhabited by the Ruffian officers and their adherents, were plundered by the mob, particularly the Ruffian generals fell a prey to the rapacious part of the lower order of the people. A number of the Ruffian foldiers, who kept themfelves concealed during the engagement, were afterwards maffacred as foon as they appeared in the ftreets. The magiftrates had affembled during the tumult; but all their endeavours to reftore tranquillity proved ineffectual. The patriots have fince fent an account of this revolution to General Kofciufko at Cracow; at the fame time inviting that general to come to their affiftance.

IRELAND.
DUBLIN, MAY 12.

Inhuman Murder.—We hear that fix men charged with moft cruel murders, were laft week committed to goal, and will be brought to trial before the prefent judges on the Leinfter Circuit. The favage deed is thus related:—A farmer having gone to a fair, thefe defperados attacked his houfe in his abfence, in order to plunder it, in which was the wife of the farmer, with a very young child, a man and a woman fervant. Having got entrance at the ftreet door, they fell upon the fervants and murdered them. The poor woman of this houfe, being above ftairs while the murders were committing, upon the firft alarm covered the child in a bed with the bed clothes, and forced herfelf for concealment, up a chimney. The ruffians, after difpatching the unfortunate fervants, fearched every part of the houfe for their miftrefs, but happily could not difcover her. Finding the child in the bed, they murdered it in a manner too fhocking to relate, by whofe cries the mercilefs monfters hoped to draw the wretched mother from her retreat; but fhe had the mortifying refolution to refift the unparalleled barbarous ftratagem, to preferve her own life.

After committing thefe murders, the barbarians plundered the houfe of a fum of money, feafted themfelves upon fome provifions they found there, and locking it up retired with their booty—but left behind them, by chance, a large dog, which belonged to one of this cruel banditti, and which was the caufe of thefe barbarians' apprehenfion.

In a fhort time after, the farmer returned to his houfe, but was aftonifhed at not being able to gain admittance into it. Upon which, he alarmed his neighbours, with whofe affiftance he broke open the door and faw the fhocking fcene we have defcribed—whofe wretched wife, when fhe heard her hufband's voice came forth from the chimney. The dog that the murderers left behind, was fecured, and a magiftrate being fent; for, a confultation was held for the purpofe of devifing the beft means for difcovering the defperadoes—It was at length agreed upon to cut off the dog's ears and part of his tail, and fet him loofe, and to purfue him as he ran, as he probably would fly to where he came from. This was accordingly done, and the plan fucceeded; for the dog flew to a houfe at a great diftance, howling with pain from the operation, into which he was followed by a perfon who found the woman of the place, uttering curfes againft thofe who maltreated fo cruelly her dog. This was enough, the fignal was given to a party that ftood at a diftance, who all entered the place, in a private room, in which they found the whole gang dividing the booty they had taken, who were all inftantly feized and dragged to goal.

DOMESTIC OCCURRENCES.

A SCHOONER has lately arrived in this port from Breft, which fhe left the 24th of May.

The Captain, a gentleman of veracity and refpectability informs, that about the 18th May, the grand fleet from Breft, confifting

confifting of 32 fhips of the line, and a number of frigates, failed from that port, in expectation of joining another fleet from Rochefort and Havre—that on the 29th of the fame month, he paffed this fleet which then confifted of fifty fail, off Cape Clear, ftretching for Cape Finifterre. The Captain alfo informs, that during his ftay at Breft, about 6 weeks, upward of 120 were brought in there, 40 of which were outward bound Jamaica men, a very valuable Dutch fhip, worth five millions of dollars, and feveral Englifh South Sea men.

The Captain further reports, that the day before he failed, a corvette arrived from the Chefapeake fleet, which he left four days before; that the Englifh fleet was not out, and in all probability faid fleet arrived foon after he failed. Provifions were very plenty at Breft. The important account of the total defeat of the Duke of York, had been received at Breft; but as the Captain faw no official account, he is not able to relate the particulars; but it was reprefented to be a complete victory on the part of the Republicans.

The French papers, by the late arrivals, contain a number of letters which have been read in the Convention, containing numerous accounts of victories gained by the Republican troops, over the armies of the defpots of Europe; among a variety of others is an account from Genoa read in the Convention of 30000 Republicans paffing through the Genoefe country, which concludes thus—" It may be eafily eftimated that the French have at leaft 30000 men on our territory; and they conftantly pafs along artillery and ammunition, by land as well as by fea; in frequent convoys of fmall veffels.—I fhould be defective in truth if I did not fay, that the French army marched with the moft edifying difcipline, and the moft exemplary conduct. The French foldiers, had they been thirty thoufand monks in their noviciate, could not have behaved with more circumfpection and civility.

CAPTURE OF THE PIGOU.

By a letter from Halifax, the following information of the capture of the fhip Pigou, an American Indiaman, by the Blanche and Huffar frigates, has been received—Thurfday returned from a cruife his Majefty's fhips Huffar and Blanche—They have brought in with them, the American India Ship Pigou, bound from the Ifle of France to Philadelphia.

ACCIDENT.

The following unfortunate accident happened at the paper-mill lately in Worcefter.—The workmen had been preffing a poft of paper; the fcrews of the Prefs which was new, when it was releafed, did not, as ufual, immediately rife; one of the workmen, Mr. *Micah Haven*, took a handfpike to ftart it back; the moment he applied the handfpike to the fcrew, it is fuppofed it rofe of itfelf, and with fuch velocity as to caufe the handfpike to make a large dent in the fide of the prefs, and rebounding, ftruck Mr. Haven in the fide of his head, and broke his fkull, feveral pieces of which were extracted—He lived till Thurfday evening, and then expired.

VIOLENT STORM.

On Monday the 1ft inftant, a terrible ftorm of rain and hail, was experienced in Lynn; the violence of it for ten minutes, was never before known in any of of thefe parts. It came in near a weft direction, beginning at Billerica, and extended about 20 miles, to the Nahant, and was in width about half a mile: Several trees 12 inches through, were blown to the ground, and great damage done to the corn, &c. The hailftones that defcended, were as large as hen's eggs, and one that was picked up fome time after the abatement of the ftorm, weighed three ounces. A pair of cattle belonging to Mr. Aaron Bowman, were killed, and the damage done to the houfes, by breaking the window glafs, &c. was very confiderable.

COMMENCEMENT.

On Wednefday 16th inft. the anniverfary Commencement at Harvard Univerfity was celebrated. The Overfeers, Corporation, and immediate Government of the Univerfity, after tranfacting the neceffary bufinefs, at 11 o'clock, A. M. proceeded to the meeting houfe, efcorted by the Candidates for Degrees, preceeded by a band of mufic. The performances appeared to give general fatisfaction to the learned, brilliant and numerous auditory who attended.

The following gentlemen received the honours of the Univerfity.

BACHELORS OF ARTS, viz.

David Abbot, Oliver Ainfworth, Timothy Alden, George Wafhington Appleton,
Charles

Charles Humphrey Atherton, John Atkinson, William Biglow, James Bowers, Thomas Bowman, Isaac Braman, Daniel Brooks, Lucas Brown, Francis Dana Channing, William Crosby, Christopher Cushing, Elijah Dunbar, Daniel Emerson, Samuel Aldridge Flagg, Jacob Flint, Thomas Geyer, James Blake Howe, Edward Jackson, David Kendall, Joseph M'Kean, Jesse Olds, Stephen Peabody, Joseph Perkins, Samuel Stearns, Hall Tufts.

And the following gentlemen to the Degree of

MASTERS OF ARTS, viz.

OUT OF COURSE.

John Chandler, A. B. 1787. Elisha Gardner, A. B. 1789. Israel Andrews, A. B. 1789.

IN COURSE.

Zabdiel Boylston Adams, Thomas Austin, Amos Bancroft, Samuel Procter Bayley, Ephraim Briggs, Ezekiel Hersey Derby, Abraham Redwood Ellery, John Harris, William Hodge, Asa King, Nathaniel Cabot Lee, John Morse, Samuel Benjamin Morse, Moses Porter Phelps, Thomas Pickman, Thomas Rice, Luther Stearns, Daniel Stone, Ichabod Tucker, Benjamin Turner, John Walton, Henry Dana Ward, David Wheaton, Calvin Whiting, Peter Whitney, Elijah Brigham, of Dartmouth College, admitted *ad eundum.*

BACHELORS OF PHYSIC.

Mr. William Ingalls, | Mr. Heber Chase,
Mr. Amos Bancroft, | Mr. Sam'l Adams.
Mr. John Walton.

DOCTORS OF DIVINITY.

Rev. David Tappan, | Rev. Joshua Toulmin, of Great-
Hollis Professor of | Britain.
Divinity.

DOCTOR OF PHYSIC.

John Haygarth, of Great-Britain.

On Thursday, the PHI BETA KAPPA Society held their anniversary meeting at Harvard University. The fraternity having previously convened and transacted the necessary business, proceeded to Harvard Chapel; where, before a respectable auditory, consisting of the Governors of the University, many of the reverend Clergy, and other gentlemen strangers, two Orations were delivered by CHARLES COFFIN, A. M. and JOSIAH QUINCY, A.M. The burst of animated approbation which these Orations received, speak their merit better than any laboured panegyric. The fraternity then returned to Mr. Warland's, and enjoyed " the feast of reason, and the flow of soul."

MARRIAGES.

MASSACHUSETTS.—*Boston,* Monf. Jacobus Pick to Miss Elizabeth Bradshaw; Mr. Samuel Dunnels to Miss Deborah Kneeland; Mr. Jeremiah Dyer to Miss Susannah Wild; John Halsey, Esq. of New York, to Miss Nancy Crafts; Mr. William Alline to Miss Rebecca Cazneau; Mr. William Kerr to Miss Nancy Hodgdon; Mr. Philip Surrell to Miss Sally Clark; Isaac Parker, Esq. to Miss Rebecca Hall; Mr. Snelling Powell to Miss Betsey Harrison; Mr. Nathan Webb to Miss Sally Leach; Mr. Leon Chappertin to Miss Bridget Colman; Mr. Lewis Lambert Macallier to Miss Lydia Fosdick.

Andover, Mr. Solomon Abbot to Miss Lucy Frye.

Bridgewater, Mr. Shepard Snell to Miss Anna Thayer; Mr. Nahum Mitchel to Miss Nabby Lazell.

Brookfield, Mr. Samuel Convers to Miss Rebecca Kitteredge.

Dracut, Mr. Moses Whiting to Miss Mary Hovey.

Framingham, Doctor Samuel Gamwell to Miss Patty Trowbridge.

Norton, L. Wheaton, Esq. to Miss Fanny Morey.

Plymouth, Mr. Dunbar to Miss Nancy Crombie; Mr. William Crombie, jun. to Miss Deborah Jackson.

Scituate, Mr. Thomas Foord to Miss Abigail Church.

Springfield, Mr. Jeremiah Hallett to Miss Edny Clark.

Weymouth, Mr. Samuel Fenner, to Miss Sukey Humphrey.

DEATHS.

MASSACHUSETTS.—*Boston,* On his passage to China, Capt. John Owen of this town; Miss Ann Willis, 63; Miss Harriet Stillman; Mr. Moses Bradley, 57; Mr. Thomas Tileston, 59; Mr. John Molineux, 38; Mr. Edward Wentworth; Mrs. Elsa Gardner, 26; Mrs. Abigail Hall.

Bridgewater, Mr. Nathan Hayward, 74; Monsieur Duchatel.

Beverly, Benjamin Jones, Esq. 78;
Brookfield, Hon. Elijah Dwight, Esq. 48.
Dorchester, Joseph Henderson, Esq.
Hampton Falls, Capt. Sandborn, 68.
Lynn, Mrs. Mary Lewis.
Roxbury, Mrs. Phebe Pratt, 46.
Pepperellborough, Josiah Fairfield, Esq. 47.
Sutton, Mrs. Amity Hayward, 27.
NEWHAMPSHIRE.—*Exeter,* Mr. James Ranlet, 65.

THE

MASSACHUSETTS MAGAZINE:

OR,

MONTHLY MUSEUM

OF

KNOWLEDGE and RATIONAL *ENTERTAINMENT.*

No. VIII.] FOR AUGUST, 1794. [Vol. VI.

CONTAINING,

WITH A HANDSOME ENGRAVING.

PRINTED AT *BOSTON*, FOR THE PROPRIETORS,
BY EZRA W. WELD AND WILLIAM GREENOUGH,
No. 49, STATE STREET.
Sold at JOHN WEST's Bookftore, No. 75, *Cornhill*, BOSTON ; and by the feveral
GENTLEMEN who receive Subfcriptions for this WORK.
MDCCXCIV.

ACKNOWLEDGMENTS to CORRESPONDENTS.

We commend the piety expreſſed in the verſification of the Lord's prayer, but we think it more ſuitable for the devotional hours of the Author than for our Magazine.

The Cenſor is too perſonal for admiſſion. Satire that has vice, not character, for its object, will always be acceptable.

Linus will be pleaſed to accept our acknowledgments for his uſeful and entertaining communications.

The Eſſayiſt, No. XI, is received. It ſhall have a place next month.

The hints of Correſpondents ſhall be complied with, as far as in our power.

The Apology of the *Duelliſt*, for private reaſons, cannot be publiſhed.

Will the daughters of the Muſes, who have favoured us with their compoſitions, condeſcend again to tune their lyres, that the Cabinet of Apollo may be filled with original pieces of ſentiment and elegance?

PRICES OF PUBLIC SECURITIES, BANK STOCK, &c.

Auguſt.	Six per Cents.	Three per Cents.	Defer'd Stock.	Maſſachuſ. State Notes.	U.S.B. Shares ab. par.	Maſſachuſ. Bank Shares.	Union Bank Shares ab. pr.	Final & L. Of. Cert. inter. fr. Jan. 1788.	Reg. Dt. with int. fr. March 4. 1789.	Indents Int. on Loan Offi. Cer. & Reg. Dt.	New Emiſſion Money.	O. Eqiſ. Mo.
	s. d.	s. d.	s. d.	s. d.	per ct.	dols.	per ct.	s. d.	s. d.	s. d.	s. d.	s.
1	18 10	10 9	11 9	14 9	17	None	6	16 6	15 6	9 0	8 0	40
2	18 10	10 9	11 9	14 9	17	at	6	16 6	15 6	9 0	8 0	40
4	18 10	10 9	11 9	14 9	17	mkt.	6 1-2	16 6	15 6	9 0	8 0	40
5	18 10	10 9	11 9	14 10	17		6 1-2	16 6	15 6	9 0	8 0	40
6	18 10	10 8	11 9	14 10	17		7	16 6	15 6	9 0	8 0	40
7	18 10	10 8	11 10	14 10	18		7	16 6	15 6	9 0	8 0	40
8	18 10	10 8	11 10	14 10	18		7	16 6	15 6	9 0	8 0	40
9	18 10	10 8	11 10	14 10	18		7	16 6	15 6	9 0	8 0	40
11	18 10	10 8	11 10	14 10	18		8	16 6	15 6	9 0	8 0	40
12	18 10	10 7	11 10	14 11	18		8	16 6	15 6	9 0	8 0	40
13	18 10	10 7	11 10	14 11	18		8	16 6	15 6	9 0	8 0	40
14	18 10	10 7	11 10	14 11	18		8	16 6	15 6	9 0	8 0	40
15	18 10	10 7	11 10	15	18		8	16 6	15 6	9 0	8 0	40
16	18 10	10 7	11 10	15	18		8	16 6	15 6	9 0	8 0	40
18	18 10	10 7	11 10	15	18		8	16 6	15 6	9 0	8 0	40
19	18 9	10 7	12	15	18		9	16 9	16	9 6	8 0	40
20	18 9	10 7	12	15	18		9	16 9	16	9 6	8 0	40
21	18 9	10 8	12	15	18		9 1-2	16 9	16	9 6	8 0	40
22	18 10	10 10	12	15	18		9 1-2	16 9	16	9 6	8 0	40
23	19	10 10	12	15	18		9 1-2	16 9	16	9 6	8 0	40
25	19	11	12	15	18		9 1-2	16 9	16	9 6	8 0	40
26	19	11	12	15	18		9 1-2	16 9	16	9 6	8 0	40
27	19	11	12	15	18		9 1-2	16 9	16	9 6	8 0	40
28	19	11	12	15	18		9 1-2	16 9	16	9 6	8 0	40
29	19	11	12	15	20		9 1-2	16 9	16	9 6	8 0	40
30	19	11	12	15 1-2	20		9 1-2	16 9	16	9 6	8 0	40
											8 0	40

JOHN MARSTON, *Stock Broker.*

FLORETTA and FLORIO.

THE

MASSACHUSETTS MAGAZINE.

FOR *AUGUST*, 1794.

The INSTANTANEOUS IMPRESSION.

[Illuftrated with a handfome ENGRAVING.]

FLORETTA poffeffed more beauty than fortune ; and though fhe was efteemed the moft amiable Shepherdefs in the Province of Lifle, fhe yet poffeffed more fenfe than beauty. A certain undefinable fweetnefs fat in every feature of her face, and charmed in every action of her mind. Like SHAKE-SPEARE's PERDITA—if fhe fung, fuch was the melody of her voice, we would have her fing for ever :—If fhe danced in the rural ring on the green, or on the upland, the Swains, with enamoured fondnefs, hung on every movement, and entreated her to dance for ever. In fhort, every incident of life ferved but as a mirror to exhibit her endowments. The fimplicity of her manners—the artlefs innocence of her mind—the warmth of her endearing and kind temper, were attractions that drew every Shepherd around her cottage, and made the little embofomed manfion like an aviary of birds—a fcene of vocal harmony and mufic. We might with voluptuous pleafure dwell on the defcription of her abode ; painting the enamelled beauties of the fcene with poetic colouring, and giving evenfrefh luxuriance to the tints of Nature. But

" ————To paint the lily,
" To throw a perfume on the violet,
" To fmooth the ice, to add another hue
" Unto the rainbow, or try, with taper light;
" The beauteousface of heaven to garnifh,
" Is wafteful and ridiculous excefs."

Her Cottage was beautified by Nature, and was tenanted by Heaven : Man, therefore, need not flatter himfelf poffeffed of abilities to enrich it by defcription. In vain did the Swains affail her with all the eloquence of erratic love : FLORETTA was too poor for a wife. In the prefent day of fafhionable extravagance, it is a melancholy truth, that no motives fo generally actuates the mind as intereft. Our luxuries and refinements beget innumerable wants, unknown in earlier times ; which force the human mind to deviate even from its moft amiable volitions, and profecute lines of conduct as mortifying as they are difgraceful. The priftine fimplici-ty ty of our plains is contaminated with a portion of the rage that has gained such entire possession of the fashionable world. The Shepherd no more invokes the inspiration of the rural Pan ; the oaten reed lies neglected ; and the purling streams flow unassociated by the wonted melody of the piping swains. In the little retired village, indeed, which gave birth to the lovely FLORETTA, a remnant may be seen of Arcadian simplicity ; but tinctured with the volatile salt of perfidious refinement, it exists in so vitiated a state, that it deserves not the name of Felicity. An incessant round of pleasure, indeed, may be foolishly conceived by the young, infatuated, and thoughtless, to be happiness. Levity, bordering on licentiousness, marks the characters of the females ; and an unbounded thirst in the pursuit of interest and pleasure, those of the men. In such a society may it not be wondered, that the lovely FLORETTA remained uncontaminated, since we know how easily, and how imperceptibly the chains of passion cling around the heart ? Gilt o'er by the sanctity of custom,. Vice loses its deformity, and assumes the most fascinating features. Never, therefore, O never let us trust ourselves one instant, in the presence of a crime. The first step towards iniquity is difficult to accomplish— the second may be painful—but the third is easy : The ladder that reaches to the abyss, becomes gradually more easy, as we descend, till at last we find pleasure in what at first gave us pain. FLORETTA is an excellent exception to this general rule. She stood the shock of association unhurt: She saw through the misleading glare of lawless pleasures, and shuddered at the danger she was daily exposed to. To the many assiduities of the village swains

she was impenetrable. They sung, they danced, and they piped in vain, She saw that they assailed her virtue, not her heart. They did not seek for connubial delights in her society, but for momentary gratifications in her seduction. Aware of their ends, she had strength and virtue enough to defeat them ; and she lived the pattern of imitation, as she was the emblem innocence.

FLORIO, the son of a farmer in the neighbourhood, returned from the Academy, where he had completed his education ;—an education not designed to render him eminent in any public profession, but such as fitted him for social intercourse, and domestic retirement. His father, possessed of happy affluence, esteemed it more eligible to station his heir in the bosom of his pastoral fields, than in the round of dissipation attendant on a town life, or in the busy, bustling, enviable road to fame. FLORIO was happily calculated for the path in which he was to walk. He was possessed of a most captivating sensibility ; tender in his nature, and with a comfortable mixture of that wit and humour which is the seasoning to the dish of life.

Strolling one day across the uplands of the beautiful and various country near his father's, he accidentally saw FLORETTA.—FLORETTA saw him. The glance was mutual, and the Impression was Instantaneous ! They felt an undescribable something take possession of their hearts : It was pleasure, mingled with pain. This mutual sensibility urged them to pass on ; but an irresistible impulse fixed them to the spot. Their eyes alternately met, and fell towards the ground : They were confounded, as their glances, in the interchange, were discovered, and from the pure ingenuousness

genuousness of their souls, a ver-million spread itself upon their cheeks.

FLORIO, however, recovering him-self from the enchantment which had chained him to the ground, advanced with the most enamoured, and yet throbbing heart, to FLO-RETTA.

"May I not (says he, with the most winning sweetness of accent) —may I not help you to tend your flock, my Shepherdess? I will be a faithful guide, and will conduct them across the hill for you, with care.—Do, pray, let me ease you of the task."

"Gentle Stranger (replies the lovely FLORETTA), it is so delight-ful a task, that I cannot agree to part with it."

"Then pray (says he), my fair one, let me enjoy but a part of the delight. I know not how it is, but I take an interest in the welfare of your flock. I think they are the finest Lambs I ever saw. But bless me (continues he, with a sigh), what have I to do with them?—They are the property of a shepherdess, whose heart, no doubt, is in the possession of some favoured Swain, and I tar-ry and gaze upon them, to my un-doing."—A momentary suspense seized them both, on this instant.— She knew not what to say; and he wished to have the doubt removed, for which the hint was thrown out. His susceptibility was touched—He read the desired answer in her blushing cheek and downcast eye. He saw the inward workings of her heart, and with a tumultuous tide of transport he snatched the fair one's hand, and imprinted on it the warm-est effusion of his soul. Recollect-ing himself, and starting at the thought of his having been, perhaps, too vehement in his address, he, with the awe that is inspired by the emo-tions of honourable love, retreated a few paces, and prayed the fair one to forgive him the effects of a trans-port which he could not smother, and which he hoped did not arise from misconception or disrespect. The language of the heart, as it is gathered from the eyes, is the sim-plest thing on earth, and did more for this enamoured pair, in two min-utes of suspense which succeeded to this apology, than all the ecclair-cissement that words could have brought about. Were we permit-ted, in imitation of the most captiva-ting Physiognomist that ever penned a History for the entertainment of Mankind, to translate the dumb lan-guage into English, it would near-ly run as follows:

"Believe me, kind swain (said FLORETTA), I am as pleased with your transports as yourself. I feel an inexpressible pleasure in your society; and would the delicacy of my sex permit, I would return your caress with equal ardour, and shew you how much your first appearance hath prepossessed me in your fa-vour."

"O Heavens! (exclaimed the enraptured FLORIO) And is it pos-sible that I have made an impression on your heart?—Is it possible, that I may be happy enough to be united to you for ever—to dwell in your society—to hang upon your sweet-ness, and, like the bee from the per-fumed floweret, distil the balmy essence from that lip, without rav-aging its beauty, or injuring its sweets?—Is it possible that I may be your's?"

"It is, my Shepherd, it is! There is an attachment in my bo-som, which, as it is fixed there, no doubt, by the hand of Providence, for the wisest ends, I do not coun-teract, which tells me I must be your's or no one's."

When

When the happy interval was paſt, which had been filled up with ſuch ſignificant intercourſe of the eyes as hath formed the ground-work for the above interpretation, they parted, without reducing it to more explicit language—but not before he had entreated to know her name.

" Floretta—a Maid whoſe only fortune is her innocence, and her occupation a Shepherdeſs."

" And I am Florio, poſſeſſed of a comfortable inheritance ; not e-nough, indeed, to anſwer the calls of Luxury, but more than ſufficient for two ſuch people as you and I are."

They parted—ſhe to conduct her ſheep to the paſture, on the brow of the hill ; and he to ſeek his father. He ſoon found him, and throwing himſelf at his feet, with an earneſt-neſs and a warmth which beſpoke at once the ardour of his affection, and the ſincerity of his heart, he be-ſought him to conſent to his union with Floretta. The father knew her—admired her ;—for every one that knew, admired her; and raiſing his ſon, with parental tenderneſs told him—the choice was worthy of his heart—He conſidered Floret-ta as the richeſt female of the Land, ſince ſhe poſſeſſed treaſures more eſtimable than lucre, in an undefil-ed and a pure heart. She would make a wife capable of rendering his journey through this life a chain of felicity, in which there would be found no intermitting link of anxiety or ſorrow.

Florio, in a few days, was join-ed to Floretta ; and at this very moment they are the happieſt couple in the Province of Liſle.

[Weſtmin. Mag.

ANECDOTE of Dean SWIFT.

DR. Swift had an odd blunt way that was miſtaken by ſtrangers for ill nature ; it was ſo odd that there is no deſcribing it* but by facts. One evening Gay and Pope went to ſee him. On their coming in, " Hey day, gen-tlemen," ſaid the Dean, " what can be the meaning of this viſit ? How came you to leave all the great Lords you are ſo fond of, to come hither to ſee a poor ſcurvy Dean ?" Becauſe we would rather ſee you than any of them. " Ay, any one that did not know you ſo well as I do, might poſſibly believe you ; but ſince you are come I muſt get ſome ſupper for you, I ſuppoſe." No, Doctor, we have ſupped already. " Supped already ! that is impoſſi-ble, why it is not eight o'clock."—Indeed we have. " That's very ſtrange ; but, if you had not ſup-ped, I muſt have got ſomething for you ; let me ſee, a couple of lob-ſters would have done very well—two ſhillings ; tarts, a ſhilling : but you will drink a glaſs of wine with me, though you ſupped ſo much before your time only to ſpare my pocket." No, we had rather talk with you, than drink with you.— " But if you had ſupped with me, as in all reaſon you ought to have done, you muſt then have drank with me ; a bottle of wine two ſhil-lings—two and two are four, and one is five ; juſt two and ſix pence a piece ;

* The late Archbiſhop of Armagh, happening to object one day in Swift's company to an expreſſion of Pope, as not being the pureſt Engliſh, Swift anſwered with his uſual roughneſs, " I could never get the blockhead to ſtudy his grammar."

a piece ; there Pope, there's half a crown for you, and there's another for you, Sir ; for I won't fave any thing by you, I am determined." This was all faid and done with his ufual ferioufnefs on fuch occafions : and in fpite of every thing they could fay to the contrary, he actually obliged them to take the money.

For *the* MASSACHUSETTS MAGAZINE.

The MEMORIALIST. No. IV.

IN whatever light we confider man, whether as a felfifh, a focial, or religious being, we ftill behold in him the traces of infinite wifdom. All the literary fciences, all the attainments in virtue and morality, are fo many rivulets which terminate in the vaft ocean of boundlefs perfection.

Next to the important confideration of religion, we may place the great principle of humanity. All civilized claffes of men, nay, even the rude barbarians, entertain fome conceptions of this important virtue. Such high ideas did the ancients have of humanity, that their elyfium itfelf was not confidered as a ftate of perfect happinefs without it. Children, according to their philofophy, met in thofe blifsful abodes the fpirits of their fathers, and enjoyed a focial communion. The Roman bards carried this principle to excefs. Virgil in particular, while he records the pleafures of the virtuous in elyfium, with language next to infpiration, reprefents them folicitous for the fate of their friends in this upper world. But while we admire the fplendor of the pagan virtues, unaffifted by revelation, well may the Chriftian exult in the fuperior excellency of his own religion.

The facred pages inculcate, in the moft emphatical terms, the doctrines of humanity. They command mutual affection, not on the comparatively narrow and felfifh principle of patriotifm, but becaufe we are all children of the fame Parent—the Father of the univerfe.— Does not this prove the divine original of Chriftianity, and fufficiently refute the cant of fophifts, and the invidious fneer of infidelity ? But the great principle of humanity, like all other paffions, will decay, if it is not cherifhed with proper care and attention. It is a tender plant, that grows only in feeling minds.

By frequently vifiting the houfe of ficknefs, and abodes of defpair ; by ameliorating the miferies, and relieving the diftreffes of our fellow men, we enkindle in our bofoms the generous flame of humanity : And if it is not prefumption to ufe the expreffion, we perform, though in a humbler fphere, the province of the Deity. If mankind would uniformly act on this motive, the world, inftead of exhibiting a horrid fpectacle of jars and diffenfions, would be fuddenly converted into a glorious millenium. And we may rationally conjecture, that if this grand period will ever be brought forth by the operation of natural caufes, it muft proceed on fome fimilar principle. Then would the barren defert of the foul bloffom with the rofes of contentment—happinefs reaffume her empire in the human breaft— and the whole face of nature be converted from barrennefs and folitude, into beauty and fertility.

Having proceeded thus far, I fhall endeavour to point out fome of
the

the moſt obvious cauſes which interrupt the growth of humanity.— Operas and maſquerades tend evidently to deaden the finer feelings of nature. Theſe were the cauſes which, by confounding all natural diſtinctions, by teaching the man to ape the manners of a woman, and by the introduction of a thouſand vicious faſhions, poured a torrent of licentiouſneſs on modern Europe. It was theſe cauſes which rouſed to oppoſition the keen irony of Swift, and the refine ᵈ humour of Addiſon. May we not with propriety aſcribe to the ſame ſources the viſible decline of genius in that country, which once was juſtly denominated the Athens of the world? I mention theſe cauſes in particular, as unfavourable to humanity, to ſuggeſt to my countrymen the propriety of effectually guarding againſt them, if they ſhould ever appear on this ſide of the Atlantic. I will now mention one principle, which accelerates the progreſs of humanity—and that is, a ſocial and frequent intercourſe with ſociety.—

How can we exerciſe thoſe feelings, which nature has implanted in us, for the benefit of mankind, if we ſhun the company of man? As I ſaid before, thoſe paſſions will die for want of exerciſe. Some few cold hearted bigots may pretend that the life of man ought to be a life of laborious virtue, independent of theſe pleaſures, and they are merely pretences. The path of our duty is ſtrewed with flowers. Why has the Deity enriched the fields with a beautiful green, and tinctured the ſkies with a lively blue, if it is not that the eye may be refreſhed when it ſlides along the vaſt landſcape of heaven and earth? Half of the beauties of nature are viſionary beauties. The reſtleſs eye of imagination catches the brilliant features as they tranſpire, and by its creative faculty, multiplies them to infinity. Here then the mind of the Deity ſhines through his creation. Let us be perſuaded, that arguments, drawn from the nature of things, cannot be refuted, and indulge freely the ſenſations of humanity.

ANECDOTE.

THE Emperor Charles V. was the great patron of Titiano, a celebrated painter. Among the other honours which he laviſhed upon him, he inveſted him with the Order of Santiago at Bruſſels, and, in 1553, conſtituted him a Count Palatine of the empire at Barcelona. Theſe favours alarmed the jealouſy of the Nobles both of Germany and Spain; but their envy drew no other anſwer from Charles, than that he had many Nobles in his empire and but one Titiano.— The artiſt, who was at ſome diſtance, employed upon a picture, overheard the retort with conſcious

ſatisfaction; and, as he made his reverence to the Emperor, dropt a pencil on the floor; the courteous Monarch took it up, and delivering it to him, confounded by this ſecond mark of his condeſcenſion, added, that, to wait on Titiano, was a ſervice for an Emperor. Charles did not only grace this eminent artiſt with the ſplendid ornaments and titles above-mentioned, he gave him more ſolid marks of his favour, appointing him rents in Naples of two hundred ducats annually each, beſides a munificent compenſation for every picture he executed.

The

The GENERAL OBSERVER. No. XLVII.

" When the obligations of morality are taught, let the fanctions of Chriftianity never be forgotten ; by which it will be fhewn that they give ftrength and luftre to each other : Religion will appear to be the voice of Reafon, and Morality to be the will of God."

JOHNSON.

IT is furprizing into what extravagances human nature will run when it has got loofe from all reftraints, and prides itfelf in being uncontroled in any of its vagaries ! Even the intelligent mind, when it feels felf fufficient, and equal to the tafk of exploring its own way, and directing its own movements, regardlefs of all prefcription, and of all regulation, human or divine, except from *the divinity that ftirs within*—often flies off eccentric, is loft in clouds, or finks grovelling in the mire, and acts very irrationally while it glories in following reafon. Look at France ! Look at her philofophers ! Look at her zealous reformers ! Look at their humble imitators, both in Europe and America !

Happy, indeed, are the followers of reafon ! But reafon is cool, and requires fedatenefs in order to attend to her dictates, and an impartial and difpaffionate temper in order to feel their force, and fubmit to their authority. In the din of contention, the directions of reafon are not heard, or not regarded. In the glow of triumph, other principles than reafon prefide and direct. In the rage of reformation, zeal takes the lead, and reafon is left far behind. In the infurrection of the paffions, reafon is dethroned, and, like other eminent characters, hurried by the rabble to the *guillotine*. When Enthufiafm, like a raving goddefs, infpires men's minds ; and when fuch inflamed minds vie with each other in a certain novelty and extravagance in thinking, in acting, and in expreffion, we are not to expect a rational and regular line of conduct ; we are not to expect an adequate well digefted form of government ; much lefs are we to look for a regular fyftem of religion. When fuch are the leading features of a nation, what rational man would call fuch a period *the reign of reafon ?* .

France exhibits an awful fpecimen and proof, that when men of warm paffions are receding from one extreme, they cannot ftop at any middle, or moderate point, but will run to the other extreme ; that when the fhackles of flavery are fuddenly thrown off, unexperienced minds, in their hafte to get away from the awe and reftraint of defpotifm, are apt to run into all the extravagances of licentioufnefs and anarchy ; and that, in their zeal to rid themfelves of prieftcraft and religious impofition, to which they have ignominioufly been fubjected, they are in danger of difcarding religion itfelf, and all its neceffary inftitutions and minifters.

When the tempeft is over ; when the elements are compofed ; and the atmofphere is ferene, then the fun of reafon will fhine out ; men will fee what confufion has been made, and begin to fet things to rights ; regular fyftems of government will be framed ; equitable forms of judiciary proceeding will be eftablifhed ; religion, without which men cannot fubfift in regular fociety, will be recalled from exile ; reafon will be coolly confulted in devifing the beft modes of worfhip ;

thip; the difcarded Bible will be hunted up and carefully examined ; impartial reafon will feel and acknowledge the force and divinity of its doctrines and precepts ; and religion, revealed religion, the Chriftian religion, will appear to be the moft reafonable thing in the world.

Religion refults from the nature and ftate of man as the creature of God, as a rational creature, and as connected with others. It comprehends, therefore, all thofe acts of piety towards God, all thofe righteous and benevolent tranfactions with men, and all that regular and becoming conduct in the various fcenes and relations of life, which unbiaffed reafon, enlightened by revelation, approves. All religion has reference to a Deity, and comprehends inward exercifes of veneration and affiance, and outward acts of religious worfhip, as well as the practice of the focial virtues from a principle of obedience. Religion in fyftem comprehends all moral obligations ; religion in practice is the faithful difcharge of thefe obligations. That religion, therefore, which leaves out any of the rational acts of piety which are more immediately due to the Supreme Being, is quite as defective

as if it left out any of the effential focial virtues. *To walk humbly with God*, is as neceffary a part of religion, and as agreeable to reafon, as *to do juftly, and to love mercy*. As man is a dependent and connected being, the religion of man confifts in paying a proper regard to all beings, in proportion to this dependence and connexion. If there is a being upon whom we are abfolutely dependent for our exiftence, fupport, and happinefs, that being claims our moft grateful and devout acknowledgments. If this being has commiffioned an auguft perfonage to bring us the overtures of peace, to prepare us for happinefs, and to remove all obftructions to happinefs which we could not remove ourfelves, moft certainly, there are peculiar duties, affections, and acknowledgments, which are due from us to this perfonage. So that the fyftem of religion, the peculiar obfervances, prefcribed by Chriftianity, muft, to impartial reafon, appear as rational, and as effential, as any of the duties which we owe to civil rulers, to our earthly parents, and to our moft generous benefactors. The reign of the pureft reafon, will be the reign of the pureft religion.

The G A M B L E R: An A N E C D O T E.

IN the days of yore, a certain young gentleman had become a notorious *inamorato* of the billiard and card table. All his hopes and enjoyment were concentrated in a kind of amufement, in which, as an adept, he had no compeer. In the wife and fortunate adjuftment of things, the *compagnon de chambre* of this gambler was a paragon of virtue. His celebrity for regularity of deportment and abhorrence of

every fpecies of vice had pervaded the country. He frequently reminded the deluded youth of the great impropriety and ruinous tendency of fuch a career. All remonftrances, however, were totally inadequate to his reformation. To effect this, the good *compagnon de chambre* was confcious that, unlefs fome method were foon adopted, his deftruction would inevitably follow. He therefore contrived one

night,

night, when the gambler was gone to pay his devoirs to the billiard table, to get a monstrous great black hog into their chamber. The morning began to dawn as he returned. All was hushed as the foot of night. He was beginning to open the door, when, to his unutterable astonishment, he was saluted with a tremendous *grunt*. Before the door was half open, his *Pandemonian majesty*, as, from his shape, colour, and language, our hero took

him to be, rushed out—broke down the door with a horrid crash—took up the gambler with irresistible force—disgorged an impetuous torrent of the salutary dialect—and sprang forward with renovated vigour, till he and our hero made a glorious pitch from the top to the bottom of the stairs.

It was happy that this expedient proved the conversion and effectual reformation of the young gentleman. Q.

On DUELLING.

[From BOSWELL'S Life of Dr. JOHNSON.]

ON —— I dined with Dr. Johnson at General Oglethorpe's, where we found Dr. Goldsmith.— The question was started whether duelling was consistent with moral duty. The brave old General, fired at this, said with a lofty air, " Undoubtedly a man has a right to defend his honour." Dr. Johnson entered on the subject. " As men become in a high degree refined, various causes of offence arise ; which are considered to be of such importance, that life must be staked to atone for them, though in reality they are not so. A body that has received a very fine polish may be easily hurt. Before men arrive at this artificial refinement, if one tells his neighbour he lies, his neighbour tells him he lies ; if one gives his neighbour a blow, his neighbour gives him a blow ; but in a state of highly polished society, an affront is held to be a serious injury. It must, therefore, be resented, or rather a duel must be fought upon it ; as men have agreed to banish from their society one who puts up with an affront without fighting a duel. Now, Sir, it is never unlawful to fight in self de-

fence. He, then, who fights a duel, does not fight from passion against his antagonist, but out of self defence ; to avert the stigma of the world, and to prevent himself from being driven out of society. I could wish there was not that superfluity of refinement ; but while such notions prevail, no doubt a man may lawfully fight a duel."

Let it be remembered that this justification is applicable only to the person who *receives* an affront. All mankind must condemn the aggressor.

The General told us, that when he was a very young man, serving under Prince Eugene of Savoy, he was setting in a company at table with a Prince of Wertemberg. The Prince took up a glass of wine, and, by a fillip, made some of it fly in Oglethorpe's face. Here was a nice dilemma. To have challenged him instantly, might have fixed a quarrelsome character upon the young soldier : to have taken no notice of it might have been considered as cowardice. Oglethorpe, therefore, keeping his eye upon the Prince, and smiling all the time, as if he took what his highness had done.

done in jeſt, ſaid, " Mon Prince,"
in Engliſh, " That's a good joke ;
but we do it much better in England ;" and threw a whole glaſs of
wine in the Prince's face.   An old
General who ſat by, ſaid, " *Il a bien,
fait, mon Prince, vous l'avez com-
mencé ;*" and thus all ended in good
humour.

HISTORICAL ANECDOTES.

A GENTLEMAN ſent a buck to the
celebrated Judge Hale in his circuit,
who was to have a cauſe tried before him
that aſſize ; the cauſe being called, and the
Judge taking notice of the name, aſked if
it was the ſame perſon, who had preſented
him with a buck ? And finding it to be the
ſame, the Judge told him, " He could not
ſuffer the trial to go on till he had paid
him for his buck." To which the gentleman anſwered, " that he never ſold his
veniſon, and that he had done no more to
him, than he had always done to every
Judge that came the circuit ; which was
confirmed by ſeveral gentlemen on the
bench.   But all this would not prevail upon the Judge ; nor would he ſuffer the trial to proceed till he had paid for the veniſon ; upon which the gentleman withdrew
the record, ſaying, " He would not try his
cauſe before a Judge, who ſuſpected him
to be guilty of bribery by a cuſtomary civility."   *Dr. Burnet.*

ENIGARDUS, principal Secretary of
ſtate to Charlemagne, made his addreſſes
to one of the Emperor's daughters, and ſhe
conſidering him as a perſon who had riſen
by merit, received his addreſſes, and gave
him opportunity in winter nights to viſit
her in her own apartment, where their
mutual affection was permanently eſtabliſhed.   Staying one night very late, at
his departure they ſaw a great ſnow had
fallen, which put them both into great perplexity for fear his foot ſhould be known,
and his life be endangered, for privately
viſiting the King's daughter without his
licence ; to prevent this, ſhe took the gentleman upon her back, and carried him
the length of the court to his own lodgings without ſuffering him to put his foot
to the ground ; ſo that if any inquiry had
been made next morning no footing would
have appeared but her own : It ſo happened, that Charlemagne, who was induſtrious in public affairs, was up in his ſtudy,
and ſeeing this witty contrivance, was in
debate with himſelf whether he ſhould
be angry or pleaſed.   Next day in a great
appearance of the nobility, his daughter and Enigardus being preſent, he demanded, " what puniſhment that ſervant
was liable to, who employ'd a king's daughter in the office of a mule, and made himſelf be carried on her back through the
ſnow in the night, and in very ſharp and
piercing weather ; all the Lords ſoon gave
their opinions, that ſo inſolent a wretch
ought to ſuffer a ſevere death.   The prin-
ceſs and the ſecretary were under a
dreadful ſurpriſe, looked ghaſtly upon one
another, and expected nothing elſe than to
be flead alive.   The Emperor perceiving
them under a terrible conſternation, ſmiled
on his ſecretary, ſaying, " Enigardus, hadſt
thou loved my daughter, thou ſhould have
addreſſed thyſelf to her father for his conſent, in the omiſſion of which thou haſt de-
ſerved death ; but to relieve you both from
your flights and fears, inſtead of taking
away one, I will give thee two lives ; here,
take

take thy beautiful and kind portrefs to wife, fear God and love one another." How thefe lovers were on a fudden tranfported into ecftacies of joy and happinefs. I leave the reader to imagine.

Cayfin. Hol. Court.

———————

For the MASSACHUSETTS MAGAZINE.

The REPOSITORY. No. XXIII.

WHAT abundant thanks are due to the Redeemer for the manifeftations of his tender love! How doth the affurance that his regards are univerfal, and his benignity to the creature he hath made, exhauftlefs and unbounded, fmooth the bed of pain, and remove the thorn from the pillow of the dying! How dreadful, to behold a fellow creature ftanding upon the borders of our world, and fhrinking from that leap, which, however, muft inevitably, and probably with the coming moment, be taken! Impotent is every effort; no hand can refcue, and unavailing pity can only pour its fruitlefs lamentations. 'She is gone; but oh with what reluctance fhe relinquifhed life! I beheld the laft breath quiver upon her lips, and I faw the agonies of her parting foul. I entered her chamber; I approached her bed; I found that the king of terrors was indeed making fwift advances; the cold dews of death diffufed itfelf over the whole expiring frame, and not a veftige of hope remained! She lifted up her languid eyes, examining, alternately, with heart affecting earneftnefs, the faces which furrounded her. At length, with a voice of inconceivable terror, fhe exclaimed, Am I dying? am I dying? Oh fpeak, and eafe my burfting heart! She was made to underftand that it was conceived fhe was. Oh then, fhe rejoined, I cannot die, I have no God, no Chrift, no Saviour! Her accents, ftill found terrific in my ear. I was inexpreffibly fhocked. For fome moments fhe remained filent, until once more lifting up her dying eyes, fhe addreffed herfelf to me: What fhall I do? I have no Saviour, to whom in this tremendous moment, to make application! I took this reference for a permiffion to fpeak; it was with difficulty that I had refrained. Why, my friend, give place to fuch fhocking apprehenfions? Why conceive that you have no Saviour? Tell me, is the arm of the Lord fhortened? Is his ear heavy that he cannot hear? And doth not falvation ftill belong to him? O yes, I know that all power indeed belongeth unto God; but I have no proof of my intereft in a Redeemer, no manifeftation that I am the purchafe of Emmanuel's fufferings! What proof, I returned, do you require? Are you not a finner? Were you not loft? And is not Jefus Chrift the Saviour, the benign, the compaffionate Redeemer of finners? Did he not come to *feek that which* was loft? And fhall he feek in vain? Shall he not find? Is your fpirit the breath of God? And will God doom to eternal mifery his own breath, efpecially when it has coft him fo many pangs to refcue it from deftruction? I am fenfible, I added, that you will fufpect my teftimony; you have fuppofed me entangled, wrapped about in clouds of error. But, my dear friend, in the word of our God there can be

no ·

no deception : The declarations of Jehovah are furely worthy of all acceptation ; and his records proclaim the univerfality of his love, and his power ; the reftitution of all things, and the wiping of every tear from off every face.

The furrounding individuals remained filent ; they were willing to let the heretic, if in her power, foothe the agonized mind of her departing friend ; nay, their countenances were defcriptive of approbation ; a gleam of hope feemed alfo to light up the face of the dy-

ing ; but it was only the meteor of the moment, her fears returned, and defpair enwrapped her foul. —Yet few perfons were more worthy. In life fhe was ufeful, benevolent, and amiable. How important is an acquaintance with the great and confolatory truths of our moft holy religion !

Penetrated with the goodnefs of my God, and wrapped in the robe of Emmanuel's righteoufnefs, I proftrate at the feet of the Moft High.

CONSTANTIA.

ALEXIS : Or, The COTTAGE in the WOODS.

(Continued from the 399th page.)

PART SECOND.

Alexis paffes a twelvemonth in the Cottage.—He is forced to leave it.

CHAPTER II.

THE LESSON OF MUSIC.

AURORA had difpelled night, and the fun began to gild the tops of the trees, a cloudlefs azure fky proclaimed a ferene day, and foon the balmy frefhnefs, inftilled by Zephyr in the brilliant pearls of the dew, was going to yield to the ardent fires of the meridian ; all nature was beauteous and tranquil ; but the heart of Alexis was not.

Pale, trembling, bewildered, he waited the fatal doom of death ; already had he recommended himfelf to the mercy of the Supreme Being : Prayer, in fome manner, reftored the calm of his fenfes ; he juft rofe from his knees, when a gentle voice calls him ; " Alexis, are you awake ?"—" Yes," exclaimed he, " yes, I am, and prepared for all events !"—" It is Candor," replied the voice, " he comes to open your door and to embrace you !"

To embrace you !—Alexis was quite aftonifhed : Was this a new fnare ? Did his judgment deceive him ? He made a thoufand conjectures, when Candor opens the door, enters, and is ftruck with the perplexity of his friend. He looks at him, lays hold of his hand, and, with fuch an air of penetration and truth, that Alexis cannot help liftening to him, and makes him blufh at his errors ; he fays, " What have you, my fon—what means the trouble in which I fee you ?—Is it becaufe I have kept you laft night in a kind of captivity ?—My friend, you would have wronged me, not to confide in your Candor ?—I cannot believe it :—I would be afhamed to think—compofe yourfelf, hear your father, and conquer that childifh fear which cannot but grieve me.

" You were locked up laft night, and every future night I muft obferve the fame precaution, which is more effential to me than you imagine.—It ought not to alarm you, becaufe, the whole day I fhall give

you

you a thoufand proofs of my fincere friendfhip; but I infift upon your not endeavouring to penetrate into that fatal fecret. It is all I cherifh, it is all I poffefs, do not tear it from me! My Alexis, did you but know!—Deferve my confidence, be always fubmiffive, tender, and regardful; and foon I will difclofe you my condition and misfortunes. Make yourfelf worthy of that confeffion!—I will not conceal it from you; nay, I expect of you a moft fignal fervice—but a fervice founded upon juftice and gratitude, which, if you love me, will never affect your delicacy. I am old, Alexis, I have been inhumanly betrayed; I was deprived of what I held moft dear on earth. You fhall be mine avenger.—You fhall deferve the charming recompenfe, which I have deftined for you; the charming recompenfe which will be dear to your heart! —Urge me not to fay more—I conjure you, let me keep my fecret for a while—one day I will depofit it in your bofom—you will know me then; but as yet, I am compelled to reftrain your curiofity; I do not conftrue it into a crime, it is natural to your age. Every night permit me to lock you up, I beg it as a favour!—On thefe terms live with us, difpel all cares and anxiety, and be truly perfuaded that your innocence is in no kind of danger in this folitary abode: we all cherifh religion, wifdom, and virtue!"

This difcourfe, and the venerable appearance of the old man, rid Alexis of all perplexity. The balm of confolation defcended into his heart, and ferenity enlivened again his countenance. His foul was frank and honeft; he communicated his foolifh panic to Candor, fmiled and embraced him. Cla-

ra's father was fome time confufed when he heard that Alexis had feen his nocturnal ceremony; but foon he recovered himfelf, laid hold of his arm, and both went below to Clara, who had juft rifen, and had as bad a night as her young friend, but from a caufe of a quite oppofite nature. Love, which began to enter her heart, the happinefs which awaited her, and her own flattering notions, had kept her awake all night long; but it only ferved to add new energy to her charms; her eyes betrayed an air of languor, for which her father chid her, and fhe blufhed with fo much grace, as made Alexis quite contrite for having doubted a fingle minute the fincerity of that lovely child.

Soon after, Germain joined them, and they all three requefted their new gueft to give them a fpecimen of his abilities on the harpfichord. Alexis, with eager compliance, fung his romance, and the audience could not forbear fhedding tears.

Clara performed after him, and though her fkill was not equal in point of perfection to that of Alexis, he was enraptured with her performance, efpecially with a fong fhe added to it. She had compofed it during night, and the mufic was fo fweet and melodious, as to leave Candor much in doubt of its being of her own compofing.

A SONG.

PEOPLE fay that at my tender age,
The fmart of love no tongue can tell,
 I know it well,
 And will as well
Elude his fnares, and fcorn his rage:
A man by fate is hither drove,
I guefs he is a lovely lad,
 To him I'm kind—and what of that?
Sure, fure, 'tis no fuch thing as love!

His prefence always gladdens me,
His fmiles for crowns I would not fell,

I

I know it well,
And forefee well,
His heart will prove as true to me.
    In his eyes, with joy, I fee move
    The flame which within him doth burn,
    To me he is kind in his turn;
Sure, fure, 'tis no fuch thing as love!

When Cupit's dart does wound the
    breaft,
The heart is fore, and never well;
    I feel it well,
    And roundly tell,
His malice ne'er fhall fteal my reft.

All feelings in me fweetnefs prove,
Inftead of gloom I feel defpair,
I am blythe like May, and light like
    air—
Then fure 'tis no fuch thing as love!

Thus the day was fpent in pleafing amufement. At night Alexis
was locked up, but felt no uneafinefs, and enjoyed a found fleep.

It had been determined that A-
lexis fhould begin his leffons with
Clara on the day following ; he
of courfe went to her apartment.
Candor and Germain went to cultivate their garden, and did what
was neceffary to be done in the
houfe, while our young mafter was
left alone with his pupil. The reader will judge, from a fketch I fhall
give of this leffon, all thofe which
Candor's daughter received afterwards. Let us enter the mufic
room, and hear without interrupt-
ing.

Alexis. Clara, I find the fong
you fung yefterday very pretty ;
have you compofed it for me ?

Clara. For whom elfe ? Is there
more than one Alexis in the world ?

Alexis. You are juft like me : I
have feen many women, yet never
but one Clara.

Clara. You joke : I have no
charms, no drefs !—

Alexis. Drefs is the refult of art,
charms are the gift of nature ; you
poffefs thofe, and join to them a
foul, a heart !—

Clara. If I have a heart, I have

only perceived it two days fince ;
when I faw you, it is quite natural.

Alexis. What, did it never beat
for your father ?

Clara. Yes, it did, but that is a
quite different fenfation !—Now I
will afk him to explain me thofe
two fentiments.

Alexis. Will you afk your father ?

Clara. Yes, I will. Why fhould
I conceal from him what I feel ? I
want no other confidant than him !
Now mind, Alexis, when we walk
or repofe together in the grove, or
fay a hundred times a day, we love
one another, I tell him our converfation every night.

Alexis. Ah heaven ! take care !

Clara. What makes you be fo
much furprifed ? my father is very
glad to fee me content ; if I am
pleafed with you, why fhould he be
angry ?

Alexis. Did he never enter into
any difcourfe with you about love ?

Clara. Yes, that he did, and
very often too ! He told me a hundred times that love is a fatal paffion, which confounds reafon and
fenfe, and makes people jealous, uneafy, raving !—Oh ! you cannot
imagine how he forbade me to give
way to that cruel fentiment.

Alexis. Well, Clara, do you
think he will approve of ours ?

Clara. Of ours !—you are miftaken : It is not love I feel for you.
I feel nothing of what my father
hath told me ! Oh ! I fhould be
very forry if ever I did.

Alexis. What innocence ! O my
Clara, preferve then that pure fentiment, and always be upon your
guard of not falling in love, or at
leaft if you do, don't difcover it to
Candor !

Clara. Nay, Alexis, I fhall like
you no more, if you hinder me from
placing my confidence in fo refpect-

able a father!—He fhall always know not only the moft fecret thoughts of my heart, but I will even communicate them to his old friend Germain.

Alexis. Oh! oh! to all the world, if you pleafe!—Clara, Clara, how unhappy fhould I be, if—

Clara. Only fee! you take the alarm at every thing!—Well, let us drop that fubject, and take leffon!—

Alexis. You do not underftand me!—Did you but know people—

Clara. People! my father is not people!—

Alexis. He certainly is fo kind, fo generous!—But pray do you know his misfortunes?

Clara. No, but Germain does.

Alexis. Have you known your mother?

Clara. Yes; oh how fhe loved me!—how I loved her!

Alexis. What is become of her?

Clara. I can't tell. I was brought up in a convent till I was eight years old; my mother came often to fee me! During the latter part of my ftay, I could hear no more of her, and my father made me come hither, where he fince told me a hundred times, that his fpoufe and fon (my brother whom I never faw) were both near us; that he faw them every day, and I fhould fee and embrace them too when I fhould be a few years older. They muft be very unfortunate too, becaufe Candor and Germain never fpeak of them without tears.

Alexis. Did you never afk any farther queftions?

Clara. It is my father's fecret, and I refpected it too much, to force it from him—yet I know that he goes every night into the cave below and takes Germain with him: There they remain about an hour, and then return to their apartment.

Vol. VI. G

They fix every year, a certain day, on which they perform a kind of ceremony, quite ftrange to me, at the bottom of the great poplar, in the garden. I could never follow them, becaufe every night I am locked up, like you.

Alexis. This very ceremony frightened me much the other night.—I can guefs part of his misfortunes.—Alas! his fon, his fpoufe, fell victims to treachery.

Clara. Do you believe they are dead?

Alexis. Can you doubt it?

Clara. Why, I am to fee them one day—what can that be?

Alexis. In me he fhall find an avenger!—I will efpoufe his caufe, he fhall know his Alexis.

Clara. Ah, my fweet friend! he loves you!

Alexis. He is a wonderful father.

Clara. He told me already:— My daughter, if your heart is to feel, if you are to love, place your affections in Alexis, who, I believe, is worthy of you: But let him deferve you firft. Be the recompenfe of the great fervice I expect him to do me. If he loves you, he will accomplifh all my wifhes.

Alexis. O heaven! did he fay this?

Clara. They are his very words: don't you think it would be horrible to betray his confidence?

Alexis. Ah, what a man!—Let us love each other, my dear creature, let us love, and may a father, by his bleffing, rivet bands as facred as thofe in which we might be joined before the altar, did our manfion not deny us that facred ceremony.

The whole time allotted for the leffon was almoft fpent in amorous topics and confidences. But Alexis, anxious for the progrefs of his pupil, was more ready afterwards,

wards, and Clara, in a little time, became a real adept in mufic and drawing; fhe got even proficient in the abftract fciences, fuch as the mathematics, phyfic, and aftronomy.   *(To be continued.)*

ANECDOTES of Sir THOMAS MOORE.

WHEN Sir Thomas Moore was firft made a privy counfellor, he oppofed a motion at the board made by Cardinal Wolfey, which all the reft of the council affented to; upon which the Cardinal in great paffion faid, " are not you afhamed, being the meaneft perfon here, to diffent from the opinion of fo many wife and honourable perfons? certainly you prove yourfelf a great fool for your pains." To which Sir Thomas replied, " Thanks be to God, I rejoice to hear that the King has but one fool in his Right Honourable Privy Council."

When he was Lord Chancellor, he decreed a gentleman fhould pay a large fum of money to a poor widow he had wronged, to whom the gentleman faid, " then I hope your lordfhip will grant me a long day to pay it in ;" " I grant your motion," faid the Chancellor, Monday next is St. Barnabas day, which is the longeft day in the year, pay it the widow that day, or I will commit you to the fleet." ·

His lady, though an excellent houfe wife, was too much given to chiding the fervants for trivial offences, for which he often greatly reproved her; and one day coming from confeffion, fhe faid to her hufband, " Be merry, Sir Thomas, for this day I have difburthened my confcience, and will leave my old fhrewifhnefs" —yes, fays Sir Thomas, and begin anew.

Vita Tho. Mor.

For the MASSACHUSETTS MAGAZINE.

The GLEANER. No. XXVII.

Indulgent Nature yields that plaftic glow,
From which unnumber'd foft endearments flow;
About the heart her kindred ties fhe flings,
And clofely twines the fympathetic ftrings;
Her filver cord with touch magnetic draws,
Reflection all her mellowing powers employs;
Motives for amity her fingers trace,
Bleft lineaments—which few can e'er efface.

THE multifarious ligaments which bind families together, being the handy work of nature, and effentially or clofely interwoven with our exiftence, that fhock muft be indeed violent, that can burft them afunder. It is true that a long continued feries of difobligation may obfcure the vivid glow of thofe images, which nature and habit have impreffed upon the intellect. Unkindnefs is the opaque body, which intercepts the funny beams of luminous, and inborn tendernefs; but the eclipfe is feldom total, and the cheering influence of affection, is frequently invigorated, and often becomes the more tranfcendent, scendent, for the momentary obstruction, by which it seemed well near inveloped. Surely that heart must be strangely deficient, which the pleasing sensations, that are attendant upon the first stage of being, hath not indelibly impressed ; and, that mind is unwarrantably implacable, which, intrenched by inexorable inflexibility, is incapable of being roused to the tenderness of recollection ; which is not softened by the remonstrances of nature, furnished with arguments, drawn from a series of endearing, and substantially beneficial proofs, of a generous attachment. Yet I know that there are a variety of combustibles, which although perhaps not radically natives of the human soil, having, however, obtained a growth therein, and once taking fire, it is difficult to say where the conflagration may end. I am aware that there are injuries which pride and self estimation, consider as unpardonable. It is a melancholy truth that there are obdurate hearts, and, it may be, that the strong winds of passion may obliterate, or uproot from the bosom, every proper sensation of the soul. Yet, granting that the empoisoned plant may become rampant in the rancorous breast, the Gleaner, while engaged in the routine of his profession, hath at no moment bound himself to select the noxious weed ; he confesses that he is fond of culling the flowers of humanity, and with these, as often as may be, he is solicitous to furnish and adorn his page.

To the well regulated mind, the contemplation of family harmony is inexpressibly pleasing. The philanthropic speculator views the little society unalterably attached, bound together by the strong cords of mutual affection, and rising superior to the adverse influence of

separate, or selfish claims, as a miniature of that vast family of man, which futurity shall see collected under the protecting auspices of a benignant and paternal God. Order, unbroken confidence, celestial tenderness, energetic love ; in this vast assembly, these shall all triumphantly officiate. Peaceful angels shall hover round ; discord shall find no entrance there ; offences shall be no more ; but truth, sky robed innocence, unimpeached integrity, unblemished virtue, and undeviating holiness, shall be established, *from everlasting to everlasting, and of their dominion there shall be no end.* Yes, it is pleasing to trace the striking resemblance which is exemplified in the animated sketch. Mild, affectionate, and *judiciously* indulgent parents ; duteous, and confiding sons, and daughters, mutually complacent, and unequivocally attached brothers and sisters. The royal bard of Israel, strikingly, feelingly, and poetically delineates the family of love, " Behold how good, and how pleasant it is for brethren to dwell together in unity"—well might the sacred poet summon the aid of a splendid fancy, and arrest the most expressive figures to image the fine effects, and pleasing utility of domestic complacency ; the rich perfumes which consecrated the anointed priest of the Hebrew tribes, the fertilizing dew descending upon Hermon's verdant summit, and resting with genial influence upon the adjacent eminence ; these but shadow forth the sublimity of that union, upon which our God hath commanded a blessing, which originates a dignified and blissful immortality. Yes, it is pleasing to trace the striking resemblance which is exemplified in the animated sketch. The contemplation of domestic harmony soothes and elevates the mind, and although it is undeniably true, that the philosopher will extend his regards from the little group which constitutes his relative circle, to friends, to country, to the universe at large, until he commences a citizen of the domain of heaven ; yet he will not refuse to acknowledge those ardors, those hopes, and those fears, which upon his opening mind, in the white winged hours that marked his dawn of being, were, by the strong hand of nature, irreversibly engraved.

Affection is very properly said to descend, and it is generally true, that while we venerate with pious duty the authors of our being, while our hearts are warmed for them by inmingling love, and reverence, we are in the same moment impelled to acknowledge for our offspring, augmented and more energetic tenderness. Doubtless nature hath implanted these superior and irresistible sensations, for the purpose of nerving our efforts for the preservation, and cultivation of the infant candidate for our favour ; but the fact is indubitable, in whatever wise regulations it may have originated. Family ties, of every description, are variously respectable, and variously estimable, in their various departments. I was lately a silent attendant upon a disquisition, which aimed at deciding what relative character deserved the preference—the investigation was rather curious than important ; but it served, however, to amuse, during a vacant hour, which might have been worse appropriated. The attachment of a well informed and tender father, to an amiable, and grateful daughter, has been said to resemble that which is experienced by a guardian angel, to the being who is committed to his charge—

tender, delicate, and divested of all that can debase, the paternal eye regards with immeasureable complacency, his beauteous, his dependant child ; and the finest feelings of his soul become embodied. To protect her from every ill he is sedulously attentive ; his judicious cautions hover round her inexperienced steps ; his protecting arm would present the invulnerable shield ; and his auspices are those of wisdom. Ever vigilant, ever upon his guard, to save her, even from the imputation of dishonour, he would consider his life as a comparatively trivial sacrifice. It is true that he is impassioned, but his ardours are those of virtue ; his affections are pure, innocent, laudable, elevated, and refined ; originating in nature, originating in God, they will be perfected in heaven. All this is irrefragably just, and yet I take leave to observe, that the *fraternal* department, when filled by a good and virtuous mind, more exactly answers the ideas which I have indulged, of that attendant cherub, ordained to tread with holy vigils, the destined path of the expecting voyager. In contemplating the character of a father, however beneficial its offices, we can hardly forbear recollecting, that having produced the being which is cherished, the consequent attachment may be the result of that *selfish principle* which so universally, more or less, actuates the human mind ; and, it is undeniably true, that the operation of a *selfish principle* essentially diminishes the lustre of the most beneficial and exemplary action. A brother, it hath been divinely observed, is born for adversity ; a gentle and confiding female can hardly boast a more agreeable, or *disinterested* relation ; the general arrangements of nature, authorizes a hope, that his
protection

protection will continue coeval with her mortal career, and if he fulfills the duties of the fraternal name, he will ftill continue a natural, patronizing, and confolatory refource. What eye is not charmed by a view of the marked, and delicate attention, which is paid by an elegant young man, to the gentle and accomplifhed maiden, who is the daughter of his father and of his mother. Grant that opportunities of this kind are extremely rare, the fenfations derived therefrom, are neverthelefs pleafing in a fuperior degree. The attachment of a brother to a fifter, if it is genuine and fincere, if it correfponds with the defignation of unadulterated and upright nature, partakes the exquifite delicacies and refinements of love, devoid of its tumultuous caprices, or intcrefted and ungovernable fervors ; with a confcious glow of ineffable fatisfaction it yields that protection, to which nature and education combine to give the fex a claim ; it is not ftinted in its regards, it is tender, elevated, and refined ; it is generous and communicable ; it is fympathetic and permanent. A true brother unites the duties of the *paternal*, with the more equal, fweet, and focial pleafures of the *fraternal* intercourfe ; the heart of a brother hefitates not to acknowledge the bland, endearing, and indiffoluble ties of amity. A true brother is at all times a guardian friend ; he rejoiceth in his fraternity, and, I repeat, that his attachment may claim kindred with thofe fentiments, which may be fuppofed to actuate the tenderly watchful feraph, who commiffioned by the high court of heaven, enters with the firft moment of our exiftence upon his truft, and fulfils his celeftial miffion, by attending thro' every ftage of life, his progreffing charge.

Richardfon exhibits the character, proper to a brother, in the moft vivid and glowing hues ; but if his Gradifon originated not in fiction, the portrait doubtlefs owes many embellifhments to the incomparable pen of that inimitable writer. It is a melancholy fact, that eminent virtue, of whatever defcription, is a gem that the hand of nature, however indulgent, hath too feldom produced. Yet, for the honour of humanity I cannot deny myfelf the gratification of affirming, that I at this moment contemplate, with fublime pleafure, the character of a gentleman, with whom I am perfonally acquainted, who is entitled to rank in the fame grade with Richardfon's finely imagined brother. I am not authorized to name the benevolent example, that I feel myfelf, neverthelefs, impelled to produce. The emblazoning voice of fame might probably tinge his cheek with the hue of difapprobation. It is true, that genuine merit " *does good by ftealth, aud blufhing finds it fame ;*" but if, while fketching the outlines of a character fo admirable, its fingularity fhould induce the finger of perception to point out the man, the Gleaner flatters himfelf that he fhall not be made refponfible, for a confequence fo natural ; that his folicitude to pleafe, by an exhibition of tranfcendent excellence, will apologize for the freedom of his pen, and that this, his motive, may obtain his pardon for prefenting to the public eye, a man, whofe name, to borrow a metaphor, " deferves to be written by the rays of the fun on the furface of the heavens."

Reader, on the faith of my veracity, I pledge unto thee my facred word of honour, that I am not prefenting thee with the hero of a romance, that I hold not the

pen

pen of the novelift in the fketch which I am about to attempt ; and that *truth* and not *fancy* is the motto of the prefent page.

Fraternus received his birth in a fmall town within the jurifdiction of the ftate of Maffachufetts ; a clergyman, dignified by the integrity of his heart, the clearnefs of his underftanding, and the humane and indulgent liberality of his fentiments, was the author of his being. His mother, fuperior to the generality of women, hath contributed much to the emolument, and elevation of her family ; fhe poffeffes a mind capacious and highly cultivated ; few perfons can exprefs themfelves with more elegance, precifion, or fluency, upon any fubject ; her language is the language of propriety, and fhe adds a grace to every fentiment which fhe utters ; the candour and opennefs of her difpofition, is equalled only by that franknefs, which is confpicuous in the manners, and gentlemanlike deport, of her venerable coadjutor in the voyage of life. Such were, fuch are, for they ftill live to witnefs the falutary effects of efforts dictated by the principles of propriety, the parents of Fraternus.

They have reared to maturity a numerous family of fons and daughters ; they have wept over the untimely grave of one gentle, and uncommonly meritorious child ; fhe was truly amiable in her life ; fhe was rendered exemplary through a long period of fufferings, and fhe continued, during the hour of her emancipation, divinely tranquil.— Yet they have fwelled no murmuring figh ; with holy refignation they have fubmitted to the decrees of heaven ; nor have they, in any inftance, violated the honour of that facred function, which the father of Fraternus hath been called to fill ;

they have fupported with uniform propriety the Chriftian and facerdotal characters, and they are in poffeffion of that applaufe, which fhould invariably attend the benevolent and the good. Regularity hath prefided in their family ; each morning hath ftill been ufhered in, by the devout breathings of their cheerfully folemnized fpirits, and the return of fober fuited evening, hath witneffed their grateful and pious orifons. Well have they difcharged the various duties of humanity, and their leifure hours have been uniformly devoted to the cultivation of the minds of thofe children, whom they have defigned ufeful and ornamental members of the community.

Thus educated, and thus fafhioned by the hands of polifhed rectitude, thus formed to virtue, Fraternus embarked, at an early age, upon that vaft ocean of contingencies, on which the bufy fons of commerce, if not arrefted by the pointed rock, or treacherous fands, are rapid borne. Integrity is not alway hereditary, but Fraternus joined to the inftructions which were fealed upon his youthful bofom, an innate probity, and great benevolence of foul. His firft onfet was happy ; his early engagements threw open the road to wealth ; his enterprifes have generally been fuccefsful, and he now ranks among the moft opulent defcription of merchants, in a certain celebrated emporium. A citizen of the world, his brethren in every line, according to their feveral exigencies, and his abilities, have experienced his beneficence, but his extenfive family, of whom he is juftly confidered the pride, and the ornament, derives from his good fortune the moft important advantages. One amiable fifter fhall fuffice

as

as an example of the arrangements, which he has established, relative to those of his blood.

This lady joins to a pleasing exterior, great vivacity, exquisite sensibility, and genuine goodness of heart. United to the man of her choice, for many years she continued an ornament to the married state; but he to whom fate had yielded her hand, possessing all the eccentricities of original genius, neglected to employ his superior talents, in making that provision for a rapidly increasing family, that prudence invariably directs; and the sister of Fraternus saw herself at the age of thirty six, the widowed mother of four sons and three daughters. She possessed not a shilling of property, and the state of insolvency upon which she was precipitated, became to her upright spirit, a source of inexpressible regret. Here was an ample field for the exercise of those virtues which Fraternus so eminently possessed. In the solacing offices of benignity he engaged with ardour, and his arrangements more than answered the most sanguine expectations, to which his well known munificence had given birth. His sister has not been degraded from her rank as mistress of a family; her children and domestics are continued about her exactly in the wonted train; not only the necessaries, but even the elegances of life are *liberally* bestowed; and, lest she should have a real or a fancied want unsupplied, delicate pretences are ingeniously furnished, to place in her hands generous sums, for which the only compensation that is required is her *silent* acceptance. There is but one point that Fraternus has been known to contend with his sister: As she has no request to make, he is induced to suspect a want of that unbounded confidence in his affection, which he has been solicitous to authorize. But what is left for her to ask, whose wishes have, in every instance, been regularly prevented or anticipated? Fraternus enters into all those exquisitely tender sensations which make up the aggregate of the maternal feelings. Various friends would have severally appropriated the children of his Adelaide; but with a delicacy almost unexampled, without referring to her the invidious task of objecting, he humanely interposed his caveat—" It will be best, my love, that thy children should remain with thee; nature hath ordained thee their revered monitress, their tenderly interested guide; and since the demise of their father, complicated duties have devolved upon thee: We will watch their various propensities, and the simple and unadulterated indications of their opening minds, shall point their future destination."—Mean time no attention is wanting; the best of schools are provided; the girls will figure with the most accomplished females, and the sacred walls of Harvard, or the more busy scenes of commercial life, as unerring nature shall direct, are destined to complete the education of the boys. Yet Fraternus has a young and increasing family of his own; but his Lydia is the counterpart of himself, she seconds, in every instance, his benignant plans, and, systematical in the exercise of that well judged economy, without which even a princely fortune might soon be reduced, she thus enables Fraternus to pursue the generous purposes of his munificent heart.

Liberal minded and amiable pair, may the first of blessings be yours; may your offspring imitate your virtues; may you still enjoy

joy

joy the felicity of beſtowing competency ; may you never loſe that zeſt for Godlike pleaſures which you ſo eminently poſſeſs ; and may your means of communicating good be continued coeval with the lateſt period of your exiſtence.

CLAUDINE: *A Swiss Tale.*

[From the French of M. de FLORIAN.]

(Concluded from the 433d page.)

" CLAUDINE, ſurpriſed to find any one who did not deſpiſe her, kiſſed his hands without ſaying a word. He ſpoke to her in the moſt friendly manner, and inquired after his good brother the curate : He dwelt with pleaſure on the good deeds of that worthy man, and obſerved, that one of the moſt pleaſing duties of their miniſtry was to conſole the unhappy, and heal the brokenhearted. Claudine liſtened with reſpectful gratitude, he appeared to her as an angel ſent from heaven to comfort her. After ſupper ſhe retired to bed in a calmer ſtate of mind, and if ſhe did not ſleep, ſhe at leaſt reſted.

" On the morrow, the good curate ſearched through Salenches for a little chamber where Claudine might lie in. An old woman, called Madam Felix, offered an apartment, and promiſed ſecrecy. Claudine repaired thither in the evening, the curate paid three months rent in advance, the old Lady paſſed her for a niece lately married at Chambery, and every thing was ſettled. Indeed it was high time ; for the fatiguing journey, and the agitation of mind that Claudine had ſuſtained, brought on her labour pains that very evening ; although only ſeven months gone with child, ſhe produced a boy beautiful as the day, whom Madam Felix cauſed to be baptized by the name of Benjamin.

" The curate was deſirous of immediately putting the child out to nurſe, but Claudine declared with tears in her eyes, that ſhe would rather die than be ſeparated from Benjamin : She was allowed to keep him for the firſt few days, and at the end of theſe days her maternal fondneſs had increaſed. The curate reaſoned with her ; repreſented to her, that ſuch conduct deprived her of all hopes of ever returning to Chamouny, or of being reconciled to her father. Claudine's only anſwer was to embrace Benjamin. The time ſlipt on, Claudine nurſed her child, and remained with Madam Felix, who loved her with all her heart.

" The fifty crowns from her father, and the little money Nanette had put into her bundle, had hitherto paid her expenſes. Nanette did not dare to come to ſee her, but ſhe ſent her all ſhe could ſpare, and thus Claudine wanted for nothing. She employed her time in learning to read and write of the old lady, who had formerly kept a ſchool at Bonville, and in taking care of Benjamin. Claudine was not unhappy, and little Benjamin grew charming. But ſuch happineſs could not laſt. One morning the Curate of Salenches came to pay her a viſit.

" My

"My dear girl," said he, "when I received you under my protection, when I covered your faults with the mantle of charity, my defign was to take care of your child, to enable him to gain his bread ; and I hoped, during that interval, to have appeafed the anger of your father ; to have prevailed with him to receive you once more into his houfe, where your repentance, your modefty, your love of virtue, and of labour, might gradually have induced him to forget the diftreffes of which you had been the fource. But this plan you have yourfelf oppofed. With what eyes could Simon look upon this child? He muft neceffarily remain a lafting monument of your mifconduct and difgrace. I can difcern by your eyes that your choice is made ; but you ought to confider that you cannot always remain with this good woman, whofe circumftances, however defirous fhe might be of befriending you, render it impoffible. The money that Nanette fends you, is taken from the fupport of herfelf and family. Nanette labours the ground while you carefs Benjamin, and Nanette has been guilty of no fault. You have but one refource, which is, to go into fervice either at Geneva or Chambery ; but I doubt whether without feparating from your child, you would eafily find a place. I allow you two days to reflect coolly on thefe matters. You will then inform me of your determination, and, depend on it, I will do every thing in my power to affift you." Claudine was fenfible of the truth of all the curate had faid, but fhe found it impoffible for her to live without Benjamin. After paffing a day and a night in reflecting on what fhe ought to do, fhe at laft refolved, and after writing a letter

to the curate, acknowledging all his kindnefs, which fhe left on her table, fhe made a bundle of her clothes, tied up twenty crowns which ftill remained in a handkerchief, and taking Benjamin in her arms, fhe departed from Salenches.

"She took the road to Geneva, and flept that night at Bonville ; for on account of little Benjamin, fhe could not travel far. The fecond day fhe arrived at Geneva. Her firft care was to fell all her female attire, and provide herfelf with a fuit of man's clothes : She even fold her fine black hair, and bought a knapfack, into which fhe put her clothes. She faftened the ring, which fhe had always hitherto worn on her finger, round her neck. Thus clad like a young Savoyard, with a ftout ftick in her hand, her knapfack on her back, atop of which, Benjamin was feated, clafping his hands round her neck, fhe fet out from Geneva on the road to Turin.

"She was twelve days in croffing the mountains, and people were fo much pleafed with the air and appearance of this handfome little Savoyard, and of the child whom fhe carried on her back, and called her little brother, that fhe was hardly allowed to pay any thing, but commonly difcharged her reckoning by amufing the company with fome of the little beautiful fongs peculiar to her country ; fo that when Claudine arrived at Turin, fhe had ftill fome of her money left, with which fhe hired a little garret, bought a brufh and blacking, and followed by little Benjamin, who never left her, fhe fet up a little ftall for blacking fhoes, in the Palais Royal, under the name of Claude.

"During the firft days fhe gained but little, becaufe fhe was awkward,

ward, and took a good deal of time to gain a penny ; but the foon became expert, and the work went on well. Claude, intelligent, active, alert, ran all the errands of the quarter. Benjamin, during her abfence, fat upon and guarded the ftool. If there was a letter to be carried, a box to be removed, or bottles to be conveyed to the cellar, Claude was called in preference to any other. She was the confidant and affiftant of all the lazy fervants in the neighbourhood, and in the evening often carried home a crown as the gains of the day. This was fully fufficient to fupport her and Benjamin, who every day increafed in ftature and in beauty, and became the favourite of all the neighbourhood.

" This happy life had lafted for more than two years, when one day Claudine and her fon being bufy arranging their little ftall, with their heads bent towards the ground, they faw a foot appear upon the ftool. Claudine took her brufh, and without looking at the mafter of the fhoe, immediately began her operation. When the moft difficult part was done, fhe raifed her head.—The brufh fell from her hands, fhe remained immoveable ; it was Mr. Belton whom fhe beheld. Little Benjamin, who was not at all affected, took up the brufh, and with a feeble hand attempted to finifh the work of Claudine, who ftill remained motionlefs, with her eyes fixed on Mr. Belton. Mr. Belton afked Claudine, with fome furprife, why fhe ftopped, and fmiled at the efforts of the child, whofe figure pleafed him. Claudine recovering her fpirits, excufed herfelf to Mr. Belton with fo fweet a voice, and fuch well chofen words, that the Englifhman, ftill more furprized, afked Claudine feveral quef-

tions about her country and fituation. Claudine anfwered, with a calm air, that fhe and her brother were two orphans who gained their bread by the employment which he faw, and that they were from the valley of Chamouny. This name ftruck Mr. Belton, and looking attentively at Claudine, he thought he recognifed her features, and inquired her name. " I am called Claude," faid fhe.—" And you are from Chamouny ?" " Yes, Sir, from the village of Prieure." —" Have you no other brother ?" —" No, Sir, only Benjamin."— " Nor any fifter ?"—" Pardon me, Sir ?"—" What is her name ?"— " Claudine."—" Claudine ! and where is fhe ?"—" Oh, I do not know, indeed, Sir."—" How can you be ignorant of that ?"—" For many reafons, Sir, which cannot intereft you, and which it would make me weep to tell." Claudine, with the tears ftarting in her eyes, told him fhe had done. Mr. Belton, who did not go away, put his hand into his pocket, and gave her a guinea. " I cannot change you," faid Claudine.—" Keep the whole," faid the Englifhman, " and tell me, would you be forry to quit your prefent employment, and accept of a good place ?"—" That cannot be, Sir." —" Why not ?"—" Becaufe nothing in the world would make me quit my brother."—" But fuppofe he were to accompany you ?"— " That would be another matter." —" Well, Claude, you fhall be with me ; I will take you into my fervice, you will be very happy in my houfe, and your brother fhall accompany you."—" Sir, anfwered Claudine, a little embarraffed, " favour me with your addrefs, and I will call upon you tomorrow."— Mr. Belton gave it her, and bade her not fail to come.

" It was well for Claudine that the conversation now terminated, for her tears almost suffocated her ; she hastened to her chamber, and there shut herself up to reflect on what she ought to do. Her inclination and her affection for Benjamin prompted her to enter into the service of Mr. Belton ; but his past treachery, and the promise she had made to the curate of Salenches, never to do any thing which might endanger her virtue, made her hesitate : But the welfare of Benjamin preponderated ; she resolved to go to Mr. Belton, to serve him faithfully, to make him cherish his son, but never to tell him who she was.

" This point being settled, the next morning she waited on Mr. Belton, who agreed to give her good wages, and ordered her and her brother clothes immediately. Mr. Belton now wished to renew the conversation of yesterday, and to inquire further concerning her sister. But Claudine interrupted him.— " Sir," said she, " my sister is no more : She is dead of misery, chagrin, and repentance. All our family have lamented her unhappy end; and those who are not our relations, have no right to renew such melancholy reflections." Mr. Belton, more than ever astonished at the spirit of Claude, desisted from further inquiry ; but he conceived a high esteem and a sincere friendship for this extraordinary young man.

" Claude soon became the favourite of his master ; and Benjamin, towards whom Mr. Belton found himself attached by an irresistible impulse, was for ever in his chamber. The amiable child, as if conscious that he owed his existence to Mr. Belton, loved him nearly as well as Claudine ; and he told him so with such sweet innocence and simplicity, that the Englishman could not do without Benjamin. Claudine wept for joy, but she concealed her tears. But the dissipation of Mr. Belton afflicted the heart of Claudine, and made her fear that the hour of discovery would never arrive.

" By the death of his parents, Mr. Belton had, at the age of nineteen, been left master of a very large fortune, which he had hitherto employed in wandering over Italy, stopping wherever he found it agreeable to him, that is, wherever he met with agreeable women whom he could deceive and ruin. A lady of the court of Turin, rather advanced in life, but still beautiful, was his present mistress : She was lively, passionate, and very jealous of Mr. Belton. She required that he should sup with her every evening, and write to her every morning. The Englishman did not dare to refuse. Notwithstanding all this, they had many quarrels : For the smallest cause she would weep, tear her hair, seize a knife, and play a thousand fooleries, which begun to tire Mr. Belton. Claude saw and felt all this, but she suffered in silence. Mr. Belton gave her every day fresh marks of confidence, and often complained to her of the unpleasant life he led. Claude now and then risqued a little advice, half joke and half serious, which Mr. Belton heard with approbation, and promised to follow tomorrow ; but when tomorrow came, Mr. Belton returned to the lady, more from habit than inclination ; and Claude, who wept in private, affected to smile, while she accompanied her master.

" At length there arose so violent a quarrel between the Englishman and the marquise, that he resolved never again to go near her ; and in order to prevent it, connected himself with another lady of the same place,

place, no better than the former. In this change, Claudine saw only a new subject of affliction. All that she had done was to begin again; but she resigned herself to it without complaining, and continued to serve her master with the same fidelity as ever. But the marquise was not of a disposition so easily to yield up the heart of her English lover. She had him watched, and soon discovered her rival; she exhausted every stratagem of intrigue to make him return; but in vain. The Englishman did not answer her letters, refused her appointments, and ridiculed her threats.—The marquise, now in despair, thought only of revenge.

"One day, when Mr. Belton, followed by Claudine, was as usual, coming out of the house of his new mistress about two o'clock in the morning, and, already displeased with her, was telling his faithful Claudine that he had thoughts of setting out immediately for London, suddenly four desperadoes fell with poniards on Mr. Belton, who had hardly time to throw himself against the wall with his sword in his hand. Claudine, on sight of the assassins, sprang before her master, and received in her bosom the stroke of a poniard aimed at Mr. Belton: She instantly fell. The Englishman set furiously on the man who had wounded her, and soon stretched him on the pavement; and the three others finding themselves furiously attacked, quickly fled. Mr. Belton did not pursue them; he returned to his domestic, raised him, embraced him, and called on him with tears; but Claudine did not answer, for she had fainted. Mr. Belton took her in his arms, carried her to his house, and laid her in his own bed, while others at his desire ran for a surgeon. Mr. Belton,

impatient to see the nature of the wound, unbuttoned Claudine's vest, drew aside the shirt covered with blood, looked, and beheld with astonishment, the bosom of a woman.

"During this, the surgeon arrives, and examines the wound, which he declares not to be mortal, as the weapon had struck against the bone. The wound is dressed, and stimulatives applied, but still Claudine does not recover. Mr. Belton, who supported her head, perceives a ribbon round her neck; he pulls it and discovers a ring. It is his own; the same that he had left on Montanverd to the beautiful shepherdness whom he so cruelly abandoned. Every thing is at once evident. He sends for a nurse, who undresses Claudine, and lays her in her own bed; and the poor girl at length recovering her senses, throws her eyes around, and sees with astonishment, the nurse, the surgeon, her master, and Benjamin, who, awaked by all this noise, had risen, and run half naked to his brother, whom he embraced with tears.

"Claudine immediately endeavoured to console Benjamin; then calling to mind what had happened, seeing herself in a bed, and reflecting with inquietude that she had been undressed, she quickly put her hand to the ribbon which held her ring. Mr. Belton, who watched her, saw in her looks the pleasure with which she found it was still there.. He then made every body leave the room, knelt down by the side of the bed, and taking the hand of Claudine,—"Do not be alarmed," said he, "my sweet friend: I know every thing, and it is for the happiness of us both. You are Claudine, and I am a monster. There is but one way that I can cease to be so,

and

FOR AUGUST, 1794.   **477**

and that depends upon you. I owe you my life, and I wish to owe my honour to you, for it is I who have loft it, not you. Your wound is not dangerous; and as foon as you can go out, you fhall beftow on me the name of hufband, and pardon me a crime which I am far from pardoning myfelf. I have long ftrayed from the paths of virtue, Claudine: but they will be the more agreeable when I am reftored to them by you." Imagine the furprize, the joy, the tranfports of Claudine. She would have fpoke, but her tears prevented her. She then perceived little Benjamin, who had been turned out with the reft, and who, anxious about his brother, had foftly opened the door and thruft in his pretty face to fee what was going forwards. Claudine fhewed him to Mr. Belton, faying, " There is your fon, he will anfwer you better than I can." He flew; Benjamin covered him with kiffes, and carrying him to his mother, he paffed the remainder of the night between his wife and his child with a fatisfaction of mind to which he had long been a ftranger.

" In fifteen days Claudine was well. She had informed Mr. Belton of all that had happened to her. This endeared her to the Englifhman, who was now fonder of her than the firft time he faw her. Claudine, now dreffed as a woman, but with great plainnefs, entered the coach of the Englifhman with Benjamin, and all three went ftraight to Salenches, to the houfe of the curate. The good man did not at firft know Claudine; but at length recollecting her, he ran to old Madam Felix, who was ftill alive, and who almoft died of joy when fhe beheld Claudine and Benjamin. The next day they fet out for Chamouny, where Mr. Belton, who was a cath-

olic, wifhed that the marriage might be publicly folemnized in the parifh church of Prieure.

" In the evening, the curate of Salenches was fent to demand the hand of his daughter, of the terrible M. Simon. The old man received him with great gravity, heard him without teftifying any joy, and gave his confent in very few words. Claudine came to throw herfelf at his feet; he allowed her to remain a few feconds, raifed her without a fmile, and faluted Mr. Belton with great coolnefs. The good Nanette laughed and cried at the fame time. On the road to church, fhe carried Benjamin on one hand, and held her fifter with the other: The two curates walked before, and old Madam Felix behind with M. Simon; all the children of the village followed finging fongs.

" In this order they reached the church, where the ceremony was performed by the curate of Salenches. Mr. Belton had tables covered on the banks of the Arva, where every gueft was welcome, and the whole village danced during eight days. He bought fome good eftates for old M. Simon, but he refufed to accept of them. Nanette was not fo impracticable. She accepted of an eftate, and a handfome houfe which Mr. Belton gave her, and is now the richeft and the happieft woman in the parifh. Mr. and Mrs. Belton went away in about a month, carrying with them the benedictions of every body. They are now at London, where I underftand Benjamin has five or fix brothers and fifters.

" Such is their hiftory; which I could not fhorten becaufe I tried to tell it you in the words of the curate, whom I have often heard repeat it. If it has not pleafed you, you will excufe me."

I

I thanked Francis Paccard, af-
furing him that his tale had interefted me much. I defcended from
Montanverd, with my head full of
Claudine; and during my return
to Geneva, I wrote this ftory as
Paccard had told it me, without
trying to correct the many faults
of ftyle which the critics will no
doubt difcover in it.

The PARSON: An ANECDOTE.

A CERTAIN *divine* in one of the *Weſt-
India* iſlands, collateral perhaps in
point of conſanguinity with the celebrated
Sphintext, read the pfalm one Sunday, and
fat down, as uſual, while it was fung.
Whether unmindful of his facred function,
or overplied by the labours of the day, the
legend fayeth not; but, while his devotional hallelujah choir was paying a tribute to
the *Sovereign of all*, the charitable *parſon*
threw in his mite to the *Morphean god*.

The muſick at length was finiſhed, and
the people were waiting for the word,
while the venerable *diſpenſer* was in a found
fleep. As foon as the *deacons* obferved the
fad cataſtrophe, one of them turned to the
parſon, and with an audible voice faid to
him, *it is out*, (meaning the pfalm.) *Is it?*
faid the parſon, half waking—*well, fill
it up again, and charge it to Jim Bowers.*

Q.

ANECDOTE.

A N Engliſh Nobleman once aſked Dr.
Johnſon, what was become of the
gallantry and military ſpirit of the old Engliſh nobility? He replied, why my Lord,
I'll tell you what is become of it; it is gone
into the city to look for a fortune.

ADELISA: *A Tale.*

[By Mr. Cumberland.]

A DELISA, poſſeſſed of beauty,
fortune, rank, and every elegant accompliſhment that genius
or education could beſtow, was
withal ſo unſupportably capricious,
that ſhe ſeemed born to be the torment of every heart, which ſuffered
itſelf to be attracted by her charms.
Though her coquetry was notorious
to a proverb, ſuch were her allurements, that very few upon whom
ſhe thought fit to practice them had
ever found refolution to refift their
power. Of all the victims of her
vanity, Leander ſeemed to be that
over whom ſhe threw her chains
with the greateſt air of triumph; he
was, indeed, a conqueſt to boaſt of,
for he had long and obſtinately defended his heart, and for a time
made as many repriſals upon the
tender paſſions of her ſex, as ſhe
raiſed contributions upon his: Her
better ſtar at length prevailed; ſhe
beheld Leander at her feet, and
though her victory was accompliſh-
ed at the expenſe of more tender
glances than ſhe had ever beſtowed
upon

upon the whole fex collectively, yet it was a victory which only piqued Adelifa to render his flavery the more intolerable for the trouble it had coft her to reduce him to it. After fhe had trifled with him, and tortured him in every way that her ingenious malice could devife, and made fuch public difplay of her tyranny, as fubjected him to the ridicule and contempt of all the men who had envied his fuccefs, and every woman who refented his neglect, Adelifa, avowedly difmiff- ed him as an object which could no longer furnifh fport to her cruelty, and turned to other purfuits with a kind of indifference as to the choice of them, which feemed to have no other guide but mere caprice.

Leander was not wanting to him- felf in the efforts he now made to free himfelf from her chains ; but it was in vain ; the hand of beau- ty had wrapped them too clofely about his heart, and love had riv- etted them too fecurely, for rea- fon, pride, or even the ftrongeft ftruggles of refentment, to throw them off ; he continued to love, to hate, to execrate, and adore her. His firft refolution was to exile himfelf from her fight ; this was a meafure of abfolute neceffity, for he was not yet recovered enough to abide the chance of meeting her, and he had neither fpirits nor incli- nation to ftart a frefh attachment by way of experiment upon her jealoufy. Fortune however befriended him in the very moment of defpair, for no fooner was he out of fight, than the coquetifh Adelifa found fome- thing wanting which had been fo familiar to her, that Leander, though defpifed when poffeffed, when loft was regretted. In vain fhe culled her numerous admirers for fome one to replace him ; contin- ually peevifh and difcontented,

Adelifa became fo intolerable to her lovers, that there feemed to be a fpirit conjuring up amongft them, which threatened her with a gene- ral defertion. What was to be done ?—Her danger was alarming, it was imminent :—She determined to recal Leander :—She informed herfelf of his haunts, and threw herfelf in the way of a rencontre ; but he avoided her :—Chance brought them to an interview, and fhe began by rallying him for his apoftacy : There was an anxiety under all this affected pleafantry that fhe could not thoroughly con- ceal, and which he did not fail to difcover. He inftantly determined upon the very wifeft meafure which deliberation could have formed ; and he combated her with her own weapons ! He put himfelf apparent- ly fo much at his eafe, and coun- terfeited his part fo well, as effec- tually to deceive her ; fhe had now a new tafk upon her hands, and the hardeft as well as the moft hazardous fhe had ever undertaken : She attempted to throw him off h's guard by a pretended pity for his paft fufferings and a promife of a kinder ufage for the-future.

He denied that he had fuffered any thing, and affured her that he never failed to be amufed by her humours, which were perfectly a- greeable to him at all times.—"Then it is plain," replied fhe, " that you never thought of me as a wife, for fuch humours muft be infupporta- ble to a hufband."—" Pardon me," cried Leander, " if ever I fhould be betrayed into the idle act of mar- riage, I muft be in one of thofe very humours myfelf : Defend me from the dull uniformity of domeftic life ! What can be fo infipid as the tame ftrain of nuptial harmony everlaft- ingly repeated ?—Whatever other varieties I may then debar myfelf of, of, let me at leaſt find a variety of whim in the woman I am to be fettered to."—" Upon my word," exclaimed Adeliſa, " you would almoſt perſuade me we were deſtined for each other."—This, ſhe accompanied with one of thoſe looks, in which ſhe was moſt expert, and which was calculated at once to inſpire and betray inſenſibility. Leander, not yet ſo certain of his obſervations as to confide in them, ſeemed to receive this overture as raillery, and affecting a laugh, replied— I do not think it is in the power of deſtiny herſelf to determine either of us ; for if you was for one moment in the humour to promiſe yourſelf to me, I am certain in the next you would retract it ; and if I was fool enough to believe you, I ſhould well deſerve to be puniſhed for my credulity :—Hymen will never yoke us to each other, nor to any body elſe ; but if you are in the mind to make a very harmleſs experiment of the little faith I put in all ſuch promiſes, here is my hand : It is fit the propoſal ſhould ſpring from my quarter, and not your's ; cloſe with it as ſoon as you pleaſe, and laugh at me as much as you pleaſe, if I vent one murmur when you break the bargain.—" Well then," ſaid Adeliſa, " to puniſh you for the ſaucineſs of your provoking challenge, and to convince you that I do not credit you for this pretended indifference to my treatment of you, here is my hand, and with it my promiſe ; and now I give you warning that if ever I do keep it, it will be only from the conviction that I ſhall torment you more by fulfilling it, than by flying from it."—" Fairly declared, cried Leander, and ſince my word is paſſed, I'll ſtand to it ; but take notice, if I was not perfectly ſecure of being jilted, I ſhould think myſelf in a

fair way to be the moſt egregious dupe in nature."

In this ſtrain of mutual raillery, they proceeded to ſettle the moſt ſerious buſineſs of their lives, and whilſt neither would venture upon a confeſſion of their paſſion, each ſeemed to rely on the other for a diſcovery of it. They now broke up their conference in the gayeſt ſpirits imaginable, and Leander at parting, offered to make a bett of half his fortune with Adeliſa, that ſhe did not ſtand to her engagement, at the ſame time naming a certain day as the period of its taking place. —" And what ſhall I gain," ſaid ſhe, " in that caſe, by half your fortune, when I ſhall have a joint ſhare in poſſeſſion of the whole ?"—" Talk not of fortune," cried Leander, giving loose to the rapture which he could no longer reſtrain, " my heart, my happineſs, my life itſelf is yours."—So ſaying, he caught her in his arms, preſſed her eagerly in his embrace, and haſtily departed.

No ſooner was he out of her ſight than he began to expoſtulate with himſelf upon his indiſcretion :—In the ecſtacy of one unguarded moment he blaſted all his ſchemes, and by expoſing his weakneſs, armed her with freſh engines to torment him. In theſe reflections he paſſed the remainder of the night ; in vain he ſtrove to find ſome juſtification for his folly ; he could not form his mind to believe that the tender looks ſhe had beſtowed upon him were any other than an experiment upon his heart, to throw him from his guard and reeſtabliſh her tyranny. With theſe impreſſions, he preſented himſelf at her door next morning, and was immediately admitted. Adeliſa was alone, and Leander immediately began by ſaying to her, " I am now come to receive at your hands the puniſhment,

ment, which a man who cannot keep his own secret, richly deserves: I surrender myself to you, and I expect you will exert your utmost ingenuity in tormenting me ; only remember that you cannot give a stab to my heart, without wounding your own image, which envelopes every part, and is too deeply impressed for even your cruelty totally to extirpate."—At the conclusion of this speech, Adelisa's countenance became serious ; she fixed her eyes on the floor, and after a pause, without taking any notice of Leander, and as if she had been talking to herself in soliloquy, repeated in a murmuring tone :—" Well well, it is all over ; but no matter."—" For the love of Heaven," cried Leander in alarm, " what is all over ?"—" All that is most delightful to woman," she replied ;—" All the luxury which the vanity of my sex enjoys in tormenting your's : Oh Leander ! what charming projects of revenge had I contrived to punish your pretended indifference, and depend upon it, I would have executed them to the utmost rigour of the law of retaliation, had you not in one moment disarmed me of my malice by a fair confession of your love. Believe me, Leander, I never was a coquette but in self defence ; sincerity is my natural character ; but how should a woman of any attractions be safe in such a character, when the whole circle of fashion abounds with artificial coxcombs, pretenders to sentiment, and professors of seduction ! When the whole world is in arms against innocence, what is to become of the naked children of nature, if experience does not teach them the art of defence !—If I have employed this art more particularly against you, than others, why have I so done,

but because I had more to apprehend from your insincerity than any other person's and proportioned my defences to my danger ! Between you and me, Leander, it has been more a contest of cunning, than an affair of honour, and if you will call your own conduct into fair review, trust me you will find little reason to complain of mine. Naturally disposed to favour your attentions more than any other man's, it particularly behoved me to guard myself against propensities at once so pleasing and so suspicious. Let this suffice in justification of what is past ; it now remains that I should explain to you the system I have laid down for the time to come :—If ever I assume the character of a wife, I devote myself to all its duties ; I bid farewel at once to all the vanities, the petulances, the coquetries of what is falsely called a life of pleasure ; the whole system must undergo a revolution, and be administered upon other principles and to other purposes : I know the world too well to commit myself to it, when I have more than my own conscience to account to, when I have not only truths but the similitudes of truths to study ; suspicions, jealousies, appearances to provide against ; when I am no longer singly responsible on the score of error, but of example also :—It is not therefore in the public display of an affluent fortune, in dress, equipage, entertainments, nor even in the fame of splendid charites my pleasures will be found ; they will center in domestic occupations ; in cultivating nature, and the sons of nature, in benefiting the tenants and labourers of the soil that supplies us with the means of being useful ; in living happily with my neighbours, in availing myself of those numberless opportunities,

tunities, which a refidence in the country affords of relieving the untold diftreffes of thofe who fuffer in fecret, and are too humble, or perhaps too proud to afk."—Here the enraptured Leander could no longer keep filence, but breaking forth into tranfports of love and admiration, gave a turn to the converfation, which it is no otherwife interefting to relate, than as it proved the prelude to an union which fpeedily took place, and has made Leander and Adelifa the fondeft and worthieft couple in England.

For the MASSACHUSETTS MAGAZINE.

The INVESTIGATOR, No. I.

In this wide world what varying objects rife?

HAPPY is that man, who is free from *envy;* who is content with his condition, and complains not of the deeds of Providence ; but, though unfortunate himfelf, rejoices at the profperity of thofe around him ; whofe eyes moiften at the tale of forrow, and whofe fympathetic breaft beats in unifon with the fufferer ; who from his little ftore beftows a generous mite to the children of poverty : Happinefs is moft certainly his companion, and the ills of life reft lightly on his head. The morfel which he eats, is fweet and nourifhing ; the water which he drinks, is cool and refrefhing ; and the ftraw which fupports his limbs, foothes him in foft forgetfulnefs. He is beloved by all who know him ; careffed where ever he goes, and fought after by the good and generous. When he vifits his neighbours in trouble, fuch benignity fets upon his countenance, that the eye of forrow wears a fmile, and the perturbed breaft ceafes to heave a figh. He, like a minifter of peace, is received among them, and his words affect them as the oil of confolation. How infinite, how extenfive muft be his felicity ! Surely he, above all the reft of mankind, partakes of heaven below, of blifs which none but faints and angels ever claim. He becomes, by his deeds, an honour to human nature, and a bleffing to mankind.

But the *envious man* is a plague to fociety, a torment to himfelf, and a difgrace to humanity. Envy is of fuch a poifonous, corrofive nature, that it fefters the mind and corrupts the foul. All the tender, fympathetic feelings, are by it deftroyed, and its poffeffor is rendered unfit to perform the deeds of this world, and to undergo the troubles concommitant with man. It mars all his enjoyments, extirpates tranquillity from the mind, and ruins domeftic and conjugal happinefs. The pleafures of friendfhip and converfation are entirely cut off. Society, the boon of heaven and choiceft gift of God, is by it rendered abortive, without which, who can travel life's dull and weary round ?

The envious man is of all men the moft miferable ; he is the moft pitiful object in nature, for if he happens to fall into company, like a true cynic, he fhows the colour of his mind by the features of his face. The wrinkled frown upon his brow, and the fneering crook of his nofe, are things which plainly mark *the man.* If the topic of converfation happens to run upon men and

and public measures, he *is* pleafed, for then he can and *will* join the confab' by uttering the moft bitter epithets and virulent remarks upon the charaɛters above him. His envy poifons all he fays or does, it diffufes itfelf into every word which he utters, and corrupts even his retired thoughts.

While he is receiving the bleffings of health and riches from the hand of his merciful Creator, he *fits* repining at the hardnefs of his lot. He exclaims againft Providence while he is living on his bounty. He curfes the food which he is eating, becaufe it is the fame which nourifhes and fupports thofe around him. There is nothing which he fo much dreads, and which fo much vexes his foul, as the profperity of his neighbours. With forrow and indignation he beholds their fields waving in luxuriant pride, their mountains covered with herds, and their paftures moving with cattle. That they fhould merit the fmiles of God more than himfelf; that they fhould be fuperior to him in knowledge, or riches, are ideas too fhocking for his conception, too degrading to his nature, and things which he wifhes to conceive as impoffibilities.

The life which he leads, is wretched beyond defcription. To fay he poffeffes any peaceful moments, no one can, unlefs thofe can be called fuch, which he expends in trying to deftroy the good fame and charaɛter of his fellow beings. His time rolls heavily along, bringing with it fomething produɛtive of heartfelt uneafinefs, which to others (though not becaufe they rejoice in his afflictions) is the fource of pleafure and happinefs. He eats his beft food without relifh, and drinks his wine as if it partook only of the fournefs of the grape. He rifes from his table unfatisfied, and unrefrefhed; and after roving in fome folitary place, till the fun has declined the weft, he returns peevifh and morofeful, having thrown himfelf upon his couch, he lingers out a reftlefs night. Thus his life wears away; thus he goes curfing and curfed down to the grave; the fods of the valley cover him; the eye beholds his depofit, unmoved, and the earth tumbles upon his coffin without raifing a figh!

Happy are they who fhun this laft extreme;
Who live all mindful of fome happier foil,
Who court the bleffings of the great Supreme,
Nor think for facred blifs too much they toil.

Who view the increafe of their neighbour's ftore
With joy unmingl'd with an envious eye;
And whofe ambition leads him to that lore,
Which teaches how to live and how to die.

Singular ACCOUNT of LA MAUPIN.

[From BURNEY's Hiftory of Mufic.]

LA MAUPIN feems to have been a moft extraordinary perfonage. "She was equally fond of both fexes, fought and loved like a man, and refifted and fell like a woman. Her adventures are of a very romantic kind. Married to a young hufband, who foon was obliged to abfent himfelf from her, to enter on an office he had obtained at Provence.

Provence, fhe ran away with a fencing mafter, of whom fhe learned the fmall fword, and became an excellent fencer, which was afterwards a ufeful qualification to her on feveral occafions. The lovers firft retreated from perfecution to Marfeilles; but neceffity foon obliged them to folicit employment there, at the opera; and, as both had by nature good voices, they were received without difficulty. But foon after this fhe was feized with a paffion for a young perfon of her own fex, whom fhe feduced, but the object of her whimfical affection being purfued by her friends, and taken, was thrown into a convent at Avignon, where La Maupin foon followed her; and having prefented herfelf as a novice, obtained admiffion. Some time after, fhe fet fire to the convent, and, availing herfelf of the confufion fhe had occafioned, carried off her favourite. But being purfued and taken, fhe was condemned to the flames for contumacy; a fentence, however, which was not executed, as the young Marfellaife was found, and reftored to her friends.

"She then went to Paris, and made her firft appearance on the opera ftage in 1695, when fhe performed the part of Pallas, in Cadmus, with the greateft fuccefs. The applaufe was fo violent, that fhe was obliged, in her car, to take off her cafque to falute and thank the public, which redoubled their marks of approbation. From that time her fuccefs was uninterrupted. Dumeni, the finger, having affronted her, fhe put on men's clothes, watched for him in the Place des Victoires, and infifted on his drawing his fword and fighting her, which he refufing, fhe caned him, and took from him his watch and fnuff box. Next day, Dumeni having boafted at the opera houfe, that he had defended himfelf againft three men who attempted to rob him, fhe related the whole ftory, and produced his watch and fnuff box in proof of her having caned him for his cowardice. Thevenard was nearly treated in the fame manner, and had no other way of efcaping her chaftifement, than by publicly afking her pardon, after hiding himfelf at the Palais Royal during three weeks. At a ball given by Monfieur, the brother of Louis XIV. fhe again put on men's clothes, and having behaved impertinently to a lady, three of her friends, fuppofing La Maupin to be a man, called her out. She might eafily have avoided the combat by difcovering her fex, but fhe inftantly drew, and killed them all three. Afterwards, returning very coolly to the ball, fhe told the ftory to Monfieur, who obtained her pardon."

OBSERVATIONS on BLINDNESS, and on the Employment of the other Senfes to fupply the Loss of SIGHT.

[By Mr. BEW.—From "Memoirs of the Literary and Philofophical Society of Manchefter."]

——— tenebrafque neceffe 'ft
Non radii folis, neque lucida tela diei
Difcutiant ———   LUCRET.

AMONGST the various accidents and calamities, to which the human fpecies are fubjected, there are none that excite compaffion, or call forth our benevolent aid more powerfully, than blindnefs. The

The blind man, in all ages and countries, has ever been allowed an indisputable claim on the good offices of his fellow creatures; his necessities have generally been supplied with sacred care; and his genius, if it approached to excellence, has been respected with a degree of reverence, superior to what is usually bestowed, on such as are possessed of the faculty of sight.

The faculty of sight, indeed, is justly considered as superior to any of the other senses. Hearing, tasting, and smelling, when compared with vision, appear very limited in their powers and determinations; and though the sense of touch may possess the most general, and accurate power of conveying the ideas of the various modifications of matter to the mind; yet the comprehensiveness, together with the instantaneous celerity, with which vision displays to us the wonders of Nature, or the varieties of Art, far transcend any of the perceptions, that the touch, or the other senses are able to furnish us with. It is, perhaps, on this account, that we figuratively employ the term, *seeing*, in acknowledging the conscious evidence of reason and truth; and even extend the application, as the most expressive, to one of the distinguishing attributes of Almighty perfection.

In no part of the human fabric, or even throughout the whole of nature, with which we are acquainted, are there more evident marks of exquisite perfection and wisdom, than in what relates to the sense of seeing; whether we direct our attention to the wonderful regularity, order, minuteness, and velocity of the rays of light, which minister to this sense, or to the structure and formation of the little organ, in which this faculty is destined to reside. " With a

* Dr. Reid, p. 121.

" ball and socket, (as a learned and " and elegant philosopher* beauti-" fully observes) of an inch diame-" ter, we are enabled, in an instant " of time, without changing our " place, to perceive the disposition " of an army, the figure of a palace, " and the variety of a landscape;" and not only, as he farther remarks, to " find our way through the path-" less ocean, traverse the globe of " the earth, determine its figure and " dimensions, and delineate every " region of it:" But,

- - -" Breaking hence, take our ardent flight
" Through the blue infinite,"

ascertain the order, revolutions and distances of the planetary orbs, and even form probable conjectures on

- - - - - - - - - - - - - " Every star
" Which the clear concave of a winter's
        night
" Pours on the eye, or astronomic tube,
" Far stretching, snatches from the dark
        abyss."   THOMSON.

In contemplating, therefore, the extensive and almost unlimited properties of vision, we not only find our gratitude warmed and elevated to piety and devotion, but are, likewise, conscious of an involuntary impulse, that urges us to exert our endeavours, towards the assistance of such as are unfortunately deprived of this noble faculty, whenever they are presented to our notice.

And here, again, we have every motive to inspire us with admiration of the providential wisdom and benevolence, displayed by the divine Author of our existence. For, notwithstanding the great and comprehensive powers of sight, there is little of the actual knowledge acquired by this faculty, that may not, by attentive and patient perseverance, be communicated to the man who has been doomed to darkness from his birth.

birth. The bigot, or the enthufiaft, who condemns the refearches of philofophy, and erroneoufly pronounces them to be incompatible with religion ; perceives, with aftonifhment, the blind enabled to expatiate on light or colours ; on reflection, refraction, and on the various fubjects, from which we might naturally fuppofe they would be excluded, by the deprivation of fight ; and fatisfies himfelf with abruptly referring the whole to the immediate difpenfation of the Deity. The philofopher, on the other hand, though, with willing fubmiffion, he ultimately attributes the effects to Omnipotence ; is, neverthelefs, defirous to avoid the cenfure paffed on the fervant, " *who buried his talent in a napkin ;*" and ventures to exert the abilities with which he may be endowed in endeavouring to inveftigate the means by which the effects are ordained to be accomplifhed, to the end, that the interefts of humanity may be ferved with greater certainty.

The powerful influence of exercife and habit upon the intellectual, as well as upon the corporeal faculties, are too well known and acknowledged, to require much illuftration. The mufcles, of any part of the body, acquire peculiar vigour and fullnefs by habitual exercife ; and the fame is remarkable, though in a ftill higher degree, with refpect to the effects of exercife and habit, on the faculties of the mind. From this wife regulation, in the economy of nature, refults a train of refources, which the blind are found capable of deriving, from the exercife of the other fenfes ; and which may be fo far perfected, as to compenfate, in a great meafure, for the lofs of the darling fenfe of fight. The delicacy and precifion, with which fome eminent blind people have employed the other fenfes, particularly *hearing* and *touch*, would, indeed, exceed the bounds of credibility, were we not affured of the facts, as well from actual experience, as from undoubted authorities.

Dr. Saunderfon loft his fight by the fmall pox, fo early in his infancy, that he did not remember to have ever feen. He had no more ideas of light, than if he had been born blind. Notwithftanding this misfortune, he acquired fuch profound and perfect knowledge in the fcience of mathematics, that, by the influence of his merit only, he was appointed to the profefforfhip in the Univerfity of Cambridge. The addrefs of this celebrated philofopher was no ways inferior to the knowledge he poffeffed ; a circumftance, which we do not always meet with in thofe who have the full powers of fight. His lectures on the different branches of mathematics, natural philofophy, aftronomy, and optics, were remarkably clear and intelligible. Fully aware of the difficulties young minds have to contend with, from the abftrufenefs in which the fubjects of natural philofophy are ufually involved, his endeavours were fuccefsfully directed to obviate and remove thefe obftructions ; and to furnifh a method, at the fame time, comprehenfive, natural, and eafy to be underftood.

Dr. Saunderfon's fenfation of touch, as is ufual with blind people, was very exquifite ; and it was by means of this fenfe, that he acquired many of his principal ideas. He diftinguifhed, with aftonifhing nicety, the peculiar properties of bodies, that depended on the roughnefs or fmoothnefs of their furfaces. A remarkable inftance is given of his nice accuracy in this refpect. A feries of Roman medals, fome of which were true, and others falfe, were

were prefented to his touch. Dr. Saunderfon, by running his fingers over them, was foon able to diftinguifh the genuine antiques, from thofe that were counterfeited; tho' the latter had been executed, with fuch exactnefs of imitation, as to deceive a connoiffeur, who only judged by the eye. But, fays the profeffor, " I, who had not that fenfe " to truft to, could eafily feel a " roughnefs in the new caft, fuffic- " ient to diftinguifh them by."

The impreffion made by the approach of bodies nearer to him, or their being removed farther off; and the different ftates of the atmofphere, were diftinguifhable to him by the fame delicate fenfe of touch; and his fenfe of hearing was refined to a fimilar degree of perfection. He could readily afcertain the fifth part of a note of mufic. He not only diftinguifhed and remembered the different people he converfed with, by the peculiar founds of their voices, but, in fome meafure, places alfo. Judging by the founds of the pavements, of the courts and piazzas, and the reflection of thefe founds from the walls, he remembered the different variations, fo as to be able to recollect the places, pretty exactly, when conducted to them afterwards.

We might produce a great variety of inftances, both ancient and modern, where blind perfons have excelled in different departments of fcience; and particularly, in the feveral branches of mathematics.* But the attachment, which thefe unfortunate people difplay, for the pleafing purfuits of mufic and poetry, is ftill more general. The powerful influence of verbal expreffion, when communicated to the blind, in the form of poetry, and the congenial ideas it infpires, are really aftonifhing. Of this we have a recent proof in Dr. Blacklock, of Edinburgh. This amiable gentleman was, I believe, either born blind, or became fo very foon after his birth : Yet, we find no defects, in thofe beautiful poems he has exhibited to the world, that can be attributed to his want of fight; on the contrary, we meet with defcriptions of vifual fcenes and objects, as beautiful, expreffive, and juft, as if he had actually been poffeffed of the faculty of feeing; and had drawn his defcriptions, from an enraptured furvey of the variegated profpects of nature. Whereas, we muft be convinced, when we accurately confider the matter, that the poetic enthufiafm, which infpired him, and excited thefe imitative powers, could only be produced by the various combination of founds, which were conveyed, by words, to his imagination.

The influence of mufic is ftill more generally to be obferved than that of poetry. Mufic, almoft without exception, appears to be the favourite amufement of the blind. There is no other employment of the

* Diodotus, the preceptor of Cicero, is reprefented as attaching himfelf, with greater affiduity to the Science of Mathematics after he became blind.

" Diodotus Stoicus, cæcus multos annos, noftræ domi vixit : is vero, quod credibile " vix effet, cum in Philofophia multô etiam magis affiduè quam antea verfaretur tum " quod fine occulis fieri poffit. Geometriæ munus tuebatur, precipiens difcentibus, " unde, quo, quamque lineam fcriberent." Cic. Tufc. difp. L. V. 39.

Didymus of Alexandria is celebrated by St. Jerom and the hiftorian Caffiodorus, as a prodigy in logic and mathematics, though blind from his infancy. The latter writer, likewife fpeaks of one Eufebius, an Afiatic, who, though blind, diftinguifhed himfelf highly in all kinds of learning.

the mind, religious contemplation excepted, that seems so well adapted to sooth the soul, and dissipate the melancholy ideas, which, it may naturally be expected, will sometimes pervade the dispositions of those who are utterly bereft of sight. This, together with the beneficial influence that results from the practice of this delightful art, by quickening and perfecting the sense of hearing, is a matter that deserves the most serious attention. The celebrated Professor, just now mentioned, excelled in performing on the flute, in his youth ; and the refinement of his ear has been very justly attributed to his early attention to music. It is not, therefore, surprising that so many blind people have distinguished themselves in this science. Stanley and Parry were deprived of their sight in early infancy ; yet both these gentlemen have displayed extraordinary proofs of their abilities, not only as composers and performers of music, but, likewise, in matters that, at a first view, we might be apt to consider as peculiar to those who are fully possessed of the faculty of vision. Their separate reputations, as musicians, are sufficiently known and acknowledged. The stile of Stanley is truly his own ; and his execution on the organ, equal, if not superior to any of his cotemporary performers on that grand instrument. Parry may be revered as the British bard of modern times. The halls of the Cambrian Chief resound with the melodious vibrations of his harp, and he has united the refinements of taste and elegance to the rude, but expressive modulations of antiquity.

I pass over a number of instances, that might be offered to your notice, and proceed to give some account of Dr. Henry Moyes, the el-

egant reader on philosophical chemistry ; whose lectures, the greatest part of this society had the satisfaction of attending, and whose personal acquaintance several of us have enjoyed.

This intelligent philosopher, like the celebrated professor of Cambridge before mentioned, lost his sight, by the small pox, in his early infancy. He never recollected to have seen : " But the first traces of memory I have," says he, " are in some confused ideas of the solar system." He had the good fortune to be born in a country where learning of every kind is highly cultivated, and to be brought up in a family devoted to learning.

Possessed of native genius, and ardent in his application, he made rapid advances in various departments of erudition ; and not only acquired the fundamental principles of mechanics, music, and the languages ; but, likewise entered deeply into the investigation of the profounder sciences ; and displayed an acute and general knowledge of geometry, optics, algebra ; of astronomy, chemistry ; and, in short, of most of the branches of the Newtonian philosophy.

Mechanical exercises were the favourite employments of his infant years. At a very early age, he made himself acquainted with the use of edged tools, so perfectly, that, notwithstanding his entire blindness, he was able to make little windmills ; and, he even constructed a loom, with his own hands, which still shew the cicatrices of wounds, he received in the execution of these juvenile exploits.

By a most agreeable intimacy, and frequent intercourse, which I enjoyed, with this accomplished blind gentleman, whilst he resided in Manchester ; I had an opportunity

nity of repeatedly obferving the pe-culiar manner, in which he arrang-ed his ideas, and acquired his in-formation. Whenever he was in-troduced into company, I remarked, that he continued fome time filent. The found directed him to judge of the dimenfions of the room, and the different voices, of the number of perfons that were prefent. His dif-tinction, in thefe refpects, was very accurate ; and his memory fo re-tentive, that he feldom was miftak-en. I have known him inftantly recognize a perfon, on firft hearing him fpeak, though more than two years had elapfed fince the time of their laft meeting. He determin-ed, pretty nearly, the ftature of thofe he was fpeaking with, by the direc-tion of their voices ; and he made tolerable conjectures, refpecting their tempers and difpofitions, by the manner in which they conducted their converfation.

It muft be obferved, that this gen-tleman's eyes were not totally in-fenfible to intenfe light. The rays refracted through a prifm, when fufficiently vivid, produced certain diftinguifhable effects on them.— The red gave him a difagreeable fenfation, which he compared to the touch of a faw. As the colours declined in violence, the harfhnefs leffened, until the green afforded a fenfation that was highly pleafing to him ; and which he defcribed, as conveying an idea fimilar to what he felt, in running his hand over fmooth polifhed furfaces. Polifhed furfaces, meandering ftreams, and gentle declivities, were the figures, by which he expreffed his ideas of beauty. Rugged rocks, irregular points, and boifterous elements, fur-nifhed him with expreffions for ter-ror and difguft. He excelled in the charms of converfation ; was happy in his allufions to vifual objects ;

Vol. VI. F

and difcourfed on the nature, com-pofition, and beauty of colours, with pertinence and precifion.

Dr. Moyes was a ftriking inftance of the power, the human foul pof-feffes, of finding refources of fatif-faction, even under the moft rigor-ous calamities. Though involved " in ever during darknefs," and ex-cluded from the charming views of filent or animated nature ; though dependent on an undertaking for the means of his fubfiftence, the fuc-cefs of which was very precarious ; in fhort, though deftitute of other fupport than his genius, and under the mercenary protection of a per-fon, whofe integrity he fufpected— ftill Dr. Moyes was generally cheer-ful and apparently happy. Indeed it muft afford much pleafure to the feeling heart to obferve this hilarity of temper prevail, almoft univerfal-ly, with the blind. Though " cut off from the ways of men, and the contemplation of the human face divine ;" they have this confolation ; they are exempt from the difcern-ment, and contagious influence, of thofe painful emotions of the foul, that are vifible on the countenance, and which hypocrify itfelf can fcarcely conceal. This difpofition, likewife, may be confidered, as an internal evidence of the native worth of the human mind ; that thus fup-ports its dignity and cheerfulnefs under one of the fevereft misfortunes that can poffibly befal us. Nor is this cheerful refignation peculiar to thofe who have been blind from their birth ; we find it, alfo, generally prevail with fuch as have loft their fight, even at a more advanced age ; and who muft, undoubtedly, feel the misfortune with the utmoft anguifh. The diftreffing recollection, which memory muft prefent, of former en-joyments, we find, however, foon fubfides. Gentler and more pleaf-ing

ing reflections fucceed. Contemplation takes her refidence in her proper province, the human mind; and the blind, fubmiffively and cheerfully refign themfelves to the will of Heaven, and the benevolent protection of the lefs unfortunate of their fellow creatures. And hard, indeed, is the heart of him, who will not ftretch out his hand to fuccour the blind; or who, by injuftice, illiberality, or unkindnefs, adds a fting to the confcious dependence, to which, whilft they live, they muft ever be fubjected.

[*Remainder next month.*]

ESSAY on DELICACY of SENTIMENT.

[From "The Bee," a Scotch Periodical Publication.]

Oh! teach us—yet unfpoil'd by wealth
That fecret rare, between th' extremes to move,
Of mad good nature, and of mean felf love.   POPE.

THE character of delicacy of fentiment, fo efteemed at prefent, feems to have been unknown to the ancients. It is certainly a great refinement on humanity. Refinements are never attended to in the earlier ages, when the occupations of war, and the wants of unimproved life, leave little opportunity, and lefs inclination, for fanciful enjoyments. Danger and diftrefs require ftrength of mind, and neceffarily exclude an attention to thofe delicacies, which while they pleafe, infallibly enervate.

That tendernefs which is amiable in a ftate of perfect civilization, is defpifed as a weaknefs among unpolifhed nations. Shocked at the fmalleft circumftances which are difagreeable, it cannot fupport the idea of danger and alarm. So far from exerciling the cruelties which are fometimes politically neceffary in a rude ftate, it ftarts with horror from the fight, and at the defcription of them. It delights in the calm occupations of rural life, and would gladly refign the fpear and the fhield for the fhepherd's crook and the lover's garland. But in an unformed community, where conftant danger requires conftant defence, thofe difpofitions which delight in retirement and eafe will be treated with general contempt; and no temper of mind which is defpifed will be long epidemical.

The ancient Greeks and Romans were the moft civilized people on the earth. They, however, were unacquainted with that extreme delicacy of fentiment which is become fo univerfally prevalent in modern times. Perhaps fome reafonable caufes may be affigned. The ftoic philofophy endeavoured to introduce a total apathy, and, though it was not embraced, in all its rigidity, by the vulgar, yet it had a fufficient number of votaries to diffufe a general tafte for an infenfibility of temper. It perhaps originally meant no more than to teach men to govern their affections by the dictates of reafon; but as a natural want of feeling produced the fame effects as a rational regulation of the paffions, it foon paffed among the vulgar for what it could lay no claim to, a philofophical indifference.

That refpectful attention to women, which in modern times is called

called *gallantry*, was not to be found among the ancients. Women were looked ' upon as inferior beings, whose only duty was to contribute to pleasure, and superintend domestic economy. It was not till the days of chivalry that men showed that desire of pleasing the softer sex, which seems to allow them a superiority. This deference to women refines the manners and softens the temper ; and it is no wonder that the ancients, who admitted no women to their social conversations, should acquire a roughness of manners incompatible with *delicacy of sentiment.*

Men who acted, thought, and spoke, like the ancients, were unquestionably furnished, by nature, with every feeling in great perfection. But their mode of aducation contributed rather to harden, than to mollify their hearts. Politics and war were the sole general objects. Ambition, it is well known, renders all other passions subservient to itself ; and the youth who had been accustomed to military discipline, and had endured the hardships of a campaign, though he might yield to the allurements of pleasure, would not have time to attend to the refinements of delicacy. But the modern soldier, in the present mode of conducting war, is not compelled to undergo many personal hardships, either in the preparation for his profession, or in the exercise of it. Commerce, but little known to many ancient nations, gives the moderns an opportunity of acquiring opulence without much difficulty or danger ; and the infinite numbers who inherit this opulence, in order to pass away life with ease, have recourse to the various arts of exciting pleasure. The professions of divinity and law, leave sufficient time, opportunity, and inclination to most of their professors, to pursue every amusement and gratification. The general plan of modern education, which, among the liberal, consists of the study of the poets and sentimental writers, contributes, perhaps more than all other causes, to humanise the heart and refine the sentiments: For, at the period when education is commenced, the heart is most susceptible of impression.

Whatever disposition tends to soften, without weakning the mind, must be cherished ; and it must be allowed that delicacy of sentiment, on this side the extreme, adds greatly to the happiness of mankind, by diffusing an universal benevolence. It teaches men to feel for others as for themselves ; it disposes us to rejoice with the happy, and, by partaking, to increase their pleasure. It frequently excludes the malignant passions, which are the sources of the greatest misery in life. It excites a pleasing sensation in our own breast, which if its duration be considered, may be placed among the highest gratifications of sense. The only ill consequence that can be apprehended from it is, an effeminacy of mind, which may disqualify us for vigorous pursuits and manly exertions.

In the most successful course of life, obstacles will impede, and disagreeable circumstances disgust. To bear these, without feeling them, is sometimes necessary in the right conduct of life : But he who is tremblingly alive all over, and whose sensibility approaches to soreness, avoids the contest in which he knows he must be hurt. He feels injuries never committed ; and resents affronts never intended. Disgusted with men and manners, he either seeks retirement, to indulge his melancholy, or, weakened.

ed by continual chagrin, he conducts himfelf with folly and imprudence.

How then fhall we avoid the extreme of a difpofition, which in the due medium, is productive of the moft falutary confequences? In this excefs, as well as all others, reafon muft be called in to moderate. Senfibility muft not be permitted to fink us into that ftate of indolence, which effectually reprefses thofe manly fentiments that may very well confift with the moft delicate. The greateft mildnefs is commonly united with the greateft fortitude in the true hero. Tendernefs, joined with refolution, form indeed, a finifhed character.

The affectation of great fenfibility is extremely common. It is, however, as odious as the reality is amiable. It renders a man contemptible, and a women ridiculous. Inftead of relieving the afflicted, which is the neceffary effect of genuine fympathy, a character of this fort flies from mifery, to fhew that it is too delicate to fupport the fight of diftrefs. The appearance of a toad, or the jolting of a carriage, will caufe a paroxyfm of fear. But it is remarkable that this delicacy and tendernefs often difappear in folitude, and the pretender to uncommon fenfibility is frequently found, in the abfence of witneffes, to be uncommonly unfeeling.

To have received a tender heart from the hand of nature, is to have received the means of the greateft bleffings. To have guided it by the dictates of reafon, is to have acted up to the dignity of human nature, and to have obtained that happinefs of which the heart was conftituted fufceptible.

May a temper, thus laudable in itfelf, never be rendered contemptible by affectation, or ufelefs by neglect!

HISTORY of the Intercourfe between the Earl of CHESTERFIELD and Dr. JOHNSON.

LORD Chefterfield, to whom Dr. Johnfon had paid the high compliment of addreffing to his lordfhip the plan of his Dictionary, had behaved to him in fuch a manner as to excite his contempt and indignation : But when the dictionary was upon the eve of publication, lord Chefterfield, who, it is faid, had flattered himfeif with expectations that Johnfon would dedicate the work to him, attempted, in a courtly manner, to footh and infinuate himfelf with the fage, confcious, as it fhould feem, of the cold indifference with which he had treated its learned author ; and further attempted to conciliate him, by writing two papers in "The World," in recommendation of the work ; and it muft be confeffed, that they contain fome ftudied compliments, fo finely turned, that if there had been no previous offence, it is probable that Johnfon would have been highly delighted. Praife in general was pleafing to him ; but by praife from a man of rank and elegant accomplifhments, he was peculiarly gratified. His lordfhip in thefe papers, fays, I think the public in general and the republic of letters in particular, are greatly obliged to Mr. Johnfon, for having undertaken, and executed, fo great and defirable a work. Perfection is is not to be expected from man; but if we are to judge by the various works of Johnson already published, we have good reason to believe, that he will bring this as near to perfection as any man could do. The plan of it, which he published some years ago, seems to be a proof of it. Nothing can be more rationally imagined, or more accurately or elegantly expressed.——

It must be owned that our language is, at present, in a state of anarchy, and hitherto, perhaps, it may not have been the worse for it. During our free and open trade, many words and expressions have been imported, adopted and naturalized from other languages, which have greatly enriched our own. Let it still preserve what real strength and beauty it may have borrowed from others; but let it not, like the Tarpeian maid, be overwhelmed and crushed by unnecessary ornaments. The time for discrimination seems to be come. Toleration, adoption, and naturalization, have run their lengths. Good order and authority are now necessary. But where shall we find them, and at the same time, the obedience due to them? We must have recourse to the old Roman expedient in times of confusion, and choose a dictator. Upon this principle, I give my vote for Mr. Johnson to fill that great and arduous part. And I hereby declare, that I have made a total surrender of all my rights and privileges in the English language, as a free born British subject, to the said Mr. Johnson, during the term of his dictatorship. Nay more, I will not only obey him, like an old Roman, as my dictator, but, like a modern Roman, I will implicitly believe in him as my Pope, and hold him to be infallible while in the chair, and

no longer. More than this he cannot well require; for I presume, that obedience can never be expected, when there is neither terror to enforce, nor interest to invite.

This courtly advice failed of its effect. Johnson, who thought that " all was false and hollow," despised the honied words, and was even indignant, that lord Chesterfield should for a moment imagine, that he could be the dupe of such an artifice.—His expression concerning lord Chesterfield, on this occasion, was, " After making great professions, he had, for many years, taken no notice of me; but when my dictionary was coming out, he fell a scribbling about it. Upon which I wrote him a letter, expressed in civil terms, but such as might shew him, that I did not mind what he said or wrote, and that I had done with him."

———

The Letter.
To the Right Honourable the Earl of Chesterfield.

MY LORD,

I HAVE been informed by the Proprietor of The World, that two papers, in which my dictionary is recommended to the public, were written by your lordship. To be so distinguished, is an honour, which being very little accustomed to favours from the great, I know not well how to receive, or in what terms to acknowledge.

When, upon some slight encouragement, I first visited your lordship, I was overpowered, like the rest of mankind, by the enchantment of your address; and could not forbear to wish that I might boast myself Le vainqueur du vainqueur de la terre;—that I might obtain that regard for which I saw the world contending; but I found my attendance so little encouraged,
that

that neither pride nor modefty would fuffer me to continue it. When I had once addreffed your lordfhip in public, I had exhaufted all the art of pleafing, which a retired and uncourtly fcholar can poffefs. I had done all that I could; and no man is well pleafed to have his all neglected, be it ever fo little.

Seven years, my lord, have now paffed, fince I waited in your outward rooms, or was repulfed from your door; during which time. I have been pufhing on my work through difficulties, of which it is ufelefs to complain, and have brought it at laft, to the verge of publication, without one act of affiftance, one word of encouragement, or one fmile of favour. Such treatment I did not expect, for I never had a patron before.

The fhepherd in Virgil grew at laft acquainted with Love, and found him a native of the rocks. Is not a patron, my lord, one who looks with unconcern on a man ftruggling for life in the water, and when he has reached ground, encumbers him with help? The notice which you have been pleafed to take of my labours, had it been early, had been kind; but it has been delayed till I am indifferent, and cannot enjoy it; till I am folitary, and cannot impart it; till I am known, and do not want it. I hope it is no very cynical afperity not to confefs obligations where no benefit has been received, or to be unwilling that the public fhould confider me as owing that to a patron, which Providence has enabled me to do for myfelf.

Having carried on my work thus far with fo little obligation to any favourer of learning, I fhall not be difappointed, though I fhould conclude it, if lefs be poffible, with lefs; for I have been long wakened from that dream of hope, in which I once boafted myfelf with fo much exultation.

My lord, your lordfhip's moft humble, moft obedient fervant,

SAMUEL JOHNSON.

[*Bof. Life Johnfon.*

A N E C D O T E.

ON the 25th of October, 1694, a bowl of punch was made at the Right Hon. Edward Ruffel's houfe, when he was Captain-General and Commander in Chief of his Majefty's forces in the Mediterranean feas. It was made in a fountain in a garden, in the middle of four walks, all covered over head with lemon and orange trees, and in every walk was a table the whole length of it, covered with cold collations, &c. In the faid fountain were the following ingredients, viz. four hogfheads of brandy, eight hogfheads of water, 25,000 lemons, twenty gallons of lime juice, thirteen hundred weight of fine Lifbon fugar, five pounds of grated nutmegs, 300 toafted bifcuits, and, laftly, a pipe of dry mountain Malaga. Over the fountain was a large canopy, built to keep off the rain; and there was built on purpofe a little boat, wherein was a boy belonging to the fleet, who rowed round the fountain, and filled the cups to the company; and in all probability more than 6000 men drank thereof.

[*Weftmin. Mag.* 1778.

DESCRIPTION

DESCRIPTION of the CORAL.

[From HARRIS's Natural History of the Bible.]

CORAL* is a hard, ftony, marine fubftance, refembling in figure the ftem of a plant divided into branches. It is cf different colours; black, white, and red. The latter is the fort emphatically called coral, as being the moft common, and moft valuable, and employed in the way of ornament. It is of a fine uniform red colour throughout its whole fubftance.

This, though no gem, is ranked by the author of the book of Job xxviii. 18. with the onyx and fapphire. It muft however be owned that the fignification of the original word is altogether uncertain.

The Syrians anciently brought it from the South, and traded therein with the Tyrians. Ezek. xxvii. 16.

Mr. Bruce† thinks the fea Zuph, in our and other verfions called the Red Sea, fhould be named *the fea of coral.* " As for what fanciful people have faid of any rednefs in the fea itfelf, or colour in the bottom, the reader may affure himfelf all this is fiction, the Red Sea being in colour nothing different from the Indian or any other ocean.

" There is a greater difficulty in affigning a reafon for the Hebrew name, *yam fuph ;* properly fo called, fay learned authors, from the quantity of *weeds* in it. But I muft confefs, in contradiction to this, that I never in my life (and I have feen the whole extent of it) faw a weed of any fort in it ; and, indeed, upon the flighteft confideration it will appear to any one that a narrow gulf,

under the immediate influence of monfoons blowing from contrary points fix months each year, would have too much agitation to produce fuch vegetables, feldom found but in ftagnant waters, and feldomer, if ever, found in falt ones. My opinion then is, that it is from the *large trees,*‡ or *plants, of white coral,* fpread every where over the bottom of the Red Sea, perfectly in imitation of plants on land, that the fea has obtained this name."

While I am making this extract, a learned friend§ ftrengthens, by his ingenious criticifms, this opinion of Mr. Bruce. He obferves that the word *fuph* means fometimes *poft,* or *ftake,* to which the large branches of coral may bear fome refemblance. Dr. Shaw fpeaks of them as fo confiderable that they tied their boats to them. The fea is at this day called *Bahrfuf,* and the vegetation it produces *fufo.* And Calmet produces the authority of Don John de Caftro, Viceroy of the Indies for the King of Portugal, who believes likewife that it has its name, *yam fuph,* from the great quantity of *coral* found in it.

If after this I might hazard a conjecture of my own, I would contend that it means the *extreme,* or *boundary fea ;* my reafons for which I will produce after accounting for the name it now bears. It is certain that the books of the old teftament invariably call it *the fea zuph.* And I am inclined to believe that the name *red* was not given to it till after

---

* Vaft groves of it grow on the rocks in the Red Sea, Perfian gulf, &c. See Chryfoft. ex Strab. geogr. l. 16. p. 213. ed. Hudfon, and Shaw's travels, p. 384, &c.

† Travels, p. 246. 8vo.

‡ I faw one of thefe, which from a root nearly central, threw out ramifications in a nearly circular form, meafuring twenty fix feet diameter every way.

§ Rev. Mr. Weft, of New Bedford.

after the Idumeans [or Edomites] had spread themselves from Eaſt to Weſt till they came to border upon and poſſeſs this ſea. They had long the property and uſe of it for their ſhipping. Then it came to be called by the name of the *ſea of Edom,* which the Greeks tranſlated *thalaſſe Erythrea, the ſea of Erythras* (the ſame as Edom) Edom ſignifying *red*. ‖ In 1 Kings, ix. 26, and 11 Chron. viii. 17. *the ſea of ſuph* is mentioned as in the land of Edom, which may be conſidered as a confirmation of this conjecture.

This ſea is twice mentioned * expreſsly as the *limit* or *extreme boundary,* of the poſſeſſions of the Iſraelites: And in ſeveral inſtances † is implied, or included, in the boundary. The original and moſt general meaning of *ſuph* is *end, limit, extremity,* or *hinder part.* § This has induced me to believe it originally called by the Jews *the further boundary ſea.* That it was not named *ſuph* becauſe abounding in *coral.* I apprehend from this circumſtance that that marine production is mentioned in ſcripture by an entirely different name. It is ſpoken of in Job xxviii. 18. and Ezek. xxvii. 16. as a precious ſtone, and is called *ramut,* from a verb, whoſe primary and uſual ſignification is *to lift,* or *raiſe up,* and in Iſai. ii. 13. x. 33. *to have lofty branches.* Coral, as we have before obſerved, lifts itſelf many yards above the water; and therefore might very properly be called, *ramut, the branching ſtone.*

‖ Gen. xxv. 30. Buxtorf. Taylor.
* Exod. xxiii. 31. and Numb. xxxiv. 3.
† Deut. xi. 24. Joſhua 1. 4. 1 Kings, iv. 21, 24. Pſal. lxxii. 8.
§ See Buxtorf, and Taylor.

Remarkable ANECDOTE of the BARON DE MIZELANDWITZ.

HE was one of the Swediſh Senate deprived of all power by the preſent king, upon the memorable revolution in the Government which changed it to an abſolute monarchy; he was poſſeſſed of an eſtate equal to one worth 10,000l. a year in England, and upon the event fled his country, ſaying, he would ſuffer the moſt wretched exile abroad rather than to remain a ſlave where he had a right to freedom. He took up his reſidence at Hamburg, where he has lived ever ſince in great poverty, lodging in a very miſerable apartment, and waiting entirely on himſelf. The King has written twice to him in the moſt flattering terms, inviting him to return to his eſtate and honours; but he never took any notice of his letters; and, upon his Majeſty's ſending him a remittance to enable him to live more comfortably, he refuſed it, ſaying, " I will die rather than receive a dollar at the hands of one who has enſlaved my country!"

[*Weſtmin. Mag.* 1780.

HISTORICAL TRAITS.

IT is remarkable, that in Catholic countries the Sunday is almoſt every where a day of irregularity. In Paris no leſs than fourteen feſtivals in the year have been recently ſuppreſſed, which was taking off ſo
many

many 'days from drunkennefs and debauchery.—A cobler of that city, perceiving on Thurfday a fergeant, who was fo intoxicated, that his fupporters could hardly keep him from falling, fuddenly left his ftall, placed himfelf before the tottering man, and, after attentively looking at him, pathetically exclaimed, " Alas, this will be my condition next Sunday !"

Adriano, of Cordova, was an artift fo diffident of himfelf, that he ufed to deface or deftroy his pictures, as foon as he had executed them ; and fo general was this practice with him, that his friends took occafion to intercede with him for the prefervation of his valuable productions in the name of the fouls in purgatory, knowing his attachment to the holy offices in their behalf. By this mode of exorcifm, the deftroying fpirit, which his felf diffatisfaction had conjured up, was kept in check ; and thanks to the fouls in purgatory ! fome very valuable pictures were refcued from extinction by their influence and authority.

Apicius, the celebrated Roman Epicure, could not name all the animals that covered his table, and which were brought from every part of the world. It was his flave who enjoyed the delicacies which his own lofs of appetite prevented him from tafting. At length, he poifoned himfelf ; for, on looking over his accounts, and finding he had but 60,000 crowns left, he was apprehenfive that he fhould die of hunger.

Peter, King of Caftile, furnamed the Cruel, was faid by the Spanifh hiftorians to be a lover of juftice. The following anecdote is a very *curious* proof of it. Being fond of roving in the ftreets in the night, he once made a riot. The watch man, not fufpecting him to be more than a private man, attacked him inftantly, and was killed by the King. Search was made the next day after the prepetrator of the murder. A woman, who had been a witnefs to the fact, recollected the perfon of his Majafty, and accufed him of the crime. The Magiftrates, in a body, went inftantly to carry their complaints to the throne. The King allowed that juftice ought to be fatisfied ; and, with that view, moft gracioufly ordered his head to be ftruck off—from his own effigy. A mutilated ftatue is ftill to be feen in a corner of the ftreet where the murder was committed.

ANECDOTES of the late EMPEROR of GERMANY.

THIS amiable Prince had determined to vifit Paris in the month of January, 1777 ; but the great quantities of fnow, that had fallen in Auftria and Bavaria, had rendered the roads impracticable, and obliged his Majefty to poftpone his journey. Being told by one of his Courtiers that fome hundreds of peafants would foon clear the roads, he nobly anfwered : " I would rather facrifice every pleafure of my life, than give pain to the meaneft of my fubjects."

His Majefty often drives through the ftreets of Vienna in a chabriolet, a kind of one-horfe chaife. One day, he happened to overfet a green-ftall, and the woman, who knew him not, while fhe was gathering her cabbages and carrots, loaded him with a thoufand reproaches. The moment he had returned to the Palace, he fent a dozen ducats to the good woman,

with

with this obfervation : " I think fhe will now be fatisfied. This will repair any injury I may have done her, and fhe has had fufficient leifure to abufe me."

Before he quitted the frontiers of Auftria, the Emperor, who travelled incognito, happened to meet with one of thofe vain-glorious beings, who, in reality, are *little*, in the very proportion in which they would exalt themfelves above their inferiors ; forgetting that the virtues only form the real diftinctions between men, and that in the beginning all where equal. This fingular adventure is thus related : The Count of Falkenftein, (the title under which the Emperor travelled) had fcarce alighted at an inn, when he faw a very fplendid equipage, preceded and followed by a great number of poftillions. Inquiring what Nobleman it was who travelled with fuch parade, he was informed, that it was the Bifhop of——, who was going to Vienna, accompanied by his Grand Vicar. Certain of not being known, the Count fent to requeft the Bifhop would permit him to have the honour to fup with him. The Prelate received with great coolnefs this felf-invitation

from a man whom he thought of fuch inferior rank ; nor would he have admitted the ftranger to his table but, for the preffing inftances of his Grand Vicar. Apprehenfive, however, of doing him too much honour, the Bifhop with difficulty deigned, during the repaft, to addrefs two or three words to the illuftrious traveller ; and the converfation would have been extremely languid, but for the politenefs of the Grand Vicar, who, after difplaying a great deal of wit and good fenfe, informed the Count, that the Bifhop was going to Court, to folicit for a rich Abbey then vacant, and which he was certain of obtaining. His Majefty retired, as little fatisfied with the ridiculous vanity. of the Prelate, as charmed with the excellent qualities he had difcovered in his companion. The Bifhop had no fooner arrived at Vienna, than he repaired to the Prime Minifter, with all the certainty of fuccefs. But how great was his mortification in being informed, that this rich Abbey was difpofed of to his own Grand Vicar, at the recommendation of the Nobleman with whom he had fupped at fuch an inn.

For the MASSACHUSETTS MAGAZINE.

R E V I E W.

Sermons on various Subjects, Evangelical, Devotional, and Practical, adapted to the Promotion of Chriftian Piety, Family Religion, and Youthful Virtue. By Jofeph Lathrop, D. D. Paftor of the 1ft Church in Weft Springfield.

TO promote virtue in youth, religion in families, and Chriftian piety among all ranks and ages, is the worthieft employment in which the human faculties can be enjoyed. That thefe Sermons are well calculated to anfwer this important end, will be readily acknow-

ledged by every reader of difcernment and piety. They are not intended, nor adapted to fupport any particular fyftem—to propagate fingularities, to offend or to flatter any fect or denomination of Chriftians, but, by commending the truth as it is in Jefus, to every man's confcience

in

ight of God, *to pleafe all men
...eir good to edification,* and to
make them Chriftians in belief, in
temper, and in practice.

It is the great excellence of thefe
Sermons, that the fubjects are important and practical ; that the
thoughts naturally grow out of the
fubjects, are judicioufly arranged,
and communicated in language that
is eafy, perfpicuous, and familiar,
and at the fame time pure and elegant. Our author is happy in his
matter and method, in the concife-
nefs and clearnefs of his difcourfes.
He is equally happy in dignifying
and enriching his ftile as well as en-
forcing his matter, by introducing
with facility and pertinence the language of fcripture. The reader of
tafte as well as devotion, finds, as he
proceeds, his feelings interefted, and
his mind opened, elevated, and fatisfied. Perhaps it will not be eafy
for young ftudents in divinity to
find a better model for fermonifing.
We are perfuaded that if their difcourfes are formed after the pattern
of thefe, as to fentiment, conftruction, arrangement and language,
they will be more than popular
preachers, they will be entertaining
and ufeful. They will be intelligible to the unlearned, pleafing to the
refined, and profitable to all.

We felect a few paffages to gratify thofe who have not the volume
in their hands, and to verify our
criticifm.

SERMON I. p. 15. " We are to glorify
God for our own exiftence,

" If a happy exiftence is to be valued,
an exiftence accompanied with prefent
enjoyments, and with the means of higher enjoyments hereafter, is to be contemplated with gratitude and joy. Perhaps
in the gloom of a difcontented mind you
complain of life as a burden. Impatience
may undoubtedly draw up a long lift of
grievances. But from this lift, let your
fober reafon make proper deductions.
In the firft place, ftrike out your *imaginary*

troubles ; thofe which arife from pride,
vanity, avarice, habit, irregular paffion,
and extravagant expectation. Strike out
next the troubles which are merely *negative,* confifting only in the removal of
bleffings which you have enjoyed for a
while, and which, if you had never enjoyed them, you never would have defired. Strike out alfo your *comparative* evils,
which owe their exiftence to an apprehenfion, that your neighbours poffefs benefits derived to you—benefits you would
not have thought of, if you had not feen
them in the poffeffion of others. Make
thefe deductions, and your lift of grievances will be much reduced. Call gratitude to make the eftimate, and your bleffings will be found to exceed your troubles.
You have more days of health and comfort, than of ficknefs and pain. In a
courfe of regular induftry, you have more
fuccefs than difappointment. In your
connexions, you have many friends ; few
enemies—perhaps none. Remember alfo,
that your real troubles, rightly regarded,
are preparatives for a ftate of pure enjoyment ; and that death, which of all things
here you moft dread, is your paffage to
that ftate.

" But ftill perhaps fome will conclude,
that their exiftence is to be regretted :"
" For revelation informs us, that a great
part, yea, much the greater part of the
human race will be miferable forever. It
is then, with refpect to each one who
comes on this ftage, more probable that
he will be miferable than happy. And if
this is his ftate, what ground is there to
be thankful for exiftence ?"—" Now, without entering on the queftion, whether the
proportion of the faved will be great or
fmall, a queftion not fubject to human
calculation, we are to confider, whether
we have the means and offers of happinefs,
and whether we have them from a Being
that may be trufted ? If we have, then
there is caufe of thankfulnefs for our exiftence ; for we may be happy if we will
be wife. It is only the abufe of divine
goodnefs that makes us miferable. You
are not to confider the plan of the gofpel,
as the fcheme of a lottery, in which each
man's chance for fuccefs is according to
the proportion of prizes to blanks ; but as
a moral and rational plan, in which each
one's fuccefs will be determined by his
own choice. Be the number of the faved
ever fo fmall, this diminifhes not the probability in favour of thofe, who feek for
glory by a patient continuance in well
doing.

doing. Be it ever fo great, this gives no additional hope to thofe who neglect their falvation. To determine the probability of your fuccefs, you need not inquire how many, or how few will be faved : You are only to inquire what you yourfelves are doing. In the deftruction of the old world, Noah and his houfehold, though few, only eight fouls, were preferved. At the wedding fupper, the one unworthy gueft was caft into utter darknefs. Whatever may be the number of the righteous, or of the wicked, the Lord knoweth how to deliver the godly out of temptation, and how to referve the unjuft unto the day of judgment to be punifhed."

" Finally, we are to glorify God for the profpects which are opened before us. Here we may know fomething of God's works ; for creation is all around us and Providence is working before us. Angels and faints above know more of God's works than can be known here. They have a ftronger fight, and can look to more diftant objects. They are raifed to higher ground, and can command a more extenfive view. Their fight is not bounded by the circle of our horizon, nor their profpect terminated by the canopy of our fkies. They fee more than we can fee, and they admire and love more than we can do. But delightful is the hope, that we fhall one day be with them, and be like them ; fee as they fee, and praife as they praife."

SERMON XVI. p. 243. " As the conjugal relation is one of the moft important relations in life, to the parties themfelves, to fociety, and to pofterity, they who fuftain it, ought above all things to ftudy mutual peace. This will render the relation a blefling ; without this, it will become a vexation and a curfe. The Chriftian pair, confidering themfelves as having one common intereft, and feeling themfelves animated by one foul, will readily participate in each other's labours and forrows, and will cheerfully communicate to each other their own pleafures and joys. The rougher paths of life they will tread hand in hand, and by reciprocal fmiles of content, will beguile the tirefome walk. The pains of life they will lighten by bearing each other's burdens, and heighten every enjoyment by fharing it in common. In the education and government of the family, they will ftrengthen each other's hands ; and inftead of contending for an idle fuperiority, will combine their influence for the good of the houfehold.

Little differences of opinion will ⬛ pofed by mutual condefcenfion. ⬛ dental miftakes and trivial faults, will be overlooked, or viewed with the eye of candour. More ferious errors will be mentioned with tendernefs, and corrected with meeknefs. Real virtues and worthy actions will meet the cheering fmiles of approbation ; and worthy defigns will be encouraged by a prompt, unfolicited concurrence. Unavoidable infirmities will be viewed with the comforting eye of pity, not with the infulting eye of difdain.— Real failings will not be matter of keen reproach, but of kind expoftulation.— Under trifling inconveniences they will not teafe and vex each other by eternal complaints ; nor under fevere misfortunes will they embitter each other's fpirits by mutual upbraidings. But on the contrary, by examples of patience, cheerfulnefs, and heavenly mindednefs, they will elevate their own and each other's minds above the fmaller, and fortify them to bear the greater troubles of this changing world."

SERMON XIX. p. 299. " You muft always remember that religion is a *benevolent* and *ufeful* thing ; and that wherever it takes place, it makes men *better* than they were before. It confifts not in empty noife and vain fhow ; but in folid virtue and fubftantial goodnefs. It does not effentially confift in little niceties and trifling diftinctions, which neither influence the heart, nor concern the practice ; nor in the obfervance or rejection of particular rites and forms, which a man may ufe or difufe without prejudice to real virtue in himfelf or others ; nor in a zealous attachment to, or angry abhorrence of, this fect, or that church, in which, as in moft other fields, there are fome tares and fome wheat ; but in fomething more excellent and divine. That, in a word, is true religion, which makes a *good man*—which renders one pious toward his God—conformed to the pattern of his Saviour—benevolent to his fellow men—humble in his temper and manners—peaceable in fociety—juft in his treatment of all—condefcending in cafes of difference—ftrict in the government of himfelf—patient in adverfity—and attentive to his duty in all conditions and relations of life. When you fee fuch a character, you may believe that religion is there. When you find this to be your character, you may believe that wifdom has entered into your heart."

CABINET

CABINET OF APOLLO.

PAPER: A POEM.

Written by the late Dr. FRANKLIN.

SOME wit of old—such wits of old there
    were—
Whose hints show'd meaning, whose allu-
    fions care,
By one brave ftroke to mark all human-
    kind,
Call'd clear blank paper ev'ry infant
    mind ;
When ftill, as opening fenfe her dictates
    wrote,
Fair virtue put a feal, or vice a blot.

    The thought was happy, pertinent, and
      true ;
Methinks a genius might the plan purfue.
I (can you pardon my prefumption) I—
No wit, no genius, yet for once will try.

    Various the papers various wants pro-
      duce,
The wants of fafhion, elegance, and ufe.
Men are as various : And, if right I fcan,
Each fort of *paper* reprefents fome *man.*

    Pray note the fop—half powder and
      half lace—
Nice, as a bandbox were hisdwelling place:
He's the *gilt-paper,* which apart you ftore,
And lock from vulgar hands in the 'fcru-
    toire.

    Mechanics, fervants, farmers, and fo
      forth,
Are *copy paper,* of inferior worth ;
Lefs priz'd, more ufeful, for your defk de-
    creed,
Free to all pens, and prompt at every need.

    The wretch whom av'rice bids to pinch
      and fpare,   [heir,
Starve, cheat, and pilfer, to enrich an
Is coarfe *brown-paper* ; fuch as pedlars
    choofe
To wrap up wares, which better men will
    ufe.

    Take next the mifer's contraft, who de-
      ftroys   [joys.
Health, fame and fortune, in a round of

Will any paper match him? Yes, through-
    out.
He's a true *finking-paper,* paft all doubt.

    The retail politician's anxious thought
Deems *this* fide always right, and *that* ftark
    nought ;
He foams with cenfure ; with applaufe
    he raves—
A dupe to rumours, and a tool of knaves ;
He'll want no type his weaknefs to pro-
    claim,
While fuch a thing as *fools-cap* has a name.

    The hafty gentleman, whofe blood runs
      high,
Who picks a quarrel, if you ftep awry, ·
Who can't a jeft, or hint, or look endure :
What's he? What ? *Touch-paper,* to be fure.

    What are our poets, take them as they
      fall,
Good, bad, rich, poor, much read, not
      read at all ?
Them and their works in the fame clafs
      you'll find ;
They are the mere *wafte-paper* of mankind.

    Obferve the maiden, innocently fweet,
She's fair *white-paper,* an unfullied fheet ;
On which the happy man whom fate or-
    dains,   [pains.
May write his *name,* and take her for his
    One inftance more, and only one I'll
      bring ;
'Tis the *great man* who fcorns a little thing,
Whofe thoughts, whofe deeds, whofe max-
    ims are his own,
Form'd on the feelings of his heart alone :
True genuine *royal-paper* is his breaft ;
Of all the kinds moft precious, pureft, beft.

For the MASSACHUSETTS MAGAZINE.

An ADDRESS to the rifing SONS of AMERICA.

COLUMBIA's fons, for you fhall fa-
    cred truth
    Beam thro' corruption and direct the
      prefs,

For you bright laurels of immortal worth
  Shall bloom eternal on the brow of
    peace.

Therefore behold the great and glorious
  ftar,
  That fhines confpicuous at the helm of
    ftate ;
That led our heroes thro' tremendous war,
  And robb'd the quiver of approaching
    fate.

Copy from him the all celeftial flame ;
  The patriot's virtue and the ruler's
    guide ;
On his perfections rear a glorious name,
  And with him be your country's boaft
    and pride.

With him purfue where reafon deigns to
  lead ;
  Unaw'd by faction—conquer needlefs
    fear,
And learn to copy each heroic deed
  From the bright annals of each paffing
    year.

Firm to the caufe of lib erty remain,
  To freedom's rights, and to the rights
    of God ;
That India's commerce may enrich our
  main,
  And peace and plenty gild Columbia's
    road.

That heaven born fcience my diffufe her
  light
  Around the mind begloom'd with
    bigot zeal;
That art increafing may enchant the
  fight,
  And to the plough transform Bellona's
    fteel.

Rob of its fang, and all corrofive power
  The demon flander, ere its baneful ufe
Deftroys the bud of many an op'ning
  flower,
  And treats good nature with its curs'd
    abufe.

Full many a genius, many a freeborn
  fon
  Has felt its blaft, and from the ftroke re-
    coil'd ;   [gun,
Has—ere pure reafon had its courfe be-
  For flights of fancy been forever foil'd.

Therefore to you the prune and pen is
  given   [foil ;
  To fpread improvement o'er our infant
To keep the path, that leads to truth, to
  heaven,
  And wreft the bloffom from eternal
    fpoil.

Then immortality will blefs your names,
  And o'er your minds diffufe fuch fa-
    cred blifs,
Than when th' Archangel nature's end
  acclaims
  You'll rife triumphant to the realms of
    peace.

                ALCADOUR.

To the Editors *of the* Maffachufetts Magazine.

GENTLEMEN,

The following STANZAS, written by Mrs.
ROBINSON, *the Sappho of her age, are, with
pleafure prefented to the public eye, by an A-
merican—The unaffected fimplicity, tendernefs, and poetic beauty, which run through each
line, muft charm every reader of tafte and fentiment.*   ANNA.

BOUNDING billows,* ceafe your mo-
    tion,
  Bear me not fo fwiftly o'er ;
Ceafe your roarings, foamy ocean,
  I fhall tempt your rage no more.

Ah ! within my bofom beating,
  Varying paffions wildly reign ;
Love with proud reluctance meeting,
  Throbs by turns of *joy* and *pain.*

Joy, that far from foes I wander,
  Where their arts can reach no more !
PAIN, that women's hearts grow fonder,
  When their dream of blifs is o'er.—

Far I go where fate fhall lead me,
  Far acrofs the reftlefs deep !
Where no ftranger's ear fhall heed me,
  Where no eye for *me* fhall weep.

Proud has been my *fatal paffion* !—
  Proud my *injured heart* fhall be !
Every thought and inclination,
  Still fhall prove me *worthy thee !*

Not *one* figh fhall tell my ftory,
  Not *one* tear my cheek fhall ftain,
Silent grief fhall be my glory,
  Grief that *ftoops* not to complain !

Yet ere far from all I treafur'd
  Frederic !† ere I bid adieu !
Ere my days of pain are meafur'd,
  Take the fong that's ftill thy due.—

I have lov'd thee, *dearly* lov'd thee !
  Thro' an age of worldly woe ;
How *unworthy* I have prov'd thee,
  Let my mournful exile fhow !

                    Ten

---

* *Written on her paffage from Dover to Calais.*
† *The Prince of Wales.*

Ten long years of tender sorrow,
  Hour by hour I counted o'er ;
Looking forward till *tomorrow*,
  Every day I lov'd thee more !

Fower and splendor could not charm me,
  I no joy in wealth could see :—
Nor could threats of fears alarm me,
  Save the fear of losing *thee !*

When the storms of fortune press'd thee,
  I have wept to see *thee* weep !
When the pangs of care distress'd thee,
  I have lull'd those cares to sleep !

Think when all the world forsook thee,
  When with grief thy soul was press'd,
How to these fond arms I took thee,
  How I clasp'd thee to my breast.

Often hast thou smiling told me,
  Wealth and *power* were trifling toys,
When thou fondly didst infold me,
  Rich in love's luxuriant joys !

Fare thee well, ungrateful rover !—
  Welcome *Gallia's* hostile shore !—
Now the breezes waft me over,
  Now we part—to *meet no more !*—

To the Memory of a Taylor.

A PARODY.—Scene a Garret.

RESOUND ye walls ! resound the dismal lay !
(A taylor cries) our master dy'd to-day !
Say what avails it now our seats to keep,
Since he who feed us—Oh !—is fast asleep.
Rise, rise, my friends ! haste ! get upon
  your feet,
We lose our time if we preserve our seat :
But let us, ere we leave the garret, try,
Who best can speak his griefs, who loudest
  cry.
Begin——This charge the dying buckram
  gave,
And said—Ye workmen sing, around my
  grave !
Sing, whilst the widow'd lady sits below,
And laughs, and eats, and sips, to soothe
  her woe.
O ! Twist and Thimble, cast your work
  away,
Burn all the thread, and stitch no more to
  day,
And with your needles, now so useless
  grown,
Inscribe this verse on Buckram's tender
  stone :
Let Nature change—let heav'n and earth
  deplore,
For Buckram, best of taylors, is no more !

Twist.

'Tis done ! see Nature's various charms decay ;
'Tis dark as pitch, tho' middle of the day !
Ho ! Molly ! bring us lights, that we may
  see,
How well inanimates with us agree.
Lo ! where in hell the faded cabbage lies,
With him it flourish'd and with him it
  dies !
Were Buckram living how the dyes would
  bloom,
And suits on suits be scatter'd o'er the
  room.
Ah ! what avail'd of business his store !
He's dead ! and now enjoys the trade no
  more !

Thimble.

At morn good ale, at evening gin I prize :
At morn and evening how they cheer'd
  my eyes,
But Buckram always—Now, nor gin, nor
  beer,
Can please my soul, for Buckram is not
  here.
Oh grief ! the heated goose and I agree,
That hot with fire, and I inflam'd by thee,
Alas ! poor master, oft my thumb shall
  bleed,
For losing thee can I my stitching heed ?
Away, my needle, I will sit and roar,
For Buckram, first of taylors, is no more !

Stay-Tape.

My wretched brethren, what avails our art,
That mendeth clothes, yet cannot heal the
  heart ?
How Nature mourns ! the sun has ceas'd
  to shine,
The dogs to bark, and silent are the swine !
Ye happy pigs, that on the clean straw lie,
No more we hear ye grunt, or hear ye cry ;
O ! happy pigs, ye sleep in peace the same,
Nor heed the sorrows which our breasts
  inflame ;
But when awaken'd, O ! how ye will
  mourn
Your wash, beans, barley-meal, e'en all
  things scorn,
And, stretch'd at large upon your strawy
  bed,
Will grunt in chorus, for poor Buckram's
  dead !

Thimble.

For him the dogs shall loathe their 'custom'd
  meal,
The cats disdain the savory bit to steal,
Yet shall they scream in concert, louder far
Than when at night they urge the amorous
  war ;

No

No more, alas! their fqualling fhall for-
bear,
A fweeter mufic than their own to hear,
But, growing wild, inceffantly fhall roar,
And tell that Buckram's finging is no
more!

TWIST.

No more fhall cloth retain its wonted dyes,
And e'en, untouch'd, fhall break the
needles' eyes:
The fheers, when feiz'd by other hands
for ufe,
Shall ftubborn clofe, and cutting-out re-
fufe;   [bread,
And every journeyman fhall fcorn his
And ftarve in pity, for a taylor's dead!

STAY-TAPE.

Hark! hark! the meafures, by the pitying
wind
The fad news told, are grumbling here be-
hind!   [fire;
The grumbling meafures to the impatient
His death regrumble, and the flame burns
higher;
Th' impatient fire to embers wafted down,
Now fnaps with rage, now foars with dif-
mal moan: [plore,
The wind, the meafures, and the fire de-
For Buckram, beft of taylors, is no more!

THIMBLE.

Whilft yonder cufhion fhall our needles
hold,
His fame to future taylors fhall be told.

ALL.

Adieu our fhop-board, goofe, and hell a-
dieu!   [you!
Buckram is dead, and we muft part with

TWIST.

Refound the tale of woe, for Buckram's
dead!

ALL.

We will, as long as we can needles thread.
Here every thimbled hero fhook his
head,
Now grief grew riotous, they kick'd, they
roar'd;
At laft it broke, and all came tumbling
from the board!
[T. and C. Mag.

SONNET to the MORNING.

Extracted for the Maffachufetts Magazine.

MORN'S beaming eyes at length un-
clofe,
And wake the blufhes of the rofe,
That all night long opprefs'd with dews,
And veil'd in chilling fhade its hues,

Reclin'd, forlorn, the languid head,
And fadly fought its parent bed;
Warmth from her ray the trembling
flow'r derives,
And fweetly blufhing through its tears re-
vives.
" Morn's beaming eyes at length unclofe,"
And melt the tears that bend the rofe;
But can their charms fupprefs the figh,
Or chace the tear from forrow's eye?
Can all their luftrous light impart
One ray of peace to forrow's heart?
Ah! no; their fires her faining foul op-
prefs—
Eve's penfive fhades more footh her meek
diftrefs.

SONNET to the LILY.

Extracted for the Maffachufetts Magazine.

SOFT filken flow'r! that in the dewy
vale
Unfolds thy modeft beauties to the morn,
And breath'ft thy fragance on her wandering gale,
O'er earth's green hills and fhadowy vallies borne;

When day has clos'd his dazzling eye,
And dying gales fink foft away;
When eve fteals down the weftern fky,
And mountains, woods, and vales decay;

Thy tender cups, that graceful fwell
Droop fad beneath her chilly dews;
Thy odours feek their filken cell,
And twilight veils thy languid hues.

But foon, fair flow'r! the morn fhall rife,
And rear again thy penfive head;
Again unveil thy fnowy dyes,
Again thy velvet foliage fpread.

Sweet child of fpring! like thee, in forrow's fhade,
Full oft I mourn in tears, and droop forlorn;
And O! like thine, may light my glooms
pervade,
And forrows fly before joy's living morn.

EPITAPH on a GLAZIER.

PRECARIOUS dealer! Death, alas!
Has fnapt in two life's brittle glafs;
Keen was thy di'mond on the pane,
And well thy putty ftopt the rain;

But all thy arts were weak thro' life,
Death cut more certain with his fcythe;
And thou, fafe from a rainy day,
Art putty'd up in mother clay.
The

The Rose and the Butterfly.

A FABLE, by Cunningham.

AT day's early dawn a gay Butterfly
    spy'd
A budding young Rose, and he wish'd
    her his bride:
She blush'd when she heard him his pas-
    sion declare,
And tenderly told him—he need not
    despair.
Their faith was soon plighted as lovers
    will do,
He swore to be constant, she vow'd to
    be true.
It had not been prudent to deal with
    delay, [away,
The bloom of a rose passes quickly
And the pride of a butterfly dies in a day.

When wedded, away the wing'd gentle-
    man hies,
From flow'ret to flow'ret he wantonly flies;
Nor did he revisit his bride, till the sun
Had less than one fourth of his journey
    to run.
The Rose thus reproach'd him: "Al-
    ready so cold!
" How feign'd, O you false one, the pas-
    sion you told!
" 'Tis an age since you left me;" she meant
    a few hours;
But such we'll suppose the fond language
    of flowers:
" I saw when you gave the base vi'let a
    kiss;
" How—how could you stoop to a mean-
    ness like this?
" Shall a low, little wretch, whom we
    roses despise,
" Find favour, O love! in my Butterfly's
    eyes?
" On a tulip quite tawdry, I saw your
    fond rape,
" Nor yet could the pitiful primrose es-
    cape:
" Dull daffodils too, were with ardour ad-
    dress'd,
" And poppies ill scented you kindly ca-
    ress'd."

The coxcomb was piqu'd, and reply'd
    with a sneer,
" That you're first to complain, I com-
    mend you, my dear!
" But know, from your conduct my max-
    ims I drew,
" And if I'm inconstant, I copy from you.
" I saw the boy Zephyrus rifle your
    charms,
" I saw how you simper'd and smil'd in his
    arms;

" The honey bee kiss'd you, you cannot
    disown,
" You favour'd besides—O dishonour!—
    a drone;
" Yet worse—'tis a crime you must not
    deny,
" Your sweets were made common, false
    Rose, to a fly."

MORAL.

This law, long ago, did love's providence
    make,
That every coquette should be curs'd
    with a rake.

                   A.

STANZAS on a LAKE in SAVOY, environed with Mountains, Precipices, &c.

HOW smooth that lake expands its
    ample breast!
Where smiles in soften'd glow the sum-
    mer sky;
How vast the rocks that o'er its surface
    rest!
How wild the scenes its winding shores
    supply.

Now down the western steep slow sinks
    the sun,
And paints with yellow gleam the tufted
    woods;
While here the mountain shadows, broad
    and dun,
Sweep o'er the chrystal mirror of the
    floods.

Mark how his splendor tips with partial
    light
Those shatter'd battlements! that on the
    brow
Of yon bold promontory burst to sight,
From o'er the woods that darkly spread
    below.

In the soft blush of light's reflected power,
The ridgy rock, the woods that crown its
    steep,
Th'illumin'd battlement, and darker tower,
On the smooth wave in trembling beauty
    sleep.

But, lo! the sun recals his fervid ray,
And cold and dim the wat'ry visions fail;
While o'er yon cliff, whose pointed craggs
    decay,
Mild evening draws her thin empurpled
    veil!

How sweet that strain of melancholy
    horn!
That floats along the slowly ebbing wave,
And up the far receding mountains borne,
Returns a dying close from Echo's cave!

                 Hail

Hail fhadowy forms of ftill, expreffive
    Eve !
Your penfive graces ftealing on my heart,
Bid all the fine attun'd emotions live,
And fancy all her lovelieft dreams im-
    part.
                [*Romance of the Foreft.*]

For the MASSACHUSETTS MAGAZINE.

HYMN to CHEERFULNESS.

NYMPH of the darkly rolling eye,
    Enrob'd in fancy's tinctur'd veft,
Forth from thy fecret covert fly,
And take poffeffion of my breaft.
Now fancy's airy forms, on wing,
    Their momentary charms difplay,
    And feem to chide thy long delay,
" In number boundlefs, as the blooms of
    fpring."

Here let us join the nightly dance,
And fport on yonder flow'ry lawn,
Beneath the foft moon's filver glance,
And fhun the purple light of morn.
In midnight's folitary hours,
    O Cheerfulnefs, thy charms beftow,
    Spread o'er our minds a peaceful glow,
And breathe a fragrance on the fields and
    flowers.

Loft to all feeling, fenfe and fhame,
The mifer grafps his golden toys,
Spurns the rich honours of thy name,
And poifons all his focial joys.
How foon his fairy profpects fade,
    See haggard difappointment ftand ;
    Behold he moves his fable hand,
And clouds the landfcape with a gloomy
    fhade.

The failor quits the realms of eafe,
Forfakes, alas ! thy happy reign,
He ploughs with joy the foaming feas,
But, lo ! he ne'er returns again.
While round the howling billows rave,
    Hark ! how he fhrieks with wild affright,
    As dim he fees the *ghoft of night*,
Half viewlefs gleaming thro' the fea green
    wave !

Fair Goddefs, to thy charms divine
Thy fuppliant daily homage pays,
And lights thy confecrated fhrine
With pure affection's hallow'd blaze.
Here let me foft Contentment find,
    And far from all the din of courts,
    Amidft thefe lively rural fports
Reap the rich harveft of a virtuous mind.
                  THE HERMIT.

For the MASSACHUSETTS MAGAZINE.

The INDIAN in PRISON.

ONCE on thofe plains where nature
    gave me birth,
In mild ferenity well pleas'd I rov'd,
Tafted the fweets and fipp'd the wines of
    joy.
Freedom, that bleft prerogative of man,
Was mine : To me fhe gave unbounded
    blifs ;
Gave me to roam where fancy call'd, and
    where
The flowers of eafe, without the thorns of
    care,
Lifted, in honeft pride, their fragrant heads.

There I enjoy'd a father's tender love,
That led my youthful feet in all the ways
Which nature fhew'd and cuftom pointed
    out ;
Taught me to tame the lordly beaft, that
    fill'd
With cries the folitary wildernefs ;
Taught me to aim aright the miffive dart,
To hunt the gloomy dens, where lurks
    alone
The hoftile beaft, and fhuns the eye of day.
Paternal care inftructed me to guide
The tottering barge acrofs the ruffled pool ;
To tear the finny monfters from the deep ;
To lure the airy wanderers to my net ;
To fhun the poifon'd ferpent's deadly fting,
And the more pois'nous rage of vengeful
    man.

'Twas there a mother's fond folicitude
    I knew ;
Her care protected, and her love preferv'd
My youthful frame from all the woes of life.
When pallid ficknefs fhook my tender
    frame,
And potent death feem'd ardent for his
    prey,
Then would maternal care procure the
    fhield
That turn'd the levell'd dart afide.
  A brother's converfe there and fifter's
    love,
Beam'd like the fun upon good fortune's
    day ;
And in affliction's night, like the fair moon,
Shed heavenly comforts on its weeping
    fhades.
Together oft we've join'd the friendly
    throng,
And while the hours in fwift fucceffion
    flew,
Cheerful and bleft have fearch'd the finny
    ftream,
Or rov'd the woods and fhady groves a-
    long.
                     Such

Such was the sea of pleasure, where in youth
I swam, unconscious of the hidden rocks.
Child of the woods, by parent nature nurs'd,
I spent my youth in solitary wilds,
Slept on the rosy couch of much lov'd ease,
Heedless of thorns, those cares of riper days,
But war, dread demon, stalk'd the plains along,
While his big cry roll'd through the hollow vale,
And mighty tremblings seiz'd the hills around.
High wav'd the banners of insulting foes;
Their deadly weapons gleam'd upon the hills
Like meteors dancing in the shades of night—
Stern strode the chief in all the pomp of war,
And wav'd his sword in triumph o'er his head.
To guard the infant, to protect the sire,
To save my country from the impending storm,
I seiz'd my arms, and with the warrior band
Rush'd, like the lion, on the bloody foe.
As two dark clouds that lift their sullen brows
Above the hills, and at a distance frown,
Then meet with fury; while the angry winds
Howl o'er the hills, and roar the groves along,
Loud thunders rumble, and the lightnings blaze—
So roar'd the fight—warrior with warrior mix'd,
In horrid confusion. Five bloody youths
Lay welt'ring at my feet, ere came the blow,
That gave the cursed wound: Prone in the dust
I fell: Ah, had I dy'd in honour's cause!
A warrior ought to meet a warrior's fate.
Scarce had the battle ceas'd, when I was led,
Besmear'd with blood, into this dreary cell.
Here have I lain, o'erwhelm'd with tides of grief,
And wish'd in vain for death. No comfort here;
No consolation to my harrass'd soul!
Dire is this gloomy place. No sound I hear,
Save the sad accents of my butcher'd friends,

Who mourn in wild despair: Save when I hear
The big mouth'd bell speak sullen in the ear
Of night, and tell when comes the hour of rest:
At morning, too, his voice salutes the dawn,
Bids drowsy mortals shake off sleep, and rise.
Oft at his voice I wake; but wake, alas!
To scenes for me too awful to describe!
When will the happy moment come, when free'd
From this detested gloom, my feet shall rove,
The fields again, when gales bring health and peace!

LINUS.

For the MASSACHUSETTS MAGAZINE.

The GHOST of WARREN.

A VISION.

By the Same.

LOUD roar'd the surges of the sea
Along the rocky shore;
All darkness was the night to me,
And mirth was heard no more.

On Bunker's hill alone I stood,
High on the mossy rocks;
The tear of grief my face bedew'd;
Hoarse winds sigh'd through my locks,

Of WARREN's death, my sighing song
Told the lamented tale:
My numbers roll'd the hill along,
Borne by the passing gale.

At length, upon a gloomy cloud,
I saw great WARREN soar;
Ten thousand warriors round him bow'd,
And wav'd their swords of gore.

Borne on the pinions of the wind,
The splendid vision pass'd;
While WARREN cast a look behind,
And thus the bard address'd.

" Sweet are thy numbers, son of songs!
My shade is sooth'd to rest;
No more shall great COLUMBIA's wrongs
Disturb my tranquil breast.

To scenes, in other worlds, I go,
Where joys shall never end;
Then cease thy song, O bard of woe!
And weep no more thy friend."

He said—they mounted on the gale,
While music roll'd around;
Thro' the broad sky in pomp they sail,
To realms where joys abound.

SONG

SONG of a SPIRIT.

By Mrs. RADCLIFF.

IN the fightlefs air I dwell,
  On the floping fun beams play;
Delve the cavern's inmoft cell,
  Where never yet did day light ftray:

Dive beneath the green fea waves,
  And gambol in the briny deeps;
Skim ev'ry fhore that Neptune laves,
  From Lapland's plains to India's fteeps.

Oft I mount with rapid force
  Above the wide earth's fhadowy zone;
Follow the day ftar's flaming courfe
  Through realms of fpace to thought
    unknown:

And liften to celeftial founds
  That fwell the air unheard of men,
As I watch my nightly round,
  O'er woody fteep, and filent glen.

Under the fhade of waving trees,
  On the green bank of fountain clear,
At penfive eve I fit at eafe,
  While dying mufic murmurs near.

And oft, on point of airy clift,
  That hangs upon the Weftern main,
I watch the gay tints, paffing fwift,
  And twilight veil the liquid plain.

Then, when the breeze has funk away,
  And ocean fcarce is heard to lave,
For me, the fea nymphs foftly play
  Their dulcet fhells beneath the wave.

Their dulcet fhells! I hear them now,
  Slow fwells the ftrain upon mine ear;
Now faintly falls—now warbles low,
  Till rapture melts into a tear.

The ray that filvers o'er the dew,
  And trembles thro' the leafy fhade,
And tints the fcene with fofter hue,
  Calls me to rove the lonely glade;

Or hie me to fome ruin'd tower,
  Faintly fhewn by moon light gleam,
Where the lone wand'rer owns my power
  In fhadows dire that fubftance feem;

In thrilling founds that murmur woe,
  And paufing filence makes more dread;
In mufic breathing from below
  Sad folemn ftrains, that wake the dead.

Unfeen I move—unknown am fear'd;
  Fancy's wildeft dreams I weave;
And oft by bards my voice is heard
  To die along the gales of eve.

ODE to LIBERTY.

HAPPY the man, who, unconftrain'd
  Obeys but Nature's equal laws;
Who fears no power by might maintain'd,
  And boldly vindicates his Country's
    caufe.

Fortune's attacks fecure he braves,
  Firmly prepar'd for any chance;
None tremble at her frowns but flaves,
  Whofe daftard fears their abject hopes
    enhance.

His roving fteps, uncurb'd by dread,
  From clime to clime can freely roam;
He goes where choice or fortune leads,
  Freedom his guide, and all the world
    his home.

Confcious of worth, his generous foul
  To ftoop to lawlefs power difdains;
No threats or force his thoughts control,
  He e'en enjoys his Liberty in chains.

MUSA.

STANZAS,

*Written extempore, on feeing a beautiful Young
Lady bathing at a diftance.*

HOW fweet do Clara's charms appear,
  When bathing in yon ftream fo clear!
My foul in rapture melts away,
I feel each faculty decay,

Kind god of Love! thy aid impart,
To foothe a wretched fhepherd's heart:
O, teach the lovely, cruel fair,
The anguifh of my foul to fhare!

Or, from my tortur'd love-fick breaft,
Which knows nor joy, nor peace, nor reft!
Withdraw the cruel, deadly dart,
That fadly wounds my yielding heart.

LEANDER.

The ADVANTAGE of VIRTUE.

VIRTUE, foft balm of every woe,
  Of every gift the cure;
'Tis thou alone that canft beftow
  Pleafures unmix'd and pure.

The fhady wood, the verdant mead,
  Are Virtue's flow'ry road;
Nor painful are the fteps which lead
  To her divine abode.

'Tis not in palaces or halls,
  She or her train appear;
Far off fhe flies from pompous walls,
  Virtue and Peace dwell here.

MONTHLY

MONTHLY GAZETTE.

Summary of Foreign Intelligence.

TURKEY.

CONSTANTINOPLE, April 27.

THE people are anxious for a war with Ruffia, and as the greateft preparations are making to complete the military eftablifhment, it is confidently reported and believed that the defires of the people will be complied with. A rumour was circulated three days ago, that the Porte had ordered the French frigates to quit the Archipelago. The fact is, that the French fhips meet with the moft ample protection, and are permitted to difpofe of their cargoes, and to carry on their commerce in the fame manner as they did during the exiftence of the old government. A French brig from Smyrna has brought orders to the frigates to return to Toulon : This brig carried into Smyrna two Englifh merchantmen, which fhe had captured in her paffage from Toulon.

A member of the National Convention arrived here yefterday : His entry was magnificent, and he appeared with the bonnet rouge on his head. The object of his miffion is not yet known, but it is faid, that it is for the purpofe of pointing out to the Porte, the policy and neceffity of fupporting the Polifh patriots againft Ruffia, and of Pruffia, and promifing that if this fyftem of policy is adopted, the French will protect with their fleets, the trade of Turkey.

FLANDERS.

Camp of Eckoo, near Thielt, June 21.

I have only time to inform you of the melancholy pofture of affairs in Weft Flanders. Ypres furrendered yefterday morning; the garrifon confifting of ten battalions, much reduced in number by the fiege, are prifoners of war, and have been efcorted to Lille; the Hanoverians are at Bruges, where the Britifh, who were at Oftend, joined them laft night. General Clairfayt is at Thielt, and unlefs he receives reinforcements, muft fall back upon Ghent tomorrow.

Never was feen fuch a break up as that of yefterday at Oftend : Every body that could find the means were quiting the place. The magiftrates and people of property were all gone : When the French come, they will find nothing but magazines empty, fhops fhut up and deferted. General Steward gave leave to all the inhabitants yefterday to depart : All the fhips in the harbour were ordered out into the road, and all the baggage belonging to the ftaff, the 85th Regiment of foot, and the 8th Dragoons, was embarked ; the departure of Prince Erneft was the fignal of alarm and flight. The French came yefterday with 20,000 men to Roufelaer. A piquet of 30 men of the 8th dragoons, fent out in the morning, was furrounded and taken, before Giftell. As far as we can judge from appearances, Nieuport and Oftend will be abandoned to them in the courfe of two days, without ftriking a blow, for the inundations have not produced the expected effect. The French have again paffed the Sambre, and invefted Charleroi, with more numerous forces than before, fo that we have no affiftance to hope from that quarter, but much to fear.

FRANCE.

PARIS, *May* 28.—The National Convention have lately decreed the formation of a military fchool in the plain of Sablons, near Paris. The heads of this decree are : That there fhall be fent to Paris from each diftrict of the Republic, fix young citizens, from the age of 16 to 17 and an half, to receive, by a revolutionary education, all the knowledge and habits of a Republican Soldier. They fhall come to Paris on foot, unarmed, and travel as the defenders of the Republic : The national agents of the diftricts fhall take fuch meafures that the Eleves of their vicinity fhall march ten days after the receipt of the decree. The Eleves of the military fchool fhall be clothed, armed, and fed, at the expenfe of the Republic. They fhall be exercifed in the ufe of arms, the maneuvres of infantry, cavalry, and artillery. They fhall learn the principles of the art of war, and fortification ; they fhall be trained to fraternity, good manners,

ners, love of their country, and a hatred for Kings ; and be under the immediate infpection and management of the Committee of Public Welfare.

DEFEAT of the SPANIARDS.

Letter from the Reprefentatives near the Eaftern Pyrenuean army.

CITOYENS COLLEAGUES. We have to announce to you a great victory obtained over the Spaniards. Nothing but the infant love of country could have enabled our brothers in arms to have overcome the almoft infuperable obftacles which oppofed their fuccefs, and which fhielded their enemies. St. Elmos, fituated on an almoft inaccefible mountain, has fallen, and its garrifon, though thus fituated, have capitulated. We have this inftant been to fee, according to the terms of capitulation, 7000 flaves depofit their arms at the feet of the Republicans, and take the oath not to ferve againft the French republic during the war. The force of the Spanifh guards at Collioure and its environs, are fix battalions of Spanifh, and one regiment of little Waloon guards ; in all eleven regiments not compleat, befides artillery and cavalry. Return of prifoners, 3 Marfhals de Camp, 10 Brigadiers, 15 Colonels, 60 Lieutenant Colonels, 300 Captains and Lieutenants, 300 Sergeants, 6468 privates, and feveral companies of cavalry and artillery, 6468 mufquets, 20 ftandards, 100 chefs of tambour, all the horfes and mules, the army and equipments of the cavalry and artillery. We have fent two officers who are charged to prefent to the National Convention the fplendid trophies of this victory of republicans.

Signed,   SOUNBRAY and MILHAUD.

E N G L A N D.

LONDON, *June* 20.—The committee of American merchants had an interview with Mr. Pitt on Saturday laft, to know whether they might with confidence prepare their goods for the American markets as ufual, or whether, under the exifting circumftances, the alarm of a rupture was fufficiently grounded to make them hefitate in executing the orders they had received ? Mr. Pitt declined giving them any advice as to executing their orders ; he faid he was happy in being able to affure them, that the governments of the two countries were difpofed to preferve a good underftanding ; but it could not be concealed that Jacobin doctrines had

made their way in America to fuch an extent as to make it doubtful what would be the iffue of the differences now to be fettled. He trufted, however, that they would be guided by moderation and wifdom in the propofitions they had to make to this country, and the gentlemen, whom they had deputed on the occafion, would find his majefty's minifters earneftly difpofed to preferve the peace which fo happily fubfifted between the two countries.

June 28.—A fervant belonging to the Duke of York arrived this morning at the Secretary of State's office with difpatches from his Royal Highnefs. The particulars of the contents have not yet tranfpired ; but it is known that they confirm what has been ftated, that the army has made a movement towards Nivelles to fuccour the Prince of Orange, who was judged to be in a critical fituation, on account of the immenfe numbers of the French.

This meffenger was obliged to come by the way of Holland, which puts it beyond a doubt that the French have cut off completely for the prefent, all communication between Eaft and Weft Flanders.

Gen. Kofciufko's account of the action between the Polifh troops, and the army of the King of Pruffia, received by the Dutch mails, differs, very materially, from that given in the Berlin papers. The lofs of the Poles amount to 600 men, that of the enemy is much more confiderable. Some reports ftate the lofs of the Pruffians at 500 killed and wounded and that of the Ruffians at 400.

Yefterday Mr. Jay, the American Minifter, had a private interview with Mr. Pitt at his houfe in Dawning ftreet.

We have juft learnt that the French, having returned in great numbers to Nieuport, have retaken the town of Furnefs, and all the ports of which a part of our garrifon had poffeffed themfelves the evening before. Sixty thoufand French troops, collected from Lifle, Countray and Menin, are now furrounding the fortrefs of Ypres, the communication of which, with the other places in Flanders, is entirely cut off. The bombardment of it is carried on vigoroufly. Two attempts, it is faid, have been made to take it by affault. An attempt is meditated by the French, on Oftend. It appears that the French have fired red hot balls into Ypres, by which means they have deftroyed the convents, and many fine buildings belonging to that town. By letters received yefterday from Oftend, we have the un-
pleafant

pleafant intelligence, that Gen. Clairfayt had fuftained a defeat in his attempt to relieve Ypres on the 12th inft. In confe- quence, it is faid that Ypres had furren- dered on the 13th.

DOMESTIC OCCURRENCES.

NOVA SCOTIA.
HALIFAX, July 24.
CAPTURE of the FRENCH CONVOY.

ON Tuefday laft arrived from the Capes of the Delaware, his Maj- efty's fhips Argonaut of 70 guns, Capt. Aylmer, and L'Oifeau of 36 guns, Capt. Murray; having under their convoy the following French and American veffels : 5 fhips, 1 fnow, 6 Brigs and 1 fchooner, chiefly laden with flour, and belonging to Philadelphia and Alexandria. Thefe veffels are prizes to his Majefty's fhips under the command of Rear Admiral Murray. The Admiral failed from Ply- mouth the 19th of May, having under his command, the following fquadron, which are appointed to the American ftation, and are to rendezvous at this place.

Ships.	Guns.
Refolution,	74
Argonaut,	70
Africa,	64
Thetis,	38
L'Oifeau,	36
Celopatra,	32
Thifbe,	28
Alert,	14

It is faid that Fauchet had been for fome time collecting this provifion fleet, and that he expected the arrival of four fail of the line, which not arriving at the time appointed, and the expenfes of demurage, &c. high, he had concluded to fend them away with the above mentioned convoy.

GRAND NAVAL COMBAT.
Letter from Admiral Earl HOWE, on board the Queen Charlotte, June 2, 1794.

SIR,

THINKING it may not be neceffary to make a more particular report of my proceedings with the fleet for the infor- mation of the Lords Commiffioners of the Admiralty, I confine my communications chiefly in this difpatch, to the occurren- ces when in prefence of the enemy yefter- day.

Finding on my return off Breft, on the 19th paft, that the French fleet had, a few days before put to fea ; and receiving on the fame evening advices from Admiral Montague, I deemed it requifite to endeav- our to form a junction with the Rear Admiral as foon as poffible, and proceeded immediately for the ftation on which he meant to wait for the return of the Venus. But having gained very credible intelli- gence on the 21ft of the fame month, whereby I had reafon to fuppofe the French fleet was then but a few leagues farther to the weftward, the courfe before fteered was altered accordingly.

On the morning of the 28th the enemy where difcovered far to windward, and partial actions were engaged with them that evening, and the next day. The weather guage having been obtained in the progrefs of the laft mentioned day, and the fleet being in a fituation for bringing the enemy to clofe action the firft inftant, the fhips bore up together for that purpofe, between 7 and 8 o'clock in the morning.

The French, therefore, confifting of twenty fix fail of the line, oppofed to his Majefty's fleet of twenty five, waited for the action, and fuftained the attack with their cuftomary refolution.

In lefs than an hour after the clofe ac- tion commenced in the centre, the French Admiral, engaged by the Queen Charlotte, crowded off and was followed by moft of the fhips of his van in condition to carry fail after him, leaving with us 10 or 12 of his cripled or totally difmafted fhips, exclufive of one funk in the engagement. The Queen Charlotte had then loft her fore topmaft and the main topmaft fell over the fide very foon after.

The greater number of the other fhips of the Britifh fleet were at this time fo much difabled, or widely feparated, and under fuch circumftances with re- fpect to thofe fhips of the enemy in a ftate for action, and with which the fir- ing was ftill continued, that two or three even of their difmafted fhips attempted to get under a fpritfail, fingly, or fmaller fail raifed on the ftump of the foremaft could not be detained. Seven remained in our poffeffion, one of which however funk before the adequate affiftance could be given to her crew; but many were faved.

The

The Brunfwick having loft her mizen maft in the action, and drifted to leeward of the French retreating fhips, was obliged to put away large to the northward of them. The material injury to his Majefty's fhips, I underftand, is confined principally to their mafts and yards, which I conclude will be fpeedily replaced.

I have not yet been able to collect regular accounts of the killed and wounded in the different fhips. Capt. Montague is the only officer of his rank who fell in the action. The number of both difcriptions I hope will prove fmall, the nature of the fervice confidered ; but I have the concern of being obliged to add on this fubject that Admiral Graves had received a wound in the arm, and that Rear Admirals, Bowyer and Pafley, and Capt. Hutt of the Queen have each had a leg taken off.

REMARKS on the PRESENT SITUATION of FRANCE.

The refources of France are fo aftonifhingly great that the lofs of 25 fhips at Toulon fcarcely excited the attention of the nation. The lofs of them has not been mentioned by the National Convention, as an event in any refpect connected with the great fyftem of their revolution. Amidft this difafter they purfued their victories, and in a few months fitted out a fleet equal, according to the Englifh account, to theirs. France muft excite the aftonifhment of the world. Alone fhe is fighting the caufe of freedom, of mankind, and particularly of America. Befet with a banditti of tyrants, fhe appears like a lion, furrounded with every ravenous beaft of the foreft. Animated with the fpirit of liberty, they will roufe to the combat, and like her fifter America, who always became formidable from her misfortunes, will renew their attacks with tenfold energy. In Flanders the French are almoft uniformly victorious. The Germans are computed to have loft 60,000 men in the month of May, and are now wholly on the defenfive.

DISTRESSING CONFLAGRATION.

On Wednefday the 30th ult. a fire in this town began its devaftation in the Ropewalk owned by Mr. Howe, about twenty minutes after 4 o'clock A. M. from accident. Mr. How had kindled a fire that morning, a fpark from which caught fome hemp and tar, and inftantly communicated the flames in all directions, baffling every effort to extinguifh them. The alarm was inftantly fpread through the town ; but before any number of citizens could be collected, fuch was the quantity of the combuftibles on fire, all the walks adjacent, fix of which were fix hundred feet in length, were enveloped in the flames ; which, fed by immenfe quantities of hemp, cordage and tar, fpread with nearly the celerity of electricity. A large number of dwelling houfes in Green's Lane and in the ftreet facing the Ropewalks have been deftroyed, and, it is faid, nearly one hundred families turned out of doors by this diftreffing accident.

PUBLIC EXECUTION.

On Wednefday afternoon, 30th ult. Collins, Fertidi, and Polefki, were executed on the common in this town for piracy, agreeably to the fentence of the Circuit Court.

MARRIAGES.

MASSACHUSETTS.—Bofton, Mr. Jacob Euftis to Mifs Eliza S. Gray ; Mr. Ifaac Larkin, junior editor of the Independent Chronicle, to Mifs Nabby Clark ; Mr. William Trefrey to Mifs Mary Stimpfon ; Mr. Afa Hatch to Mifs Patty Brown ; Mr. Thomas Stepfon to Mifs Polly Hammond ; Mr. Thomas H. Kemble to Mifs Abigail Bumftead.

Dedham, Mr. Jofiah Bumftead to Mifs Abigail Baker.

Lexington, Dr. Jofeph Fifk, jun. to Mifs Betfey Stone.

Methuen, The Rev. Titus Theodore Barton to Mifs Ruth Wood.

Salem, Capt. John Fofter to Mifs Polly Burchmore.

Tewkefbury, Mr. Ruffell Meers to Mifs Sufannah Duton.

DEATHS.

MASSACHUSETTS.—Bofton, Mr. John Robinfon, 56 ; Mr. Daniel Collins, 58 ; Mifs Sally Mackay ; Capt. Jofeph Cowdin, 29 ; Samuel May, Efq. 71 ; Mrs. Frances Maud, 57 ; Mifs Phebe Harlow, 18 ; Mrs. Hannah Dinmore, 68 ; Mrs. Sarah Davis, 47 ; Mifs Mary Blake, 29 ; Capt. William Porter, 30 ; Mr. John Winniett, 70 ; Mr. John Clap ; Mr. William Eaton, 38 ; Mrs. Mary Alline ; Mr. William Foot, 44 ; Mrs. Eliza Eaton, 38 ; Mr. William Penniman, 59.

Boylfton, Mrs. Rehekah Keyes, 89.

Gloucefter, Mrs. Mary Beach, 31 ; Mrs. Deborah Melvill, 58.

Haverhill, Mrs. Prifcilla Bartlett.

Plymouth, Mrs. Nancy Jackfon, 28.

AUTUMN.

THE
MASSACHUSETTS MAGAZINE:
OR,
MONTHLY MUSEUM
OF
KNOWLEDGE and RATIONAL ENTERTAINMENT.

No. IX.]   FOR SEPTEMBER, 1794.   [Vol. VI.

CONTAINING,

WITH A HANDSOME ENGRAVING.

PRINTED AT *BOSTON*, FOR THE PROPRIETORS,
By EZRA W. WELD AND WILLIAM GREENOUGH,
No. 42, CORNHILL.
Sold at JOHN WEST's Bookftore, No. 75, *Cornhill*, Bofton ; and by the feveral
GENTLEMEN who receive Subfcriptions for this WORK.
MDCCXCIV.

ACKNOWLEDGMENTS to CORRESPONDENTS.

We drop the tear of fympathy with *Celia* on the death of her friend; fhould we publifh her elegy, we fhould occafion her, in the hour of difpaffionate reflection, additional forrow.

Effay on Juftice—under confideration.

The Stranger fhall receive due attention.

The Meffengers of David, are defired to tarry at Jerico till their beards be grown.

Preferves of Parnaffus—They do not contain a fufficiency of attic falt to preferve them from putrefaction.

Lothario is thanked for his beautiful extract—future favours are folicited.

PRICES of PUBLIC SECURITIES, BANK STOCK, &c.

September.	Six per Cents.	Three per Cents.	Defer'd Stock.	Maffachuf. State Notes.	U.S.B. Shares ab. par.	Maffachuf. Bank Shares.	Union Bank Shares ab. pr.	Final & I..Of. Cert.inter.fr. Jan. 1788.	Reg. Dt. with int. fr. March 4, 1789.	Indents. Int. on Loan Offi.	Cer.&Reg.Dt.	New Emiffion Money.	O. Emif. Mo.
	s. d.	s. d.	s. d.	r. d.	per ct.	dols.	per ct.	s. d.	s. d.	i. d.	s. d.	s.	
1	19 1	11 0	12 0	15 2	20	None	9 1-2	16 9	16	9 6	8 0		40
2	19 1	11 0	12 0	15 2	20	at	10	16 9	16	9 6	8 0		40
3	19 2	11 0	12 0	15 2	20	mkt.	10	16 9	16	9 6	8 0		45
4	19 2	11 0	12 0	15 2	22		10	16 9	16	9 6	8 0		45
5	19 2	11 0	12 0	15 2	22		10 1-2	16 9	16	9 6	8 0		45
6	19 2	11 0	12 0	15 2	22		10 1-2	16 9	16	9 6	8 0		45
8	19 2	11 0	12 0	15 2	22		10 1-2	16 9	16	9 6	8 0		45
9	19 2	11 0	12 0	15 2	22		11	16 9	16	9 6	8 0		45
10	19 2	11 0	12 0	15 2	22		11	16 9	16	9 6	8 0		45
11	19 2	11 0	12 0	15 2	22		11	17 0	16	9 6	8 0		45
12	19 4	11 0	12 0	15 2	22		11	17 0	16	9 6	8 0		45
13	19 5	11 1	12 2	15 4	22		11	17 6	16	10 0	8 0		45
15	19 5	11 2	12 4	15 4	23		11	17 6	16	10 0	8 0		45
16	19 1	11 2	12 4	15 4	23		12	18 0	14	10 0	8 0		45
17	19 1	11 0	12 6	15 4	23		12	18 0	17	10 0	8 0		45
18	19 1	11 0	12 6	15 4	23		12	18 0	17	10 0	8 0		45
19	19 1	11 0	12 6	15 4	23		12	18 0	17	10 0	8 0		45
20	19 2	11 0	12 6	15 4	23		12	18 0	17	10 0	8 0		45
22	19 2	11 1	12 6	15 4	25		8	18 0	17	10 0	8 0		45
23	19 2	11 1	12 6	15 4	25		8	18 0	17	10 0	8 0		45
24	19 2	11 1	12 6	15 4	25		8	18 0	17	10 0	8 0		45
25	19 2	11 1	12 6	15 4	25		8	18 0	17	10 0	8 0		45
26	19 2	11 1	12 6	15 4	25		8	18 0	17	10 0	8 0		45
27	19 2	11 1	12 6	15 4	25		8	18 0	17	10 0	8 0		45
29	19 2	11 1	12 6	15 4	25		8	18 0	17	10 0	8 0		45
30	19 2	11 1	12 6	15 4	25		8	18 0	17	10 0	8 0		45

JOHN MARSTON, *Stock Broker.*

the united preffure of thofe currents from all fides, into the higher regions; which funnel, as the denfity of the air leffens according to its height, and the furrounding preffure which contracts it muft decreafe nearly in the fame proportion, would more and more diverge and expand the higher it rofe above the furface of the fea. This would be attended with a moft furious blaft of wind up to, and far above the top of the atmofphere. In like manner,

6. If inftead of a pure vacuum, or a total annihilation of fuch part of the atmofphere, we fuppofe the fame to become, by any means whatever, fpecifically lighter than the furrounding regions, the effect would be the fame as above, in kind, though not in degree ; the denfer air flowing in, but with lefs rapidity, from all quarters without, expelling the lighter and fupplying its place, as in article four ; upon which alfo a large quantity of this confluent air, for the fame reafon, would be driven up with violence through a like narrow vent, yet not with the fame impetuofity, nor to the fame height as if forced through this funnel into a pure vacuum.

That the atmofphere over large tracts of fea or land may thus become fpecifically lighter than that over the furrounding regions, will be evident, if we confider, 1. That heat has a natural tendency to rarefy

and expand the air upon which it acts. 2. That the atmofphere over our head does not confift of mere elementary air, but it is an univerfal receptacle of all the heterogeneous vapors and effluvia that are perpetually exhaling from every fubftance that exift upon the face of the earth, whether animal, vegetable or mineral. 3. That, by the cafual difpofition of thefe vapours and effluvia in the atmofphere, the air which is, of itfelf, naturally enough difpofed to acquire heat from the paffage of the fun's rays through it, may become more difpofed to imbibe and retain that heat, in one region, than in another in its neighbourhood ; which from the intervention of clouds, or from its purity and freedom from thofe fteams and vapours with which the former is charged, may, in a great degree, retain its natural coolnefs and denfity, while the other becomes heated, rarefied and expanded, and is thereby rendered fpecifically lighter.

That thefe different affections of the atmofphere actually take place, and difpofe the air, at one time and in one place, even in the fame feafons of the year, to imbibe and retain the heat excited by the fun's rays, more than at another, is not a matter of mere conjecture ; but, whatever the caufe may be, is notorious to all perfons of obfervation.

ANECDOTE of the late Lord Chancellor NORTHINGTON.

[From the life of Bifhop NEWTON, prefixed to his Works.]

WHILE this great lawyer continued at the bar, he went the weftern circuit, and being of lively parts and a warm temper, he was like fome other lawyers, too apt to take indecent liberties in examining witneffes. An extraordinary inftance of this kind happened at Briftol. In a caufe of fome confequence, Mr. Reeve, a confiderable merchant, and one of the people called Quakers, was crofs-examined

by

by him with much raillery and ridicule. Mr. Reeve complained of
it at the time; and when the court
had adjourned, and the lawyers
were all together at the White Lion,
Mr. Reeve sent one of the waiters to
let Mr. Henley know, that a gentleman wanted to speak to him in a
room adjoining. As soon as Mr.
Henley had entered into the room,
Mr. Reeve locked the door, and put
the key into his pocket. " Friend
Henley," said he, " I cannot call
thee ; for thou hast used me most
scurrilously. Thou mightest think,
perhaps, that a Quaker might be in-
sulted with impunity : but I am a
man of spirit, and am come to demand, and will have, satisfaction.
Here are two swords, here are two
pistols; choose thy weapons, or fight
me at fifty cuffs if thou hadst rather ;
for fight me thou shalt before thou
leavest this room, or beg my pardon." Mr. Henley pleaded in excuse, that it was nothing more than
the usual language of the bar ; that
what was said in court should not
be questioned out of court ; lawyers
sometimes advanced things to serve
their client, perhaps beyond the
truth, but such speeches died in
speaking ; he was so far from intending any insult or injury, that he
really had forgotten what he had
said, and hoped the other would not
remember it ; upon his word and
honour he never meant to give him
the least offence, but if undesignedly

he had offended him, he was sorry
for it, and was ready to beg his
pardon, which was a gentleman's
satisfaction. " Well," said Mr.
Reeve, " as the affront was public,
the reparation must be so too. If
thou wilt not fight, but beg my
pardon, thou must beg my pardon
before the company in the next
room." Mr. Henley, after some
difficulty and some delay, submitted
to the condition ; and thus this fray
ended. No farther notice was taken on either side, till after some
years the lord chancellor wrote a
letter to Mr. Reeve, informing him
that such a ship was coming into
the port of Bristol, with a couple of
pipes of Madeira on board, consign-
ed to him. He therefore begged
Mr. Reeve to pay the freight and
the duty, and to cause the vessels to
be put into a waggon, and sent to
the Grange ; and he would take the
first opportunity of defraying all
charges, and should think himself
infinitely obliged to him. All this
was done as desired ; and the winter following, when Mr. Reeve was
in town, he dined at the chancellor's with several of the nobility and
gentry. After dinner the chancellor related the whole story of his
first acquaintance with his friend
Reeve, and of every particular that
had passed between them, with great
good humour and pleasantry, and
to the no small diversion of the company.

On AFFECTATION.

IT is commonly remarked, that
handsome people are vain and
fantastical, this is because every motion, gesture and action of their's is
more particularly observed, and envy never fails to give a disadvan-
tageous turn to every little inadver-
tency : whereas an ugly person may

be guilty of a thousand imperti-
nences which nobody will regard.

What the ladies are pleased to
call a pretty kind of woman, is a
creature little superior to a piece of
machinery, which discovers no other
signs of life but that it moves.

OBSERVATIONS

OBSERVATIONS on BLINDNESS, and on the Employment of the other Senfes to fupply the Loss of SIGHT.

[By Mr. BEW.—From "Memoirs of the Literary and Philofophical Society of Manchefter."]

(Concluded from the 490th page.)

THE blind people I have hitherto felected to fpeak of, it
may be remarked, were fuch as
had their native faculties excited
and matured by early and attentive
education. But we fhall find, even
where education has been wanting,
and the blind left, in a great meafure, to the fimple exertions of nature ; that the natural faculties
themfelves make furprizing efforts
towards fupplying the deficiency of
fight. I fhall bring forwards to
your notice a perfon, well known
in this neighbourhood, of which he
is a native. This is one John Met-
calf, who, like the gentlemen already mentioned, became blind at
a very early age, fo as to be entirely unconfcious of light and its various effects. This man paffed the
younger part of his life as a wag-
goner, and occafionally, as a guide
in intricate roads during the night,
or when the tracks were covered
with fnow. Strange as this may
appear to thofe who can fee, the
employment he has fince undertak-
en is ftill more extraordinary : It
is one of the laft to which we could
fuppofe a blind man would ever
turn his attention. His prefent occupation is that of a projector and
furveyor of highways in difficult
and mountainous parts. With the
affiftance only of a long ftaff, I

have feveral times met this man
traverfing the roads, afcending
precipices, exploring valleys, and
invefligating their feveral extents,
forms, and fituations, fo as to anfwer his defigns in the beft manner.
The plans which he defigns, and the
eftimates he makes, are done in a
method peculiar to himfelf ; and
which he cannot well convey the
meaning of to others. His abilities, in this refpect, are, neverthelefs, fo great, that he finds conftant
employment. Moft of the roads
over the Peak in Derbyfhire, have
been altered by his directions ; particularly thofe in the vicinity of
Buxton : And he is, at this time,
conftructing a new one, betwixt
Wilmflow and Congleton, with a
view to open a communication to
the great London road, without
being obliged to pafs over the
mountains.*

These inftances will, I am perfuaded, be fufficient to prove, how
effectually, by proper exercife, the
other fenfes may be refined and
perfected, fo as, in many refpects,
to fupply the lofs of fight. The
fenfations of fmell and tafte, indeed,
are fo very limited, that they do
not feem capable of yielding many
peculiar advantages to blind people : But the perceptions of hearing
and touch, as we have feen, may
be

Vol. VI. B

* Since this paper was written, and had the honour of being delivered to the
fociety, I have met this blind projector of the roads, who was alone as ufual ; and
amongft other converfation, I made fome inquiries refpecting this new road. It
was really aftonifhing to hear with what accuracy he defcribed the courfes, and
the nature of the different foils, through which it was conducted. Having mentioned to him a boggy piece of ground it paffed through, he obferved, that " that was the
" only place he had doubts concerning ; and that he was apprehenfive they had,
" contrary to his directions, been too fparing of their materials."

be applied to purpofes wonderfully extenfive.

By the nice diftinction of touch and found, the blind man not only acquires knowledge with refpect to perfons and fituations ; is not only warned from danger, and excited to pleafure ; but by means of thefe delicate faculties, he is enabled to conceive many of the vifual qualities of bodies, and to diftinguifh them with certain precifion. I do not mean to infer, that a blind man annexes the fame ideas to vifual qualities, as are excited in the minds of thofe who are poffeffed of the perfect faculty of fight. I only wifh to obferve, that he forms a general conception of their characters, by the analogy which he finds they bear to qualities he is acquainted with, by means of his other fenfes. Thus, for example, if we prefent a violet to him, and demand of him what ideas he has of its qualities ; he will be able to anfwer with great precifion refpecting its fmell, &c. which, as well as the name of the violet are foft, fweet, and pleafing. But, with regard to the colour, he will be wholly unable to conceive any idea of it, except what takes place from very diftant analogies : The plaintive melody of the flute, the foft fmoothnefs of furfaces, &c. In like manner, by oppofite affociations, he may compare the intenfe colour of fcarlet to the glow of a furnace, the noife of a trumpet, or the odour of aromatics ; becaufe they feverally affect his fenfes with intenfe excitements.

But whatever amazing information, the fenfes of hearing and touch, may afford the blind ; thefe powers would, neverthelefs, be tranfient and ineffectual, were not the impreffions and ideas they excite in the mind, preferved and ma-

tured by the affiftance of the memory. It is chiefly by the affiftance of the memory, that the blind acquire the exquifite advantages, derived from the other fenfes. In this refpect, providential benevolence feems to have determined the greateft compenfation, for the fevere deprivation of the fenfe of fight. The foul of the blind man, undiftracted by the never ceafing variety which is always prefent to the organs of vifion, when awake, purfues its internal perceptions and contemplations with unconfounded ferenity. The blind unlettered projector of roads could reply to me, when I expreffed myfelf furprized at the accuracy of his difcriminations, "that there was nothing fur-"prizing in the matter ; You, "Sir," fays he, " can have re-"courfe to your eye fight whenever "you want to fee or examine any "thing ; whereas, I have only my "memory to truft to. There is one "advantage, however," he remarked that he poffeffed. "The "readinefs with which you view "an object at pleafure, prevents "the neceffity of fixing the ideas "of it deeply in your mind, and "the impreffions, in general, be-"come quickly obliterated. On "the contrary, the information I "poffefs, being acquired with great-"er difficulty, is, on that very ac-"count, fo firmly fixed on the "memory, as to be almoft indeli-"ble." Such, indeed, is the wonderful influence, refulting from the union of exercife and habit, on the faculties of the blind, that the permanency of their knowledge in a great meafure, compenfates for the labour required in its attainment !

The inftantaneous facility, with which, by the aid of fight, we are able to afcertain the peculiarities
of

of any place we furvey, and the eafe with which we review and recognize them, renders dependence on the memory, to us, lefs neceffary. For inftance, the dimenfions of the apartment I fit in; the furniture, &c. will, by the organs of vifion, be immediately prefented to the mind of any ftranger who may call on me, fo that he will be able, in a moment, to recollect the whole whenever he repeats his vifit, to the fame place. This kind of information can only be acquired by the blind man, in confequence of the moft patient attention. He is to be led round the feveral parts of the room, his finger conducted to the furfaces of the furniture, pictures, &c. before he can poffibly form any idea with refpect to the place. But when, by means of the perceptions of touch, and a neceffary degree of information, he conceives a regular train of diftinguifhing ideas, his mind affociates them, with fuch tenacity, that he feldom has occafion to repeat his inquiries.

It is this accurate and retentive power of the memory, that enables the blind mathematician to make exact calculations and inferences; to work problems in algebra, and in infinite feries; to conceive, with precifion, the different effects that bodies muft produce to the fight, by their being nearer or farther off; by their moving in a ftrait or in an oblique line; and, that directs his inveftigation with refpect to the principles of projection, and the various rules of perfpective.

It muft here be remarked, that though the blind man may conceive the properties of figure and extenfion with certain accuracy; yet it does not follow that he would be able to diftinguifh them, with the

fame certainty, by vifion, provided that faculty were, immediately, beftowed on him. On the contrary, the queftion ftarted by Mr. Molineux, * was found to prove exactly as that philofopher expected, in the extraordinary cafe of a blind youth, whom Mr. Chefelden had the good fortune to bring to fight, by couching, at thirteen years of age. This young man, at his firft feeling the impreffions of objects on the organs of vifion, imagined every thing he faw touched his eyes; nor was he able to difcriminate one object from another, however different their forms. When things that were before known to him, by touching, were prefented to him, he confidered them attentively, in order to recognize them; but on a fudden, he felt himfelf confufed, from the multitude of objects that crowded for admiffion, and the whole was involved in obfcurity. It appears, therefore, from the above fact, as well as from a due examination of the fubject, that thofe who make ufe of their eyes, for the firft time, fee only furfaces and colours; and have no conception of the vifible effects of light and projection, until they learn it from experience. In fact, if we carefully attend to the operation of our own minds, we fhall find, that the vifible appearances of objects are feldom accurately attended to, unlefs we are employed in delineating thofe objects. The vifible appearance of things, is varied according to the direction of the light, the pofition, and the diftance, with refpect to the beholder: Yet, as we are confcious from experience, of the identity, the real figure is conceived in its actual proportion, and the vifible, or perfpective appearance is confidered only as a fign or indication.

The

The accurate painter is well aware of this operation of the mind, and in delineating his objects, and relieving them with the diftribution of light and fhade, is carefully attentive to avoid forming conclufions, before he accurately confiders the premifes. The effect produced by a well managed picture, fufficiently evinces the actual appearance of bodies, according to their point of view ; and the impreffions they muft make on the organs of fight, when employed previous to the influence of reafon, and the correction of the judgment. The painter, who exerts the imitative powers of his art to deceive the eye, does not merely draw the outline of his figure, and colour it with the exact uniform tinge it naturally difplays : He furveys it in one certain point of view, and then proceeds to delineate and adapt his tints, as if the figure were, in reality, adhering to the canvafs. It is no wonder, therefore, that the young gentleman, juft mentioned, was aftonifhed to find, on examining the pictures, prefented to him, with his finger, that they had not the fame projection, with the objects they reprefented. This, as well as the art of diminifhing a figure, and ftill preferving the refemblance, would evidently be as much an enigma, to a perfon juft poffeffed of vifion, as the circumftance of the Mirror, mentioned by M. Diderot.*

It is more than probable, therefore, that the blind man, has no ideas of colour, except, as has been already remarked, what are derived from a kind of diftant analogy, regulated by the affociating powers of the mind, and preferved by the memory ; and, indeed, moft of the perfons of this clafs I have converfed with, have frankly confeffed

themfelves wholly ignorant of its qualities. Nor is this deficiency in the forming of ideas peculiar to the fenfe of fight. A deaf man would be juft as much embarraffed, with refpect to the qualities of found ; and the fame may be obferved with refpect to the other fenfes.

In the courfe of my inquiries, however, on this fubject, it occurred to me, that I might poffibly derive fome new matter for obfervation, from the recollection of the blind man's perceptions whilft under the influence of his dreams. In the ufual filent hours of repofe, when the exercife of the memory is, in a great meafure, fufpended ; and the unfettered imagination difplays its powers, in a very peculiar manner ; I conceived it might be poffible for the blind to experience fome tranfient impreffions, relative to vifual qualities. It is true Mr. Lock gives it as his opinion, "that " the dreams of fleeping men are " made up of waking men's ideas ; " though," he allows, "they, are, " for the moft part, oddly put " together." The impreffions of dreams, it muft be acknowledged, are too fleeting to admit of much inveftigation ; and our recollection of them is liable to the greateft uncertainty : Yet, notwithftanding the opinion of this great philofopher, there are few, I am perfuaded, who have not felt themfelves fometimes affected, during their dreams, in a manner which they could by no means account for, or reconcile with any circumftance that had previoufly taken place in real life. And though I have not been able to gratify my curiofity to its full extent, yet I have gained fufficient information to convince me, that the blind feel impreffions in dreaming,

* Vid les Œuvres de M. Diderot, tom. II. Art. Lettres fur les Avcugles, &c.

ing, in some degree, similar to the visible appearances of bodies. A blind gentleman, with whom I have lately conversed, clearly proves to me, that he is conscious of the figure, though he cannot distinguish the varieties of the human countenance : And from the confused efforts he makes to explain himself, it may be perceived, that he feels himself alarmed with new sensations, that bear a strong relation to our ideas of light and colour ; but which he finds it impossible to describe, because he cannot fix on any comparative idea whereby to explain himself. These dreams, my intelligent friend informs me, are always painful, and, as may naturally be expected, the impressions are extremely transient and unsatisfactory.

But it is not the blind only, who are unable to trace the various effects produced by light and colour. There are persons, whose organs of vision are so imperfectly formed, that they cannot distinguish colours, though they see the objects perfectly. In the philosophical transactions we have an account of a man who knew no difference of colour whatever ; and there is an ingenious person, within the circle of our acquaintance, whose knowledge in perspective, as well as in the other branches of natural philosophy, is unquestionable ; yet who finds himself deficient in discerning the difference of some colours, which he knows to exist, and which are distinguishable to perfect vision. In particular, I think I have heard him mention, that the sensation he felt, from the colours of brown and green, had no obvious difference, provided they were diffused with equal degrees of intenseness.

But these speculations, however curious and entertaining, were not the principal objects I had in view when I sat down to consider the subject of blindness. It may be remarked, that in the sketches, relative to blind people, I have offered to your notice, I have purposely avoided speaking of such, as had ever possessed the faculty of vision, so as to recollect it with any degree of accuracy : And I have been the more particular in my account of Dr. Moyes, and the blind projector of roads, because I had an opportunity of availing myself of immediate information from them, with respect to such peculiarities, as it was not in my power to derive from the writings of the few authors, who have treated on this subject.* In tracing the progress, and marking the degrees of perfection, to which the most celebrated blind people have carried the exertions of the other senses, to supply the loss of sight ; I was persuaded, that farther observations and discoveries might be made, which might be applied to advantage in the education of blind children ; and also in rendering more perfect, the different inventions, that have already been devised, in order to facilitate their information, and the means of their improvement : And I flattered myself, that these matters would be deemed sufficiently important, to engage the attention of the learned members of this society. Instances too frequently occur, that most powerfully call for the generosity and compassion of mankind ; and though our abilities rarely arrive at the divine perfection

* Besides occasional hints which I have acquired from conversing with various blind people, whose names are not mentioned ; I have particular acknowledgments to make to Mr. Cheese, the organist of the collegiate church in Manchester, for the satisfaction he has afforded me in many of my inquiries.

feƈtion of *giving fight to the blind*, we ſhall always experience a conſcious benevolent ſatisfaƈtion, in miniſter- ing to their knowledge, their con- venience and happineſs.

———⋙◆⋘———

For the MASSACHUSETTS MAGAZINE.

The G L E A N E R. No. XXVIII.

Turn how we may, avoid it how we will,
Innate conviƈtion muſt attend us ſtill ;
Religion follows as our guardian ſhade,
Ardent to bleſs, though impiouſly betray'd :
Our every breath Omnipotence proclaims,
A plaſtic God all varying nature names,
The breeze is his—the uprooting whirlwind's roar,
The gentle rill—the waves of every ſhore ;
'Tis God direƈts the day—and God the night,
As erſt he ſpake, and Nature ſprang to light.

NO, Atheiſm will never do. The prime procurer and miniſter of the French arrangements, at length accedes to this axiom ; and Gallia, having guillotined her ſovereign, and blaſphemouſly ſought to dethrone and annihilate the Monarch of heaven—becomes, in her preſent reſolutions, ſolicitous to re-eſtabliſh the Deity in her ſyſtems, to inveſt the Supreme with thoſe divine honours which the language of nature haſteth to beſtow, which the diƈtates of reaſon invariably award. Oppoſed, from principle, to thoſe ſanguinary decrees, which pronouncing the death warrant of whole hecatombs of my ſpecies, fail not to let looſe the dogs of war, I will confeſs that I have not felt for the name of Robeſpierre, any of thoſe cordialities, which conſtitute the aggregate of amity. The anarchy and conſequent enormities, prevalent in France, together with thoſe licentious principles which have apparently been ſo generally embraced, I have conſidered as replete with incalculable evils, as the baleful precurſors of every ill which can affliƈt humanity !

Such my ſentiments, I expeƈted not from the report of Robeſpierre, thoſe ſtrong and glowing ſenſations, which, whenever I attend to the voice of truth, moſt delightfully expand my ſoul. But I have read, and charmed with the prevalent contour of the compoſition, the energy and beauty of the diƈtion, and the demonſtrative propriety and ſublimity of the obſervations ; while I do homage to the tranſlator, I cannot but join my ſuffrage to thoſe applauſes, by which America have marked the *new born* piety of the French politician.

It is true that, as being a member of the proteſtant community, I am neceſſitated by my creed to renounce all ſupplications made to ſaints, whatever eclat may have attended their canonization. I may not feel at liberty to cry out, " Oh ! Sanƈta Robeſpierre, ora pro nobis," yet, if he *in reality* ſhall at length purſue the *mild diƈtates* of *truth* and *reaſon* every ſentiment of my ſoul will combine to wiſh him God ſpeed. An admirer of the report in the groſs, I yet conceive that the following extraƈts can hardly

be

be too often repeated, can scarcely be too strongly inculcated, or too deeply engraven upon the tablets of reflection. " What was the wish of those, who in the bosom of the conspiracies with which we were surrounded, in the midst of the embarrassments of such a war, at the moment while the torch of civil discord was still smoaking, suddenly attacked all kinds of worship by violence, to establish themselves as the furious apostles of annihilation, and as the fanatic missionaries of atheism ? Attend only to the happiness of your country and the interests of humanity ; *cherish all opinions and institutions which console and elevate the mind ; reject* those which tend to degrade and corrupt them ; *revive* and exalt all those generous sentiments and those great moral ideas which they have wished to extinguish ; *reconcile, by the charms of friendship, and the bonds of virtue, those citizens whom they have wished to divide. Who has given thee the mission of announcing to the people, that the Deity does not exist ?* To you who are attached to this barren doctrine, and who are not animated in the cause of your country, *what advantage do you derive* from *persuading man that a blind force presides in his destiny, and strikes by chance his virtues or his vices ; and that his soul is only a transient breath which is extinguished at the tomb ? Will the idea of his annihilation inspire him with more pure or more elevated sentiments than that of his immortality ?* Will it inspire him with more respect for his fellow men, or for himself ; more attachment to his country ; more firmness in braving tyranny ; more contempt for death or pleasure ? *You who regret a virtuous friend, do you not delight to reflect that the most valuable part of him has escaped de-*

cease ? You who weep over the corpse of a son or a wife, *are you consoled by him who tells you that nothing more of them remains than a vile heap of dust ?* Unfortunate men, who expire under the stroke of an assassin, your last sigh is an appeal to eternal justice ! Innocence, on the scaffold, makes the tyrant turn pale in his triumphal car : Would it have this ascendancy if the tomb put upon a level the oppressor and the oppressed ? Miserable sophist ! from whence do you derive this right of rending from innocence the sceptre of reason, and of placing it again in the hands of vice ; *to throw a melancholy veil over nature, to drive misfortune to despair ; to* encourage vice, to afflict virtue, to degrade humanity ? *The more a man is endowed with sensibility and genius, the more is he attached to those ideas which aggrandize his being, and which elevate his mind ; and the doctrine of men of this character should become that of the universe.* Ah ! how can those ideas differ from truth ? At least I cannot conceive how nature could have suggested to man any *fictions* more useful than these *realities ;* and if the existence of a God, if the immortality of the soul, were only dreams, they would still remain the most splendid of all the conceptions of the human mind. The idea of the Supreme Being, and the immortality of the soul, is a continual invitation to justice : It is then social and republican. He who can replace the Deity in the system of social life, is, in my opinion, a prodigy of genius ; and he, who without having replaced him, only endeavours to banish him from the mind of man, appears to me a prodigy of stupidity or perversity. If the principles I have hitherto developed are errors, I am deceived in

what

what the world unite to revere. Obferve with what art Cefar, pleading in the Roman Senate in favour of the accomplices of Cataline, loft himfelf in his greffion againft the doctrine of the immortality of the foul ; fo well calculated did thefe ideas appear to him, to diftinguifh in the hearts of the judges the energy of virtue ; fo clofely did the caufe of vice appear to him, connected with that of Atheifm. Cicero, on the contrary, invoked againft the traitors both the fword of the law and the thunder of the gods. Socrates, when dying, converfed with his friends on the immortality of the foul. Leonidas, at Thermopyles, fupping with his companions in arms, at the moment of executing the moft heroic defign that human virtue ever conceived, invited them for the next day to another banquet in a new life. A great man, a real hero, efteems himfelf too much to be pleafed with the idea of his annihilation. A villain, contemptible in his own eyes, and horrible in thofe of other men, perceives that nature cannot afford him a more fplendid boon than that of his annihilation. Religion collects mankind together, and by collecting them together you will render them better ; for when men are thus affembled, they endeavour to pleafe each other, which can only be effected by thofe things that render them eftimable ; give to their reunion a great moral and political motive, and the love of virtuous things will, with pleafure, enter their hearts ; for mankind do not fee each other without pleafure."

I had but recently perufed the whole of this very excellent moral report, when one of the beft informed, and moft fentimental of my friends, put into my hands a piece felected from the London Morning Chronicle of November 29, 1793.

To the matured judgment of this friend I am in the habit of paying high deference, and he conceived, that whether we regarded the little narration as a fact, or a malevolent reflection on the conduct of the predominant party in France, it contained a fufficient quantum of good fenfe to merit prefervation. It is a proper fupplement for the celebrated report of Robefpierre, and in my office of caterer for my readers, perhaps I could not do better than to offer it to their acceptance. I fubjoin it, therefore, with an added wifh, that it may contribute as largely to their pleafures, as it did to the fatisfaction of the Gleaner.

A few days after the bifhop of Paris and his vicars had fet the example of renouncing their clerical character, a curi from a village on the banks of the Rhone, followed by fome of his parifhoners, with an offering of gold, filver, faints' chalices, rich veftments, &c. prefented himfelf at the bar of the houfe. The fight of the gold put the Convention in very good humour, and the curi, a thin venerable looking man, with gray hair, was ordered to fpeak. I came, faid he, from the village of ———, where the only good building ftanding (for the chatteau has been pulled down) is a very fine church ; my parifhoners beg you will take it to make a hofpital for the fick and wounded of both parties, they being equally our countrymen ; the gold and filver, part of which we have brought you, they entreat you will devote to the fervice of the ftate, and that you will caft the bells into cannon, to drive away its foreign invaders. For myfelf I am come with great pleafure to refign my letters of ordination of induction, and every

deed

-ieed of title, by which I have been conftituted a member of your ecclefiaftical polity. I am ftill able to fupport myfelf with the labour of my hands, and I beg you to believe that I never felt fincerer joy than I now do in making this renunciation—I have longed to fee this day; I fee it, and am glad.

When the old man had done fpeaking, the applaufes were immoderate. You are an honeft man, faid they all at once; a brave fellow, you do not believe in God; and the prefident advanced to give him the fraternal embrace. The curi did not feem greatly elated with thefe tokens of approbation; he retired back a few fteps, and thus refumed his difcourfe: Before you applaud my fentiments, it is fit you underftand them; perhaps they may not entirely coincide with your own. I rejoice in this day, not becaufe I wifh to fee religion degraded, but becaufe I wifh to fee it exalted and purified. By diffolving its alliance with the ftate, you give it dignity and independence; you have done it a piece of fervice which its well wifhers would never have had courage to render it, but which is the only thing wanted to make it appear in its genuine luftre and beauty. Nobody will now fay of me, when I am performing the offices of my religion—it is his trade; he is paid for telling the people fuch and fuch things; he is hired to keep up a ufeful piece of mummery. They cannot now fay this, and therefore I feel myfelf raifed in my own efteem, and fhall fpeak to them with a confidence and franknefs, which before this I never durft venture to affume. We refign, without reluctance, our gold and filver images and embroidered veftments, becaufe that we have never found, that looking upon gold

or filver made the heart more pure, or the affections more heavenly: We can alfo fpare our churches; for the heart that wifhes to lift itfelf up to God, will never be at a lofs for room to do it in;—but we cannot fpare our religion, becaufe, to tell you the truth, we never had fo much occafion for it. I underftand that you accufe us priefts of having told the people a great many falfehoods. I fuppofe this may have been the cafe; but till this day we have never been allowed to inquire, whether the things which we taught them were true or not. You required us formerly to receive them all without proof, and you now would have us reject them all without difcrimination. Neither of thefe modes of conduct become philofophers, fuch as you would be thought to be. I am going to employ myfelf diligently, along with my parifhoners, to fift the wheat from the bran, the true from the falfe: If we are not fuccefsful, we fhall be at leaft fincere. I do fear, indeed, that while I wore thofe veftments which we have brought you, and fpoke in the large gloomy building which we have given up to you, I told my poor flock many idle ftories. I cannot but hope, however, that the errors we have fallen into have not been very material, fince the village has in general been fober and good; the peafants are honeft, docile, and laborious; the hufbands love their wives, and the wives their hufbands; they are fortunately not too rich to be compaffionate, and they have conftantly relieved the fick and fugitives of all parties, whenever it has lain in their way. I think, therefore, what I have taught them cannot be fo very much amifs. You want to extirpate priefts; but will you hinder the ignorant from applying for inftruction, ſtruction, the unhappy for comfort and hope, the unlearned from looking up to the learned ? If you do not, you will have prieſts, by whatever name you will order them to be called; but it is certainly not neceſſary, they ſhould wear a particular dreſs, or be appointed by ſtate letters of ordination. My letters of ordination, are my zeal, my charity, my ardent love for my dear children of the village; if I were more learned, I ſhould add my knowledge; but, alas ! we all know very little ; to man every error is pardonable, but want of humility. We have a public walk, with a ſpreading elm tree at one end of it, and a circle of green round it, with a convenient bench. Here I ſhall draw together the children as they are playing round me. I ſhall point to the vines laden with fruit, to the orchard, to the herds of cattle lowing round us, to the diſtant hills ſtretching one behind another, and they will aſk me how theſe things came ? I ſhall tell them all I know or have heard from wiſe men who have lived before me ; they will be penetrated with love and veneration ; they will kneel, I ſhall kneel with them ; they will not be at my feet, but all of us at the feet of that good Being, whom we ſhall worſhip together ; and thus they will receive within their tender minds, *a religion*. The old men will come ſometimes from having depoſited under the green ſod one of their companions, and place themſelves by my ſide ; they will look wiſhfully at the turf, and anxiouſly inquire—*Is he gone forever ? Shall we be ſoon like him ? Will no morning break over the tomb ?* When the *wicked ceaſe from troubling, will the good ceaſe from doing good ?* We will talk of theſe things ; I will comfort them ; I will tell them of

the goodneſs of God ; I will ſpeak to them of a life to come ; I will bid them hope for a ſtate of retribution. In a clear night, when the ſtars ſlide over our head, they will aſk what thoſe bright bodies are, and by what rules they riſe and ſet ? And we will converſe about different forms of being, and diſtant worlds, in the immenſity of ſpace, governed by the ſame laws, till we feel our minds raiſed from what is groveling, and refined from what is ſordid. You talk of Nature, this is Nature ; and if you could at this moment extinguiſh religion in the minds of all the world, thus would it be kindled again. You have changed our holy days ; you have an undoubted right, as our civil governors, ſo to do ; it is very immaterial whether they are kept once in ſeven days, or once in ten ; ſome, however, you will leave us, and when they occur, I ſhall tell thoſe who chooſe to hear me, of the beauty and utility of virtue, and of the dignity of upright conduct. We ſhall talk of good men who have lived in the world, and of the doctrines they have taught ; and if any of them have been perſecuted and put to death for their virtue, we ſhall reverence their memories the more—I hope in all this there is no harm. There is a book, out of which I have ſometimes taught my people : It ſays, we are to love thoſe who do us hurt, and to pour oil and wine into the wounds of a ſtranger ; it has enabled my children to bear patiently the ſpoiling of their goods, and to give up their own intereſt to the general welfare. I think it cannot be a very bad book. I wiſh more of it had been read in your town ; perhaps you would not have had ſo many aſſaſſinations and maſſacres. In this book we hear of a perſon called JESUS ; ſome wor-

ſhip

hip him as a God ; others, as I am told, fay it is wrong to do fo ;—fome teach that he exifted before the beginning of ages ; others, that he was born of Jofeph and Mary. I cannot tell whether thefe controverfies will ever be decided ; but in the mean time, I think we cannot do otherwife than well in imitating him ; for I learn that he *loved the poor, and went about doing good.*

Fellow citizens, as I travelled hither from my own village, I faw peafants fetting amongft the fmoking ruins of their cottages ; rich men and women reduced to deplorable poverty ; fathers lamenting their children in the bloom and pride of youth ; and I faid to myfelf—*thefe people cannot afford to part with their religion.* But indeed you cannot take it away ; if, contrary to your firft declaration, you choofe to try the experiment of perfecuting it, you will only make us prize it the more, and love it the better. Religion, *true* or *falfe*, is fo neceffary to the mind of man, that you have already begun to make yourfelves a new one. You are fowing the feeds of fuperftition at the moment you fancy you are deftroying fuperfti-

tion, and in two or three generations your pofterity will be worfhipping fome clumfy idol, with the rights perhaps of a bloody Moloch, or a lafcivious Thamufar. It was not worth while to have been philofophers, and deftroyed the images of our faints for this, but let every one choofe the religion that pleafes him : I and my parifhoners are content with ours ; it teaches us to bear the evils your childifh or fanguinary decrees have helped to bring upon the country.

The curi turned his footfteps homeward, and the Convention looked for fome minutes on one another, before *they refumed their work of blood.*"

The Gleaner is aware, that the republifhing of the foregoing, cannot fail of unveiling him to the gentleman, from whom he received the manufcript ; but he has fuch perfect confidence in the indulgence and honour of the difpofition of his refpected friend, and in that of thofe with whom he ftands immediately connected, as to reft affured that they will not betray a fecret, which he, the Gleaner, hath delayed to reveal to the deareft of his affociates.

For the MASSACHUSETTS MAGAZINE.

A COMPARISON between DEMOSTHENES and CICERO.

DEMOSTHENES was a citizen of Athens. He was contemporary with Philip of Macedon, againft whom, by the moft vigorous and fpirited eloquence, he endeavoured to roufe the Athenians.

Cicero flourifhed at Rome. He was the moft eloquent orator in the fenate, and the moft eminent pleader at the bar, that the Roman nation ever produced. He lived in

the fame age with the notorious Cataline, whofe traitorous defigns he detected and fruftrated.

Thefe two men have been efteemed the greateft orators the world ever produced. Their merits have been extolled to the very clouds. Their names have been enrolled in the lift of fame with the moft illuftrious characters that ever exifted. They have been denominated the

princes

princes and fathers of eloquence. Their orations have stood the test of ages, and are still esteemed as the genuine works of nature, as the most excellent models of eloquence, and as the most surprising exertions of human genius and learning.

Demosthenes, unassisted by art, was entirely original. He made nature his mistress : Tutored by her hand, and guided by her principles, he gradually arose to the summit of eloquence. Many were the difficulties he had to encounter. His pronunciation was rapid, his articulation indistinct, and his gestures unnatural and awkward. But, by indefatigable diligence, he conquered those habits, and obtained that excellence which nature seemed to have denied him. Accomplished as he was, he could not, in a free state, fail of obtaining the esteem of his countrymen, and arising to the highest stations of honour. His promotion was equal to his wishes. He long possessed the esteem of a grateful country.

His eloquence, peculiar to himself, was spontaneous and sublime. Unpolished by art, it was the genuine effusions of nature : It was more forcible than persuasive ; more rapid and penetrating, than tender and attractive. He did not lull his audience to sleep : but kept their minds in a continual agitation. No one could hear him declaim, and not feel interested in the subject of his declamation. He insensibly stole the attention of his audience, and by that means accomplished whatever he designed. When he arose, it was with the dignity of age : When he spoke, it was with the fire of youth. He exerted every faculty. Not a nerve or muscle were useless. His limbs and his features were expressive of the tone of his mind. His countenance was stern,

his eyes darted lightning, and his voice shocked like the thunder of heaven. His eloquence fell upon his audience unexpected : It took them by surprize, and like the fearful whirlpool, it drew every understanding and every heart into the vortex. It was irresistible.

Cicero lived in a more enlightened age than Demosthenes. Mankind had become more polished : They had exchanged the simplicity of nature for the refinements of art. Great improvements were made in civilized life. The arts and sciences were carried to a higher degree of perfection.

Cicero, inspired with the love of fame, early determined to distinguish himself as an orator. With the greatest ardour imaginable he entered on the study of eloquence. His attention was close and unremitted ; and his improvement was rapid. After a long discipline in the school of elocution, he made his appearance in public, and astonished the Romans with his eloquence. In his first performance he was intimidated ; he felt the diffidence of youth. But he soon acquired that confidence which was necessary. Conscious of his own worth, he seemed to feel himself superior to all around him.

Cicero was endowed with a comprehensive memory, which he improved by study and reflection. He was a very great student, and his erudition was almost unbounded. He was well acquainted with law, politics, philosophy, arithmetic, mythology, and with the fine arts ; particularly poetry, in which he made a considerable proficiency.

When Cicero arose to speak, it was with an unassuming and engaging modesty. His language was smooth and magnificent ; but did not possess the energy of Demosthenes.

mofthenes. Honied mufic dropped unbidden from his lips. His voice was the voice of the charmer. His words rolled on like a deep and fmoothly flowing ftream. His lips breathed foftnefs, and fublimity fat upon his tongue. He was a model of eloquence, of which no idea can be formed but by thofe who heard him. He was a great orator, but not fo great as Demofthenes. As a reprefentation differs from the original, fo Cicero differed from Demofthenes. In fhort, Cicero feemed formed to delight, inftruct, and perfuade; but not to command.

Cicero was highly honoured by his country. By the fuffrages of free citizen, he was placed in the higheft offices of government. In a free country, true merit will unavoidably lead to eminence. In thefe offices Cicero had a grand opportunity to exercife and improve the talents nature had given him. With the eye of the vulture, he watched over the rights of his conftituents, and defended them againft the encroachments of tyrannic luft. He difplayed the ftandard of unconquered abilities, and blowed the trumpet of irrefiftible eloquence;

vice fhuddered; cruelty hid her fnaky head; and oppreffion turned pale, and fhrunk into that abject, cowardly thing, that God and nature ftamped her. Under his adminiftration, peace was promoted, and the rays of glory gilded his country.

Cicero was the mild and infinuating man; Demofthenes was the rough and commanding man. Cicero's oratory was like the gentle gale fighing through the grafs on the hill; but the oratory of Demofthenes was like the rough blaft in the woods, that overturns the fturdy oak, and bears down all obftructions. Demofthenes poffeffed the greateft genius; but Cicero the moft art. Demofthenes hurried his audience with an irrefiftible force; Cicero conducted them with an alluring dignity. Cicero often forgot his fubject and introduced himfelf; Demofthenes paffed by himfelf, and attended to his fubject folely.

I efteem both thefe orators; but, I confefs that I efteem the elaborate pomp of Cicero, lefs than the energetic fimplicity of Demofthenes.

LINUS.

ALEXIS: Or, The COTTAGE in the WOODS.

(Continued from the 466th page.)

PART SECOND.

ALEXIS paffes a twelvemonth in the Cottage.—He is forced to leave it.

CHAPTER III.

Some part of the Manufcript is wanting.

THE VOICE IN THE FOREST.

ALEXIS, happy and cherifhed in the cottage, had forgot his misfortunes. Mufic, agriculture, and fometimes the fport of the chace in the foreft took up all his

time, and left him no leifure to be difgufted.

How fweet and innocent were the pleafures of our four hermits! They had every thing they wanted, defired no more, and all nature feemed to refpect their retreat, and to co-operate in their happinefs. The thunder, which ftruck inceffantly the loftieft trees of the foreft, had never defcended on their premifes; the robbers, who were heard all

day

day long, crying and shouting about its walls, had never formed the design, perhaps impracticable, to scale them. Germain left the cottage only once a year to go to St. Marcellin, to buy corn, and, doubtless by a visible protection of heaven, he had never been attacked, except the last time, when he was relieved by Alexis. Candor had expressly enjoined Clara not to tell her young friend where she had been, on the day she met with him in the valley of Romans, because he himself intended to give one day every detail of it to Alexis, and exact from his hand a most terrible revenge, which he wished to take of his enemies, before he should go down to the grave.

In consequence of this intent, he studied daily the character and temper of Alexis, and flattered himself to see him always steady and courageous; he thanked heaven, for having sent him in his ills a being, perhaps the only one on earth, capable to execute his projects. It was with complacency he beheld the love subsisting between the young couple; he protected and even strengthened it, in hopes it would one day turn to his advantage. His daughter kept no secret from him; he calculated the progress of this passion, and waited till it had reached the highest pitch, to disclose his secrets to Alexis. In the mean time he commanded Clara, not to suffer her lover to take the smallest liberty with her: He followed them wheresoever they went, watched them carefully, and apprehending their innocence might be in danger in the little grove, he always joined them there, brought them back to the cottage, and, not sufficiently confident of his own vigilance, he made choice of Germain to assist him.

All these precautions were to no purpose; Alexis was too delicate, too virtuous to infringe upon the laws of hospitality, and Clara endowed with too much prudence and respect to disobey her father, and commit a fault, which she would never have been able to own. On the other hand, their passion was protected, and they had the promise to be united. They were at liberty to love, and declare their mutual passion before Candor. This freedom banished the very idea of crime; and if love sometimes ventured to put the blind upon their eyes, the light of truth soon shook it off, with offering to their sight the abyss in which they would plunge themselves, and a sense of shame and remorse ever ready to assail them upon leaving the grove.

Thus the two children loved one another; but their love was pure, decent, grounded upon virtue, upon self-esteem, and the voluntary consent of a father.

Sweet sympathy of the soul, unsullied by the mean impulse of sensuality, satisfied with calm sentiment and reflection, a stranger to sore remorse, to guilty secresy, to guilty diffidence, and sanctioned by paternal authority—ah! how few are the hearts destined to feel thy delights!

Alexis, who by this time perceived the scrupulous vigilance of Candor and Germain, deemed it an affront upon his principles. The sole idea of being suspected of treachery, sapped the happiness he enjoyed. Often when returned from a walk where Candor had interrupted a delicious tête-à-tête, he would go to his room, and, regardless of the tokens of love and affection which the old man continually lavished upon him, shed a torrent of tears. What should, would he exclaim, I be capable of?

—and

—and can theythink it?—I am dogged and watched as if there was any occafion to apprehend that I could fo far forget myfelf, as to betray the confidence I enjoy, and to feduce an innocent child! It feems they cannot read in my heart!— No, they will never know it; that feeling heart, fraught with gratitude and delicacy, is torn by the moft outrageous fufpicion!—Alas! will men never do me juftice!—O Candor, Candor, how you grieve me!

Candor often furprized him in thofe acceffes of a gloomy temper; he inquired for the caufe of his trouble, but Alexis remained filent; the remembrance of his misfortunes was his excufe; and the old man, who knew him to be candid and fincere, believed, comforted and engaged him to a walk in the garden, and, partly by his careffes, partly by dint of argument, diffipated the melancholy of his young friend.

* * * * * *
* * * * * *

Here a matter of twenty pages is wanting in the original manufcript. Some leaves half torn prove, however, that this deficiency, in other refpects little interefting, was filled with the pleafures and occupations of our four hermits, in the cottage; alfo with an account of the increafing paffion between the young couple. I thought it ufelefs to make fupplements of my own, as thofe paffages which are wanting, leffen by no means the merit of the work. I will, therefore, fimply begin where the narrative is continued in a fucceffive and regular order.

In this manner, Candor, Clara, Alexis, and Germain, paffed their life at the cottage. They always terminated the bufinefs of the day by a rural walk; they all four fat down in the little grove on the borders of the limpid rivulet, they returned, enjoyed a frugal meal, and tafted the fweets of a quiet fleep, from which nothing could rouze them, but the rifing of Aurora, and the concerts of birds.

At the expiration of a twelvemonth, our young couple loved no more, but adored each other. It was a violent paffion which nothing could keep within bounds, but the hope of a fpeedy union. They were determined to fpeak of it to Candor, and to crave, upon their knees, his paternal bleffing, a tie as facred in their eyes, as the auguft ceremony of wedlock, which they had no opportunity to obtain; but the old man, equally cunning and vindictive, had waited for that inftant, to lay open his projects to Alexis. He had himfelf foftered in his breaft the flames of love, and fuffered the paffion of Alexis to attain the very pitch of violence, only with a view to be convinced of his fidelity to ferve him. He was, however, unacquainted with the firmnefs and fpirit of our young hero; he intended putting them to trial, in order to be fure of his inviolable attachment, and to defer, a little longer, the ftory of his misfortunes, which he had promifed to relate.

Alexis, for his own part, always miftrufting and fufceptible, was alarmed at the delays of Candor. He had repeatedly entreated him to unite him with the object of his love, and the old man would always anfwer, My fon, it is not enough for me, that you love my daughter, and have her welfare at heart; but it is alfo neceffary that your friendfhip for her father be equal to your love to her. Clara can therefore, not be yours, unlefs

I

I have real proofs of your attachment.—Alexis, with tears in his eyes, asked which were those proofs that he required of him. Candor made no reply, squeezed his hand, and left him, with a sigh and a woeful countenance.

What a situation for our hero! It was then that his first misfortunes retraced themselves in his mind, and he sighed.

One day, going to fell some wood at the entrance of the forest, he was struck with astonishment, upon perceiving his name engraved on the bark of a lofty tree. He approaches, he discovers some other characters, and trembling, read these few lines: *Alexis, fly from Candor, fly from the perfidy of the cottage, where the most enormous crime is expected of you.*

Cruel wretch! exclaimed he, with indignation, whoever thou be, thou art an impostor!—Candor is virtuous; Candor is the most respectable of men; and this is the value I set upon thy infamous calumny! So saying, he lays hold of his ax, and with several blows effaces the odious inscription. Though he gave it not the least credit, a sensation of sadness remained in his soul; he strives to dissipate it, but without success.

What hand inimical to my rest, said he to himself; what traitor could give me such insidious advice! Unknown as I am to all the world, I am known to live in this forest.—Why should I leave it? Why destroy my peace by unjust suspicion? What do I say? I have no suspicion. Avaunt, guilty mistrust! O my father! shouldst thou design me to be criminal, thou the most wise, the most generous of men! O! why is it not in my power to extirpate with my own hand the base accuser who dared to out-rage a virtuous man! But who is he? what interest can he find to give me such dangerous advice? Does he know me? Is it my father, or Dumont? who—O God! I have not well enough examined the characters! I might perhaps have discovered—could it be you, unfortunate beings, whom I cherished so much? Could your tenderness reclaim Alexis, and wish him back to your arms? Yes, I know the characters; how unreasonable was I to efface them so soon! My father! Dumont;—could it be you? But what appearance is there? Where strays my reason?—No, I reject this too flattering idea! It is a stranger, I doubt not; I must not doubt, it is even a wretch, a ruffian, who seeks to ensnare me. Ah! I will shun him, and never leave this dear abode.—I will love and respect my generous hosts, and deem a crime, the cruel calumny which I discovered upon this tree. Blush, Alexis, thou art become an accessary to guilt, in having read it.

Alexis returned to the cottage, where Candor, who saw his trouble, chid him for his melancholy: The youth stammered, and excused himself as well as he could, his soul longed for solitude, and he took a walk by himself in the remotest part of the garden, on the borders of the rivulet. Quite lost in thought, he approached the wall, which separated the premises from the forest; he thought he heard a sweet voice, uttering his name. He looks, he listens, and soon a person in the wood, on the brink of the ditch of the habitation, addresses him with these words: " Alexis, thy sufferings are at an end. Turn thy eyes upon the rivulet which streams at thy feet, and read."

Alexis, quite motionless, looks
into

into the stream, and his astonishment increases upon seeing, tied to a branch of a bush; a letter, which the unknown person had thrown on his side, and which past through the opening that was made in the wall. He seizes the branch, unties the letter, and eagerly read the following lines, which moved him to the highest degree:

"Heaven, my Alexis, is finally appeased: Your father acknowledges you for his son. Leave the cottage, and the woods of *Chamborau*: Come to meet him at *St. Etienna*, where he, with your friend Dumont, is waiting for you. To receive you, his arms are open. When to-morrow's sun will hide itself in the water, come, alone, to the spot where the forest forms a star marked with six martlets. It is there you will find a faithful guide, who is to conduct you to the most unfortunate and most tender of fathers."

What a perusal for Alexis!— He questions the stranger, but is not answered; to all appearance he is gone.—His father waits for him, his father acknowledges him for his son!—Heaven! in what moment does he hear tidings, which, at other times, he would have considered as the greatest of blessings!—But how is he to act now? Shall he renounce love for nature? Shall he betray gratitude for filial tenderness? shall he fly from the arms of a generous friend to those of a father? What an embarrassment! what a cruel embarrassment!

Clara's lover remains for some time in the deepest gloom of reflection: He takes this adventure for an illusion; he cannot believe that what he sees, and reads, is real!— His father calls him;—how could he find out his retreat? who could have directed him here? As he knows it why does not he himself

come to fetch him, in order to see and thank the good old man who received his son in his house? Why does he fear to appear before Candor? Justice, gratitude, all makes it his duty! But does he know of the passion of Alexis for Clara? does he fear the effects of that passion? Well, if he does, the greater reason he has to prevent them by his presence. But the letter he has received is not of his father's writing: He might well have wrote himself. That mysteriousness, the stranger, the guide who waits for him, all looks very suspicious. Should it be a contrivance of the calumniator, of whom he received once a perfidious advice, engraved on the bark of the tree? Yes, yes, it must be some stratagem: He has certain secret enemies who conspired his ruin, who will tear him from this abode of peace, to devote him to destruction! All mankind is against him, and were he at the extremity of the pole, still there would be traitors, bent to persecute him!——But, after all, if it were true!—If his father and Dumont were waiting for him in the village of St. Etienne!—Who knows!— They indeed left him at Valence; but they may have discovered which way he went; people may have been set to follow him even as far as the cottage.—All this is possible.— What shall he do? What resolution ought he to take?—Here nature chides him: Can you fly the caresses of thy father?—Here love and gratitude are combined to detain him. Which of either shall he obey? Which of either is the most imperative voice, that appeals to his heart? Which of either will prove victorious?—O Alexis, Alexis, what wilt thou do! unfortunate youth, what wilt thou do!

(To be continued.)

The

For the MASSACHUSETTS MAGAZINE.

The ESSAYIST. No. XI.

The way of tranfgreffors is hard.——SOLOMON.

THE proverbs or aphorifms of Solomon are the refult of much learning, the greateft natural abilities, the pureft philanthropy, and an extenfive knowledge of mankind. They contain rules of life and manners admirably adapted to every defcription of men, interfperfed with friendly admonitions and fage reflections. They exhibit the collected wifdom of all ages prior to the time of the royal compiler, fuperadded to his own, which is faid to have been fuperior to that of any other man, and have been fanctioned by the united approbation of all fucceeding generations. From uniform obfervation and from perfonal experience, for fuch is the weaknefs of humanity in its moft perfect ftate, that even Solomon did not exhibit a faultlefs pattern of virtue, the wife king of Ifrael afferts with laconic fimplicity, that "*the way of trarfgreffors is hard.*" My prefent defign is by a few obfervations and reflections to attempt an illuftration of this concife, energetic, and demonftrable pofition.

In the firft place, "the way of tranfgreffors is hard" confidered with refpect to its origin ; or, in other words, it is difficult to enter upon the career of vice. "Whofoever committeth fin tranfgreffeth the law, for fin is a tranfgreffion of the law," fays the apoftle John. The law here intended may be either the pofitive revealed commands of the Creator, or reafon, which was given to man for a rule of conduct, or both united. Now, if it be granted, that the defign of the Deity in creation was to confer happinefs on his creatures, it muft likewife be granted, that all the laws impofed by the former upon the latter will be relative to this great end. This appears ftill further evident from that unconquerable defire of happinefs, which is implanted in every rational being, as well as from that infeparable connexion between duty and intereft difcoverable in the economy of man, which will hereafter be more particularly confidered. Now, as happinefs is the ultimate object of every human wifh, and as all the laws of the Deity have a remote or immediate reference to this great object, it muft be with the greateft reluctance and difficulty, that a man can refift this fundamental principle of his nature, this innate thirft for felicity, and counteract his own beft intereft, by deferting the loyal ftandard of rectitude, and enlifting himfelf under the rebellious banners of vice. Notwithftanding the ftrength of temptation fo often urged in palliation of faults, no man ever commenced a courfe of criminal indulgence without being firft obliged to encounter the fevereft oppofition from within himfelf. The confideration, that for a trifling and momentary gratification he is about to injure his own moft effential interefts, and to poifon that great fource of happinefs, his peace of mind and an approving confcience, muft throw almoft infurmountable obftacles in his way to vice. I might almoft venture to affert, that it is unjuft to cenfure a man for having yielded to temptation *in the firft inftance*, if he did not, every thing confidered, find it more difficult to yield than to refift. It is true, that after we have once broken over the barriers of virtue, we can turn afide into the crooked paths of immorality with much greater facility than we could before ; for such is the influence of habit upon our minds, that it can render tolerable, and even agreeable, what we once avoided with disgust and horror. But still, so powerful is the moral sense in the human breast, so deformed and hideous is vice on its first appearance, and so directly opposed to every thing, which can conduce to happiness, that the way of transgressors, with respect to the first entrance upon it, may with the greatest safety and propriety be pronounced *hard*.

In the next place, the way of trasgressors may be termed hard on account of its concomitant inconveniences and pains. Perhaps the wisdom and goodness of the Deity are not more clearly displayed in any of his works or dispensations, than in that intimate and inseparable connexion between moral and physical good and evil, which is so strikingly apparent in the admirable system of humanity. Almost every deviation from the path of virtue seems to be necessarily attended by its proper punishment. This will more evidently appear from a short survey of some of the vices most prevalent in the world, and the natural calamities, which ever accompany them.

The first example, which will be offered, is *lying*. The man, who has contracted the vile and irrational habit of detailing falsehood, finds a very severe punishment annexed to the infamous practice. He loses that relish for the sweets of truth, which affords to others a constant source of the purest satisfaction. He is deprived of all those numerous advantages and opportunities for promoting his interest and happiness arising from the approbation and esteem of his fellowmen, which the man of veracity enjoys. Be-

sides, the man, who publishes a falsehood, has undertaken a most arduous task. He must invent a second in support of the first, and a third in support of the second, and so on in an infinite series. Further, when he has once acquired the reputation of a liar, should he by accident or design stumble upon the truth, he will not have the good fortune to be believed. He must inevitably forfeit the confidence of his fellow men ; his name will be branded with infamy and scorn ; he will be banished from the company of all the wise and good ; he will expose the feelings of those, who are connected with him, to the severest mortification ; and may thank the unmerited bounties of an indulgent Providence, if he does not wander a wretched outcast from society, or even perish in the streets, as a just punishment for his inexcusable folly. Is not the way of the liar hard ?

We shall instance next in *stealing*. He, who appropriates to his own use the property of another without his consent, may fancy indeed, that he has made an easy and a profitable bargain ; but the price appears much too high to the eye of reason for a man in his sober senses to make the purchase. The arts and fatigues, which are necessary to enable the thief to effect his purpose ; the consciousness of the odious nature of the offence ; the fears and anxieties, which attend and follow the commission of the crime ; the disgrace and infamy resulting from the almost inevitable detection of the theft ; and the shame and pains of the prison, the trial, the stocks, the pillory, the post, castle island, and the gallows ; all which he will suffer a thousand times in anticipation, and a part of them once in reality ; these, I say, must be considered, as a punishment almost too severe,

severe, even for the detestable vice of stealing. Are not the ways of thievery hard?

The *drunkard* may next employ our attention. There is no vice perhaps, which so effectually transforms the man into the beast, as drunkenness. For the sordid and momentary pleasure of tickling his depraved palate, the tippling sot pours down the liquid fire, till every mental and corporeal faculty shrinks from its office, and he falls prostrate to the earth, exposed to every species of insult and injury, the shame of human nature, and the contempt and pity of all around him. These are the natural and immediate effects of a single instance of ebriety. The consequences of a *habit* of intemperate drinking are more permanent and more fatal. And we may observe by the way, that the sable skin of the Ethiopian may almost as easily be changed to white, as a habit of this kind can be eradicated. By habitual intoxication, a man is wholly disqualified for discharging the duties of social life. Instead of preserving and accumulating, he is perpetually squandering his property, and exposing himself, and perhaps a lovely partner and helpless offspring, to all the horrors of want. He is constantly liable to fall into numerous other vices as well as personal dangers, and is deprived of all the innocent enjoyments of life. He is daily impairing his health and strength, and accelerating the growth of the feeds of mortality implanted in him by nature, till a premature death snatches the goblet from his palsied hand to the great *joy* and inconsolable *grief* of all who knew him, and to his own inexpressible confusion. Surely the way of the drunkard is intolerably hard.

Intemperance in *eating* deserves a little notice. It is readily granted that excess in this particular, is not immediately attended by consequences so disagreeable, shocking and fatal, as inebriation. Many circumstances and effects are however common to both these species of vice. Take an attentive survey of the insatiable gormandizer, the pampered, gorged, gouty, glutton. Hear those groans; mark those distortions, that livid cheek, those useless feet, that helpless, cumbrous, enormous mass of flesh. Let reason decide, and she will certainly pronounce the ways of gluttony hard.

The *votary* of *Venus* must not be passed over in silent neglect. It may be urged, that the warm temperament of youth renders it next to impossible to adhere strictly to the cold precepts of rigid chastity, and therefore, that a few almost unavoidable deviations from them ought not to be ranked with those odious vices, which have now been the subject of animadversion. It is granted, that the strong propensities of nature may *in some degree* extenuate the criminality of indulgence. But, it is believed, the experience of thousands can testify, that by resolute abstinence from illicit pleasures, the passions may soon be brought under the easy dominion of reason, while gratification is perpetually adding fuel to the fire, till health, estate, reputation, peace of mind, and every innocent and rational enjoyment, are consumed in the flame. When I mention health, I have reference to the natural tendency of unlawful indulgence to impair the constitution. But when we take into consideration that most odious and shocking of all diseases, which a righteous Providence has *entailed* upon this species of vice; a disease, which, if not checked in the first
stages

stages of its operation, presents death in its most dreadful form to its subject, and if *eradicated*, which is seldom the case, is often followed by the most disagreeable consequences ; when, I say, we take this and all its concomitant evils into consideration, we must exclaim with Solomon, that " the harlot's house is the way to hell, going down to the chambers of death,"

Shall we proceed and enlarge the dismal catalogue, till it comprehend all the numerous vices, to which poor humanity is obnoxious ? Or shall we not rather avert our eyes from a scene so shocking, convinced from the specimens, which have now passed under review, that on account of the physical evils necessarily attendant on vice, the way of transgressors is intolerably hard ?

Further, the way of transgressors may be termed hard on account of those painful *reflections*, which necessarily result from a consciousness of having broken the divine laws and the rules of right reason ; of having wantonly abused our talents and the gifts of an indulgent Providence ; of having essentially injured our connexions and society in general ; and of foolishly neglecting our best interest by turning aside from the delightful path of virtue, which is accompanied by present, and leads directly to future and eternal felicity, into those crooked ways of vice, which are replete with thorns, with present difficulties and dangers, and terminate in endless and remediless ruin.

Finally, the way of impenitent transgressors will be inexpressibly hard at that dreadful hour, when " every work will be brought into judgment with every secret thing, whether it be good, or whether it be evil ;" when a much greater discrimination will be made between

the virtuous and the vicious, than that very striking one, which we now behold ; when " the righteous shall go away into life eternal," and the incorrigibly wicked shall be subjected to the pains of the fretting tooth of the worm of conscience, that never dies, and of that fire of unutterable remorse, which never can be quenched.

Thus it appears, that the way of transgressors is hard, considered with respect to the difficulty of first entering upon it ; its concomitant physical evils ; its dreadful immediate, and its more dreadful, remote and eternal consequences. Let us now make a few reflections.

What reason have we to thank and adore the goodness of that Being, who has fenced in the road to happiness with such almost insuperable barriers ; who has so strongly connected our duty and interest, that we cannot neglect the former without directly counteracting the latter ; who has given us reason for our pilot, and happiness for our pole star ; and who, if we strictly adhere to the dictates of these our guides, has promised us a prosperous voyage across the ocean of life, and a safe arrival at our destined haven of immortal felicity ! On the other hand, what language can express the folly and madness of those, who strive against the wind and current of their nature, their duty, and their interest, to drive their fragile barks upon the fatal quicksands of immorality ! We readily denominate that man a fool, who rushes voluntarily into fire or water to the injury of his person or the loss of his life. But the ideot is indisputably a sage compared with the reasoning votary of vice.

Let us make it our constant aim to follow virtue, if not " for virtue's sake," at least on account of our
own

own eafe, convenience, and fecurity. Let us not engage in the arduous and vexatious bufinefs of vice. Life is fhort and uncertain. Let us fnatch the prefent moment and be happy while we may. Convinced that " *the way of tranfgreffors is hard,*" let us fteadily purfue the plain, the flowery, the delightful path of virtue, which alone can conduct us to happinefs in this world, and to everlafting felicity in that which is future. May we all know by happy experience, that " *the ways of wifdom are ways of pleafantnefs, and that all her paths are paths of peace.*"

For the MASSACHUSETTS MAGAZINE.

The REPOSITORY. No. XXIV.

May 31ft, 1777, Saturday Evening.

A WHITE day this. I have hailed Cleora the joyful mother of a fecond pledge of her connubial love ; it is a fweet fmiling girl, her infant countenance prognofticates future lovelinefs, and the lines of her pretty face already unfold a number of latent beauties. How enchanting is innocence, how fweetly interefting, how endearingly prepoffeffing ! The fcene at Cleora's hath been replete with joy ; it was about four o'clock in the afternoon that the God of our falvation gave us this caufe for rejoicing ; with what tranfport did I fly to gratulate the tender fair one, and to hail the new born ftranger ; alternately we preffed the lovely infant to our bofoms, while the gentle matron appeared abforbed in extatic contemplation, and her every wifh, in that delicious moment, feemed amply gratified. The partner of her life was in a delirium of joy ; nor knew he to which to addrefs himfelf, the tender female who had thus bleft him, or the little infenfible pledge of their mutual loves. For Cleora, a virtuous blufh fuffufed her pale countenance as the father of her children approached ; her eyes proclaimed him the man of her heart, and every feature was expref- five of the unutterable tendernefs with which her fond foul is replete. Happy, thrice happy Cleora—filken are the bands by which thou art holden. Their firft hope, their eldeft bloffom, was introduced ; here was a new fource of pleafing fenfations. The child appeared loft in pretty innocent wonder ; I congratulated him upon the birth of his fifter ; fpoke to him of her mamma, &c. In a hafty manner he demanded, " who is her mamma ?" I pointed to the bed, but as the female there confined was confeffedly his mamma, he could not comprehend how fhe could be the baby's alfo ; fuddenly he quitted the room, but foon returned, bearing a number of toys, which with great earneftnefs he endeavoured to make the new born notice, faying he would certainly give them all to her. What pleafures were apparent in the revered countenances of my father, and my mother ; but it were in vain to attempt a defcription of the various fenfations which were difplayed in the features of parents, grand parents, and each felicitating relation and friend. Many are the felicities of fuch a hymen. Thou art happy, Cleora—may thy lot be ftill diftinguifhed by every bleffing.—

What

What a melancholy contrast doth the childlefs wife exhibit ! Is fhe feparated from the lord of her wifhes, for the abfençe of her kindred foul her tears muft ceafelefs flow. A folitary, a childlefs wife, how dreary the idea ; no fweet infant to foothe her cares, to clafp to her bofom, to receive and to beftow the kifs of love. Did fome pretty prattler fill her arms, with what delight would fhe dwell upon every feature, and how might fhe trace the likenefs of the man fhe loved, till all the father ftood confeffed !

CONSTANTIA.

For the MASSACHUSETTS MAGAZINE.

BATHMENDI: *A Persian Tale.*

[Tranflated from the French of Monfieur de FLORIAN.]

T. A.

UNDER the reign of a certain Perfian king, a merchant of Balfora was ruined by his unfortunate enterprizes. He collected the gleanings of his fhattered fortune, and retired to the extremity of the province of Koufiftan.

He there purchafed a fmall country feat, and a farm, which he cultivated but indifferently, as he was ever regretting the time, when he was not obliged to labour. Difappointment and vexation curtailed the days of the merchant.

Being fenfible of his approaching diffolution, he called his four fons together, and addreffed them in the following manner. " My children, all the property I have to leave you confifts in this little cot, and in the knowledge of a fecret, which it was my duty not to reveal to you, till the prefent moment. In the time of my opulence, the *genius Alzim* was my friend. He promifed to take you into his care after my deceafe, and to divide a *treafure* among you. This *genius* dwells at the diftance of many miles hence in the great foreft of *Kom.* Go to him and demand this treafure ; but, *be very cautious of believing"* —— —— here death put a period to his life.

The four fons of this merchant,

after having bewailed the lofs of their father, and decently interred him, gained the foreft of *Kom.* They readily found the manfion houfe of the *genius Alzim.* Alzim was known to all the country. He received kindly all who came to fee him. He heard their complaints, adminiftered confolation, and lent them money when they ftood in need of it. Thefe favours, however, were on this condition, that thofe who participated them, fhould blindly follow the counfel he gave. This was his *mania.* None were fuffered to enter his palace, till they had given oath to follow his counfel.

This oath was no obftacle with the three eldeft fons of the merchant. The fourth, whofe name was Taï, confidered this ceremony as very ridiculous. To obtain the treafure, it was abfolutely requifite to go through the formality. Accordingly, he fwore, as did his three brothers. Reflecting on the hazardous confequences of this foolifh oath, and recollecting that his father, who frequently vifited this palace, had fpent his life in unwife undertakings, he was anxious to fcreen himfelf from all danger without the imputation of perjury. To this end, while on his way to the genius,

genius, he ſtopped his ears with o-
doriferous wax. Fortified by this
precaution, he proſtrated himſelf
before the throne of Alzim.

The genius directed the four ſons
of his ancient friend to riſe. He
embraced them, converſed with
them reſpecting their father, dropped a tear to his memory, and ordered a capacious coffer, replete with
darics, to be preſented. Here, ſaid
he, is the treaſure, which I have ſe-
cured to you. I will divide it a-
mong you, and then I will point
out to each of you the route you are
to take in order to obtain perfect felicity.

Taï heard not a word, which the
genius ſpake ; but he obſerved him
with attention, and ſaw in his eyes
and on his face an air of *fineſſe*, and
of malignity, which led him to think
not a little ; yet he received with
gratitude the part of the treaſure ap-
portioned to him.

Alzim, after having loaded them
with riches, aſſuming a very affectionate tone, addreſſed them in this
manner. " My dear children, your
fortunate, or unfortunate deſtiny depends on your meeting ſooner or
later a certain being known by the
name of *Bathmendi*, of whom every
body has ſomething to ſay—but,
whom very few know. The unhappy part of mankind grope in darkneſs for this being. But I, who
love you, I will in a whiſper reveal
to each the place where you ſhall
find him.

Immediately Alzim took Bekir,
the eldeſt of the four brethren. My
ſon, ſaid he, you are endued with
great talents for war. The king of
Perſia is about to ſend an army a-
gainſt the *Turks*. Join this army.
It is in the Perſian camp you will
be able to find *Bathmendi*. *Bekir*
thanks the *genius*, and already burns
to depart.

Alzim beckoned to the ſecond
ſon to approach. His name was
Meſrou. You have ſenſe, ſaid he to
him, addreſs, and a great diſpoſition
for lying. Go to *Iſpahan*. It is at
court you are to ſeek *Bathmendi*.

He then called the third brother,
whoſe name was *Sadder*. You,
ſaid he, are endued with a lively
and fertile imagination. You ſee
objects, not as they are, but as you
wiſh them to be. You have often
genius, but not always *common ſenſe*.
You ſhall be a poët. Take your
way to *Agra*. It is among the wits
and belles of this city you may find
Bathmendi.

Taï advanced in his turn ; and,
thanks to the balls of wax, heard
not a ſyllable. It has ſince been
found that Alzim counſelled him to
become a *dervis*.

The four brethren, after having
thanked the beneficent genius, returned to their habitation. The
three eldeſt prepared to go in ſearch
of *Bathmendi*. Taï unſtopped his
ears, and heard them propoſe ſelling
their little cot the firſt opportunity,
in order to ſhare the money. Taï
requeſted permiſſion to purchaſe it.
He made an eſtimate of the houſe
and farm, paid each of the brothers
his reſpective portion, wiſhed them
the higheſt degree of proſperity, embraced them tenderly, and took up
his ſolitary abode in the humble paternal cot.

Then it was he undertook to put
in execution a project, on which he
had long been meditating. He was
ſmitten with young *Amina*, the
daughter of a neighbouring farmer.
Amina was beautiful and chaſte ;
ſhe had the management of her father's houſehold affairs. She ſolac-
ed his old age, and requeſted of God
but *two things*. The *firſt* was, that
her father might live long ; and the
ſecond, that ſhe might become the
wife

wife of *Taï*. These wishes were granted. Taï sued for, and obtained her. The father of *Amina* came and dwelt with his son in law, and taught him the art of making the earth yield bountifully to her cultivators. Taï had still some part of his portion, which he laid out in enlarging his farm, and in purchasing a flock of sheep. The farm doubled its worth; the fleeces were sold ; abundance reigned in the house of Taï ; and as he was industrious, and his wife economical, every year augmented their revenue. Amina had a child every ten months. Children, which are the ruin of the rich idlers of cities, are the riches of industrious farmers.

At the end of six years, Taï, the father of seven children, the prettiest in the world, the husband of a good and virtuous wife, the son in law of an old man still lively and amiable, the master of many slaves, and possessor of two flocks, was the happiest and the richest farmer of *Koufistan*.

In the mean time his three brothers were in pursuit of *Bathmendi*. *Bekir* had arrived at the *Persian* camp. He presented himself to the *grand vifier*, and requested to serve in the company which was the most exposed. His figure, and his good will, pleased the *grand vifier*, who, therefore, admitted him into a troop of cavalry.

After a few days a bloody battle was given. *Bekir* there effected prodigies. He saved the life of his *general*, and with his own hand took away that of the *general* of the enemy. The praises of *Bekir* were echoed from every quarter. The soldiers all called him the hero of Persia. The *vifier*, in gratitude to his deliverer, raised him to the rank of *general*. *Alzim* was right, says *Bekir* to himself; here fortune has

waited for me. All conspire in announcing that I am on the point of meeting *Bathmendi*.

The glory of *Bekir*, but especially his elevation, excited envy and murmurings among all the satraps. Some came to ask him respecting his father, complaining that they had suffered by his bankruptcy. Others pretended to have had his mother for a slave. In fine, all refused to serve under him, because they were his superiors. Bekir, unhappy even through his success, lived alone, always upon his guard, always in danger of abuse, which he well knew how to revenge, but not to prevent. He regretted the time in which he was only a soldier, and waited with impatience the end of the war, when the Turks, reinforced by new troops, and directed by a new general, came to attack the division which Bekir commanded.

At length opportunity presented, as the *satraps* of the army had for a long time expected. They employed a hundred times more force to subdue their chief, and to prevent being overcome, than they had during their life before.

Bekir defended himself like a lion ; but was neither obeyed nor seconded. The Persian soldiers attempted in vain to resist. Their officers restrained them, and never directed them except in flight. The brave *Bekir*, abandoned, covered with wounds, overwhelmed by the number, was taken by the *Janissaries*. The *Turkish* general had the baseness to load him with irons as soon as he was able to carry them, and sent him to *Constantinople*, where he was thrown into a hideous dungeon. Alas ! cried he in prison, I begin to believe that Alzim has deceived me ; for I can never hope to find *Bathmendi* here !

The war continued fifteen years,

Vol. VI.   E   and

and the fatraps ever prevented the exchanging of *Bekir.* His prifon was not opened till peace.

He went, as foon as liberated, with all fpeed to *Ifpahan,* to fearch out the *vifier* his protector, whofe life he had faved. For three weeks he could not fpeak to him. At the end of this term he obtained audience. Fifteen years imprifonment changes, not a little, the figure of a beautiful young man. It was *Bekir's* unhappinefs to be no more known : Therefore, the vifier knew nothing of him.

At length, calling to mind the different epochs of his glorious life, he recollected that *Bekir* had formerly rendered him a little fervice. —Yes, yes, my friend, faid he, I recognife you. You are a brave man ; but the ftate is greatly in debt. A long war, and expenfive feafts, have exhaufted our finances. However, come again,—— and I will endeavour —— I will fee —— Ah ! my lord, I have no bread ; and for fifteen days I have been waiting for an opportunity to fpeak to your highnefs. I fhould have died with mifery, but for one of the foldiers on duty, my old comrade, who fhared his pay with me ! It is very well from that foldier, anfwered the vifier. How then !—that is affecting— I will inform the king of him.—— Come to fee me again, you know that I love you.——As he fpake thefe words, he turned his back upon him.

Bekir returned the next day, and found the gate fhut. In defpair he went from the palace and the city, refolved never to enter it again.—

He fell down at the foot of a tree, on the bank of the river *Zenderou.* There he reflected on the ingratitude of the vifier, on all the misfortunes which he had experienced, and on thofe which ftill threatened him ;

and, being no longer able to fupport thefe difmal ideas, he arofe in order to plunge himfelf into the river.——At this inftant, he found himfelf embraced by a beggar, who bedewed his face with tears, and with a fob, cried, " It is my brother, it is my brother *Bekir !*" Bekir looked upon him, and recognifed his brother *Mefrou.*

Every man, without doubt, experiences fome pleafure in finding a long loft brother. But an unfortunate man, who, without refuge, without friend, is about to put a period to his days through defpair, believes he fees an angel from heaven, when he finds a beloved brother. This is the fentiment, which *Bekir* and *Mefrou* then felt. They mutually embraced each other and mingled tears. The firft moments were devoted to tender fenfibility. They then beheld one another with eyes which equally befpoke their wonderment and affliction. Art thou unhappy too ? exclaimed Bekir——This, replied *Mefrou,* is the firft inftance of felicity, which I have enjoyed fince we parted. At thefe words, the two unfortunate brothers again embraced. *Mefrou,* then feated nigh his brother, began his hiftory.

You remember that fatal day, on which we went to *Alzim.* This perfidious *genius* told me I fhould find at court this *Bathmendi,* of which we were fo defirous. I followed his dire counfel, and prefently arrived at *Ifpahan.* I became acquainted with a young flave, which belonged to the miftrefs of the firft fecretary of the *grand vifier.* This flave loved me, and introduced me to her miftrefs, who finding me younger and handfomer than her galant, gave me lodgings in her houfe by making me pafs for her young brother. Prefently

ently the *young brother* was present-ed to the vifier. Some days after he obtained an employment in the palace.

I had nothing to do, but to re-ceive the favours of fortune, and a-bove all to recollect the road by which I had gained them. I left not this road; and as the fultana dowager was aged, ill favoured, and powerful, I failed not to make court to her with affiduity. She dif-tinguifhed me, and took me into a friendfhip as intimate as that be-tween me and the flave and miftrefs had been.

From this moment riches and honours began to rain down upon me. The fultana caufed all the money of the treafury to pafs into my hands by the fofa, and all the dignities of ftate were heaped upon me. The monarch himfelf gave marks of affection for me. He was fond of talking with me, becaufe I flattered him with addrefs, and al-ways counfelled him to what he was anxious to perform. This was the method of fecuring what I wifhed. It never failed. At the end of three years, I faw myfelf at once the firft minifter, the favourite of the king, the lover of his mother, with the power of nominating and removing the grand vifier. Deciding every thing by my influence, and receiving every morning the grandees of the empire, who attended my levee, in order to obtain of me a fmile of pro-tection.

In the midft of my glory and for-tune, I was furprifed not to find Bathmendi, whom I was in purfuit of. Nothing, faid I, is wanting to me; why is Bathmendi wanting to me? This idea, and the horrid tor-ture in which I paffed my life, poi-foned all my pleafures. The older the fultana grew, the more exigent fhe became, and the more painful

my gratitude. The tendernefs which fhe had for me, became my punifh-ment. Befides, there were paffion, fits, imputations of ingratitude, then tears, and then careffes a hundred times worfe. On the other hand, my fituation brought me a hundred troublefome courtiers, and a hun-dred thoufand powerful enemies. At any favour I granted, fcarcely a fingle mouth thanked, while a thou-fand curfed me. The generals I appointed, were beaten, and then complaints were made. The good which the king did, redounded to his honour, while all the evil was at-tributed to me. The people deteft-ed me—all the court abhorred me. A thoufand libels defamed me. My mafter frequently grumbled at me. The fultana dowager was ev-er abufing me, and Bathmendi feem-ed to be feparated from me forever.

The paffion of the king for a young *Mingrelian* at length com-pleted my misfortune. The whole court turned on that fide, with the hope that the miftrefs would banifh the minifter. I guarded againft this, however, by getting into the good graces of the *Mingrelian*, and flattering the love of the king. But the attachment became fo vio-lent, that the monarch, determined to marry his miftrefs, afked my ad-vice. I put him off by evafive an-fwers for feveral days. The ful-tana dowager, who was afraid of lofing her credit by feeing her fon married, declared to me, that unlefs I broke this match fhe would caufe me to be affaffinated on the day of the ceremony. An hour after, the Mingrelian came and fwore to me, that if I did not caufe the king to marry her by the next day, I fhould be ftrangled the day after. My fituation was truly em-barraffing. I muft choofe either the dagger, the rope, or flight. I
chofe

chofe the laft. I put myfelf in difguife, and fled from the palace with
a few diamonds in my pocket,
which will fubferve for our fubfiftence in a corner of *Indoftan*, far
from fultana dowagers, *Mingrelians*,
and the court.

After this recital, *Bekir* recounted
his adventures to *Mefrou*. They
both were decidedly of opinion
that it would have been as well for
them not to have traverfed the
world, and that the wifeft thing
they could now do, would be to return to Koufiftan, and fettle with
their brother T·aï, where the diamonds of *Mefrou* would procure an
eafy living, After this refolution
they fet off, and travelled many
days without any fingular adventure.

As they paffed through the province of *Farfiftan*, they came to a
little village towards night, where
they purpofed to tarry till the next
day. It happened to be holiday.
In entering the village they faw
good many children returning from
a walk, conducted by a poorly clad
mafter, who walked with his head
caft down, and had a penfive melancholy air. The two brethren
approached this mafter, they looked at him, they thought———
But what was their furprife !—It
was *Sadder* !—It was their brother
Sadder, whom they embraced !———

Alas, my friend, faid *Bekir* to
him, is it thus that *genius* is recompenfed ! You fee, replied *Sadder*,
that it fares but a little better, than
bravery. But philofophy here finds
a noble fubject of reflection, and
that is a great confolation. As he
faid this he made all his children
repair to their refpective fathers,
conducted *Bekir* and *Mefrou* into his
little cottage, prepared a little rice
for their fupper, and, after having
heard them relate their hiftories,

gave them his own, as follows.

The *genius Alzim*, who, as I conceive, delights in the mifery of
others, counfelled me to fearch this
introuvable Bathmendi in the great
city of *Agra* among the wits and
belles. I arrived at *Agra ;* and
before I was known to the world I
had a mind to announce myfelf by
a work of eclat. At the end of a
month my performance appeared.
It was a complete courfe of all human fciences in a little volume of
60 pages divided into chapters.—
Every chapter was a ftory, and ev-
ry ftory comprehended a fcience.

The fuccefs of my book was aftonifhing. Certain reviewers criti-
cifed on it, and faid that it was too
diffufe in fome places ; but the genteel part of the world purchafed it,
and I rofe fuperior to their criticifms. My book and myfelf were
altogether in fafhion. I was court-
ed, and invited into all focieties,
which piqued themfelves on their
abilities. Every thing I did was
charming. The converfation of
people was altogether refpecting
me, and my company was highly
gratifying to all. The reigning
fultana wrote me an unorthographi-
cal billet with her own hand, requefting me to come to court.

Go on, faid I to myfelf, Alzim
has not deceived me. My glory is
at its zenith. I will go to court,
there I fhall maintain myfelf by
means, more certain, than thofe of
intrigue. I fhall pleafe, I fhall feduce, I fhall find *Bathmendi*.

I was perfectly welcome in the
palace of the great *Mogul*. The
reigning fultana declared herfelf in
the ftrongeft terms my protectrefs.
She prefented me to the emperor,
befpoke verfes, gave me a penfion,
admitted me at her petits foupés,
and fwore to me a hundred times a
day an indiffoluble friendfhip. On

my

my part, I gave myself up to gratitude with all the vivacity of my heart. I promised to spend my days in singing and celebrating my benefactress. I wrote in honor of her a poem, in which, the splendor of the sun, in comparison of her eyes, was but a false brilliance; the ivory, coral, and pearls of the Persian gulf, lost all their beauty and magnificence when set in competition with her visage, mouth and teeth. These fine spun delicate commendations, secured me her permanent support.

I believed myself on the verge of meeting Bathmendi, when my protectress had a falling out with the vizier respecting the government of a province which he had refused the son of the favourite's confectioner. The sultana, outrageous with audacity, insisted to the emperor on the banishment of the innocent minister; but the emperor, having a great regard for his vizier, denied her request. An intrigue was then set on foot for the destruction of the vizier. I was concerned in the affair, and received orders to compose a bloody satire against the minister, and to circulate it throughout the country. The satire was soon completed; that was easy enough. It was good, and that was easy enough too. It was read with avidity, and that was a necessary consequence.

The vizier well knew that I was the author of it. He goes to the favourite, carries her the commission, which he at first had refused to: He ordered a hundred thousand darics, from the royal treasury, and requested no other recompense, than permission to put me to death in a dungeon. That is a trifle, replied the favourite, and I am very happy to have it in my power to do something, which shall be agreeable to you. I will go, if you please, and send directly for this insolent

man, who has dared to insult you in spite of my express order, and I will deliver him into your hands. Fortunately, a slave belonging to the favourite was present, and came immediately after to give me information. I had scarcely time to save myself.

Since this memorable epoch I have traversed all *Indostan*, and have procured with difficulty my subsistence by writing romances, making verses, and labouring for booksellers, who cheated me, and who, more difficult for my talent than for their consciences, said my style was not sufficiently pure. While I had a profusion of money my publications were master-pieces; but as soon as I was reduced to indigence my writings were worse than indifferent. At length, disgusted at teaching the universe, I chose to teach the peasant's children to read, and have been made a preceptor in this village, where I live upon brown bread, and never expect to find Bathmendi.

You have it now in your power to quit this situation, said *Mesrou*, and return with us to *Koufistan*, where some diamonds, which I have with me, will insure us a sweet and tranquil living. There was no difficulty in gaining *Sadder's* assent to this proposal. On the following day the three brothers departed from the village and took their way to Koufistan.

They were on their last day's journey and were near the little house of their brother Taï. This idea afforded considerable consolation; but their hope was mingled with fear. Shall we find our brother? We left him very poor. He cannot have found Bathmendi, since it has not been in his power to go in quest of him.

My dear friend, said Sadder to them, I have reflected much on this
Bathmendi,

Bathmendi, of whom Alzim fpake to us; and frankly, I believe that the genius has impofed upon us, Bathmendi does not exift, and never has exifted; for, fince brother Bekir has not been able to find him, even when he commanded half the Perfian army; fince Mefrou has heard nothing of him, although he was once the favourite of the great king, and fince I myfelf have been unable even to guefs what this was when I was loaded with riches and glory, it is evident that *Bathmendi* is an imaginary being, an illufion, a chimera, after which all men are running, becaufe they are enamoured of chimeras, and becaufe men love to wander about.

He was going on to prove that Bathmendi had no habitation in the world, when a troop of thieves fallied forth from fome adjacent rocks, encircled the three travellers, and ordered them to ftrip themfelves. Bekir attempted to refift; but he was foon difarmed, and four of thefe affailants holding a dagger at his breaft, took every thing from him, while their comrades ferved Mefrou and Sadder in the fame manner.

After this ceremony, which was an affair of a moment, the chief of the robbers wifhed them a good journey, and left them all three naked in the midft of the high way.

This corroborates my propofition, faid Sadder, looking on his brethren. Ah! the cowardly fellows, exclaimed Bekir, have taken away my fword. Ah! my poor diamonds! anfwered Mefrou, weeping.

It was night. The three unfortunate brothers preffed on to reach their brother's houfe. They arrived there; the view of this houfe made their tears to flow. They ftopped at the gate; they dared not to knock. All their fears and uncertainties began again. While they were confidering what to do, Bekir rolled up a large ftone and got upon it; and finding a flit in the window fhutter, he looked into the chamber, and perceived it to be properly, but in a fimple manner furnifhed. His brother Taï was at table in the midft of feventeen children, who ate, laughed, and prattled all at once. Amina was feated at the right hand of Taï, and cut off little pieces for her youngeft fon; and at his left was a little old man of a pleafant and cheerful countenance, who poured out liquor for Taï. Bekir, at this fight, throws himfelf haftily into his brothers' arms, and knocks at the door with all his might. A fervant came to open it. He cried out for fear at feeing three men naked. Taï runs to the door. One embraces him; one fays, my brother, the other bedews him with tears. He is confounded at firft; but prefently recognifes Bekir, Mefrou, and Sadder. His brotherly love fwallows up his fenfibility. All the children run to this fingular fpectacle. Amina comes, but fhe with her daughters retire at the fight of three naked men. There was none, except the old man, who left not the table.

Taï gives his brothers fome clothes, introduces them to his wife, and makes them kifs his children. Alas! faid Bekir, overwhelmed with fenfibility, thy happy lot confoles us of all we have fuffered. Since the moment of our feparation, our life has been a continual concatenation of misfortunes, and we have not fo much as had a glimpfe at this *Bathmendi*, in queft of which we have fo long toiled.

I believe it, faid the old man, who remained all this while at the table, I have not been a ftep from here.—How, cried Mefrou, are you! —— I am *Bathmendi*, replied

moſt eminent advantages. I appeal to common experience, if bodily caſtigation does not rouſe the principle of revenge? Inſtead of exciting remorſe, it obdurates the heart, and ſteels the mind againſt the arrows of conviction. What friend of humanity would not wiſh to ſee it aboliſhed? It may be proved to a demonſtration, that governments, by the exerciſe of this arbitrary prerogative, inſtead of promoting the peace and harmony of ſociety, prompt the criminal to deſperate meaſures. How indeed can can it be otherwiſe when the credit of the delinquent is gone, and when the ſtern viſage of public contempt frowns upon him? Is he not driven to the commiſſion of more enormities, I had almoſt ſaid by an inevitable neceſſity? Another ſource of public calamities may be mentioned no leſs remarkable than the former. Idleneſs is the mother of iniquity. When a criminal is confined and left to his own reflections, he employs them in planning future ſchemes of miſchief, and when releaſed from his cuſtody, he is let looſe like the tiger of the deſert, on the theatre of action. How many evils have ariſen from cauſes as apparently inſignificant! Towns and cities have been laid in duſt; the fields of the huſbandmen deſolated; nay, even the lives of citizens made the ſport of a wanton multitude. The pen of the hiſtorian has recorded theſe melancholy facts in characters of blood. It is then the duty of the legiſlature to watch theſe evils with a careful eye, and to ſtifle them in the firſt ſtage of their exiſtence. Nothing will more effectually accompliſh this deſirable purpoſe, than a reformation in the penal code of Engliſh juriſprudence. Labour might not unfreqnently be ſubſtituted in the place of death and corporal puniſhment. Criminals are often made more from neceſſity than choice. The want of ſome honeſt occupation or employment drives them into exceſſes. Certainly then, if they were placed under the inſpection of a ſevere tutor, and taught how to follow ſome uſeful calling, they might again be reclaimed to the paths of virtue.

Then, inſtead of horrid imprecations, we might hear the ſong of content reſound through the walls of a priſon; and inſtead of the peſtilential fumes of a dungeon, the eye would probably find dwellings of induſtry and neatneſs. It is rare to find criminals ſo obſtinately bent on deſtruction, as not to liſten to the voice of ſelf intereſt, and here it evidently invites them. It is then natural to preſume, that after the time of their confinement had expired, they would quit the place, and once more become honeſt and reputable citizens.

Whatever legiſlature will firſt undertake this glorious revolution, amidſt all their difficulties they will have one conſoling reflection, that they are the firſt champions in this cauſe of humanity.

ANECDOTES of the late JOSEPH, EMPEROR of GERMANY.

THIS prince was a moſt ſingular character; his abilities were certainly very great, but they were ſtrangely perverted. It is well known to what a ſtate he reduced his dominions, yet his meaſures

ures were fuch as promifed aggran-
difement inftead of diminution,
glory inftead of difgrace. Certainly no prince ever did fo well, with
fuch ill fuccefs ; fortune continually
fought againft him. We muft add
to this, that he had many faults ; his
principal ones appear to have been
irrefolution, and obftinacy ; fome
of the following anecdotes exhibit
him as a man in the moft deteftable
light.

The Emperor being at fupper at
Paris, with Count de Vergennes,
the French minifter, and difcourfing of French affairs, he advifed
the Count to announce a national bankruptcy, in order to clear
France of all her debts ; to this he
was anfwered—" Should fuch an
event take place, your majefty's
own fubjects in Brabant would lofe
more than eighty millions." " Do
not let that deter you, anfwered
Jofeph, give me half that fum, and
you fhall have my affent."

At the time of the affair with
the Dutch concerning the Schelt,
which terminated fo fhamefully for
Jofeph, talking with his head gardener, the gardener afked permiffion to write to Haarlem for a few
flips of flowers, which he wanted.
The Emperor ftarted from his feat ;
his eyes flafhing fire—" No, faid
he, you fhall not write. Within
fix weeks I will fetch them myfelf
from Haarlem, at the head of my
army." Within that time the affair was finifhed with difgrace. So
pofitive was he of fuccefs, and fo
fure always to fail.

He was naturally cruel ; in his
childhood, when he could get at
one of his fifter's canary birds, he
would pluck off its feathers, break
its legs, and put it into the cage
yet alive. To torture animals, a-
bove all, to ride horfes to death,
and cudgel dogs, were his chief a-

mufements. Even when Emperor,
he would go to Saxenburgh, to the
falcony, at five o'clock in the morning, when the birds were to be fed,
would take the pigeon deftined
for that purpofe alive, in his hand,
turn it upon its back, and let the
falcon devour it from the belly upwards, whilft he obferved with
fmiles every convulfive motion of
the fuffering victim : This was to
him the fupreme enjoyment of life.

The Emperor Francis, his father, died fuddenly in his arms of
an apoplexy. As he lay on his left
arm, in the agonies of death, he
took the keys out of his pocket
with his right hand, fmiling, and
too impatient to wait till he had
breathed his laft.

When his mother Therefa, lay
on her death bed, fhe gave him
fuch a fevere lecture on the badnefs
of his heart, that he flung himfelf
on the floor, wept, and rolled himfelf about in feeming defpair. Six
hours after the Emprefs died, immediately he repaired to the apartment of the chief governante, who
was prefent at the foregoing fcene,
and faid to her with a fmiling
countenance, and jefting mien,
" Countefs, that was a fine fight a
few hours ago ; it was an excellent
joke.—Did you really believe me
in earneft ?" This circumftance at
firft fight feems to difplay a moft
unpardonable want of feeling and
natural affection : yet, upon confideration, the guilt will appear to
be not fo great. It muft require a
great effort to feign fo well a contrition which he did not experience ; and it was the intention of
the mother to awaken this contrition, the behaviour of the fon muft
certainly give her more fatisfaction
than if he had heard her with contemptuous neglect, or fullen difdain.

CHARACTER

To the EDITORS *of the* MASSACHUSETTS MAGAZINE.

GENTLEMEN,

If you deem the following biographical sketches, extracted from Holt's Charac-
ters of English Sovereigns, with notes Historical, worthy the perusal of your
readers, you will please to give them insertion, and oblige your's, &c. A.

CHARACTER of ANNE.

THE Queen continued to dose in a lethargic insensibility, with very short intervals, till the first day of August, in the morning, when she expired, in the fiftieth year of her age, and in the thirteenth of her reign. Anne Stuart, queen of Great-Britain, was in her person of the middle size, well proportioned ; her hair was of dark brown colour, her complexion ruddy, her features were regular, her countenance was rather round than oval, and her aspect more comely than majestic : Her voice was clear and melodious, and her presence engaging ; her capacity was naturally good, but not much cultivated by learning ; nor did she exhibit any marks of extraordinary genius, or personal ambition ; she was certainly deficient in that vigour of mind, by which a prince ought to preserve her independence, and avoid the snares and fetters of sycophants and favourites ; but, whatever her weakness in this particular might have been, the virtues of her heart were never called in question ; she was a pattern of conjugal affection and fidelity, a tender mother, a warm friend, and indulgent mistress, a munificent patron, a mild and merciful princess ; during whose reign, no blood was shed for treason. She was zealously attached to the church of England, from conviction rather than from prepossession ; unaffectedly pious, just, charitable and compassionate— she felt a mother's fondness for her people, by whom she was universally beloved with a warmth of affection, which even the prejudice of party could not abate. In a word, if she was not the greatest, she was certainly one of the best and most unblemished sovereigns that ever sat upon the throne of England, and well deserved the expressive, though simple epithet of, " the good queen Anne." SMOLLETT.

She died in 1714.

Observations on the character of Anne.

When elevated rank is embellished by propriety of conduct, and this too manifested in the several stations of " friend, mother and wife," how extensively useful may such a character become to the public at large, by the force of so splendid and amiable an example. Anne " was a pattern of conjugal affection, a warm friend, an indulgent mistress, a munificent patron, a mild and merciful princess."

Any one of these enumerated good qualities, distinctly and separately considered, are praiseworthy, and in the estimation of many, might cover a multitude of faults. But as there appears no one virtue more becoming the frailty of human nature than *mercy ;* and since it is not always found in the character of princes, we will make it the subject of our present reflections ; for " Anne was a merciful mistress."

Youth brought up in affluence, and under the hand of indulgence, scarcely know the meaning of such a term, although they may be the object of so many mercies ; and yet, how easy for a friend or parent to inculcate this lesson in a few words, upon many occasions. As there is no duty more becoming mankind, considered

considered as frail creatures, dependent on each other ; so one should imagine it would manifest itself more especially among the weaker sex, who have so much need of protection, if it were not notorious, that they are more prone to detraction, and less merciful towards the individuals of their own sex, than the men, insomuch that a certain writer has wittily observed, that "women are to each other like Turkey fowls, which, when any one has the least conspicuous blemish the whole flock combine to pick and lacerate the wound without *mercy*, aggravating the first misfortune, till they have completed their vengeance by the death of the sufferer."

Since the female character is liable to injury, even from the least breath of defamation, and since there are circumstances, where the most unblemished can hardly escape censure ; let us recommend to you, my fair friends, to escape this reproach, by adopting the maxim of Sophia. "Sophia never talks of women, but to express the good she knows of them ; of others, she says nothing."

If the wounded in spirit, who has somewhat deviated from the strict line of duty, should, with a penitent heart say, "I will arise and return to my father ;" but is withheld from these good intents, through apprehension that he who felt no pity would shew no mercy ; or that the taunts of her own sex, as satirically exemplified above, would be too much for her feelings to support on past sufferings ; what gladness of heart would it afford, if some protecting hand would step forth, and look upon such with partiality whom the world eyes with prejudice ; let us conceive such an one addressing her patroness in the following language :

"May that grace and favour which your good fortune has thrown upon you, be turned to make up the coldness and indifference that is manifested towards me, and then the good and generous will have an eye of kindness for me for my own sake, and the rest of the world will regard me for yours. As the rich can make rich without parting with any of their store, and the conversation of the poor makes men poor, though they borrow nothing of them ; so there is a happy contagion in an established character, as well as destructive one in lost reputation ; for the estimation of the world follows us according to the company they keep." Who, that has the least bowels of compassion, but would mercifully wish to save that soul alive ?

The quality of mercy is not strained ;
It droppeth like the gentle rain from
  heaven,
Upon the place beneath. It is twice
  blessed,
It blesses him that gives, and him that
  takes ;
'Tis mightiest in the mightiest ; it becomes
The throned monarch better than his
  crown ;
His sceptre shows the force of temporal
  power,
The attribute of awe and majesty,
Wherein doth sit the dread and fear of
  kings ;
But mercy is above this sceptred sway,
It is enthroned in the hearts of kings ;
It is an attribute of God himself ;
And earthly power doth then shew likest
  Gods,
When mercy seasons justice.

             Merchant of Venice.

HISTORICAL NOTE.

The union of the Kingdoms of England and Scotland.

A. D. 1706.—This important transaction was finally completed at the close of this year, after their crowns had been united one hundred and four years before, in the
            person

person of James the firſt. This great Union had been ſeveral times before attempted, in different reigns, but had been as often obſtructed, by various objections ſtarted, and not ſeriouſly and ſteadily endeavoured to be removed. National prejudices are with difficulty eradicated ; and lucrative offices under the State, which muſt of neceſſity be ſunk under ſuch an Union had no ſmall influence in obſtructing the incorporation ; but an able miniſtry in both nations, joined to a more moderate way of thinking than formerly, at length got the better of every obſtruction : And preparatory laws being made in both kingdoms, the parliament of Scotland firſt agreed to the articles of this famous Union, which were ratified by a ſolemn act of Engliſh parliament. The articles were twenty five in number— It may be ſufficient to mention the fourth and fifteenth articles, by which it was enacted, that all the ſubjects of the united kingdom of Great-Britain ſhould, from and after the Union, have full freedom and intercourſe of trade and navigation to or from any port or place within the ſaid united kingdoms, and the dominions and plantations thereunto belonging ; and that there ſhould be a communication of all other rights, privileges and advantages which do or may belong to the ſubjects of either kingdom, except when it is otherwiſe expreſsly agreed in theſe articles. By the article XV. it was agreed, that Scotland ſhould receive an equivalent for what the ſubjects of that kingdom ſhall be charged towards payment of the

debts of England contracted before the Union, for which the ſum of three hundred ninety eight thouſand and eighty five pounds, ten ſhillings, was granted by the Parliament of England. This Union took place on the 1ſt of May, 1707 ; the advantages of which to England are, that many thouſands of brave men from that country ſupply our fleets and armies. England has the abſolute uſe thereby of many good ports ; a more extenſive fiſhery, a ſupply of black cattle, and ſundry other advantages.

Scotland, in return, enriches herſelf, by a participation of commerce with England's foreign plantations, factories, &c. alſo a ſale for her coarſe woollen ſtuffs and ſtockings, and her more valuable linen manufactories, not only in England but America. Nature, in ſhort, intended theſe two for one, by being ſeparated by the ocean from the reſt of mankind ; ſo that it is wonderful that they ſhould not ſooner have purſued their mutual intereſts : And the ſame may be obſerved by poſterity with regard to the preſent commercial treaty between England and France ; ſince probably the next generation may, with equal aſtoniſhment, ſurvey the prejudice which guided the judgments of former politicians, by clogging with heavy duties, amounting to a prohibition, a mutual commerce with two neighbouring kingdoms, that would have been highly beneficial to both. But we are told, " There is a time for all things."

[*Holt's Royal Characters.*]

———————

ABUSEI and THAIR : An Eaſtern APOLOGUE.

IN the winter ſo remarkable for the great revolutions which happened at the court of Nourad-din, Abuzei ſaid unto Thair, "Congratulate me, my father ; I am the ſultan's favourite, his ſiſter's lover, and

and tomorrow her highnefs and I are to hunt together."——

" O, my fon," anfwered Thair, " the favour of kings; the fmiles of women, and the fine days of winter; are three things on which we ought but little to depend !"

The event juftified the fage obfervation of the venerable Thair ; for, the next day, the rain prevented the hunt, the princefs changed her mind from caprice ; and the fultan, at his fifter's inftigation, difgraced Abuzei.

For the MASSACHUSETTS MAGAZINE.

The INVESTIGATOR. No. II.

Since 'tis with us to choofe immortal blifs;
Or all the ills, that wait on man below ;—
Let's then unfurl the ftandard of our peace,
And lofe by reafon what we gain by wo.
For, to remain in bigotted fufpenfe,
And view creation on the fombre fide,
Too plainly marks the fcarcity of fenfe,
And all the follies of illit'rate pride.

IF it is counted ridiculous in man, to be continually complaining of that mifchief, of which he is the fole, and deliberate author ; why then do *we* complain of the ills of life, when we do not attempt to extricate ourfelves from them ? A queftion, I acknowledge, too intricate for the Inveftigator, and which I beg leave to fubmit to the more experienced and philofophic. In the mean time I fhall attempt to paint and point the errors we have run into, and the manner, by which we can enjoy ourfelves and thofe around us.

That God created man for terreftrial happinefs and immortal blifs, appears fully evident from the fuperiority of his fituation, the majefty of his form, and the noblenefs of his mind. He is exprefsly declared, by the Deity himfelf, to be lord and fovereign of all below ; for which reafon, the beafts, that graze the fields, the fowls, that fcale the air, and the fifhes, that fill the deep, are fubject to his control. The fun, the moon, and ftars, thofe glorious luminaries, rife to adorn and beautify his abode ; to revive and continue in life him and the things that are at his difpofal. The earth vegetates for man alone ; Spring, Summer, and Autumn, all unite to make him happy. But gloom and forrow fet on his countenance ; grief rangles in his heart, and difappointment fwells his breaft. And why ? Becaufe he views nature on the fombre fide, and will not ftudy nature's God. It arifes from his miftaken ideas of life, and his ignorance of himfelf; from his neglect of virtue and propenfity to vice. He looks upon his pilgrimage as a burden, and his reafon the fource of all his mifery ; without allowing it thofe noble qualities, which alone place him fo near his Creator. He confiders his fellow beings as enemies and rivals, whereas he fhould view them as beloved brethren, as children of the fame father and fubjects of the fame God. From hence arifes all his pain and wretchednefs.

If he could be brought to look upon life as a blefling, and reafon the key to happinefs—peculiarly pleafing and almoft adorable would be his

his fituation. It was not for the happinefs of the Creator that man was formed, but for the creature; who then lofes by man's neglect?

" As a man thinketh, fo will he conduct;" is the affertion of ancient and great philofophers. If fuch indeed is the cafe, how eafy is it for us to enjoy ourfelves! we have only to employ that reafon, which we fo foolifhly pervert; that noble key, which unlocks creation, and prefents it to the mind in all its variety, in all its wonder. Reafon firft begins by teaching man how to fupport his animal part; therefore leads him to furvey earth and its productions; afterwards to trace out the caufes and effects of things more immediately before him. When it arrives to a ftate of refinement, its poffeffor contemplates the grand and more aftonifhing works of the Deity; he views the heavens, the fun, moon, and ftars, not as a man, but as a philofopher; not as things ornamental, but as ufeful and requifite in the fyftem of nature. From thefe works and contemplations he foars to the Deity himfelf; the knowledge of whom, though it never can be perfect; yet as far as the underftanding can reach, fo far and in fuch proportion we admire and adore him; and almoft immediately reconcile things, which at firft appeared as oppofite.

The more a man gains acquaintance with his Creator, the more fenfible he is of his own ignorance and weaknefs, and the more confcious he becomes of the truth of this affertion, " that what ever is, is right," as it refpects creation. Therefore I may juftly conclude that the greater part of our forrow and mifery arifes from bigotted ignorance, vice and idlenefs. For as foon as we undertake rightly to think, fo foon will grief and depreffion of mind vanifh, as the morning clouds before the rifing fun.

At prefent, the greater part of mankind crawl to the valley of death through a cloud of fears; and as they go moping through exiftence, curfe the world, becaufe it cannot make them happy againft their own inclinations. Others delight to brood over the ills concomitant with humanity, and make thofe which never exifted but in their own deluded imaginations. For my part I conceive " that fufficient to the evil is the day thereof;" and I am fure that we cannot add a moment to our pleafure, nor extract a minute from our pain, by fobbing and complaining. The Deity does neither pity, nor efteem the perfon, who is continually fighing about his felf-made deplorable condition, fo much as the man, who confcious of his iniquity, by private fupplication, and open manly behaviour, endeavours to ward off the impending curfe; for being the effence of holinefs, noblenefs and glory, he delights in the things that appertain thereunto. Therefore let us look upon this life as defigned for the pleafure and happinefs of man. Let us view it as we ought to, the road to heaven. In fo doing we fhall do wifely; we fhall conduct as men, and live as Chriftians: We fhall enjoy ourfelves and thofe around us. The journey of life will be pleafant and delightful; we fhall arrive at the gate of death, (which opens to eternity) ferene and compofed; and when we bid the final adieu to earth and its inhabitants, it will be in the language of reafon and religion, which, though it fhould call forth a tear from the eye, will adminifter comfort to the mind.

ANECDOTE

MASSACHUSETTS MAGAZINE,

ANECDOTE of M. LAVATER.

THIS gentleman having afferted, in the fecond part of his Treatife on Phyfiognomy, that fhoemakers have generally a fickly appearance and weak conftitutions, and that at Zurich, of twenty four children born of parents exercifing that profeffion, feven only were boys, all the *craft* of that place rofe up againft him, about fix years ago, in a riotous manner. M. Lavater, finding it neceffary to quell the tumult as amicably as poffible, declared publicly that he had been miftaken, for that the juft proportion was twenty eight males to thirty of the other fex. He begged, however, that the fhoemakers would permit him to ftand godfather to all the males; and they cheerfully accepted his offer.

EXTRAVAGANCE.

LUCIUS CASSIUS, the celebrated orator, confeffed that a great part of his filver plate ftood him in fix thoufand feftirces, or 48l. 15s. fterling per pound, becaufe of the workmanfhip. He had two filver goblets engraved by Mentor, which coft him 812l. 10s.

Old Efop, the player, dreffed up a difh of finging birds, which ftood him in 4143l. 10s.

ANECDOTE.

PUBLIUS BELLIUS POLLIO, originally a Roman flave, but afterwards a knight, carried luxury to its greateft extravagance. He kept lampreys in a pond where he fed them with human flefh; the ordinary punifhment inflicted on his flaves, even for trivial faults, was to have them thrown hands and legs together, into that pond to feed thofe voracious animals.

For the MASSACHUSETTS MAGAZINE.

REVIEW.

An attempt to tranflate the prophetic part of the Apocalypfe of St. John into familiar language, by divefting it of the metaphors in which it is involved. By James Winthrop, Efq.——8vo. price 1f6.

THE obfcurity of the revelation of St. John has puzzled the greateft critics in biblical literature. Several very learned divines have publicly confeffed their inability to unfold this book, and others,

ers, who attempted it, have failed. Voltaire, *in his vein*, obferved, that " Sir Ifaac Newton wrote his comment upon the revelation to confole mankind for the great fuperiority he had over them in other refpects." The witty Dr. South, in one of his fermons, fays, " This book always finds a man mad, or leaves him fo."

Mr. Winthrop, perfuaded " that the apocalypfe was not written at random, like the reveries of a difturbed imagination, but that it was eftablifhed in truth," and not difcouraged by the failure of preceding commentators, has attempted to explain and apply the predictions of St. John. The work before us has the merit of *originality*, and it difcovers the profound erudition and extenfive reading for which its author is eminently diftinguifhed.

He fuppofes that the predictions of this book were communicated in the form of hieroglyphic pictures; and that John defcribed the emblems in each picture, as the leaves of the prophetic volume were unfolded to him. The method of explanation is, firft to affume definitions of the emblems, and then to apply them to the events of hiftory—in the manner that picture hiftory is decyphered. The great object of the prophecy, on fuppofition, is, civil government formed on the principles of Chriftianity. To this his definitions or terms are made to apply. In their application to the events of time, he begins with the converfion of the Roman empire, to the Chriftian religion, under Conftantine, and ends with the period at which Chriftianity fhall be made the bafis of equal government. And " from which men fhall derive wealth, wifdom, power, and all the advantages of fociety."

To enable thofe of our readers who have not feen the work, to form an adequate idea of our author's plan, we think it expedient, in this place, to give a fpecimen of his definitions, and of the manner of their application.

(To be continued.)

SPECIMEN.

NECESSARY DEFINITIONS.

1. ABADDON ; commonly interpreted the Deftroyer. Bryant's etymologies give Great Lord of Light, which accords with the appellation of *The Prophet* given to Mahomet by his followers.

2. *Abyfs* or *Bottomlefs Pit*; a diforderly ftate arifing from faction and lawlefs force, or from having never formed into a ftate of civil fociety.

3. *Angel*; any remarkable interpofition of divine Providence, as war, revolutions, epidemic difeafes, &c. It does not neceffarily include an eminent character for a leader, but may arife from the ftate of fociety. 2. In a fubordinate fenfe it means officers of government.

4. *Angel of bottomlefs pit*; a government or perfon rifing to importance by means of the factions in the country.

5. *Angel of fire*; the Holy Spirit as our director and purifier.

6. *Angel of water*; the Holy Spirit as our comforter.

7. *Four Angels bound in the Euphrates*; the true believers who were to be freed from the Papal Government by various revolutions.

8. *Angel with a fickle*; reprefents time.

9. *Four animals, beafts,* or *living things*; the four Prætorian Præfectures or great Judicial departments into which Conftantine divided the empire. Each had three vice Præfects, reprefented by three pair of wings. The whole twelve pair did not fill the empire ; but Egypt, Syria, and the neighbouring provinces, though fubject to the præfects, were governed by the Auguftan præfect of Egypt, and the Count of the Eaft. Thefe two jurifdictions feem to include the country allotted by Ezekiel to the Jews at their reftoration. The twelve vice præfectures were divided equally among the præfects. 1. The eaft containing Thrace, Afiana, and Pontica, befides the foregoing exception. 2. Illyricum, comprehending Pannonia, Dacia, Macedonia and Greece. This was defignated by the *calf*, as the former was by the *lion*. 3. Italy, with the neighbouring iflands, Rhetia as far as the Danube, and the

the countries now called Tunis, Tripoli, and Algiers on the African fhore. The emblem is a *man*. 4. Gaul contained all weft of the Alps, and reached from Atlas to the Rhine. This was the *Eagle.* The eyes of the præfects were the lawyers and official agents, who were fupported by the government to give the neceffary effect and fyftem to the Judicial department; it being the object of Conftantine to eftablifh a permanent government of laws, inftead of the loofe one of force.

10. *Armageddon* or *Mt Megiddo; fuppof*ed to reprefent figuratively a perfecuting power which fhould afflict the faints.

11. *Babylon;* Rome, chiefly as an idolatrous feat of empire.

12. *Balance;* the counterpoife which Julian endeavoured to eftablifh between the Chriftians and heathens, when he fet up an heathen hierarchy, and paid them out of the Chriftian funds.

13. *Beaft wild;* any governments affuming power to control the maxims of the gofpel for political caufes. It is applied in chap. xiii, to the firft of the three antichriftian powers, and in other places to each of them. The connexion muft determine as in any other cafe.

14. *Candle;* an high prieft.

15. *City* or *Great City;* the dominions of the three antichriftian States collectively. It is alfo ufed for the Empire or the Country under confideration.

16. *Cities of the Gentiles;* the empire of the Image, or third antichriftian power.

17. *City beloved;* the church.

18. *Cloud;* a great multitude.

19. *Dens and Caves,* or *Holes in Mountains;* the protecting hand of great and influential men.

20. *Death;* private life, alfo heathen darknefs or in general obfcurity.

21. *Death and Hell;* obfcurity and mifery under heathen rulers.

22. *Devil;* human force not regulated by religious principles, whether in legal Governors or feditious leaders.

CHAP. IV.—*Defcription of a Chriftian Empire, fuppofed to be the Roman, under Conftantine and his fucceffors.*

TRANSLATION.

AFTER writing thefe epiftles, I faw the way prepared for the government to be converted to Chriftianity, and I received fufficient affurances, that the vifion was prophetic.

2 And in the vifion I* faw an imperial throne, and the prince feated upon it.

3 And he was adorned with the emblems of majefty, and his throne was uncommonly magnificent, and his reign glorious.

4 And about the throne were the feats of twenty-four counfellors of ftate. They were diftinguifhed for their integrity, and ranked as princes.

5 And before the emperor were difcuffed all queftions of magnitude, whether relating to legiflation, adminiftration of juftice, or war, and fuitable decrees were paffed. There were alfo feven confidential minifters of the palace, fignified by feven lamps, which alfo typify feven general revolutions.

6 And the Emperor had conftantly in view the eftablifhment of an equal government upon the principles of Chriftianity. And he divided his dominion into four præfectures or judicial departments, which were all fubject to his revifion, and were furnifhed with all neceffary means for information.

7 And the firft præfecture was diftinguifhed by the emblem of a lion, the fecond by that of a calf, the third by that of a man, and the fourth by an eagle with expanded wings.

8 And each of the præfects or chief juftices, had under him three vicepræfects, who were alfo furnifhed by government with all the means for obtaining the neceffary information in their refpective districts. And they were continually employed in the execution of thofe orders, that fhall promote the glory of God.

9 And when the præfects make report to the emperor of the fuccefs attending their endeavours to eftablifh the Chriftian fyftem,

10 The Council of State give thanks to God from whom their honour is derived, faying,

11 Thou art worthy, O Lord, to receive glory, and honour, and power; for thou haft created all things, and for thy pleafure they are and were created.

* *The Apoftle in this inftance, fpeaks* individually; *in fome others he feems to perfonate the* church. *I have not always been careful to diftinguifh the different ufes of the firft perfon, having fometimes ufed it, when the collective term would apply as well. But the connexion will enable the moft carelefs reader to determine the meaning.*

CABINET of APOLLO.

To *the* Editors *of the* Maſſachuſetts Magazine.

GENTLEMEN,

THE Stanzas in your laſt Magazine were not, as there inſerted, addreſſed to the Prince of Wales, by Mrs. Robinſon, but to Colonel Tarleton, whom ſhe emphatically ſtiles " BAYARD," *after a great* military *character of a former age ; and the perſon who tranſcribed thoſe lines from the European Magazine, was guilty of a miſtake, by placing the name of "Frederic," where that publication left a blank ; as Mrs. R's connexion with the Prince was of ſhort duration, and diſſolved in conſequence of her infidelity to him and her attachment to Tarleton, the ſtanza "Ten long years," &c. is moſt inapplicable ; but it is a well known fact that her love poems are addreſſed to this gentleman, that he has been ſupported by her for many years, and though a man of univerſal gallantry, is ſtill the object of her tendereſt attachment. The following elegant verſes, being the moſt delicate production of her pen, were firſt publiſhed in England, in the year ninety-one, and addreſſed*

To Col. BANASTRE TARLETON.

LOTHARIO.

OH ! think no more that life's deluſive
  joys,
 Can charm my thoughts from friendſhip's dearer claim ;
Or wound a heart, that ſcarce a wiſh employs,
 For age to cenſure, or diſcretion blame.

Tir'd of the world, my weary mind recoils
 From *ſplendid ſcenes*, and tranſitory joys,
From *fell ambition's* falſe and fruitleſs toils,
 From hope that flatters, and from bliſs
  that cloys.

With THEE, above the taunts of empty
  pride,
 The rigid frowns to *youthful error** given,

* Youthful error probably alludes to her quitting her huſband, Mr. Robinſon, an attorney,

Content in ſolitude my griefs I'll hide,
 Thy voice my counſellor, thy ſmiles
  my heaven.

With *thee* I'll hail the morn's returning ray,
 Or clime the dewy mountains bleak
  and cold ;
On the ſmooth lake obſerve the ſunbeams play,
 Or mark the infant flowers their buds
  unfold.

And when I ſee thy warm unſpotted
  mind,
 Torn with the wound of broken friendſhip's dart ;
When ſickneſs chills thy breaſt with
  pangs unkind,
 Or ruthleſs ſorrow preys upon thy
  heart—

The taſk be *mine* to ſooth thee to repoſe,
 To check the ſigh, and wipe the trickling tear,
Or with ſoft *ſympathy* to ſhare thy woes ;
 O proudeſt tranſport of the ſoul ſincere.

When fate's ſtern hand ſhall cloſe my
  weeping eye,
 And ſeal at length, my wandering ſpirit's doom,
Oh may *kind friendſhip* catch my parting
  ſigh,   [tomb.
And cheer with hope the terrors of the

who is ſtill living, and by whom ſhe has a daughter of ſuperior beauty, and accompliſhment.

For the MASSACHUSETTS MAGAZINE.

LE BOUQUET des ROSES.

Written by the Authoreſs of the Bouquet of Lilies, in the Magazine of June laſt.

SWEET flowers ! that erſt upon your
  parent buſh
 Bloom'd to the enraptur'd eye ſo freſh
  and gay,
Your fragrance fled, and faded your ſweet
  bluſh,
 Drooping ye haſten to your ſad decay !
     Ah !

Ah ! why thus evanefcent that fine hue—
   Which once fo lovely—grac'd yon dear
      retreat ?
Bouquet of Rofes—ah ! Heaven's fofter-
      ing dew,
   And cheering fun, no more revive your
      fweets.

Yet ftay one moment—from the babling
      rill
   I'll bring frefh moifture to reflore your
      charms,
And court bright Phœbus to afford you
      ftill
   That fmile, which foon fhall banifh thefe
      alarms.

Inhaling vigour thence—long fhall ye live,
   And bloom more frefh, more fragrant
      than before,
And to your fond reftorer grateful give
   The tribute of your odours, o'er and
      o'er.

For the MASSACHUSETTS MAGAZINE.

L I N E S,

*Written by a Lady, who was queftioned refpeɛt-
   ing her inclination to marry.*

WITH an heart light as cork, and a
      mind free as air,
Unfhackled I'll live and I'll die, I declare ;
No ties fhall perplex me, no fetters fhall
      bind,
That innocent freedom that dwells in my
      mind.

At liberty's fpring fuch draughts I've im-
      bib'd,
That I hate all the doɛtrines by wedlock
      prefcrib'd ;
Its laws of obedience could never fuit me,
My fpirit's too lofty, my thoughts are too
      free.

Like an haughty republic my heart with
      difdain,
Views the edicts of Hymen and laughs at
      his chain,
Abhors his tyrannical fyftems and modes,
His baftiles, his fhackles, his maxims and
      codes ;

Inquires why women confent to be tools,
   And calmly conform to fuch rigorous
      rules ;
Inquires in vain, for no reafons appear,
Why matrons fhould live in fubjeɛtion and
      fear.

But round freedom's fair ftandard I've ral-
      lied and paid,
A vow of allegiance to die an old maid.

Long live the republic of freedom and
      cafe,
May its fubjeɛts live happy and do as they
      pleafe.

For the MASSACHUSETTS MAGAZINE.

S I M I L E.

By J. W. Efq.

YOU fay, fir, once a wit[*] allow'd
   A woman to be like a cloud ;
Accept a *fimile*, as foon,
Between a *woman* and the *moon* ;
For, let mankind fay what they will,
The fex are *heavenly bodies* ftill.

Grant me to mimic human life,
That SUN and MOON are man and wife ;
Whate'er kind Sol affords to *lend* her
Is fquander'd upon *midnight fplendor.*

And when to reft he *lays him down,*
She's up and ftar'd at, thro' the town !
From him her beauties clofe confining,
And only in his *abfence fhining :*

Or, elfe, fhe looks like fullen tapers,
Or, elfe, fhe's fairly in the *vapours ;*
Or owns at once, a wife's ambition,
And fully glares in *oppofition.*

Say, are not thefe a modifh pair—
Where each for other feels no care ?
Whole days in *fep'rate coaches* driving,
Whole nights to keep *afunder* ftriving—

Both in the dumps in gloomy weather,
And lying *once a month* together ;—
In one fole point, unlike the cafe is,
On *her own head,* the *horns* fhe places.
                                          A.

[*] *Dean Swift.*

For the MASSACHUSETTS MAGAZINE.

An AUTUMNAL PIECE.

AS rambling in the folitary wood,
   When folemn filence through the
      yellow grove,
Invites my mufing, philofophic ftep,
A fmooth unruffled calm pervades my
      foul,
And foothes each lift'ning fenfe to tafte
The various beauties of autumnal fcenes.
When thro' the loaded orchard ambling
      flow,
I pluck the faireft fruit from ev'ry tree ;
The frequent found of apples falling off
From branches overburden'd with their
      ftore,
Awakes attention, looking for the fwain,
Whom fancy eager thinks to find engag'd
In fhaking from the tree the full ripe fruit.
                                          But

But now the swain appears beside his cart,
Well fill'd with baskets, and a jovial train
Of children, raising their vocif'rous mirth.
The fields resound with glee of female voice,
And male, in sweet, harmonious task engag'd.
The aged peasant now with hook in hand,
And looks of satisfaction in his face,
From tree to tree shakes off the choicest fruit,
While in the pride of manhood's nervous limbs,
His rugged sons spring up the branching tree,
With muscles vig'rous from salubrious toil,
They shake the lab'ring branches; when forthwith,
A clust'ring show'r descends with thund'ring sound,
And with luxuriant sweetness clothes the ground.
With screams of glee the younger tribe beneath,
In sweet contention for the fairest fruit,
With laughter loud now vex the hapless wight,
Who on his head receiv'd the pelting show'r,
And now with rueful face declares his hurt,
Avers his head is broke and brains beat out,
With hand uplifted soothes his aching crown.
The cart well fill'd now homeward moves along,
Fraught with the richest store; and oft returns,
Till round the creaking mill th' extended heap,
In variegated plenteousness is seen,
Which soon compress'd distils the cheering juice, [swain;
The wholesome bev'rage of the hardy
Whose lusty sinews feel its genial force,
And glow with warmth that scorns the winter's cold.

He, not such pleasure feels, whose costly store,
Of choice Madeira sparkles on his board;
Him, with his dainties in his spacious dome,
The peasant pities;—quaffs his orchard wine,
That cheers, but not inebriates the soul;
And while the necessaries of life he finds,
Feels not the loss of delicates unknown;
Or known—despis'd, as sweets for children made.

He with the plainest food enjoys content;
By constant labour from the spleen set free,
That clouds with deepest gloom the sons of wealth;
Whose sickly palates and weak wayward minds
Forever crave unsatisfying joys,
That fleeting, yet forever in their view,
Lead them life's round in quest of airy forms,
Phantoms of vain, imaginary good,
That mock them with the view—then disappear.

BLANDULUS.

Extracted for the MASSACHUSETTS MAGAZINE.

Composed on reading Shakespeare's Midsummer Night's Dream.

TITANIA to her LOVE.

O! FLY with me through distant air,
To isles that gem the western deep!
For laughing Summer revels there,
And hangs her wreath on ev'ry steep.

As through the green transparent sea
Light floating on its waves we go,
The nymphs shall gaily welcome me
Far in their coral caves below.

For oft upon their margin sands,
When twilight leads the fresh'ning hours,
I come with all my jocund bands
To charm them from their sea-green bow'rs.

And well they love our sports to view,
And on the ocean's breast to lave;
And oft, as we the dance renew,
They call up music from the wave.

Swift hie we to that splendid clime,
Where gay Jamaica spreads her scene,
Lifts the blue mountain—wild—sublime!
And smooths her vales of vivid green.

Where throned high, in pomp of shade,
The *power of vegetation* reigns,
Expanding wide, o'er hill and glade,
Shrubs of all growth—fruit of all stains:

She steals the sun beams' fervid glow
To paint her flowers of mingling hue
And o'er the grape the purple throw,
Breaking from verdant leaves to view.

There, myrtle bow'rs, and citron grove,
O'ercanopy our airy dance;
And there the sea breeze loves to rove
When trembles day's departing glance.
And

And when the falfe moon fteals away,
Or ere the chafing morn doth rife,
Oft, fearlefs, we our gambols play
By the fire worm's radiant eyes.

And fuck the honey'd reeds that fwell
In tufted plumes of filver white ;
Or pierce the cocoa's milky cell,
To fip the nectar of delight !

And when the fhaking thunders roll,
And lightnings ftrike athwart the gloom,
We fhelter in the cedar's bole,
And revel 'mid the rich perfume !

But chief we love beneath the palm,
Or verdant plantain's fpreading leaf,
To hear, upon the midnight calm,
Sweet Philomela pour her grief.

To mortal fprite fuch dulcet found,
Such blifsful honrs, were never known !
O ! fly with me my airy round,
And I will make them all thine own !

For the MASSACHUSETTS MAGAZINE.

AN EPISODE.

Verfified from the Poems of Offian.

COMAL was Albion's fon ; the chief
of fwains ;
His hungry deer fed on a thoufand plains.
A thoufand rocks that fpread their arches wide
An echo to his fhrill voic'd hounds reply'd.
His ruddy face with youthful mildnefs beam'd,
And in his hand the fate of heroes gleam'd.
One was his love and fhe was all his care;
Mild as the morning beam, appear'd the fair.
Her charms held Comal in a ftrong embrace :
She oft attended in his hunting chafe.
Full oft their eyes of love tranfporting meet ;
Their fighs were tender and their paffions fweet ;
But cruel Gormal, Ardvan's gloomy chief,
Lov'd the young maid and pin'd with fecret grief.
He watch'd her lone fteps on the filent heath,
And madly meditated Comal's death.
One pleafant day they chas'd the foreft beafts
Till eve came on with darknefs, clouds and mifts.
Then Comal, with a gentle paffion fir'd,
To Ronan's cave with Galvina retir'd.

This lonely cave was Comal's wonted feat,
When oft from toil he fought a calm retreat.
The rock was carv'd with deeds of former times,
And fill'd with rarities of other climes :
An hundred bucklers hung upon the wall,
An hundred helmets grac'd the facred hall.
Here reft, he faid, thou light of Ronan's cave,
And read the actions of the ancient brave.
On Mora's brow I feek the bounding deer ;
But foon I fhall return and meet thee here.
I fear, faid fhe, dark Gormal's bloody dart
Will find a paffage to thy lovely heart.
Yet go ; impatient here I'll wait thy ftay,
And mufe the folitary hours away.

Comal departs, and on high Mora's brow
Purfues the deer with dogs and bended bow—
The penfive Galvina, her fkill to try,
Laid all her robes and golden tiffues by ;
Put on the glittering armour of the brave,
And ftrode majeftic out from Ronan's cave.
Comal return'd and met the maid of fnow,
And rafhly deem'd her his inveterate foe :
He ftopp'd : His colour chang'd : His heart beat high :
He drew his bow ; he let his arrow fly,
Lo ! haplefs Galvina in crimfon fell !
Comal in hafte repairs into the cell,
And calls to Galvina his long lov'd maid :
But calls in vain—no Galvina reply'd—
He went—he look'd—he mark'd her bleeding heart—
Beating with pain againft the mortal dart.
O Conloch's daughter ! Is it thou ? he cry'd—
Then funk upon her bloody breaft and figh'd.

The early hunters found the haplefs pair,
Galvina dead and Comal in defpair.
In fullen grief he trod the lonely grove,
Round the dark dwelling of his buried love.
The fleet of Ocean came ; he met their pride ;
The ftrangers fell ; their valiant heroes dy'd.
He fought for death ; but, death could not be found :
No dart could give the much defired wound.

At

At length the hero threw his shield away
And rush'd more furious to the mad affray,
A fatal arrow found his manly breast
And sent his soul to everlasting rest.
With his fair Galvina he sleeps secure
Where yonder billows lash the hollow
shore.
Their solitary tombs, in grassy green
By the bold mariners are often seen:
With sympathetic grief they point and
cry,
" There hapless Galvina and Comal lie."
LINUS.

To the Editors of the Massachusetts Magazine.

GENTLEMEN,

As the author of the following lines very seldom
attempts poetical writing, imperfections will be
more excusable.

" With gen'rous candour read these artless
lays, [praise."
And kindly pardon, though you cannot

To the MEMORY of WILLIAM HOL-
BROOK, Milton.

AS the fair morning of the op'ning
spring,
When roses bloom on ev'ry fruitful spray,
Bursts from the night, and neighb'ring song-
sters sing,
Such was thy morn, sweet youth, too short
thy day.

In the first dawning of thy infant age,
Thy parents view'd thee with increasing
joy,
Active and fair, thou didst their hearts engage,
Thy sister's kindness was their sweet employ.

Thus, in their fondling arms, encircled
round,
Time gently roll'd, till ev'ry setting sun;
The night descending, joy did still abound,
Around each neck, dear little William
hung.

Caress'd, belov'd, the little youth rejoic'd;
His teacher's heart his fond affection won,
His praise resounded with an echoing
voice,
And expectation hail'd her fav'rite son.

Thus, like the morning sun, he gently rose,
And promis'd rising to meridian height,
But dire diseases quickly interpos'd,
And wav'd around the gloomy veil of
night.

E'en then, what anguish wrung the parents'
breast, [pain;
To see their fav'rite wrack'd with tort'ring

A wasting fever broke his balmy rest,
And prayers, and tears, and sighs were all
in vain.

Increasing paleness seiz'd his comely face,
And ling'ring sickness wore his strength a-
way;
Grim death receiv'd him to his cold em-
brace;
May Angels guide him to eternal day.

There dwell, sweet youth, death's power
is overpast,
His shafts no more shall pierce thy tender
breast;
In the bright world, where joys forever
last,
There reign in mansions of eternal rest.

How long, dire monster! shall thy fury
rage,
And scatter havock through the sons of
men?
O spare our children! spare the hoary
sage!
To this, let all repeat a long amen.

But ah, dread tyrant! hear this sacred
truth,
The years roll on, the time approaches
nigh;
When thou, who spar'dst not, e'en the
blooming youth,
Ev'n thou thyself, grim " death, shalt die."

Milton, Sept. 17, 1794.

For the MASSACHUSETTS MAGAZINE.

DAPHNIS and EVELINA.

WHEN midnight stretches out her
shade,
And clouds of darkness wrap the skies;
Then will I go to view the glade
Where now my much lov'd Daphnis lies.

Form'd with a mind above the pride
And glitt'ring splendor of the great,
He ventur'd not on pleasure's tide,
But sought repose in humbler state.

A lonely cottage he possess'd,
Contented there in peace to dwell;
The poor, the sickly and oppress'd
Found shelter in his humble cell.

White handed peace and rosy joy,
And virtue always smiling fair,
Bright pleasures form without alloy,
And ever blooming health was there.

But Evelina, fairest maid,
Would visit oft that humble place,
In native innocence array'd,
Her mind unspotted as her face.

Her winning form, her foft addrefs,
Kindled in Daphnis love's pure flame ;
He felt the pangs of fweet diftrefs,
And Evelina felt the fame.

How foon their pleafures end in pain,
For fate the promis'd blifs denies,
Their parents turn with four difdain,
Forbid the match, and Daphnis dies.

Around thy melancholy tomb
The fweeteft flowers of fpring fhall blow,
And cover with their purple bloom,
The facred fod that lies below.

There haplefs Evelina ftands,
Her bofom throbs with pain fevere ;
Behold ! She wrings her feeble hands,
And dews the turf with many a tear.

Oft fhall the filver ftar of eve,
While mounting in the clear blue fky,
Paufe o'er the fpot awhile to grieve,
And hide in clouds his twinkling eye.

Dear fhade, accept thefe feeble lays,
Which flow fincerely from a friend,
Who knew thy worth in early days,
And now laments thy haplefs end.

THE HERMIT.

Extracted for the MASSACHUSETTS MAG-
AZINE.

MORNING, on the SEA SHORE.

WHAT print of fairy feet is here
On Neptune's fmooth and yellow fands ?
What midnight revels airy dance,
Beneath the moon-beams' trembling
glance,
Has bleft thefe fhores ?—What fprightly
bands
Have chas'd the waves uncheck'd by
fear ?

Whoe'er they were they fled from morn,
For now all filent and forlorn
Thefe tide-forfaken fands appear—
Return, fweet fprites ! the fcene to cheer !
In vain the call !—till moonlight's hour
Again diffufe its fofter pow'r,
Titania, nor her fairy loves,
Emerge from India's fpicy groves.

Then, when the fhad'wy hour returns,
When filence reigns o'er air and earth,
And ev'ry ftar in ether burns,
They come to celebrate their mirth ;

In frolic ringlet trip the ground,
Bid mufic's voice on filence win,
Till magic echoes anfwer round—
Thus do their feftive rites begin.

O fairy forms ! fo coy to mortal ken,
Your myftic fteps to poets only fhewn,
O ! lead me to the brook, or hallow'd glen,
Retiring far, with winding woods o'er-
grown !

Where'er ye beft delight to rule ;
If in fome foreft's lone retreat,
Thither conduct my willing feet
To the light brink of fountain cool,
Where, fleeping in the midnight dew,
Lie fpring's young buds of ev'ry hue,
Yielding their fweet breath to the air ;
To fold their filken leaves from harm,
And their chilheads in moonfhine warm,
To bright Titania's tender care.

There, to the night-bird's plaintive chaunt
Your carols fweet ye love to raife,
With oaten reed and paft'ral lays ;
And guard with forceful fpell her haunt,
Who, when your antic fports are done,
Oft lulls ye in the lily's cell.
Sweet flow'r ! that fuits your flumbers well,
And fhields you from the rifing fun.

When not to India's fteeps ye fly
After twilight and the moon,
In honey'd buds ye love to lie,
While reigns fupreme light's fervid noon ;
Nor quit the cell where peace pervades
Till night leads on the dews and fhades.

E'en now your fcenes enchanted meet my
fight !
I fee the earth unclofe, the palace rife,
The high dome fwell, and long arcades of
light
Glitter among the deep embow'ring
woods,
And glance reflected from the trembling
floods !

While to foft lutes the portals wide unfold,
And fairy forms, of fine etherial dyes,
Advance with frolic fteps and laughing
eyes,
Their hair with pearl, their garments
deck'd with gold ;
Pearls that in Neptune's briny waves they
fought,
And gold from India's deepeft caverns
brought.

Thus your light vifions to my eyes unveil,
Ye fportive pleafures, fweet illufions, hail !
But ah ! at morn's firft blufh again ye
fade !
So from youth's ardent gaze life's land-
fcape gay,
And forms in fancy's fummer hues ar-
ray'd,
Diffolve at once in air at truth's refplen-
dent day !

T†

To DELIA, on her approaching
NUPTIALS.

HAIL, happy nymph! indulgent heav'n,
  To thee, her richeft gifts has giv'n,
    And fortune has in ftore,
Her greateft dainties ftill for thee,
Love, friendfhip, joy, and harmony,
    Await the approaching hour.

To thee belongs enchanting blifs,
The panting breaft, the balmy kifs,
    The bright and fparkling eye,
The lips that quiver as they fpeak,
The ruddy rofe-enamell'd cheek,
    That emulates the fky.

Bleft is thy Damon! happy he!
A happier fwain can never be
    Enclos'd in Hymen's band,
Nor could the niceft wifh infpire,
The gentle youth once to defire,
    A fairer lady's hand.

The arch coquet may fickle be,
The rake may fwear he will be free,
    By all the powers above,
Not fo with Damon's gen'rous foul,
He feels with rapture thy control,
    And fondly cries, " 'Tis love."

Hail, happy Delia! lovely fair,
Bleft nymph! the gods' peculiar care,
    And happy Damon's choice;
Th' impartial world muft all agree,
In yielding praife to love and thee,
    With one accord and voice.

Grateful, let Damon thank the care
Of Cupid, who did firft prepare
    Thy breaft for Love's alarms,
Soft'n'd by him, thou firft gav'ft ear,
His tender moving tale to hear,
    And melted in his arms.

Phœbus, hafte down the northern fkies,
Dart through the night, and quickly rife,
    'To bring th' aufpicious morn;
When the fond couple, fide by fide,
The happy bridegroom, lovely bride,
    The nuptial rites adorn;

Then fhall the neighb'ring nymphs and
    fwains,
Join in epithalamium ftrains,
    To give the fair one joy:
And may the fwain forever prove,
Conftant in friendfhip, true in love,
    In love that ne'er can cloy.

May pleafure crown each circling year,
And ev'ry day an hour appear,
    An hour unknown to ftrife;
And may the products of your joys,
Be pretty girls, and handfome boys,
    To blefs the loving wife.
Sept. 21. Q.

VERSES
Addreffed to a gentleman on feeing at his houfe a
very excellent print of the head of a Human
Skeleton.

  —Omnes una-manet nox,
  Et calcanda femel via lethi.   HOR.

WHILST you, my friend, to whom
      the power is given
To practife ev'ry virtue under heaven;
With eye ferene the ghaftly form behold,
Which oft in fcenes of death hath fhook
    the bold;
And yet much oft'ner pafs'd unheeded by,
Or elfe, perhaps, juft claims a tranfient
    figh:
To me 'tis given, not in profe to rail,
But vice to fcourge in moralifing tale.

  My lady, and Sir John, a happy pair,
As ever breath'd in gay St. James's air,
One fummer feafon left the vacant town,
And to their country manfion rambled
    down;
Not that to them the country charms
    could yield,
The gloomy foreft, or the verdant field;
But all they wanted was to change the
    fcene,
For learned doctors faid, it cas'd the
    fpleen;
One fober ev'ning, having nought to do,
Call'd on the vicar, with a " How do
    you do,"
The vicar kept them, 'till the clock ftruck
    nine,
And then difmifs'd them with a glafs of
    wine:
The glimmering twilight juft fupply'd the
    day
As through the church yard drear they
    took their way;
It chanc'd the fexton, whiftling o'er his
    fpade,
Juft in the path a human fkull had laid;
My lady ftarted, and Sir John took fire,
On his pale checks was feen vindictive
    ire;
He curs'd the fellow as he pafs'd along,
Who only anfwer'd with a ruftic fong;
Then to his trembling lady thus began
To eafe her fears, and prove himfelf a
    man;
" You know, my dear, I never fear'd to
    die,
Once at Almack's I gave a lord the lie;
My lord was prudent, and the affront
    forgave,
And from that hour, the world pro-
    nounc'd me brave."

To

To this, my lady, in soft sounds reply'd,
" In men their courage is their greatest
    pride ;
As for myself, I must confess my fear,
Death strikes at distance, but is dreadful
    near ;
Oh, awful thought ! we must resign our
    breath !
But if I think, I shall be hipp'd to death ;
Suppose, my love, we call on dear Spadile,
And see and make a party at quadrille :"—
This noble resolution pleas'd the knight,
And so in cards and mirth they spent the
    night.

From hence, my friend, these truths at
    least are plain,
That heaven forewarns, and wisdom calls
    in vain :
Trifles, and toys, each little mind employ,
The laugh of folly, and the dance of joy ;
But soon the laugh, and soon the dance is
    o'er,
And then this world knows the gay croud
    no more !   T. C.

For the MASSACHUSETTS MAGAZINE.

SUNRISE: A SONNET.

OFT let me wander, at the break of
    day,
Thro' the cool vale o'erhung with wav-
    ing woods ;
Drink the rich fragrance of the budding
    May,
  And catch the murmur of the distant
    floods ;
Or rest on the fresh bank of limpid rill,
  Where sleeps the vi'let in the dewy
    shade,
Where op'ning lilies balmy sweets distil,
  And the wild musk-rose weeps along
    the glade :
Or climb the eastern cliff, whose airy head
  Hangs rudely o'er the blue and misty
    main ;
Watch the fine hues of morn thro' ether
    spread,
  And paint with roseate glow the chrys-
    tal plain.
Oh ! who can speak the rapture of the
    soul,
  When o'er the waves the sun first steals
    to sight,
And all the world of waters, as they roll,
  And heaven's vast vault unveils in liv-
    ing light !
So life's young hour to man enchanting
    smiles,
  With sparkling health, and joy, and fan-
    cy's fairy wiles !

For the MASSACHUSETTS MAGAZINE.
SONNET.

HOW sweet is love's first gentle sway,
   When crown'd with flow'rs he softly
    smiles !
His blue eyes fraught with tearful wiles,
Where beams of tender transport play :
Hope leads him on his airy way,
   And faith and fancy still beguiles—
   Faith quickly tangled in her toils—
Fancy, whose magic forms so gay.
The fair deceiver's self deceive—
   How sweet is love's first gentle sway ;
Ne'er would that heart he bids to grieve,
   From sorrow's soft enchantments stray—
Ne'er—till the god, exulting in his art,
Relentless frowns, and wings th' enven-
    om'd dart !

A THOUGHT on WAKING.

SLEEP by night, and cares by day
   Wear my fleeting life away.
Lo ! in yonder eastern skies
Sol appears, and bids me rise :
Tells me life is on the wing,
And has no returning spring :
Death comes on with steady pace,
And life's the only day of grace.
Shining preacher ! shining morning !
Let me take th' important warning.
Rouze then all my active pow'rs,
Well improve the coming hours ;
Let no trifles kill the day,
(Trifles oft our heart betray)
Virtue, science, knowledge, truth,
Guide the inquiries of my youth.
Wisdom, and experience sage
Then shall sooth the cares of age.
They with time shall never die ;
They will lead to joys on high ;
They the path of life display,
Shining with celestial day.
Blissful path, with safety trod,
That leads the virtuous soul to God.

EPITAPH on GEN. WOLFE.

*On the death of General Wolfe, a premium be-
ing offered for the best written epitaph on that
brave Officer, a number of poets of all descriptions started as candidates. Amongst the rest,
there was a poem sent to the Editor of the
Public Ledger, from which the following curious stanza is selected :*

" HE marched without dread or fears
   " At the head of his bold grenadiers ;
" And what was more miraculous—nay,
   very particular,
" He climbed up rocks that were perpen-
    dicular."

MONTHLY

MONTHLY GAZETTE.

Summary of Foreign Intelligence.

ITALY.

Turin, June 7.

ON the 4th inst. the Chevalier de St. Amour was shot; he was a Savoyard by birth, and commandant of the almost impregnable fortress of Saorgio. He was accused and convicted of treachery for abandoning the above fortress in a scandalous manner, against the advice of the imperial officers, instead of defending it according to the orders he received.

MILAN.

We have accounts that the execution of the conspirators at Turin, has commenced, for which purpose two foreign executioners had been hired. The king and royal family are gone to Montcallier, to be out of the way during the affecting scene.

GERMANY.

Frankfort, June 14.

Near 6000 French prisoners have passed through here, within a few days past, mostly good looking men and national guards. They go to Gunsburg, and from thence by water to Hungary. By the express command of the Emperor no volunteer officers are to be admitted into the army of the empire. Numbers of oxen, horses, &c. are still sent from the Austrian States into France, by way of Switzerland. The French army between Basel and Landau does not exceed 40000 men.

Berlin, June 21.

A messenger arrived here yesterday morning from the head quarters of the king, with the agreeable account that Cracow surrendered to his Majesty's forces under Major General Van Elsner, on Sunday the 15th of this month.

Altena, July 3.

Letters from Holland of the 28th June, say, that Clairfait, on the 24th, was defeated not far from Bruges. Bruges was taken by the French the 25th, and Ghent the 26th; the garrison of those places, having evacuated them on the approach of the French. Nineteen Hanoverians that were taken in the battle of the 24th, were shot, agreeable to the decree of the Convention. The French took Charleroi on the 24th, and the garrison were made prisoners of war.

Prince Cobourg has given orders to evacuate Valenciennes, Conde, Quesnoy and Landrecies. The body of Emigrants that were in Ypres, by means of a disguise in women's or peasant's clothes, chiefly escaped before the surrender of the place. Brussels and Ostend were said to have fallen into the hands of the French.

POLAND.

Warsaw, June 11.

We yesterday received the news of the action which took place on the 7th inst. at some distance from Malagofzee, between General Kosciusko and the combined Russian and Prussian troops. General Kosciusko's account runs thus. "That notwithstanding the enemy's superiority in regular troops, by the junction of the Prussians and their heavy artillery, the Polish commander was on the point of obtaining a complete victory. The enemy had already begun to give way, after having lost five cannon, when a ball took off the Polish General Grochowski. This occasioned some disorder, which was encreased by a general report prevailing throughout the army, that it was General Kosciusko, who was killed; and that General to undeceive his troops exposed himself to the greatest danger. The enemy, in the interim, failed not to profit by this accident, and rallied. General Kosciusko perceiving that one of his battalions of infantry was unable to resist the shock of the enemy's cavalry, and that on the other hand the corps of pikemen did not seem inclined to do their duty, would not risk a decisive action. He retired to Malagofzee, carrying with him his dead and wounded, but left two cannon in the hands of the enemy. The loss of the Poles is about 600 men; that of the enemy must be far more considerable. Some accounts state the loss of the Prussians at 500 killed and wounded, and that of the Russians at 400.

June

JUNE 21.

Kofciufko, notwithftanding his defeat, fpeaks in a very high tone. In a circular letter which the fupreme council have iffued on the 21ft, by his orders, it is faid that the Poles will proceed now no longer on the defenfive, but mean to act offenfively, and Kofciufko promifes therein liberty to all the Pruffian and Ruffian prifoners, provided the infurgents can penetrate into thefe provinces, and provided likewife that thefe foreign provinces are fond of Polonian liberty.

The Polifh General Jafinfki has iffued a proclamation to the people of Lithuania, which contains the following fentiment.

Citizens,

" The earth on which we live cannot be taken from us by the enemy—They may burn your thatched dwellings, and rob you of your goods ; but foon will the booty you will get from the enemy enable you to build more comfortable houfes, and you may live more happily when the land is freed by your valour. Then, citizens, let us attack the enemy in their own country, and treat them as they have treated us ; fhowing, however, mercy to thofe who have not injured you ; revenging your wrongs on thofe who have fought your ruin by the moft unwarrantable exceffes. Let us be confident in our ftrength; but that ftrength muft be exerted, and our country calls upon us for a defperate effort.

IRELAND.
DUBLIN.

The Emprefs of Ruffia has abfolutely demanded 24000 auxiliaries from the Emperor, according to treaty. Ruffia being attacked by the Poles.

BRITISH ARMY.
LONDON, July 24-25.

In our prefent pofition, (at Kontigh) there is fuch a fcarcity of water that all the men in the army, who have been accuftomed to fink wells, or to any fimilar employment, are immediately to fet about the digging of fome, that the troops may be fupplied with water.

Yefterday we were informed that the enemy had taken Louvain ; and we have alfo learnt that for thefe two days paft they have been bombarding Eclufe and Saf-de-Gand. Should they gain poffeffion of thefe, they will immediately pafs into Dutch Flanders In fhort, every operation of the enemy fhews that they are determined to lofe no time in completing the conqueft of this country.

We hear a heavy firing on the fide of Malines, commonly called Mechlin, the enemy, as we are informed, having attacked that place. The Earl of Moira, with a great part of his army, has marched to its relief.

The force which the enemy carried againft Malines, amounted to between 6 and 7000 men and 5 pieces of cannon, with which they kept up a brifk fire on the town, for fome time. They however began to retreat before Lord Moira's army could reach the place. On this occafion, a Capt. of O'Donnel's corps was killed. One fubaltern, with about thirty men, were killed or wounded ; and feven houfes were damaged by the fhot of the enemy. At the commencement of the attack, the garrifon, with that precipitation and terror, which have but too confpicuoufly marked the conduct of fome of our allies on different former occafions, fet fire to the bridge acrofs the canal immediately in front of Malines, although it turned on a pivot, and could be withdrawn in an inftant, by which they have deprived themfelves of the only means they had either to purfue the enemy or reconnoitre their fituation. The French may now approach the town in the fmalleft parties with impunity, as they know that the garrifon has no mode of croffing the canal to moleft them, either in their approach or retreat.

The prefent pofition of the Duke of York and the Earl of Moira's armies, though a pofition neceffary to be occupied by fome troops, is the moft unfavourable that can be conceived for Britifh to act in, the country being fo completely interfected by woods and hedges, that ground can hardly be found to encamp or draw a fingle battalion upon. Our formidable cavalry would be entirely ufelefs where we now are ; and even the bravery and difcipline of our infantry would avail them little, where every paltroon, who can fire from behind a tree or a hedge, becomes the equal of an intrepid foldier. The weather has been hot in the extreme, for fome days paft, from which circumftance, and the fcarcity of water, the troops have fuffered exceedingly.

JULY 14.

We are beginning to fend off our heavy baggage ; and all our fick at Antwerp, about 1200 men, are embarking on board transports

transports to be conveyed to Flushing, which induces us to believe that we shall shortly sail back from this into Holland. Indeed, as this country is now completely lost to the allies, the sooner we quit it the better ; for any action in our present situation, however successful we might be, could not be productive of any one benefit to the allies.

The Earl of Moira's army are still without tents ; but though they are hutted very indifferently, there is not a single murmur among the troops, who every day witness their commander, whom they venerate, almost to admiration, subjecting himself to the same hardships with themselves ; sleeping on his cloak on sandhills, or in a wretched hut of straw, and not better accommodated than the lowest soldier in his army.

The enemy having succeeded in their attempt to cross the canal, have taken Malinet, and are now advancing two miles on this side of it, close to the bridge of Waelhem, within four miles of our camp. Lord Moira's army is at this moment drawn up on the banks of the river, to oppose any attempts of the enemy to cross it ; and the bridge is covered with combustibles ready to set fire to, the moment the enemy shall approach. We do not, however, expect that the enemy will attempt any thing farther to night ; but to-morrow it is probable they will ; from dispositions however, which are now making, we have reason to believe that, by that time we shall have retreated to Antwerp.

A general impress has taken place on the river, by which, all the ships were stripped of their hands. A number of seamen, by this mean, are procured for the men of war, under orders for immediate service.

The French and Prussians had a smart skirmish on the Golgenberg on the 15th. The Leyden Gazette observes, that the efforts which it costs to resist the advances of the enemy in Flanders, are not to be regarded with surprise, as it was determined in the committee of Public Safety, in the month of May last, and shortly after the capture of Landrecy, to augment the force of the army of the north, joined to that of the Ardennes to 300,000 effective men.

The French cartridges used in the late engagements with Lord Howe, were in general made of writings of estates, and genealogies of French families.

DOMESTIC OCCURRENCES.

PITTSBURG INSURGENTS.
VIRGINIA.

BY late accounts from the westward, we are told, that the rioters of Pennsylvania, do not confine their operations to their own State : They have visited Morgan town, and ordered the collector there residing, to resign his office and papers, or they would come and destroy them with all his property. They also sent him a letter with a fictitious signature, informing him, that on such a night they would pay him a visit ; on such repeated threats, the collector, with the advice of his friends, judged it prudent to decamp ; which he did, bringing with him his records, &c. Agreeable to their notice, a number visited his house the night preceding that appointed ; but luckily were disappointed of their intended object.

We are happy to hear, that a very few only of the Virginians approve these rebellious proceedings of their neighbours ; and it is to be hoped their prudence will continue to guard them from associating in measures that must terminate in the punishment of those persons who are guilty of such illegal conduct.

By the report of the commissioners, who were sent by the executive of Pennsylvania, to negociate an accommodation with the Pittsburg insurgents, dated August 22 ; it appears they had then some prospect of restoring order, without the effusion of blood. They had proposed conditions to he committee appointed to confer with them, on the acceptance of which, they, conformably to power vested in them, promised an act of free and general pardon and oblivion for all that had taken place ; and they conclude their report by saying, " Just now we have received an answer in writing to our propositions which does not come up quite to our wishes ; but we expect, from what has been said, that we shall be able to accommodate the business with them." It must be observed however, that proceedings since bear a quite contrary appearance,

MISCELLANEOUS

MISCELLANEOUS PARAGRAPHS.

It is underftood that the fiege of Sluys, in Dutch Flanders, has recommenced with redoubled vigour ; and that the place is as vigorouſly defended. It is completely inundated on the fide on which the attack is made.

Liege is almoft wholly deferted. All the nobles and clergy have fled towards Germany, and the religious have quitted their convents. More than four hundred boats loaded with valuable property in the town, had dropped down the Meufe, and the utmoft confternation prevailed.

A letter from Amfterdam has this paffage in it, " So great is the apprehenfion of an infurrection in this city, that a body of 600 Huffars have been fent for, and more are expected.

The peace the Dutch have concluded with the Dey of Algiers, on the 27th of March laft, was bought by the former, at the price of 150,000l. befides a fubfidy which is to be paid annually of the fum of 10,000 ducats.

WAYNE's ARMY.

By a gentleman from Fort Stanwix, we learn, that news has been received there from the Miamis, ftating that General Wayne, with the American army, had begun his march into the Indian country ; that he had defeated the Indians in a battle near the rapids of the Miamis, and on his arrival at the fort erected by Governor Simcoe, at the foot of the rapids, he fent peremptory orders to the Britifh garrifon to evacuate the place in 15 minutes, and in cafe of their compliance, they would be permitted to return to Detroit or Niagara in peace, but that if they hefitated, he would immediately ftorm the fort. The Britifh not thinking it prudent to difpute the matter with the hero of Stony Point, marched off within the time limited.

In New-Jerfey, Pennfylvania, Maryland and Virginia, every thing has the appearance of military buftle and active preparation. The commiffioners of peace have returned to give place to the commiffioners of war. All the troops required from New Jerfey, Maryland and Virginia, are on the march, and Governor Mifflin has taken the field in perfon, as commander of the Pennfylvania volunteers.

The Prefident of the United States has augmented the troops deftined to act againft the Pittfburg white boys to 15000 men ; the addition will be compofed of Virginia riflemen.

ACCIDENT.

The following melancholy accident happened on Thurfday laft. As Mr. Benjamin Peters, with his grandfon, Henry Peters, and Nero Paine, a black man, were in a boat, a little below Beverly bar, a fudden guft of wind overfet it, and the unfortunate perfons above mentioned were all drowned. Search was immediately made for the bodies. The two former were found the next day on Weft Beach, Beverly fide ; the latter has not yet been found.

MARRIAGES.

MASSACHUSETTS.—*Bofton*, Maj. Ebenezer Kent, of Watertown, to Mifs Charlotte Vinall, of this town ; Mr. Jofeph Howe to Mifs Patty Gridley ; Mr. Edwin Locke to Mifs Matilda Traſk.

Dorchefter, Mr. John Mears, of Roxbury, to Mifs Sarah Robinfon.

Marblehead, Mr. Jofeph Chapman to Mifs Sufannah Lee ; Mr. Sylvanus Gray to Mifs Charlotte Gallifon ; Edward Fettiplace, Efq. to Mrs. Sarah Bowden.

Newburyport, Mr. Jofeph Brown to Mifs Sally Newell ; Mr. Silas Francis to Mifs Nancy Steele.

Portfmouth, Mr. George Froft to Mifs Sally Boles ; Mr. John Sawyer to Mifs Sally Stagpole ; Mr. John Daniels to Mifs Hannah Tuttle.

Springfield, Mr. Thomas Dickman, of Greenfield, printer, to Mifs Nancy Church.

DEATHS.

MASSACHUSETTS. *Bofton*, Mrs. Lucy Tilefton, 35 ; Mrs. Martha Thwing, 86 ; Mrs. Charlotte Gleafon, 27 ; Mrs. Sufannah Faxon, 43 ; Mrs. Rebecca Bodge, 57 ; Mifs Hannah French, 21 ; Mr. William Cunningham, 47 ; Capt. John White, 54 ; Mr. Jofeph Hovey ; Mr. William Hinkling, 29 ; Mrs. Ann Barbara Bender, 48 ; Mr. Thomas Greene, 79 ; Mrs. Hannah Moore, 39.

Charlton, Mr. Ebenezer Twifs, 85.

Concord, Lois Whitney, 25.

Columbia, S. C. James Green Hunt, Efq.

Blooming Vale, Mofes Dewitt, Efq.

Haverhill, Mr. John Goodridge, 55 ; Mrs. Sufannah Remick, 58.

Keene, Mifs Betfey Blake.

Long Ifland, Dr. John B. Ricker, 57.

Newbury, Mrs. Mary Johnfton, 32 ; Mrs. Elizabeth Jenkins ; Capt. Michael Bifhop, 49 ; Mrs. Lucy Fletcher, 39.

Portfmouth, Mr. Stephen Sumner.

Wilmington, Mr. James Broom, 81.

THE

MASSACHUSETTS MAGAZINE :

OR,

MONTHLY MUSEUM

OF

KNOWLEDGE and RATIONAL ENTERTAINMENT.

No. X.]   FOR OCTOBER, 1794.   [Vol. VI.

CONTAINING,

WITH A HANDSOME ENGRAVING.

PRINTED AT *BOSTON*, FOR THE PROPRIETORS,
BY EZRA W. WELD AND WILLIAM GREENOUGH,
NO. 42, CORNHILL.
Sold at JOHN WEST's Bookftore, No. 75, *Cornhill*, BOSTON ; and by the feveral
GENTLEMEN who receive Subfcriptions for this WORK.

MDCCXCIV.

ACKNOWLEDGMENTS to CORRESPONDENTS.

Alkmas is adviſed to ſuſpend the attempt to write for the entertainment of the public till his junior year.

Proteus's communications are under conſideration, future attention will be paid them.

Our Charleſtown correſpondent is informed, that the numbers of the Speculator have been omitted by neceſſity ; our copy was miſlaid; we ſhall continue their publication.

Lines to Olivia, too incorrect and unfiniſhed for publication.

The Charade—is deficient in ſenſe as well as verſification.

We ſolicit the favour of an ode on the cloſe of the year from ſome of our poetic correſpondents.

Crates's ſyſtem of Education is under conſideration. If he ſhould think proper to continue his obſervations, we beg leave to recommend a different mode of conveyance ; as communications for the magazine ought never to be taxed with heavy poſtage.

The *General Obſerver*, the *Memorialiſt*, and ſeveral other pieces, came too late for inſertion in the preſent number—It is requeſted, that all compoſition intended for the Magazine, may be ſent early in the month.

PRICES of PUBLIC SECURITIES, BANK STOCK, &c.

October.	Six per Cents.	Three per Cents.	Defer'd Stock.	Maſſachuſ. State Notes.	U.S.B. Shares. ab. par.	Maſſachuſ. Bank Shares.	Union Bank Shares. ab. pr.	Final & L. Of. Cert. inter. fr. Jan. 1788.	Reg. Dt. with int. fr. March 4, 1789.	Indents. Int. on Loan Offi.	Cer.&Reg.Dt. New Emiſſion Money.	O. Emiſ. Mro
	s. d.	s. d.	s. d.	s. d.	per ct.	dols.	per ct.	s. d.	s. d.	(s. d.	s. d.	s.
1	19 2	11 1	12 6	15 4	25	None	8	18 0	17	10 0	8 0	45
2	19 2	11 1	12 6	15 4	25	at	8	18 0	17	10 0	8 0	45
3	19 3	11 2	12 8	15 4	25	mkt.	8	18 0	17	10 0	8 0	45
4	19.3	11 2	12 8	15 4	25		8	18 0	17	10 0	8 0	45
6	19 3	11 2	12 8	15 6	25		8	18 0	17	10 0	8 0	45
7	19 3	11 2	12 8	15 6	25		8	18 0	17	10 0	8 0	45
8	19 3	11 2	12 8	15 6	25		8	18 0	17	10 0	8 0	45
9	19 3	11 2	12 8	15 6	25		8	18 0	17	10 0	8 0	45
10	19 3	11 2	12 8	15 6	25		8	18 0	17	10 0	8 0	45
11	19 3	11 2	12 8	15 6	25		8	18 0	17	10 0	8 0	45
13	19 3	11 2	12 8	15 6	25		8	18 0	17	10 0	8 0	45
14	19 3	11 2	12 8	15 6	26		8	18 0	17	10 0	8 0	45
15	19 3	11 2	12 8	15 6	26		8	16 0	17	10 0	8 0	45
16	19 4	11 2	12 8	15 6	26		8	18 0	17	10 0	8 0	45
17	19 4	11 2	12 8	15 6	26		8	18 0	17	10 0	8 0	45
18	19 4	11 2	12 8	15 6	26		8	18 0	17	10 0	8 0	45
20	19 4	11 2	12 8	15 6	26		8	18 0	17	10 0	8 0	45
21	19 4	11 2	12 8	15 6	26		8	18 0	17	10 0	8 0	45
22	19 4	11 2	12 8	15 6	26		8	18 0	17	10 0	8 0	45
23	19 4	11 2	12 8	15 6	26		8	18 0	17	10 0	8 0	45
24	19 4	11 3	12 8	15 6	26		8	18 0	17	10 0	8 0	45
25	19 4	11 3	12 8	15 6	26		8	18 0	17	10 0	8 0	45
27	19 4	11 3	12 8	15 6	26		8	18 0	17	10 0	8 0	45
28	19 4	11 3	12 8	15 6	26		8	18 0	17	10.0	8 0	45
29	19 4	11 3	12 8	15 6	26		8	18 0	17	10 0	8 0	45
30	19 4	11 3	12 8	15 6	26		8	18 0	17	10 0	8 0	45
31	19 4	11 3	12 8	15 6	26		8	18 0	17	10 0	8 0	45

JOHN MARSTON, *Stock Broker.*

ACKN
Alkmas is ad·
lic till his innie

sta. Mag. 1794.

One of the dasels ils full size & shape.

The great Tetraodon Mola, *or* Sun Fish.

THE
MASSACHUSETTS MAGAZINE.
FOR *OCTOBER*, 1794.

For the MASSACHUSETTS MAGAZINE.

DESCRIPTION of the MOLA TETRAODON, or OBLONG SUNFISH.

(Accompanied with an ENGRAVING.)

THIS rare and fingular fifh was left by the tide on Dorchefter flats on the beginning of laft Auguft, and was brought afhore and exhibited to the examination of the curious. It refembled in form a bream or fome deep fifh cut off in the middle. Its length was four feet nine inches, its width two feet, and its thicknefs through the middle about one foot and a half. Its weight was fuppofed to be between three and four hundred pounds.

The mouth was very fmall; meafuring only three inches over. Each jaw contained two broad teeth with fharp edges.

The eyes were placed about nine inches diftant from the tip of the fnout. Before each of thefe was a fmall femilunar aperture, two inches round; within which were the gills. There were feveral other orifices in the head, the ufe of which has never been afcertained by any naturalift, though Willoughby fuppofes that two of them correfpond to the organs of hearing in other animals.[*]

The pectoral fins were placed immediately behind the eyes. They were fmall and of a roundifh fhape. Each meafured feven inches in length, and the fame in width at the infertion.

The dorfal and anal fins were placed high, and at the very extremity of the body. Each meafured two feet in length, and one in width at the infertion. The tail fin was irregularly femicircular, and filled up the whole abrupt fpace between them.

On each fide of the fifh, near the extremity, by the bottom of the larger fins, were about thirty fmall taffels. Thefe were formed of a ftrong ligament, of the fize of a large pack thread; about three inches in length, and were furnifhed with

[*] Icthylogia, p. 151.

with a tuft, or a thick pencil of hairs at the end.

The colour of the back was dufky, and dappled ; the belly filvery. The fifh was not coated with fcales, but covered with a thick and hard fkin, and rough as fagri.

I had not an opportunity of examining any of the inteftines but the liver, which was large and heavy, and would probably have yielded a confiderable quantity of oil. It was of a bright yellow colour.

The meat of the fifh was of the moft delicate whitenefs ; but rather rank and unfavoury. Writers on natural hiftory fay, that, when boiled it has been obferved to turn into a glutinous jelly, refembling ftarch after it is cold, and ferved the purpofes of glue on being tried on paper and leather. The fifh I am defcribing was preferved fo long for fhew that it was unfit for this experiment.

They are faid to feed on fhell fifh.

This fifh is called by Ray and others, the *Sun fifh*, as being round and emitting a kind of fplendor in a dark room ; by others, with Rondolet, the *Moon fifh*, becaufe not only round and fhining by night, but from having the fhape of the crefcent betwixt the pectoral fin and eye.

" But what is moft remarkable in this creature, fays Mr. Borlace,* is that fo large a fifh fhould have fuch little fins, and thofe moftly on its hinder parts. This is one confpicuous inftance how artfully nature adapts the inftruments of motion to the form of the body which is to be moved. It is fo long, fo thin, and flexile, that a large fin in the former part would hinder its fwiftnefs ; being itfelf but one thicker fin ; it wafts itfelf forward in a great meafure by the mere bending of its back from fide to fide, whilft its wedge-like form and fharp-pointed head eafily cut their way. But the chief momentum is from behind, where the tail fin is fixed like a rudder and an oar too, reaching from top to bottom, to keep the whole body on its edge more fteadily, as well as further and guide its progrefs. At each end of this fingular appendix is a fin, the upper one raifing itfelf above the body, and the under one tending below, it both by their fpread increafing the force of thefe parts, co-operating with the wavy flexures of the body, and accelerating its progrefs, in the fame manner as an oar working at the ftern of a boat drives forward and directs the whole machine."

Dorchefter, Octo. 1794.

* Nat. Hift. of Cornwall, p. 267.

The PILGRIM's STORY.

[From Mrs. ROBINSON's *Vanienza.*]

" MY eyes firft opened to the viciffitudes of life, in the city of Avignon. My father was a general in the French fervice ; and my mother the only offspring of her noble, but indigent parents. They were united by difinterefted affection, and as their happinefs centered in each other, they were above the envy or malice of mankind. My father's fortune, though not competent to procure the luxuries of the world, was, by my mother's economy and exemplary prudence, fufficient for the enjoyment of every comfort.

" I was

" I was the only fruit of their un-sullied attachment. My amiable mother survived but a few minutes after she gave me being. She embraced me, and clasping me to her bosom, resigned her gentle soul to endless happiness : But, alas ! her helpless offspring was reserved to struggle through a wilderness of woe, the destined victim of relent-less sorrow.

" My father, whose profession called him from Avignon when I was scarcely three years old, committed the care of my education to the Abbe de Versac, a distant relation of my mother. He was a man celebrated for his profound erudition and brilliant talents : He instructed my young mind in all the elegant acquirements of a scholar and a gentleman. The labours of his anxious hours were repaid by my close application to the precepts he wished to inculcate.

" My learned and enlightened tutor, was a cynic in manner, though a philanthropist in principle ; his soul was replete with all the sublime sensations of pity and generosity ; he considered flattery as a baleful weed, upon which fools thrive and wise men sicken. He laughed at the wretched arrogance, too often the associate of wealth, and considered the man, born to an exalted rank in life, as one, afflicted with an incurable disease, that infected all who approached him with the poison of duplicity.

" What," has he often said, " can be a more miserable situation, than that of a man who at the first dawn of reason, finds himself surrounded by slaves, subservient to his caprices, commending his follies, concealing his imperfections, and impregnating his docile mind with the absurd idea, that because he is highly born he is virtuously

supreme ! The poor and unprotected mechanic, toils on, from youth to age, with industry and humility for his only associates ; he dreads a deviation from the paths of rectitude, because he knows he has no title, but his good name ; he is taught to examine his own heart, and correct its errors ; because he moves in a sphere, where truth is not hoodwinked by interest, or fulsome applause extorted from the trembling tongue of fear : He has no ermined robe to guard him from the blasts of reproach ; no dazzling mask to hide him from the prying eye of justice ; he cannot, like the possessor of worldly power, laugh at the pointing finger of scorn, and trample on the vassal, whom nature formed his equal! " Know," said he " my little pupil, you are born the proudest work of your Creator ! He has given you faculties to support the dignity of your birthright, and intrepidity of soul, to stem the overwhelming torrents of insolent oppression. Look to yourself for superiority, and from every example of fallen depravity, extract a lesson of morality. Flatter not the weaknesses of the base and degraded, neither meanly withhold the tribute of applause, where the perfections of the heart demand it of you ; above all, remember you are a human being ! endowed with intellects, and placed in a garden of luxuriant blessings, that only require your hand to cultivate them for your use and pleasure."

" Such were the precepts of Abbe de Versac; my observations through a life of perplexing vicissitudes, have invariably convinced me of their truth and propriety.

" At the age of seventeen I had acquired a competent knowledge of the classics, and had already composed many successful pieces in
imitation

imitation of the Greek and Latin poets. The rocks of Vaucluse, consecrated by the inspiration of the Muses had often echoed with my matin song, and the celestial form of the immortal Laura, frequently blessed in visionary dreams the slumbers of the evening !

" I felt rapt, inspired, as I traversed the deep valley, or mused beneath the laurelled bower, dedicated to love and virtue ! I wandered on the margin of the shallow rivulets that were once dear to the faithful Petrarch ; their murmurs soothed my pensive heart ; and as I dropped a tear upon their bubbling surface, I experienced the conscious delight of having paid the tender tribute due to his memory and his sorrows ! Often did I cast my listless form upon the sod made sacred by the footsteps of the wandering lover. These were my happy moments—transient indeed they were, for they now almost appear to have been the phantoms of a bewildered fancy. The subduing hand of misery has nearly erased the very shadows of my early hours ; the bright delusions of youth's glowing day are sunk in cold oblivion, as the glorious sun sets in the border of the dark and troubled ocean !

" Filled with romantic inspiration, my mind was softened like the tempered wax, and ready to receive the tenderest impressions.

" In the vicinity of Avignon, beneath the shades of an embowering wood, devotion had long performed her sacred orison at the monastery of saint Teresa; the lofty walls were inaccessible, except on the fifteenth of June ; when, at the celebration of the Fete de Dieu, the grates were thrown open, and every eye was permitted to view the solemn ceremony of the high mass.

" Curiosity, more than zeal, led me to be a spectator : The holy sisters arranged in the chapel of the convent, sung their choral anthems, replete with seraphic harmony ; the vaulted arches repeated the thrilling sounds, while the fumes of heavenly incense curled around a thousand quivering tapers. Among the vestals, my every sense was fascinated by one, whose beauty far surpassed all I had yet conceived of mortal woman ! A sweet melancholy gave inexpressible softness to features exquisitely regular, and the meek blush of unaffected modesty heightened a complexion beauteous and glowing as the rays of morning. Her age pronounced her but newly initiated in holy duties, and her every look declared she was formed for that world from which she was secluded, in the deep and cheerless gloom of monastic apathy. I gazed upon her with a devotion more warm, more chaste, than even piety itself could have suggested. Her eye encountered mine. I fancied a thousand childish things; my earnest attention seemed to perplex her ; the crucifix fell from her trembling hand ; she rose and left the chapel.

" I returned to Avignon. The image of this pearless angel never forsook me ; I beheld her in my midnight slumbers ; her voice vibrated on my enraptured ear, and awoke me to all the agonies of despair. Often did I wander, when the sun sunk beneath the horizon, to watch its last beam that illuminated the vanes of her lonely habitation. Often did I listen whole hours beneath the hated walls that enclosed the treasure of my soul, to catch the distant and imperfect sound of the holy evening song. I fancied I could distinguish her voice from every other, and my heart

heart panted fadly refponfive to every fwelling note.

" I remained feveral months in this ftate of perfect wretchednefs, when an accident opened to my diftracted mind a gleam of tranfitory comfort. The Abbe de Verfac, difgufted with the depravity of mankind, having entered into the moft rigid ftate of holy bondage, was frequently employed in the pious office of confeffor to the Nuns of Saint Terefa. A fudden indifpofition prevented his ufual attendance, I embraced the opportunity that prefented itfelf ; and, in the habit of a monk, bore to the abbefs of the convent a letter, containing a fpecious recommendation of myfelf, deputing me as worthy of the facred confidence. I was readily admitted into the cell of ghoftly admonition, and fortune directed the heavenly Louifa to the footftool of contrition !

" The purity of her life fcarcely left her a fingle error to acknowledge ; my penance was as gentle as her foul was fpotlefs : I requefther to perufe a leffon I had written for her, and to abide by the injunctions it contained ;· fhe thanked me, then with the voice of meeknefs and humility, implored my benediction, and departed.

" My fafety required that I fhould inftantly withdraw from the facred walls, left the impofition fhould be detected, and at once deftroy my reputation and my hopes. The tranfaction was foon made public, and I frequently heard eternal vengeance denounced againft the daring perpetrator of fo vile a fraud. The abbefs offered an immenfe reward for apprehending the facrilegious hypocrite, and every tongue united to condemn me. My letter acquainted her of my name, quality, and fortune ; which, by my father's death, was not inconfiderable ; I implored her compaffion for my fufferings, and earneftly requefted her decifive anfwer. I told her, in the language of defpair, that nothing fhould induce me to furvive her refentment, and concluded my frantic prayer by informing her that I fhould watch ten fucceffive nights beneath the walls that immured her, to receive the fiat of my irrecoverable deftiny.

(To be continued.)

CONSIDERATIONS addreffed to the FAIR SEX.

WHILE I view the irrefiftible charms of the fair fex in general, their fymmetrical features, their animated countenances, the graces of their divine perfons, and the mild complacency of their manners : I yet cannot forget, amid the contemplation of thefe perfections, that the beauties of their perfons will not palliate the defects of their minds. Beauty is but of fhort duration. Virtue alone is of a permanent nature ; that teaches us moderation in profperity, fortitude in adverfity, and even excites homage from the vicious. Confcious, then, of the truth of this affertion, nothing can more excite my aftonifhment than the melancholy reflection that incredible numbers inceffantly deviate from the paths of virtue, which are the only real paths of pleafantnefs, to tread thofe of vice, which, after many perplexed windings, involve them in a labyrinth of perpetual mifery.

The

The diversified amusements which continually engage the attention of the fair, although they are of a volatile nature, may yet be tempered with discretion, and, in lieu of operating as incentives to vice, be rendered entirely innocent, and even beneficial. By a rigid adherence to rectitude, we are not to understand an exclusion of mirth. Innocent festivity gives a relish to life, and vivacity in a female is a charm universally acknowledged and felt. Let not this, however, be indulged at another's expense. Even women of sense are too frequently addicted to the pernicious vice of detraction—a vice which, if encouraged in the smallest degree, gains imperceptibly a greater influence, until it ultimately biasses the judgment. By attempting to depreciate the good qualities of another, we by no means enhance our own. The failings of an individual will excite compassion in a generous mind, and not an accumulation of bitter reproaches.

There are many sprightly girls who, corrupted by the irreligious deportment of a coquette, fall insensibly into the same error. Religion in females, far from depreciating them in the eyes of the world, will, on the contrary, endear them to every person endowed with sense and judgment. Let my fair readers try the experiment, and a little experience will shew them the truth of my remark. It is not the decorations of dress, the airs of coquetry, or the animated glance of the eye, that can secure them happiness :—these may for some time procure adulation, and flatter the vanity of the person who receives it ; but unless the mental faculties are duly cultivated, and our hopes are solidly erected on the permanent base of virtue, misery must be our portion ; and, when we come to look back on our past life, remorse and sorrow will rend our souls, while we reflect on the folly and futility of our conduct when it is to late for a compensation to be made. Therefore, let both the fair, and those who have less claim to boast of their personal charms, reflect on the folly of dissipation and vice ; and, while they remark the defects of others, be careful to amend their own.

MARRIAGE RITES in MODERN GERMANY.

THEIR women in general are of a tolerable complexion, but more corpulent than the rest of their neighbours, except the Netherlanders. They are very obsequious to their husbands, have less command in their houses than English or French woman, and are not allowed the upper end of the table. They account it rude to salute a woman with a kiss, except they have been bred in such countries where it is practised ; so that their way of greeting is by a mutual touch of the hand.

Their marriages and funerals are very expensive, so that sometimes an ordinary man is scarce able to recover the charge of his father's funeral, or of his own wedding in seven years. The entertainment frequently lasts a month, during which they keep open house, and send the bell-man about to invite all their neighbours, who usually send in wine or some other provisions.

ESSAY

ESSAY on CUNNING.

IT has been confidered by moralifts as an excellent piece of juftice in the general difpenfation of
things in this fublunary world, that
covetoufnefs, which is one of the
moft odious of all vices, carries its
own punifhment along with it. The
Romans were fo fenfible of this,
that to be wretched and covetous
were fynonymous terms in their
language; but moral writers in
general have inadvertently fet a
brand upon this vice as the only
one in the long catalogue of human
failings that in this obvious manner
punifhes and avenges the world of
itfelf; fince there is another criminal quality of the mind equally o-
dious, and equally pernicious to fociety, and which likewife carries its
own punifhment with it; this is that
fpecies of art, which we, to diftinguifh it from prudence, whofe form
it affumes, commonly call *Cunning*.
The vulgar often miftake this fhadow of wifdom for the fubftance; and
the bafe fuccefsful villain is too often faid to have raifed himfelf to
honours and riches by his wifdom
and prudence.

The event, however, ufually dif-
tinguifhes thefe as it crowns all
other actions; and the world as feldom fails to fee the fhort continuance of the benefits produced from
difhoneft Cunning, as the unfading
duration of thofe which are the rewards of honeft wifdom: The wife
and good, while they are rifing gradually to fame or honour, would
have all the praifes juftly beftowed
on them in the end, doubled in the
progrefs of their purfuits, could the
world fee every ftep by which they
rofe; while the dark fcenes of villainy, by which the cunning man
has made his way to greatnefs and
affluence, could any one of them

be fully laid open, he muft fall the
victim of the foul difcovery. Men
are but men, and great crimes cannot be perpetrated alone; the fecret
is fafe enough in the hands of the
mafter knave; but the accomplices
in black deeds, having lefs reward,
often difcover the whole; and the
fmalleft part alone being fufficient
to prove fatal to the exalted and
feemingly happy chief, his continual apprehenfions of fuch a cataftro-
phe, and his alarms on the leaft
coolnefs or diftance of his companions in iniquity, keep fufpicion conftantly awake, and plant daggers
every hour in his wretched heart.

Hiftory has given us a thoufand
inftances of this in high life, and
daily experience furnifhes a thoufand more in every rank and order
of men in fociety: Nor is the mifery
lefs even in the breaft of the moft fuccefsful of the race of cunning fharp-
ers, who efcape external punifhment, and in the world's eye, make
a happy exit after a very long life.
The fear of that which might have
happened every day, though fortunately for him it never came to pafs,
muft have kept him in continual anguifh, and length of life muft have
been to him a painful duration of
torture. How wretched muft be
that greatnefs, which it is in the
power of the meaneft dependent to
deftroy, which the poffeffor knows
he is not fecure of one day after a-
nother. How embittered the enjoyment of ample fortune amaffed by
low Cunning, which conftantly im-
plies fraud, by the fear of being o-
bliged by legal means to make reftitution of ill-gotten wealth! How
immenfe then is the difference between greatnefs acquired by honeft
wifdom, and that which is purchafed by this mean vice!

B The

The higheft and the lowest of the people have their fhare of *Cunning*, and very often are undiftinguifhed in the events of it. Sometimes both flourifh long, and fometimes blind chance performs the office of judge and executioner, and punifhes both on the fpot, in the very act of villainy. The fubtle Spaniard, who feeing great part of the wealth of Peru falling into his father's coffers, and who eager to fucceed to him in an office of fuch emolument, bribed his miftrefs to poifon him, and then ftabbed her to prevent difcovery, was fcarce feated in his place, when a popular commotion arofe, his houfe was befet, and in a few minutes he was torn to pieces.

The Egyptian annals on the contrary, prefent us a very romantic hiftory of *Cunning*, fuccefsful through a feries of events, and long miftaken even by the perfon injured, for wifdom, but the final iffue proved it to be otherwife.

RHAMPSINITUS had accumulated a greater ftore of wealth than any of the kings of Egypt, his predeceffors, and being defirous to depofit it in fome fecure place, he commanded a treafury to be built for that pnrpofe. The architect of this work placed one of the ftones fo artfully, that it might be taken out and put in again by one man, intending to fhare the riches of the place. But, about the time that the treafure was lodged in it, he was taken ill, and finding himfelf at the point of death, he fent for his two ſns, declared to them the whole artifice, and gave them the moft exact directions for the management of the bufinefs. The father died, and the fons, impatient to take advantage of the difcovery, repaired foon after to the treafury ; and having with great cafe removed the ftone, carried ●ff a great fum, and repeated the

theft every night. Rhampfinitus going to view his ftores, found a vifible diminution of his treafure, and was the more furprifed as the feal on the door was whole. The two brothers fuccefsively continued their nocturnal pilferings, till the king perfectly fenfible that his wealth decreafed very faft, ordered fnares to be fet round the veffels that contained the money. The next time the two brothers came, one of them was caught in the fnare near a veffel of filver, and finding it impoffible to get loofe, he earneftly entreated his brother to come in and cut off his head, that he might prevent a difcovery and fave his own life. The brother, reluctantly, yielding to the neceffity of the cafe, complied with his requeft, and putting the ftone in its place again, took away the head. The king went the next morning to fee if his project had produced any effect, and finding a man in the fnare without a head, he was fo aftonifhed, that he hurried out in the greateft confufion ; but as foon as he was recovered from his furprife, he ordered the body to be expofed to publick view, charging the guard to obferve the countenances of the fpectators, and to bring before him all fuch perfons as appeared to be affected at the fpectacle. The mother of the deceafed threatened her furviving fon, if he did not procure his brother's body to be interred, that fhe would inform the king who had robbed him. The young man finding it in vain to remonftrate on the impracticability of complying with her requeft, at length gratified her by the following cunning ftratagem. He loaded a number of mules with fkins of wine, and driving them to the place where the body was expofed, as foon as he reached the guards, he privately opened one of the fkins, skins, and striking his breast, when the wine began to run out, counterfeited the grief of a man utterly undone. The soldiers in the mean time strove to save the liquor for themselves, which he seeing, reviled them for the pleasure they took in his misfortunes, instead of offering him any assistance; but upon their speaking to him fair, he pretended to be pacified, and in the end offered to give them the remainder of the wine; upon this they gathered round him, and pressed him to stay and partake of it, he readily complied, and when they wanted more, opened another skin, till in the end, they became so intoxicated, that he found means to steal away the body in the dead of the night, while they were asleep, and having fastened it across one of his mules, he shaved the left cheek of each soldier, by way of derision, and then made the best of his way home.

The news of this adventure reached the palace early in the morning, and afforded fresh matter of wonder to the incensed king. Determined, if possible, to find out the cunning thief, he ordered his daughter, a beautiful princess, to submit to the embraces of every person promiscuously, in a certain apartment, but under this restriction, that she should previously require from each a confession of the most ingenious, and the most wicked actions of their lives. The young man was the first who accepted of these conditions, but resolved to perplex the king more and more: He procured the arm of a dead body quite fresh, and concealing it under his cloak, he boldly entered the apartment of the princess, and being interrogated by her, confessed, that the most wicked action he had ever committed was cutting off his brother's head in the treasury, and the most ingenious was stealing the body from the guard. The princess upon this discovery attempted to secure him, but he presented to her the dead arm, which she grasped for his, and taking to his heels, he escaped by favour of the night.

The king's rage being now converted into admiration of the boldness and ingenuity of the man, he ordered it to be proclaimed through every street, that if the person would discover himself, he should not only be pardoned but rewarded. The young man confiding in the royal word, went to the palace and presented himself to the king, who declared, he thought him superior in wisdom to any man then living, and as a reward gave him his daughter in marriage.

But mark the end! Successful Cunning, like avarice, is never satisfied: He could not stop here, but imagining that the same wicked ingenuity and audacity which had raised him thus high, would advance him one step higher, he formed a plot for murdering the generous king, in order to succeed him on the throne; a slave betrayed him, and excruciating tortures, too horrid for relation, put an end to a life, whose prosperity had not its source in virtue or true wisdom.

[Lond. Mag.

CHASTITY: A Remarkable Story.

THUANUS relates a beautiful example of chastity, and of an uncommon return to a sense of honour. In 1578, during the civil wars in the Low Countries, one of the Spanish officers would have forced

forced the daughter of an advocate of Lifle, at whofe houfe he lodged. This young perfon, in defending herfelf, feized the poniard of her ravifher, plunged it in his bofom, and inftantly fled. The Captain, perceiving his wound to be mortal, called for a confeffor, and, impreffed with the deepeft remorfe, entreated his attendants to bring this virtuous young woman to him. " I earneftly implore you," fays he, " to pardon my atrocious attempt. To make you all the reparation in my power, I now declare myfelf your hufband. Since my crime and your virtue have rendered it impoffible for me to be united to fuch excellence, receive, at leaft, with my name, the rights of my wife to all my fortune. Let thofe who fhall be informed of the violence I would have committed learn, at the fame time, that, by an honourable marriage, I have expiated my odious attempt to difhonour you, and have recompenfed the courage with which you have defended yourfelf." On finifhing thefe words, the noble Spaniard, with the confent of her father, and in prefence of his confeffor, efpoufed the virgin. He expired foon after ; leaving all in doubt which moft to admire—the magnanimity with which he had atoned for his crime, or the courage which the virtuous girl had difplayed in the defence of her honour.

GREAT FIRE in Moscow.

IN 1713, there happened a great and dreadful fire, which confumed the greateft part of the city, efpecially the wooden houfes ; the fire broke out in a maiden monaftery without the town, and a ftrong weft wind blew the fire upon the city, which fet it all on a blaze : The only method they ufe, to ftop the progrefs of a fire, is, by pulling down houfes at a diftance before it, as it is impoffible to ufe fire-engines ; the ftreets being all of timber, burn at the fame time with the houfes. On this occafion, a poor fuperftitious man feeing the fire advancing to confume his all, took a picture of St. Nicholas, and holding it between him and the fire, prayed fervently for that Saint's protection, but in vain, for the flames foon feized his houfe, for which he became fo enraged at the Saint that he threw him into the fire, faying, fince he would not fave him, he might now fave himfelf : This coming to the ears of the clergy, the poor man was fentenced to be burnt alive. All the brick buildings, fuch as churches, and other religious houfes, noblemen, and gentlemen's houfes, efcaped this conflagration, only the roofs of the latter were burnt without being otherwife damaged, for all the houfes of three or four ftories high are arched to the top, and their ftreet doors and window fhutters are of iron.

An inftance of the fuperftition of the people, and power of the clergy, happened fometime before this fire. A young man, whom the Czar had fent to Leyden for his education, having finifhed his ftudies in phyfic, returned a graduated phyfician, and at a merry meeting with his friends, they queftioned him concerning his religion : He being then in his cups, told them, he was as much of the Greek church as ever, but that he had loft all his faith in Saints' pictures, and to prove what he faid, he took one down from the wall, and threw it in the fire ; whereupon he

was

was immediately feized, and put into the hands of the clergy, who very foon fentenced him to the flames, and burnt him in a moft cruel manner ; laying the fire at fome diftance from him to keep him the longer in torment. The Czar, being informed of the cruelty of the clergy, as he had formerly abolifhed the dignity of patriarch, took this opportunity to deprive them of the power of life and death, and made a law that all the clergy fhould apply themfelves to ftudy, allowing them five years for that end ; after which they were to undergo an examination, and thofe who were found capable to perform their functions were to be promoted, the others to be difcarded. And as three fourth parts of the year were holidays in commemoration of fome Saint or other, whereby the people were for the moft part idle, he made a law that no holiday fhould be kept but in commemoration of our Saviour, the Virgin Mary, the twelve Apoftles, and St. Andrew, and St. Nicholas, the tutelar Saints of Ruffia. And as there were in the empire many thoufand convents full of lazy monks, who lived in idlenefs, he reftricted the number of thefe houfes to fifty, each houfe to contain no more than fifty monks, each monk to be above forty years of age ; the reft of them to be appropriated to hofpitals for fuch of the army and navy as were become unfit for fervice, and other indigent perfons not able to maintain themfelves ; and their revenues for their fupport : And the monks who had been bred to no handicraft, and were fit for fervice, to be employed in the army.

The OBSERVER.

[By Mr. CUMBERLAND.]

AMONGST the variety of human events, which come under the obfervation of every man of common experience in life, many inftances muft occur to his memory of the falfe opinions he had formed of good and evil fortune ! Things which we lament as the moft unhappy occurrences and the fevereft difpenfations of Providence, frequently turn out to have been vouchfafements of a contrary fort ; whilft our profperity and fuccefs, which for a time delight and dazzle us with gleams of pleafure, and vifions of ambition, turn againft us in the end of life, and fow the bed of death with thorns, that goad us in thofe awful moments, when the vanities of this world lofe their value, and the mind of man being on its laft departure, takes a melancholy review of time mifpent, and bleffings mifapplied.

Though it is part of every good man's religion to refign himfelf to God's will, yet a few reflections upon the worldly wifdom of that duty will be of ufe to every one, who falls under the immediate preffure of what is termed misfortune in life. By calling to mind the falfe eftimates we have frequently made of worldly good and evil we fhall get hope on our fide, which, though all friends elfe fhould fail us, will be a cheerful companion by the way : By a patient acquiefcence under painful events for the prefent, we fhall be fure to contract a tranquillity of temper that will ftand us in future ftead ; and by keeping a fair face to the world we fhall by degrees make an eafy heart, and find innumerable

merable refources of confolation, which a fretful fpirit never can difcover.

I wonder why I was fo uneafy under my late lofs of fortune, faid a very worthy gentleman to me the other day, feeing it was not occafioned by my own mifconduct; for the health and content I now enjoy in the humble ftation I have retired to, are the greateft bleffings of my life, and I am devoutly thankful for the event, which I deplored.—

How often do we hear young unmarried people exclaim—What an efcape have I had from fuch a man, or fuch a woman!—And yet perhaps they had not wifdom enough to fuppofe this might turn out to be the cafe at the time it happened, but complained, lamented, and reviled, as if they were fuffering perfecution from a cruel and tyrannic Being, who takes pleafure in tormenting his unoffending creatures.

An extraordinary example occurs to me of this criminal excefs of fenfibility in the perfon of a Frenchman named Chaubert, who happily lived long enough to repent of the extravagance of his mifanthropy. Chaubert was born at Bourdeaux, and died there not many years ago in the Francifcan convent; I was in that city foon after this event, and my curiofity led me to collect feveral particulars relative to this extraordinary humorift. He inherited a good fortune from his parents, and in his youth was of a benevolent difpofition, fubject however to fudden caprices and extremes of love and hatred. Various caufes are affigned for his mifanthropy, but the principal difguft, which turned him furious againft mankind, feems to have arifen from the treachery of a friend, who ran away with his miftrefs, juft when Chaubert was on the point of mar-

rying her; the ingratitude of this man was certainly of a very black nature, and the provocation heinous, for Chaubert, whofe paffions were always in extremes, had given a thoufand inftances of romantic generofity to this unworthy friend, and repofed an entire confidence in him in the matter of his miftrefs: He had even faved him from drowning one day at the imminent rifque of his life, by leaping out of his own boat into the Garonne and fwimming to the affiftance of his, when it was finking in the middle of the ftream: His paffion for his miftrefs was no lefs vehement: So that his difappointment had every aggravation poffible, and, operating upon a nature more than commonly fufceptible, reverfed every principle of humanity in the heart of Chaubert, and made him for the greateft part of his life the declared enemy of human nature.

After many years paffed in foreign parts he was accidentally brought to his better fenfes by difcovering that through thefe events, which he had fo deeply refented, he had providentially efcaped from miferies, of the moft fatal nature: Thereupon he returned to his own country, and entering into the order of Francifcans, employed the remainder of his life in atoning for his paft errors after the moft exemplary manner. On all occafions of diftrefs Father Chaubert's zeal prefented itfelf to the relief and comfort of the unfortunate, and fometimes he would enforce his admonitions of refignation by the lively picture he would draw of his own extravagancies; in extraordinary cafes he has been known to give his communicants a tranfcript or diary in his own hand-writing of certain paffages of his life, in which he had minuted his thoughts at the time
they

they occurred, and which he kept by him for such extraordinary purposes. This paper was put into my hands by a gentleman who had received much benefit from this good father's conversation and instruction ; I had his leave for transcribing it, or publishing, if I thought fit ; this I shall now avail myself of, as I think it is a very curious journal.

" My son, whoever thou art, profit by the words of experience, and let the example of Chaubert, who was a beast without reason, and is become a man by repentance, teach thee wisdom in adversity and inspire thy heart with sentiments of resignation to the will of the Almighty!

" When the treachery of people, which I ought to have despised, had turned my heart to marble and my blood to gall, I was determined upon leaving France and seeking out some of those countries, from whose famished inhabitants nature withholds her bounty and where men groan in slavery and sorrow ! As I passed through the villages towards the frontiers of Spain, and saw the peasants dancing in a ring to the pipe or carousing at their vintages, indignation smote my heart, and I wished that heaven would dash their cups with poison, or blast the sunshine of their joys with hail and tempest.

" I traversed the delightful province of Biscay without rest to the soles of my feet or sleep to the temples of my head. Nature was before my eyes dressed in her gayest attire :—Thou mother of fools, I exclaimed, why dost thou trick thyself out so daintily for knaves and harlots to make a property of thee ? The children of thy womb are vipers in thy bosom, and will sting thee mortally, when thou hast given them their fill at thy improvident

breasts.—The birds chaunted in the groves, the fruit-trees glistened on the mountain sides, the water falls made music for the echoes, and man went singing to his labour :—Give me, said I, the clank of fetters and the yell of galley-slaves under the lashes of the whip—and in the bitterness of my heart I cursed the earth, as I trode over its prolific surface.

" I entered the ancient kingdom of Castile, and the prospect was a recreation to my sorrow-vexed soul : I saw the lands lie waste and fallow; the vines trailed on the ground and buried their fruitage in the furrows; the hand of man was idle, and nature slept as in the cradle of creation ; the villages were thinly scattered, and ruin sate upon the unroofed sheds, where lazy pride laid stretched upon its straw in beggary and vermin. Ah ! this is something, I cried out, this scene is fit for man, and I'll enjoy it.—I saw a yellow half-starved form, cloaked to the heels in rags, his broad-brimmed beaver on his head, through which his staring locks crept out in squalid shreds, that fell like snakes upon the shoulders of a fiend—Such ever be the fate of human nature ! I'll aggravate his misery by the insult of charity. Harkye, Castilian, I exclaimed, take this pisette ! it is coin, it is silver from the mint of Mexico; a Spaniard dug it from the mine, a Frenchman gives it you : Put by your pride and touch it !—Curst be your nation, the Castilian replied, I'll starve before I'll take it from your hands.—Starve then, I answered, and passed on.

" I climbed a barren mountain ; the wolves howled in the desert, and the vultures screamed in flocks for prey ; I looked, and beheld a gloomy mansion underneath my feet, vast as the pride of its founder,

gloomy

gloomy and difconfolate as his foul; it was the Efcurial.—Here then the tyrant reigns, faid I, here let him reign; hard as thefe rocks his throne, wafte as thefe deferts be his dominion!—A meagre creature paffed me; famine ftared in his eye, he caft a look about him, and fprung upon a kid, that was browfing in the defert, he fmote it dead with his ftaff, and haftily thruft it into his wallet.—Ah, facrilegious villain!— cried a brawny fellow; and, leaping on him from behind a rock, feized the hungry wretch in the act; he dropped upon his knees and begged for mercy—Mercy! cried he that feized him, do you purloin the property of the church and afk for mercy? Take it!—So faying, he beat him to the earth with a blow, as he was kneeling at his feet, and then dragged him towards the convent of Saint Lawrence: I could have hugged the mifcreant for the deed.

" I held my journey through the defert, and defolation followed me to the very ftreets of Madrid; the fathers of the inquifition came forth from the cells of torture, the crofs was elevated before them, and a trembling wretch in a faffron-coloured veft, painted with fiames of fire, was dragged to execution in an open fquare; they kindled a fire about him, and fang praifes to God, whilft the fiames deliberately confumed their human victim: He was a Jew who fuffered, they were Chriftians who tormented.—See what the religion of God is, faid I to myfelf, in the hands of man!

" From the gates of Madrid I bent my courfe towards the port of Lifbon; as I traverfed the wildernefs of Eftremadura, a robber took his aim at me from behind a corktree, and the ball grazed my hat upon my head.—You have miffed your aim, I cried, and have loft the merit of deftroying a man.—Give me your purfe, faid the robber.— Take it, I replied, and buy with it a friend, may it ferve you as it has ferved me!

" I found the city of Lifbon in ruins; her foundations fmoked upon the ground; the dying and the dead laid in heaps; terror fate in every vifage, and mankind was vifited with the plagues of the Almighty, famine, fire, and earthquake—Have they not the inquifition in this country? I afked; I was anfwered they had.—And do they make all this outcry about an earthquake? faid I within myfelf, let them give God thanks and be quiet.

" Prefently there came fhips from England, loaded with all manner of goods for the relief of the inhabitants; the people took the bounty, were preferved, then turned and curfed their prefervers for heretics. —This is as it fhould be, faid I, thefe men act up to their nature, and the Englifh are a nation of fools; I will not go amongft them. —After a fhort time behold a new city was rifing on the ruins of the old one! The people took the builders tools, which the Englifh had fent them, and made themfelves houfes: I overheard a fellow at his work fay to his companion—Before the earthquake I made my bed in the ftreets, now I fhall have a houfe to live in. This is too much, faid I; their misfortunes make this people happy, and I will ftay no longer in their country—I defcended to the banks of the Tagus; there was a fhip, whofe canvafs was loofed for failing.—She is an Englifh fhip, fays a Galliego porter; they are brave feamen, but damned tyrants on the quarter deck.—They pay well for what they have, fays a boatman, and I am going on board
her

her with a cargo of lemons.——I threw myself into the wherry, and entered the ship : The mariners were occupied with their work, and nobody questioned me why I was amongst them. The tide wafted us into the ocean and the night became tempestuous, the vessel laboured in the sea and the morning brought no respite to our toil.—Whither are you bound ? said I to the master.—To hell, said he, for nothing but the devil ever drove at such a rate !—The fellow's voice was thunder ; the sailors sung in the storm, and the master's oaths were louder than the waves ; the third day was a dead calm, and he swore louder than ever.—If the winds were of this man's making, thought I, he would not be content with them.—A favourable breeze sprung up as if it had come at his calling.—I thought it was coming, says he, put her before the wind, it blows fair for our port.— But where is your port ? again I asked him. Sir, says he, I can now answer your question as I should do ; with God's leave I am bound to Bourdeaux ; every thing at sea goes as it pleases God.—My heart sunk at the name of my native city. I was freighted, added he, from London, with a cargo of goods of all sorts for the poor sufferers by the earthquake ; I shall load back with wine for my owners, and so help out a charitable voyage with some little profit, if it please God to bless our endeavours.——Heyday ! thought I, how fair weather changes this fellow's note !—Lewis, said he to a handsome youth, who stood at his elbow, we will now seek out this Monsieur Chaubert at Bourdeaux, and get payment of his bills on your account.—Shew me your bills, said I, for I am Chaubert.—He produced them, and I saw my own

Vol. VI. C

name forged to bills in favour of the villain who had so treacherously dealt with me in the affair of the woman who was to have been my wife.—Where is the wretch, said I, who drew these forgeries ?—The youth burst into tears.—He is my father, he replied, and turned away. —Sir, says the master, I am not surprised to find this fellow a villain to you, for I was once a trader in affluence, and have been ruined by his means and reduced to what you see me ; I can earn a maintenance, and am as happy in my present hard employ, nay happier than when I was rich and idle ; but to defraud his own son proves him an unnatural rascal, and, if I had him here, I would hang him at the mizen yard.

" When the English master declared he was happier in his present hard service than in his former prosperity, and that he forgave the villain who had ruined him, I started with astonishment, and stood out of his reach, expecting every moment when his phrensy would break out ; I looked him steadily in the face, and to my surprise saw no symptoms of madness ; there was no wandering in his eyes, and content of mind was impressed upon his features.—Are you in your senses, I demanded, and can you forgive the villain ?—From my heart, answered he, else how should I expect to be forgiven ?—His words struck me dumb ; my heart tugged at my bosom ; the blood rushed to my face. He saw my situation and turned aside to give some orders to the sailors ; after some minutes he resumed the conversation, and advancing towards me, in his rough familiar manner, said—It is my way, Mr. Chaubert, to forgive and forget, though to be sure the fellow deserves hanging for
his

his treatment of his poor boy his son, who is as good a lad as ever lived, but as for father and mother ——Who is his mother ? What was her name ? I eagerly demanded. Her name had no fooner paffed his lips than I felt a fhock through all my frame beyond that of electricity ; I ftaggered as if with a fudden ftroke, and caught hold of the barricade ; an involuntary fhriek burft from me, and I cried out—That woman——Oh ! that woman—Was a devil, faid the mafter, and if you knew but half the mifery you have efcaped, you would fall down upon your knees and thank God for the bleffing ; I have heard your ftory, Mr. Chaubert, and when a man is in love, do you fee, he does not like to have his miftrefs taken from him ; but fome things are better loft than found, and if this is all you have to complaiu of, take my word you complain of the luckieft hour in your whole life. He would have proceeded, but I turned from him without uttering a word, and fhutting myfelf up into my cabin furrendered myfelf to my meditations.

" My mind was now in fuch a tumult, that I cannot recal my thoughts, much lefs put them in any order for relation : The fhip however kept her courfe, and had now entered the mouth of the Garonne ; I landed on the quay of Bourdeaux ; the mafter accompanied me, and young Lewis kept charge of the fhip : The firft object that met my view was a gibbet erected before the door of a merchant's compting houfe : The convict was kneeling on a fcaffold, whilft a friar was receiving his laft confeffion ; his face was turned towards us ; the Englifhman glanced his eye upon him, and inftantly cried out—Look,

look, Mr. Chaubert, the very man, as I am alive ; it is the father of young Lewis.—The wretch had difcovered us in the fame moment, and called aloud—Oh Chaubert, Chaubert ! let me fpeak to you before I die !—His yell was horror to my foul ; I loft the power of motion, and the crowd pufhing towards the fcaffold, thruft me forward to the very edge of it ; the friar ordered filence, and demanded of the wretch why he had called out fo eagerly, and what he had farther to confefs. Father, replied the convict, this is the very man, the very Chaubert of whom I was fpeaking ; he was the beft of friends to me, and I repaid his kindnefs with the blackeft treachery ; I feduced the woman of his affections from him, I married her, and becaufe we dreaded his refentment, we confpired in an attempt upon his life by poifon.—He now turned to me and proceeded as follows—You may remember, Chaubert, as we were fupping together on the very evening of Louifa's elopement, fhe handed to you a glafs of wine to drink to your approaching nuptials ; as you were lifting it to your lips, your favourite fpaniel leaped upon your arm and dafhed it on the floor ; in a fudden tranfport of paffion, which you were ever addicted to, you ftruck the creature with violence and laid it dead at your feet. It was the faving moment of your life—the wine was poifoned, inevitable death was in the draught, and the animal you killed was God's inftrument for preferving you ; reflect upon the event, fubdue your paffions, and practife refignation ; Father, I have no more to confefs ; I die repentant ; let the executioner do his office."

The

For the MASSACHUSETTS MAGAZINE.

The REPOSITORY. No. XXV.

CURIOSITY is undoubtedly one of the moſt active principles of the ſoul. What degree of curioſity is compatible with ſound philoſophy, may be a queſtion, but that it is of general utility, muſt, I think, remain indiſputable. Curioſity is ſaid to predominate in a ſuperior degree in the female boſom. I know that curioſity is not aſcribed to us as a virtue ; no, by no means ; it is rather pointed out as a reprehenſible excreſcence. But with all due deference to thoſe who are fond of ſearching out, and of reporting the ſuppoſed blemiſh, I take leave to ſay, that if curioſity was confined to us, then would the lords of the creation be indebted to us, for all thoſe improvements of which humanity hath been found ſuſceptible ; we ſhould then become the ſource of information, and by conſequence it is we who muſt be inveſted with the honorary bays.— Suppoſe the principle of curioſity had been from the beginning dormant in the ſoul ; ſuppoſe the human being wholly incurious, altogether averſe from inveſtigation— in what profound ignorance would mankind have been wrapped ?— Where would have been all the aſtoniſhing diſcoveries which we owe to the ſublime genius of a Newton ? Void of this ſtimulative, his reſearches would have been at an end ; or rather they would never have commenced ; and it is, therefore, to this noble incitement, that the world is indebted for the pleaſing knowledge of the great balance of nature, the idea of gravitation, the order of the planets, with many other uſeful, delightful, and elevating ſpeculations, which once were latent. Suſpend for a time the operation of this ſame curioſity, and, during ſuch ſuſpenſion, ſcience is at a ſtand, genius hath loſt its prime movement, and the progreſs of every improvement is effectually arreſted. Thus it is a fact, that thoſe who ſo laviſhly attribute curioſity, in ſo large a proportion to *the ſex*, very evidently, although perhaps they are not aware thereof, aſcribe to females a ſuperior degree of that noble incentive, which is the origin of every mental acquiſition. Let then curioſity, *female curioſity*, ceaſe to be conſidered a term of reproach ; and let the levellers of female abilities, take a more certain aim at that worth, which they aſſay to proſtrate.

CONSTANTIA.

ESSAY on HAPPINESS.

——————— Alas ! where ſhall we find
Some ſpot to real happineſs confin'd ?   GOLDSMITH,

THIS penſive inquiry has not been confined to the breaſt of the ingenious poet from whom my motto is taken. In the hours of diſappointment and adverſity, it has been the general language of mankind. Beings who poſſeſs faculties capable of enjoyment unattainable in the preſent ſtate of exiſtence, naturally extend their ideas to a better life. This longing after ſomething unpoſſeſſed, is the wiſh of every mind conſcious of its immortality.

But the complaint frequently ſprings from cauſes of an inferior nature.

nature. It has often arifen from real, and ftill oftener from imaginary, infelicity. This hath been often increafed, and fometimes wholly proceeds from making a falfe eftimation of human happinefs. Men are apt to place an higher value on every bleffing not in their poffeffion than on thofe which they enjoy. The profpect of every diftant good is embellifhed with charms which lofe their luftre on a nearer approach, or pall with familiarity.

It is not unufual with us to imagine the condition of others preferable to our own : We change our fituation, but find not the happinefs we expected ; and yet remain unconvinced of our folly. We purfue, vainly purfue, the phantom which the fervor of hope raifes in the diftempered imagination, although difappointment attend us at every ftep, and mock every endeavour. We either find the objects of our wifhes recede in proportion to our advances towards them, or that, if gained, they prove inadequate to our expectations.

One of the moft deceitful bubbles, that ever danced before the eye of human vanity, is wealth. It glitters at a diftance, and appears replete with all the requifites effential to earthly felicity. It attracts the attention of numbers from every other object, and kindles in the breafts of its votaries an inextinguifhable thirft to acquire it. By weak minds it is confidered as the fummum bonum of fublunary bleffings, and therefore, in the attainment of it, fuch think to exclude every want, to enjoy every fatisfaction.

But alas! wealth often flies before the purfuer ; and, in the end, leaves him tired, languid, and

difappointed. To fome indeed fhe grants her favors with peculiar liberality : But are thefe in " a fpot to real happinefs confined ?" No furely : They find, by unprofitable experience, that the enjoyments derived from riches fall far fhort of their expectations.

Riches are not able to confer that happinefs they promife ; or to avert thofe evils which they are fuppofed to cure. They feldom fill the grafp of avarice, or limit the ardour of defire. They are infufficient to guard the avenues through which afflictions enter. To

" The branch that blooms with vegetable gold,"

Death pays no regard.

The poffeffion of wealth introduces wants not lefs numerous than thofe we complain of in a ftate of poverty. They are indeed different in kind, but not lefs deftructive of that felicity we vainly feek for in this imperfect ftate of being. We are apt to conclude, that thofe are exempt from unhappinefs on whom profperity beams her radiance. In the erring eftimation of fuperficial minds, " their lines are caft in pleafant places ;" but a little reflection will convince us, that they are often " encompaffed with many forrows." View thofe who have free accefs to the temple of riches, and you will not find them happier than other men. They not only feel numerous wants increafing with their acquifitions ; but are often a prey to ftill more numerous fears, arifing from thofe very poffeffions to which men in humbler ftations are ftrangers. Some find their defires ftrengthened by the increafe of their poffeffions : The more they inherit, the more unbounded is their grafp. Were it poffible for

fuch

fuch to accumulate all the treafures of the earth, they would ftill be unfatisfied, and, like Alexander, weep becaufe there was no other world within their reach to plunder. Others, who appear contented with their prefent poffeffions, are not lefs unhappy. Men cannot effentially poffefs more than they enjoy : The reft, like a cypher on the left hand of a figure, is of no value, unprofitable to any ufeful purpofe. It is only as barren fplendor, which, like the glare of a comet, may indeed fhine at a diftance, and create awe in vulgar minds ; but affords no warmth to invigorate him who gazes upon it. The poffeffor may contemplate it with barren admiration, but cannot render it fubfervient to the ufeful purpofes of life. Such, therefore, who poffefs more wealth than is fufficient to furnifh their reafonable wants, are generally employed in a laborious fearch after pleafures yet untafted, in which they hope to find an increafe of happinefs. In general they are difappointed.

There is indeed one fource of refined pleafure, which the enjoyment of wealth affords to a rational mind. The extenfion of help to the helplefs, of relief to mifery, and of comfort to thofe who dwell in the vale of adverfity, are employments in which we feel the pureft fatisfaction. To awaken joy in countenances ftrongly marked with the gloom of forrow is attended with the moft refined fenfations of delight, and attunes the foul to harmony. This is the nobleft ufe to which wealth can be applied ; the effential end for which Heaven has difpenfed it. But, amongft the great and opulent, how few are there who exercife themfelves in fuch a courfe of

benevolence and virtue ! How few whofe minds are fufficiently elevated to feek for the fatisfaction arifing from a conduct fo truly eftimable ?

The generality of the rich fpend their time and fubftance in a courfe of falfely eftimated pleafure, which, while it affords a momentary gratification to fome defires, creates others more difficult to fatisfy. Every indulgence of the paffions beyond the limits of reafon and temperence either excites the appetite for more criminal enjoyments, or cloys with a languid fatiety. Thefe ⬤ effects equally deftructive of true happinefs. In this dilemma the mind of a man of pleafure is perpetually toffed like a veffel without a rudder in the fury of a ftorm. Still hurried along by the gales of paffion, he purfues fomething yet untried, which he fuppofes more capable of conferring happinefs ; but this when attained leaves him equally diffatisfied, and at a diftance from true felicity.

Thus, through the diverfified paths of error, men purfue, with unremitting ardour, that happinefs, which, for want of a better regulated judgment, they cannot attain ; till, tired with reiterated difappointments, they quit the ftage of life and their fruitlefs fearch together.

It would be a mark of wifdom in us to confider fuch examples as proper objects for our inftruction. Viewed in this light, they may be ufeful warnings, and teach us to avoid the folly fo ftrongly exhibited in their conduct. Let their errors and confequent difappointments excite others to purfue a different plan ;—a plan more likely to be attended with fuccefs.

Complete happinefs is not the produce

produce of a terrestrial soil. While we tread the paths of human life, and are incompassed with human frailties, the avenues through which happiness beams on the soul will not in a sufficient degree satisfy or fill up our intellectual capacities : But still such a portion of it is within our reach as will render this state of existence easy and tranquil. The Sovereign Lord of universal nature has wisely ordained, that, amidst the highest gratifications we can enjoy in this world, some alloy should be experienced. By these means the mind is led to aspire after the attainment of that more perfect bliss, which, in the wise determinations of his counsel, we were formed to enjoy, when time and its illusive scenes shall vanish for ever.

The terms, on which this superior happiness is declared by the voice of wisdom to be attainable, are, such as, if complied with, will tend greatly to the increase of our present felicity. We are told in the volume of sacred truth, that " Godliness is profitable to all things ; having the promise of the life that now is, and also of that which is to come." The experience of wise and good men in all ages has proved its validity. The more we withdraw our affections from perishing delights, and endeavour to fix them on celestial objects, the more acute, pure and refined, will our perceptions be of present pleasures. They will not be pursued to satiety, or abused with a wanton ingratitude.

Those joys, which the visible creation affords, will not be relied upon as a substantial lasting good, but rather considered as the lower steps of that ladder by which we may ascend from earth to heaven. By the " good things that are seen"

and which we are favoured to enjoy here, we shall be excited to seek after " those that are invisible," in that state where the aspirations of hope will end in certainty ; and desire, in the complete fruition of eternal blessedness.

It is undoubtedly a mark of wisdom in us to seek, by every prudent means, for the attainment of that happiness which, in the wise order of Providence, we were formed to enjoy in the present life. Our passions are ever calling for fresh gratification ; they are clamorous, and not easily silenced : But we know that, if indulged without restraint, they would soon precipitate us into irretrievable ruin. It is therefore the province of reason to regulate them, to curb the rovings of the will, and to point out those boundaries of action which we ought never to pass.

Whenever we thus submit to her wise restrictions, the commotions in our breasts will cease ; our desires will be circumscribed ; and, instead of repining at our lot, we shall be convinced the blessings we have received are infinitely beyond our deserts. This sense produces gratitude and humility, and thence spring true contentment and lasting peace : We are satisfied with those blessings which the munificent Author of our being has showered down upon us, and are most solicitous to make suitable returns for his unmerited bounty.

In this disposition of mind the purest happiness of this life is found ; and herein we are best capable of becoming successful candidates for that superior felicity which will be the portion of the wise and virtuous in the realms of immortality.

[*Universal Mag.*
The

For the MASSACHUSETTS MAGAZINE.

The GLEANER. No. XXIX.

Eafy the burden, lightly borne, appears,
Content her poppies ftrews—a wand fhe bears—
Whofe magic influence can new joys unfold,
Changing the *iron*—to an age of *gold*.

THE value of an equal and accommodating difpofition, cannot, I conceive, be too highly appreciated, too energetically inculcated, or too often expatiated upon. Such, and fo frequent are the vicifitudes of life, that an unbending mind, refufing to yield to that neceffity which is impofed upon its exiftence, is broken by the boifterous winds which are abroad, and too frequently proftrated by thofe calamities, or adverfe tranfitions, to which an acquiefcent fpirit finds it wifdom, with humble patience, to fubmit. "The burden becomes light by being well borne." I have not forgot that this is an old adage, but I repeat, that its antiquity doth not deduct the fmalleft particle from its rationality ; thefe venerable old faws frequently contain the very pith and effence of fentiment, and I have often thought that the pen appropriated to the pointing out their excellence might be *much worfe* employed. Say, thou difcontented and repining mortal, what emolument haft thou derived from continually tracing the dark fhades in the picture ? Haft thou received injuries, and doft thou find thy recompenfe in eternally brooding thereon ? Do fuch contemplations meliorate thy virtues, or promote the funfhine of the foul ? Are the genial and falutary airs of tranquillity originated, or wafted forward, by reflections, which wound the mind, and fire the bofom with indignation ?

Health of body, ferenity of foul, fweet complacency, fprightly mirth, all thefe are among the victims of *cherifhed, gloomy* and *corroding refentment !* The foul of the vindictive is the region of horror, and the moft black and baleful paffions harbour there. What are the pleafures of the angry man ? It is undeniably true that he is his own tormenter, and if he throws the reins upon that implacability, and inveterate revenge, which fo fearfully predominate in his breaft, his moft uniform or confirmed enemy could hardly devife means more adequate or better calculated for the deftruction of his felicity. Have not the attentions which I have received been commenfurate with that merit, with which my felf-partiality hath invefted me ? Have I to complain of cold indifference or neglect from thofe upon whom nature, circumftances, or amity, had furnifhed me with indifputable claims ? Have I not only been defrauded of thofe dues to which the inviolable laws of fociety hath entitled me, but hath infult, and even outrage been alfo added ? Well, it is really a pity-moving fituation, and I would certainly turn as often as poffible from the view. Canft thou derive either fatisfaction or profit from an enumeration of thy grievances ? I pity the malignant fpirit which can delight to prey upon food on which the fiends affembled in Pandemonium might joy to riot ! Reader, if thou wert ever angry, then haft thou experienced the ravages which the war of the paffions maketh upon thy peace, like all other wars, defolation follows in the train, and reafon can never eftimate their profit ; yet, if upon a fair calculation, the fum total proves thee a fingle drachm, or even a half drachm, nay, the hundredth part of a ·fcruple the gainer ; I will then confent that thou fhalt in future vex thyfelf to a fkeleton more hideous than the brain of fertile poefy e'er conjured up, though fickening envy, or yellow jealoufy, or fell revenge, ftalked full in view— " Yes," cried Maria, " the fenfations which are attendant upon the contemplation of a virtuous action, are undoubtedly divine ; I would pafs by a thoufand fuppofed injuries, but I would dwell for ever upon the contemplation of genuine worth. The reflections which are the accompaniments of offences do not exercife, they do not invigorate the finer feelings of the foul. I liftened to the pleafing matron," continued Maria, " I liftened with rapture, for her tongue expatiated upon the philanthrophy of Alberto."

" My fon, faid fhe, was on a voyage, he was a ftranger, and he took rank among the loweft grade which made up the fhip's company—my fon fell fick ; he was dangeroufly ill ; gloomy was his fituation ; but Alberto commanded the fhip ; he fought out my fon ; he foothed his woes ; he lodged him in his own cabin ; he attended him in perfon, and my fon was reftored to health. Immeafurable are my obligations to Alberto and his name, next to that of the Supreme, is entitled to my utmoft veneration. Alberto is my brother ; I am many years

his fenior ; I have known him the moft beauteous of infants, and he gladdened the hearts of his parents. How fweet are the praifes of a brother ! Alberto, dear Alberto, for this, and many fimilar anecdotes of thy fhort life, I will remit unto thee all, and every one of the peccadilios, which, fhading thy character, do but to render thy virtues the more confpicuous. Yes, the genuine benignity of thy foul fhall ferve as a fpunge wherewith to obliterate all recollection of thofe afperities, that the rough contour of thy inborn integrity, fo frequently prefents." The election of Maria exemplified her accuftomed penetration, for reiterated obfervation of proper and becoming actions, has upon the heart the moft falutary effect. Was I called upon to delineate the path which would moft affuredly lead to as great a fhare of happinefs as is compatible with humanity, I fhould dictate to the candidate for felicity, a frequent recurrence to the fair fide of perfons, circumftances and events ; almoft every thing may be viewed in different mediums, and even the various emphafizing of any given narration, may furnifh the fame fact with features directly oppofite. Refolve then to view every occurrence in the very beft poffible light, and if there is a pleafing conftruction, feize with avidity the fuppofition which points to complacency. Make, I befeech thee, the experiment, determine to be pleafed for one week, and then tell me how fmoothly fled the hours. Here I am aware of an objection ; misfortunes may await, the preffure of which may fink *even fortitude itfelf*, but let it be remembered that I have not at prefent reference to the real calamities of life, and although it is und ubtedly
true,

true, that every evil may be mitigated by patience, yet at this moment, in endeavouring to rouse to refolution, I had only in view that fretful ennui, which is commonly the offspring of indolence, and ftrongly marks the want of thofe efforts which are fo proper to a rational being. Murmuring, repining, captious difcontent, invidious cavilling, thefe are the fiends which are armed at all points againft our repofe ; difagreeable recollections, wounding farcafms, irritating recriminations—thefe are hunted after, as if they were fome hidden treafure, and they ftab our choiceft comforts ; they are the dark affaffins which, aiming at the vitals of tranquillity, fatally deftroy our peace ! Of what confequence is it who was the aggreffor ? humanity is fubjected to error, and that immaculate Being, to whom alone belongeth undeviating rectitude, hath given us a dignified example of forgivenefs. Take the advice of a friend ; make the moft of life, enjoy with avidity ; reverence virtue ; make it the goal of thy wifhes ; purfue and overtake, cultivate philanthrophy ; give ample fcope to every benignant fuggeftion ; take not upon thyfelf the character of a *public accufer, or cenfor ;* but leaving this invidious office to thofe to whom it may *legally belong,* accuftom thyfelf to expatiate upon the *good qualities* of thy affociates, upon the *benefits* accruing from an intercourfe with thy connexions, upon the *eligibles of life :* Tread lightly upon offences ; if thou fhouldeft awake the fleeping mifchief, it will fting thee to the foul, its envenomed fhafts will find their way to the deepeft receffes of thy fpirit. Do not magnify or even inveftigate the ill offices which have been done thee ; few circum-

ftances can juftify the perturbating fcrutiny ; anger will grow in thy bofom. How fhocking, how deforming is anger ! Seneca's defcription of anger is not too high coloured, and it is juft as true at the prefent day, as it was near eighteen hundred years fince. Seneca, upon anger, may not be in your library ; I take leave, therefore, to tranfcribe an extract from his admired page. " He was much in the right, whoever he was, that firft called anger a' fhort madnefs ; for they have both of them the fame fymptoms ; and there is fo wonderful a refemblance between the tranfports of choler and thofe of phrenfy, that it is a hard matter to know the one from the other. A bold, fierce and threatening countenance, as pale as afhes, and in the fame moment as red as blood ; a glaring eye, a wrinkled brow, violent motions, the hands reftlefs and perpetually in action, wringing and menacing, fnapping of the joints, ftamping with the feet, the hair ftarting, trembling lips, a forced voice ; the fpeech falfe and broken, deep and frequent fighs and ghaftly looks ; the veins fwell, the heart pants, the knees knock ; with a hundred difmal accidents that are common to both diftempers. Neither is anger, only a bare refemblance of madnefs, but many times an irrecoverable tranfition into the thing itfelf. How many perfons have we known, read, and heard of, that have loft their wits in a paffion, and never came to themfelves again ? It is therefore to be avoided not only for moderation fake, but alfo for health. Now, if the outward appearance of anger be hideous, how deformed muft that mind be that is harraffed with it ? for it leaves no place either for counfel or friendfhip, honefty or good manners ;

ners ; no place either for the exercife of reafon, or for the offices of life. If I were to defcribe it, I would draw a tyger bathed in blood ; fharp fet and ready to take a leap at its prey, or drefs it up as the poets reprefent the furies, with whips, fnakes and flames. It fhould likewife be four, livid, full of fcars, and wallowing in gore, raging up and down, deftroying, grinning, bellowing, and purfuing ; fick of all other things, and moft of all of itfelf. It turns beauty into deformity, and the calmeft counfels into fiercenefs : It diforders our very garments, and fills the mind with horror. How abominable then is it in the foul ! Is not he a mad man who hath loft the government of himfelf, and is toffed hither and thither by his fury, as by a tempeft ; the executioner of his own revenge, both with his heart and hand ; and the murderer of his neareft friends ? The fmalleft matter moves it and makes us unfociable, and inacceffible. It does all things by violence, as well upon itfelf as others ; and it is in fhort the mafter of all paffions." Say, my fair friend, doth the portrait difguft thee ? fly then, lovely Sentimentalift, from the very firft approaches of the fell deftroyer ; rude and mifshapen, it affimilates into its own frightfully fhocking afpect the fineft features, and, beneath its horrid and imperious fway, proftrate beauty fades and is extinct ; its depredations on the fweet tranquillity proper to thy fex, are marked with the moft aggravating and unnatural circumftances. Gentle woman fhould ftudioufly fhun that queftionable path which may remotely terminate in the moft diftant approximation to the hell-born fiend ; for every mild, every bland and focial virtue, fhould conftitute the aggregate of the female character. How charming is the funfhine of the foul ; how friendly to the growth of mental life is the milk of human kindnefs ! how divine is the precept—" Bear one another's burdens, and fo fulfil the royal law of love." But ftop, I prefume not to invade the province of the preacher ; the fact is, that thought hath followed thought, until having overfhot my purpofe, I have widely deviated from my original plan : Indeed, the want of regularity, is not the leaft of the inconveniences which are the accompaniments of the vagrant tribe, but my humble pretenfions muft at all times be my apology.

My defign was to have devoted this Gleaner to the confideration of the utility, of fupporting with equanimity, the unavoidable misfortunes incident to life : And I was furnifhed with an exemplification of the advantages which I had in view to delineate, during a tour which I lately made through the out-fkirts of one of the eaftern ftates. Thus it is, the eccentricity of my occupation not feldom deranges my moft favorite views, and I am neceffitated to admit the multifarious produce of an excurfive, or fugitive imagination, yet, although thrown from my courfe, I will not be prevented from prefenting my example ; I think it cannot fail of ftriking agreeably, and it may poffibly give birth to thofe very identical reflections which it was my wifh to embody. It was upon a beautiful morning of April laft that, feeking the pleafures of folitude, I wandered from the company at our little inn, and mounting my horfe, I threw the reins upon his neck, determining to leave to chance the direction of my ramble. We were equally ftrangers to the road, and a few miles in a country hardly emerging from a state of nature, conducted us to a thick wood, when, securing my horse to the trunk of a tall tree, I prepared to penetrate a coppice which presented the only vestige of the wants, or ingenuity of man, which the eye could trace : Almost lost in contemplation, I proceeded onward to the extremity of the wood, which bordered a few acres of ground, equally remarkable for the sterility of its soil, and the persevering patience, and uncommon industry of its proprietors. I was roused from my reverie by a number of voices, which arresting my attention, immediately drew me forward to the place from whence they proceeded. I suspected the employment of our rustics, and least I should interrupt operations so proper to the season, I made my advances with care. The opening scene presented a poor built cottage, which, in language unequivocal, proclaimed industrious poverty ; the healthy appearance of the grounds, evinced the stinted produce, with which they repaid the master's culture ; a few sheep, and a single cow, whose thin forms demonstrated the scanty pittance on which they fed, stood forth additional vouchers of the partial penury of nature. But a fertilizing stream, which murmured by, and bore in its bosom various descriptions of the finny tribe, diversified the view, and gave birth to the pleasures of hope. A well looking man was busily employed in turning up, and shaping the glebe, a sentimental carol vibrated upon his tongue, and his features were expressive of content. A graceful female at a little distance, round whom no less than eleven children, of different ages, were collected,

was directing the eldest boy, a rosy cheeked youth, in setting some plants, while she herself committed to the prepared sod, those seeds from which she cheerfully anticipated the distant harvest. The vestments of the family, were the vestments of penury, and if they could be considered as garments, they were entitled, for so respectable an appellation, to that unwearied diligence, which following still the well worn robe, had so repeatedly repaired each time-made breach, as to render it impossible to decide of what hue or texture it was originally possessed. Yet the voice of gladness echoed round, and the colour of every feature seemed descriptive of heart-felt age. With folded arms, and grateful admiration, I contemplated the uncommon group. The face of the matron was not immediately turned toward me, neither had the shepherd observed me, but the children had begun to amuse themselves with my figure, when their mother, having finished her employ, was drawn by their innocent mirth to the spot on which I was fixed. I have already confessed mingling surprise and pleasure, at the gay tranquillity which was so apparently the appendages of a scene so barren of good, and so remarkably devoid of the eligibles of life, but no language can express my astonishment, when in the countenance of the penuriously garbed matron, I recognized the once opulent, truly amiable, and highly deserving Flavilla ! Gracious God ! spontaneously I exclaimed—Is it possible ; do I in reality behold the once idolized, and ever charming Miss Kneller ? Flavilla, long accustomed to the vicissitudes, and caprices of events, uttered no perturbed exclamation, but with that genuine dignity, which

which nature not feldom confers upon a confcioufnefs of innate worth, with a grace and manner which I have not often feen equalled in a drawing room, prefenting her hand ; fhe exprefled her fatisfaction in an interview fo unexpected, and leading me to her humble abode, we were foon joined by Evander, and the little family. I had known Flavilla from early youth : She was born to affluent fortune, and her education had been in the firft line. Her parents Mr. and Mrs. Kneller, had no other child, and this daughter, promifing in every view, was of courfe regarded as an ineftimable treafure. Evander was the man of her heart, and her union with the youth fhe loved, and who reciprocated her attachment, received the cheerful fanction of the authors of her being. Soon after the marriage of Mifs Kneller, her parental friends payed the great debt of nature, and Evander and Flavilla poffeffed an ample fortune. But from this period thick clouds began to gather, and they experienced a moft diftrefling reverfe of circumftances. The *career* of their misfortunes was ufhered in by a dreadful conflagration, in which their manfion houfe, containing many valuable articles, was reduced to afhes ; a feries of calamities fucceeded, until at length, of all their vaft poffeffions, fcarce a veftige remained ; yet a principle of rectitude triumphed in their fouls ; of their inborn integrity the malice of their fate could not diveft them, and difcharging, with intereft, the laft farthing, for which they were indebted, with the poor pittance which was left, they retired, like Thompfon's Lavinia, " *far from thofe fcenes that knew their better days,*" far from their native place, the much-loved fcene of their early

pleafures, and purchafed in this remote fpot—*'twas all they could*— the barren grounds from which they have ever fince obtained a fcanty, and hard earned fubfiftence. Their original ftock confifted of thirty fheep, one cow, and a yoke of oxen ; the fheep were almoft immediately deftroyed by the wolves, the cow fell a victim probably to the fteril foil to which fhe was confined, and, in an attempt to level a tall tree, one of their oxen was killed upon the fpot. Succeeding years has reduced to the loweft ftate the neceffaries which made up their perfonal and family wardrobe, and it has not been in their power to poffefs themfelves of the fmalleft fupplies : Yet, ftrange to tell, neither time, or forrow, hath been able to infix their deadly fangs in the bofom of Flavilla ; health dances in her veins, and beauty glows upon her cheek; her fmiles ftill difplay the dimples of youth, and in her mildly expreffive eye corrected vivacity yet beams. It was impoffible that I could forbear expreffing my aftonifhment, and my admiration ! and I inquired by what means they had, Flavilla efpecially, fupported fuch an uncommon meafure of tranquillity in the midft of fuch a calamitous reverfe of circumftances : " It is fimply this," replied Flavilla, " we have confidered the brevity of life, and the certainty of our removal to another, a better, and a more permanent ftate of being ; we have adopted, realized, and reduced to practice the fentiment of an admired poet ; we have been taught by experience that " *earth born cares are vain ; that man wants but little here below,*" we have fully known, and we do not expect to want " *that little long.*" To contribute to the relief of Flavilla, or her family, is impoffible, for
                                           fince

since the discovery of her retirement, in regard to which she hath injoined the strictest secresy, however ingenious, I have been in my attempts to augment their finances, I have still found myself with a firmness almost unexampled, uniformly repulsed. To have put Flavilla, in possession of every thing which her situation seemed to claim would have been the highest luxury which benevolence could have tasted ; but while I regret as an individual, her steady rejection of all pecuniary assistance, I cannot but admire the genuine elevation of her high-souled sentiments. She listened, it is true, to those remonstrances with which, after more indirect methods had failed, I ventured to address her ; but she listened only to ascertain her rejection ; " No, Sir," with all the calmness of inborn superiority, she replied, " I am but too much obliged in receiving your munificent proposals, but no one shall say that he hath enriched either Flavilla, or her family. Flavilla and her family will depend only upon Nature and Nature's God ; habit hath reconciled us to our situation, we are resigned, we are contented—besides, my friend, the prospect now gradually brightens upon us ; by rigid economy, we have replaced our stock ; our children are growing up about us ; my boys will assist their father ; we have already laid the foundation of a little tenement, in which we expect to meet a tranquil close to waneing life. Labour will ameliorate even the steril earth ; many hands will bear from some more friendly spot the rich manure ; the increase of our own fields shall yet spread us a plenteous board. See yonder flax, already it assumes a promising and healthy aspect. The finest threads are spun by my girls, and even by myself. Lydia has made herself mistress of the weaving business ; William has a fine mechanical genius, his looms are nearly complete, and the well made web, the product of our own industry, will ere long furnish us with decent and becoming vestments."

Happy, deservedly happy woman ; felicity hast, from the discordant spirit of the captious murmurer, although the child of affluence, and enveloped in gold and purple, it hasteth to the bosom of contentment ; it seeketh shelter in the breast of equanimity, bestowing on its votaries, although dwelling in a humble cottage, the choicest of its blessings.

ALEXIS : Or, The COTTAGE in the WOODS.

(Continued from the 537th page.)

PART SECOND.

Alexis passes a twelvemonth in the Cottage.—He is forced to leave it.

CHAPTER IV.

THE SUBTERRANEOUS TEMPLE.

THE dawn of gay morning had risen from the east, the feathered tribe saluted it with the most melodious concern ; all nature brilliant, and displayed, seemed to rejoice at the beneficent rays of the sun. Alexis, who used every morning to contemplate and adore this magnificent scene, paid not the smallest attention to it. All night a prey to the most painful reflections, he no sooner perceived Aurora, than

than, running to the window, he surveyed, with a countenance expressive of grief, the vast expanse of the forest. Sighs heaved his bosom, his veins beat precipitately, his over-burdened heart seemed to be willing to force its way through his breast, to repair to the spot where he knew his father waited for him. Alexis could not see the village of St. Etienne, but he guessed its situation, and said to himself: Romans lies to the south; St. Marcellin on this side; and St. Etienne facing the mountain covered with woods. Yes, St. Etienne lies there, my father and Dumont are near me! O why cannot my eyes pierce through the obstacles which part us! Why not see and examine them!— What do I say? Their image is in my soul.—There they are, sitting by one another: They sigh, and say, Will Alexis come to join us?—Will Alexis prefer his father to his mistress?—Will nature have greater command over his heart than love? Will it be in vain for me to hold out my arms to him and to call him aloud!—Ah! my son! come, come, my mouth smiles at you; my eyes only wait for your bosom, to pour in it a flood of tears; my heart longs to feel the beating of your's. Will you come my Alexis, will you come?—Yes, I will, my father; yes, I'll embrace your knees; my soul shall be united with your's.—O Alexis! O most ungrateful of all men! could'st thou hesitate, could'st thou waver? descend into your heart, it will prescribe your duty, and tell you, what is a lover, what is a benefactor. Are they above a father? Can friendship, can gratitude, equal paternal fondness! O sacred names of a father, of a son, are you not holier than those of a lover and a friend!—I am resolved this evening, I will leave the cottage, I will quit

for ever Candor and Clara.—For ever!—great God!—for ever!— beings so generous, so virtuous!— O my father, what a sacrifice do you exact of me!—it is above my power; yes, I feel it will be impossible for me to consummate it.—But, cruel parent, why did not you come yourself? Why did you write by a hand not your own? That letter, that stranger, that guide, who is to conduct me—yes, that guide!— should it be yourself—yes, my father, it is you—I shall meet you in the forest: My heart tells me so; it cannot deceive me! O sun, hasten thy career, behold what happiness awaits me when it is completed! restore a son to his father, and thy setting will be more beautiful for Alexis than thy meridian glory.

Alexis, enlivened by the idea of meeting his father in the guide of the forest, was shedding tears of joy. Soon calm cheered his soul, and serenity animated his countenance. He went down to Clara, gave her a lesson of music; they repaired to Candor, of whom he begged leave to go a hunting in the afternoon; the latter granted it, embraced him closely, and called him his dear son, which entirely disconcerted our hero: His firmness failed him, his resolution vanished, his heart was distressed, and he fell into his former state of irresolution.

Clara, whom he joined, finished putting him into the most anxious perplexity and confusion: Alexis, said she, rejoice, my father is going to grant thee thy wishes; he said to me just now, to night you and I shall know his secrets. O my God! how I long for that blessed moment! —But what ails you? It seems as if you was sorry at these tidings?— Don't you love my father? don't you love—me? how often have you declared and sworn you did?—

In

In faith, Alexis, could I but think you ungrateful, I would esteem you no more.—Oh, how you look at me!—you weep now.—No, sir, no, be not sorry, I believe there is nothing bad in what I told you.—

Alexis endeavoured to answer, but his grief would not permit him: He only pressed her hand, and then retired. Clara, who had never seen him so downcast, saw him go; her beautiful eyes were filled with tears: She, mechanically, followed as it were, the traces of her young friend, and stopping on the banks of the rivulet, near the bridge that leads to the grove, she was highly amazed to see Alexis write some characters upon the bark of the great poplar. She hid herself behind an antique willow, and watched attentively every motion of her lover, intending, as soon as he should be gone, to read the inscription he made on the tree. Alexis, at certain times, interrupted his task, lifted his hands towards heaven, and uttered the most woful moans. Soon after, he kissed the characters which he had traced, and with a slow pace returned to the cottage, not without turning round, and coming back upon his footsteps.

No sooner Clara saw him at too great a distance to be perceived by him, than she ran trembling to the great poplar. What became of her, when upon it she read these words!

"O you tender friends, objects of my thoughts, that ought to expect a more grateful return, accuse not my heart of a forcible flight! one day you will see me again."

Clara attempts to read the fatal lines again; but her eyes cannot see; a cloud of darkness covers them; her tongue denies its office, she drops down senseless upon the turf and remains in that condition, which nobody could guess, without the smallest succour. She however gradually recovered her senses, and her unfaithful remembrance hides from her the cause of her perturbation; she rises, sees herself, with astonishment, open her eyes again to light: Soon the happy darkness which covered her soul vanished; she repents not having followed the traces of her lover, and quickly enters the cottage, where she cries with a loud voice, Alexis! Alexis! ungrateful man, it is Clara who calls you! answer me, oh, answer me!—Alexis could hear no more, in consequence of Candor's having given him leave to go a hunting; he had just left the cottage; he was in the forest, he looked at the draw bridge which had just shut itself behind him, and doubting whether he should have it let down again, he could neither advance, nor return. What a situation for his feeling heart! What, exclaimed he, Candor, the respectable Candor, who does not suspect my project, and has just given me tokens of the most tender friendship—should I leave him!—Oh God! how ungrateful! —And Clara, poor Clara! what will she become, if she reads my last farewel upon the great poplar? She will see that I was forced to go, she will see that I am to return one day.—Yes, I will return, my generous friends, you will see me again; and will to-morrow hinder me from coming here with my father and Dumont.—Oh! they will not be able to disapprove of my project; they will follow me; to-morrow I shall embrace Candor, he will pardon me. How delightful a hope is this to my heart!—It quite enlivens me; I will go, I will proceed on my journey, embrace father who waits for me at a little distance. Heaven be praised for

this

this favour, it baffles all expreſſion !

Alexis turned his face towards the cottage, he ſhed tears, then took his road as he was directed by the letter : He had now walked half a league in the foreſt, when the ſky was imperceptibly overcaſt with clouds, the lightning rent the air, the thunder roared, whole cataracts of water poured down from the irritated elements, and the blackeſt darkneſs covered all nature. Alexis, moved at the dreadful ſcene, felt his knees tottering ; terror ſeized his ſoul, he was almoſt convinced that heaven, provoked at his ingratitude, would ſhiver him into atoms, he had almoſt ſuccumbed under the weight of his grief, when a ſpacious cavern preſents itſelf to his ſight. He enters to avoid the heavenly wrath ; he ventures to ſtep a little forward ; all of a ſudden an involuntary horror makes him tremble, his hair ſtands at an end, he thinks to ſee ſpectres that purſue and ſtop him ; he believes he hears the voice of Clara and Candor ; it is they, it is their voice ; they load him with reproaches and curſes. Heaven ! where is he to ſeek refuge ? The phantoms purſue him wherever he goes ; on all ſides ſighs and ſhrieks reſound in his ears. Let us for a moment leave him in this critical ſituation, and ſee what paſſes in the cottage.

Clara, after ſhe had read the words, written on the great poplar, ran back to the cottage in hopes to find Alexis ; but what was her ſurprize, when her father informs her that he is not there, but went out a hunting in the foreſt.—" A hunting !" cried Clara ; " ah, my father, he flies from you, he leaves you forever !"—" What do you ſay, my daughter ?"—" Yes, the ungrateful Alexis is gone !—We ſhall

ſee him no more."—" But how do you know this ?"—" Liſten, my father, liſten to me, and know all his treachery."

Here Clara told Candor and Germain the adventure of the poplar tree, and begged her father to ſend Germain after him ; not to bring him back, but to upbraid him, in the blackeſt terms, with his ingratitude.—Candor heard patiently Clara's report, and ſhewed her that the project ſhe had conceived was quite impracticable. Which way indeed, could he ſend in purſuit of him ? Which way did he go ? A whole hour at leaſt, had elapſed ſince his departure.—Beſides, in ſuch weather !—would it be worth while to brave tempeſt and lightning to run after a traitor ? No, my dear Clara, continued he, it is uſeleſs to give ourſelves any trouble ; you ſhall ſee your Alexis, you ſhall ſee him again ; but he ſhall pay dear for the torments he cauſes Clara !—Withdraw, for a while, to your apartment, and leave me to conſult with Germain upon what can be done.

Clara kiſſed her father's hand, and repaired to her apartment, where ſhe wept bitterly. Thus ſhe ſpent the beſt part of the evening and night without ſeeing either Candor or Germain ! the latter finally came to open her priſon (for ſhe had been under key ;) " Clara," ſaid he, " follow me, you will ſee him again."—" Who ? Alexis ?"—" Himſelf, he is here."—" O heaven ! ſhall I—yes, I will—let us go, Germain, conduct me to the traitor !—will he be able to ſtand my preſence ?"

Thus ſhe—Germain immediately laid hold of her hand, and made her go down into the place where ſhe had never been before ; but let us not dwell upon a deſcription of
it,

it, which we shall give hereafter; but let us see how Alexis was conducted to it.

We left him in a cavern of the forest, haunted by remorse and fantastic apparitions. He was now an hour in it, when he thought he heard a voice at the bottom of the subterranean; he listens, the voice utters his name; it is no vision, a feeble light glimmers at a distance before him. Is it a snare? shall he go and follow that voice which may make him tumble into some abyss? Yes, Alexis, prompted by a supernatural courage, risks the adventure. Whosoever you be, (calls he out to the man who carried the light, whose features he could not distinguish) whosoever you be I will follow you boldly; but what do you want of me?—No answer is given. He advances, and the light disappears before him.—What intrepidity in a young man of eighteen; to be sure, so extraordinary an adventure was worth his no[ita-] Alexis thought he saw spec[: he] he trembled—now he fol[no rea-]man, and his firmness [try; but] frightful illusions often[perate a] more than credulity. [neart, and]

He therefore walke[erm of all] guide, and distance alw[] him from recognizing [is kind and] passage took up abc[Duverly with] he remarked a [made him the offer] this grotto; [use his home as long] faction off[. Duverly gratefully] then a lit[is proposal, and I re-]layers hanks to my father. The him, soon became so fond of my to k[as to blazen forth his merits] Ihout reserve, and to make him, every thing, the pattern of my onduct: we both studied the pro-ession of the law, for which Duerly manifested more disposition and taste than myself. He became also daily more grave and serious.

his way, and his astonishment became so great as not to permit him to think. At last he saw himself in a splendid temple, whose door shut itself after him. The floor and columns were of black marble, and on the ceiling hung a lamp which cast a deadly gleam. In the centre of the temple several steps led to a magnificent tomb; above it he saw a picture, representing a woman with a child in her lap. Alexis, struck with all these things, had no doubt of the portraits being that of the persons set by the tomb. But what place could it be? Who was he that conducted him to it? His guide had disappeared, he was alone, shut up, and nobody came to let him out.—Alexis [you well.] repent his too [... and it being] when, lo! [... that he could not] abl[... ue with regard to Duver-]...y esteem for the latter height. [...]ed, and I tried every thing in my power to re-obtain his confidence, which I thought I had forfeited by my failings.

My father was very intimate with an old baroness, whose name was Myrsange: she was the widow of an officer of horse, and a few years since came to live at Grenoble with her only child, an adorable charming young lady, whom I could not see without emotion. My father, my friend, and I, were used to spend the evening at the baroness' house, and the too lovely Adela made every day so great a progress in my affections, that I soon was able to discern the nature of my sentiments. I made this confidence to Duverly, who, surprised and astonished, received my avowal with such a kind of indignation as intimidated me from making further confidence. What, said he, do you love Miss Myrsange! You—only think, Dorance! Think that she is but a sort of adventurer, whose family

and

depended on. O treacherous Alexis! you have opened my eyes but too much!—I see I have lost all in this world, as there is not one single friend left to me.—Ah! my father, cried Alexis, throwing himing himself at his feet, ah! my generous benefactor! yes, you speak the truth, it was a trial too hard for my heart.—But did you know what conflicts and torments I endured!—Ah! pardon me, and be persuaded that it wanted nothing less than filial tenderness that could balance that you have inspired me with.

Candor was going to reply, when a door opened—it is Germain, it is Clara, who came to load the unweight of Alexis with their recavern presents immortified with He enters to avoid the youth, wrath; he venters to step a their forward; all of a sudden an involuntary horror makes him tremble, his hair stands at an end, he thinks to see spectres that pursue and stop him; he believes he hears the voice of Clara and Candor; it is they, it is their voice; they load him with reproaches and curses. Heaven! where is he to seek refuge? The phantoms pursue him wherever he goes; on all sides sighs and shrieks resound in his ears. Let us for a moment leave him in this critical situation, and see what passes in the cottage.

Clara, after she had read the words, written on the great poplar, ran back to the cottage in hopes to find Alexis; but what was her surprize, when her father informs her that he is not there, but went out a hunting in the forest.—" A hunting!" cried Clara; "ah, my father, he flies from you, he leaves you forever!"—" What do you say, my daughter?"—" Yes, the ungrateful Alexis is gone!—We shall

est; if he has been your guide hither without your being able to know him; in short, if I receive you for the first time in this dismal place, it is merely to disclose a great design which I have conceived, and to exact from your arm a vengeance, which my own, withered by age, cannot take upon the cruel enemy who has caused all my misfortunes. Behold this mysterious cave, which I have concealed from you till now, and in which lays deposited what makes both my despair and the treasure of my heart!—Here lies my spouse—she was guilty, but—my poor son!—Permit me to let flow my tears!—Here you see his image; this is his portrait; alas! a barbarous monster has murdered them both—would you believe it, my son, that monster stands before you? I am the monster!—yes, I am he who sacrificed them!—O shame! O remorse! O despair! must my old age be haunted by the remembrance of so atrocious a while—No, I will have no commerce to · children; my tears will wash off the blood with which Clara tied my hands!"

and repa man wept for a while, where she by degrees, and comspent the history of his misforand night Clara herself heard Candor or Germme. nally came to ope, she had been under k v. said he, " follow me, him again."—" Who? of his rihim again."—" Who? A " Himself, he is here."—" my faen! shall I—yes, I will—Lerlia- Germain, conduct me to the iv.' tor!—will he be able to stand? presence?"

Thus she—Germain immediately laid hold of her hand, and made her go down into the place where she had never been before; but let us not dwell upon a description of where I unfortunately made the acquaintance of a traitor, the chevalier Duverly. Like me, young, brifk, and fiery, his temper bore fo much refemblance to mine, that, in a little time, we became fo intimate, that we could hardly be feparated for one moment. He was an orphan, and his education entrufted to the care of a guardian, who was to reftore him his whole property when he fhould come to be of age.

I fhall not expatiate upon the particulars of our intimacy, nor the circumftances which cemented it: it will be fufficient for you to know, that upon leaving the college, where we had ftudied the *humanities* together, I requefted him to come and fpend fome time with me at Grenoble at my father's houfe, to whom I had many times wrote in a very flattering manner, about my friend's conduct, and alfo expreffed a defire of getting more particular knowledge of him. Duverly at that time complied with an invitation, that quite charmed him: he loved me, or, I had at leaft no reafon to think to the contrary; but his paffions were foon to operate a change in his perfidious heart, and to infect it with the fperm of all vices.

My father, who was kind and generous, received Duverly with cordiality, and made him the offer to make his houfe his home as long as he pleafed. Duverly gratefully accepted his propofal, and I returned thanks to my father. The latter foon became fo fond of my friend as to blazen forth his merits without referve, and to make him, in every thing, the pattern of my conduct: we both ftudied the profeffion of the law, for which Duverly manifefted more difpofition and tafte than myfelf. He became alfo daily more grave and ferious.

He had no more for me that confidence, nor made thofe friendly effufions which I fo often experienced from him in his youth; in a word, I found him more referved and deliberate. Whatever alarmed me in his conduct; whatever I confidered as an evident change in his friendfhip to me, my father looked upon as an energy of mind and a difcretion of character entitled to his admiration. Behold, faid he, often to me, behold your friend! he fhows not that levity fo confpicuous in your character; he is grave, reafonable, thinking, and folid. Endeavour to preferve always his friendfhip, and to follow his advice, for I am certain he wifhes you well. I liftened to my father, and it being congenial to me, that he could not miflead me with regard to Duverly, my efteem for the latter heightened, and I tried every thing in my power to re-obtain his confidence, which I thought I had forfeited by my failings.

My father was very intimate with an old baronefs, whofe name was Myrfange: fhe was the widow of an officer of horfe, and a few years fince came to live at Grenoble with her only child, an adorable charming young lady, whom I could not fee without emotion. My father, my friend, and I, were ufed to fpend the evening at the baronefs' houfe, and the too lovely Adela made every day fo great a progrefs in my affections, that I foon was able to difcern the nature of my fentiments. I made this confidence to Duverly, who, furprifed and aftonifhed, received my avowal with fuch a kind of indignation as intimidated me from making further confidence. What, faid he, do you love Mifs Myrfange! You—only think, Dorance! Think that fhe is but a fort of adventurer, whofe family and

and property are equally unknown to every body. She and her mother, I grant you, make a tolerable figure in this town ; but whence come they ? Who are they ? it is now three years they have refided here ; is that enough to know well perfons, who perhaps have been banifhed or expudiated ? Open your eyes, Dorance—acknowledge your folly—your faher will never confent to it, believe me. No, he will never confent : I know him. He will, I fuppofe, make inquiries, and fhould they not prove fatisfactory, you know yourfelf the confequence —in other refpects he repofes great truft in me ; and if he afks my advice, in faith, I will be candid with you, refent it if you choofe, yet, I fhall never give my opinion in favour of fuch a match.—O heaven ! what, Duverly !—no : depend upon it : I profefs too much attachment to your well-being, not to fuffer you to throw yourfelf blindly and headlong into a precipice : the day would come, when you would reproach me with having promoted your ruin.—My ruin ! by all means ; have not you dived into the character of that little body? Oh ! I know her better than you. I can fwear—firft of all I believe fhe is a haughty, imperious, flandering coquet. She has wit, I won't deny her that ; but a deceitful, malicous and farcaftic wit, you yourfelf know it—My dear Dorance is it poffible !—ah, did you know how painful this confeffion of your's is to me ! painful on your account ; for were you not my friend, it would be very indifferent to me, whether you have her or another— Come, promife me to follow my advice, and to conquer a foolifh paffion, which fhould never have rofe in your heart.

This difcourfe of Duverly afton-

ifhed me to fuch a degree, that I was at a lofs to make a reply—I remained motionlefs, my heart was heavy ; I was going, I believe, to fhed tears, when my father by his entering the apartment, interrupted our converfation, and took us with him to the court, where a caufe highly interefting was to be pleaded; it was a couple who had married by inclination and without the confent of their parents : fix months having paft, they became equally odious to one another, and fued for a divorce. They made ufe of as many invectives as they formerly had made of tender and pious expreffions, and adduced in their behalf facts fo atrocious, as would have provoked the moft indelicate ear.

This fuit ftruck me with horror, and Duverly, who preceived it, was pleafed to add to my confufion, by pufhing me at every quotation made by the counfellors, and expatiating with a low voice, upon the dangers of an ill-concerted marriage, which each of the couple depicted with equal energy.

Upon my return, I made the moft cruel reflections. I did not fufpect my friend of any fecret motive to oppofe my paffion : moreover, my father efteemed him much, and entertained the moft flattering notions of his fpirit and judgment : this was a fufficient reafon for me to refpect him blindly.

Of all the fears Duverly had caufed me, none feemed to me well founded ; they were confined to vague fufpicions, without proofs, and of no alarming nature. What could I think of Duverly ! He had appeared much moved at the confidence I made him of my paffion : was it his concern for me, which—Oh ! yes, it was doubtlefs his concern, his friendfhip alone, which

which made him fpeak to me. He was perhaps too timid, too prying into futurity; but all this reflects honor upon his heart; he was attached to me; he loved and refpected my father, and was afraid left he fhould fee unfortunate, fome day, the family he cherifhed.

I did abide by thefe reflections, and intended to ftudy Mifs Myrfange's character, and to renounce her hand, if ever I fhould difcover in it the faults which my friend had pointed out.

My father, however, frequently afked me what I thought of Adela? I dared not difclofe to him my real fentiments on that head, left they fhould kindle his wrath. One day he explained himfelf to me in a more diftinct manner. Dorance, faid he, I perceive the daughter of the baronefs is not indifferent to you; anfwer me, my fon, open your heart, and thou wilt perhaps not repent.—My father—you love her; come, out with the word— Yes my father, I do love the charming Adela; yes, I do adore her, were you even to load me with all the weight of— O load you !— what means that, my fon? You accomplifh my wifhes and thofe of her mother;—know that we both defire to fee love rife in your breaft!—how ! —Adela is your's, Adela fhall be your fpoufe upon condition—What condition? fpeak father. What condition? That you go to Paris to ftudy law, to receive inftruction, and enable yourfelf to take the function of my charge, which I fhall not refign but in favour of that marriage. To go to Paris, my father! Could not I ftudy here, as well as in Paris?—Undoubtedly, but there is no place like Paris for young people to get inftructed. Befides I will recommend you to my beft friend, Mr. de Calenzieux;

he is a counfellor of parliament, and will perhaps take better care of your education than I can do; he is an old fenator, replete with genius and knowledge: go to him my fon, go to draw from his advice that prudence and wifdom, fo neceffary to him who is to be the judge of his equals: and as you are to fucceed me in office, give me the fatisfaction to think, when I defcend to the grave, that I leave my fellow citizens a virtuous and equitable magiftrate. You fhall fet off tomorrow with Duverly, who, I have no doubt (for Mr. de Calenzieux will receive you both with equal pleafure, and he tells me fo in his anfwer) will accompany you; then return in a twelve month: yes, in a twelvemonth you fhall poffefs Adela, and fulfil the hope of my old age !

I embraced my father, and retired with the greateft joy. I was however determined not to mention any thing about the project of my marriage to Duverly, fearing he might try to alter my father's mind, and I only informed him of our intended journey to Paris. I perceived that this news was highly vexatious to him; he turned pale, oppofed the meafure for fome time, and when he made me perceive that he began to feel the weight of the links of our friendfhip, my father, much occupied that day, had only time to fay a few words to him; he requefted him to accompany me to Paris, and to be my mentor. My dear Duverly, faid he, you are a man of found and folid parts, be vigilant over my fon, grant him always your friendfhip and your advice, which I command him to follow and to refpect as mine own. Let him pay attention to you, and he will accomplifh all my wifhes. Duverly anfwered only ftammering;

ing ; I obferved him to be down-caſt that whole day. At night we went to take our leaves of the bar-onefs and her daughter : the latter gave me a very cold reception, caſt down her eyes, and I thought I perceived ſhe had been weeping. I paid her a compliment which ſhe did not return : I preſſed her hand without her ſeeming to be moved. Her coldnefs affeſted me ; I could eaſily difcover that ſhe did not love me ; an involuntary bluſh diffuſed itſelf over my face, and I let drop ſome tears. The mother, who per-ceived my perplexity, endeavoured to allay it : ſhe opened her arms and called me her ſon, I obtained leave of her to embrace her daugh-ter ; but feeing the latter averſe to grant the parting kifs, ſhe was or-dered to comply. Well ! my daugh-ter, ſaid the baronefs, well !—that may be granted to a perſon who takes his leave—come, comfort him, that poor traveller : he is, you ſee, ſorry to leave us !—Adela o-beyed with ſeeming reluſtance, and I embraced her trembling. With regard to Duverly, the baronefs was much more referved ; but the per-fidious Adela had not the leaſt ob-jeſtion to embrace him ; ſhe made half the advances to it : I was not ſurpriſed : ſhyneſs might have made her more moderate with me, and, having ſuffered me to take that lib-erty, it would have been the groſſeſt inſult to my friend, not to grant him the ſame indulgence. We ſet out early on the next morning, and, during the whole journey, Duverly was ſad, uneaſy, grieved, and even ſnappiſh ; he ſometimes ſighed, looked up to heaven, and exclaim-ed, I am very unfortunate ! What is the matter, dear friend, aſked I ? Why, nothing, anſwered he ; my health, which I ſee decline day by day, gives me ſome uneaſinefs—I

feel ſuch depreſſions and palpita-tions of heart, which robs me of reſt both day and night. Aye, it is the vapours. The vapours, ſir ! you call it the vapours ! you are very inhuman, very hard !—I beg your pardon my friend, I did not wiſh to—you are happy !—ev-ery body ſmiles at you ! you are al-ways ſucceſsful ! what, you ! you are as hardy as Hercules !—you enjoy the careſſes of a father, of a moſt excellent father ! but I, who, have no parents, nobody in the world. I am left alone to myſelf ! —Alone—to yourſelf—when you have friends !

Duverly made no anſwer to this : he had a relapſe of his melancholy, and I was ſorry to ſee him in ſuch a ſituation ; as to his health having been worſe for ſome time, it was true, he had no ſleep, he could not eat, and fell into a ſtate of languor, which would bring on a dangerous diforder.

It was not long before it happen-ed. We had now been two months at the houſe of the counſellor, when Duverly was taken ill. The phy-ficians who were confulted upon his cafe, gave it as their opinion, that the young man had ſome inward grief which preyed upon him, and if it was poſſible to remedy its in-fluence, his life might eaſily be fav-ed. Judge what impreſſion this re-port made upon me. I, who loved Duverly, believed to poſſefs his con-fidence ! he concealed his grief from me. Ah ! my feeling heart could not bear that idea ; I was de-termined to try all poſſible means to get from him that fatal ſecret, and to reſtore him to health, even at the riſk of my life. As I ſat up by him regularly every night, I took the opportunity of a moment when he was calm and ſettled, to ad-drefs him as follows : Duverly, you

will

will die; you will conceal from me the cause of your death—ah! what an outrage to my heart! could you pry into it; could you but see!—entrust me with your sorrows, my dear Duverly; entrust me with them—if it was in my power to redeem your life, doubt not, I will do every thing!—Yes, Dorance, it is in your power :—yet—speak, in the name of heaven, speak—your friend does conjure you!—I am afraid the service which I require of you will hurt your feelings.—No matter: if I can do it without trespassing the laws of honour, cost what it will, I am prepared for all.—O my friend! were I sure of you; but—Duverly! Duverly! how can you thus grieve me? Well, I will make an entire confession—but how can I?—Ah' hear me, and pardon if I conceal certain particulars, which—You must disguise nothing!—I should should not for my own sake, but for—the person I love.—You love! you!—O heaven, do you really love?—Yes I do love, I do burn!—attend to me; pray, attend.

Duverly upon this prepared to digest in his head the little fable he was going to relate. Alas! my friends, had he then unravelled to me the truth, all would have been over : I would have made him welcome to Adela's hand; I would have made that effort, and not have suffered a series of misfortunes, of which he was the sole author, and which will never cease but with my life.

Know then, said he, that the first day of our arrival at Grenoble, I paid a visit to a relation of the name of Mrs. des Roches. I never mentioned that lady before, because she is the only source of my unfortunate adventure, and I—hesitated to let you into any fatal secret. I met at her house with a respectable old man, who came there upon a visit with his daughter, a girl of about sixteen : no, my friend, thou never hast seen so much allurement, brown (observe, my children, that Adela was fair) brown, sprightly, full, replete with wit, graces, and accomplishments ; I could not see her, without falling desperately in love. When she had left the house, I made bold to tell my relation what impression the young lady had made upon my heart. Beware, Duverly, answered she, of harbouring such a passion. Rosina's sole dependence is on a wealthy and very amiable father. A young colonel now in town, has solicited her hand, and promise was made on both sides.— O heaven! and does Rosina love him?—Alas! no, the poor child has fits quite averse to that marriage ; but the will of a father is a law!—How soon is her marriage to take place?—I do not know : the colonel expects the consent of his family, may arrive tomorrow.

Mrs. des Roches made me also the confidant of many other circumstances : the most pleasing to me was to hear that Rosina came every day quite alone to see her, and staid for whole hours. The father, pursued she, has every possible friendship for me, and is never more pleased than when he knows his daughter is at my house.

I begged leave of Mrs. des Roches to permit me to see the beautiful Rosina at her house, to which she at first thought proper to refuse : but when she saw that I persisted in my intreaties, and dropping down upon my knees, and a torrent of tears gushed from mine eyes, she was at last finally prevailed upon to comply. Thus I had the good fortune to see fair Rosina every day, to declare my passion to her, and to find her soon moved with pity for her distracted

diftracted lover. What a difference (continued the traitorous Du-
verley) what a difference between
my Rofina and your Adela!—Ah!
if I was as free as you, I would
marry her without delay. If her
mother, her father, I fay, would
give me their confent, as the baronefs gives you her daughter!—but;

no, the father, a hard and cruel father, is fo overfond of his colonel,
that he will make Rofina a facrifice
to intereft and rank!—Ah! my
friend, you fee my difafterous fate!
I muft renounce the moft beauteous, the moft amiable young lady!
—Oh! how I am to be pitied!
(To be continued.)

A PICTURE of VIRTUE in DISTRESS.

TURNING the corner of a
ftreet I met a young woman
who begged me to give her fomething, it would be a great charity.
She wept bitterly, her diftrefs affected me; I examined her with attention, and I found in her face
much fweetnefs and many charms,
though fhe was extremely dejected,
and feemed to be embarraffed.—
Notwithftanding her clothes were
worn out, there was fomething in
her appearance, which commanded refpect. "Why do you weep?"
faid I. "Alas! fir, I am in a
moft miferable condition," fhe replied; but in a tone of voice which
chilled my blood, and which fhewed
anguifh and defpair. I was almoft
tempted to leave her without inquiring any farther, to fpare myfelf the painful intereft that fhe began to infpire me with; but I could
not get the better of the pity I felt
for her fufferings; it would have
required more refolution than I
was mafter of; and had I given
way to caution, I fhould have been
more uncomfortable, than if I had
been ever fo much affected by her
misfortunes. I took her to a place
where I might hear her ftory without being interrupted. "You appear to me, madam, to be very unhappy," (faid I, giving her money)
" may I beg to know the caufe of

fo much affliction?" She only anfwered at firft with fighs, her tears
flowed fafter than before; at length,
being a little pacified—" Since you
you have the goodnefs to be interefted in my fufferings," (faid fhe) " I
will make you acquainted with the
circumftances that have occafioned
them. I am of a good family, my
father had a confiderable place under government in one of the provinces, he died about three years ago,
gaming had impaired his fortune,
and my mother became a widow
with three daughters to provide for,
of which I am the eldeft.

" My mother and I came to Paris, after having fold all our effects,
in order to put an end to a law-fuit,
which, had we gained, might have
re-eftablifhed our affairs. We have
been here eighteen months, the perfon we are at law with has great
intereft, he knows that the decifion
of the court cannot be favorble to
him, and has influenced the Judges
to defer paffing fentence; in confequence of this delay we have been
obliged to difpofe of every thing we
had. In this extremity we have
been induced to throw ourfelves at
the feet of our Judges, to implore
their juftice: But in court we have
always found them furrounded with
clients, among whom we did not
dare to intrude ourfelves in the fhab-
by

by condition we are. When we waited upon them at their houſe, whether it was that our appearance did not attract the attention of their ſervants, or that we went at improper hours, we were always told their maſters were buſy, or not at home. By which means we have nobody to defend our cauſe ; our affairs are neglected becauſe we have no longer any money. At length, the miſery to which we are reduced, our ſufferings, the unwholeſome air we breathe, and the obſcurity of the place we live in, the pain that my mother endures on my account, and her great age, render her incapable of ſupporting ſuch an accumulation of diſtreſs. She is very ill, and is in want of every thing. I am in deſpair to ſee her in this ſituation ; I muſt beſides reſiſt my love and compaſſion for her. If I liſten to them I am ruined. A rich merchant has offered me every poſſible aſſiſtance ; but what aſſiſtance, ſir ! he would ſave the mother's life at the expenſe of the daughter's honour. This is my ſituation, can you conceive one more horrible ?

I love my mother, and ſhe has the greateſt affection for me ; ſhe is dying, which makes me tremble for us both ; in my affliction I have made her acquainted with the offers of the man which I mentioned to you. I thought when ſhe had heard my ſtory, ſhe would have expired in my arms ; ſhe bathed me with her tears, and gave me a look expreſſive of the greateſt deſpair, then turned her face from me without ſaying a ſingle word. I do not know why I did not urge her to ſpeak to me. It ſeemed as if this virtuous woman's courage entirely failed her, and that ſhe ſunk under the weight of our misfortunes. For my part, I would die to be relieved from the danger of ſeeing her.

Every good man will feel how much the diſcourſe of this young woman muſt have affected me. I gave her what money I could ſpare, to which I added the moſt ſalutary advice her ſituation ſuggeſted, and returned home almoſt as much afflicted as ſhe was.

[New Lady's Mag.

LETTER of Dr. Johnson's to a Friend, on the Death of his Wife.

DEAR SIR,

AT a time when all your friends ought to ſhew their kindneſs, and with a character which ought to make all that know you your friends, you may wonder that you have yet heard nothing from me.

I have been hindered by a vexatious and inceſſant cough, which this day ſeems to remit.

The loſs, dear ſir, which you have lately ſuffered, I felt many years ago, and know therefore, how much has been taken from you,

and how little help can be had from conſolation. He that outlives a wife, whom he has long loved, ſees himſelf disjoined from the only mind that has the ſame hopes, and fears, and intereſt. From the only companion with whom he has ſhared much good or evil ; and with whom he could ſet his mind at liberty, to retrace the paſt, or anticipate the future.

The continuity of being is lacerated ; the ſettled courſe of ſentiment

ment

ment and action is stopped ; and life stands suspended and motionless, till it is driven by external causes into a new channel. But the time of suspense is dreadful.

Our first recourse in this distressed solitude, is, perhaps, for want of habitual piety, to a gloomy acquiescence in necessity. Of two mortal beings, one must lose the other; but surely there is a higher and better comfort to be drawn from the consideration of that Providence which watches over all, and a belief that the living and the dead are equally in the hands of God, who will reunite those whom he has separated, or who sees that it is best not to reunite.

I am, dear sir, &c.

SAM. JOHNSON.

Biographical Sketch of JOSEPH MARIA PANCRAZI.

" Wits live obscurely, men know not how ; or die obscurely, men know not when."

ASCHAM.

" FORTUNE has rarely condescended to be the companion of merit. Even in these enlightened times men of letters have lived in obscurity, while their reputation was widely spread ; and have perished in poverty, while their works were enriching the bookfellers.

That generous warmth of soul which encouragement might have enlivened into gratitude, or bounty elevated to ambition, has too frequently been extinguished by the tears neglect has caused it to shed. Want and dependence check the flights of genius, obstruct every noble effort of the mind, and " chill the genial current of the soul."

A person endowed with superior mental faculties in distress, was, by the antients, very aptly shadowed under the emblem of Minerva in a poor habit, having her right hand chained to a huge stone lying on the ground, whilst her left hand, which is furnished with a pair of wings, is held aloft ; signifying the ardor with which GENIUS aspires to the noblest things, whilst unhappiness of condition restrains its endeavours and prevents the accomplishment of its desires.

A little memorandom by the late Thomas Hollis Esq. (the munificent benefactor to Harvard university) led to these humilitating remarks.

There was something very affecting in the fate of Father Pancrazi. The learning and the merit of this excellent and hospitable man were known and admired throughout Italy. Yet these empty applauses, sometimes leavened with malignant envy, were the only rewards obtained from his industrious application to literary pursuits, his extensive erudition, and bounteous generosity. Wholly engaged in his studies and his devotions he took no thought for the necessary supplies of life. His resources, every day lessening in acts of charity and hospitality, and in the purchase of rare and valuable books, were at length exhausted. He became extremely poor. It was now, however, that he began his much admired work on the Antiquities of Sicily :* This he composed, as the celebrated Johnson says he did his dictionary, " with little assistance from the learned, and without any patronage of the great ; amidst inconvenience and distraction,

---

* Antichita Siciliane. Napol. 1751. 2 vol. fol.

diſtraction, ſickneſs and ſorrow;" and much of his time was unavoidably ſpent in making proviſion for the day, which was paſſing over him. Many who read his book with admiration knew of his neceſſities, yet no one relieved them. "In the autumn of 1752, ſays Mr. Hollis,* he lodged in a Theatin convent, the convent of his order, at Naples. There he was attacked by a violent fever, which impaired and broke his conſtitution. In that feeble ſtate, however, he applied to his work; and, in order more ſpeedily to publiſh the third volume of it, found means, in the year 1753, to ſell a few rare medals which he had collected, to the king, by whom he had the honour to be perſonally known and reſpected. The ſuperior of the convent ſomehow got intelligence of that tranſaction, claimed the money ariſing from the ſale of the medals for the uſes of the convent, and obtained it. When Father Pancrazi became apprized of the event he went diſtracted directly; and after languiſhing, with intervals, miſerably ſome years, at length ended his wretched life."

* See a note in his own hand writing, in the firſt volume of the above work in the Library of Harvard Univerſity: to which Mr. Hollis makes this addition, "this good man rendered me hoſpitality, and by his letters I travelled throughout Sicily and Malta."

A CURIOUS FACT.

[From a Delaware Paper.]

I SEND you an account of a curious fact, which I have often heard aſſerted, but which never came fully under my notice till very lately. During ſeveral weeks of laſt ſummer, one of my milch-cows very frequently gave clotted blood from one of her teats, which, whenever this was the caſe, appeared much ſcratched and inflamed. The milkmaid inſiſted ſhe was ſucked by a ſnake, and ſaid it was frequently the caſe in Maryland. I paid but little attention to her remark at firſt. Obſerving the animal ſo affected, I had her put into a ſeparate paſture, and then no accident happened for ſeveral days. Thinking ſhe might now be ſuffered to graze with the other cattle, ſhe was put into her former paſture, and immediately her milk and teat was affected as above. I determined to have her watched; ſhe ſeemed very uneaſy towards evening, always repaired to the ſame ſpot of the field about that time, and lowed violently as if ſhe had loſt her calf. One evening, as I was walking towards her, I ſaw a large black ſnake very near her: It ſlipped away on preceiving me, to an adjoining graſs field, and we could not find it again. The cow was removed to a different paſture ſoon after, and nothing uncommon was obſerved either in her milk or teat. Early this ſpring ſhe was put with other cattle, into the field where the ſnake was ſeen laſt Auguſt. She began to low as calling her calf: and a little girl who was watching her, ſaw the ſnake near her. It fled to a ſtump upon ſeeing her. She ran home to call one of the men, who immediately accompanied her to the ſpot, found the ſnake, killed it, and brought it home. It meaſured near four feet; was of the black kind, and reſembled exactly the one I ſaw near the cow laſt ſummer. I cannot help concluding

cluding from thefe circumftances, that it was the fame fnake ; and if the cow fhould not be affected in the fame manner during the courfe of this fummer, I think we may reafonably fuppofe that the uncommon appearance of her milk and teat, muft have arifen from her being fucked by this reptile.

ANECDOTE of Dr. JOHNSON.

A RUDE cuftom prevailed for thofe who failed upon the river Thames to accoft each other in the moft abufive and fatirical language. A fellow having in this fituation attacked Dr. Johnfon with fome coarfe raillery, he anfwered, " Sir, your wife, under pretence of *keeping a bawdy houfe,* is a receiver of ftolen goods.

For the MASSACHUSETTS MAGAZINE.

A SERMON.

GENESIS III, 16.

Thy defire fhall be to thy hufband, and he fhall rule over thee.

UPON a furvey of the material world, the great Architect pronounced it good. To partake of the bleffings of creation, God formed numberlefs claffes of beings and endowed with powers that fitted them for their refpective ftations. To contemplate the beauties of creation ; to rule the animal world, and to enjoy the pleafures of reafon and virtue. He formed man out of the duft of the ground, and breathed into him the breath of life. To man he imparted a fpark of his own intelligence, and inftamped upon him his image. Compaffionating his folitary condition, he gave him a companion poffeffed of all the graces and fenfibilities of beauty, modefty and innocence. With her he was to enjoy the rich and various bleffings of heaven, and to participate in all the endearments of focial life.

In a difcourfe from the paffage of fcripture before us.—I fhall illuftrate the following propofitions.

1. The defign of woman's creation was, that fhe might devote herfelf to the concerns of domeftic life. Thy defire fhall be to thy hufband.

2. That woman ought to be fubject to the direction of man, he, *thy hufband,* fhall rule over thee.

1. The defign of woman's creation was, that fhe might devote herfelf to the concerns of domeftic life.

The defign of every being may be learned from the conftitution of his nature.

Man was formed out of the duft of the ground. His nerves are vigorous, and his general frame is robuft and hardy : Hence his aptitude for the bufy fcenes of the world, his fondnefs for the noife and buftle of fociety, his ambition for places of difficulty and danger.

Woman was not made of rough materials. The clay that formed
for

man was a fecond time fublimated for the compofition of woman. She is therefore a lefs fimple, but a more refined being than man. Her delicate frame is not fuited for the more laborious and perplexing fcenes of human life; like the fenfative plant, fhe fhrinks from the rougher impreffions of difficulty and danger. She was taken from the head to fuperintend and direct the important affairs of fociety; fhe was not taken from the limbs of more immediate action to be the flave of man and to execute his lordly mandates; but fhe was taken from the fide, the feat of the tender affections. In her are concentred all the nicer feelings, the more refined fenfibilities of human nature. She is formed for the foft and tender relations of a friend, a wife and a mother. Obfervation will confirm this reafoning upon the female frame : Solomon declares, and who can difpute the experience of Solomon, Solomon declares that a man among a thoufand he had found averfe to the endearments of domeftic life, but a woman he had never found. Univerfal hiftory gives its teftimony to the truth of this maxim of the wife man. While men tread the theatre of ambition for empty frame, or grovel in the duft,their native foil,for paltry gold, women collect for the focial amufements of the tea table or the affembly-room. While the phlegmatic conftitutions of men fuffer them to fet like ftatues torpid and dumb, the more delicate nerves of women vibrate at fight of each other, and the ingenuoufnefs of their hearts gives perpetual volubility to their tongues. While we are fpeaking of the general propenfity of women for fociety, I would notice a *particular bias*, arifing from the perpetual tendency of the matter of which

they are compofed, to reunite to its original fubftance.

I pafs to confider the fecond head of our fubject, viz.

2. Women ought to be fubject to men. He, *thy hufband*, fhall rule over thee.

This propofition is a confequence of the former.

The bufinefs of man is to enter into ferious action, that he may acquire the means of amufement and pleafure to women--While therefore women ftimulate men, by all the arts of perfuafion, to exertion, they muft allow them to judge of the extent of their abilities, and to determine the extent of the fupplies which they can furnifh for recreation and amufement.

A few practical reflections will clofe the difcourfe.

1. Since the concerns of domeftic life are the peculiar province of women, they have at leaft in thefe relations equal privileges with man; yet the tyrannic cuftoms of the world forbid them to make the firft overtures, and many a fine woman is obliged alone to tread the dreary path of life, the chief defign of her exiftence unaccomplifhed. And in this place I muft bring into view that infignificant,inanimate, worthlefs animal, I can't find words to exprefs my contempt—an old bachelor. Whether he be more the object of fcorn than of pity is not eafy to determine, fo we will leave him in the arms of infenfibility, which is the moft congenial to his difpofition.

2. Let women be content to move in that fphere, which nature has marked out to them. Let them not lofe the fofter traits of female delicacy in the mafculine airs of the other fex. May not placid features be diftorted by anger, nor nativecharms,in themfelvesirrefiftable,

ble, be rendered ridiculous by vanity and affectation. Strive not to teaze and vex that being, to promote whose happiness, was one reason of your formation ; but may purity of sentiment, refinement of expression, and dignity of manners ever be the attendants of beings on earth, the most accomplished, the most perfect. But should any of the sex fall from this delicacy of behaviour, load her not with that weight of abuse and infamy which will prevent her reascending the seat of virtue, while you permit the criminal agent of her ruin to go unpunished, and perhaps to glory in his shame. Combine to brand the man with infamy who can treat you with dishonour, and in this way bring impudence and villainy into disgrace.

And thou, O man ! who boastest of thy superiority, act agreeably to thy arrogant pretensions. Recoil from the thought of baseness and cruelty, to beings placed in any degree dependent on thee.

Give not pain to the breast that was formed to be the seat of softness and humanity. Aim not to ensnare the heart that has been taught to look up to thee for support and protection. By your behaviour prove that you are worthy of confidence.

To conclude.

May the courage and strength of one sex protect the innocence and beauty of the other. As you, O man ! are indebted to the female sex, for the refinements and the happiness of social life, do you repay them, by the cheerful performance of the laborious offices of society, and strive to render those acts of attention and benevolence, pleasant, which their station obliges them to receive from you.

As man labours, O woman ! that the fruits of his toils may administer to your convenience and pleasure, condescend to soothe his afflictions, to soften his cares, and to render his fatigues light and easy. Thus may you mutually endeavour to make the road of life pleasant and happy.

DIGNITY of the British HOUSE of COMMONS.
[From Boswell's Life of Dr. Johnson.]

I TOLD Dr. Johnson that I was engaged as counsel at the bar of the House of Commons, to oppose a road-bill in the county of Stirling, and asked him what mode he would advise me to follow in addressing such an audience ? "Why, sir, you must provide yourself with a good deal of extraneous matter, which you are to produce occasionally, so as to fill up the time ; for you must consider, that they do not listen much : If you begin with the strength of your cause, it may be lost before they begin to listen.

When you catch a moment of attention, press the merits of the question upon them." He said, as to one point of the merits, that he thought " it would be a wrong thing to deprive the small landholders of the privileges of assessing themselves for making and repairing the high roads ; *it was destroying so much liberty, without a good reason, which was always a bad thing.*" When I mentioned this observation next day to Mr. John Wilkes, he replied, "What ! does *he* talk of liberty ? *Liberty* is as ridiculous

diculous in *his* mouth, as *religion* in *mine*." Mr. Wilkes's advice, as to the beft mode of fpeaking at the bar of the Houfe of Commons, was not more refpectful to the Senate, than that of Dr. Johnfon. " Be as impudent as you can, and fay whatever comes uppermoft. Jack Lee is the beft heard there of any counfel ; and he is the moft impudent dog, and always abufing us."

CHARLOTTE, or the Power of Virtue.

CHARLOTTE was fixteen, and very pretty ; fhe had loft her mother, and being deprived of her affiftance, was reduced to keep a flock of fheep. One day fhe went to offer her cuftomary tribute to her mother's fhade, a cup of pure water and the choiceft flowers. When the young orphan in the biternefs of her woe, had three times walked round her tomb in filence, under the fhade of the cyprefs trees that furrounded it ; fhe fat down and exclaimed, " O thou moft affectionate of mothers! may thy example, which is ever prefent to my imagination, caufe me to admire the power of virtue; yes, it is the remembrance of thee, who art ftill fo dear to me, that has refcued my innocence from the fnares of a feducer : May I ever follow thy footfteps. Know then the dangers by which I have been fo much alarmed : In what other breaft could I give vent to my tears ? Nothing fhall be concealed from thee. Fatigued from the noife of Athens, the lord of this country came to feek that tranquillity which is to be found upon the banks of thefe rivulets : The other day he accofted me, and with an air of great kindnefs, admired the flock entrufted to my care, and paid me many handfome compliments : When he looked at me, his eyes feemed to fparkle with inexpreffible joy. I faid to myfelf, " how good our mafter is ! " The rich are happy, they deferve to be fo ; I cannot in the leaft contribute to the bleffings he already enjoys but at the foot of the altar in this rural temple, I will ever offer up my prayers for him : But how fimple are we villagers! The next day I met him by accident not far from the grove, " ftop," (faid he) " and receive this pledge of my affection ;" he then put a gold ring on my finger, I blufhing caft my eyes upon the ground. "Doft thou fee, "(faid he,) " that pretty child upon the ring who has wings, and fmiles like thee ?" It is in his power to make thee happy ; he preffed my hand, and his voice found its way to the bottom of my heart. He loves thee, Charlotte, and has more than a father's tender care for thee ; " but," faid I to myfelf, in what manner couldeft thou have merited the kindnefs of fo great a nobleman ? Thefe, my dear mother, were then the reflections of thy daughter. The gods are witnefs how I was deceived, and how far I was from fufpecting the danger which I was in ; that morning he called me into the orchard, I cannot think of it without horror ! I haftened there to him : He took my hand, and gently preffing it, " come," faid the charming beauty, " leave thy flock for a moment, I am very fond of flowers, will you have the goodnefs to bring

me

me fome into this arbour?" Being credulous, I gathered the fineſt I could find, and joyfully ran to prefent him with them. "What grace," he exclaimed, "how much more charming are thefe rofes from the hands of Charlotte!" then giving way to the paffion with which he was inflamed——immortal gods! I tremble at it yet; he feized me, and fuddenly taking me in his arms, he preſſed me to his bofom with great violence; he made ufe of the moſt tender arguments, that love could fuggeſt. I trembled and burſt into tears; too weak to refiſt a feducer, I implored his pity, but in vain;—muſt I at length declare, that had it not been for thee, thy daughter would have been forever unhappy. At that inſtant I thought I faw thy avenging ghoſt; I immediately found my ſtrength redoubled, and by a great effort I efcaped from the arms of Myfis, and am come to offer thee tears of joy for my deliverance. O deareſt mother, for fo great a benefit, deign to receive my warmeſt gratitude; yes, it is the remembrance of thee who art ſtill fo dear to me, that has refcued my innocence from the fnares of a feducer. Ah! if ever I forget the kind advice thou gaveſt me, in thy laſt moments; if the torch of thy wifdom ſhould ceafe to direɭt my laſt ſteps, may I be left in this wicked world alone, forfaken by thee, and may the gods no longer keep me under their proteɭtion: fo young, alas! how great is my misfortune to lofe thee! Muſt I be, ye gods, like the tender flower, which, for want of fomething to fupport it, droops its head and falls? Thy ſhade from heaven defcended will divert the ſtorm that threatens my youth. May the fear of the gods, wifdom, and modeſty, reign in my heart, and may they be refleɭted in my countenance." She fpoke; and her eyes yet moiſt with her tears, ſhe had that graceful timidity which modeſty gives to beauty. A delightful glow animated her face, which might be compared to the heavens refuming their ferenity after a ſtorm; more fatisfied and not lefs captivating, Charlotte left this melancholy place. Myfis fuddenly appears, tears of contrition fall from his eyes; ah, pardon me thou moſt amiable of women, it is the moſt fincere remorfe that brings me into thy prefence; when thou wert in converfation with thy mother, this thicket hid me from thy view. I have heard every thing, deign to forget my great fault: Thy modeſty and goodnefs have covered me with confufion. I admire thee as much as I love thee, I triumph over my own inclinations, and it is thou that art intitled to the reward for it. Preferve thy beauty and be happy: the half of the flock under thy care, the cottage and the field adjoining to it are thine, do not refufe them; I aſk no other return but the heartfelt pleafure of rewarding a young woman, in whom I find fo much perfeɭtion. May a huſband worthy of thy love complete thy happinefs, and may each day pay homage to thy virtue.

A N E C D O T E.

AN Engliſh gentleman mentioned, that he was born in Moorfields, and was educated in Grub-ſtreet. One prefent replied, Sir, you have been regularly educated.

For the MASSACHUSETTS MAGAZINE.

The INVESTIGATOR. No. III.

Whate'er we do, let *honour* us control,
It shields our virtue and secures us fame;
Gains us the wife man's praise, the good man's prayer,
And makes us happy in a life's review.

BY Honour, I mean that, which prompts us to perform things consistent with the laws of God and society; things, which enrich the performer without injuring either his neighbour, or his country. It is a pair of scales suspended in the mind, and guarded by conscience; in which every man should weigh his thoughts, words and actions. It is as necessary for us so to conduct, as to exist: Not only for the benefit, which will accrue to us as individuals, but as a community.

There is nothing which ennobles a government so much as the freedom and honour it possesses. It is from that only you can calculate its increase and perpetuity. Riches are of no further use to a nation, or people, than this. That they are thereby rendered able to oppose the hostile attacks of its tyrannical neighbours. It cannot promote the happiness of a people, unless applied to initiate them in the useful arts and sciences. For this reason, the first aim of a free people should be, to improve themselves in the knowledge of divine law and human frailty. By this means, like a good general, they would know where to place the strongest guard. They should so compile the laws of their country, and so connect them with those of their Creator, that a violation of one would be an infringement upon the other. In so doing, they would be few, clear and righteous. The minds of the people would be easy and enlarged; confusion and enthusiasm would subside, and each would rely upon the hon-

our of the whole. Honour, thus considered, would be the greatest bulwark, the greatest security a nation could have. They need neither fear disturbances abroad, or commotions at home; but may rest assured of the smiles of God and the blessings of heaven.

I would not, however, be understood, in using the word honour as a modern; no, far from that; we, unhappily, have confounded and mixed its meaning with that of *pride* and *self-conceit*. So synonymous have become these terms, that when a modern's pride is injured, he immediately demands satisfaction for the wound his *honour* has sustained. Such also is the case with the self-conceited, arrogant fool.

For these reasons I have undertaken the subject before me. It is from the prostitution of that noble epithet, that exalted title, that vice is triumphant, and virtue neglected, that men grow negligent, and sinners become plenty.

Such is the state of man, that he cannot injure himself without injuring the community; he cannot commit a vice without corrupting his mind, and one corrupted mind, like a foul stream, too often tends to corrupt the whole body. This, I should conceive, was sufficient to excite men to honour, if it were only for honour's sake.

What is the condition of that person, who has lost his reputation, but the most wretched, the most detestable? and, what is reputation but honour? No person, according to my idea of man, would wifh to live miftrufted, detefted, and defpifed ; and fuch furely is the cafe with him, who has loft his honour, who has, as it were, feparated himfelf from the laws of God and fociety. Like the robber, he depends upon the weaknefs and innocence of his opponents ; and like the robber, not fo eafily detected.

They fap the foundation of domeftic and national happinefs ; deftroy the confidence, which man places in man, which confidence arifes from the noble ideas we entertain of our brethren. This is moft certainly weakened, when thofe upon whom we rely are found without principle, or honour. The more this takes place, the more diftruftful we grow ; and the more diftruftful we grow, the more unhappy and miferable we are. The more private faith and public confidence is doubted, the more jealous and uneafy individuals are forced to be.

Curfed then be the man, who by his vicioufnefs and depravity fetches a curfe upon his country. Like Haftings, let him be damned in his own name, and all the people fay, amen.

Honour is the nobleft characteriftic of a nation, the greateft ornament of a people, and higheft comment, that can be beftowed on man. For which reafon, *honourable*, in a free country, is beftowed on thofe, who have been confpicuous in promoting the caufe of Chriftianity ; in guarding and defending the rights and privileges of that country. For fuch then let it be preferved, and merit and patriotifm will receive their reward ; virtue will be encouraged, and vice detefted.— The people will increafe and flourifh ; the temple of difcord will be fhut, and on it fealed *eternity*. Riches will be efteemed as only ferviceable to preferve the body, whereas they are now the greateft road to honour and preferment.

As this is the age of reafon and improvement, I feel a fatisfaction in hoping to add the " age of honour ;" an age, which no country will arrive to fooner than America.

'Tis for her fons, to them 'tis kindly given,
To be both great below, and great in heaven.

For the MASSACHUSETTS MAGAZINE.

R E V I E W.

An Apology for Chriftianity. In a feries of Letters, addreffed to Edward Gibbon, Efq. author of the Hiftory of the Decline and Fall of the Roman Empire. Being a neceffary and inftructive Appendix thereto. By R. Watfon, D.D. F.R.S.   Price 4/6.

THE prefent edition has been committed to the prefs, at the inftance of fome, who, though not called by Providence to the public defence of the Religion of Jefus, yet efteem it their ineftimable treafure, and ardently pray for the diffemination of its principles and bleffings among mankind.

This volume will be found entertaining and improving to thofe who are ftrangers to Mr. Gibbon, as containing a happy arrangement of fome of the leading arguments in fupport of Chriftianity ; and of rational replies, combating the fophifms and ungenerous infinuations which have been uttered againft it.

The readers and admirers of the hiſtorian, will conſider it as a neceſſary and inſtructive Appendix to the Decline and Fall of the Roman Empire. It diſcovers deep thought, and extenſive reading, and breathes a calm, a manly, and a Chriſtian temper. The poliſhed ſtyle of Dr. Watſon is compared by Mr. Gibbon himſelf to the ſmoothneſs of the Ionic dialect.

But the ſubſequent candid acknowledgment of the hiſtorian, who in defending himſelf againſt other antagoniſts, declined a public controverſy with our author, will make further obſervations unneceſſary.

"When Dr. Watſon gave to the "public his Apology for Chriſti-"anity in a ſeries of letters, he ad-"dreſſed them to the Author of the "Decline and Fall of the Roman "Empire, with a juſt confidence, "that he had conſidered this impor-"tant object in a manner not un-

"worthy of his antagoniſt, or of "himſelf. Dr. Watſon's mode of "thinking, bears a liberal and phi-"loſophical caſt ; his thoughts are "expreſſed with ſpirit, and their "ſpirit is always tempered by po-"liteneſs and moderation. Such "is the man whom I ſhould be hap-"py to call my friend, and whom I "ſhould not bluſh to call my antag-"oniſt. But the ſame motives which "might tempt me to accept, or e-"ven to ſolicit a private and ami-"cable conference, diſſuaded me "from entering into a public con-"troverſy with a writer of ſo re-"ſpectable a character ; and I em-"braced the earlieſt opportunity of "expreſſing to Dr. Watſon himſelf, "how ſincerely I agreed with him "in thinking, that ' as the world is ' now poſſeſſed of the opinion of us ' both upon the ſubject in queſtion, ' it may be, perhaps, as proper for ' us both to leave it in this ſtate,'*

* Gibbon's Vindication of ſome paſſages againſt ſeveral opponents.

An attempt to tranſlate the prophetic part of the Apocalypſe of St. John into familiar language, by diveſting it of the metaphors in which it is involved.— By James Winthrop, Eſq.——8vo. price 1/6.

(Concluded from page 564.)

OUR author illuſtrates ſome of his definitions by coins and other devices. The reader may judge of the ſupport derived from theſe alluſions, by the following example—" Coloured horſes repreſent the different ſituations of the church, after the converſion of the empire ; being devices choſen by Conſtantine, and his immediate ſucceſſors, and ſerving as chronological diſtinctions."—" This definition is ſupported by the following coins—When Conſtantine ſucceeded his father, A.D. 306, he ſtruck a coin, in which he appeared on horſeback, treading down his enemies, with a glory about the head

of his horſe, and one of his enemies preſenting him with a crown of laurel, and at the ſame time receiving the point of his ſpear. This is the only inſtance of the radiated horſe, and agrees to the white horſe of the firſt ſeal.

" The ſecond period, or that of the red horſe, laſted twenty years, and comprehends the reign of the ſons of Conſtantine, till A.D. 360. The device of an horſeman treading down his enemies, without thoſe marks of glory peculiar to Conſtantine, expreſſes, as well as can be done on metals, the red horſe, whoſe rider had power to take peace from the earth. The third
period

period is the short and inglorious reign of Julian, from A.D. 360 to 564. Constantine's white horse was represented with a glory—Julian, by way of insult, reversed the figure, and represented the horse stumbling, and the footman triumphing over him. This circumstance, and the natural connexion between darkness and stumbling, point out the black horse." Most of the definitions have less support—to us they appear arbitrary.

The definitions are applied with uniformity through the work, and the whole series of prophesies are in such a manner translated, as to form a plain and connected meaning. The stile is perspicuous and classical. In some instances, our author has not preserved the dignity of the original, nor equalled the common version. The flowing language of the 2d verse of the 14th chapter, he has translated— And the government made a proclamation for a general thanksgiving.

Mr. Winthrop supposes that there cannot be " two systematic readings of the whole book, radically different from each other." We conceive that much less ingenuity and learning than he possesses, would be sufficient to invent definitions of the terms and emblems, which would apply to some profession or occupation of civil life, with as great uniformity as his apply to civil government on the basis of Christianity; and the result be a meaning as plain and connected.

Should no wit apply to Mr. W. the sarcasm of M. Voltaire upon Sir Isaac Newton, yet we apprehend he will swell the catalogue of unsuccessful commentators upon the apocalypse of St. John. It is with diffidence we give this opinion; the pamphlet, we unreservedly recommend to general perusal, as the work of the scholar, the philosopher, and the Christian.

We select the history of the reformation in Germany, under Luther, &c.

TRANSLATION.

13 And at the beginning of the sixth period the cry for a reformation became general in the Christian church.

14 And the believers, who had been restrained by the Papal hierarchy, demanded liberty of conscience.

15 And the progress of reformation was limited in its operation to somewhat more than 391 years; which term is divided into one year, thirty years, and three hundred and sixty years, in which space a third part of the Papal empire shall be taken off.

16 And the number of the reformers was very great.

17 And they were armed with truth, sagacity, and severity; and they proceeded with courage, and defended themselves with truth and the severity of wit.

18 And by these qualities in their preaching was a third part of the Papal empire detached from its allegiance to its federal head:

19 For the power of the reformers consisted in their preaching, which left a lasting wound on their adversaries like the sting of a serpent.

ANECDOTE of POPE.

POPE pretended to hate kings, but professed great esteem for the then prince of Wales. His Royal Highness asked him, *how he could love a prince, while he disliked* kings? Pope answered, the young lion is harmless and even playful; but when his claws are full grown, he becomes cruel, dreadful, and mischievous.

CABINET

CABINET OF APOLLO.

For the MASSACHUSETTS MAGAZINE.

On HOPE.

*Humbly inscribed to Miss H—— by her friend
and admirer,* LINUS.

COME, gentle hope; descend celestial
   maid,
In all the robes of happiness arrayed:
Without thy smiles, without thy quicken-
   ing breath,
All action ceases, and each thought is
   death!
Without thy aid, creation veils her face,
And beauty loses its attractive grace;
Despair ensues; blood starts through eve-
   ry pore;
The world expires; existence is no more.
Thou canst all future into present bring,
And glad the soul with one continued
   spring;
Bid all *Parnassus* pass before our eyes,
Whose glories charm and soar above the
   skies.
There dwell the *Muses*, there *Apollo* reigns,
Lord of the summit and surrounding
   plains.
Castalian springs their bubbling waters roll,
To raise the genius and exalt the soul.
New wonders rise to view in every age,
Exalt the man, and dignify the page:
The summit's bottom darkens into shame,
But, on the top, there stands eternal fame:
Promotion waves her silken banners
   round;
Undying honours tread the hallowed
   ground;
There dwells in radiant dress attractive
   truth,
There pleasure brightens in eternal youth.
Make man your study and peculiar care,
'Tis this and books will only mount you
   there.
Books are the steps by which we must a-
   rise,   [wise;
Abhorred by fools, companions of the
One source from which the streams of
   knowledge run,
As fire at first descended from the sun.

Mount with a steady step, nor let the way,
Tho' steep at first, retard you, or dismay:
Combat each obstacle with manly force,
Nor start astonished at your destined
   course:
Hope still continue;—rise! ye females,
   rise,
Ascend the summit and out-top the skies;
There, with Apollo, and the tuneful nine,
Both learn in rapture and in death re-
   fine.
How grand the prospect which is viewed
   from thence!
And, oh! how pleasing to the mental
   sense!
The *Druid* dancers blow the *Cyrian* string,
Old *Rome* and *Athens* from their ashes
   spring;
Patriots and heroes from their dust arise,
And gathering thunder sparkle in their
   eyes:
Carthage appears! oh, Rome, thy dread-
   ed foe,
And *Hannibal* with lightning on his bow.
The ancient victors from remotest days,
Who fought for virtue and who died for
   praise:
The happy few, who studied to impart
Fair learning's store and civilize the
   heart;
Who roused each latent spark, until the
   flame
Blazed into honours and undying fame;
Who touched each tender feeling till they
   roll,
In streams of love, fast binding soul to
   soul.
Far nobler wonders still immerge in sight,
The starry system each a world of light;
The planets running their harmonious
   round,
And comets blazing thro' the vast pro-
   found.
The sun, like Atlas, standing in his might
And cheering distant regions with his
   light;
How natural causes their effects produce,
And *nature's* varied properties and use.

From

From hence we view all nature as it lies,
And MAN, that little world below the
    skies;
Then turn aloft and view the living foul,
Who moves and governs and directs the
    whole.
This is the height; come, let us all af-
    pire;
Ye female bosoms catch the generous fire.

Extracted for the MASSACHUSETTS MAG-
AZINE.

The PHILOSOPHER and the COX-COMB.

Written by the late Mr. CAWTHORN.

A COXCOMB once in Handel's par-
    lour found;
A Grecian lyre, and try'd to make it
    found;
O'er the side stops his awkward fist he
    flings,
And rudely presses on the elastic strings:
Awaken'd difcord fhrieks and fcolds, and
    raves,
Wild as the diffonance of winds and
    waves,
Loud as a wapping mob at midnight
    bawls,
Harfh as ten chariots rolling round St.
    Paul's;
And hoarfer far than all th' extatic race,
Whofe drunken orgies ftun'd the wilds of
    Thrace.
Friend, quoth the fage, that fine machine
    contains
Exacter numbers and diviner ftrains.
Strains, fuch as once could build the The-
    ban wall,
And ftop the mountain torrent in its fall;
But yet to wake them, roufe them, and
    infpire,
Afks a fine finger, and a touch of fire,
A feeling foul, whofe all expreffive powers,
Can copy nature as fhe finks or foars;
And, juft alike to paffion, time, and place,
Refine correctnefs into eafe and grace.
He faid—and flying o'er each quiv'ring
    wire,
Spread his light hand, and fwept it on the
    lyre,
Quick to his touch the lyre began to glow,
The found to kindle, and the air to flow,
Deep as the murmurs of the falling floods,
Sweet as the warblers of the vocal woods;
The lift'ning paffions hear, and fink, and
    rife,
As the rich harmony, or fwells, or dies,
The pulfe of AVARICE forgets to move,
A purer rapture fills the breaft of LOVE;

DEVOTION lifts to heaven a holier eye,
And bleeding PITY heaves a fofter figh.
Life has its eafe, amufement, joy and fire,
Hid in itfelf, as mufic in the lyre;
And, like the lyre, will all its pow'rs im-
    part,
When touch'd and manag'd by the hand
    of art:
But half mankind, like Handel's fool, de-
    ftroy,
Through rage and ignorance, the ftrain of
    joy;
Irregularly wild their paffions roll
Through nature's fineft inftrument, the
    SOUL.
While men of fenfe, with Handel's happier
    fkill,
Correct the tafte, and harmonize the will,
Teach their affections, like his notes, to
    flow,
Not rais'd too high, nor ever funk too low,
Till ev'ry virtue, meafur'd and refin'd,
As fits the concert of the mafter mind,
Melts in its kindred founds, and pours a-
    long
The according mufic of the moral fong.

For the MASSACHUSETTS MAGAZINE.

LINES,

*Addreffed to a mother, occafioned by the death of
her amiable little daughter—from her fympathetic friend,*   LINUS.

ACCEPT an ardent with to heal
    The wounds, maternal paffions feel;
My tender breaft with pity glows,
And pants to mitigate your woes.
But, ah! methinks I hear you fay,
" What comfort can my grief allay?
What can affuage the thrilling fmart,
And eafe the anguifh of my heart?
How often has the parent fmiled,
When fhe beheld her darling child?
With what delight thefe tender arms
Embraced the lovely infant's charms?
With what maternal fondnefs paft,
The fmiling beauty to my breaft?
But, ah! thefe pleafing fcenes are o'er,
And the fweet babe is now no more!
The cold remains the grave receives,
While the fad figh my bofom heaves,
What then can mitigate my pain?
I mourn, I weep, alas, in vain!"

Yet let kind fympathy apply
Her balm, to check the rifing figh:
Her foft, her foothing language hear,
To wipe the unavailing tear.
Affliction is no cafual thing,
Nor from the duft do forrows fpring.

                    To

To trouble we are born, my friend,
As certain as the sparks afcend.
What numerous ills our lives annoy!
How lafting grief! How tranfcient joy!
New objects of delight we fee,
And chafe the phantoms as they flee:
How foon are all our comforts fled!
How foon fhall friends pronounce us dead!
Death fnatched the child from your em-
  brace,
To lodge it in a happier place:
Now in a gracious Saviour's arms,
It calmly fmiles fecure from harms.
I fee, or feem to fee, the child,
Her lovely face divinely mild;
In robes of fpotlefs white fhe ftands,
Celeftial palms adorn her hands:
While liftening fancy hears her fay—
" O, ceafe, fond poet, ceafe your lay;
And tell my parents I'm fecure,
Where pain and death fhall come no more.
Here God the judge of all difplays,
His glorious, uncreated blaze;
Here the adored Redeemer lives,
Whofe matchlefs grace our fins forgives;
Here happy faints and angels dwell,
In blifs no mortal words can tell."

Thus fpeaks thy child, and fweetly fings
The praifes of the king of kings.
O! then let faith divine engage,
And point you to the facred page:
There read, and there this truth behold,
More precious than the choiceft gold.
He who prefides in heavenly light,
Ordains all things wife, good, and right;
He gives, and he refumes again,
Then blefs, forever blefs, his name.

An ODE to TRUTH.

SAY, fhall no white-robed fon of light,
  Swift darting from his heavenly
    height,
Here deign to take his hallowed ftand;
Here wave his amber locks; unfold
His pinions clothed with downy gold;
Here fmiling ftretch his tutelary wand?
And you, ye hofts of faints, for ye have
    known
Each dreary path in life'sperplexing maze,
Tho' now ye circle yon eternal throne
With harpings high of inexpreflive praife,
Will not your train defcend in radiant ftate,
To break, with mercy's beams, this gath-
    ering cloud of fate?

'Tis filence all. No fon of light
Darts fwiftly from his heavenly height,
No train of radiant faints defcend;
" Mortals, in vain ye hope to find,

If vice, if guilt has ftain'd your mind,
Or faints to hear, or angels to defend."
So truth proclaims; I hear the facred
    found
Burft from the centre of his burning
    throne;
Where aye fhe fits with ftar-decked luftre
    crowned,
A bright fun lights her adamantine zone,
So truth proclaims; her awful voice I
    hear;
With many a folemn paufe it flowly
    meets my ear.

Attend, ye fons of men, attend and fay,
Does not enough of your refulgent ray
Break thro' the veil of your mortality?
Say, does not reafon in this form defcry
Unnumbered, namelefs glories that fur-
    pafs
The angel's floating pomp, the feraph's
    glowing grace?

Shall then your earth-born daughters vie
With me? fhall fhe whofe brighteft eye
But emulates the diamond's blaze,
Whofe cheek but mocks the rofe's bloom,
Whofe breath the hyacinth's perfume,
Whofe melting voice the warbling wood-
    lark's lays;
Shall fhe be deemed my rival? fhall a
    form
Of elemental drofs, of mouldering clay,
Vie with thefe charms imperial? The poor
    worm
Shall prove her conteft vain. Life's little
    day
Shall pafs, and fhe is gone; while I ap-
    pear;
Flufhed with the bloom of youth thro'
    heaven's eternal year.

Know, mortals, know, ere firft ye fprung,
Ere firft thefe orbs in ether hung,
I fhone amidft the heavenly throng;
Thefe eyes beheld creation's day,
This voice began the choral lay,
And taught archangels their triumphant
    fong.
Pleafed I furveyed bright nature's gradual
    birth,
Saw infant light with kindling luftre
    fpread,
Soft vernal fragrance clothe the flowering
    earth,
And ocean heave on his extended bed;
Saw the tall pine afpiring pierce the fky,
The tawny lion ftalk, the rapid eagle fly:
Laft MAN arofe erect in youthful grace,
Heaven's hallowed image ftamped upon
    his face,

And

And as he rose the high behest was given,
That I alone of all the hosts of heaven,
Should reign protectress of the god-like
  youth ;—
Thus th' Almighty spake : he spake, and
  called me TRUTH.

For the MASSACHUSETTS MAGAZINE.

To the HERMIT.

NIGHT robed in sober gray began to
  reign :
Hushed was the melody of ev'ry plain.
Each wearied beast retired to early rest,
And every bird sunk silent in his nest.
Uncommon lustre from the full-moon
  beamed,
Half changed to noon the lonely midnight
  seemed.
No noise was heard, save the unfrequent
  gale,
And distant dogs that hunted in the vale.
  Such was the night, when to the grove
  I strayed,
To meditate beneath the silent shade.
A rock I found, that reared its lofty brow,
And looked contemptuous on the plains
  below ;
A small, smooth stream, that kissed the
  rock's low base,
Smiled thro' the rushes with unruffled
  face.
Here, while I sat upon the time-worn rock,
And o'er my head high hung the verdent
  oak,
The great renown of bards of former days,
Their lettered relics of eternal praise,
Employed my mind. Homer, the bard
  of Greece,
Who sung the feats of war and scenes of
  peace :
Virgil, who softly struck the Roman shell,
And sung how Trojan heroes fought and
  fell :
Milton, seraphic bard, whose numbers scan
The war of angles and the lapse of man ;
Old Ossian too, poetically wild,
The boast of genius, nature's happy child ;
Who loved to sing the fall of warring hosts,
To sound their fame and sooth their angry
  ghosts.
While these old bards employed my drow-
  sy mind,
My weary limbs upon the rock reclined,
Sudden a sound came floating on the gale,
And swelling, sweetly rolled along the vale;
Seraphic harps and heavenly-softened
  tongues
In sweetest concert, joined their happy
  songs.

I looked : A cloud in majesty serene,
Far o'er the dusky desert now is seen.
Slowly it rises; lo! an angel stands,
The book of fate high lifted in his hands.
A host of angels circle him afar,
And ride sublime upon the cloudy car.
His countenance seems brighter than the
  sun,
And ten-fold glories round the vision run.
Hoarse o'er the hills the winds begin to
  rise,
Loud as ten thunders rumbling thro' the
  skies ;
The trees uprooted twirl along the plain ;
The shattered cottage scours the air a-
  main ;
Egyptian darkness fills the dread profound,
And the big thunder rolls his voice around.
With sun-like blaze the forked lightnings
  fly,
And day and night alternate reign on
  high :
The mountains shake, the hills uplifted
  move,
And storms seem rushing from the world
  above.

  To yonder mount the awful cloud re-
  tires,
And on its summit lifts its winding spires :
High on the top th' angelic chief appears,
A sage he seems of wisdom and of years ;
At well-known distance round their leader
  stand,
In seraph smiles, the heaven descended
  band.
And now the chief, with ever-winning
  grace,
Rises, and bids the war of nature cease.
Hush, as the house of death, all nature
  seems,
And double glory from the vision beams.
The mighty angel silent stands awhile ;
Then bowing with a love-endearing smile,
Thus the throng harangues :
  " Ye guardians of virtue and art here
    below,   [flow !
From whom all the pleasures of harmony
Attend to the mandates which now I shall
    give,   [you receive.
And conceal in your breasts every word
From the regions of bliss, the worlds of
  delight,
Again to the earth I have taken my flight,
To cull from his sons a youth of renown,
And to place on his head the poetical
  crown.
Thro' all the wide world for this youth
  have I sought ;
A period at length to my searching is
  brought :
                              The

The youth have I found : now, ye angels,
rejoice
And raife to the heavens the notes of your
voice.
Among all the nobles that fhine on the
earth,
Diftinguifh'd by honour, by talents or
birth,
There's none like the HERMIT, that mu-
fical fage,
The pride of his friends and flower of his
age.
Let him be your charge, ye Guardians of
fame,
Inftruct him in virtue and honour his
name.
Like a fun, let him light the poetical
world ;
Let the banners of glory o'er his head be
unfurl'd.
AMERICAN HOMER, the youth fhall
be call'd,
And his name with the greateft of fages
enroled.
Watch over his ways : give him pleafure
and health,
The bleffing of friends and a plenty of
wealth.
For fcience renown'd and in honefty bold,
Let his glory eclipfe all the fages of old ;
Go, feraphs, preferve him and teach him
to rife
'Till his fame fills the earth and his glory
the fkies."

He fpake ; and all the feraphs quickly flew
To guard the youth : they to their charge
are true.
The godlike form that on the dark cloud
ftood
Soared to the fky his high ferene abode.
All things again their ufual figure took,
And early morning o'er the mountain
broke.   LINUS.

For the MASSACHUSETTS MAGAZINE.

The PLEASURES of FANCY.

SWEET attic warbler of the fpray,
 Awhile fufpend your pleafing lay;
Ye gales your gentle breaths forbear,
 And, hufhed in filent foft repofe,
Attend a while, and you fhall hear,
 The pleafures which the hermit knows.

When the rich mantle of the morn
 Begins its fplendor to unfold,
m ark, upon the bending thorn,
 The lively dew-drop ting'd with gold.
Forth from my lave I view the light,
Rejoicing o'er the fhades of night,

While my fond thoughts with rapture roll,
With all the energy of foul.

But when the cheerful day is gone,
And darkfome night moves flowly on,
When with a melancholy grace,
Pale Luna lifts her fober face,
Then whifpers foft fome unknown power,
'Tis Contemplation's fav'rite hour.

If chance the rainy torrent falls,
And patters on my cottage walls,
Secure I hear the tempeft roar,
And howl for entrance at the door :
On the bright bow with joy I gaze,
Where mimick diamonds feem to blaze.

If from the north ftern winter blows
His driving cataracts of fnows,
In dark'ning ftorms and tempefts dreft,
 Fair fancy drops her cherub wing,
Reclines on April's dewy breaft,
 And hails the fymphony of fpring.

When fummer comes, with grandeur
crown'd,
Difpenfing light and glory round,
I feek the heaven-afpiring hill,
Or wander where the murmuring rill
Rolls over fragrant beds of flowers,
And there I pafs the noon-tide hours.

Nor fhall fweet autumn come in vain,
'Tis then I count the ftudious train,
Or haunt the mufes' facred grove,
Where fancy's footfteps love to rove.

And when the trees ftand dark and bare,
No cheerful mufic warbling there,
My breaft with tender pity heaves,
I read my fate in falling leaves.

O nature ! all-fufficient maid,
 Teach me thy won'drous works to read;
Infpire me with thy powerful aid,
 And tune with joy my fimple reed.
          The HERMIT.

A SONG.

*From a Lover to his Miftrefs, upon her fmiling
foon after having fhed tears.*

THE rofe that weeps with morning
 dew,
 And glitters in the funny ray,
In tears and fmiles refembles you,
 When love breaks forrow's cloud away.

The dews that bend the blufhing flower,
 Enrich the fcent—renew the glow ;
So love's fweet tears exalt his pow'r,
 So blifs more brightly fhines by wo !
          The

For the MASSACHUSETTS MAGAZINE.

The HERMIT and WREN.

A SENTIMENTAL FABLE.

*Originally written several years since, to an opu-
lent, learned, and eminent friend, who had retired into solitude, and to whose sentiments and
situation it was thought applicable.**

PALEMON on a desert isle,
    Fled public clamor guilt and toil ;
Spontaneous nature gave him food,
Who spurn'd the cruel thirst of blood ;
With no inflaming liquors curs'd,
The silver streamlet slak'd his thirst ;
His days in meditation spent,
He hop'd in vain to find content.

One morn he trod a rocky plain,
That overlooks the boundless main ;
The rising sun, with golden beam,
Seem'd dipping in the briny stream ;
Fair shone the glossy surface o'er,
And ting'd the hills remote on shore.
A sail, it seem'd, he could descry,
In farthest verge of sea and sky ;
He walk'd the height in tho't profound,
And view'd the ample scene around.

And now a wren engag'd his view,
Who to her callow nestlings flew,
And fed them, piteous of their cry,
An agonizing butterfly.
This wrung Palemon's tender breast,
Who thus the listening wren address'd :—

" Unfeeling bird, is this thy joy,
Thy fellow creatures to destroy ;
To needless, feast thy callow train,
On members shiv'ring still with pain,
While luscious fruitage earth affords,
For summer's food and winter's hoards,
Thine is the range of all the plain,
And choice of all my stores contain ;
Of this thy rapine, whence the cause,
This breach of nature's gentle laws ?
Yet, though the harmless you destroy,
No guilty cares your peace annoy ;
You sweetly warble on the spray,
And chaunt the jocund hours away,
And seem to hold, devoid of pain,
The happiness I've sought in vain.
Though science lent her fairest ray,
Though reason's son hath led my way,
Though virtue hath my soul inspir'd,
And common love my actions fir'd ;
For while I trod life's busy round,
My soul no satisfaction found ;
There virtue is an empty name,
And caprice holds the trump of fame ;

* *The author regrets that an unfinished copy of
this fable has been published, some years since, still
more incorrect, in his opinion, than the present one.*

There slanders every tongue employ,
And friendship flatters to destroy,
Proud witlings modest worth deride,
And learning paints the plumes of pride ;
Or men to vain researches bend,
To seek with toil the circle's end ;
Religion proves all reasoning vain,
By unconcatenated chain ;
And governments preclude desert,
While blind devotion kneels to art.

For honest calm, in bloom of age,
I left the fulsome busy stage,
To question with my soul apart,
Enjoy myself and mend my heart :
And here three lonely years have spent,
Nor 'scap'd the fiend of discontent.
Is reason, studiously refin'd,
But given to discompose the mind ?".

The wren, vivacious, chirp, and gay,
Responsive said, or seem'd to say—
" Though held to mute attention long,
Thy partial reas'ning moves my tongue :
Nature, I grant, hath bless'd our plains
With luscious fruits, and wholesome grains,
The sweetest of thy dainties rare,
I from thy tender bounty share ;
Who near thy own my house hast rear'd,
And kept me with a kind regard :
But fruits alone are not the food,
Adapted to my tender brood ;
He who with fruits supplies our need,
On various creatures bids us feed,
And prompts us to select the right,
By instinct and by appetite ;
Bids each his sustenance pursue,
With form adapted thereunto.

The hawk's tremendous fangs and beak,
His prowling appetite bespeak ;
The howling wolf, with deathful jaws,
The panther's horrid teeth and claws.
Yet all whereon each creature lives,
The universal Father gives ;
Though you and I the suff'rers are,
Self-preservation be our care.
He who can fathom nature's laws,
May tax the universal cause.

Your gentle heart hath rightly chose,
All wanton slaughter to oppose ;
But nature flesh and fruits has blest,
And both in reason suits you best.

The fates all animals ordain
To die, and many to be slain.
This prov'd, on every larger kind
You by your grosser optics find :
But had you my more subtil eye,
Minuter objects to descry,
What varied swarms would strike your view,
What evidence would teem anew ;
No rising tide the margin laves,
But drowns whole millions in its waves,
              Nor

Nor falling nut the forefts yield,
Nor fhining fruitage of the field,
Shook off by zephyr's gentle breath,
But crufhes fome to inftant death.

  To fhun all flaughter doft thou think ?
Then ftir not hence, nor eat nor drink,
Left thoufands die beneath thy tread,
Left death at every motion fpread ;
Eat not the plum, the grape, the pear,
Their habitants humanely fpare,
Nor let the ftream thy thirft fupply,
Left in the draught an hundred die.
Reverfe the order nature gave,
And ftarve thyfelf their lives to fave.

  The hidden reafon wouldft thou fee,
Why fortune fhowers her blifs on me ?
Why I the happinefs attain,
That wifer thou haft fought in vain.
Contentment cheers my humble way,
By no ambition led aftray ;
That reftlefs fire, that various blaze,
That into mad confufion ftrays,
That trifles vain too deep explores,
And from its fphere eccentric foars.

  My mate, the deareft of the throng,
Improves my joy and aids my fong ;
We feek out food, attend our young,
And freely chaunt the groves among.
The little toil that nature claims,
Does but invigorate our frames ;
No ufelefs cares our peace deftroy,
That ftill the human kind annoy ;
Yet they who fcorn our humble ftate,
Exclufive reafon arrogate.

  And though you have, with noble mind,
Shun'd many errors of your kind,
Yet ftudies have your foul depreft,
And made you wretched o'er the reft.
Had you a lab'ring hind been rear'd,
Nor wealth, nor baneful grandeur fhar'd,
You might, in humble thoughtlefs way,
Have plodded out your peaceful day ;
Or ufeful acquifition made
Of fcience in the rural fhade ;
And free from high ambitious ftrife,
Have prov'd the tender joys of life :
But grandeur fails, with fcience join'd,
To happify a modeft mind,
Loft to the humble fweets of life,
Among the vain at fruitlefs ftrife ;
By few devoid of intereft priz'd ;
For fingularity defpis'd ;
The tedious melancholy day,
To torpid indolence a prey.

  From ills innumer'd fuch as thofe,
A fad relief you here have chofe ;
To fhun the vain, the worthlefs crew,
You have forfook the virtuous few ;
To be from common errors freed,
Have fhun'd the means of virtuous deed

To live recluse from public ftrife,
Have fhun'd all focial joys of life ;
Your mind to melancholy prone,
Small recreation here hath known ;
And fed on fruits three tedious years,
Your frame a fkeleton appears.

  You who the laws of nature plead,
Her plaineft characters mifread,
Elfe by your form you might define,
You deviate from your true defign :
And he who from his orbit ftrays,
In painful pennance waftes his days.

  Were man for folitude defign'd,
Then why his focial gifts of mind ?
His oral pow'rs, his various frame,
His focial agency proclaim ;
Temper'd and organiz'd to prove
The melting joys of gentle love ;
With variable vifage bleft,
Where every paffion is expreft,
And eye all eloquent t' impart
Each emanation of the heart.

  If his formation were defign'd
For labours merely of the mind,
Why did the Architect divine
In him fuch ufeful members join ?
Who flight this hint, in fpite of pride,
From real comfort wander wide ;
*Nor frame nor mind, is blefs in floth,
'Tis action vigorates them both ;*
What though inactive fome you find,
Whofe lucubrations light mankind ;
Long painful days and nights are their's,
Unlike the joy the lab'rer fhares.

  Then wouldft thou wifh for comfort's ray,
To cheer the remnant of thy day,
With yonder veffel fkim the main,
To focial life return again ;
There feek thee out an humble feat,
Remote from circles of the great,
With juft enough of fruitful land
For cultivation of thine hand ;
The neighbours, fociably inclin'd,
Of gentle and induftrious kind,
From thefe felect a virtuous fair,
Thy joys and toils of life to fhare,
Whofe mind thy prudent tho'ts approve,
Whofe modeft charms infpire thy love ;
Connubial comforts wifely tafte,
While yet their deareft feafon laft.

  Domeftic joys and cares you'll prove,
Will vapours of the brain remove ;
Of flefh and fruits partake the beft,
Your toil will mod'rate meals digeft,
Difpel by night each troubled dream,
And but a recreation feem,
For human labour need be fmall,
To anfwer nature's every call,
Were man to reafon's ftandard brought,
And real comfort wifely fought.

So shall your studious hours succeed,
From clouds of melancholy freed,
Unvext with metaphysic flight,
To reason out of reason's sight ;
Contemning needless search abstruse,
And prizing science but for use ;
Thy soul unbiggoted, unaw'd,
Successful seek the parent God ;
Nor dull theories tire thy brain,
To thee an irksome fulsome train ;
Nor toils of pride, nor follies strife,
That waste the little span of life.

So shall thou glide in social ease,
Along the humble vale of peace ;
From scenes of courtly art retir'd,
By simple virtue be admir'd ;
Thy spouse shall every art employ,
To soothe thy cares, to crown thy joy ;
With fortitude together bear,
Such ills as human kind must share ;
Together shall your ravish'd eyes
Behold your hopeful offspring rise,
Together blest with many days,
You'll steal to rest by slow decays."

Here ceas'd the strain. The sage reclin'd,
And thus he question'd with his mind—
" Vain pomp and state I've long deny'd,
As bart'ring happiness for pride ;
False learning dark, fastidious, vain,
I've found true useful reasons bane.
Yet by their wildering maxims taught,
A false relief I've idly sought ;
They blind our course through life's dark
maze,
Like candle-light 'mid luna's rays.
We seek o'er fairy lands astray,
For bliss that borders on our way.
They spurn the life that crowns the swain,
Sweet, healthful, simple, social, plain,
On pompous art our minds engage,
And soil our view of nature's page,
That scarce a tint can meet the eye,
But through the mirror they apply.
And am I thus from error's night,
By nature's simplest child set right ?

Dame nature leads her children dear,
Each wisely round his proper sphere,
And soundest lessons there impart,
In silent language to the heart :
'Twas not the wren I seem'd to hear,
'Twas reason 'woke the mental ear ;
'Tis nature beckons me away,
And lo her summons I obey."

He said, and wav'd a signal high,
And soon the gallant ship drew nigh ;
In her his native shore he sought,
And took the measures lately taught ;
His tranquil pleasures never cloy'd,
Not AGLAUS more content enjoy'd.
HOMO.

Extracted for the MASSACHUSETTS MAG-AZINE.

To the NIGHTINGALE.

CHILD of the melancholy song !
O yet that tender strain prolong !
Her lengthen'd shade, when ev'ning flings,
From mountain-cliffs and forest green,
And sailing slow on silent wings
Along the glimm'ring west is seen ;
I love o'er pathless hills to stray,
Or trace the winding vale remote,
And pause, sweet bird ! to hear thy lay
While moon-beams on the thin clouds
float,
Till o'er the mountain's dewy head
Pale midnight steals to wake the dead.

Far through the heav'ns ætherial blue,
Wafted on spring's light airs you come
With blooms, and flow'rs, and genial dew,
From climes where summer joys to
roam,
O, welcome to your long lost home !
" Child of the melancholy song !"
Who lov'st the lonely woodland-glade
To mourn, unseen, the boughs among.
When twilight spreads her pensive shade,
Again thy dulcet voice I hail !
O, pour again the liquid note
That dies upon the ev'ning gale !
For fancy loves the kindred tone ;
Her griefs the plaintive accents own.
She loves to hear thy music float
At solemn midnight's stillest hour,
And think on friends forever lost,
On joys by disappointment crost,
And weep a-new love's charmful pow'r !
Then mem'ry wakes the magic smile,
Th' impassion'd voice, the melting eye,
That won't the trusting heart beguile.
And *wakes again* the hopeless sigh !
Her skill the glowing tints revive
Of scenes that time had bade decay ;
She bids the soften'd passions live—
The passions urge again their sway.
Yet o'er the long regretted scene
Thy song the grace of sorrow throws ;
A melancholy charm serene,
More rare than all that mirth bestows.
Then hail, sweet bird ! and hail thy pen-
sive tear !
To taste, to fancy, and to virtue, dear !

MOTTO for a WATCH.

HOW short a span
Is life, O man !
Then why so fond of pleasure ?
In time lay by,
'Gainst 'ternity,
A fund of lasting treasure.
MONTHLY

MONTHLY GAZETTE.

Summary of Foreign Intelligence.

GERMANY.

FRANKFORT, July 20.

THE French at Rheignheim, Oggerheim, and Kircheim, are threatening every where to break through and make a defcent.

Prince Hohenloe is at Pforzheim, near Worms. The greateft part of the magazines of Frahential and Lautorn are loft. A moft violent cannonade has been heard during the whole of this morning. The Pruffians have loft a great many men all along their line, without recovering their generals Schladem, Vofs and Ruchell, who are wounded. Schladem, Mannftem, and Romberg, fuffered moft—Upwards of a hundred Pruffian officers are either killed or wounded. Had the Pruffians attempted to have maintained Lautern, they would have rifked a lofs of 20,000 men, and of being cut off.

Dutch Brabant, Bois le Duc. The governor of our city having received orders to put the place in a ftate of defence, has ordered all the fluices to be opened to effect an inundation—This meafure has fucceeded partially, the want of rain having left the waters very low—The fame attempt has been made with as little fuccefs, at Heuden, Capelle, and Breda.

HOLLAND.

FLUSHING, July 28. The French, for thefe two or three days, have been in the neighbourhood of Sluys, without coming near enough to the town to be annoyed by the garrifon; but this morning it feems, they began in earneft their labour, the effect of which was the complete routing of all the Dutch troops that were placed both there and in this place, with batteries at the entrance of the oppofite fide of the Scheldt.

Their retreat was cut off from Sluys, fo that they were obliged to fly to this place, where they arrived at four o'clock this morning. We difcern very plainly the Carmagnols working at the batteries, which they attempt to conftruct all along the fhore: a Dutch armed brig has been all the morning firing at them, and they return the fire.

Yefterday we faw very diftinctly from this place acrofs the water, which is only four miles, a very large body of the French horfe and foot marching for Sluys: this was about a quarter paft 9 o'clock. About 12 a very heavy cannonade commenced; the refult no one here is acquainted with: The French were about 10,000 according to the beft judges. The Mynheers began to examine their guns upon the ramparts, and a brig in the offing fired at the Carmagnols as they paffed along the Sands.—Sir S. Smith and Lord Moira are here—There are 400 pieces of brafs cannon in Sluys; but there are not 2000 men to defend it. We feem all panic ftruck and every place given up; for as the French paffed over the plain, they took a fort mounted with 50 pieces of cannon with only 12 fhot fired.

ENGLAND.

LONDON.

All the accounts that have been received from the continent concur in ftating that the French are collecting an immenfe force in the Netherlands for the purpofe of invading Holland—The defence of that republic will moft probably be undertaken by the Dutch and Britifh troops only.—The fuccefses of the French on the Rhine are fo complete, that Frankfort, Manheim, and Mentz are in danger, and feveral of the inhabitants have retired with their effects: Others, who were preparing to follow their example, have been prevented by a proclamation iffued by the French General, who promifes that no one fhall be molefted in his property.

The attack which the French lately made upon the Pruffians in the neighbourhood of Kaiferflautern was perhaps the moft defperate and bloody of the whole campaign—They followed it up from the 9th of the month, day after day, till Sunday the 13th, from which time, till Wednefday, following, the Pruffians had not a moment's refpite, day or night. The numbers of the French increafed to 180,000 at leaft, and in their larger attack they rufhed up to the Pruffian cannon, with as much indifference as if they had not been loaded, carrying the whole at the point of the bayonet, killing or wounding every artillery officer, except one, and almoft completely annihilating the Pruffian army.

Letters

Letters from Stockholm mention, that there has been a warm difpute between the Ruffians and Swedes near Swenkfund, on an attempt by the latter to raife a fmall fortification. The Ruffians contended, that the territory belonged to them. It does not appear that any blood was fpilt upon the occafion.

The French are faid to have marched into Antwerp at 3 o'clock, P. M. on Wednefday the 23d ult. The Duke of York marched from it nearly about the fame time. There is an account received by the way of Frankfort, that Landrecy furrendered to the French on the 14th of laft month.

The French have a garrifon of 3000 men at Nieuport—at Oftend they have only 2000; but at Ghiftel, near Oftend, they have a camp of about 4000.

Difpatches from the Hague have lately been received at the Dutch Ambaffador's, which, it is faid, are not of the moft confoling nature.

The French forces deftined to act againft Holland confifts of about 80,000 men. The combined armies under the command of his Royal Highnefs the Duke of York, are only 42,000 ftrong, of which 18,000 are Britifh; but a communication will be obferved between them and the Dutch troops, commanded by the Prince of Orange. It appears by the laft advices from the Britifh army, that they were expected to march in a day or two from the neighbourhood of Breda, in order to take an advantageous pofition between Bois le Duc and the river Scheyfke.

Since the fall of Robefpierre we have no accounts of executions in Paris, except thofe members of the commune, and officers of police, who abetted him in refifting the decree of accufation. The long lifts of convictions by the Revolutionary Tribunal, were fome days prior to the execution of Robefpierre.

FRANCE.
Decapitation of Robefpierre, &c.

PARIS, *July* 30. The day before yefterday were led to the place of execution, and executed, the following perfons, viz. Maximilian Robefpierre, aged 35. He had defended himfelf in a fracas, which had happened in the commune, with a knife, which took off one half of his face, after which he was carried to the Convention, and was refufed to be admitted; he was then fent to the prifon of theConciergerie where he was detained until his execution—his head was fhewn to the people.

The brother of Robefpierre, who had broken both his legs, as he attempted to efcape.

Couthon, aged 38. St. Juft, 26. General La Valette. Dumas, Prefident of the Revolutionary Tribune—his head was fhewn to the people.

Fleuriot, the mayor of Paris. Payen, a national agent; and twelve members of the Commune of Paris.

The very remarkable circumftances which occafioned the downfal of Robefpierre, who had arrived at the fupreme power by the moft cruel and bloody means, deferves a particular detail. It is obfervable, however, that the principal caufe of that extraordinary event, is yet buried under the veil of darknefs.

The committee of public fafety, compofed of Robefpierre and his adherents, had poffeffed themfelves of the fovereign power, and exercifed it with unheard of tyranny; a tyranny to which the convention itfelf was no proof. No deputy dare exprefs his fentiments freely, without being immediately threatened with prifon or death. This occafioned a general diffatisfaction, which produced a fecret coalition of feveral members of the committee of public fafety itfelf. Collot d'Herbois and Billaud Varennes, who felt themfelves oppreffed by Robefpierre, refolved, fupported by a great number of the members of theConvention, to oppofe the further progrefs of this new Cromwell.

To fupport himfelf againft fo powerful a party, Robefpierre fought affiftance with the Jacobins, in behalf of himfelf and partifans; and the whole club appeared at the bar of the Convention on the 25th, and informed them of their fears refpecting the new intrigues carried on by foreigners, to annihilate the revolution, to calumniate the moft fincere patriots, to divide them among themfelves, and make the decrees of the Convention fufpected, efpecially that which acknowledges the exiftence of a Supreme Being. All this had not the effect which Robefpierre had expected.

On the 26th Robefpierre mounted the roftrum. He made a long fpeech on the revolution, in which he endeavoured to juftify himfelf of the views which were imputed to him of afpiring at the dictatorfhip—He faid, that ever fince he had lately proclaimed the exiftence of a Supreme Being, the partizans of Herbert and Danton had been let loofe upon him. He likewife ftrove to juftify himfelf of the report which had been fpread of his wifhing to get 30 more members of the Convention

vention guillotined. He added, that the Committee of Public Safety and *Surveillance* were the two pillars of liberty; but that the majority were often deftroyed, and that fome were endeavouring to give another form to the Republic. The decree againft the Englifh had never been executed—The fyftem of Dumourier was obferved in the low countries—Trees of liberty were planted every where—that it was urgent to fuffer the fmall ramifications to fprout out ; but that it was of the utmoft importance to watch them clofely. Freron replied, " when we wifh to give birth to liberty, the freedom of fpeech ought to be eftablifhed ; who would dare to fpeak freely, if he were conftantly furrounded by the fear of being arrefted ?"

Several emiffaries of this new Cromwell were declared outlawed ; and on the 25th in the evening, in the midft of acclamations of *Vive la République* fell the head of Robefpierre.

NEW POLICE OF FRANCE.

NATIONAL CONVENTION, *Aug.* 5.
CAMBON, after expofing the arts by which the tyrant ROBESPIERRE, aided by the *Jacobins*, had continued to accumulate all power in the hands of the committee of Public Safety ; and fhewing the errors in the organization of the various committees, prefented the following decree, which was adopted by the Convention.

DECREE, &c.

ARTICLE I. The Committee of Public Safety fhall affume the name of " *The Central Committee of Government.*" It fhall be compofed of twelve members, to be renewed every month, and not eligible again till after the interval of a month.

II. This committee fhall be under the direct infpection of the " *Commiffion of Foreign Affairs,*" and cannot difpofe of any of the public funds except for the fecret fervices of government. For this purpofe it fhall have upon the national treafury a credit of ten millions. The credit which it had formerly, and is hitherto unemployed, is hereby withdrawn.

III. The committee of Surety and Superintendence, fhall take the name of " *The Committee of the General Police of the Republic.*" It fhall confift of fifteen members. It fhall, independently of the Convention, have alone the power of arrefting citizens. For iffuing warrants of arreft againft public functionaries, it fhall act in concert with the committee charged with the fuperintendence of the adminiftration

to which fuch functionary may belong.

IV. It fhall neither fend to trial thofe who have been arrefted, nor liberate thofe fentenced by the Popular Commiffions without being in concert with the Central Committee of Government.

V. The Commiffion of Civil Affairs of Police, and the tribunals, fhall make to it a daily report of the police and the interior fecurity of the republic.

VI. It fhall have under its immediate infpection, the Police and armed force of Paris, the Revolutionary Tribunal, the Committees of Superintendence of the Republic, and the Popular Commiffions.

VII. The National Treafury fhall credit it for nine hundred thoufand livres, for extraordinary and fecret expenfes.

VIII. A fifth part of the members of the committee fhall be changed every month, and not re-eligible till the interval of one month.

IX. All other committees, or commiffions of the Convention, now in exiftence, are abolifhed.

X. The following twelve committees fhall be eftablifhed :—

1. One to fuperintend the Commiffion of Agriculture and Arts, compofed of five members.
2. One to fuperintend the Commiffion of Public Inftruction, to confift of five members.
3. To fuperintend the Commiffion of Commerce and Provifions, five members.
4. To fuperintend the Commiffion of Expreffes, Poft-Offices, and Poft-Houfes, five members.
5. To fuperintend the Commiffion of Arms and Powder, fix members.
6. To fuperintend the Commiffion of the movement of the Armies, fix members.
7. To fuperintend the Commiffion of the Marine and Colonies, five members.
8. To fuperintend the Committee of Public Succour, five members.
9. To fuperintend the Commiffion of Public Works, five members.
10. For the fuperintendence of the public expenfes and revenues, there fhall be four fections:—the firft, confifting of five members, fhall fuperintend the Commiffion of the Public Treafury; the fecond of ten members, the national revenues ; the third of ten members, the general liquidation ; and the fourth of ten members, the office of accounts.
11. A Committee of Legiflation, compofed of fifteen members, fhall have the fuperintendence of the Commiffion of civil Adminiftration, the Police and Tribunals,

Tribunals, according to the report of the Tribunals and Administrative Bodies, shall be charged with the revision and classification of the laws, and the details respecting the territorial divisions of the Republic.

12. A Committee of Inspectors of the Proces-Verbeaux, consisting of fifteen members, is charged with superintending the transcription of the Acts of the Convention in its offices and archives, the National Press, and the Commission of Civil Administrations.

ART. XI. There shall also be a Committee of Inspectors of the Hall, composed of fifteen members, exclusively, charged with the Police within the limits of the Convention, the Committees, and the National Garden. It shall regulate the expenses of the National Convention and its archives, as well as those of the Committees, also the travelling expenses of the Representatives of the People sent to the departments, or the armies.

XII. It shall verify and adjust the accounts relative to the aforesaid expenses; and the resolution of that Committee, declaring its verification of the expenses of the Representatives of the People, amounting to such a sum, shall be allowed as an admission of that account.

XIII. The National Treasury shall give it credit for three millions, to be employed in such expenses in the aforesaid payments; and all former credit, hitherto unemployed, is withdrawn.

XIV. Every Executive Commission shall give a daily account of its proceedings to the Committee charged with its inspection, and shall propose to it the difficulties to be surmounted, and the means of removing them. It shall also submit, for the approbation of the Committee, the agents nominated for the execution of its order.

XV. The Commissioners shall every day lay before the Committee for inspecting the Public Expenditure and Revenue, a detailed account of the expenses incurred in the course of the day.

XVI. The Committees shall directly propose to the Convention, all legislative objects, after having previously communicated them to the Central Committee of Government. They shall concert with that Committee through the medium of one of its members, who shall be charged to report the executive objects discussed in the Committee.

XVII. All executive objects shall be definitely settled by the Central Committee of Government; which shall be responsible for the resolutions it may take. These resolutions shall be signed by at least six members of the Central Committee, and by the Commissioner of the Committee who shall make the report. The resolutions shall be sent to be executed by the Commissions, and an account of them shall then be laid before the Convention.

XVIII. Should there be any difference of opinion in the Central Committee of Government, the affairs to be discussed and decided by a meeting composed of one Commissioner from each of the Committees.

XIX. In cases of urgency, where expedition is required, the Central Committee of Government may call upon one or more of the Committee charged with the superintendence of the matter in question, and the result of their deliberation shall be carried into execution. But the members who shall assist in such deliberations, shall make an immediate report of it to the General Committee.

XX. The Convention shall itself nominate the Representatives of the People to be sent on any commission, the Generals, the members of the Executive Commission, the members of the Revolutionary Tribunal, and Popular Commissions, on the proposition of the Central Committee of Government, united with the Committee charged with what relates to that particular object.

XXI. The National Convention alone has power to recal the Representatives of the People sent upon commission. The Central Committee of Government, in concert with the Committee charged with that particular affair, may remove the Generals, the members of the Executive Commissions, and other public functionaries, of which a report is to be made to the Convention.

XXII. All the Committees shall have a fifth of their members changed every month.

XXIII. All the Committees and Commissions within the Convention shall continue to exercise their functions till the Committees that are to replace them are perfectly organized.

The Committee of *Public Welfare* at Paris is now composed of the following persons: Barrere, Lolloi, Tallien, Thuriot, Collet D'Horbois, Treithard, Billaud, Varrenes, Carnot, Effecherau, sen. Prieur, Breaid, and Lindet.

The domestic occurrences of this month are necessarily omitted.

THE

MASSACHUSETTS MAGAZINE:

OR,

MONTHLY MUSEUM

OF

KNOWLEDGE and RATIONAL *ENTERTAINMENT.*

No. XI.] FOR NOVEMBER, 1794. [Vol. VI.

CONTAINING,

WITH A HANDSOME ENGRAVING.

PRINTED AT *BOSTON,* FOR THE PROPRIETORS,
By EZRA W. WELD AND WILLIAM GREENOUGH,
No. 42, CORNHILL.
Sold at JOHN WEST's Bookftore, No. 75, *Cornhill,* BOSTON ; and by the feveral
GENTLEMEN who receive Subfcriptions for this WORK.

MDCCXCIV.

ACKNOWLEDGMENTS to CORRESPONDENTS.

Senex is unreservedly thanked for his advice. No attention can poffibly be paid to his plan till the commencement of the new year.

Veritas—his epigrams are too pointed and particular. Wit and fatire are always acceptable, but perfonal abufe will never be admitted.

W. L.—his letter on tafte is not original—We are grateful for judicious extracts, but we muft refufe their admiffion when impofed in the form of originality.

Inquifitus—his queries are better calculated for his own amufement than for our magazine.

Reflections on general Thankfgiving, are devotional, and fuited to the prefent feafon, but for reafons, with which their author muft be well acquainted, we beg to be excufed from publifhing them.

PRICES of PUBLIC SECURITIES, BANK STOCK, &c.

November.	Six per Cents.	Three per Cents.	"Defer'd Stock.	Maffachuf. State Notes.	U.S.B. Shares ab. par.	Maffachuf. Bank Shares.	Union Bank Shares ab. pr.	Final & L. Of Cert. inter. fr. Jan. 1788.	Reg. Dt. with int. fr. March 4, 1789.	Indcats. Int. on Loan Offi.	Cer. & Reg. Dt.	New Emiffion Money.	O. Emif. Mo.
	s. d.	s. d.	s. d.	s. d.	per ct.	dols.	per ct.	s. d.	s. d.	s. d.	s. d.	s.	
1	19 4	11 3	12 8	15 6	26	None	8	18 0	17	10 0	8 0	45	
3	19 4	11 3	12 8	15 6	26	at	8	18 0	17 6	10 0	8 0	45	
4	19 5	11 3½	12 8	15 6	27	mkt.	8	18 0	17 6	10 6	8 0	45	
5	19 5	11 3½	12 8	15 6	27		8	18 0	17 6	10 6	8 0	45	
6	19 5	11 3½	12 8	15 6	27		8	18 0	17 6	10 6	8 0	45	
7	19 5	11 3½	12 8	15 6	27		8	18 0	17 6	10 6	8 0	45	
8	19 6	11 4	12 9	15 6	28		9	19 0	17 6	10 6	8 0	45	
10	19 6	11 4	12 9	15 6	28		9	19 0	17 6	10 6	8 0	45	
11	19 6	11 4	12 9	15 6	28		9	19 0	17 6	10 6	8 0	45	
12	19 6	11 4	12 9	15 6	28¼		9	19 0	17 6	10 6	8 0	45	
13	19 6	11 4	12 9	15 6	28½		9	19 0	17 6	10 6	8 0	45	
14	19 6	11 4	12 9	15 8	29		9	19 0	17 6	10 6	8 0	45	
15	19 6	11 4	12 9	15 9	29		9	19 0	17 6	10 6	8 0	45	
17	19 8	11 4	12 9	15 9	30		9	19 0	17 6	10 6	8 0	45	
18	19 8	11 4	12 9	15 9	30		10	19 0	17 6	10 6	8 0	45	
19	19 9	11 4	12 9	15 9	30		10	19 0	17 6	10 6	8 0	45	
20	19 9	11 4	12 9	15 9	30		10	19 0	17 6	10 6	8 0	45	
21	19 9	11 4	12 9	15 9	31		10	19 0	17 6	10 6	8 0	45	
22	19 10	11 4	12 9	15 9	31		10	19 0	17 6	10 6	8 0	45	
24	19 10	11 4	12 9	15 9	31		10	19 0	17 6	10 6	8 0	45	
25	19 10	11 4	12 9	15 9	31		10	19 0	17 6	10 6	8 0	45	
26	19 10	11 4	12 9	15 9	31		10	19 0	17 6	10 6	8 0	45	
27	20	11 5	13 2	16	32		10	19 0	17 6	10 6	8 0	45	
28	20	11 5	13 2	16	32		10	19 0	17 6	10 6	8 0	45	
29	20	11 4	13 2	16	32		11	19 0	17 6	10 6	8 0	45	

JOHN MARSTON, *Stock Broker.*

y
le,
er-
en-
fo
m-
pe.
er
— to
uld
rn,
to
ght
on-
pa-
en
hat
h

iron
one,
ecef-
liver-
Johnson
happened

The Fatal Alternative.

T,HE

MASSACHUSETTS MAGAZINE.

FOR *NOVEMBER*, 1794.

The FATAL ALTERNATIVE.
A TALE.

[Embellifhed with a handfome Engraving.]

THE force that eloquence gives to the precepts of virtue, and the fecurity that rank brings to the prefervation of character, are alike feeble in the conflict of paffions, and alike unavailing in thofe hours of trial, which the confent of mankind has in lenity called *unguarded*. The fuperiority of mind, the dignity of character, the awe of virtue, and the tenor of fixed principles, are but words of courfe " when ftrong temptations try," when impulfes are felt which cannot be refifted, and allurements are propofed whofe effects are not underftood.

It was not want of underftanding, it was not want of education, it was not the power of feduction, but it was a perverfity of thinking, formed of all thefe wants, which reduced Laura Belfont from an enviable rank among the good and the happy, to a ftate at which the happy fhuddered, and the virtuous were appalled. The comfort of her parents, the delight of their eyes, and the pride of their heart, the admiration of one fex, and the envy of

the other. Laura's days promif length and happinefs ; the mornii of life arofe with fplendour a beauty ; it bid fair for a glorious day but the dawn was fcarcely vifible, when the thicknefs of darknefs overfhadowed the profpect, and the evening of that day which promifed fo fmilingly, haftened on without calmnefs, without ferenity, without hope.

She had married the man of her artlefs heart, but not of her *choice.*— Love only decidedly gave colour to the fate of a life which it would have required judgment to adorn, and tendernefs and fidelity to lengthen. Under the well wrought difguife of affection, her lover concealed the only paffion he was capable of enjoying, *avarice*, and when by the poffeffion of her fortune that was gratified, the poffeffion of h perfon loft the only charm it He did not become carelefs, i t iron rent and brutal—He only thr ftone, the mafk, and appeared in hi necefcharacter, without love, age diverprinciple, without tender hen Johnfon yet not of her : fenfual happened with her beauties ; ambitious, yet not of her affection ; he renewed his criminal correfpondence with a woman who had long triumphed over the boafted fidelity of the male fex, and had rendered her own vices a fource of advantage and pride to herfelf.—She had no character to lofe ; fhe envied every woman who poffeffed what, to her, was irrecoverably loft.

The gay, and fprightly Laura, for fuch fhe was in better times, was now foftened down to the penfive tenant of a melancholy abode, in a lonely and remote part of the country, where all accefs to the confolations of friendfhip was denied her, and where fhe had full leifure to combine the worft reflections of the paft with the moft agonizing prof- pects of the future.   She feldom faw · · hufband, and knew no generofity om him, but that he allowed, and ,at barely, the neceffaries of life ; but to all its pleafures fhe was in every fenfe of the word, cruelly mortified.   He infulted her by the company of abandoned women, who were the companions of his licentious hours, and with whom he fquandered the fortune fhe had brought him, and wafted the affection fhe alone ought to have enjoyed.   Vice had corrupted his mind, and all the finer feelings were warped by a narrow fenfuality, which was alike infatiable and impotent, and gratified by a repetition of pleafures that left no fatisfaction, and only prepared for the days of remorfe and defpair.

Laura was friendlefs—fhe had 29 rvived her parents ; fhe was far (ˉved from her inmates ; fhe was ded by creatures of her huf- ˉs providing, whofe hearts had fince forgot to beat in the caufe ' innocence.—She was in a ˉere philofophy prefcribes

refignation, but where nature yields to forrow.—She was not formed for the afperities of life : alas ! fhe had none to calm the tumult of her breaft ; fhe had none to fpeak peace to a mind already troubled beyond the power of being allayed.

It was in one of thofe miferable hours, when hope forfook her and fled—at a time when a dead infant, the only tie which connected her with her hufband, lay ftretched on her bed—when all the events of her life came in review before her, that fhe wandered into a park near her habitation, feparated from the road by a river—It was there fhe fat herfelf down on the grafs, and indulged in agonies of grief, which were to be no longer fuppreffed.

All the horrors of her fituation appeared in review before her—the fad contraft between the days of youth and happinefs, of admiration and vanity, and thofe miferable days and nights fhe had fince fuffered were active in her imagination. Putting her hand into her pocket for a handkerchief to dry thofe tears, which once the proudeft would have been happy to dry up, fhe found a letter addreffed to her by her father on the firft news of her intended marriage ; there he, though gently, upbraided her with want of confidence, fuggefted fufpicions of the real character of her lover, and painted in lively colours the feelings of a parent and the duty of a child.— This only was wanting to give fury to that fpeechlefs agony which now poffeffed her whole foul—and furrounded as fhe was by horrors which cannot be defcribed, fhe fought relief, where it is to be feared the miferable feek it in vain—fhe plunged into the river near her, and funk in a moment to rife no more !

But this unhappy fair one was not unobferved—Two perfons on horfeback

horfeback on the road had obferved her, though at a confiderable diftance, and one of them put fpurs to his horfe, beckoning the other to follow.—They foon arrived at a place where the river was fordable, but arrived too late for the relief of Laura.—They procured affiftance in finding the body, and conveyed it to her lonely abode.—The wretched hufband was not unmoved by the news of this, which was fpeedily conveyed to him, but he objected only that impulfe which guided all his actions.—He fummed up all his crimes in one, and by an unfought facrifice to the memory of his wife, he rufhed into the prefence of his Maker, with the guilt of his own and her blood on his devoted head.

The conclufion of this narrative is perhaps no more than has often been inculcated, but it is what ought often to be repeated, that "Though vice is conftantly attended by mifery, virtue itfelf cannot confer happinefs in this world, except it is animated with the hopes of a better, where complete juftice fhall be done and where complete happinefs fhall have no end."

Laura ought to have yet fuftained evils which, however great, cannot without long experience, be deemed hopelefs. But her mind, originally not ftrong, was driven, by the impatience of wrong, to the *fatal alternative*—to fuffer yet more, or to end all by precipitating herfelf into an untimely grave.

SINGULAR INSTANCE of LIBERALITY.

THE people of the Eaft, who are generally more volatile than the reft of mankind, carry their virtues and vices to extremes.

A man who was liberal even to profufion, refided in Bagdad, under the reign of the Caliph Mamoun: His prodigality prefently difperfed an immenfe fortune. One day, Afmai, a poet, who had fhared very confiderably in his profufion, came and knocked at his door as ufual, fuppofing him to be ftill a rich man; the porter refufed him admittance: Afmai, chagrined at this treatment, wrote fome verfes to

the following effect: *What difference is there between a mifer and a generous man, if the latter keeps his door fhut?* He gave thefe lines to the porter, defiring he would prefent them to his mafter. He did not ftay long for an anfwer, for the fervant immediately returned with the fame paper, on the back of which was written two lines to the following purport——*When a generous man has given away his all, he does right to keep his door fhut, that he may not have the mortification of refufing to grant a favour.*

ANECDOTES of Dr. JOHNSON.

THERE were two fingularities in this genius, which have efcaped the refearches of all his biographers. In the centre of the market place at Litchfield where

he was born, there is a great iron ring, fixed by a ftaple in a ftone, which formerly ferved as a neceffary inftrument in the favage diverfion of bull-baiting. When Johnfon happened

happened in his walks, for he paid an annual vifit to Litchfield, to pafs by this fpot, he would frequently in the midft of thofe feveries in which he feemed to be involved, ftep afide, and ftooping down, lay hold of the ring, and pull it about, as if he had been trying whether he had been able to extricate it from the ftone to which it was fixed.

The other remarkable particulars concerning Johnfon, which has not been mentioned by his numerous biographers is, that he made it a point, when he paid his annual vifit to the place of his nativity, to call on every perfon in that city, with whom he had the leaft acquaintance ; but that the inftant he knocked at the door, he would, without giving time for the opening of it, pafs on to another, where he would do the fame thing ; fo that it frequently happened that two or three fervants would be running after the doctor, requefting that he would return to their mafters or miftreffes houfes, who were waiting to receive him.

Ludicrous Anecdote of FRENCH GALLANTRY.

[From Mariti's Travels through Syria and Palestine.]

I VISITED the wells of Ras-Elein, in the company of two French gentlemen, one of whom was a phyfician—from the fummit of a little hill, we had a view of the furrounding plains, and perceived, at a fmall diftance, a group of Arab women on the brink of a rivulet, in which fome of them were wafhing their clothes, and others bathing ; but they were all perfectly naked. This fpectacle produced fuch a fudden effect on one of the French gentlemen, as plainly fhewed he was of a very warm temperament. He wifhed immediately to defcend the hill, in order, as he faid, to obferve thefe people a little clofer ; and he requefted me to accompany him. Knowing better than my companion the difpofition of the orientals, I pointed out the dangers to which he was going to expofe himfelf, either from the women themfelves, or the Arabs that he might meet : But all my remonftrances were ineffectual ; for he was determined to gratify his curiofity, even at the hazard of his life.

Finding that I would not comply with his requeft, he endeavoured to prevail on the phyfician to accompany him, but he had as little courage as I. Our companion was then no longer able to contain himfelf ; he ftamped on the earth with his foot, curfed his bad fortune that he had not at leaft brought his fpy glafs with him, and even reproached nature with having placed fuch a diftance between the hill and the rivulet.

Hurried away by his vivacity, he did not even fpare us, whom he confidered as pufilanimous beings, and infenfible to female charms. In fhort, he burft from us with fo much velocity, that he had reached the borders of the rivulet before we well knew of his departure.

I was much furprifed to fee all the women come forth from the water, and, advancing towards him, naked as they were, invite him to take a place among them. Our French friend then redoubled his compliments, and employed the moft expreffive figns to fhew his gratitude. He was eagerly received, and almoft immediately furrounded by a circle a circle of thefe females; but their careffes were only a fnare to enable them to punifh his prefumption. They attacked him all at once, fome tearing his hair, while others mauled him with their fifts; and, I am perfuaded, that he would have fallen a victim to their fury, had not his courage delivered him from their hands. He afterwards avoided, as well as he could, a fhower of ftones, difcharged after him; fome of which,

notwithftanding his activity, were not without effect.

This tragi-comic fcene excited both laughter and compaffion, while the amorous Frenchman was obliged to folicit the aid of the phyfician, to drefs his wounds. Senfible of his folly, he promifed to behave with more prudence in future, and, indeed, we gave him full credit for his refolution.

SENTIMENTAL REFLECTIONS.

WHY is the mind of man, when endued with what is called tafte, delighted with extravagant flights in poetry, extraordinary metaphors, exceffes in grammar, cromatics in mufic, &c? How come we to be charmed with things which offend common fenfe, or fhock the natural ear? And from what turn of caprice does it proceed, that the very errors and faults of fome of the arts and fciences, are efteemed beauties? Nay, to fhew that tafte is not only above, but even fometimes averfe from rational admiration, we need but recollect the pleafure we receive from viewing fome of the deformities of nature, as rocks, precipices, &c. and at the fame time remember, that we are fenfible of a cerain horror during the contemplation.

LIFE is a picture; fortune the frame, but misfortune the fhade—the firft only its extrinfic ornament, but the latter, if well fuftained, forms the intrinfic merit by giving a bolder relief to the figures.

THE critic lives too much in his ftudy; and the difference between fuch a perfon, and thofe who con-

verfe familiarly in the world, may be compared to the upper fod, and the under fpit of the earth—the latter may have intrinfically the fame powers of vegetation, but wants the action and impregnation of the atmofphere, to fee its fixed falts at liberty to exert themfelves.

IS not a child's grief for the lofs of his dinner more fincere than a man's? In proportion as our reafon improves, and our fentiment refines, the poignancy of difappointment appears more blunt. There is an alleviating refource, a kind of felf-foothing confolation, in the very diftreffes of delicate minds, the refinement of which would be but poorly exchanged for

" The broadeft unfeeling folly wears."
But the difappointment of mere natural appetite has no refource, no alleviation; how much more to be pitied then!

THERE is a certain reftleffnefs and impatience in our minds, that refufes pleafure from a continued enjoyment, or contemplation of the fame objects, or ideas; and our nature thirfts for variety, from the cradle to the grave. The feveral
feafons

seafons of life open with novelty, to childhood, to youth, to manhood, and *fenefeince*. We find ourfelves ftill, as we approach thefe advancing æras, attracted by different views, paffions, and purfuits; and quit the former fcene without regret ; not becaufe the fhifting one will afford us better entertainment, for as yet we have had no experience of it, but which does as well, becaufe we have made fufficient trial of the foregoing, have effayed its pleafures, and exhaufted its variety. At length the vaffalage of ignorance and fubjection is paft ; we have now arrived at the long wifhed-for throne of man's eftate, and would maintain the flattering empire of health, vigour, and reafon, during the remainder of our reign. But when we have chimed over all the changes on the few notes of this pitch of life, how fhall we be able to relieve that *tiædium vitæ*, that fatiety of life, fo generally complained of already, even in the prefent contracted portions of our time, which numbers have found fo irkfome, that they have had recourfe to drunkennefs, or fuicide, to rid themfelves of ?

———

THE fucceffion and alternation of manly bufinefs, fports, and pleafures, are truly rational amufements to the mind ; the chafte alliances, the tender connexions, the generous friendfhips, the charitable dependencies of this ftate of life (the youthful), are, indeed, additional fources of moral happinefs, and heart-felt tranfports. But continued to a certain period, only fatiety fucceeds, too often repeated joys ; and pleafures ftill running in a circle, lag, when we begin the well known courfe again. Were vigorous manhood to remain, the fame paffions and purfuits would ftill

fubfift, with baffled hopes, and difappointed wifhes ; novelty would grow ftale, and variety lofe its change, while curiofity would urge, and impatience refent the palled fruition ; till we fhould at length, cry out with a fmall alteration, in the language of Milton,

" Each feafon and its change difpleafe alike."

A thoufand untried follies would be then attempted ; premiums preferred by wearied libertines, as was once done by a Roman emperor, by the invention of new pleafures ; caprice, debauchery, and vice, would vifit, and clofe our lives in madnefs or defpair. Happily in relief to our unftable nature, our vigour declines, our paffions fubfide ; curiofity grows weary, our defires are fatisfied, and indolence fucceeds. A different train of ideas infenfibly form themfelves, by degrees, in our minds—health, peace, and eafe become then our wifer wifh. We have feen the vanities, and felt the follies of life ; nor would we try again with feeble mind, and relaxed finews,

" To feek, with erring ftep, contentment's obvious way."

Laftly, death, that in vigour would have been our fear, in decay becomes our hope.

———

A mediocrity in writing is quicker perceived in poetry, than any thing elfe. I would rather *buoy* in the furface fometimes, than always *anchor* in the mud.

———

HOW cruel a cafe is it, after a perfon has fpent his life in attaining a good repute, that fome capricious jealoufy arifing in our minds, or any malicious infinuations from another hand, fhall deprive him of the credit of it ? A man may have honour and fell iron at the fame time.

HERALDRY

For the MASSACHUSETTS MAGAZINE.

HERALDRY HIEROGLYPHICS.—A FRAGMENT.

THE hiſtory of the *cruſades* affords a ſtriking picture of the folly and enthuſiaſm of mankind, when left to the blind impulſe of a heated and deluded imagination. It is to theſe, however; we are indebted for that perfection to which heraldry, as a ſcience, has been carried.

Heraldry is a ſcience ſo eſtimable and amuſing, that many of the nobility and virtuoſos of every nation have, for ſeveral centuries, deemed it worthy their ſtudious application.

Kings and princes have derived entertainment from the inveſtigation of the nobility, alliances, and power of their anceſtry, in the hieroglyphics of this curious ſcience. Others, of inquiry and enterpriſe, although confined to a humbler ſphere of action, have been equally gratified in finding that their progenitors were dignified with royal favour. Their pleaſure has been heightened, when; by their induſtrious ſcrutiny into the mazes of heraldry, they have diſcovered that a reſpectable number of their anceſtors were enrolled in the liſt of fame for ſome diſtinguiſhing literary acquirement, military prowefs, a ſhining virtue, or ſome ſingular patriotic ſervice.

In a coat of arms we have a conciſe, but comprehenſive hiſtory of the heroic deeds, which raiſed the anceſtry of the bearer to eminence. Arms, properly blazoned, ſerve to point out the deſcent of the bearer, and to mark the various ſteps by which his anceſtors arrived at celebrity. They diſtinguiſh the multiplied branches proceeding from the ſame original ſtock, and ſhow the relationſhip between families.

In this, as in moſt other ſciences, there have been abuſes. Several armoriſts, fond of the marvellous, wiſhing to give themſelves an importance, by the profundity of their reſearches and diſcoveries, or perhaps actuated by an entailed portion of the cruſaders' ſpirit, have been diſguſtfully prolix on the nature, properties, and myſtic alluſions of heraldic tinctures. The pretenders to this myſterious knowledge, we readily grant, have an indefeaſible right to a province in the cabaliſtic empire.

It is with heraldry, in ſome meaſure, as with the *maſoretic notes.* Theſe ſubſerve the purpoſe of determining the original pronunciation of the Hebrew and ſome other oriental languages. Heraldry ſubſerves the purpoſe of giving birth and rank their due precedence, according to the ideas of former times. This modern age has guillotined them both.

The ſcribbler of this paper is as high and wiggified a devotee to liberty and equality, under *rational reſtrictions,* as ever graſped *pen* or *ſword;* yet, it is his creed, that there is an incontestible foundation in nature for diſtinctions. This ſentiment is ſanctioned by the invariable diſpoſition of the parts throughout the three kingdoms of nature, and by the high beheſt of God himſelf.

The noble have been diſtinguiſhed from the ignoble by external badges, time immemorial. The breaſtplate, ephod, mitre, and veſtments of curious workmanſhip, were the levitical characteriſtics. Crowns and diadems have ever been thoſe of monarchs and emperors. In peruſing Homer, Virgil, and other claſſics, we find their heroes diſtinguiſhed by the various figures

figures of their fhields. Homer has given a very pompous account of the fhield of Ulyffes. Alexander the great permitted his chiefs to wear certain badges on their armour, pennons and banners, that their perfonages might be eafily known and fuitably revered. He firictly enjoined that no potentate throughout his dominions fhould confer fuch badges of honour. This prerogative he claimed as his independent right, and all kings and fovereign princes, from that period to the prefent, have, in this particular, made him their pattern.

Hieroglyphic characters have been in vogue from the remoteft ages.* The Egyptians brought this myfticel fpecies of writing to very confiderable perfection. Converfant with the natural world, favoured with a fituation friendly to fcientific inveftigation and improvement, and bleffed with a brilliant imagination, they felected the figures of fuch objects as in fome particulars bore the moft ftriking refemblance to the things they wifhed to defcribe. Thofe figures, their importance eftablifhed, fubferve the purpofe of writing. They are in fact a kind of fterography. With a fmall number of thefe the Egyptians could exprefs, on a little piece of papyrus, what a modern fcribbler would fpin into the extent of many folio pages.

The morning, which has been the fubject of fo many elaborate, fublime, and beautiful poetic productions, is unfolded to view by the fimple figure of the *crocodile's eye*. Job probably knew the import of this hieroglyphic ; for, in fpeaking of this monftrous animal, he fays, "his eyes are like the eyelids of the morning." Could it be proved that this fymbol was in ufe prior to the days of Job ; that he had it in his mind when he penned this would hardly remain problematical. The fymbol is very natural, for,

———"When his burnifh'd eyes
"Lift their broad lids, the morning feems
   to rife."

      ,   MODENA.

* The curious may be highly entertained with the writings of the late learned and ingenious *Count de Gebelin*, on hieroglyphics.

For the MASSACHUSETTS MAGAZINE.

The REPOSITORY. No. XXVI.

REFLECTIONS occafioned by reading an account of a ludicrous exit.

I DO not like this apparent gaiety, this ebullition of facetious wit, in the hour of diffolution ! Methinks an air of levity but ill becomes a departing fpirit ; and there is a decent, a compofed folemnity, which, while it elevates the mind, in the fame moment, beft accords with propriety. If my head is, upon the coming hour, deftined to the block, refignation, and prefence of mind, with manners fedately dignified, is fortitude : but licentious jefting, and ludicrous comments, upon an occafion fo awfully ferious, are truly fhocking. At fuch a period, *recollection* is furely neceffary—at leaft, it is *natural* ; an *affectation* of unconcern is defpicable ; and if it is *real*, it announces a mind devoid of fenfibility. Exertions of native fuperiority, evinced by calm compofure, are defcriptive of equanimity ; but boifterous mirth can never
           be

be confidered as the fmalleft indication of heroifm. Were we to rufh, with a familiar air, or fupercilious ftep, into the prefence of that being, whofe brow was encircled by the wreath of merit, or upon whofe head glittered even an earthly crown, we fhould be juftly chargeable with temerity ; but when we are about to prefent ourfelves before an omnipotent, and a felf-exiftent Creator, from whom we originate, and upon whom we muft eternally depend, perturbation, even in the *extreme*, may be *tolerated*—and the moft profound veneration, and deep-felt awe, is but a proper acknowledgment of the immenfity of Deity. It is furely incumbent upon the foul, to clothe itfelf in the garments of humility, to affume its utmoft purity, and if it joys in its approach to the divine, the benignant Author of its exiftence, let its joy partake of folemnity—let it be chaftifed by ferious propriety. I envy not the felicity of that *actor*, who, being apprized that he hath but a few hours to continue in the prefent fcene, devotes the interval to *drefs*, and *fancy ;* to *bows*, and compliments. When the period of my diffolution is at hand, let me

employ my powers in meditating upon an opening heaven—in grafping at ideas fuitable to that auguft affembly, which I am fo foon to join, and in an effort to diveft my fpirit of every earth-born care.—The change is affuredly great—it is of immeafurable importance.—Of our deftination we can have little idea, and although, from the philanthropy of our God, from the atonement made for our offences, and the price paid for our redemption, we may rationally conclude, that happinefs is our defignation ; yet, there is a variety of confiderations that are, at fuch a moment, abundantly fufficient to fill, and exercife the ftrongeft, and moft capacious mind ; and we fhould be careful to clofe the fcene with becoming decency. Even the atheift, I fhould imagine, except he hath, by continued anticipation, become habituated to the comfortlefs profpect of annihilation, muft acknowledge the period which is to terminate his exiftence, but ill-fuited to *expreffions of mirth*—and the probability is, that he bids adieu to pain and pleafure, with fenfations of folemn regret.

CONSTANTIA.

For the MASSACHUSETTS MAGAZINE.
The MEMORIALIST. No. VI.

ALCANDOR was a youth endowed with all the charms of beauty ; but his outward form feemed only an index to the fuperior graces of his mental accomplifhments. His artlefs behaviour, and the complacency of his difpofition, gained him the efteem of his neighbours, and prepoffeffed the hearts of ftrangers in his favour. Even in the ftages of his infancy, while childifh amufements employed his atten-

tion, there feemed in him that noblenefs of fpirit above his playfellows, which is the fure indication of an early genius. *Natural* objects only for a fhort time could fatisfy his ambition—he panted to climb the fteeps of fcience. But nurfed in humble obfcurity—a ftranger to the politenefs of a court—where fhall he find a Mæcenas ? He grieved, but carefully concealed the caufe of his grief from his parents. Often, by by the secret rock and the tree, would he retire, to lament the parsimony of fortune. The parent at length found out the cause of his son's melancholy, but was unable to relieve it. Resignation was the only cordial which could afford relief to their souls : But capricious fortune looks with an eye of pity upon their situation. A stranger, stopping accidentally at the cottage to take some refreshment, was delighted with the simple neatness of the mansion, the industry of the parents, but much more with the conversation of young Alcandor. He discovered their penurious circumstances, and conceiving a strong affection for their son, proposed to take him under his own care, which proposal was cheerfully accepted. It is needless to say any thing of the joy which his parents expressed—it is easier felt than described. The benevolent stranger beheld with pleasure the uncommon genius of Alcandor, and sent him to an university for his education.

We are now to contemplate Alcandor rambling in the fields of science, and enriching himself with all the stores of intellectual knowledge. We must consider him, not merely indulging himself with the pictures of fancy, but with making that improvement of science, which brings home useful instructions to the heart. After the common time allotted for education had elapsed, Alcandor quits the walks of his study and enters on the threshold of the world, with his mind well guarded against the seductions of vice. It is natural to presume, that he would choose that profession which will infallibly lead merit into public attention. He remains to this day the pride and ornament of his country.

From the imperfect sketch here given of the character of Alcandor, the importance of the establishment of public schools is fully illustrated. Had not a benevolent stranger beheld this youth, he would have sunk unnoticed into oblivion. So true are the words of the poet :

" Full many a gem, of purest ray serene,
The dark unfathom'd caves of ocean bear ;
Full many a flower is doom'd to blush unseen,
And waste its sweetness on the desert air."

Thus a diamond may often lie neglected in its crust, which, if polished by the hand of an artificer, would be a gem of inestimable value. But it is answered, that much of the public money must be squandered away to no purpose, as many children would attend the schools, who could reap no advantage from study. Aside from the natural weakness of this remark, and the presumption that we are dealing with a nation of misers, let us see if this assertion is founded on fact. History informs us, that the most valuable discoveries, in every art and science, were made principally by men, who, to speak in the fashionable stile, were of low birth and family. From whence arose that illustrious group of statesmen, of poets, and orators, the admiration of antiquity, and whose works have been hung out as examples to modern ages ? Unquestionably they sprung from the common mass of the people. By such characters the credit of a nation is established, and thus the public are more than doubly repaid for their expenses. But even if this statement is nothing but a falacy, it does not injure, in the least, the validity of the argument. No one will contest but what the property of individuals is as well expended in the establishment of schools, as in the purchase of gewgaws and the fripperies of fashion.

It

It will check the progrefs of luxury, which is the bane of public felicity. It is then the duty of the legiflature to interpofe ; but the good fenfe of the citizens of the different ftates, forbids us to doubt, but what this ufeful fcheme of a general education, will finally be adopted. The example of Maffachufetts will doubtlefs be followed, and, in this manner, the way may be opened for the complete emancipation of the human mind from the flavery of ignorance.

The GLEANER. No. XXX.

Apparent fecrecy fufpicion nerves,
And fcrutiny is nurtur'd by referve ;
While the fweet flow of confidence bequeaths,
That treafur'd peace, a rich perfume which breathes.

DISGUISES are frequently the convenient afylums of villainy ; and as they are always queftionable, they are with propriety always fufpected. To trace the labyrinth of folly, into which the flagitious delinquent is precipitated, requires more than human penetration. Many are the windings and doublings of the proficient in error ; all his paths are intricate, he is fruitful in fubterfuges, and he is enveloped in myftery. I do not fay that virtue hath never worn a veil, or that integrity may not fuppofe it neceffary to hold up falfe lights ; but I contend that the *practice* of *deception*, being an expedient that muft be acknowledged *extremely hazardous*, it ought never to be reforted to but in the *laft extremity :* and I am free to own, that I have found a fingular pleafure in indulging a hope, that truth and innocence will generally bear their own weight. The fmooth furface of the limpid ftream out-fpreads its azure flow to the moft curious inveftigation ; the orient luminary of day emits a flood of light ; it iffues forth a tranfcendent body, elevated in itfelf, and to every eye confeffed ;

and the upright ancient, wifhed for a glafs in his breaft, that the *poffibility* of concealment might be thus erafed from the catalogue of his abilities. Ambiguity cafts a veil over the moft irreproachable life ; it originates the *invidious ardours* of *fpeculation ;* and it gives to the features of virtue the contour of folly. I confefs that I am charmed by franknefs of foul ; ingenuity and integrity of manners, carry with them their title to my unreferved efteem, and upon the honeft fincere man, reafon, unbiaffed by fafhion, or habit, is ever ready to pronounce a eulogy. I abhor duplicity in every form, doubtful meanings, double entenders, playing upon words, with every bagatelle of this defcription, are, in my opinion, at leaft inelegant; and unbecoming ; nor can I allow that they make any part of *manly fenfe, true wit,* or *genuine humour.* In a fair, open, confiftent manner of thinking, converfing and acting, there is both dignity and propriety, and an elevated reputation is the well earned reward of perfevering, and unequivocal worth. We liften, with unreftrained pleafure, to the man of unimpeached honour ; to
him,

him whofe upright foul hath never been entangled in the wilds of deceit, who hath never debafed himfelf by an alliance with falfehood, nor fported with the credulity of his affociates ; who, worfhipping at the fhrine of truth, hath ftill held her inviolate, regarding all her inftigations as facred, and difdaining to purchafe the *fmile* of *levity at the expenfe of that jeft which borrows its humour from a breach of veracity ;* and it is then that we confer upon him the moft honourary diftinction, when, with unlimitted confidence, we repofe upon his word the moft unhefitating faith ; it is dangerous to amufe ourfelves with the *femblance* of *vice ; the habit* of uttering *merry falfehoods,* will foon blunt the fine edge of our feelings, and we fhall eafily flide into the moft *ferious* and *capital violations of truth.* Integrity dignifies a character ; franknefs is truly amiable, and if the offence is not highly enormous, foftened by the ingenuity of a candid acknowledgment, we are ready to prefs the offender to our bofoms, we allow him a fecond leafe of our efteem, and it depends altogether upon himfelf, whether we fhall ever again ferve upon him a writ of ejection. A moment of concealment is a moment of humiliation ; and although circumftances may fometime render it neceffary, yet, it is certain, that when the *paths* of *innocence are encompaffed by ambiguity ;* the luftre of her crown is dimned ; her blooming honours *feem* to *wane,* and we hefitate, while uttering thofe applaufes which fhould be referved to enwreath the brow of *unequivocal merit.* Myfterious arrangements excite fufpicion; conjecture is afloat ; jealoufy is roufed; the ærial mifchief feeds upon the thineft diet, and peace evaporates in its grafp. Monimia is perturbed and agitated ; not an hour in the day but a variety of tormenting ideas fucceed each other in her mind ; and the moft vexatious inquietude, is the defpot of her dreams. Monimia once boafted of her felicity, and her prefent fufferings are the offspring of conjecture ; delicacy forbids her to queftion, and yet her tranquillity will never be reftored, until fhe learns to what fair hand her loved Eugenio was indebted for the *expreffive device* fo elegantly enwreathed, and fo curioufly cut, which hath recently come into his poffeffion, and which he carefully preferves in the cover of his watch.   Clariffa is agitated and unhappy ; fhe accidentally difcovered in the efcritoir of Horatio, a lock of hair ; it was beautifully gloffy ; fhe is pofitive that it never made a part of her own auburn treffes ; it was neatly folded in fome lines, fweetly pathetic, and tenderly poetical : Perhaps the rape of that immortalized lock, which Dan Pope has fo fweetly fung, although it interefted the celeftials, was not productive of more *real anguifh*—and I perfuade myfelf that every fufceptible fair one will drop a tear over the forrows of Clariffa. Cordelia, whofe attachment to her nuptial lord is ftill unbroken, hath paffed *months of diffatisfaction,* occafioned by her incertitude, relative to the difpofal of a pair of fleeve buttons, which fhe formerly prefented to her Henry as a pledge of love. But thefe are all unjuftifiable fources of inquietude—they are the imbecilities of the mind, and originating in the *caprice* of affection, they are of too fmall moment to merit attention ; and they are, befides, too reprehenfible to be countenanced. I grant that they are at prefent *comparatively* fmall ; yet if I am unhappy, I am unhappy, whatever may have produced the evil ;

and

and when the peace of a family, or even of an individual, is involved, a full explanation, with every attempt to soothe, is as neceſſary as it is generous ; and it ſhould always be remembered, that the unextinguiſhed flame, which, raging with increaſing violence, purſues its deſolating career, and iſſues in the moſt diſtreſſing conflagration, was once a lambent ſpark, whoſe genial warmth might eaſily have been ſuppreſſed, and whoſe agency, under a judicious direction, might have produced the moſt beneficial effects. Yes, the peace of families is too often ſacrificed to falſe delicacy, and to an ill-judged ſilence upon facts, and circumſtances, which ought to have been ſcrupulouſly narrated, and critically examined. Inviolable ſecreſy, preſerved for any conſiderable length of time, ſuppoſing it of importance to thoſe with whom we are intimately connected, is hardly within the chapter of poſſibilities ; a word, or even a look, accidentally tranſpiring, will give the alarm ; the truth, however latent, is in part divulged ; curioſity commenceth the purſuit, and a clue is obtained, which may be juſt ſufficient to introduce the intereſted perſon into a labyrinth, from which, never being able to extricate himſelf, he may be deſpoiled of all that treaſured ſerenity, which he had vainly hoped, would ſerve as a fund, for the ſupport of a life of rational enjoyment. A lovely woman at this moment ruſhes upon my recollection ; ſhe is not perſonally known to me, but although the vaſt Atlantic rolls its waves between us, yet, with reiterated pleaſure, I have frequently traced the lineaments of her fair mind, as I have ſeen it portrayed in many a well-written page, the product of her inimitable pen. She hath, I am told, a pleaſing exteri-

or, and her underſtanding is elevated much above the level of mediocrity. Nature, when ſhe beſtowed upon her uncommon parts, endowed her alſo with an exquiſite tenderneſs of ſoul. Her imagination was lively and fertile, and ſhe had a taſte capable of diſtinguiſhing, and highly zeſting, the beauties of poetry. Early enliſting in the ſervice of the Muſes, ſhe became one of their moſt ſucceſsful votaries ; and, from the beautiful parterres which ornament the parnaſſian grounds, ſhe hath ſkilfully and happily combined many an elegantly fancied bouquet. She was always a nymph of the ſober-ſuited train, and to airs the moſt penſively melodious her lyre was uniformly attuned. Sweet Eliza, in the enchanting walks of poeſy thy feet have ceaſed to ſtray ; that confirmed melancholy, which the ſunny beams of hope can no longer impreſs, will no more ſwell the neglected chords, the voice of the chantreſs is forever mute, and the lovely minſtrel hath forgotten to charm. Unhappy fair one, the flowers of fancy thou haſt refuſed to cull, the roſe of thy tranquillity is blighted, and *thy violets, alas ! have all withered.* It is to the ill-fated ſilence of Eliza, and her maternal parent, that her misfortunes muſt be imputed. The ſtory of her life is ſimple ; I owed unreturnable obligations to her father, for it was to him that I was indebted for that ſyſtematic, and rational mode of thinking, which has conſtituted the moſt tranquil, and refined moments of my exiſtence. He was a man in the literary line ; his writings are copious, and energetic ; and for ſtrength of argument, perſpicuity of diction, and ſelf-evident demonſtrations, he hath never yet been ſurpaſſed : but having attained, in his favourite pursuit, to the highest possible grade, he was so absorbed in those contemplations, in which originated so large a part of his felicity, as to become reprehensibly inattentive to every consideration which he deemed of lesser moment. It too often happens that real, or original genius, although possessed of every other excellence, and distinguished by the most shining qualifications, is nevertheless found destitute of those very necessary requisites, which can alone bestow a capability of a beneficial intercourse with mankind. Mr. Mortimor, the father of Eliza, made his nuptial choice with so little discretion, as to exchange the marriage vow with a woman, who, at the very moment that she met him at the altar, knew herself to be the wife of another! With this perfidiously abandoned ingrate, he lived in total ignorance of her criminal connexion, and lavishing upon her every proof of an attachment almost unexampled, until the perjured miscreant, having stripped him of every valuable article which he possessed, found means to abscond with the paramour of her choice, at a period when the treacherously betrayed Mortimor was engaged in the discharge of some benevolent offices, which his philanthropic disposition had imposed upon him as duties. It was not until after her elopement, that the turpitude of her life was disclosed to him, and yet he could not even then al-though convinced of her atrocity, be persuaded to take measures calculated to bring her to condign punishment! Many years elapsed before the wound that he had received admitted a cure ; his tenderness of soul, and his innate sense of rectitude, still combated his peace, and reason, for a long time, plead in vain. At length, however, the

lenient hand of assuaging years, aided by the intellectual accomplishments, and the prepossessing exterior, of a truly deserving female, effectuated the most salutary change. Hope once more dawned in his bosom, it gleamed like some heavenly visitant athwart the melancholy region of his benighted soul ; by degrees it obliterated the gloomy ideas which hovered there, and he again asserted the native dignity of his character. To the sweet soother of his sorrows, his hours of leisure were invariably devoted ; a sentimental intercourse commenced ; it was ameliorated by the strictest amity, and it terminated in an attachment of the tenderest kind. Hymen once more lit for Mortimor his sacred torch, and had he attended to some legal steps, which should previously have been taken, the auspices under which he entered into this second engagement, would have been most happy : Yet those arrangements, which flower souls would have deemed indispensible, must have occasioned delays ; the process of the law was tedious ; Mortimor had many enemies, obstacles might be interposed, and if, upon application, he should not be able to obtain the necessary form of divorce, the happiness of his life would be defeated. What was to be done ; concealment was a ready resource, and wrapping himself about in the veil of secrecy, in his own privately retired apartment, in the presence only of the holy priest, and a few select friends, he plighted his willing faith. Mrs. Mortimor, still received merely as the friend of her husband, retained her family name ; and although many might suspect, those only who were bound to secresy, could decisively pronounce. At length, however, revolving months

months ufhered into the world the infant Eliza, and impenetrable myftery ftood fentinel at her birth ; fhe was produced in fociety under the name of Montague ; and her parents introduced her as the orphan daughter of deceafed relatives : Indeed, having conducted their engagement with fo little obfervance of forms, however innocent in intention, and in fact, the parties in reality were, the fevere penalty annexed by the laws of England, againft that irregularity, or breach, a defcription of which would undeniably involve their connexion, rendered it incumbent upon them to avoid, by every means, an explanation.

Eliza was educated with the moft fcrupulous care, fhe was nurtured by the hand of elegance, fhe was trained to the obfervance of every virtue, and fhe was, as I have already obferved, an uncommonly accomplifhed woman. As early as her opening reafon authorifed a confidence fo important, under the ftrongeft injunctions of inviolable filence, fhe was made acquainted with the fecret of her birth, and that difcretion, armed by filial piety, with which fhe guarded a communication, on which hung the life of her father, abundantly juftified the repofing a truft of fuch a nature, in fo tender a bofom. Fifteen happy years were paffed by Eliza, amid the foft endearments of parental tendernefs ; by new proofs of provident care, each cheerful dawn was ufhered in, and the feathery hours were all marked by fage precepts, gentle admonitions, tender cautions, well judged advice, and bland careffes ; and, clafped in the loved embrace, returning evening ftill faw her encircled by thofe arms, and preffed to the faithful bofoms of thofe who fealed upon her balmy

lips, their wifhes for the repofe of the night, always concluding their pious benediction, by fo natural an avowal of feelings which were the genial offspring of that affection, which perhaps cannot be furpaffed. How fatal for Eliza was the hour, that juft at this period, robbed her of a father, who, actuated by a fpirit of univerfal benevolence, and breathing forth the mildeft, and moft benignant expreffions of philanthropy, glowed with uncommon tendernefs for a daughter, whom, in his moft unimpaffioned moments, he could not but acknowledge as highly deferving, every way amiable, and comprifing in herfelf the fum total of a father's wifhes.

The demife of Mr. Mortimor prefented a moment, in which it would have been wifdom to have opened upon fociety, with a full, and unequivocal ecclairciffement. Death had placed the victim, that the law would have demanded, beyond the reach of its penalties, and, clothed in the habiliments of confciousintegrity, *they had then nothing to hazard by an explanation.* The prieft, who joined the hands of the parents of Eliza, could at that juncture have been produced, and the chofen friends, who were prefent at the marriage, were ftill in exiftence.— Alas, alas, they are now all numbered with the dead ! and, ftrange to tell, letting flip the golden feafon of opportunity, Mrs. Mortimor was ftill known by the name of Laughton, while Eliza was addreffed by that of Montague !

It is certain that referves, *except impofed by neceffity,* are never juftifiable ; and the neceffity of myftery ceafed with the death of Mr. Mortimor. From this period, five fucceeding years performed their annual round, ere the difcreet Eliza

felected

selected from the circle of those, who respectfully presented themselves as candidates for her election, a youth, with whom her gentle heart could unhesitatingly consent to inweave the silken bands of tender, conjugal, and indissoluble amity : But her choice once made, she deferred not to banish from the bosom of him she approbated, that perturbed suspense, that so fatally corrodes each promised joy ; and although her every step was pointed by virgin delicacy, yet did she skilfully enwreath therewith, a noble and dignified franknefs, which hushed that tumultuous whirlwind of the paffions, which hath shipwrecked the peace of many a manly breast. Pity that she was not permitted to be uniformly explicit, but the maternal prohibition was strangely, and unaccountably interposed, and her nuptials were solemnized under that disguise, which, although justifiable for a time, was most imprudently continued, and should never have been worn in the presence of a man, whom, in every other respect, she had honored by the most unbounded confidence ; but she remained perseveringly silent, reprehensibly silent ! and this silence hath been fatal to her peace. The first years of her wedded life were uncommonly serene ; she bore to Altamont many fine children, and none but tranquil days seemed written for her. How precarious are terrestrial joys ! An untoward accident suddenly reverfed the scene. A paper, written by herself, and addressed to her mother, breathing the language of ambiguity, deeply fraught with mystery, and yet obscurely hinting at the truth, unfortunately met the eye of Altamont ! To the nicest sense of honor Altamont is exquisitely alive, the soul of ingenuity

is his, and the delicacy of his sentiments refuseth to tolerate the most distant appearance of deception. He drank in the contagious lines ; every word operated as an envenomed draught, and while he shrunk from the fearful contents, they became, in effect, like those subtil poisons, which are said to procure immediate death; for they infixed their deadly fangs in the very vitals of that tranquillity, which he had fondly hoped was beyond the malice of fate. Instantly the fiend, despair embodied its ministers ; they were busy about his heart ; complacency was chased from his bosom; the benignant smiles of benevolence are no more ; a deep and settled melancholy lowers upon his brow ; and the sullen silence which he obstinately observes, effectually bars an ecclaircissement. His house, once the seat of social happiness ; now, alas ! dire suspicion, dark conjecture, and baleful jealousy, hover there ; and although months and years have revolved, no beam of elucidation hath yet illumined those heartfelt glooms, by which he is enveloped. The tear is upon the cheek of Eliza ; her dream of happiness, of terrestrial happiness, is gone forever. The deep melancholy which impressed the mind of Altamont, was immediately succeeded by the most alarming estrangement; his temper seems totally ruined ; he eyes her with a mistrustful kind of indignation; she has lost his confidence ; she has every reason to believe that she no longer possesses his affection ; and the probability is, that was she now to come forward with a full and undisguised explanation, it would produce no salutary effect. The clergyman, who joined the hands of her parents, now sleepeth quietly in the narrow house, and all
those

those vouchers, which she might once have produced, at this period repose also in the dust. Altamont is haughty, and implacable, and Eliza, having once indisputably deceived him, it is to be feared that he will yield her no future credence.

ERRATA.—In p. 603, 1st c. l. 29, for *healthy* r. *heathy*—in 2d c. same p. l. 18, for *colour* r. *contour*—in l. 20, for *age* r. *glee*—in p. 605, 2d c. l. 25, for *baft*, r. *bafteth*.

For the MASSACHUSETTS MAGAZINE,

The GENERAL OBSERVER. No. XLVIII.

How many sink in the devouring flood,
Or more devouring flame!   THOMSON.

WERE those, who are inclined to scepticism, to confine their attention to the apparent irregularities of nature and providence, to the unaccountable events which take place from time to time, their doubts would be apt to increase, and their infidelity be confirmed. And were timid Christians to pore upon the evils of life, upon the afflictions which often wring the hearts of the best of men, upon the overwhelming calamities, the sudden and unlooked for disasters which ruin individuals, or spread distress and consternation all around, their hearts would sink in despondency, and they would lose their confidence in the great Superintendent of the universe. But happy for poor mortals! things are so arranged in nature, and events in general are so ordered in providence, as to strike this conviction into every impartial mind, and to convey this consolation into every humble heart— *verily there is a reward for the righteous ; verily there is a God who judgeth in the earth !*

Still it cannot be denied that many things in the divine proceedings are hard to be accounted for, and hard to be borne. It is agreeable to our ideas of a wise, good, and impartial God, that every creature of his hands should be fitted for the circumstances of his habitation, and that the circumstances of his habitation should be suited to his nature and wants. This in general holds true in the case of man. But it is evident that many individuals are of a constitution too delicate, of a frame of mind too refined, and of a set of feelings too sensible and tender, for the roughening scenes, the thorny paths, and the rude tempests, through which they are forced to pass. Their natures have not strength, their minds have not fortitude, adequate to the weight of evils under which they are forced to groan. How often does a storm burst upon a prosperous individual, or a prosperous family, while a cloud is not seen to arise, and their most vigorous hopes are torn up, and their most promising prospects destroyed in the tornado? The case is not uncommon in the country, for a man to toil and sweat to secure the last shock of grain, or the last load of hay, and then to see his full barn, containing all the produce of his fields and meadows, consumed in a moment by a flash of lightning.

How many enterprizing geniuses have, for the hope of gain, traversed the seas, and by trading from country to country, for several years, have accumulated riches sufficient

to

to support a family in splendor and independence? They send word to their friends that they may soon expect them loaded with treasure. They purchase a ship, freight it with all their abundance, and take passage for their native country. They sail prosperously till within sight of their paternal shores; when, lo! they are suddenly intercepted by a dreadful tempest, and the vessel and precious cargo are overwhelmed in the deep.

It is difficult to conceive how nature can meet with a greater shock, or the powers of the soul be put to a severer trial, than by being startled out of sleep by the crackling flames of our dwelling. Multitudes have gone to bed in security, slept soundly and in peace, and awaked not till they felt the suffocating smoke or the scorching blaze. The sudden flight, the cutting anxiety for their own safety, and for the safety of their family, not to mention the sense of the loss of their all, is enough to unhinge the mind, and put it out of possession of itself.

These cases are so distressful, that, where persons escape thus naked from a burning house, or a sinking vessel, the hearts of friends, neighbours, and strangers, are opened to relieve their sufferings, and to repair their losses. A dwelling is erected for the houseless sufferer, and provision is made for the comfort of the child of want. O charity! thou offspring of heaven! Thou noblest of the virtues! How wretched would mankind be without thee!

and how happy wouldest thou make the world, if thy influence were universally felt! Happy the breast that cherishes thee, and happy the objects upon whom thou sheddest thy tears and thy blessings!

But there is one case that is attended with circumstances of distress almost equal to the foregoing, which, nevertheless, does not excite equal commiseration, nor is admitted to equal relief. A young woman, with the consent of her parents, connects herself with a young man, against whose character or circumstances there appears no reasonable objection. They live in credit and fashion several years. But imprudences or misfortunes, which he conceals from every body as long as possible, reduce him to bankruptcy. All at once his credit is lost, his creditors seize his effects, the house is stript, the family is broken up, the husband absconds, and the deserted and impoverished wife returns forlorn and depressed, with three or four helpless children, to the house of her father, or some other friend, where, perhaps, she lingers out the rest of her days in mortification and dependence.

What a striking comment do these instances give us upon the reflection of the wise man—*Vanity of vanities! all is vanity!* And how strongly do they enforce the advice of him that was wiser than Solomon, —*Lay not up for yourselves treasures upon earth, but in heaven, where neither moth nor rust corrupt, and where thieves do not break through and steal.*

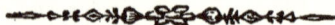

A N E C D O T E.

MISS Hannah More expressed her surprise to Dr. Johnson, that a poet, who had written Paradise Lost, should write *poor* sonnets,

The doctor answered—" Milton, madam, was a genius that could cut a colossus from a rock, but could not carve heads upon cherry stones."

The

For the MASSACHUSETTS MAGAZINE.

The INVESTIGATOR. No. IV.

Many the fcenes of forrow and diftrefs
This world affords.
Sad, fick'ning thought ! and yet deluded man,
A fcene of crude disjointed vifions paft,
And broken flumbers, rifes, ftill refolv'd,
With new flufh'd hopes, to' run the giddy round.——THOMSON.

IT appears almoft impoffible, in our firft view of nature, that fuch a thing fhould exift, as a young and rifing charaƈter ; one, whofe mind is garnifhed with every claffic accomplifhment, whofe foul fwells with benevolence and exults in humanity—falling a prey to the gilded allurements of luft and the impious incitement of the drunkard and gamefter. Yet fo it is, and the volume of experience unfolds its ample pages to prove the affertion. Ourfelves have beheld, and (perhaps) been connected with promifing charaƈters, who have been gradually degenerated and finally fell victims to thefe delufive pleafures. No doubt but we have dropped a tear at the recollection of their failings ; but have we ufed the language of reafon in trying to correct them ? Have we, like the confiderate parent and real friend, ever ftretched forth the willing arm to prevent their falling ; or fo much as pulled them by the fleeve, when harkening to the deceptive infinuations of artful hypocrify ? Have we, in the days of youth and flexibility, opened to their view the beauty of virtue, and in the clofet revealed to them our moft rational ideas of man and manners—painted in their glaring deformity the fons of vice and depravity ; or filled their glowing imaginations with romantic images of pleafure and happinefs ? Perhaps we have fledged them with the follies of fafhion and tipped their wings with the drofs of *etiquette*, opened to their view, as a fource of blifs, the crowded fcenes of life, and made them to underftand that the perfon who bows the loweft and talks the moft, is their beft friend, and deferves their unlimitted confidence ; by which means they fell from the humble path of rectitude into the gorgeous fepulchre of pallid vice.

The fault is furely in fome one, and the eye of reafon looks fufpicious on the parent and inftructor. It is from them ideas and manners are fuppofed to originate ; from them the mind receives its firft and lafting impreffions ; and by them the youth is conducted to the path he purfues. For, according to the alement we receive from childhood to puberty, our charaƈter is moft generally eftablifhed.

The Inveftigator hopes his mentioning thefe things will lead the reflective part of fociety to an examination of their conduct towards thofe, entrufted to their care. It being upon their fhoulders, the weight of government and the cultivation of manners muft ere long devolve. To them, generations to come will look for inftruction and example. The eye of ambition will view them as models worthy of imitation. Of courfe you ought to conclude, that whatever befals them will be charged to your account. That Being, who prefides at the helm of nature, is both *juft* and

and *righteous*, and will accordingly punish every one for the crimes by him *produced*.

I now pass to a picture of society as it now is, from whence you may conclude what it will be, if a reform in manners is not speedily adopted.

Friendship, with all its heavenly influence, is but pencil-work on the robe of hypocrisy. Good nature has become the foot-ball of impudence ; and Charity, the wastebook of slander. The world has so refined itself in cunning and deceit ; so mystical are its aims, that we must live in it twice before we can avoid its entanglements, much less partake of its enjoyments. The days of contentment are over, so far as it respects civilized society ; that goddess, which has been the theme of millions, now slumbering in the tomb, and the subject of thousands, who unsuccessfully pursue her, has either fled the habitable globe, or wanders with the unrefined part of creation through the lonely forest ; where riches are not found to pollute, or avarice to destroy. The accumulation of wealth is now the only spur to action ; it prompts many to perform the most servile offices that pride can invent, and its magnetic power draws them through all the despicable labyrinths of vice and corruption. In fine, riches has become the household god of every nation, and receives more adoration than the Being, who protects them. Wit, if we may so call it, has taken the chair, once occupied by sound judgment, from whence it deals its insipid compound through clubs of sociability. Where simple innocence entertained her honest companions, loquacious slander rears her baleful head, and corrupts the stream of discourse with a *damning* description of things and people. The multitude, fearful of losing a single syllable, attend with gaping mouths, joyful eyes, and widened ears. These same *good* people, when summoned to attend the ordinances of religion, have always at hand some frivolous excuse, or go with demure faces, in hopes of catching something worthy of *bitter* observation. We read of the cardinal virtues ; but, rarely see them practised. We hear of the *good old man* bending with virtue to the mouldering tomb ; but are seldom so fortunate as to partake of his company.

" I saw, (says a friend of mine, who had just returned from his tour of Europe,) in the city of London, a gentleman, whose visage bore the traits of piety and godliness ; his hair hung in silver ringlets on his shoulders and approached in vagrant locks his forehead, wrinkled with years and wisdom. His demeanor was grave and respectful ; his language solemn and impressing ; such as would inspire devotion in the breast of a deist. A black cloak concealed all but his face from the eyes of the beholder ; even that was sufficient to afford a gaze of astonishment. A damsel sat in a chair opposite the venerable father ; a gleam of beauty was visible through the meanness of her apparel ; yet depression clouded her countenance, and a tear oft stole from her eye, as she turned her head to the window. I felt for her, but was interrupted from more attentively viewing her person by the elegant harangue of her guide, who was descanting on the depravity of the times. No subject could be more applicable to my feelings, or more congenial with my thoughts ; so I attended with wonder and delight. A glow of divinity irradiated his countenance as he emphasized fized on the beauty of virtue, and the happinefs attendant on a life of innocence. He had wound my feelings to a pitch of ecftacy indefcribable, when the clock ftruck twelve, which intctrupted and ended his difcourfe. His hat was in his hand, and my folicitations could not prevent his departure. I waited upon him to the door, where I ftood gazing with aftonifhment, until he, fupported by the damfel, had turned a corner, which fairly hid him from my view. Returning to the landlord, with great importunity, I began to inquire who that venerable perfonage was, that had juft left us. A loud laugh fucceeded the requeft, which fo irritated my heated imagination, that I lifted up my cane with a determination to level a blow at the impudent rafcal; but a perfon, who ftood juft behind me feized the uplifted weapon and wrenched it from my hand; then, with due fubmjffion, begged to pacify me. Unable, by my paffion, to reafon, and by my defencelefs condition to chaftife, I haftily walked from the bar-room to the parlour, where, after two or three turns, filled with contemplative vengeance, I was interrupted by the perfon who had poffeffion of my cane. " Sir, fays he, you are a ftranger; forgive my intrufion, it being to afford you the fatisfaction you defired; or at leaft to clear up the caufe of your treatment." This was fomewhat pacifying, fo I bade him go on. " The hoft, I allow,

was rather unfeafonable in his laughter, but the confcioufnefs of your deception was the caufe. It was this, that urged me to the impolitenefs, which drove you from the room. The *venerable perfonage*, as you are pleafed to call him, is as complete a knave and hypocrite as every drew the breath of nature; and under that fanctified form lurks matchlefs villainy and complicated vice." What! that man a villain? " Yes fir, as great a fcoundrel as treads the earth. Not content with cheating every one he deals with, he has, fir, by the property he poffeffes, debauched numberlefs daughters of poverty and innocence. Did not you obferve the young woman that was with him?—She, fir, is the daughter of one of his tenants, whom he has gained over to his inclinations by threats and bribery. Shocking as it may feem to you, yet fo it is; and though tottering to the grave, he cannot forfake his vicious practices; they have become fo habitual and neceffary to his depraved inclinations. Hundreds, fir, in this city are his companions in vice and corruption." Struck with horror and deteftation at what he recited, I forgave him and left the houfe."

Yet this is the age of profound literature and deep philofophy. This the period that approaches the glorious millennium, when the lion fhall lie down with the lamb, and nature rejoice in the groves of innocence.

ANECDOTE of CHARLES FOX.

DR. JOHNSON, obferved of Fox—He is a moft extraordinary man; he has divided the kingdom with Cæfar, fo that it was a doubt whether the nation fhould be ruled by the fceptre of George the third, or by the tongue of Fox.

ALEXIS:

ALEXIS: Or, The COTTAGE in the WOODS.

(Continued from the 616th page.)

PART SECOND.

CHAPTER VI.
THE STORY OF DORANCE CONTINUED.

ON the night previous to our departure from Grenoble, a departure which, you will eafily conceive, has grieved me much—I faw her. "My dear Duverly," faid fhe, melting in tears, "all is over, we are wretched for ever !—My father has given me formal notice, that I muft refolve to be the colonel's in a twelvemonth—that very man whom I deteft, whom I abhor!"—"In a twelvemonth !" "Yes, becaufe the young man is gone to make a campaign, and is to be married to me upon his return."—"Ah ! my Rofina, what a blow !"—"Cruel indeed, Duverly ! but I am under the control of a mother, and fhe muft be obeyed.— She muft be obeyed !—Conceive, Dorance, only conceive my grief ! Your father then requefted me to accompany you to Paris : I could not refift his defire ; I fet out, but I leave you to think, whether I would not have preferred ftaying at Grenoble ! My rival was not there; I might have been a whole year with my charming Rofina, I would have been at liberty to fee her every day at Mrs. des Roches' ! Ah, how happy would have been my lot !" Duverly was filent for a moment, though the confidence he had juft made, really wounded my feelings, and made me confider Mrs. des Roches as a vile, defpicable woman. I would not, by delivering my true fentiments, aggravate my freind's fuffering condition. He then continued as follows :

"At my departure from Grenoble, Rofina promifed to write to me, and I have actually received a letter of her's a fortnight ago. It is this letter, Dorance, which has given me a mortal blow. Here it is : I fhall read it to you, and from it you will judge all the extent of my mifery."

I did not, my children, know Adela's hand writing. Duverly, who was fure of that, rifked nothing to fhew it me : but he took care not to let me perufe it, as he had a mind to change fome expreffions, which would have otherwife undeceived me.[*] He began, therefore to perufe it very flowly, for fear of making a blunder :

"Pardon me, my dear Duverly, for not having written fooner. My *father* is teazing me continually ; and fince the *Colonel's* departure, *he* does hardly give me a minute's time to fee Mrs. des Roches. But, O frefh misfortune !—did you only know what facrifice is exacted from poor *Rofina* !—My *father* is abfolutely determined to put me into a convent, till the return of the *Colonel* !—Alas ! I have put off, as long as I could, the moment of that fatal captivity—but *he* plagues, *he* perfecutes me, and I fhall at laft be forced into compliance. Oh, let me often hear of you, my gentle friend ! there is no other comfort on earth for *Rofina*."

"This letter, (continued Duverly) this cruel letter, which informs me that my dear Rofina is to be fhut up for a twelvemonth in an obfcure retreat, where I find it will be impoffible for me, if the event takes place, to write to her ; this fatal letter

[*] The expreffions which Duverly changed in reading Adela's letter, are printed in Italics.

letter has troubled my fenfes, the ague has inflamed my blood, and a furious phrenfy quite fhook my brains; this, Dorance, this is the real caufe of my difeafe."

When he had done fpeaking, I remarked fuch fire in his eyes, as made me fenfible that it was not feafonable then to give him advice. Neverthelefs he ftood in need of the beft of advice; for, what could be the aim of his paffion for an object which was unknown to me? and that Mrs. des Roches, who made herfelf fubfervient to fo fhameful an intrigue; Oh! that character was odious and indignant to me! Nay, had I known that my Adela was the object in queftion; that the letter which had been read to me was from Adela; that the colonel and pretended rival was myfelf—great God! what would have become of me! but his fable was fo well conceived, fo well difguifed; and as yet, he had fpoke fo ill of Mifs Myrfange, that I thought fhe could not be the perfon. I had even not the leaft idea of it in my mind; and, had I not explained it, my children, you would not have gueffed better than I did then. As to Mrs. des Roches, fhe was no relation of Duverly, as he gave out, but one of thefe violent go-betweens, whofe only pleafure is to hatch plots, and with whom we meet with every where to promote diforder. And yet, I will not have you believe that her houfe was a place of debauchery, but only a place moft convenient for lovers whofe bufinefs is fhort. Mrs. des Roches was a woman of *fecond-hand* principles, willing to ferve in all intrigues, the intent of which did not, to a certain point, affect her delicacy. My father and the baronefs were perfectly ignorant of the acquaintance Adela had contracted with that

woman. It was Duverly who had appointed her that rendezvous, whither fhe made it convenient to repair, to enjoy the company of her gallant.

All thefe particulars, my children, I unluckily heard, but long afterwards; but I was obliged to expofe them to you, in order to fhew how much I have been deceived. Grant me your whole attention, you fhall fee the moft perfidious and as well framed a plot as ever entered the head of man, to betray the good faith of his equals.

"My friend," faid I to Duverly, "your fituation is very cruel! You are now fenfible that love is not eafily controlled, and you can no longer blame me for harbouring that paffion, for adoring, I fay, the charming Adela, in fpite of your wife perfuafions and the faults you find in her."—"Do you love her ftill?" faid he, with a kind of emphafis—"Yes, you do, I feel it but too well!—and, although this object of your affection would never have made any impreffion upon me, yet, as you obferve, love knows no control! My dear friend, you fee I am not in a condition to write; will you favour me to write the anfwer to this letter? I will dictate it: take pen and ink—oblige me in this!—you cannot refufe a dying friend!" I hefitated for fome time how I was to act: but his entreaties—he was dying—what could I do?—I placed a table clofe to his bed-fide, and he dictated to me the following letter:

"Oh! how much has your letter affected me, my fweeteft love! You in a convent—you in a twelvemonth, in the arms of a rival! What rival; how dangerous is he!—Did you know!—but no matter; as we love one another, death alone can part us!—The obftacles, however, which I find in my way, have been very likely to coſt me my life. I was, a few days ago, at the very brink of the grave; but a ſincere friend, a friend whoſe heart is excellent, has withheld me. I entruſted him with the ſecret of our correſpondence: he is another myſelf; he ſhares my ſufferings and your own, yet he does not know you! It is he who traces theſe characters, which fell ſickneſs denies my debile hand. Yes, when you receive this letter, O my love! think on me; think on him, and behold the expreſſions of love written by the hand of friendſhip!

"When the term of my ſufferings ſhall be paſt, when heaven ſhall have reſtored my health, I intend going directly to Grenoble, I—"

Here I interrupted him, to aſk what he meant by this, but he begged me to go on, and he would explain afterwards the phraſe which made me ſtop.

"I ſhall go to Mrs. des Roches, in whoſe houſe I mean to hide myſelf for ſome time. There I ſhall ſee you, there I ſhall ſwear a thouſand times the moſt tender, the moſt conſtant attachment. O my charming Adela!—this hope gives me a new life: my ſufferings vaniſh!—I think on you, I ſuffer no more!"

Duverly uſed his utmoſt endeavours to ſign his name in a legible manner: I then folded up and ſealed the letter, when he deſired me to put upon it the following direction:

"A Madame
Madam des Roches, Rue Perrierre, Grenoble."

One might have ſaid the balm of comfort had been poured into his breaſt: his eyes became a little ſerene, his cheeks fluſhed with the blooming tokens of health, and he preſſed my hand in a manner expreſſive of ſentiment. "My friend,"

ſaid he, "this is not the only favour I have to beg of you. It is in your power to reſtore me to life; but you muſt pledge your word of honour to perform what I ſhall require. Suffer me to return to Grenoble: I ſhall hide myſelf; I ſhall ſee my Roſina, and be happy! You will therefore write to your father, to let him know that I am much better; that we always do buſineſs as uſual, &c. &c. I will even ſend you letters for him, and which you will encloſe in your own. My friend, reſtore me to life, as it will coſt ſo little.

This project excited my indignation, which I expreſſed by a plain refuſal. Had you but ſeen the traitor weep, ſigh and ſupplicate! he even fainted; and I was afraid it would be his laſt. "Wretch!" ſaid I, within myſelf, "what a paſſion! what a phrenzy!—Alas! he is a madman who muſt be taken care of againſt his own ſelf!—But were my father to diſcover him at Grenoble! were he to detect me as an impoſtor!—I expoſe myſelf to his anger!—Well, I will fall down at his feet, and deſcribe the condition my friend was in: I ſhall confeſs my weakneſs, and he will grant me his pardon. Beſides, Duverly is not my ſlave, he has a right to act as he pleaſes!—And what right have I to hinder him?—Well! imprudent as it will be of me, my imprudence will ſave his life, it will reſtore my friend!"—"Yes, Duverly!" exclaimed I, "Yes, I will do all to ſerve you; only live and let this be my reward."

Here the patient embraced me; he wept, laughed, was moved, and fell aſleep. I left him at day break, and jealous of keeping my word, went immediately to carry the letter to the poſt-office.

Don't you admire my complaiſance?

fance ?—Oh ! we are not come to the point yet ; you will fee me act a part—a part that will make me blufh all my life time ; it proves my imprudence and my foolifh-nefs ;—but I muft go on.

The chevalier got well in about a week. It is ufelefs for me to tell you how often, during that time, he talked of his love, and the pleaf-ures he was going to enjoy at Gre-noble !—At laft, impatient to wait for his full and perfect recovery, he embraced me, and departed, in-forming the counfellor, that he was to take poffeffion of a confiderable eftate in Auvergne, to which he had fucceeded by a legal right of inheritance ; and that his abfence fhould not exceed two months at furtheft.

" It would be to no purpofe," faid he, " for you to inform Mr. Do-rance, the father, of my departure; for he, having entrufted me with the conduct of his fon, might be of-fended at my lofing fight of him for fome time ; but he is no longer a child; and moreover, in what houfe, fir—in what houfe more refpectable than your's could he be ?—Are you not a real father to him.—Ah ! with you, he wants no Mentor !"

The counfellor, whofe felf-love was interefted, promifed not to write to my father; and Duverly fet out, promifing to let me fre-quently know his fufferings or his fuccefs, and requefting me to an-fwer his letters, under cover, and direct them to Mrs. des Roches.

A long period of time paffed be-fore I heard of him ; I received at laft the following letter, two months after his departure !

" Can you believe it, my friend ! —I am the happieft of mortals ;—Rofina loves me ftill !—fhe has fhown fo much repugnance to the convent, that her father would not

perfift any longer in his former de-cree. Yet, there is another old Cerberus, the colonel's father, who follows her like his own fhadow—Cupid, however, difcomfits fecretly the Argufes of Minerva—Rofina comes occafionally to vifit Mrs. des Roches, where I have been lodged ever fince my arrival. Not a foul has feen me yet in this town ; the houfe of my relation is a real her-mitage, and is richly provided with all the fweets of life.—Here I may enjoy the pleafure of a walk in a de-lightful garden, adorned with little woods, and the moft delicious groves.—Groves ; can I utter this word without retracing to my mind the happinefs I enjoyed yefterday ! —Durft I make this avowal to my friend ! will his delicacy hot be of-fended ?—O no, he loves, he muft excufe the errors which love makes one apt to commit !—Yefterday, Rofina and I, being in one of thofe groves—they are fo dangerous !—Love put his blind over the eyes of reafon ; it vanquifhed the refiftance of Rofina—and I obtained a victo-ry—alas ! a cruel victory, as it coft her tears, and me regret !—Oh, my friend ! lend me all your eloquence to confole the fair I have feduced ! Reftore me my innocence to bring back the alarmed modefty which I have difpelled, and to re-plant a flower which I have nipt in her firft bloom, in her firft frefhnefs ;—Alas ! Rofina now accufes me of her misfortune !—How will fhe dare to offer her hand to a hufband ! with what countenance will fhe kin-dle the torch of Hymen, having yielded her all to love ! This cauf-es her defpair, this brings upon me, on her part, the keeneft re-proaches !—Dorance, my dear Do-rance, oh ! pity me, write, I crave your advice !—

" I cannot conclude this without fpeaking

fpeaking of your Adela.—They fay
fhe changes every day in a moft
fingular manner ; and is torn by a
grief whofe fource is unknown.
Her phyfical parts are as much affected at her moral ones. She becomes fluttifh, pouting, even ill-na-
tured: fhe fcolds at every body.
There are fuch fcenes paffing between her and her mother !—My
friend, I cannot blame you for being in love ; but if you were not to
meet with equal return, oh ! how
unfortunate would you be! Adieu,
reflect."

The perufal of this epiftle put
me to the bluth, for the part I had
acted in this intrigue. "Yes," faid
I, "it is I who am the author of
that crime ! it is I !—Had I not
confented to Duverly's fecret departure, would he have feen Rofina,
would he have been able to feduce
her youth and virtue? O imprudent ! what have I done ?—Would
to God, I knew the colonel who is
to be her hufband !—I would confefs my fault, difcover the blow
which his honour has received ; in
fhort, hinder an honeft man from
being fo bafely deceived! I fhall
know him ; I fhall tell him ; he
fhall hear all, I will have nothing
to reproach myfelf with, as having
been the inftrument of the mifery
of his life.—What do I fay !—Vile
agent to the moft fhameful intrigue,
I had rather be filent. It behoves
me to bury it in the deepeft oblivion, and repent all my life of a conduct equally difgraceful to the dictates of honour and virtue."

I anfwered Duverly's letter, but
in the moft ferious manner; I made
him fenfible of his wrongs, and the
bafenefs of the part he had made
me act. I defired him to look out
for another confident, and concluded with conjuring him never to mention again an intrigue in which I

was afhamed to have been inftru-
mental.

What effect this fevere letter had
upon him I fhall not decide. During four months I never heard of
him, and at the expiration of that
time, I had the misfortune to receive a letter from the baronefs,
bringing the bad tidings of my father's death.

I made the utmoft difpatch to
Grenoble, where I found every
body belonging to my father's family in mourning and confternation.

I had only fome very diftant relations in that town, and was refolved to leave it, as foon as I fhould
have obtained Adela's hand, which
her mother, jealous of the promife
fhe had made my father, was always difpofed to grant me.

I hoped to find Duverly prepared to confole me, and to fhare my
grief ! Judge of my aftonifhment,
when I could not get the leaft intelligence of him. I went to Rue
Perrierre, to that Mrs. des Roches,
where I knew he lodged, and to my
utmoft furprize, was informed that
Mrs. des Roches had left town a
week ago, and that the place fhe
had chofen for her refidence was
unknown. I had not the leaft
doubt of Duverly and his infamous
accomplices having carried off the
unfortunate Rofina, and that the
former would not let me know the
matter, for fear of incurring my
father's difpleafure. But, what often puzzled me was, that nobody at
Grenoble had known Rofina, or her
father. Indeed, not knowing the
old man's name, I could not make
proper inquiries about the family.

Thus my friend was gone : he
had forfaken me ; he had broken
the firft ties of our friendfhip ! I
for fome time regretted him, but
foon after confidering his perverfe
morals, I made an effort to forget
him,

him, and fucceeded: fo true it is that vice muſt be hateful to honeſt and virtuous hearts, and that with them it outweighs all other confiderations.

In the mean while I ſaw every day my Adela, who was faithful to the portrait Duverly had drawn of her in his laſt; her mother, however, before whom ſhe conſtrained herſelf, infiſted on her giving me her hand; it was my father's laſt will; I was determined to receive it; yet without—love! This paſfion weakened in me every day, and I acted barely with paſſive obedience to the baronefs, becauſe I foreſaw the abyſs which threatened my ruin. I often attempted to try Adela's ſentiments toward me, and I found, that though ſhe had no liking to me, ſhe was not againſt accepting my hand. At laſt, being perſuaded to marriage on all ſides, when the fatal day fixed for the ceremony was come, I conducted mifs to the altar, and brought her back without joy as without ſadnefs; but with a ſentiment of inquietude, which I could not account for. Arrived at home, my ſpoufe demanded to ſpeak in private with me and her mother; we complied with her requeſt, and faw her with ſurprife, throw herſelf at our feet, and make the following fingular ſpeech: " Mother, you have forced me to marry this gentleman! You know the ſtruggles I went through, and how often you have rejected me from your boſom; give me, for heaven's fake, give me time to know him, to acknowledge his real merit, and to render myſelf worthy of the tendernefs he condefcends to have for me!—I only beg leave for two

months to retire to Mrs. Reigny's, my aunt, at St. Marcellin. There I ſhall have leiſure to deliberate better; there I will do every endeavour to deferve the affection and love of the man who merits to find more gratitude in me! Oh, my mother, and you, ſir, grant me this favour! I beg it on my knees! Alas, can you deny me?—"

The baronefs was going to load her daughter with reproaches and threats; but I was fo moved, the voice of Candor appealed fo loud to my heart, that I thought it would be cruelty to refuſe fo fingular a demand, which was nigh to have affected the life of the unfortunate Adela. Joining, therefore, my entreaties to her own, we at laſt obtained her mother's confent. At the ſame time ſhe loaded her with curfes and imprecations, and fwore never to fee her again. "Sir," added ſhe, " I have no farther rights upon her: do with her what you advife beſt: for my own part, I will no more hear of her; no, no more!—She is the fcourge of my old age!"

The baronefs ſuddenly left the room, and would not even fo much as give her a letter for Mrs. Reigny. I was as much perplexed as my ſpoufe: I fent a truſty ſervant with her, ſhe ſtept quickly into the carriage with her woman, and arrived that very day at St. Marcellin. My ſervant returned the next day, with a letter from Adela, in which ſhe thanked me for the permiſſion I had granted her, aſſuring me, that a trait fo generous would never be erafed from her memory, and that ſhe could already promife me the poſſeſſion of her heart.

(To be continued.)

The PILGRIM's STORY.

(Concluded from page 583.)

AT the twilight hour of the seventh day, when every breeze was hushed, and nature seemed to pause in melancholy silence, musing beneath the trees that encircled the prison of my idol, my ear was suddenly enchanted by the melody of a female voice. I drew near to the spot from whence the sound proceeded, and distinctly heard the words of her complaint : They pierced my very heart—attuning every heart to sympathetic pity.

Elvira hinted a wish that he would endeavour to recollect them; he complied with her desire, and thus began :

" Within this dear and silent gloom,
The lost Louisa pines unknown ;
Fate shrouds her in a living tomb,
And heaven relentless hears her groan :
Yet midst the murky shades of wo,
The tear of fond regret shall flow.

" Yon lofty wall, that mocks my grief,
Still echoes with my ev'ning pray'r ;
The gale that fans the trembling leaf,
Shall waft it through the realms of air.
Till prostrate at the throne of heav'n,
Unpitied love shall be forgiv'n !

" Or if to endless sorrow born—
If doom'd to fade a victim here ;
Still pining, friendless, and forlorn,
Ah ! let religion drop one tear ;
Like holy incense shall it prove,
To heal the wounds of hopeless love.

" Ye black'ning clouds that sail along,
Oh, hide me in your shade profound ;
Ye whisp'ring breezes, catch my song,
And bear it to the woods around !
Perchance some hapless petrarch's feet
May wander near this dread retreat.

" Ah ! tell him love's delicious strain
No rapture yields, no joy inspires,
Where cold religion's icy chain
Has long subdu'd its quiv'ring fires ;
No ray of comfort gilds the gloom,
That marks the hapless vestal's tomb !

" The ruby gem within my breast
Now faintly glows with vital heat ;
Each warring passion sinks to rest :
My freezing pulses slowly beat.
Soon shall these languid eye-lids close,
And death's stern mandate seal my woes.

" Then, when the virgin's matin song
Shall 'midst the vaulted roof resound,
Haply the tuneful seraph throng
Shall whisper gentle pity round ;
While virtue, sighing o'er my bier,
Shall drop unseen—a fainted tear !"

From that moment I determined to release the beauteous Louisa, or perish between the flinty confines of her prison ; the difficulties attending such an undertaking, and the dreadful punishments that would be inflicted on the perpetrators of such a crime, rendered every precaution necessary to ensure success.

Chance, however, completed what years of indefatigable industry might not have accomplished : the abbess of Saint Terese was suddenly attacked by an alarming indisposition, her life was supposed to be in extreme danger ; and as the lady Louisa was of the highest rank among the holy sisterhood, she was entrusted with the entire government of the convent, and unlimitted possession of the rights of a superior. It was not difficult, under these circumstances, to accomplish her wish ; my letters were delivered without creating the smallest suspicion, and the rapturous hour was appointed for her escape from misery.

Her heart was susceptible of the finest passions ; she relied on my honour, and I never deceived her. She had long considered herself as a victim doomed to eternal solitude ; the extraordinary and unexpected change my propositions presented, the prospect of happiness that opened ed to her foul, gave energy to hope, and ftrength to refolution ; I provided horfes, and a convenient difguife : Heaven fmiled upon the deed, and gave to my fond arms the beautiful Louifa. We traverfed the wood for fome miles, and taking the route towards Marfeilles, in three days reached that port in fafety.

There we were united in holy bands. The miftrefs of my affections became the wife of my bofom ! and I became the proud poffeffor of a treafure, worlds could not have purchafed !

Having procured a veffel, we fet fail for Florence ; the winds were propitious, we arrived unmolefted at Leghorn, and from thence proceeded to the moft beautiful city in the univerfe !

My adored Louifa, whofe early days had been devoted to religious duties, evinced not the fmalleft defire to relinquifh the delights of retirement ; her mind, accuftomed to an uninterrupted fcene of tranquillity, dreaded to engage in the tumultuous buftle of the bufy world. We hired a beautiful little villa in the vicinity of Florence ; and bleft in the full poffeffion of all that mutual affection and mental gratification could afford, looked down with pity on the proudeft diftinctions in the power of any earthly monarch to beftow !

Three delicious years of perfect happinefs cemented the bonds of undeviating attachment, when a regutta, in celebration of the Pope's acceffion, awoke the attention, and excited the curiofity of all ranks of people.

My Louifa was tempted to partake of the amufement ; and in the midft of delightful feftivity, when every heart bounded with rapture—mine alone received the dreadful fiat of eternal anguifh.

The arno was beautifully ferene; the filvery furface reflecting, as in a gently moving mirror ; the verdant banks floping to the margin, enamelled with flowers, and crouded with fpectators. Thoufands of little boats, decorated with variegated ftreamers, were feen fkimming along the lucid current ; fome containing the moft dulcet harmony, and others lightly fhading with their filken awnings, the fparkling eyes and rofeate blufhes of enchanting beauty.

My Louifa was charmed with this new and fancinating fpectacle, Our *barchetta*, which was decorated with feftoons of myrtle, was gently rowed by youths dreffed in the habits of Arcadian fhepherds. The mind, foothed to repofe by the enchanting fcene, funk into that fweet indolence, which, like the flumbers of wearied and exhaufted nature, replenifhed its faculties, and awaken its perfections to renovated luftre ! My Louifa reclined her gentle form upon a matrafs of yellow taffety ; the warmth of the evening heightened the glow upon her lovely cheek, and threw a delicious languor on her eyes, that rendered her the object of univerfal admiration !

My heart was full of rapture—I beheld my precious treafure with more delight than language can defcribe. The univerfe had nothing to beftow on me beyond what I poffeffed ; and my enchanted fenfe could fcarcely conceive any thing more divine, even in the regions of celeftial happinefs !

We arrefted our oars to gratify the foul with the exquifite harmony proceeding from a magnificent barge moored near the margin of the river ; when, on a fudden, a young man, of athletic form, and noble mien, darted forward, and, feizing my beloved Louifa, was

bearing

e

bearing her in his arms to a boat along fide of us.

Every nerve that quivered round my heart, throbbed at this unexpected outrage ; the ftranger committed his prize to the care of his companions, then advancing towards me while the lightnings of revenge flafhed from his indignant eyes, drew a ftiletto from his fleeve, and aimed a ftroke at my unguarded breaft. I warded off the blow, and turned his daftard weapon on himfelf.—The point entered his heart—he funk breathlefs at my feet.

Louifa opened her beauteous eyes to all the horrors of defpair and death !—She had only time to exclaim, " My brother !" when the life-blood rufhing from her convulfive lip—fhe hid her icy cheek on my diftracted bofom—and inftantly expired !

Frenzy now feizing on my tortured brain, fuggefted the foul crime of felf-annihilation ; but juftice, like a pitying cherubim, fnatched the dire weapon, reeking with kindred blood, from my affaffin hand. I was torn from the lifelefs victims of impatience, and thrown into the dungeons of horror and repentance. —The Count de Clairville, the brother of my murdered angel, was the only relation relentlefs fate had left her ;—her name is now extinct— but her virtues are immortal ! She had been compelled to take the veil, from a bafe and little pride, which too frequently facrifices the younger female branches of illuftrious, but indignant families, to a barbarous and perpetual imprifonment.

The unfortunate De Clairville was returning from his travels ; deftined to a military life, he had lately received a commiffion, and was haftening to join his regiment then at Lyons. He had long given up

the fruitlefs fearch after his adored fifter—Fate brought her to his view —then clofed his eyes forever.

The Count having given the firft affault, my punifhment was mitigated ; my doom, ten years imprifonment : and afterwards perpetual banifhment from a country, whofe laws I had violated, and whofe annals I had ftained with blood. The former part of my fentence expired in days of weeping, and in nights of anguifh—until the excefs of grief produced a fullen ftupor, that rendered me infenfible to every calamity.

Time gave again to my fad eyes the cheerful light of heaven, and with it, all the pangs of fatal recollection. Driven from fociety— an alien to my native country—an outcaft from every hope of future happinefs—alone, unfriended, loft, forgotten—I knew not whither to direct my courfe : One half of my little fortune was forfeited to the ftate, and meagre poverty ftretched forth her icy fangs to feal my deftiny. By perfeverance through a long and painful journey, I arrived in Spain, a wanderer and unknown, labouring under all the agonies of confcious mifery.

I have from that hour refided among the mountains in the vicinity of Madrid. My little hovel was too obfcure to excite curiofity, and its folitary tenant too poor to dread interruption. Poverty and forrow are the ftrongeft fecurities againft the intrufions of mankind ; let adverfity guard your threfhold, and you may linger through an uninterrupted life of mournful feclufion.

Yet, I do not prefume to repine ; for, alas, every hour convinces me, that prayers and tears are not fufficient to expiate my crimes. The penance I have impofed on myfelf, is a fad and tedious pilgrimage to

Loretto,

Loretto, and the firſt inſtance I experience of divine benignity, is the
benevolent hoſpitality I now enjoy
in the foreſt of Vancenza.

The pilgrim, riſing from his wic-
ker chair, bowed reſpectful to his
lovely auditors. Elvira gave his
ſorrows a tributary tear—it fell upon his hand that reſted on his ſtaff,
as ſhe ſtood near him—he preſſed it
to his lips—it revived his mournful
heart—for it was the holy tear of
commiſerating virtue !

Before the ſun roſe from its eaſtern canopy, the pilgrim reſumed his
toilſome journey of penitence and
ſorrow. The following melancholy verſes were found upon the table
in the chamber where he had paſſed
the night :

O'ER deſerts untrodden, o'er moſs-cov-
    er'd hills,
I have wander'd forlorn and alone ;
My tears I have mingled with flow-
    winding rills,
And the rocks have repeated my groan.

I have ſeen the wan moon from her ſilver
    veil peep,
    As ſhe roſe from her cloud-dappled bed ;
I have heard the dread hurricane yell
    midſt the deep,
    As the lightning play'd over my head.

When the tempeſt ſubſided, I ſaw the
    faint dawn
    O'er the eaſtern cliff meekly appear ;
While each king-cup that droop'd on the
    dew-ſpangled lawn,
    From its golden lids dropp'd a ſoft tear.

I have ſeen the bright day-ſtar illumine
    the earth,
    I have hail'd the proud ſovereign of fire ;
I have mark'd the pale primroſe, ſcarce
    waken'd to birth,
    Ere I ſigh'd to behold it expire.

How oft have I pitied the plaint of the
    dove,
    How I've mus'd near the nightingale's
    neſt !
For, ah, when the minſtrel ſung ſweetly
    of love,
    'Twas ſoft ſympathy thrill'd thro' my
    breaſt.

I have ſeen the tall foreſt o'erſhadow the
    glade,
    And extend its broad branches on high, .
But how ſoon I have mark'd its rich can-
    opy fade,
    And its yellow leaves whirl'd to the ſky ;

I have ſigh'd o'er the ſod where ſome lov-
    er was laid ;
    I have torn the rude weeds from his
    breaſt ;
I have deck'd it with flow'rets, and oft
    have I ſaid,
    " How I envy thy pallet of reſt !"

I have trac'd the long ſhades of the wave's
    ſilky green,
    When the ſtorm gather'd over the main ;
I have gaz'd with delight on the landſcape
    ſerene,
    When the ev'ning-bell toll'd on the
    plain.

Exulting and gay, I have ſmil'd to behold
    Proud nature luxuriantly dreſt ;
I have wept when I ſaw her uncover'd
    and cold,
    And the winter-blaſt howl'd o'er her
    breaſt.

Since ſuch are the ſcenes of this valley of
    care,
    Since each pleaſure is mingled with pain ;
Still let me the raptures of ſympathy ſhare,
    And my boſom ſhall ſcorn to complain.

Tho' deſtin'd to wander o'er mountains of
    ſnow,
    Vancenza, oh, manſion divine !
The pilgrim ſhall ſmile at his journey of wo,
    And his heart, his warm heart, ſhall be
    thine.

For the MASSACHUSETTS MAGAZINE.

PHILANTHROPY.

IT is faid by philofophers that the fize of the globules, which float in the vificles of animalcules, is at fuch an inconceivable remove below that of an elephant, that the globe we inhabit is found fcarcely large enough for a third proportional.

When we confider the tranfitory pleafures of fenfual gratification, in comparifon with the exquifite delight, which refults from acts of benevolence, reafon approves, while the former are compared to the globules, and the latter to the globe.

The fons of *Epicurus* have rioted in the lap of pleafure, indulged in a tide of luxury, defpifed the cultivation of the mind, trampled on the liberal arts, been the ruin of once flourifhing kingdoms and empires, and never contributed to the happinefs of man, except when they gave up the ghoft. *O cæcas hominum mentes ! O pectora cæca.*

LUCRETIUS

THE life of the late, JOHN HOWARD was diftinguifhed, in an unparalleled degree, by a feries of benevolent, arduous exertions for the relief of the indigent neighbour, and of the fick, helplefs, dying prifoner, in his own country, and in almoft every other under heaven. HOWARD, by his unbounded humanity, has eftablifhed a name more durable than the *Andes.*

Thefe fhall totter, melt, and fink in endlefs
Ruin ; but thy name, thou deareft friend
of man,
Shall fuperfede the wreck of time; fhall, by
Th' angelic hoft be caught, and re-echoed
With never-ending and encreafing plaudits,
Through heaven's vaft concave.

MODENA.

HISTORY of ARNAUD LA LUC.
[From the " ROMANCE of the FOREST."]

IN the village of Leloncourt, celebrated for its picturefque fituation at the foot of the Savoy Alps, lived Arnaud La Luc, a clergyman, defcended from an ancient family of France, whofe decayed fortunes occafioned them to feek a retreat in Switzerland, in an age when the violence of civil commotion feldom fpared the conquered. He was minifter of the village, and equally loved for the piety and benevolence of the Chriftian, as refpected for the dignity and elevation of the philofopher. His was the philofophy of nature, directed by common fenfe. He defpifed the jargon of the modern fchools and the brilliant abfurdities of fyftems, which have dazzled without enlightening, and guided without convincing their difciples.

His mind was penetrating ; his views extenfive ; and his fyftems, like his religion, were fimple, rational, and fublime. The people of his parifh looked up to him as to a father ; for while his precepts directed their minds, his example touched their hearts.

In early youth La Luc loft a wife, whom he tenderly loved. This event threw a tincture of foft and interefting melancholy over his character, which remained when time had mellowed the remembrance
· brance·

brance tha occafioned it. Philofophy had ftrengthened, not harden-
ed, his heart; it enabled him to refift the preffure of affliction, rather
than to overcome it.

Calamity taught him to feel with
peculiar fympathy the diftreffes of
others. His income from the parifh was fmall, and what remained
from the divided and reduced eftates of his anceftors did not much
increafe it; but though he could
not always relieve the neceffities of
the indigent, his tender pity and
holy converfation feldom failed in
adminiftering confolation to the
mental fufferer. On thefe occafions the fweet and exquifite emotions of his heart have often induced him to fay, that could the vo-
luptuary be once fenfible of thefe
feelings, he would never after forego " the luxury of doing good."
——" Ignorance of true pleafure,"
he would fay, " more frequently
than temptation to that which is
falfe, leads to vice."

La Luc had one fon and a daughter, who were too young, when
their mother died, to lament their
lofs. He loved them with peculiar tendernefs, as the children of
her whom he never ceafed to deplore; and it was for fome time
his fole amufement to obferve the
gradual unfolding of their infant
minds, and to bend them to virtue.
His was the deep and filent forrow
of the heart; his complaints he
never obtruded upon others, and
very feldom did he even mention
his wife. His grief was too facred
for the eye of the vulgar. Often
he retired to the deep folitude of
the mountains, and amid their folemn and tremendous fcenery would
brood over the remembrance of
times paft, and refign himfelf to
the luxury of grief. On his return from thefe little excurfions he

was always more placid and contented. A fweet tranquillity, which
arofe almoft to happinefs, was diffufed over his mind, and his manners were more than ufually benevolent. As he gazed on his children, and fondly kiffed them, a
tear would fometimes fteal into his
eye, but it was a tear of tender regret, unmingled with the darker
qualities of forrow, and was moft
precious to his heart.

On the death of his wife he received into his houfe a maiden fifter, a fenfible worthy woman, who
was deeply interefted in the happinefs of her brother. Her affectionate attention and judicious conduct
anticipated the effect of time in
foftening the poignancy of his diftrefs, and her unremitted care of
his children, while it proved the
goodnefs of her own heart, attracted her more clofely to his.

It was with inexpreffible pleafure that he traced in the infant features of Clara the refemblance of
her mother. The fame gentlenefs
of manner and the fame fweetnefs
of difpofition foon difplayed themfelves, and as fhe grew up, her actions frequently reminded him fo
ftrongly of his loft wife as to fix
him in reveries, which abforbed all
his foul.

Engaged in the duties of his parifh, the education of his chidren,
and in philofophic refearch, his
years paffed in tranquillity. The
tender melancholy with which affliction had tinctured his mind was,
by long indulgence, become dear
to him, and he would not have relinquifhed it for the brigheft dream
of airy happinefs. When any paffing incident difturbed him, he retired for confolation to the idea of
her he fo faithfully loved, and yielding to a gentle, and what the world
would call a romantic, fadnefs,
gradually

gradually reaffumed his compofure. This was the fecret luxury to which he withdrew from temporary difappointment—the folitary enjoyment which diffipated the cloud of care, and blunted the fting of vexation—which elevated his mind above this world, and opened to his view the fublimity of another.

The fpot he now inhabited, the furrounding fcenery, the romantic beauties of the neighbouring walks, were dear to La Luc, for they had once been loved by Clara ; they had been the fcenes of her tendernefs, and of his happinefs.

His chateau ftood on the borders of a fmall lake that was almoft environed by mountains of ftupendous height, which, fhooting into a variety of grotefque forms, compofed a fcenery fingularly folemn and fublime. Dark woods intermingled with bold projections of rock, fometimes barren, and fometimes covered with the purple bloom of wild flowers, impended over the lake, and were feen in the clear mirror of its waters. The wild and alpine heights which rofe above, were either crowned with perpetual fnows, or exhibited tremendous crags and maffes of folid rock, whofe appearance was continually changing as the rays of light were varioufly reflected on their furface, and whofe fummits were often wrapt in impenetrable mifts. Some cottages and hamlets, fcattered on the margin of the lake, or feated in picturefque points of view on the rocks above, were the only objects that reminded the beholder of humanity.

On the fide of the lake, nearly oppofite to the chateau, the mountains receded, and a long chain of alps was feen ftretching in perfpective. Their innumerable tints and fhades, fome veiled in blue mifts,

fome tinged with rich purple, and others glittering in partial light, gave luxurious and magical colouring to the fcene.

The chateau was not large, but it was convenient, and, was characterifed by an air of elegant fimplicity and good order. The entrance was a fmall hall, which opening by a glafs door into the garden, afforded a view of the lake, with the magnificent fcenery exhibited on its borders. On the left of the hall was La Luc's ftudy, where he ufually paffed his mornings ; and adjoining was a fmall room fitted up with chymical apparatus, aftronomical inftruments, and other implements of fcience. On the right was the family parlour, and behind it a room which belonged exclufively to Madame La Luc. Here were depofited various medicines and botanical diftillations, together with the apparatus for preparing them. From this room the whole village was liberally fupplied with phyfical comfort ; for it was the pride of Madame to believe herfelf fkilful in relieving the diforders of her neighbours.

Behind the chateau rofe a tuft of pines, and in front a gentle declivity, covered with verdure and flowers, extended to the lake, whofe waters flowed even with the grafs, and gave frefhnefs to the acacias that waved over its furface. Flowering fhrubs, intermingled with mountain afh, cyprefs, and ever-green oak, marked the boundary of the garden.

At the return of fpring it was Clara's care to direct the young fhoots of the plants, to nurfe the budding flowers, and to fhelter them with the luxuriant branches of the fhrubs from the cold blafts that defcended from the mountains. In fummer fhe ufually rofe with the

fun,

fun, and vifited her favourite flowers while the dew yet hung glittering on their leaves. The frefhnefs
of early day, with the glowing colouring which then touched the
fcenery, gave a pure and exquifite
delight to her innocent heart.
Born amid fcenes of grandeur and
fublimity, fhe had quickly imbibed
a tafte for their charms, which tafte
was heightened by the influence of
a warm imagination. To view the
fun rifing above the alps, tinging
their fnowy heads with light, and
fuddenly darting his rays over the
whole face of nature—to fee the
fiery fplendour of the clouds reflected in the lake below, and the rofeate
tints firft fteal upon the rocks above
—were among the earlieft pleafures
of which Clara was fufceptible.
From being delighted with the obfervance of nature, fhe grew pleafed
with feeing her finely imitated, and
foon difplayed a tafte for poetry
and painting. When fhe was about
fixteen fhe often felected from her
father's library thofe of the Italian
poets moft celebrated for picturefque beauty, and would fpend
the firft hours of morning in reading them under the fhade of the
acacias that bordered the lake.
Here too fhe would often attempt
rude fketches of the furrounding
fcenery, and at length, by repeated
efforts, affifted by fome inftruction
from her brother, fhe fucceeded fo
well as to produce twelve drawings
in crayon, which were judged worthy of decorating the parlour of the
chateau.

Young La Luc played the flute,
and fhe liftened to him with exquifite delight, particularly when he
ftood on the margin of the lake, under her beloved acacias. Her voice
was fweet and flexible, though not
ftrong, and fhe foon learned to
modulate it to the inftrument. She

knew nothing of the intricacies of
execution; her airs were fimple,
and her ftyle equally fo, but fhe
foon gave them a touching expreffion, infpired by the fenfibility of
her heart, which feldom left thofe
of her hearers unaffected.

It was the happinefs of La Luc to
fee his children happy, and in one of
his excurfions to Geneva, whither
he went to vifit fome relations of his
late wife, he brought Clara a lute.
She received it with more gratitude
than fhe could exprefs; and having
learned one air, fhe haftened to her
favourite acacias, and played it a-
gain and again till fhe forgot every
thing befides. Her little domeftic
duties, her books, her drawing,
even the hour which her father dedicated to her improvement, when
fhe met her brother in the library,
and with him partook of knowledge, even this hour paffed unheeded by. La Luc fuffered it to pafs.
Madame was difpleafed that her
niece neglected her domeftic duties,
and wifhed to reprove her, but La
Luc begged fhe would be filent.
" Let experience teach her her
error," faid he; " precept feldom
brings conviction to young minds."
Madame objected that experience
was a flow teacher. " It is a fure
one," replied La Luc, " and is not
unfrequently the quickeft of all
teachers; when it cannot lead us
into ferious evil, it is well to truft
to it."

The fecond day paffed with Clara
as the firft, and the third as the
fecond. She could now play feveral tunes; fhe came to her father
and repeated what fhe had learnt.

At fupper the cream was not
dreffed, and there was no fruit on
the table. La Luc inquired the
reafon; Clara recollected it, and
blufhed. She obferved that her
brother was abfent, but nothing was
faid.

faid. Towatd the conclufion of the repaft he appeared ; his countenance expreffed unufual fatisfaction, but he feated himfelf in filence. Clara inquired what had detained him from fupper, and learnt that he had been to a fick family in the neighbourhood with the weekly allowance which her father gave them. La Luc had entrufted the care of his family to his daughter, and it was her duty to have carried them their little allowance on the preceding day, but fhe had forgot every thing but mufic.

"How did you find the woman ?" faid La Luc to his fon. "Worfe, Sir," he replied, "for her medicines had not been regularly given, and the children had had little or no food to-day."

Clara was fhocked. "No food to-day !" faid fhe to herfelf, "and I have been playing all day on my lute, under the acacias by the lake !" Her father did not feem to obferve her emotion, but turned to his fon. "I left her better," faid the latter ; "the medicines I carried eafed her pain, and I had the pleafure to fee her children make a joyful fupper."

Clara, perhaps for the firft time in her life, envied him his pleafure ; her heart was full, and fhe fat filent. "No food to-day !" thought fhe.

She retired penfively to her chamber. The fweet ferenity with which fhe ufually went to reft was vanifhed, for fhe could no longer reflect on the paft day with fatisfaction. "What a pity," faid fhe, "that what is fo pleafing fhould be the caufe of fo much pain ! This lute is my delight, and my torment !" This reflection occafioned her much internal debate ; but before fhe could come to any refolution upon the point in queftion, fhe fell afleep.

She awoke very early the next morning, and impatiently watched the progrefs of the dawn. The fun at length appearing, fhe arofe, and, determinng to make all the atonement in her power for her former neglect, haftened to the cottage.

Here fhe returned to the chateau, her countenance had recovered all its ufual ferenity. She refolved, however, not to touch her lute that day.

Till the hour of breakfaft fhe bufied herfelf in binding up the flowers, and pruning the fhoots that were too luxuriant, and fhe at length found herfelf, fhe fcarcely knew how, beneath her beloved acacias by the fide of the lake. "Ah !" faid fhe, with a figh, "how fweetly would the fong I learned yefterday, found now over the waters !" But fhe remembered her determination, and checked the ftep fhe was involuntarily taking towards the chateau.

She attended her father in the library at the ufual hour, and learned, from his difcourfe with her brother on what had been read the two preceding days, that fhe had loft much entertaining knowledge. She requefted her father would inform her to what this converfation alluded ; but he calmly replied that fhe had preferred another amufement at the time when the fubject was difcuffed, and muft therefore content herfelf with ignorance.

"You would reap the rewards of ftudy from the amufements of idlenefs," faid he ; "learn to be reafonable—do not expect to unite inconfiftencies."

Clara felt the juftnefs of this rebuke, and remembered her lute. "What mifchief has it occafioned !" fighed fhe. "Yes, I am determined not to touch it at all this day. I will prove that I am able to control my inclinations when I

fee

fee it is neceſſary ſo to do." Thus re-
ſolving, ſhe applied herſelf to ſtudy
with more than uſual aſſiduity.

She adhered to her reſolution,
and towards the cloſe of day went
into the garden to amuſe herſelf.
The evening was ſtill and uncommonly beautiful. Nothing was
heard but the faint ſhivering of the
leaves, which returned but at intervals, making ſilence more ſolemn,
and the diſtant murmurs of the torrents that rolled among the cliffs.
As ſhe ſtood by the lake, and watched the ſun ſlowly ſinking below the
Alps, whoſe ſummits were tinged
with gold and purple ; as ſhe ſaw
the laſt rays of light gleam upon
the waters, whoſe ſurface was not
curled by the lighteſt air, ſhe ſighed, " Oh, how enchanting would
be the ſound of my lute at this moment, on this ſpot, and when every
thing is ſo ſtill around me !"

The temptation was too powerful
for the reſolution of Clara : ſhe ran
to the chateau, returned with the
inſtrument to her dear acacias, and
beneath their ſhade continued to
play, till the ſurrounding objects
faded in darkneſs from her ſight.
But the moon aroſe, and, ſhedding
a trembling luſtre on the lake, made
the ſcene more captivating than
ever.

It was impoſſible to quit ſo delightful a ſpot ; Clara repeated her
favourite airs again and again.—
The beauty of the hour awakened
all her genius ; ſhe never played
with ſuch expreſſion before, and ſhe
liſtened with increaſing rapture to
the tones, as they languiſhed over
the waters, and died away on the
diſtant air. She was perfectly enchanted. " No ! nothing was ever
ſo delightful as to play on the lute
beneath her acacias, on the margin
of the lake, by moonlight !"

When ſhe returned to the chateau, ſupper was over. La Luc
had obſerved Clara, and would not
ſuffer her to be interrupted.

When the enthuſiaſm of the hour
was paſſed, ſhe recollected that ſhe
had broken her reſolution, and the
reflection gave her pain. " I prided myſelf on controling my inclinations," ſaid ſhe, " and I have weak-
ly yielded to their direction. But
what evil have I incurred, by indulging them this evening ? I have
neglected no duty, for I had none
to perform. Of what then have I
to accuſe myſelf ? It would have
been abſurd to have kept my reſolution, and denied myſelf a pleaſure,
when there appeared no reaſon for
this ſelf-denial."

She pauſed, not quite ſatisfied
with this reaſoning. Suddenly re-
ſuming her inquiry, " But how,"
ſaid ſhe, " am I certain that I
ſhould have reſiſted my inclinations,
if there *had* been a reaſon for oppoſ-
ing them ? If the poor family,
whom I neglected yeſterday, had
been unſupplied to-day, I fear I
ſhould again have forgotten them,
while I played on my lute on the
banks of the lake."

She then recollected all that her
father had at different times ſaid on
the ſubject of ſelf-command, and
ſhe felt ſome pain.

" No," ſaid ſhe, " if I do not conſider that to preſerve a reſolution,
which I have once ſolemnly formed,
is a ſufficient reaſon to control my
inclinations, I fear no other motive
would long reſtrain me. I ſeriouſly determined not to touch my lute
this whole day, and I have broken
my reſolution. To-morrow perhaps I may be tempted to neglect
ſome duty, for I have diſcovered
that I cannot rely on my own prudence. Since I cannot conquer
temptation, I will fly from it."

On

On the following morning she brought her lute to La Luc, and begged he would receive it again, and at least keep it till she had taught her inclinations to submit to control.

The heart of La Luc swelled as she spoke. " No, Clara," said he, " it is unnecessary that I should receive your lute ; the sacrifice you would make proves you worthy of my confidence. Take back the instrument ; since you have sufficient resolution to resign it when it leads you from duty, I doubt not that you will be able to control its influence now that it is restored to you."

Clara felt a degree of pleasure and pride at these words, such as she had never before experienced ; but she thought, that to deserve the commendation they bestowed, it was necessary to complete the sacrifice she had begun. In the virtuous

enthusiasm of the moment, the delights of music were forgotten in those of aspiring to well earned praise, and when she refused the lute thus offered, she was conscious only of exquisite sensations. " Dear sir," said she, tears of pleasure swelling in her eyes, " allow me to deserve the praises you bestow, and then I shall indeed be happy."

La Luc thought she had never resembled her mother so much as at this instant, and tenderly kissing her, he for some moments wept in silence. When he was able to speak, " You do already deserve my praises," said he, " and I restore your lute as a reward for the conduct which excites them." This scene called back recollections too tender for the heart of La Luc, and giving Clara the instrument, he abruptly quitted the room.

HOSPITALITY and GRATITUDE : An Historical
ANECDOTE.

IN the latter part of the reign of Queen Ann, the Duke of Ormond, whose family name was Butler, was appointed Lord Lieutenant of Ireland. On his passage to assume the reigns of government, he was shipwrecked, and took refuge in the house of a poor curate, whose Christian name was Joseph : Here he was entertained with the greatest hospitality. On his departure the Duke expressed a sense of the goodness of his host, and promised an ample reward. Weeks and months passed, and the curate heard nothing of his noble guest. His wife urged him to visit the Duke at the seat of his government—he replied, " the expenses of the journey will but increase our poverty. His grace

is too much taken up with the concerns of the public, and the parade of greatness, to attend to me."— Her entreaties at last however prevailed. The curate made a journey to Dublin, and obtained an introduction to the clergyman of the church at which the Duke attended public worship. He was invited to preach, and took the following words for his text—" Yet did not the chief butler remember Joseph, but forgat him." The text, and observations upon it, engaged the particular attention of his grace. After service he sent for the preacher, and asked him if any previous occurrence gave rise to the text, and to the sermon. An explanation took place. " You could not," said the Duke,

Duke, " have made your vifit at a more fortunate time, a living of 500l. per annum is now vacant, I cannot do better than to beftow it on you." The curate, with the glad tidings, returned to his wife and family, and foon removed to tafte the bleffings of a richer cure. At the acceffion of George I. the Duke of Ormond fled into voluntary exile, to avoid the profecution of the whig adminiftration. He was attainted, and his eftate feized. The good curate forgot not his benefactor in adverfity. He obferved to his wife, " now, my dear, we have an opportunity to exprefs our gratitude. 200l. per annum is an ample fupport for us—300l. will fecure his grace from want." And for years the Duke was fupported by the bounty of the curate.

For the MASSACHUSETTS MAGAZINE.

The ESSAYIST. No. XII.

On the influence of example in forming the characters of men.

THE pureft joys, which man can tafte below,
From focial intercourfe and friendfhip flow.
The hermit *feels*, though loath the truth to own,
That *'tis not good for man to be alone.*
Even blifsful Adam, heaven's peculiar care,
Sigh'd for a mate his happinefs to fhare ;
Heaven pitying heard, and bade him ceafe to grieve,
And for one rib exchang'd the beauteous Eve.
  To every rank the principle extends ;
Each individual knows his faithful friends ;
When joy expands, or grief diftracts his heart,
Thefe fhare his blifs, or kind relief impart
For grief divided lofes half its weight,
But joys, when fhar'd, ftill greater joys create.
  Hence focial circles through the world abound ;
Hence fcarce a friendlefs wretch on earth is found.
  But man, to imitate, by nature prone,
From others' manners ever forms his own.
When from the diftant woods the rough hewn clown,
With many an aukward ftare is brought to town,

At firft he gazes round with wondering eyes ;
Here palaces and gilded fpires arife ;
There unaccuftom'd founds his ears invade,
By noify crouds and rattling coaches made.
The joftling throngs, that on each other prefs ;
Their unfelt compliments ; their brilliant drefs ;
Their pert vivacious looks ; their ftrutting gait ;
And all the fplendid vanities of ftate,
Strike the untutor'd lad with ftrange furprife,
He ftares, and gapes, and fcarce believes his eyes.
But foon each object is familiar grown ;
He foon becomes accuftom'd to the town ;
Approves thofe manners, which at firft feem'd odd ;
Affumes the cit and lays afide the clod ;
Improves his air, refines his tafte and wit,
And imperceptibly becomes polite.
  But not to manners only is confin'd
Example's mighty influence on mankind ;
We think and act, we fpeak, we joy and grieve,
Deteft and love, like thofe, with whom we live.
Thofe crimes, which fhock at firft, no more offend,

Seen oft, and through the medium of a
  friend ;
His vices firſt look hideous, and we hate,
Indulge them next, then love, then imitate.
  Then, ſince on virtue happineſs depends,
And both together on the choice of friends,
Thrice bleſt are they, who only ſuch ob-
  tain,   [reign ;
Whoſe paſſions yield to reaſon's gentle

Whoſe morals, piety, and learning join,
To mend the heart the manners to refine ;
Whoſe pure examples with refiſtleſs power
Allure their devious feet to wiſdom's
  bower ;
Who every virtue, every grace diſplay ;
Who point the road to heaven and lead
  the way.

DESCRIPTION of MANNA.

[From Harris's Natural Hiſtory of the Bible.]

MANNA was the food of the children of Iſrael, which God gave them in the deſerts of Arabia, during their continuance there for forty years, from the eighth encampment in the wilderneſs of Sin.

The manna mentioned by Moſes was a little grain, white like hoar froſt, round, and of the bigneſs of a coriander ſeed.* It fell every morning upon the dew ; and when the dew was exhaled by the heat of the ſun, the manna appeared alone, lying upon the rocks or the ſand.† It fell every day, except on the ſabbath ; and this only around the camp of the Iſraclites.‡ It fell in ſo great quantities, during the whole forty years of their journey, that it was ſufficient to feed the whole multitude, of above a million of ſouls.

Every one of whom gathered the quantity of an omer§ for his ſhare every day. It maintained the whole multitude ; yet none of them found the eating it, attended with any inconvenience. Every ſixth day there fell a double quantity, and though it putrified and bred maggots when it was kept any other day, yet on the *ſabbath* it ſuffered no

ſuch alteration. And the ſame manna, which was melted by the heat of the ſun, when it was left in the field, was of ſo hard a conſiſtence, when it was brought into the houſe, that it was uſed to be beaten in mortars, and would even endure the fire ; was made into cakes and baked in pans.

To commemorate their living upon omers, or tenth deals, of manna, one omer of it was put into a golden vaſe, and preſerved for many generations by the ſide of the ark.‖

Our tranſlators, and others, make Moſes fall into a plain contradiction, in relating the ſtory of the manna ; which they render thus, *and when the children of Iſrael ſaw it, they ſaid one to another, it is manna, for they wiſt not what it was :* Whereas the ſeptuagint, and ſeveral authors, both ancient and modern, have tranſlated the text according to the orginal : *The Iſraelites ſeeing this, ſaid one to another, what is it ? For they knew not what it was.* For we muſt obſerve that the word by which they aſked the queſtion was in their language *man hu,* which ſignifies likewiſe *food ready prepared ;* and therefore it was always afterwards called *man,* or *manna.*

          The

* Exod. xvi. 14.   † Numb. xi. 7.   ‡ Exod. xvi. 5.

§ About two quarts and a pint, of our meaſure.   ‖ Exod. xvi. 32.

The fcripture gives to manna the name of *the bread of heaven,* and *the food of angels.* Which are undoubtedly figurative allufions to its origin and its value. The author of the book of wifdom fays* that it fo accommodated itfelf to every one's tafte, that it proved palatable and pleafing to all. And ftill at this day, there falls manna in feveral places of the world: In Arabia, Poland, Calabria, Mount Libanus, Dauphine, and elfewhere. The moft famous is that of Arabia, which is a kind of condenfed honey, to be found in fummer upon the leaves of the trees, the herbs, the rocks, or the fand of Arabia Petrea. It is of the fame figure that Mofes defcribes. That about Mount Sinai is of a very ftrong fmell, which is communicated to it by the herbs upon which it falls. It very eafily evaporates, infomuch that if thirty pounds of it were to be kept in an open veffel, there would hardly ten of it remain at the end of fifteen days. Salmafius thinks this of the fame kind with that which fed the children of Ifrael. Several moderns are of the fame opinion. It is true that the Arabian manna has a medicinal quality: But they pretend that if one fhould make it habitual, the ftomach might be accuftomed to it, as we know that people may be brought to fuch a diet as is naturally but little convenient for maintaining health. But we ought alfo to acknowledge that the manna

fpoken of by Mofes, had miraculous qualities, not to be found in the common; and which probably lafted no longer than while the Ifraelites were fed with it. However, we fhall prefent the opinion of the learned Michaelis,† and with it conclude this interefting article.

"Manna bears a very near refemblance to the dew. Its origin is the very fame; the only difference being that it remains, whereas dew evaporates. From this reafon it is that in the countries, where manna is found, they have imagined that, like dew, it fell from above, and this conceit has got footing in the languages.

There is another kind which the Arabs, by way of diftinction, term *celeftial manna.* In the holy fcripture we read that the manna fell along with the dew, and by the fame figure which the profane poets made ufe of in calling the latter a gift of heaven, the truly infpired poet has called the manna *bread from heaven.* Thefe expreffions, to which the orientals were accuftomed from their early years, have confirmed them in the opinion that the manna defcended. It was not till the middle of the 16th century that the falfity of that opinion began to be feen into, and that in Italy manna was found to be no more than a gum exuding from plants, trees, and bufhes, on being pierced by certain infects."

* Ch. xvi. 20, 21.   † On the influence of opinions or language, 4to, p. 56.

ESSAY on FRIENDSHIP.

Addreffed to the Ladies.

THE ancients ranked Friendfhip in the fecond clafs of human virtues; and many are the inftances recorded in hiftory, where its energy has produced effects almoft divine. Confidered in its perfect

fect strength and beauty, it certainly is the most sublime, because the least selfish, affection of the soul.

Honour is its very essence; courage, frankness, and generosity, its unalienable properties. Such is the idea delivered down to us of this noble sentiment, by its cotemporary writers, "who together flourished, and together fell:" for some centuries have elapsed, since this exalted phænomenon has deigned to appear among the degenerate sons of men; and, like a mutilated statue, it is now become rather an object of admiration to a few virtuosi in philosophy, than a subject for general emulation.

Montaign, among the moderns, seems to have felt a stronger emanation of this virtue, than any author I am acquainted with; and, though the utmost stretch of his warm imagination gives us but a faint ray of its ancient lustre, yet even this slight resemblance appears too strong for our weak eyes, and seems rather to dazzle than attract our regards.

Our cotemporary, Dr. Young, has left us several very beautiful descriptions of friendship, which, though deficient in that fire which not only blazed, but burned, in this ancient virtue, are, however, sufficient to form both our theory and our practice upon:

" True friendship warms, it raises, it transports,
Like music pure the joy, without allay,
Whose very rapture is tranquillity."

This is a very pleasing and just description of friendship in the abstract; but it wants that energy which particular attachments add to all our sentiments, and without which, like a winter's sun, they shine, but not warm.

The same author has given us a more interesting, though, perhaps,

less elevated idea of this affection of the mind, in his address to a particular person:

Lorenzo, pride supprefs, nor hope to find
A friend, but what has found a friend in thee."

This is a new, and I think a just light, in which we may consider this sentiment; for, though love may be formed without sympathy, friendship never can. It is, even in its degenerate state, an affection that cannot subsist in vicious minds; and, among the most virtuous, it requires a parity of sentiment, manners, and rank, for its basis. Of all the nice ties and dependencies which constitute the happiness or misery of life, it is the most delicate, and even the most fragile. Wealth cannot purchase, nor gifts ensure, its permanence. " The chirping of birds in cages bears as much resemblance to the vocal music of the woods, as bought courtesies to real friendship." The great, alas, rarely enjoy this blessing ! vanity and emulation prevent its growth among equals; and the humiliating condescension with which superiors sometimes deign to affect friendship for their inferiors, strikes at the very foundation of the sentiment; from which there can only arise a tottering superstructure, whose pillars, like those of modern composition, bear the gloss, but want the durable quality of the mental marble, sincerity. Yet there have been instances, though rare, of real friendship between persons of different ranks in life, particularly Henry the fourth and Sully; but the virtues of the latter placed him on a level with monarchs, and the magnanimity of the former made him sensible of their equality.

Yet how often are complaints uttered by disappointed pride, against
the

the ingratitude of thofe whom they have *honoured* with the title of friend, nay, and have even ferved and o-bliged as fuch, without refieaing that obligations to a generous mind are infults, when accompanied with the leaft flight or mortification.

On the other hand, we, perhaps, too willingly attach ourfelves to our fuperiors. Our felf-love is flattered by their approbation, as it natural-ly imagines it can only be for our good and amiable qualities, that they like or diftinguifh us. But, though " love, like death, makes all diftinaion void," friendfhip has no fuch levelling power. Superi-ority of rank or fortune is general-ly felt by the perfon who poffeffes either ; and they are entitled to fome degree of praife, if they do not make others feel it alfo.

Let thofe, then, who have deli-cate minds, remember, that equal-ity is the true bafis of friendfhip ; let them fet a juft value on their own worth, as well as on the inebri-ating fmiles of greatnefs, and not expofe their fenfibility to the pangs it muft fuftain, on difcovering that neither virtues nor talents can al-ways keep the fcale of friendfhip fteady, when oppofed to the adven-titious circumftances of high birth, or great fortune.

Thus far my remarks upon this fubjea are general. Let me now apply them to more particular ufe, by earneftly recommending it to every young married woman, to feek the friend of her heart in the hufband of her affeaion. There, and there only, is that true equal-ity, both of rank and fortune, ftrengthened by mutual interefts, and cemented by mutual pledges, to be found. There only conde-fcenfions will not mortify, as they will be conceffions but of kindnefs, not of pride. There, and there on-ly, will fhe be fure to meet with, re-ciprocal confidence, unfeigned at-tachment, and tender folicitude, to footh her every care. The ties of wedded love will be rivetted by the bands of friendfhip : the virtues of her mind, when called forth by oc-cafion, will unfold themfelves by degrees to her hufband's perception, like the opening rofe before the morning ray ; and, when its bloom-ing colour fades upon her cheek, its fweetnefs fhall remain within the very foldings of his heart, from recolleaion of her fenfe and worth. Happy are the pairs fo joined ; yea, bleffed are they who are thus doubly united !

As the word friendfhip is at pref-ent generally underftood to be a term of little import, or at moft that extends merely to a preference of liking, or efteem ; I would by no means exclude my fair readers from that kind of commerce which is now accepted under that title, in fociety. But even this fort of con-neaion requires much caution in the choice of its objea ; for I fhould wifh it might be reftrained to one ; and that one ought to obtain this preference from the qualities of the heart, rather than thofe of the head. A long and intimate acquaintance can alone difcover the former ; the latter are eafily and wil-lingly difplayed ; for love with-out efteem is as a fhower foon fpent. The head is the fpring of affeaions, but the heart is the refervoir.

For this reafon it always appears to me a proof of mutual merit, when two fifters, or two young women, who have been brought up together, are ftrongly attached to each other : and I will admit, that, while they remain unmarried, fuch a conneaion is capable of forming a pure and difinterefted friendfhip, provided that the fympathy of their affeaions affections does not tend to make them like or admire the same male object ; for, though love may, friendship cannot exist with jealousy :

" Reserve will wound it, and distrust destroy."

That great master of the human heart, Shakespear, has shewn us, that maidenly attachment is no match for the stronger passion of love :

" Is all the counsel that we two have shar'd,
The sister vows, the hours that we have spent,
When we have chid the hasty-footed time
For parting us—O ! and is all forgot ?
All school-days friendship, childhood innocence ?
We, Hermia, like two artificial gods,
Created with our needles both one flower,
Both on one sampler, sitting on one cushion,
Both warbling of one song, both in one key,
As if our hands, our sides, voices, and minds
Had been incorp'rate."

Midsummer's Night's Dream.

If such an almost instinctive affection as that between Hermia and Helena was so quickly dissolved by the intruder Love, I fear there are but few female friendships that will better stand the test. And to a delicate mind it may appear a breach, perhaps, of those " sister vows," when one of the parties enters into another and more forcible engagement ; for love is an imperious and engrossing tyrant ; of course the gentler *affection* must give way and retire within itself, as the sensitive plant shrinks back, oppressed by too intense an heat.

In my small experience, I have never seen the same degree of attachment subsist between two ladies after marriage as before, excepting they were sisters. The bands of natural affection are not loosened by new engagements ; but those of choice or casualty necessarily become relaxed by the addition of a new object, as extension lessens strength.

The minds of most young women seem, and indeed ought to do so in reality, to acquire a new bent after marriage : scenes, different from those to which they had been accustomed, open to their view ; different objects engross their attention ; every state has its cares ; and, from the Queen to the peasant, every wife has duties to fulfil. Frivolous amusements are, or should be, renounced, for the more pleasing and respectable avocations of an affectionate wife, a tender mother, and a beloved and honoured matron of a family.

I hope it is impossible that I should be so far misunderstood, as to be thought to exclude married women from any innocent pleasure or rational amusement that is suited to their age, rank, or fortune. I would not only ensure but augment their happiness, and shall therefore say with Othello,

" Where virtue is, these are most virtuous."

But still there is, or should be, a difference in the enjoyment of their pleasures : between the thoughtless gaiety of girls, and the decent cheerfulness of married women. The first is bright and transient, as the youthful glow of health and vivacity that blooms upon the cheek ; the latter should express that tranquil joy which flows from true content.

Here I cannot but observe, that, as the characters and conduct of
even

even her common acquaintance reflect honour or difgrace upon a young married woman, fhe will be an inevitable fharer in that degree of refpect or contempt which her *chofen* friend poffeffes in the efteem of the world : And though its cenfures may fometimes involve the innocent with the guilty ; yet, in general, there is no fairer way of forming our opinions of perfons we do not know, than from their intimate affociates.

There is fomething ftill more alarming to be dreaded for a young woman who is thoughtlefs enough to form indifcriminate friendfhips. There is a lightnefs of mind and manners in many women, who, though free from actual vice, have loft that delicate fenfibility which heaven has placed in female minds as the out-guard of modefty. The rofy blufh that gives the intuitive alarm to decency, even before the perceptions of the mind are awake to danger, glows not upon their cheek ; the fnowy purity of innocence beams not upon their dauntlefs forehead, though it may ftill retain its whitenefs. Their minds may be coarfe, however delicate their form ; and their manners un-

feminine, even without being mafculine.

An intimacy with fuch perfons is, of all others, the moft dangerous. The franknefs and livelinefs of their converfation render them too generally agreeable, and they frequently undermine the principles of virtue, before we find it neceffary to ftand upon our guard.

As the platonic fyftem has been long exploded, it is almoft unneceffary to warn my fair readers againft particular intimacies with the other fex, when not clofely connected with them by the ties of blood or affinity. The whole fyftem of nature muft change, and the tyger and the lamb live peaceably together, before a fincere and difinterefted friendfhip can fubfift between an amiable young woman and a man not nearly related to her, who has not paffed his grand climacteric. A man of fuch an age, poffeffed of fenfe and virtue, may perhaps be a kind and ufeful mentor ; but, if a married woman is happy enough to meet with a proper and affectionate return from the firft object I have recommended to her choice, fhe cannot ftand in need of any other friend.

ESSAY on FORTITUDE.

Illuftrated with curious emblematical Devices.

IT is allowed that all men are equally defirous of happinefs, but that few are fuccefsful in the purfuit. One chief caufe of this failure is the want of ftrength of mind, which might enable them to refift the temptations of prefent eafe and pleafure, and carry them forward in the fearch of more diftant profit and enjoyment. Our affections, on a general profpect of

their objects, form certain rules of conduct, and certain meafures of preference of one above another : and thefe decifions though really the refult of our calm paffions and natural propenfities, are yet faid by a current abufe of terms to be the determinations of pure reafon and reflection. But when fome of thefe objects approach nearer to us, or acquire the advantages of favourable

ble lights and pofitions, which catch the heart or imagination; our general refolutions are frequently confounded, a prefent enjoyment is preferred, and lafting fhame or forrow entailed upon us. And however poets may employ their wit and eloquence in celebrating prefent pleafure, and rejecting all diftant views to fame, health or fortune; it is obvious that this practice is the fource of all diffolutenefs and diforder, mifery and repentance. A man of ftrong and determinate temper adheres tenacioufly to his general refolutions, and is neither feduced by the allurements of pleafure, nor terrified by the menaces of pain; but ftill keeps in view thofe diftant purfuits by which he at once infures his happinefs and his honour.

The fortitude of a man who reftrains his prefent defires to the obedience of his reafon, is confpicuous, and carries with it a dignity into the loweft ftate imaginable.— Poor Conftantius, who now lies languifhing in a moft violent fever, difcovers, in the fainteft moments of his diforder, fuch a greatnefs of mind, that a perfect ftranger, who fhould behold him, would indeed fee an object of pity, but would at the fame time perceive that it was lately an object of veneration. His gallant fpirit refigns, but refigns with an air that fpeaks a refolution which could yield to nothing but fate itfelf. This is conqueft in the philofophic fenfe; but the empire over ourfelves is in truth no lefs laudable in common life, where the whole tenor of a man's carriage is in fubfervience to his own reafon, and in conformity to the good fenfe of other men.

Marcellus is perfect mafter of himfelf in all circumftances. He has all the fpirit that a man can have, and yet is as regular in his conduct and behaviour as a machine. He is fenfible of every paffion, but is ruffled by none. In converfation he frequently feems to be lefs knowing, to be more obliging, and choofes to be on a level with others, rather than opprefs with the fuperiority of his genius. In friendfhip he is kind without profeffion; in bufinefs, expeditious without oftentation. With the greateft foftnefs and benevolence imaginable, he is impartial in fpite of all importunity, even that of his own good nature. He is ever clear in his judgment, but in complaifance to his company, fpeaks diffidently; and never fhews confidence in argument, but to fupport the fenfe of another. Did fuch an equanimity of mind regulate the behaviour of mankind in general, how fweet would be the pleafures of converfation! he that is vociferous, dogmatical, and vehement, would underftand, that it is then time to call a conftable; and know that fpoiling good company is a moft unwarrantable way of breaking the peace.

Thus much relates to the common intercourfe of fociety; but as above hinted, the man of true fortitude meafures his actions by principles of his own. The fenfe of other men ought to weigh with us in things of lefs confideration; but not in concerns where truth and honour are engaged. When we fearch to the bottom of things, we often find principles, that appear paradoxical at firft, to be evident truths; and maxims, which, before they are duly weighed, feem to proceed from a romantic kind of philofophy, and ignorance of the world, after a little reflection appear fo reafonable, that nothing lefs than direct madnefs could induce us to walk by any other rules. Thus to contradict our defires, and to conquer

quer the impulfes of ambition, when they do not coincide with thofe fentiments our cool judgment approves ; is fo truly our intereft, and fo abfolutely effential to our real happinefs, that to contemn all the advantages the world offers to us, where they ftand in competition with a man's honour, is the exercife of the virtue called fortitude.

Did we confider the mind of man as the man himfelf, it would appear to be the moft unnatural fpecies of felf-murder to facrifice the fentiments of the foul, to gratify the appetites of the body. Is it not aftonifhing, that when the neceffities of life are fupplied, a man would flatter to be rich, or circumvent to be powerful ! When we meet a poor wretch, urged by hunger and cold, fuing for an alms, we are apt to think this a ftate we could rather ftarve at once, than remain in ; but yet how much more defpicable is his condition, who being above neceffity, can yet refign his reafon and his integrity to purchafe fuperfluities ? Thefe are both abject and common beggars ; yet it is furely lefs meannefs to beg a fupply for hunger than for vanity ! But general prepoffeffions and cuftom fo far prevail over the bulk of mankind, that thofe neceffitous creatures who cannot relifh life without applaufe, attendance and equipage, are fo far from being defpifed, that diftreffed virtue is lefs efteemed than fplendid vice. But if in cafes that regard true honour, a man's appeal

were made to his own foul ; there would be a bafis and ftanding rule for our conduct : and to be honourable would be the aim of our endeavours, rather than to appear honourable. Mr. Collier, in his Effay on Fortitude, has treated this fubject with great accuracy. "What," fays he, " can be more honourable, than to have courage enough to execute the commands of reafon and confcience ; to maintain the dignity of our nature, and the ftation affigned us ? To be proof againft poverty, pain, and death itfelf, fo far as not to do any thing fcandalous or finful to avoid them. To ftand adverfity under all fhapes, with decency and refolution. To do this is to be great above title and fortune : This argues the foul of a heavenly extraction, and is worthy the offspring of the Deity !"

What a generous ambition has this writer pointed out to us ! When men have fettled in themfelves a conviction by fuch noble precepts, that there is nothing honourable that is not accompanied with innocence, nothing mean, but what is tainted with guilt ; when they have attained this mode of thinking, though poverty, pain, and death, may ftill have their terrors, yet riches, pleafures, and honour eafily lofe their charms, if they ftand between us and our integrity. Steady and happy in ourfelves, nothing external will ruffle our tempers, and fortune will point her arrows againft us in vain.

The STROKE of DEATH.

[From a Britifh Magazine.]

I AM now worth a blumb, faid old Gregory, as he afcended a hill, part of an eftate he had juft purchafed—I am now worth a blumb, which I have earned by ftrict attention to bufinefs ; and I will purchafe

chafe a feat in the commons for my fon, and procure a peer to marry my daughter—I am now worth a blumb, and am but fixty five years of age, healthy and robuſt in my conſtitution, fo I'll eat and I'll drink and live merrily all the days of my life—I am now worth a blumb, faid old Gregory, as he attained the fummit of a hill, which commanded a full profpeſt of his eſtate ; and here, faid he, I'll build a manſion, and there I'll plant an orchard, and on that fpot I'll have a pinery—Yon farm houfes ſhall come down, faid old Gregory, they interrupt my view. Then what will become of the farmers ? aſked the ſteward who attended him. That's their bufinefs, anſwered old Gregory. And that mill muſt not ſtand on the ſtream, faid old Gregory. Then how will the villagers grind their corn ? aſked the ſteward. That's not my bufinefs, anſwered old Gregory—fo old Gregory returned home—eat a hearty fupper—drank a bottle of port—ſmoked two pipes of tobacco, and fell into a profound ſlumber, from which he never awoke.—The farmers refide on their lands, the mill ſtands upon the ſtream—and the villagers all rejoice at the *ſtroke of death.*

AGRICULTURE.

[From Dr. WILLIAMS's Hiſtory of Vermont.]

THE body of the people in Vermont are engaged in agriculture. In a new country where the fettlements are yet to be made, agriculture puts on a very different appearance from that, which it bears in the ancient and well cultivated fettlements. There, the bufinefs is to cultivate and improve the farms, which have been already greatly improved : To increafe the produce, by the application of more labour and cultivation, and thus to derive a greater profit from the land. In a new fettlement, the firſt bufinefs of the hufbandman is to cut down the woods, to clear up the lands, to fow them with grain, to erect the neceffary buildings, and open the roads ; and thus to connect and form a communication between the fcattered fettlements, and make the moſt of his labour.—Amidſt the hard living and hard labour, that attends the forming a new fettlement, the fettler has the moſt flattering profpects and encouragements. One hundred acres of land in a new town, does not generally coſt him more than he can fpare from the wages of one or two years. Befides maintaining himfelf, the profits of his labour will generally enable a young man, in that period of time, to procure himfelf fuch a tract of land.—When he comes to apply his labour to his own land, the produce of it becomes extremely profitable. The firſt crop of wheat will fully pay him for all the expenfe he has been at, in clearing up, fowing, and fencing his land; and at the fame time, increafes the value of the land, eight or ten times the original coſt. In this way, every day's labour fpent in clearing up his land, receives high wages in the grain which it procures, and adds at the fame time a quantity of improved land to the farm. An acre of land, which in its natural ſtate, coſt him perhaps the half of one day's labour, is thus in one year made of that value, that it will afterwards annually produce him from fifteen to twenty buſhels of of wheat; or other kinds of produce, of equal value. In this way, the profits attending labour on a new fettlement, are the greateft that ever can take place in agriculture; the labourer conftantly receiving double wages. He receives high wages in the produce of his corn or wheat; and he receives much higher wages of another kind, in the annual addition of a new tract of cultivated land to his farm. This double kind of wages, nature with great benevolence and defign, has affigned to the man of induftry, when he is firft making a fettlement in the uncultivated parts of America: and in two or three years, he acquires a very comfortable and independent fubfiftence for a family, derived from no other fource but the earth, and his own induftry.

In every country, agriculture ought to be efteemed, as the moft neceffary and ufeful profeffion. The food and the raiment by which all orders of men are fupported, muft be derived from the earth. Agriculture is the art by which this is effected; and of confequence the art which fupports, fupplies, and maintains all the reft. It ought therefore to be efteemed the primary, the fundamental, and the moft effential art of all; that which deferves the firft and the greateft confideration, and encouragement.—The wealth drawn from agriculture, is permanent and durable; not fubject to the uncertainties attending that, which is derived from commerce; and not dependent upon the inclinations, the difpofitions, or the regulations of other kingdoms and countries. The people that thus live by their own agriculture, are independent of other nations, and need not be affected by their wars, revolutions, or convulfions; but may always have the means of fup-

port and independence, among themfelves. While they have that which is drawn from the cultivation of the land, they will have every thing that nature and fociety can need or have made valuable.

The other profeffions, thofe efpecially of the liberal arts, are of great utility, and of high importance, and they are what fociety could not flourifh without. But they derive their importance and utility from the imperfections of man, and of fociety; and do not of themfelves, add any thing to the wealth of nations. The phyfician, the lawyer, the divine, the ftatefman, and the philofopher, are engaged in employments of great utility to mankind. But there is not one of them, that adds any thing to the wealth and property of the community: They muft all derive their fupport, from the cultivation of the land. Of all arts and profeffions then, agriculture ought to be efteemed the moft ufeful, and the moft important. It is the art which produceth, and nourifhes all the reft. The other arts teach how to preferve the health, the property, and the morals of men; to enlarge their underftandings, and to give a right direction to their minds: But this provides food, raiment, and fupport for them all.

In no way has the glory of nations been more expanded, than by their attainments, and difcoveries in fcience. The mathematicians have meafured, and fettled the dimenfions of the folar fyftem: But the new fettler, has in fact, enlarged the bounds of the habitable creation. The philofophers have expanded our minds with the ideas, and evidence, that the other planets are inhabited; but the fimple and honeft farmer has made the earth the place for more inhabitants than

it

it ever had before. And while the astronomers are so justly celebrating the discoveries, and the new planet of Herschel, all mankind should rejoice, that the simple peasant in the wilderness, has found out a way, to make our planet bear more men.

Those employments which are the most necessary, and the most useful to men, seem to be the most nearly connected with morality and virtue. Agriculture appears to be more nearly allied to this, than any of the arts. The man that is constantly pursuing the business, which nature has assigned to him, seems to have but little to corrupt him.

In the many histories of corruption, there is not any account, that the body of the husbandmen ever became a corrupt, venal, and debauched generation. They must first be led to desert their employments, or they must be blinded and deceived, before they can be made fit tools for politicians to corrupt, and manage. Their profession tends to render them an industrious, hardy, incorrupted, and honest set of men. It is never in the body of the husbandmen, but among the speculators, politicians, and leaders of mobs, that we look for a settled trade, and high attainments, in venality and corruption.

AVARICE PUNISHED.

AN usurer having lost a hundred pounds in a bag, promised a reward of ten pounds to the person who should restore it. A man having brought it to him, demanded the reward. The usurer, loath to give the reward, after he had recovered his bag, alleged, after he had opened it, that there were an hundred and ten pounds in it when he lost it. Gripus being called before the judge, unwarily acknowledged that the seal was broke open in his presence, and that there were no more at that time, but a hundred pounds in the bag. "You say," cried the judge, "that the bag you lost, had a hundred and ten pounds in it?" "Yes, my lord." "Then this cannot be your bag, as it contained but a hundred pounds: therefore the plaintiff must keep it till the true owner appears; and you must go and look for your bag where you can find it."

[Hist. Mag.

The WITTY PAINTER.

SIR William Lely, a famous painter in the reign of king Charles the first, agreed beforehand for the price of a picture he was to draw for a rich London alderman, who was not indebted to nature either for shape or face. The picture being finished, the alderman endeavoured to beat down the price, alleging, that if he did not purchase it, it would lie on the painter's hand. "That's your mistake," says sir William; "for I can sell it at double the price I demand." "How can that be," says the alderman, "for 'tis like nobody but myself?" "True," replied sir William; "but I will draw a tail to it, and then it will be an excellent monkey!" Mr. Alderman, to prevent being exposed, paid down the money the painter demanded, and carried off the picture.

[Hist. Mag.

CABINET

CABINET of APOLLO.

For the MASSACHUSETTS MAGAZINE.

The CLOSE of the WEEK at COLLEGE.

THE tedious studies of the week
  To rest at length give place;
Amusement now, instead of Greek,
  Fills up the little space.

In friendly groups the students sit
  Around the social fire;
While pleasant tales and harmless wit
  Their hearts with mirth inspire.

Some wander to yon towering hill,
  Or range the distant wood,
Or stray along some purling rill
  Near Charles's gentle flood.

Eas'd of their toils, they now prolong
  The pleasant healthful walk;
The hours unheeded steal along,
  Beguil'd by cheerful talk.

Others, with smart vivacious look,
  Brush'd coat and powder'd hair,
To see the world, or—buy a book,
  To Boston straight repair.

Some to a neighboring village ride
  To see a friend and dine;
While some the fleeting hours divide
  With songs, and chat, and wine.

Some while away the lazy time
  As cards or books invite;
While some, like me, too fond of rhyme,
  Rack their dull brains to write.

C A M.

For the MASSACHUSETTS MAGAZINE.

REFLECTIONS

On viewing the Seat of Jos. BARRELL, *Esq.*

WHERE once the breastwork mark'd
  the scenes of blood,
When freedom's sons inclos'd the haughty
  foe,
Rearing its head majestic from afar
The venerable seat of *Barrell* stands.

Like some strong English castle much it
  seems,
When the great Barons of the feudal
  times
Had num'rous vassals waiting their com-
  mand,
And each rais'd armies in his own do-
  main.
Those times for free urbanity were known,
And gen'rous hospitality renown'd.
The doors were ever open to the poor—
The wand'ring pilgrim was a welcome
  guest,
And found refreshment in the plenteous
  hall.
But—
Such is the wisdom of these later days,
Free hospitality's turn'd out of doors,
Among the meaner virtues; out of date
With all the rich and mighty of the earth.
Banish'd from courts and palaces long
  since,
It sought for refuge with the middle ranks,
And humbler walks of life. With these
  alone
The faint and weary traveller finds re-
  pose,
And hearty welcome to the lowly cell.
  The rich support the rich, but grind the
  poor,
And spurn the needy stranger from their
  gate.
True Christian charity dwells not with
  them,
Who, blest with plenty by a bounteous
  God,
Are stewards of his houshold, if aright
They use the goods which Providence
  hath giv'n.
But thou, whose stately castle overlooks
The briny wave to Boston's crowded
  shores,
And where yon bridge superb extends its
  length,
(That proudly seems, when tides o'erflow
  the Charles,
Across the ocean thrown)
Be thou excepted from the common herd
Of

Of felfifh, full blown opulence and pride.
Love thou the virtues that once deign'd
  to dwell
In ancient years, beneath a roof like thine.
And in defpite of modern won'dring eyes,
Bring back old fafhion'd cuftoms to our
  view,
The lib'ral train of virtues that adorn'd
The former ages of the Englifh realm.

        BLANDULUS.

For the MASSACHUSETTS MAGAZINE.

The SONGS

*of the five Bards, who fung by night : verfified
from the notes of M'Pherfon's Offian, by*

        LINUS.

NOW all the people to the hall repair :
  The foftly-founding fhells of feaft
  are there.
Ten harps are ftrung; five bards by turns
  declaim ;
And feek the glory of no vulgar name.
Their burning fouls they pour fourth in
  the fong,
While anfwering harps the melody pro-
  long.
Of night they fing : and cheer the feftive
  hall :
Their lays re-echo from the hollow wall.
While all the people filent fat around
The firft of bards thus raifed the filver
  found.

      FIRST BARD.

The hours of lonely night are dark and
  ftill :
The black clouds roll along the diftant
  hill.
No ftar with trembling beam appears on
  high ;
No moon looks fmiling from the azure fky.
I hear the blaft that hoarfely-fweeping
  moves :
But diftant far I hear it in the groves.
I hear the murmurs of the valley ftream ;
But lonely, fad, remote the murmurs feem.
From yonder yew where fleeps our fa-
  ther's clay,
The owl is heard long howling from the
  fpray.
I fee a dim form on the plain arife :
It is a ghoft ! Alas ! it fades—it dies,
Some folemn fun'ral foon fhall pafs yon
  road ;
Some pallid meteor points the dark a-
  bode.
  From yonder hut that tops the gray-
  browed height,
The furly houfe-dog bays the ghofts of
  night.

The ftag is on the mountain mofs reclined;
And at his fide fecurely refts the hind.
Shrill in her branchy horns the rough
  winds found,
She hears the noife and ftartles from the
  ground.
  The roe lies filent on the rocky hill ;
Beneath his wing the heath-cock hides
  his bill.
No wild beaft roves, no bird now flits the
  air ;
None but the owl and fox abroad appear.
She with her howl the gloomy foreft fills ;
He in a cloud bounds o'er the dufky hills.
Dark, panting, trembling, loft the travel-
  ler ftrays
O'er rugged heaths and unfrequented
  ways.
Thro' fhrubs, thro' thorns, along the gur-
  gling rill ;
Now in the vale, now on the cloudy hill.
He fears the fen and rock's ftupendous
  height ;
He fears the ghoft that wanders in the
  night.
The old tree groans beneath the angry
  gale ;
The falling branches found along the vale.
The furious winds that through the mead-
  ows pafs,
Drive the clung withered burs along the
  grafs.
Hark, hark, he fees a ghoft—his tread how
  light !
He looks, and trembling fears amidft the
  night.
  Now cold winds blow, and angry tem-
  pefts lower,
My friends receive me from this difmal
  hour.

      SECOND BARD.

The wind is up, the fhower defcends in
  ftreams,
The diftant fpirit of the mountain fcreams.
The tall firs fall, the tufted hut is torn,
The mifts divided o'er the hills are borne.
The tempeft howls, loud roar the falling
  woods,
And diftant far refound the growing
  floods.
To pafs the ford the weary trav'ler tries ;
Hark, hear that fhriek ! he falls, he finks,
  he dies.
  Swift pours the rain, the winds with fu-
  ry blow,
And from the hill defcends the horfe and
  cow :
They tremble as the dark'ning tempeft
  roars,
And dread the billows on the rocky fhores.

In his lone hut as loud the hoarse winds
    sweep,
The drowfy hunter startles from his fleep;
He wakes the fire: his wet dogs smoke a-
    round;
He fills with heath the chink; he hears
    the found
Of mountain streams that loud and fullen
    roar,
And meet and foam before his cottage
    door.
    Sad on the hill the wand'ring shepherd
    roves;
The trees refound; the streams roar thro'
    the groves.
He chides the lingering moon and bids it
    come
And lend her aid to guide him to his
    home.
Ghosts ride the clouds and wave their
    skirts behind:
Sweet is their voice between the fqualls of
    wind.
Of other worlds they fing: they mount
    on high
And guide the storm along the gloomy
    sky.
    The rain is past—streams roar—the dry
    winds blow—
The windows flap: the stars more bril-
    liant glow.
But, fee the darkning clouds again arife;
Gloomy and dread appear the western
    skies.
What dreadful tempests in the concave
    lower!
My friends, receive me from the midnight
    hour.
        THIRD BARD.
The fqually wind founds o'er the woody
    hill;
And thro' the graffy rock it whistles still.
The burning stars look thro' the broken
    cloud;
The melancholy ghosts scream wildly
    loud.
The meteor bright portending dreadful
    doom,
Flies sparkling thro' the folitary gloom;
Far in the bofom of the grove it dies,
No more to dance along the nightly skies.
    The withered fern, the dark brow'd
    rock I fee;
But who is shrouded underneath yon
    tree?
Now on the lake dark-tumbling billows
    roar,
And foam and lash upon the rocky shore.
The boat brimfull is floating to the land,
The broken oars are fcattered on the
    strand.

A maid fits fad beneath yon aged tree,
And kens the stream as far as eye can fee.
Her lover promifed that he'd meet her
    there;
She fits—she waits—but, fees no lover
    near.
Far on the lake she faw his light boat
    bound,
Ere night unfriendly spread her gloom a-
    round.
Is this his boat? Ah, yes: what groans I
    hear!
Are thefe his groans? Are thefe his oars?
    They are.
    Hear how the hail malignant rattles
    round;
The fnow defcends and whitens o'er the
    ground.
But now the storm is hushed; no hoarfe
    winds blow,
The clouds are fled, the hill-tops shine
    with fnow.
Such changing glooms the moonlefs night
    o'ercast;
My friends, receive me from the chilling
    blast.
        FOURTH BARD.
The night is starry, calm and fair and
    lone;
The howling winds with all their clouds
    are gone.
Juft o'er the hills appear their finking
    heads;
While the broad moon a filver twilight
    sheds.
The tall trees shine; the floods o'er rough
    rocks gleam;
Bright rolls the lake and bright the valley
    stream.
    I fee the corn o'erturn'd along the
    plain;
The wakeful hind rebuilds the shocks a-
    gain.
He marks what ruin had defpoil'd the
    groves;
And shrilly whistles as the field he roves.
    Settl'd and fair is night: its storms are
    fled;
Who comes refplendent from the mighty
    dead?
She comes with robes of fnow and bluthes
    fair;
With starry eyes, white arms and dark-
    brown hair!
Lo! 'tis the daughter of our mighty chief!
She comes! she comes! magnificent in
    grief!
Ah! let us view thee, daughter of the
    night!
Thou who haft been the Hero's chief de-
    light,

Before the blaft the empty phantom flies;
White without form, it mounts towards
   the fkies. -
  Now foftly breathes the foul-delighting
   gale,
And drives the mifts along the narrow
   vale :
It mounts the hill, and lifts its head on
   high,
And fhuts the bright moon from the
   wakeful eye.
The night is fettled, blue, ferene and
   bright,
My friends, receive me not from lovely
   night.
    (The remainder next month.)

To the Editors *of the* Maffachufetts Magazine.

GENTLEMEN,

*I do not remember to have feen Father Abbey's
Will publifhed in any late periodical work.—
It was compofed by Mr. Seccombe, formerly
minifter of Harvard, in this commonwealth,
and who lately died, at an advanced period of
life, in Nova-Scotia. I think it worth preferving in your magazine.*

FATHER ABBEY's WILL.

To which is added, a *letter* of *courtfhip* to
  his amiable and virtuous *widow.*

CAMBRIDGE, December, 1736.

" *Some time fince died here, Mr.* MATTHEW
ABBEY, *in a very advanced age : He had
for a great number of years ferved the college
in quality of* bed-maker *and* fweeper :
*Having no child, his wife inherits his whole
eftate, which he bequeathed to her by his laft
will and teftament, as follows, viz.*"

TO my dear wife,
  My joy and life,
I freely now do give her,
  My whole eftate,
  with all my plate,
Being juft about to leave her.

  My tub of fope,
  A long cart-rope,
A frying-pan and kettle,
  An afhes pail,
  A threfhing flail,
An iron wedge and beetle.

  Two painted chairs,
  Nine warden-pears,
A large old dripping platter,
  This bed of hay
  On which I lay,
An old fauce-pan for butter.

  A little mug,
  A two-quart jug,
A bottle full of brandy,

  A loooking-glafs,
  To fee your face,
You'll find it very handy.

  A mufket true,
  As ever flew,
A pound of fhot and wallet,
  A leather fafh,
  My calabafh,
My powder-horn and bullet,

  An old fword-blade,
  A garded fpade,
A hoe, a rake, a ladder,
  A wooden can,
  A clofe-ftool pan,
A clyfter-pipe and bladder.

  A greafy hat,
  My old ram-cat,
A yard and half of linen,
  A woolen fleece,
  A pot of greafe,
In order for your fpinning.

  A fmall-tooth comb,
  An afhen broom,
A candleftick and hatchet,
  A coverlid
  Strip'd down with red,
A bag of rags to patch it.

  A ragged mat,
  A tub of fat,
A book put out by *Bunyan,*
  Another book,
  By *Robin Cook,*
A fkein or two of fpun'yarn.

  An old black mufF,
  Some garden-ftuff,
A quantity of burage,
  Some devil's weed
  And burdock feed,
To feafon well your porridge.

  A chafing difh,
  With one falt-fifh,
If I am not miftaken,
  A leg of pork,
  A broken fork,
And half a flitch of bacon.

  A fpinning-wheel,
  One peck of meal,
A knife without a handle,
  A rufty lamp,
  Two quarts of famp,
And half a tallow candle.

  My pouch and pipes,
  Two oxen tripes,
An oaken difh well carved,
  My little dog,
  And fpotted hog,
With two young pigs juft ftarved.

  This is my ftore,
  I have no more,
I heartily do give it,

My years are spun,
My days are done,
And so I think to leave it.

Thus father ABBEY left his spouse,
As rich as church or college mouse,
Which is sufficient invitation,
To serve the college in his station.

"Newhaven, *Jan.* 1731. *Our sweeper
having lately buried his spouse, and hearing of the death and will of his deceased
Cambridge brother, has conceived a violent passion for the relict. As love softens
the mind and disposes to poetry, he has eased
himself in the following strains, which he
transmits to the charming widow, as the
first essay of his love and courtship.*"

MISTRESS Abbey,
To you I fly,
You only can re'eve me,
To you I turn,
For you I burn,
If you will but believe me.

Then gentle dame,
Admit my flame,
And grant me my petition;
If you deny,
Alas! I die,
In pitiful condition.

Before the news
Of your dear spouse
Had reach'd us at *Newhaven*,
My dear wife dy'd,
Who was my bride,
In anno eighty-seven.

Thus being free,
Let's both agree
To join our hands; for I do
Boldly aver
A widower
Is fittest for a widow.

You may be sure
'Tis not your dower
I make this flowing verse on;
In these smooth lays
I only praise
The glories of your person.

For the whole that
Was left by *Mat,*
Fortune to me has granted:
In equal store,
I've one thing more,
Which *Matthew* long had wanted.

No teeth, 'tis true,
You have to shew,
The young think teeth inviting,
But silly youths!
I love those mouths
Where there's no fear of biting.
Vol. VI.

A leaky eye,
That's never dry,
These woful times is fitting,
A wrinkled face
Adds solemn grace
To folks devout at meeting.

Thus to go on,
I would pen down
Your charms from head to foot,
Set all your glory
In verse before ye,
But I've no mind to do't.

Then haste away,
And make no stay,
For soon as you come hither,
We'll eat and sleep,
Make beds and sweep,
And smoke and talk together.

But if, my dear,
I must move there,
Tow'rds *Cambridge* strait I'll set me,
To towze the hay
On which you lay,
If age and you will let me.

Extracted for the MASSACHUSETTS MAG-
AZINE.
From a work lately published in Scotland.

To a MOUSE,
*On turning her up in her nest with the plough,
November, 1785.*

WEE sleek it, cowrin, tim'rous beas-
tie,
O, what a panic's in thy breastie!
Thou need na start awa sae hasty!
Wi bickering brattle!
I wad be laith to rin an' chace thee,
Wi mud'ring pattle.

I'm trully sorry man's dominion
Has broken Nature's social union,
An' justifies that ill opinion,
Which makes thee startle,
At me thy poor earth-born companion,
An' fellow-mortal!

I doubt na, whyles, but thou may thieve;
What then? poor beastie thou maun live!
A daimen icker in a thrave
'S a small request;
I'll get a blessin wi' the lave,
An never miss't!

Thy wee-bit housie, too, in ruin!
It's silly wa's the win's are strewin!
An' naething, now, to beg a new ane,
O' foggage green!
An' bleak December's winds ensuin,
Baith snell an' keen!

Thou saw the fields laid bare an' waste,
An' weary winter comin fast,
An'

An' cozie here, beneath the blaft,
    Thou thought to dwell,
Till crafh ! the cruel coulter paft
    Out thro' thy cell.

That wee-bit peap o' leaves an' ftibble,
Has coft the monie aweary nibble !
Now thou's turned out, for a' thy trouble,
    But houfe or hald,
To thole the winters fleety dribble,
    An' cranreuch cauld !

But, moufie, thou art no thy lane,
In proving *forefight* may be vain :
The beft laid fchemes o' mice an' men
    Gang aft a-gley,
An' lea'e us nought but grief an' pain
    For promis'd joy !

Still thou art bleft, compar'd wi' me ! .
The *prefent* only toucheth thee :
But Och'e I *backward* caft my e'e
    On profpects drear !
An' *forward* tho' I canna fee,
    I guefs an' fear !

Extracted from a Britifh publication.

SUNSET.

SOFT o'er the mountains purple brow
  Meek twilight draws her fhadows grey;
From tufted woods, and vallies low,
  Light's magic colours fteal away.
Yet ftill amid the fpreading gloom,
  Refplendent glow the weftern waves
That roll o'er Neptune's coral caves,
  A zone of light on ev'nings dome.
On this lone fummit let me reft,
  And view the forms to fancy dear,
'Till on the ocean's darken'd breaft
  The ftars of ev'ning tremble clear ;
Or the moon's pale orb appear,
  Throwing her line of radiance wide,
  Far o'er the lightly curling tide,
  That feems the yellow fands to chide.
No founds o'er filence now prevail,
  Save of the dying wave below,
Or failor's fong borne on the gale,
  Or oar at diftance ftriking flow.
So fweet ! fo tranquil ! may my ev'ning
    ray
Set to this world—and rife in future day !

LINES,

To the Memory of Dr. LEVETT. *By Doctor*
Johnfon.

CONDEMN'D to hope " delufive mine,
  As on we toil from day to day,
By fudden blafts or flow decline
  Our focial comforts drop away.

Well try'd through many a varying year,
  See Levett to the grave defcends,

Officious, innocent, fincere,
  Of ev'ry friendlefs name the friend.

Yet ftill he fills affection's eye,
  Obfcurely wife, and courtly kind ;
Nor lettered arrogance, deny
  Thy praife to merit unrefin'd.

When fainting nature call'd for aid,
  And hov'ring death prepar'd the blow,
His vigorous remedy difplay'd
  The power of art, without the fhow.

In myftery's darkeft caverns known,
  His ready help was always nigh,
Where hopelefs anguifh pour'd his groan,
  And lonely want retired to die.

No fummons mock'd by chill delay,
  No petty gain, difclaim'd by pride ;
The modeft wants of every day
  The toil of every day fupply.

His virtues walk their narrow round,
  Nor brade a horfe, nor left a void,
And fure th' Eternal Mafter found
  His fingle talent well employ'd.

The lovely day, the peaceful night,
  Unfelt, uncounted glided by ;
His frame was firm, his powers were
    bright,
Though now his eightieth year was
    nigh.

When, with no throbs of fiery pain
  No cold grandations of decay,
Death broke at once the vital chain,
  And freed his foul the neareft way.

Extracted from a Britifh publication.

NIGHT.

O'ER the dim breaft of ocean's wave
  Night fpreads afar her gloomy wings,
And penfive thought and filence brings,
Save where the diftant waters lave ;
  Or where the mariner's lone voice
Swells faintly on the paffing gale,
  Or when the fcreaming fea-gulls poife
O'er the tall maft, and fwelling fail.
Bounding the gray gleam of the deep,
  Where fancy'd forms aroufe the mind.
  Dark fweep the fhores, on whofe rude
    fteep
Sighs the fad fpirit of the wind.
  Sweet is its voice upon the air
At ev'nings melancholy clofe,
While the fmooth wave in filence flows !
  Sweet, fweet the peace it's ftealing ac-
    cents bear !
Bleft be thy fhades, O Night ! and bleft the
    fong
Thy low winds breathe the diftant fhore
    along !

MONTHLY

MONTHLY GAZETTE.

Summary of Foreign Intelligence.

PRUSSIA.

BERLIN, *Aug.* 9.

HOWEVER certain it feems that the Poles will not be able to make a long refiftance againft the combined forces of Pruffia, the unexpected delay in military operations, occafioned by the backwardnefs of the Pruffians, is accompanied by many inconveniences, at leaft difagreeable, if not fatal to the Pruffian army. Private letters complain not only of the extreme dearth of all neceffaries, but alfo of a real fcarcity of provifions in the Pruffian camp, which is fuffering for want of good water. A great number of the Pruffian troops have died with the dyfentery; and the prince of Pruffia himfelf was attacked by this ficknefs, but is now recovered.

THORN, *Aug.* 16. The entrenched camp of Kofciufko, before Warfaw, confifts properly of four camps, whofe beginning and end touch upon the Viftula, and from whence they fire very brifkly, one of their fix pounders having the kitchen tent of the King of Pruffia.—Kofciufko himfelf is in Mokawto, and has Madufifky with him, and the generals Dambrowfky, Mokronowfky and Zagazeek, command under him in the camps. Above the river Bux, the Poles took from the Pruffians a whole bridge of Pontoons, and upwards of 100 oxen. The Pruffian colonel Tolftoy, who paffed thro' here for the Pruffian camp, informs, that the Pruffian Prince Repni is marching 40,000 men into Poland. A report that the Pruffians had taken Wilna by ftorm, and with the lofs of a great many men on both fides, wants confirmation. Another report, that the Turks had made an attack upon Cammieck, is totally groundlefs.

HOLLAND.

HAGUE, *Aug.* 12. The ftates of Holland, who muft contribute more than two thirds towards the whole expenfes of the war, and the exigencies of the republic in general, have declared anew, on the laft inft. that they will facrifice life and property in the defence of the Republic, and therefore have adopted two new means of finances, having opened, (befide the loans of laft year and this year, which remain open) a new voluntary and unlimitted loan at 5 per cent. intereft, where bullion, and manufactured filver and gold will be accepted.—The ftates moreover, declare their full expectation, that every inhabitant will richly contribute towards it.

DOMESTIC MISCELLANY.

An account of the political ftate of feveral of the powers of the ELDER WORLD.

Of CHINA—The American public cannot be indifferent to the commercial events in fo vaft and rich an empire as that of China, which contains 50,000,000 inhabitants, and abounds with every article of commercial traffic. We are therefore happy in informing, that the fplendid embaffy of Lord Macartney, from the Britifh court to the Emperor of China, has completely failed of fuccefs, and that his Lordfhip has returned to England. The object of this embaffy was to effect, as far as poffible, a monopoly of the trade of China with the Chriftian world, to the Britifh flag. To give weight to the embaffy, Lord Macartney carried with him the moft valuable prefents, which the wealth, ingenuity and workmanfhip of England would produce. To thefe were added immenfe gifts from the Indian powers fubordinate to the 'Eaft India company. Thefe valuables, as was to be expected, where cordially received by the Chinefe Emperor; who in return gave the Ambaffador feveral fets of china, and prefents of tapeftry and filks, but fet his face againft any acquiefcence in the commercial propofitions made by his Lordfhip. Thus ended the miffion, to the fatisfaction, no doubt, of the mercantile world.—Americans particularly muft feel happy in the picture of a fpeculation, which might materially have affected a confiderable portion of their commerce.—

In

In Canton, the American flag is admitted on the same conditions as the most favored nation. And here we cannot help mentioning, that to their so favorable admission, the United States are much indebted to the exertions of our late fellow townsman, *Samuel Shaw, Esq.* when Consul in China.

Of TURKEY.—To the Ottoman empire, the politics of which are so often affected by the contests of Europe, and the ambition of the sovereigns, some attention must be given. A rupture between it and Russia has been for some time expected; as not long since the Russian Ambassador at Constantinople delivered an official note to the Turkish Res Effendi, in which the empress demands, "That *the Porte should not intermeddle with the affairs of Poland: that it should grant a free passage to Russian frigates thro' the canal of Constantinople, and that it should treat with less rigor, the Greek princes and subjects of Moldavia and Wallachia.*" The Grand Signior answered these demands with firmness, refused compliance therewith, and declared he would not suffer any foreign power to interfere either in the external or internal affairs of the empire. Finding the Turkish government thus determined, the Russian relaxed in his demands; and from the tone of the communications which have since passed, there is a probability of the continuation of peace for some time: But neither the policy nor the interest of the Ottoman court can be reconciled to the annihilation of the independence of Poland. A considerable naval equipment has been made in Turkey—The Turkish government having admitted an ambassador from the French republic, a correspondence has taken place between the Res Effendi and the British minister on the subject. But in the answers of the Turk, a determination appears to support the independence and neutrality of the Porte. The French have been allowed to celebrate a national festival.

Of POLAND.

This Republic interests every friend to liberty and national justice. The American reader has already learnt by what " indirect and crooked ways" the voracious Empress of Russia, and the perfidious Frederick William, of Prussia, have conspired to cut it up, and bring it under despotic sway. Tired of reiterated usurpations, and roused by repeated insults, the gallant Poles, with a patriot king, and a virtuous nobility at their head, have risen in arms, to oppose their oppressors. They have called to their chief command, the intrepid Kosciusko, the pupil of *Washington,* and the brave defender of the liberties of America. They have formed a revolutionary government, and altho' at the moment of their rising, some excesses were committed at Warsaw, they appear nevertheless to have adopted those principles of government which are most likely to effect their leading object, the independence and liberty of Poland.—Success and disaster have alternately awaited their military operations. On one side they have to contend with the numerous troops of Russia, while on the other they are assailed by the veterans of Prussia; the latter headed by their king, have advanced to the vicinity of Warsaw; (some accounts say, they have actually bombarded the city) before which the brave Kosciusko lies with his army; and the king of Prussia has summoned the unfortunate Stanislaus to surrender.

CONGRESS.
House of Representatives, Nov. 19.

This day, at 12 o'clock, The President of the United States met both houses of the legislature, in the hall of the house of representatives, and delivered the following ADDRESS.

Fellow-citizens of the senate, and of
the house of representatives,

WHEN we call to mind the gracious indulgence of heaven, by which the American people became a nation; when we survey the general prosperity of our country, and look forward to the riches, power, and happiness, to which it seems destined; with the deepest regret do I announce to you, that, during your recess, some of the citizens of the United States, have been found capable of an insurrection. It is due, however, to the character of our government, and to its stability, which cannot be shaken by the enemies of order, freely to unfold the course of this event.

During the session of the year 1790, it was expedient to exercise the legislative power granted by the constitution of the United States, " to lay and collect excises." In a majority of the states, scarcely an objection was heard to this mode of taxation. In some, indeed, alarms were at first conceived, until they were banished by reason and patriotism. In the four western counties of Pennsylvania, a prejudice, fostered and embittered by the artifice of men, who labored

labored for an afcendancy over the will of others, by the guidance of their paffions, produced fymptoms of riot and violence. It is well known, that congrefs did not hefitate to examine the complaints which were prefented, and to relieve them, as far as juftice dictated, or general convenience would permit. But the impreffion which this moderation made on the difcontented, did not correfpond with what it deferved; the arts of delufion were no longer continued to the efforts of defigning individuals.

The very forbearance to prefs profecutions, was mifinterpreted into a fear of urging the execution of the laws; and affociations of men began to denounce threats againft the officers employed.—From a belief that, by a more formal concert, their operation might be defeated, certain felf-created focieties affumed the tone of condemnation. Hence, while the greater part of Pennfylvania itfelf were conforming themfelves to the acts of excife, a few counties were refolved to fruftrate them. It was now perceived, that every expectation, from the tendernefs which had hitherto been pur ued, was unavailing, and that further delay could only create an opinion of impotency, or irrefolution in the government. Legal procefs, was, therefore, delivered to the marfhal, againft the rioters and delinquent diftillers.

No fooner was he underftood to be engaged in this duty, than the vengeance of armed men was aimed at his perfon, and the perfonal property of the infpector of the revenue. They fired upon the marfhal, arrefted him, and detained him for fome time as a prifoner. He was obliged, by the jeopardy of his life, to renounce the fervice of other procefs, on the weft fide of the Alleghany mountain; and a deputation was afterwards fent to him to demand a furrender of that which he had ferved. A numerous body repeatedly attacked the houfe of the infpector, feized his papers of office, and finally deftroyed, by fire, his buildings, and whatfoever they contained. Both of thefe officers, from a juft regard to their fafety, fled to the feat of government; it being avowed, that the motives of fuch outrages were, to compel the refignation of the infpector; to withftand, by the force of arms, the authority of the United States, and thereby to extort a repeal of the laws of excife, and an alteration in the conduct of government.

Upon the teftimony of thefe facts, an affociate juftice of the United States notified to me, that, " in the counties of Wafhington and Alleghany, in Pennfylvania, laws of the United States were oppofed, and the execution thereof obftructed, by combinations, too powerful to be fuppreffed by the ordinary courfe of judicial proceedings, or by the powers vefted in the marfhal of that diftrict."—On this call, momentous in the extreme, I fought and weighed what might beft fubdue the crifis. On the one hand, the judiciary was pronounced to be ftripped of its capacity to enforce the laws: crimes, which reached the very exiftence of focial order, were perpetrated without control, the friends of government were infulted, abufed, and over-awed into filence, or an apparent acquiefcence; and to yield to the treafonable fury of fo fmall a portion of the United States, would be to violate the fundamental principle of our conftitution, which enjoins, that the will of the majority fhall prevail. On the other, to array citizen againft citizen—to publifh the difhonor of fuch exceffes—to encounter the expenfe, and other embarraffments of fo diftant an expedition, were fteps too delicate—too clofely interwoven with many affecting confiderations, to be lightly adopted. I poftponed, therefore, the fummoning the militia immediately into the field: but I required them to be held in readinefs, that if my anxious endeavors to reclaim the deluded, and to convince the malignant of their danger, fhould be fruitlefs, military force might be prepared to act, before the feafon fhould be too far advanced.

My proclamation of the 7th of Auguft laft, was accordingly iffued, and accompanied by the appointment of commiffioners, who were charged to repair to the fcene of infurrection. They were authorifed to confer with any bodies of men or individuals. They were inftructed to be candid and explicit, in ftating the fenfations which had been excited in the executive, and his earneft wifh to avoid a refort to coercion; to reprefent, however, that without fubmiffion, coercion muft be the refort; but to invite them, at the fame time, to return to the demeanor of faithful citizens, by fuch accommodations as lay within the fphere of the executive power—pardon, too, was tendered to them by the government of the United States, and that of Pennfylvania; upon no other condition, than a fatisfactory affurance of obedience to the laws.

Although

Although the report of the commissioners marks their firmness and abilities, and must unite all virtuous men, by shewing that the means of conciliation have been exhausted; all of those who had committed, or abetted the tumults, did not subscribe the mild form, which was proposed, as the atonement; and the indications of a peaceable temper were neither sufficiently general, nor conclusive to recommend or warrant a further suspension of the march of the militia.

Thus, the painful alternative could not be discarded. I ordered the militia to march, after once more admonishing the insurgents, in my proclamation of the 25th of September last.

It was a task, too difficult to ascertain with precision, the lowest degree of force competent to the quelling of the insurrection. From a respect, indeed, to economy, and the ease of my fellow-citizens, belonging to the militia, it would have gratified me to accomplish such an estimate. My very great reluctance to ascribe too much importance to the opposition, had its extent been accurately seen, would have been a decided inducement to the smallest efficient numbers. In this uncertainty, therefore, I put into motion fifteen thousand men, as being an army, which, according to all human calculation, would be prompt, and adequate in every view, and might perhaps by rendering resistance desperate, prevent the effusion of blood. Quotas had been assigned to the states of New-Jersey, Pennsylvania, Maryland and Virginia; the governor of Pennsylvania having declared, on this occasion, an opinion which justified a requisition to the other states.

As commander in chief of the militia, when called into the actual service of the United States, I have visited the places of general rendezvous, to obtain more exact information, and to direct a plan for ulterior movements. Had there been room for a persuasion that the laws were secure from obstruction—that the civil magistrate was able to bring to justice such of the most culpable as have not embraced the proffered terms of amnesty, and may be deemed fit objects of example; that the friends of peace and good government were not in need of that aid and countenance which they ought always to receive, and I trust, ever will receive against the vicious and turbulent, I should have caught with avidity the opportunity of restoring the militia to their families and home. But succeeding intelligence has tended to manifest the necessity of what has been done; it being now confessed, by those who were not inclined to exaggerate the ill conduct of the insurgents, that their malevolence was not pointed merely to a particular law; but that a spirit, inimical to all order, has actuated many of the offenders. If the state of things had afforded reason for the continuance of my presence with the army, it would not have been withholden: but every appearance assuring such an issue as will redound to the reputation and strength of the United States—I have judged it most proper to resume my duties at the seat of government, leaving the chief command with the governor of Virginia.

Still, however, as it is probable, that in a commotion like the present, whatsoever may be the pretence, the purposes of mischief and revenge may not be laid aside; the stationing of a small force, for a certain period, in the four western counties of Pennsylvania, will be indispensable, whether we contemplate the situation of those who are connected with the execution of the laws or of others, who may have exposed themselves by an honorable attachment to them.

Thirty days from the commencement of this session, being the legal limitation of the employment of the militia, congress cannot be too early occupied with this subject.

Among the discussions, which may arise from this aspect of our affairs, and from the documents which will be submitted to congress, it will not escape their observation, that not only the inspector of the revenue, but other officers of the United States in Pennsylvania, have—from their fidelity in the discharge of their functions, sustained material injuries to their property. The obligation and policy of indemnifying them, are strong and obvious. It may also merit attention, whether policy will not enlarge this provision to the retribution of our citizens, who, though not under the ties of office, may have suffered damage by their generous exertions for upholding the constitution and the laws. The amount, even if all the injured were included, would not be great; and on future emergencies, the government would be amply repaid by the influence of an example, that he, who incurs a loss in its defence, shall find a recompense in its liberality.

While there is cause to lament that occurrences

currences of this nature should have disgraced the name, or interrupted the tranquility, of any part of our community, or should have diverted to a new application, any portion of the public resources, there are not wanting real and substantial consolations for the misfortune. It has demonstrated that our prosperity rests on solid foundations ; by furnishing an additional proof, that my fellow-citizens understand the true principles of government and liberty ; that they feel their inseparable union, that, notwithstanding all the devices that have been made use of to sway them from their interest and duty, they are now as ready to maintain the authority of the laws against licentious invasions, as they were to defend their rights against usurpation. It has been a spectacle, displaying to the highest advantage the value of republican government, to behold the most and least wealthy of our citizens standing in the same ranks as private soldiers ; pre-eminently distinguishing, by being the army of the constitution ; undeterred by a march of three hundred miles over rugged mountains, by the approach of an inclement season, or by any other discouragement. Nor ought I to omit to acknowledge the efficacious and patriotic co-operation which I have experienced from the chief magistrates of the states to which my requisitions have been addressed.

To every description, indeed, of citizens, let praise be given ; but let them persevere in their affectionate vigilance over that precious depository of American happiness, the constitution of the United States. Let them cherish it too, for the sake of those, who, from every clime, are daily seeking a dwelling in our land. And when, in the calm moments of reflection, they shall have retraced the origin and progress of the insurrection, let them determine, whether it has not been fomented by combinations of men, who, careless of consequences, and disregarding the unerring truth, that those, who rouse, cannot always appease a civil convulsion, have disseminated, from an ignorance or perversion of facts, suspicions, jealousies, and accusations of the whole government.

Having thus fulfilled the engagement which I took, when I entered into office, " to the best of my ability to preserve, protect and defend the constitution of the United States," on you, gentlemen, and the people by whom you are deputed, I rely for support.

In the arrangements to which the possibility of a similar contingency will naturally draw your attention, it ought not to be forgotten, that the militia laws have exhibited such striking defects, as could not have been supplied but by the zeal of our citizens. Besides the extraordinary expense, and waste, which are not the least of the defects ; every appeal to those laws is attended with a doubt on its success.

The devising and establishing of a well regulated militia, would be a genuine source of legislative honor, and a perfect title to public gratitude. I therefore, entertain a hope, that the present session will not pass, without carrying to its full energy, the power of organizing, arming and disciplining the militia ; and thus providing, in the language of the constitution, for calling them forth to execute the laws of the union, suppress insurrection, and repel invasion.

As auxiliary to the state of our defence, to which congress cannot too frequently recur, they will not omit to inquire whether the fortifications which have been already licensed by law, be commensurate with our exigencies.

The intelligence from the army under the command of General WAYNE, is a happy presage to our military operations against the hostile Indians north of the Ohio. From the advices which have been forwarded, the advance he has made must have damped the ardor of the savages, and weakened their obstinacy in waging war against the United States, and yet, even at this late hour, when our power to punish them cannot be questioned, we shall not be unwilling to cement a lasting peace, upon terms of candor, equity, and good neighborhood.

Towards none of the Indian tribes have overtures of friendship been spared. The Creeks in particular are covered from encroachment by the interposition of the general government, and that of Georgia. From a desire also to remove the discontents of the six nations, a settlement, meditated at Presq' Isle, on Lake Erie, has been suspended ; and an agent is now endeavoring to rectify any misconceptions into which they may have fallen. But I cannot refrain from again pressing upon your deliberations, the plan which I recommended at the last session, for the improvement of harmony within our limits, by the fixing and conducting of trading houses, upon the principles then expressed.

Gentlemen

Gentlemen of the house of representatives,

The time which has elapsed since the commencement of our fiscal measures, has developed our pecuniary resources, so as to open a way for a definitive plan for the redemption of our public debt. It is believed, that the result is such as to encourage congress to consummate this work without delay. Nothing can more promote the permanent welfare of the nation, and nothing would be more grateful to our constituents. Indeed, whatsoever is unfinished of our system of public credit, cannot be benefitted by procrastination, and as far as may be practicable, we ought to place that credit on grounds which cannot be disturbed, and to prevent that progressive accumulation of debt, which must ultimately endanger all governments.

An estimate of the necessary appropriations, including the expenditures into which we have been driven by the insurrection, will be submitted to congress.

Gentlemen of the senate, and of the house of representatives,

The mint of the United States has entered upon the coinage of the precious metals, and considerable sums of defective coins and bullion have been lodged with the director by individuals. There is a pleasing prospect, that the institution will, at no remote day, realize the expectation which was originally formed of its utility.

In subsequent communications, certain circumstances of our intercourse with foreign nations, will be transmitted to congress; however, it may not be unseasonable to announce, that my policy, in our foreign transactions, has been, to cultivate peace with all the world—To observe treaties with pure and absolute faith—to check every deviation from the line of impartiality—to explain what may have been misapprehended—and correct what may have been injurious to any nation; and having thus acquired the right, to lose no time in acquiring the ability, to insist upon justice being done ourselves.

Let us unite, therefore, in imploring the Supreme Ruler of nations, to spread his holy protection over these United States, return the machinations of the wicked to the confirming of our constitution—to enable us at all times to root out internal sedition, and put invasion to flight—to perpetuate to our country that prosperity which his goodness has already conferred, and to verify the anticipations of this

government being a safeguard to human rights.

GEO. WASHINGTON.
United States, Nov. 19, 1794.

MARRIAGES.

MASSACHUSETTS.—*Boston,* Mr. Simon Hastings to Miss Mindwell Andrews; Mr. Joseph Balch to Miss Hannah Pope; Capt. Ezekiel Burroughs to Miss Sally Torry; Mr. Joseph Bond, of Watertown, to Miss Ruth Chittendon, of Scituate.

Dorchester, Mr. John Clapp, of Roxbury, to Miss Sukey Robins of Dorchester.

Hingham, Mr. Zeabilon Hall to Miss Patty Beals.

Salem, Mr. John Kettle, of Danvers, to Mrs. Ann Smith of Beverly.

Springfield, Mr. Pelatiah Bliss to Miss Polly Stebbins.

Watertown, Mr. John Williams to Miss Rhoda Willington.

Kittery, Mr. Joseph Keen to Miss Hannah Berald.

NEW-HAMPSHIRE.—*Concord,* Lieut. Ebenezer Durton to Miss Betsey Bryant.

Portsmouth, Mr. Joseph Dearborn to Miss Sally Seavey; Mr. Robert Oliver to Miss Mary Rand; Mr. John Libbey to Miss Comfort Noble; Mr. George Ham to Miss Joanna Beck; Mr. Walter Weeks to Miss Sarah Talton.

NEW-YORK.—Mr. Benjamin Shaw, of Boston, to Miss Charity Smith.

DEATHS.

MASSACHUSETTS.—*Boston,* Capt. John Phillips, late of Canada, 58; Mrs. Mary Phillips, Mr. John Armstrong, 46; Mrs. Eunice Walner, 87; Mrs. Hannah Baxter 67; Mrs. Mary Gore, 39; Miss Hannah White, 22; Mrs. Sarah Sweetzer, 83.

Ipswich, Mr. Benjamin Fellows.

Shrewsbury, Mr. Simeon Parker.

RHODE-ISLAND.—*Cumberland,* Mr. E. Dexter.

Warren, Dr. Isaac Barras, 34.

VERMONT.—*Currituck,* Col. Hollowell Williams and his Lady.

CONNECTICUT.—*Hartford,* Miss Sally Olcot.

Norfolk, Capt. W. Bell.

VERMONT.—*Nansemond,* Solomon Shepherd, Esq.

PENNSYLVANIA.—*Philadelphia,* Mr. Samuel Downe, of the yellow fever.

Between Forts HAMILTON and RECOVERY, by the Indians, Mr. Elliot.

WEST-INDIES, Mr. John Adams, 23, son of Mr. Elijah Adams of this town.

THE

MASSACHUSETTS MAGAZINE:

OR,

MONTHLY MUSEUM

OF

KNOWLEDGE and RATIONAL *ENTERTAINMENT.*

No. XII.] FOR DECEMBER, 1794. [Vol. VI.

CONTAINING,

WITH TWO HANDSOME ENGRAVINGS.

PRINTED AT *BOSTON*, FOR THE PROPRIETORS,
BY EZRA W. WELD AND WILLIAM GREENOUGH,
No. 42, CORNHILL.
Sold at JOHN WEST's Bookstore, No. 75, *Cornhill*, BOSTON ; and by the several GENTLEMEN who receive Subscriptions for this WORK.

MDCCXCIV,

TO THE PUBLIC.

THE Proprietors of the MASSACHUSETTS MAGAZINE, for a confiderable increafe of patronage, during the year, fince they purchafed the copyright of their predeceffors, feel grateful to the liberality of a literary community. At the fame time, they regret, that the remiffnefs of their fubfcribers, at a diftance from the metropolis, the appreciation of journey-work, and the enhanced price of paper, will neceffitate them to omit the publication of the Magazine, for three months after the completion of the prefent volume. This interval, they flatter themfelves, will enable them to collect their outftanding debts, and to revive their Monthly Mufeum, on an improved plan, which fhall more equally repay *them* for their *labour*, and the *public* for its *patronage*.

PRICES OF PUBLIC SECURITIES, BANK STOCK, &c.

December.	Six per Cents.	Three per Cents.	Defer'd Stock.	Maffachuf. State Notes.	U.S.B. Shares. ab. par.	Maffachuf. Bank Shares.	Union Bank Shares. ab. pr.	Final & L. Of. Cert.inter.fr. Jan. 1788.	Reg. Dt. with int.fr. March 4, 1789.	Indents. Int. on Loan Offi. Cer. & Reg. Dt.	New Emiffion Money.	O. Emif. Mo.
	s. d.	s. d.	s. d.	s. d.	per ct.	dols.	per ct.	s. d.	s. d.	s. d.	s. d.	s.
1	20	11 4	13 2	16	32	None	11	19 0	17 6	10 6	8 0	45
2	20	11 4	13 2	16	32	at	11	19 0	17 6	10 6	8 0	45
3	20	11 4	13 2	16	32	mkt.	11	19 0	17 6	1c 6	8 0	45
4	20	11 4	13 2	16	32		11	19 0	17 6	10 6	8 0	45
5	20	11 4	13 2	16	32		11	19 0	17 6	10 6	8 0	45
6	20	11 4	13 2	16 1	32		11	19 0	17 6	10 6	8 0	45
8	20	11 4	13 2	16 1	31		11	19 0	17 6	10 6	8 0	45
9	20	11 4	13 2	16 1	31		11	19 0	17 6	10 6	8 0	45
10	20	11 4	13 2	16 2	31		12	19 0	17 6	10 6	8 0	45
11	19 10	11 3	13	16 2	30		12	19 0	17 6	10 6	8 0	45
12	19 10	11 3	13	16 2	30		12	19 0	17 6	10 6	8 0	45
13	19 10	11 3	13	16 2	30		12	19 0	17 6	10 6	8 0	45
15	19 10	11 3	13	16 3	30		12	19 0	17 6	10 6	8 0	45
16	19 10	11 3	13	16 3	30		12	19 0	17 6	10 6	8 0	45
17	19 10	11 3	13	16 3	30		12	19 0	17 6	10 6	8 0	45
18	19 10	11 3	13	16 3	30		12	19 0	17 6	10 6	8 0	45
19	19 10	11 3	13	16 3	30		12	19 0	17 6	10 6	8 0	45
20	19 10	11 3	13	16 3	30		12	19 0	17 6	10 6	8 0	45
22	19 4	11	12 9	16 3	30		12	19 0	17 6	10 6	8 0	45
23	19 4	11	12 9	16 3	30		12	19 0	17 6	10 6	8 0	45
24	19 4	11	12 9	16 3	30		12	19 0	17 6	10 6	8 0	45
25	19 4	11	12 9	16 3	30		12	19 0	17 6	10 6	8 0	45
26	19 4	11	12 9	16 3	30		12½	19 0	17 6	10 6	8 c	45
27	19 4	11	12 9	16 3	30		12½	19 0	17 6	10 6	8 0	45
29	19 4	11	12 9	16 3	30		12½	19 0	17 6	10 6	8 0	4 5
30	19 4	11	12 9	16 3	30		13	19 0	17 6	10 6	8 0	4 5
31	19 4	11	12 9	16 3	30		13	19 0	17 6	10 6	8 0	4 5

JOHN MARSTON, *Stock Broker.*

WINTER.

THE
MASSACHUSETTS MAGAZINE.
FOR *DECEMBER*, 1794.

W I N T E R.

[The annexed PLATE is an emblematical reprefentation of WINTER.]

THE wifdom and the power of the great Architect of the univerfe are not more confpicuous, in the worlds, which to the aftronomer's view, rife on world, than is his goodnefs in the fupport furnifhed for the creatures that inhabit the earth. The natural caufes, which occafion the froft and the ftorms of winter, give all the inhabitants of the earth, in turn, the beauties of Spring, the warmth of Summer, and the bounty of Autumn. Should the prefiding Deity withdraw his hand from the fyftem of nature, the heavenly bodies would interfere, and the beautiful ftructure of the folar fyftem would return to its former chaos. Should the earth meet with obftruction in its diurnal motion, we might be fcorched with the inftant blaze of the fun, or left in perpetual froft and darknefs. But uniform is the operation of the great principle of nature, benevolent is its Author, and with devout gratitude we may exclaim, Allelujah, the Lord God emnipotent reigneth.

" Nature! great parent! whofe unceafing hand

Rolls round the feafons of the changeful year,

How mighty, how majeftic are thy works!

With what a pleafing dread they fwell the foul!

That fees aftonifh'd! and aftonifh'd fings!

Winter, that apparently is the deftruction of vegetable life, fertilizes the ground.

" At prefent the earth is buried under ice and fnow—the inhabitants of the foreft howl more hideoufly—the wild beafts are preffed with hunger, the whole world appears dead : But under this appearance of death, God watches over fainting nature, and calls to exiftence things which are not yet in being."

Remember, ye wealthy and affluent, the fons and daughters of affliction and diftrefs ! Think of thofe, into whofe fhattered dwellings poverty enters to increafe the inclemency and the horrors of the prefent feafon. Diftribute bread to the hungry, and clothes to the naked.

Be

the minifters of heaven to the
or and the forrowful, God will
cept the tribute as the moft pleaf-
ng facrifice, and the bleffing of
thofe who were ready to perifh fhall
come upon you———

————————"Thought fond man
Of thefe, and all the thoufand namelefs ills,
That one inceffant ftruggle render life,
One fcene of toil, of fuff'ring, and of fate,
Vice in his high career would ftand ap-
    pall'd,
And heedlefs, rambling Impulfe, lean to
    think ;
The confcious heart of Charity would
    warm,
And her wide foul Benevolence dilate;
The focial tear would rife, the focial figh;
And into clear perfection, gradual blifs,
Refining ftill, the focial paffions work."

As pafs the feafons of the year,
fo pafs the periods of human life.
" 'Tis done ! dread winter fpreads his lat-
    eft glooms,
And reigns tremendous o'er the conquer'd
    year.

How dead the vegetable kingdom lies !
How dumb the tuneful ! Horror wide ex-
    tends
His defolate domain. Behold, fond man !
See here thy pictur'd life ; pafs fome few
    years,
Thy flow'ring fpring, thy fummer's ardent
    ftrength,
The fober autumn fading into age,
And pale, concluding winter comes at laft,
And fhuts the fcene. Ah, whither now
    are fled
Thofe dreams of greatnefs ? thofe unfolid
    hopes
Of happinefs ? thofe longings after fame ?
Thofe reftlefs cares ? thofe bufy buftling
    days ?
Thofe gay fpent, feftive nights ? thofe veer-
    ing thoughts,
Loft between good and ill, that fhar'd thy
    life ?
All now are vanifh'd. Virtue fole fur-
    vives,
Immortal, never failing friend of man,
His guide to happinefs on high.

For the MASSACHUSETTS MAGAZINE.
The INVESTIGATOR. No. V.

The tune of my Colin, has ceas'd
  To roufe up the fmile of content ;
He once had my forrow appeas'd,
  But now can no forrow prevent.

I feel that my riches are gone,
  I know that my Colin is poor;
Then how can my nature be fhown,
  When poverty knoc at the door?

When the poor little child of defpair,
  All naked and wretched appears,
With form, that's enchantingly fair,
  Yet wafh'd with the tide of her tears.

But, ah, I have nothing to give ;
  Yet, how can I turn her away ?
How fee the fweet innocent grieve ?
  Or hear fhe is gone to decay.

WHILE we allow *keen fenfibility* to be one of the fineft
and moft amiable traits in the character of man ; one of the greateft
ources of benevolence and humanity ; we muft, though ever fo unwilling, pronounce the caufe of
wretchednefs and affliction to many
f its poffefors. It is an indubitable fact recorded in legible characters on the death-roll of every nation.

May we not with propriety, in
our reflections on human nature,
fet it down as a matter of doubt
which is the happieft of the two ;
the man who poffeffes a delicate
formation of nerves, who melts at
the

the tale of forrow; fhudders at the found of affliction, and as far as in him lies, pours the oil of confolation into the wounds of mifery; or the man, who jogs on through life with honefty and good nature for his companions; though little affected at any, fave his own bodily infirmities, yet willing, if neceffity required, to lend a liitt " in helping a fallen brother, but awkward at weeping with the child of fenfibility, and willing to bear the appellation of phlegmatic? Some, at firft view, may be led to pronounce in favour of the former, and even allege it is beyond a doubt, that he is he happieft." To fuch we would recommend the ftudy of human nature, and a dofe of reflection which like elixir-afmatic has, hapily, the power of quieting the nerves of inconfiderate impetuofity and of flopping the mouth of impudent folly.

Th pleafure of that man, whofe every eeling is alive, being founded o a peculiarity of incidents; beingclofely connected with the fituaon and circumftances of thofe arourd him, and particularly dependit on the intereft he poffeffes; that very little occurrence affects him materially. If he fees an obº charity, his happinefs depends upon alleviating his mifery; the accomplifhment of which is not optional, but dependent on the property of him, who has a defire to beftow. Now, if he is poor, he will neo only have the pain, which arifes fom viewing a fellow mortal in direfs, but the reflection of his impoffility to affift him.

The fatisfiction and delight he experiences, b they ever fo great, are of fo nice nd frail a nature, fo peculiarly metal, that the clofet of retirement ims to be the chief place of enjoyrnt. His paffing

by a fcene of riot and diffipati (if a man of morality,) upon i return from vifiting an expirin wretch, whom he had in vain attempted to relieve; muft awake in his mind fenfations truly diftreffing; fuch fenfations, as the clofet, inftead of diminifhing, would greatly increafe.

An inadvertent remark on fome character prefent, though contrary to the knowledge of the man of feeling; a remark trivial in itfelf, feparate from its being made on a character, fuppofed to be abfent, would unfit him for the pleafure of the fociety he was in, and afford ample reflection for the night enfuing.

The phlegmatic perfon, though he does not poffefs thefe finer feelings, is far from being brutal, ftupid, or unthoughtful. The above mentioned incidents, it is true, affect him, but not fo materially; they do not raife that difquietude in his mind, which operates fo powerfully on the other, but give a pang like the electric fhock, which is foon over. The time, which the other fpends in viewing the minute occurrences of nature; he occupies in furveying the grand and mighty whole. His ideas are certainly more enlarged, though perhaps not fo correct; while the other is gazing his life-time on a fingle planet, to trace out the finger of Deity, he looks on the fea, earth and heavenly bodies, with rapture and aftonifhment, as the works of God.

Though the pleafures of the phlegmatic are not fo delicate and refined, they are more fubftantial, and unaccompanied with that anxiety, which gives a zeft to thofe of the man of feeling. Is he not as beneficial to his neighbours as the former? They are generally of the fame caft with himfelf: Now, if he

ch I think is beyond a doubt,
is valuable a member of society.
he endearments of life to him
ar greater : he feels more con-
ed with his condition ; for it is
that he expects his greatest enjoyments ; the most solid happiness,
and the only corporal pleasure.
As to honesty and religion, they
have an equal claim, for they are
by no means connected with either,
that is, it does not require honesty
or religion to make a man keenly
sensible, or truly phlegmatic. It is
true he has an idea of heaven, and
supposes it a place of solemn holiness, real virtue, and unending
bliss ; but cannot relish those fine
poetic descriptions, which awake
the lively imagination to ecstacy of
delight, and elevate the soul to a
foretaste of those celestial regions.

"Where all united praise the eternal One,
As from the orient rolls the radiant sun ;
All join in concert, all in sacred praise
Attune their harps, and strike celestial lays,
Unceasing glory swells the holy space,
And little cherubs hymn eternal peace."

The man of keen sensibility, if
poor, is miserable for life, without
benefitting the meanest of creation.
To the rich it opens a vein of happiness, not to be enjoyed by himself
so much as by the sons of misfortune, who claim his protection,
or inhabit his neigbbourhood. Its
perations on the mind are so di-
ersified, and lead to actions so en-
rely different in themselves, that it
impossible oftentimes to distin-
uish its subjects from those of folly.
n Harley's munificence to the
eggar, and attention to the unfortunate Miss Atkins, we behold its
divine operations, and instinctively
admire the man. But when we
see " The Ghost, or oddish man"
pinching the ear of a favourite lap-

dog, for laying in a chair, once occupied by this beloved and deceased
friend, we may laugh at the action, but lose all respect for the
character. Yet both of these were
men of the tenderest feeling and
keenest sensibility ; their former
actions evinced it—it was indisputable.

There are many things in life
the generality of mankind look upon as trifling and unworthy attention, which to men of feeling, are
materially pleasing or disgusting.
It is with minds as with bodies ;
some can walk over stones and bri-
ers without feeling in the least in-
commoded, while a pebble in the
shoe of Harley unfits him for pleasure.

A kind of lunacy is ever attendant on people of this tender description ; they appear continually
in a state of listlessness, always aiming at something new and ideal,
which gives not only unhapiness
to themselves, but renders them disagreeable to those who are their
companions in life. They generally view the world on its sombre
side ; and sorrow cuts them with
its sharpest edge. This makes
them cry out with Goldsmith —

And what is friendship, but a name
A charm, that lulls to sleep ;
A shade, that follows wealth, or fame,
But leaves the wretch to weep ?

The phlegmatic person is pretty
easy and contented ; willing to suppose others as good as himself ; and
if ever we hear him break forth
in rapturous language, it is with
Edwin, in this beautiful stanza.

Then, pilgrim, turn, thy cares forego ;
For earth-born cares are wrong :
Man wants but little here below,
Nor wants that little long,

The

For the MASSACHUSETTS MAGAZINE.

The ESSAYIST. No. XIII.

A V A R I C E.

——*Quid non mortalia pectora cogis,*
Auri sacra fames !   VIRG.

Insatiate avarice, cursed thirst for gain !
What age, what nation has not own'd thy sway !
Despair and horror wanton in thy train ;
Crimes, pains, and slaughters, mark thy dreadful way,

MANY and various are the passions, which reign in the human heart. Of these, no one, perhaps is more despicable, with respect to its object, or more pernicious in its consequences, than avarice. The mischiefs, which it has occasioned in the natural, civil, and moral world, deform the faithful page of history, and mark with blood the annals of man.

For one dreadful example let us turn our eyes to the conquest of Mexico and Peru. We there see the Spaniards, instigated by an insatiable thirst for gold, encountering the most incredible hardships, fatigues, and dangers ; bursting every sacred band of virtue, religion, and humanity ; and wading to boundless wealth, through the blood of millions. The shocking barbarities exercised on those, who had nothing barbarous but the *name*, and whose only crime was *to be rich*, have stamped indelible infamy on the characters of the brutal conquerors of the new world, and will never be forgotten, nor cease to be deplored, while the least spark of benevolence remains in the breast of man.

But the unhappy subject of this despotic passion suffers in himself greater miseries, if possible, than those, which he occasions to others. He must therefore be allowed to possess *one virtue*, if he can boast no other. He loves his neighbour and himself with equal affection. He is perfectly disinterested in all his dealings, for he never consults his own happiness. Though immersed in gold, the miser is wasted with anxiety still to accumulate. The poorest beggar has infinitely more real enjoyment, than this self-tormentor. His affections know no object but riches ; he adores no god but gold. He is guilty of the worst of frauds ; he cheats himself. He grudges the scanty pittance, which is necessary to support his attenuated frame. In short, he is an enemy to himself, a plague to his connexions, a pest to society, and a disgrace to humanity.

At this dear rate do misers purchase gold ?
For glittering dust is every pleasure sold ?
Is honest fame with all its charms resign'd,
Which feeds, which fills, which fires the
    high-born mind ?
Must social joys, and friendship's sacred
    ties,
To sordid avarice fall a sacrifice ?
Is innocence, and heaven and virtue lost,
That here a useless treasure they may
    boast ?
Then farewel, gilded poison, farewel
    wealth !
Give me, kind heaven, but peace, content,
    and health ;
Enough to spare, the beggar's suit to grant ;
Relieve the widow's and the orphan's
    want ;
Enough to cheer the fainting heart of grief,
And yield to modest suffering worth relief ;
I ask no more ; the rest let others share ;
For more would be the poverty I fear.

GALLANTRY :

GALLANTRY: An Anecdote.

THE following is an account of the courageous behaviour of one Gillet, a French quarter master, who, going home to his friends, had the good fortune to save the life of a young woman, attacked by two ruffians. He fell upon them, sabre in hand, unlocked the jaw of the first villain, who held a poinard to her breast, and at one stroke pared the nails of the other (who was armed with a pistol) just above the wrist. Money was offered by the grateful parents; he refused it; they offered him their daughter, a young girl of 16, in marriage ; the veteran, then in his 73d year, declined, saying, " Do you think that I have rescued her from instant death, to put her to a lingering one, by coupling so lively a body with one worn out with age ?" This action has been recorded by one of the best painters in Paris, and was exhibited, not long since, in the royal gallery at the Louvre. Several of the spectators wished to see the hero of the tale ; after some researches, the modern Perseus was found in the infirmary within the college of invalids, where he had been for three months, without having uttered a word of his adventure. Monsieur de —— president of the parliament, brought him to the Louvre, where he was received amidst the applause and congratulations of persons of the first rank, who were all eager in offering him money ; but this he absolutely refused to accept of. The Governor of the college obtained of the then Minister, that the annuity of 200 livres, should be continued to him during life, though that kind of half pay generally ceases when a veteran accepts of a retreat in the invalids.

REMARKABLE PHENOMENON.

[Related in a letter from a gentleman at Smyrna to his friend in London.]

IN the night of the 5th of last June, the inhabitants of the island of Tenedos, in the Archipelago, were very much alarmed by several very severe shocks of an earthquake. In the morning, to their great surprise, they discovered a small island, about half a mile in circumference, emerged from the sea, between them and the Asiatic shore. In the center was observed a small volcano, out of which issued smoke of a reddish hue. When I heard this extraordinary account, I was determined to be an eye witness of it, and therefore hired a small vessel, which soon conveyed me there. I was told it had increased much since the night it first sprung, and still continued doing the same.

As the inhabitants are very ignorant and superstitious, they were afraid to venture near it ; I therefore set out for the spot with my servant : We tied the boat to a rock of the new island, and proceeded upon it. I observed several branches of coral dispersed upon the island ; likewise, different sorts of shellfish. A most wonderful noise proceeded from the volcano, resembling the rumbling of waggons.

System

System of WAR among the INDIANS.

[From Dr. WILLIAMS's History of Vermont.]

THE civil regulations of the savages were all designed to qualify and prepare them for war. Among the causes that lead to this, an opposition of interests, was the most common and powerful. No people ever had more clear, or more just ideas of their own rights and property, than the Indians. They not only understood their own perfonal rights, but they were perfectly well acquainted with the rights and property, that were vested in the tribe. Each tribe claimed the foil in their own domains. This right was viewed as complete, perfect, and exclusive: Such as entitled them to the full and entire poffession; and to oppofe by force and violence, all encroachments upon the foil, or game, in any part of the their territories. The bounds of thefe territories were extenfive, and ill defined. Real or fuppofed encroachments and injuries, were conftantly taking place. Hence arofe innumerable fubjects of difpute and controverfy, which eafily inflamed the fiercenefs of the favage temper, and brought on mutual injuries, reproaches, hoftilities, and war. In this ftate, moft of the Indian tribes were found. Intereft had become a fource of difcord, among the neighbouring tribes. From this caufe, arofe moft of their inveterate and perpetual wars.

The manner in which the Indians carry on their wars, is very different from that of civilized nations. To defend themfelves againft an enemy, they have no other fortification but an irregular kind of fortrefs, which they call a caftle, or fat. It confifted of a fquare, without baftions, furrounded with palifadoes. This was erected where the moft confiderable number of the tribe refided, and was defigned as an afylum for their old men, their women, and children, while the reft of the tribe were gone out to war.—The weapons of the Indian were a club made of hard wood, a bow and arrow. Thus armed, the Indian takes with him a fmall bag of corn, and is completely equipped for a campaign. When he takes the field, it is with fuch a number of warriors as the tribe can fupply. During their march, they are difperfed in ftraggling companies, that they may better fupply themfelves by hunting. When they approach near to the enemies' frontiers, their troops are more collected: All is then caution, ftratagem, fecrefy, and ambufcade. Their employment as hunters has taught them great addrefs and vigilance, in following and furprifing the game. Their mode of war is the fame, as that of hunting. With great ingenuity, they will find and follow the track of their enemies: With a furprifing patience and perfeverance, they will wait for the moment, when they find him the leaft able to defend himfelf. And when they can find an enemy unprepared, they make their attack with great fury, and with pretty fure fuccefs. In their battles, they always endeavour to fecure themfelves behind the trees or rocks, and never meet their enemy in the open field, or upon equal terms, if they can avoid it. The method of the Europeans, of deciding a battle in the open field, they regard as extreme folly and want of prudence. Their eftablifhed maxims are to obtain a fuperiority in fituation, numbers, concealment, or fome other circumftance before the battle:

In this way, to preserve the lives of their own party, and destroy their enemies, with as little loss as possible to themselves. A victory obtained with the loss of many of their own party, is a matter of grief and disgrace, rather than of exultation : And it is no honour to fall in the field of battle, but viewed rather as an evidence of want of wisdom, discernment, and circumspection.—When the attack is to be made, nothing can excede the courage and impetuosity of the savage. The onset begins with a general outcry, terminating in a universal yell. Of all the sounds that discord has produced, the Indian warwhoop is the most awful and horrid. It is designed and adapted to increase the ardour of those who make the attack, and to carry terror and horror into the feelings of those, on whom the attack is made. The Indians immediately come forward, and begin the scene of outrage and death. All is then a scene of fury, impetuosity, and vengeance. So great is the rage of the savage, that he has no regard to discipline, subordination, and order. Revenge, takes an entire possession of his soul: Forgetful of all order, regardless of discipline and danger, he aims only to butcher and destroy.—If the Indians remain masters of the field, they always strip and scalp the dead. Leaving the bodies of their enemies, naked, unburied, and often mangled, they carry off the plunder and scalps, and make a very swift and sudden retreat. Upon their approach to their own tribe, a herald is sent forward to announce the event : The tribe is collected, and the conquerors make their entry with their ensigns of triumph : The scalps stretched upon a bow, and elevated upon a pole,

are carried before them, as the tokens of their valour and success, and monuments of the vengeance they have inflicted upon the enemies of their country.

The prisoners which they have taken, make an important part of their triumph. The savages are anxious to take as many of these as possible. During their march, they are generally treated with a degree of humanity and kindness ; but the greatest care is taken to prevent their escape. When they arrive at the place of their destination, the old men, women, and children of the Indian tribe, form themselves into two lines, through which the prisoners must run the gantlet to the village. If the prisoner is young, active, and a good runner, he makes his way through the lines without receiving much injury. If he is weak, old, and infirm, he receives much damage by the blows, stripes, and bruises, he receives. When this scene is finished, the prisoners are conducted to the village, treated with apparent good humour, and fed as well as the Indians' fare admits.

To the village, thus assembled, the head warrior of the party relates every particular of the expedition. When he mentions their losses, a bitter grief and sorrow appears in the whole assembly. When he pronounces the names of the dead, their wives, relations, and friends, put forth the most bitter shrieks, and cries. But no one asks any question, or interrupts the speaker with any inquiry. The last ceremony is to proclaim the victory. Every individual forgets his own loss and misfortune, and joins in the triumph of his nation. Their tears cease, and with one of the most unaccountable transitions in human nature, they pass at once

from

from the bitternefs of forrow to all the extravagance of joy. The whole concludes with a favage feaft, fongs, and dance.

The fate of the prifoners is next to be decided. The elders and chiefs affemble and deliberate concerning their deftiny. The women and children are difpofed of, according to the pleafure of their captors ; but they are feldom or never put to torture, or death. Of the men, fome are appointed to fupply the places of fuch Indians as have fallen in battle. Thefe are delivered to their friends and relations, and if they are received by them, they have no fufferings to fear : They are adopted into the family, and fucceed to all the privileges of the deceafed ; and are efteemed as friends, brothers, and near relations. But if they are not received and admitted into the family, or if they are deftined to be put to death, a moft diftreffing and horrid fcene enfues.

A ftake is fixed firmly in the ground. At the diftance of eight or ten feet, dry wood, leaves, and faggots, are placed in a circle round the ftake : And the whole village is collected, to bear their part in the tragedy, which is to enfue. The prifoner is led to the ftake, and tied to it by his hands, in fuch a manner that he may move freely round it. Fire is fet to the wood, that as it runs round the circle, the unhappy victim may be forced to run the fame way. As the fufferings of the prifoner begin to become fevere, the acclamations of the fpectators begin. The men, women, and children, ftrive to exceed each other, in finding out new and keener methods of torment. Some apply red hot irons, others ftab and cut with their knives, others mangle and tear off the flefh,

others again bite off the nails and joints, or twift and tear the finews. Every fpecies and degree of cruelty, that favage rancour and revenge can invent and apply, is tried upon the wretched fufferer. But great care is taken that the vital parts may not be fo injured, as to bring the torments of the victim to a fpeedy end.—In this horrid fituation, the fufferer is undaunted and intrepid. He reviles and infults his tormentors. He accufes them of cowardice, meannefs, and want of fpirit ; as ignorant, unfkilful, and deftitute of ingenuity and invention in the art of tormenting. Not a groan, a figh, a tear, or a forrowful look, is fuffered to efcape him. To infult his tormentors, to difplay undaunted and unalterable fortitude in this dreadful fituation, is the moft noble of all the triumphs of the warrior. With an unaltered countenance, and with the decifive tone of dignity and fuperior importance, the hero proceeds with great calmnefs to fing the fong of his death—" Intrepid and brave, I feel no pain, and I fear no torture. I have flain, I have conquered, I have burnt mine enemies ; and my countrymen will avenge my blood. Ye are a nation of dogs, of cowards, and women. Ye know not how to conquer, to fuffer, or to torture. Prolong and increafe my torments, that ye may learn from my example how to fuffer and behave like men !" With fuch unconquerable magnanimity and fortitude, the fufferer perfeveres under ever method of torment and torture. Wearied with cruelty, and tired with tormenting the man whofe fortitude they cannot move, one of the chiefs, in a rage, concludes the fcene, by knocking the prifoner on the head, or ftabbing him to the heart.

Thefe fcenes, however, were not

common. They seem to have been kind of honours, reserved for the warriors; and were the trials of their courage and fortitude. And nothing was esteemed more base and ignominious, than to shrink from them, or to shew any sense of fear or pain under them.

When the prisoners were adopted into the tribe of the conquerors, nothing could exceed the kindness and affection, with which they were treated. All distinction of tribes was forgot; they held the same rank as the deceased person, whose place they filled; and were treated with all the tenderness due to the husband, the brother, the child or friend. And it was generally the case, that the savages avoided abuse and cruelty to the women and children, that fell into their hands.

The Indian method of carrying on a war, was so contrary to the maxims and customs of all civilized nations, that some of the European writers, judging from their own customs, have concluded it was founded on cowardice, and arose from an ignoble and timid spirit, afraid to meet its opposers on equal ground, and depending wholly on craft, and not at all on courage and firmness of mind. No conclusion was ever further from the truth. When placed in a critical and dangerous situation, no people ever discovered more valour, firmness, and intrepidity. When subdued, an Indian was never known to ask for his life. When compelled to suffer, the Indian bore it with a steadiness, a fortitude, and a magnanimity, unknown to all other nations; and of which, there are no examples in the history of war.—His method of war did not arise from a sense and fear of danger; he was well acquainted, and always in the midst of this; but it

arose, from his situation and employment, and was perfectly well adapted to it. From his situation and employment as an hunter, he acquired the art of ambuscade and surprise; and the method with which he could best succeed in taking his game, he found to be the most successful to ensnare and overcome his enemy. The situation and state of the country, overspread with thick forests, lead to the same method. The situation of the tribe, scattered and dispersed in the woods, suggested the same idea. The method of fighting could not be in the open fields, but among the trees. And he wisely placed the point of honour, in the public good; where the prospect and the probability of his success lay. Had the honour of the Indian warrior been placed, in courting fame and victory in the open field, the whole tribe would have been destroyed by the effusion of blood that must have succeeded. His maxims, therefore, were better chosen, and they were such as every circumstance in his situation and employment, naturally led him to: Not in an useless ostentation of daring courage and boldness, but in the public utility and advantage. So far as an enterprize depended on secresy, subtlety, surprize, and impetuosity, the Indian method of war seems to have been fully equal to the European. The Spaniards, the French, the English, and the states of America, have had many and painful proofs of their address and prowess in this method. But when a fort was erected, or a small fortification to be carried, the Indian method of war wholly failed. Neither their arms, their arts, or their customs, were of any avail here. Wholly unacquainted with the art of fortification, they could neither erect, or or take a fort of any strength.— When the Europeans had once got possession of any part of their country, and erected a small fortification in their territories, they held it by a sure possession. The savages were wholly unable to dispossess them by their method of war, and nothing was left for them but to retreat further into the forests.— In this way, the English and French were making constant advances into their country; and their art of war afforded them no sufficient means, either to prevent or to redress it. But when the Europeans followed them into the woods, where their strength and art might be employed to advantage, the Indians generally surprised and defeated their armies, with great havoc and slaughter.

For the MASSACHUSETTS MAGAZINE.

The REPOSITORY. No. XXVII.

AN *undue* elevation must always be painful to an ingenuous mind. The trembling spirit, perturbed and anxious, surveys the picture, by a luxuriant fancy portrayed; it beholds it upon a lofty eminence; it compares it with the original; even self-love hesitates to acknowledge a striking conformity of lineaments, and honest veracity will hardly admit a resemblance. The delicately susceptible subject of too high wrought panegyrick, catches a glance at the star-wreathed summit, on which imagination hath placed him; he snatches an agitated look; the conscious blush is upon his cheek, and, all abashed, he sinks to the valley below. It is true that praise is undoubtedly sweet to the ear: It is like the gently murmuring stream, to the traveller emerging from the desert, who, spent by a fatiguing march through a long, barren, and sandy waste, blesses the limpid flow of the restoring waters. Yet *reason* assures us, that time will awake our eulogist; that we shall not always be viewed through false opticks, but that sooner or later, our abilities being impartially appreciated, our genuine character, with all its *real powers*, *yea*, and all its *imbecilities too*, will in its proper colours be disclosed.

CONSTANTIA.

The CONSTANT LOVERS: Or, the Adventures of PEDRO and CELESTINA.—*A Tale.*

[By the Chevalier de FLORIAN.]

CELESTINA, at seventeen, was the most admired beauty in Grenada. She was an orphan and heiress to an immense fortune, under the guardianship of an old and avaricious uncle, whose name was Alonzo, and who passed his days in counting ducats, and his nights in silencing serenades, nocturnally addressed to Celestina. His design was to marry her, for the sake of her great fortune, to his own son, Henriquez, who had studied ten years in the university of Salamanca, and was now able to explain Cornelius Nepos tolerably well.

Almost

Almoft all the cavaliers of Grenada were in love with Celeftina. As they could only obtain a fight of her, at mafs, the church fhe frequented was filled with great numbers of the handfomeft and moft accomplifhed youths of the country.

One of the moft diftinguifhed among thefe was Don Pedro, a captain of cavalry, about twenty, not very rich, but of one of the firft families. Handfome, polite, and witty, he drew on himfelf the eyes of all the ladies of Grenada; though he himfelf paid attention to none but Celeftina ; while fhe, not infenfible to his attachment, began, on her part, to take confiderable notice of her admirer.

Two months paffed away without the lovers daring to fpeak, though, neverthelefs, they filently faid a great deal. At the end of that time Don Pedro, found the means of conveying a letter to his miftrefs ; which informed her of what fhe knew before. The referved Celeftina had no fooner read this letter, than fhe ordered it to be fent back to Don Pedro ; but as fhe poffeffed an excellent memory, fhe retained every word, and was able to return a very punctual anfwer a whole week afterwards.

A correfpondence was now fettled between the two lovers. Don Pedro was defirous to be ftill more intimate. He had long folicited permiffion to converfe with Celeftina through her latices ; fuch is the cuftom in Spain ; where the windows are of much more ufe during the night than the day. They are the places of rendezvous. When the ftreet is vacant and ftill, the lover wraps himfelf up in his cloak, and, taking his fword, invoking love and night to favour him, proceeds to fome low latice, grated on

the fide next the ftreet, and fecured on the infide by fhutters.

He waits not long before the windows opens, foftly, and the charming maid appears. She afks, in a tremulous voice, if any one is there. Her lover, tranfported at her condefcenfion, endeavours to difpel her fears : They talk in a whifper, and repeat the fame thing a hundred times. The gratings cannot hinder their interchanging vows ; though they may prevent their kiffes. The lover curfes the envious bars, while his miftrefs thanks them for their friendly interpofition. Day, at length, approaches, and they muft feparate. They are an hour in taking leave ; and part, at laft, without having faid half the tender things they intended.

Celeftina's latice was on the ground floor, and opened into a narrow paffage, where the houfes were ill built, and only inhabited by the lower clafs of people. Don Pedro's old nurfe happened to occupy a tenement directly oppofite the window of Celeftina. Pedro, therefore, repaired to his nurfe. My good woman, faid he, I have been much to blame to fuffer you to live fo long in this miferable habitation ; but I am determined to make you amends by giving you an apartment in my own houfe. Come and refide in that, and leave me to difpofe of this.

The honeft woman could not refrain from tears ; and, for a long time, refufed ; but, at laft, overcome by his folicitations, fhe confented to the exchange, with every expreffion of gratitude, for the kindnefs of her benefactor.

Never did any monarch enter his palace with more fatisfaction than Don Pedro took poffeffion of the hovel of his nurfe.

Early in the evening Celeftina
appeared

appeared at her latice. — She promised to repair thither every other day, and she kept her word. These delightful interviews served only to increase the flame of love; and, very soon the lovers' nights were passed in pleasing conversation, and their days in writing passionate epistles.

At length they both arrived at that intoxication of delight and anxiety which is the last period of the passion of love.

Just at this time, Henriquez, the intended husband of Celestina, arrived from Salamanca; bringing with him a declaration of his passion in latin, which had been written for him by the head of the college. The lovers consulted each other on this event at the latice; but in the mean time the old guardian had drawn up a contract of marriage, and a day was fixed on for the celebration of the nuptials of Celestina and Henriquez.

Every one must perceive. that, under such circumstances, the only remedy was to fly into Portugal. This was determined on, and it was also settled that the two lovers, on arriving at Lisbon, should first marry, and afterwards have recourse to the law against the guardian.

Celestina was to carry with her a box of jewels which had been left her by her mother. These were very valuable, and would be sufficient to maintain the happy couple till their law-suit should be decided in their favour. No plan could ever be laid with more prudence.

Nothing was now wanting but to contrive how to effect this escape; and, for this purpose, it was necessary to procure the key of the latice. In this Celestina succeeded.

It was therefore resolved that the next night, at eleven, Don Pedro, after having ordered horses to wait

without the city, should come and fetch Celestina, who should descend from the window into the arms of her lover, and immediately set off for Portugal.

Don Pedro spent the whole day in preparations for his departure. Celestina, on her part, was equally busy in getting ready the little box she was to take with her. She was very careful not to omit securing in it a very fine emerald, which had been given her by her lover.

Celestina and her box were ready by eight in the evening; and before ten, Don Pedro, who had already provided carriages on the road to Andalusia, arrived at the appointed spot; his heart beating with preturbation and hope.

As he approached the place, he heard persons calling for help, and perceived two men attacked by five assassins, armed with swords and bludgeons. The brave Pedro forgot his own affairs to defend the lives of the assaulted. He wounded two, and put the other three assassins to flight.

What was his surprise, on more attentively considering those he had delivered, to perceive they were no other than Henriquez and Celestina's guardian, Alonzo! Some desperate young cavalier of the city, who was in love with Celestina, knowing it was intended that Henriquez should espouse her, had hired bravoes, a species of rascals but too common in Spain, to assassinate them; and had it not been for the valour of Don Pedro, the young scholar and the old miser would have found it no easy matter to have escaped with life.

Pedro did his utmost to avoid their grateful acknowledgements, but Henriquez, who piqued himself on having learned politeness in Salamanca, swore he should not

leave

leave them that night. Pedro, in despair, had already heard the clock strike eleven. Alas! he knew not the mischief that had happened.

One of the bravoes, whom he had put to flight, had passed, muffled up in his cloak, near the latice of Celestina. The night was extremely dark, and the unfortunate fair, having opened the window, imagining him to be Don Pedro, she presented him the box with joyful impatience,

Take our diamonds, said she, while I descend.

At the word *diamonds*, the bravo suddenly stopped, took the box, without speaking a word, and, while Celestina was coming down from the window, fled with the utmost precipitation.

Imagine the surprise of Celestina, when she found herself alone, in the street, and saw nothing of him whom she had supposed to be Don Pedro. She thought, at first, he had left her to avoid raising suspicion or alarm. She, therefore, hastily walked to a little distance, looked round on every side, and called in a low voice. But no Pedro could she see; no lover could she hear.

She was now seized with the most alarming apprehensions. She knew not whether it was most adviseable to return home, or endeavour to find the horses and attendants of Don Pedro, that were waiting out of town. She continued to walk forwards, in the utmost uncertainty and distress, till she had lost herself among the streets; while her fears were redoubled by darkness and silence.

At length she met a person, whom she asked if she were far from the gate of the city. The stranger conducted her thither, but she found nobody waiting as she expected.

She dared not yet accuse her lover of deceiving her: still she hoped he was at no great distance. She therefore, proceeded along the road, fearful at every bush, and calling Don Pedro at every step; but the farther she walked the more she was bewildered; for she had come out of the city on the side opposite to the Portugal road.

In the mean time, Don Pedro found himself unable to get away from the grateful Henriquez and his father. They would not suffer him to leave them for a moment, but obliged him to enter the house with them, to which Pedro, fearful of betraying his intent, and frustrating his dearest hopes, and imagining too that Celestina might be soon satisfied why he thus delayed, most reluctantly consented.

Alonzo hastens to the chamber of his ward, to inform her of the danger he had just escaped. He calls, but receives no answer; enters her apartment; and finds the latice open; his cries collected the servants, the alarm is immediately given, Celestina is missing.

Pedro, in despair, immediately offered to go in quest of her. Henriquez, thanking him for the concern he expressed, declared his resolution of accompanying him. Pedro suggested that the probability of finding her would be greater if they took different roads. Accordingly, he hastened to rejoin his domestics; and not doubting but Celestina had taken the road to Portugal, put his horses on at full speed. But their swiftness only removed him farther from the object of his love; while Henriquez galloped towards the Alpuxarian mountains, the way Celestina had actually gone.

In the mean time, Celestina continued to wander disconsolate, along the road that leads to the Alpuxares, seeking her lover. Anon
she

She heard the clattering of approaching horses; and, at first, imagined it might be her beloved Pedro: but, afterwards, fearful of discovery, the violence of travellers, or, perhaps, robbers, she concealed herself trembling behind some bushes.

Here she presently saw Henriquez pass by, followed by a number of servants. Shuddering at the danger of being again in the power, and dreading a second time to submit to the redoubled tyranny of Alonzo, if she continued in the high road, she turned aside, and took refuge in a thick wood.

The Alpuxares are a chain of mountains which extend from Grenada to the Mediterranean. They are only inhabited by a few peasants. To these, fear and terror conducted the unfortunate maiden. A dry and stony soil, with a few oak trees, thinly scattered, some torrents and echoing catteracts, and a number of wild goats, leaping from precipice to precipice, are the only objects which present themselves to the eyes of Celestina, as soon as day begins to break. Exhausted; at length, with weariness and vexation, her feet being torn by the rugged stones over which she had passed, she sat down under a rock; through the clifts of which a limpid water gently oozed.

The silence of this grotto, the wildness of the landscape around, the hoarse and distant murmur of several cascades, and the noise of the water near her, falling drop by drop into the bason it had hollowed beneath, all conspired to convince Celestina she was alone in the midst of a desert, abandoned by her lover, who to her was the whole world.

She sat herself down on the edge of this stream, to vent her grief in tears, reflecting on the miseries that seemed to threaten her; but, above

all, on her lost Don Pedro, whom, at moments, she still flattered herself she should one day regain.

It certainly was not him, said she, whom I saw carry off my diamonds. I must have been mistaken. Yet, how was it possible that my heart should not have informed me of the truth? No doubt he is now far hence, seeking me with anxiety and distraction; while I, as far distant from him, here am perishing.

While mournfully thus she ruminated, she heard, at the bottom of the grotto, the sound of a rustic flute.

Upon searching, she found a young goat-herd sitting at the foot of a willow, his eyes bedewed with his tears, and fixed on the water as it issued from its rocky source. In his hand he held a flageolet, and by his side lay a staff and a little parcel.

Shepherd, said Celestina, have pity on one abandoned, and shew me my way among these mountains, to some village, or habitation, where I may procure, though not repose, at least sustenance.

Alas! madam replied the goat-herd; I wish it were in my power to conduct you to the village of Gadara, behind these rocks; but you will not ask me to return thither, when you are informed my mistress is this day to be married to my rival. I am going to leave these mountains, never to behold them more: and I carry nothing with me but my flute, a change of dress, which I have in this parcel, and the memory of the happiness I have lost.

This short account suggested a new project to Celestina.

My friend, said she to the goatherd, you have no money, which you will certainly want, when you have left this country. I have a few pieces of gold; thefe I will divide with you, if you will let me have the drefs you fay is in your parcel.

The goat-herd accepted the offer, Celeftina gave him a dozen ducats, and, having informed herfelf which was the road to Gadara, took her leave of the defpairing lover, and returned into the grotto, to put on her newly purchafed difguife.

She came out habited in a veft of chamois fkin, with a fhepherd's wallet hanging by her fide, and on her head a hat ornamented with ribbons. In this attire fhe appeared yet more beautiful than when adorned with brocades and jewels. She took the road to the village, and, ftopping in the market place, inquired of the peafants if they knew of any farmer who wanted a fervant.

The inhabitants furrounded her, and furveyed the ftranger with admiration. The girls expreffed their furprife at the beauty of her flowing ringlets; her elegant form, her graceful manner, the brilliancy of her eyes, even though dejeded, their fuperior intelligence and mild benignity, aftonifh and delight all beholders. No one could conceive from whence came this beautiful youth. One imagines him a perfon of high diftindion in difguife; another, a prince, in love with fome fhepherdefs, while the fchool mafter, who was at the fame time the poet of the village, declared it muft be Apollo, fent down, a fecond time, to keep fheep among mortals.

Celeftina, who affumed the name of Marcelio, was not long in want of a mafter. She was hired by an aged alcade of the village, efteemed one of the worthieft men in the whole province.

This honeft countryman foon contraded the warmeft friendfhip for Celeftina. He fcarcely fuffered her to tend his flocks for a month before he gave her an employment within his houfe, in which the pretended Marcelio behaved with fo much propriety and fidelity, that he was equally beloved by mafter and fervants.

Before he had lived here half a year, the alcade, who was more than eighty, left the entire management of all he poffeffed to Marcelio: he even afked his opinion in all the caufes that came before him, and never had any alcade decided with fo much juftice as he, from the time he permitted himfelf to be guided by the advice of Marcelio. Marcelio was beloved, and propofed as an example to all the village: his affability, his pleafing manner, and his good fenfe, gained every heart. See the excellent Marcelio, cried the mothers to their fons, he is continually with his mafter, he is perpetually employed in rendering his old age happy, and never negleds his duty, like you, to run after the fhepherdeffes.

Two years paffed away in this manner. Celeftina, whofe thoughts where continually employed on her lover, had fent a fhepherd, in whom fhe could confide, to Grenada, to procure information concerning Don Pedro, Alonzo, and Henriquez. The fhepherd brought word back, that Alonzo was dead, Henriquez married, and that Don Pedro had not been feen or heard of for thefe laft two years.

Celeftina now loft all hopes of ever again beholding her lover, and, happy in being able to pafs her days in that village, in the bofom of peace and friendfhip, had refolved to bid an eternal adieu to
love,

love, when the old alcade, her mafter, fell dangeroufly ill. Marcelio
attended his laft moments with all
the affection of a fon, and the good
old man behaved to him like a
grateful father ; he died, and left all
he poffeffed to the faithful Marcelio.
But his will was by no means a
fufficient confolation to his heir.

The whole village mourned for
the alcade, and, after funeral
rites had been celebrated with
more forrow than pomp, the inhabitants of the place affembled to
choofe a fucceffor. In Spain, certain villages have the right of nominating their own alcade, whofe
office it is to decide their differences, and take cognizances of greater crimes, by arrefting and examining the offenders, and delivering them over to the fuperior judges, who generally confirm the fentence of thofe ruftic
magiftrates ; for good laws are
generally perfectly confonant to
fimple reafon.

The villagers, being met, agreed,
with one voice, that no one could
be fo proper to fucceed the late alcade, as the youth whom he feemed
to have defigned for his fucceffor.
The old men, therefore, followed
by their fons, came with all the
ufual ceremonies to offer Marcelio
the white wand, the enfign of the
vacant office. Celeftina accepted
it, and fenfibly touched by fuch a
proof of efteem and affection from
thefe good people, refolved to con-
fecrate to their happinefs a life fhe
had formerly intended to dedicate
to love.

While the new alcade is bufied
with the duties of her office, let us
return to the unfortunate Don Pedro, whom we left galloping towards Portugal, and continually
removing farther from her he fo
anxioufly fought.

He arrived at Lifbon, without
obtaining any intelligence of Celeftina, and immediately returned by
the fame road, to refearch every
place he had before in vain examined ; again he returned to Lifbon,
but without fuccefs.

After fix months ineffectual inquiry, having affured himfelf that
Celeftina had never returned to
Grenada, he imagined fhe might
perhaps be at Seville, where he
knew fhe had relations. Immediately he haftened to Seville, there
he found the relations of Celeftina
had juft embarked for Mexico.

Pedro no longer doubted but his
miftrefs was gone with them, and
directly went on board the laft fhip
which remained to fail. He arrived
at Mexico, where he found the relations, but alas, no Celeftina ! they
had heard nothing of her : he,
therefore, returned to Spain. And
now the fhip is attacked by a violent ftorm, and caft on the coaft of
Grenada : himfelf, and a few of the
paffengers, fave themfelves by fwimming ; they land, and make their
way to the mountains, to procure
affiftance, and, by chance or love,
are conducted to Gadara.

Don Pedro, and his unfortunate
companions, took refuge in the firft
inn, congratulating each other on
the danger they had efcaped. While
they were difcourfing on their adventures, one of the paffengers began to quarrel with a foldier, concerning a box, which the paffenger
afferted belonged to him.

Don Pedro, defirous to put an
end to the contention, obliged the
paffenger to declare what it contained, opening it at the fame time
to difcover whether he fpoke truth.
How great was his furprife to find
in it the jewels of Celeftina, and,
among them, the very emerald he
had given her. For a moment he
ftood

ſtood motionleſs, examining attentively the caſket; and fixing his eyes, ſparkling with rage, on the claimant, how came you by theſe jewels? ſaid he, with a voice of terror.

What does it ſignify, replied the paſſenger, haughtily, how I came by them! it is ſufficient that I am poſſeſſed of them.

He then endeavoured to ſnatch the caſket from Don Pedro; but he, puſhing him back, inſtantly drew his ſword. Wretch, ſaid he, confeſs your crime, or you die this moment. So ſaying, he attacked him with great fury: his antagoniſt defended himſelf with equal bravery, but preſently received a mortal wound, and fell.

Don Pedro was immediately ſurrounded, and ſeized by the people of the houſe. They take him to priſon, and the maſter of the inn ſends his wife to fetch the clergyman of the pariſh, that he may adminiſter ſpiritual comfort to the dying man, while he runs himſelf to the alcade, to carry the caſket, and inform him of the whole adventure.

How great was the ſurpriſe, the joy, and the anxiety of Celeſtina, on perceiving her diamonds, and hearing the behaviour of the noble ſtranger. She immediately haſtened to the inn, the miniſter was already there, and the dying man, induced by his exhortations, declared in preſence of the alcade, that, two years before, as he was one night paſſing through a ſtreet in Grenada, a lady had given him that box, through a latice, telling him to hold it till ſhe came down, but that he immediately made off with the jewels; for which theft he aſked pardon of God, and the unknown lady, whom he had injured. Immediately after this confeſſion, he

expired, and Celeſtina ran to the priſon.

How did her heart palpitate with expectation! ſhe could no longer doubt but ſhe ſhould again ſee Don Pedro, but ſhe feared ſhe ſhould be known by him; ſhe therefore pulled her hat over her eyes, wrapped herſelf up in her cloak, and, preceded by her clerk and the goaler, entered the dungeon.

No ſooner had ſhe got to the bottom of the ſtairs, than ſhe perceived Don Pedro. Her joy almoſt deprived her of ſpeech; ſhe leaned againſt the wall, her head ſunk on her ſhoulders, and the tears ſtreamed down her cheeks. She wiped them away, ſtopped a moment to take breath, and endeavouring to ſpeak with firmneſs, approached the priſoner.

Stranger, ſaid ſhe, diſguiſing her voice, you have killed your companion.—What could induce you to ſo horrid an action? Theſe few words were all ſhe could utter, and ſeating herſelf on a ſtone, ſhe concealed her face with her hand.

Alcade, replied Don Pedro, I have committed no crime; it was an act of juſtice; but I beg for death. Death alone can end the continual miſeries of which the wretch I have ſacrificed to my revenge was the firſt cauſe. Condemn me, I will not to make a defence. Deliver me from a life which is hateful to me, ſince I have loſt what alone could render it delightful; ſince I can no longer hope to find——

He was unable to conclude, and his voice faintly expreſſed the name of Celeſtina.

Celeſtina trembled on hearing him pronounce her name. She could ſcarcely conceal her tranſports, but was ready to riſe and throw herſelf into the arms of her lover.

lover. The presence, however, of so many witnesses, restrained her. She therefore turned away her eyes, and faintly requested to be left alone with the prisoner; she was obeyed.

Giving a free course to her tears, she advanced towards Don Pedro, and, offering him her hand, said to him, in a most affectionate tone, do you then still love her who lives for you alone?

At these words, at this voice, Pedro lifts his head, unable to believe his eyes. Oh, heaven! is it—is it my Celestina! or is it some angelic being, assuming her form? Yes, it is she, I can no longer doubt it, cried he, clasping her in his arms, and bathing her with his tears. It is my love, my life, and all my woes are ended.

No, said Celestina, as soon as she could recover speech, you are guilty of bloodshed, and I cannot free you from your fetters; but I will repair to-morrow to the superior judge, will inform him of the secret of my birth, relate to him our misfortunes, and, if he refuses me your liberty, I will return and end my days with you in this prison.

Marcelio immediately gave orders for the removal of Pedro from the subterraneous dungeon, to a less hideous place of security; took care that he should want for nothing, and afterwards returned home to prepare for his journey, the next day, when a most alarming event prevented his departure, and hastened the delivery of Don Pedro.

Some Algerine galleys, which had for several days pursued the ship on board of which Don Pedro was, arrived on the coast some time after the shipwreck; and willing to repay themselves for the trouble they had taken, had determined to land during the night. Two renegadoes, who knew the country, undertook to conduct the barbarians to the village of Gadara, and fulfilled their promise but too well.

About one in the morning, when labour enjoys repose, and villainy wakes to remorse, the dreadful cry of *to arms*, was heard.

The Moors had landed, and were burning and slaughtering all before them. The darkness of the night, the groans of the dying, and the shrieks of the terrified inhabitants, filled every heart with consternation. The trembling wives caught their husbands in their arms: and the old men sought succour from their sons. In a moment the village was in flames, the light of which discovered the goary scymitars and white turbans of the Moors.

Those barbarians, the flambeau in one hand, and the hatchet in the other, were breaking and burning the doors of the houses; and making their way through the smoking ruins, to seek for victims or for plunder, returned covered with blood, and loaded with booty.

Nothing is held sacred by these monsters. They force their way into the temples of the Most High, break the shrines, strip off the gold, and trample the holy relics under foot. Alas! what avail to priests their sacred character, to the aged their gray hairs, to youth its graces, or to infancy its innocence? Slavery, fire, devastation, and death, are every where, and pity is fled.

On the first alarm and tumult the alcade made all possible haste to the prison, to inform Don Pedro of the danger. The brave Pedro demanded a sword for himself and a buckler for the alcade. He takes Celestina by the hand, and makes his way to the market-place. There he addresses the fugitives.

My

My friends, cries he, are ye Spaniards, and do ye fly and abandon your wives and children to the fury of the infidels?

He stops them, collects them round him, inspires them with his own valour, and, more than human, for he is a lover and a hero, rushes, sabre in hand, on a party of the Moors, whom he breaks and disperses. The inhabitants recover their recollection and their courage, enraged behold their slaughtered friends, and hasten in crowds to join their leader.

Pedro, without quitting Celestina, and ever solicitous to expose his life in her defence, attacks the barbarians, at the head of his brave Spaniards, and, dealing destruction to all who make resistance, drives the fugitives before him, retakes the plunder and the prisoners, and only quits the pursuits of the enemy to return and extinguish the fires.

The day began to break, when a body of troops, who had too late received information of the descent of the infidels, arrived from a neighbouring town. The governor had put himself at their head, and found Don Pedro surrounded by women, children, and old men; who, weeping, kissed his hands, with unfeigned gratitude for having preserved their husbands, their fathers, or their sons.

The governor, informed of the exploits of Don Pedro, loaded him with praises and caresses; but Celestina, requesting to be heard, declared to the governor, in presence of the whole village, her sex; giving at the same time a relation of her adventures, the death of the bravo by Don Pedro, and the circumstances which rendered him excusable.

All the inhabitants, greatly af-fected with her story, fell at the feet of the governor, intreating pardon for the man to whom they were indebted for their preservation. The request was granted, and the happy Pedro, thus restored to his dear Celestina, embraced the governor, and blessed the good inhabitants. One of the old men then advanced. Brave stranger, said he, you are our deliverer, but you take from us our alcade; this loss, perhaps, outweighs your benefit. Double our blessings, instead of depriving us of our greatest; remain in this village; condescend to become our alcade, our master, our friend. Honour us so far as to permit nothing to abate our love for you. In a great city, the cowardly and the wicked, who maintain the same rank with yourself, will think themselves, your equals; while, here, every virtuous inhabitant will look on you as his father; next to the Deity himself, you will receive from us the highest honour; and, while life remains, on the anniversary of this day, the fathers of our families will present their children before you, saying, behold the man who preserved the lives of your mothers.

Pedro was enchanted while he listened to the old man. Yes, cried he, my children; yes, my brethren, I will remain here. My life shall be devoted to Celestina and to you. But my wife has considerable possessions in Grenada. Our excellent governor will add his interest to ours, that we may recover them, and they shall be employed to rebuild the houses which have been burnt by the infidels. On this condition alone will I accept the office of alcade; and though I should expend in your service, both my riches and my life, I should still be your debtor; for it is you who have

have reſtored me my Celeſtina.

Imagine the tranſports of the good villagers, while Don Pedro ſpoke. The governor was a perſon of great power, and undertook to arrange every thing to his wiſh; and two days afterwards, the marriage was celebrated between Celeſtina and her lover.

Notwithſtanding the late misfortunes, nothing could exceed the joy of the inhabitants.

The two lovers long lived in unexampled felicity; and, happy and virtuous themſelves, made the whole diſtrict happy and virtuous likewiſe.

For the MASSACHUSETTS MAGAZINE.

The G L E A N E R. No. XXXI.

Ten thouſand ills from falſe concluſions ſpring,
Inveſtigation ſtill new lights ſhould bring;
Explore the probable—the doubtful ſearch,
Through poſſibilities inquiring march;
Suſpend the judgment and delay to grieve,
For ſure, full oft, *appearances deceive.*

I HAVE, for many weeks back, been largely in arrears to correſpondents; and I have frequently contemplated a Gleaner, which ſhould be wholly occupied by their various addreſſes, obſervations, and complaints. But ſuch of my friends, whoſe letters have been long ſince received, will have the goodneſs to forgive my publiſhing thoſe, which have more recently come to hand, when they obſerve, that the intereſting ſubjects, which they take up, require immediate attention. And, in the interim, I give them my word of honour, that my firſt unappropriated eſſay ſhall be devoted to their ſervice.—Proceed we now to bring forward three explanatory epiſtles:

L E T T E R I.

To the GLEANER.

Liberty Hall, Dec. 15, 1794.

UPON my word, Mr. Gleaner, I believe you are a ſly old fellow, after all. Let me tell you, ſir, it ill ſuits with your *aſſumed gravity,* to be thus foiſting yourſelf into the ſecrets of all the young, handſome, married women, of your acquaintance. Mighty fine, mighty fine, truly. *Delicacy, forſooth, forbid Monimia to queſtion her huſband;* but *delicacy,* it ſeems, did not think proper to interfere, while ſhe contrived to pour her pity-moving tale into the boſom of *nobody knows who—one who is here, and there, and every where, and very poſſibly not of much importance any where. A perfect Proteus to the imagination, aſſuming a thouſand fantaſtical forms, and becoming ſtationary in no one reſpectable character; a bird of paſſage, emigrating from ſtate to ſtate, and picking up a ſcanty pittance, after a whole month's toil, which but ill repays the labour of travelling through the dull pages, which he is ſo ſtudious to litter.—* You may think me ſevere, Mr. Gleaner, but I ſhall have the ſatisfaction of knowing, that I am *juſt;* and, I add, that you might have gone on with your itinerant gleaning, to the end of the chapter, for me, if you had not rouſed the feelings of an injured huſband, by thus palpably inſinuating, that you are
a greater

a greater favourite with his wife, than he is himself. Really, Mr. Morality, you make a very pretty, confiftent, heterogeneous figure, and I fhould like vaftly to have your motley image ftuck up in a print fhop, by way of relief to the ftudies of the chubby-faced fchool boy, as he trudges along the academical way to his daily labours.

The wife man fays, that laughter doeth good, like a medicine; and it is undeniably true, that the ludicrous is a wonderful fpecific in every intellectual complaint. But let me whifper you, good Mr. Prig, you are a coxcomb, and you may blefs your ftars that I am not able to collect the trio, which you have huddled together in your laft Gleaner; for, if I could name my fellow fufferers, we would unite together in toffing your worfhip in a blanket; but you are fuch a doughty hero, and, withal, fo evanefcent a fprite, that you elude the grafp of common exertions.

How you became acquainted with Monimia's tale of forrow, is an enigma, of which it will be conceived, that _delicacy_ forbids me to feek an explanation! The probability is, that you have practifed upon her fimplicity, and infinuating yourfelf into the good graces of the afflicted fair one, by fome illicit methods, you have at length obtained her confidence; and, as I am one of the beft natured men in the world, extending the fceptre of my clemency, I fhall view, with proper indulgence, the _imbecilities_ of _nature_. Doubtlefs I could have reftored the tranquillity of my wife, without troubling either you or myfelf with my obfervations; but, befides that, I conceive your temerity merits chaftifement, as you have impertinently precipitated me, and an affair which was wholly mine,

upon the public view, I am induced to believe, that the ecclairciffement hath thus acquired a kind of right to publicity.

Monimia will remember, that I not long fince paid a vifit to my relations at B——. My kinfman, S. has a daughter, _who hath not yet rounded her twelfth year_—Mifs S. is very ingenious, and handles her fciffors to admiration; _fhe cut my watch paper, and fhe will be proud of furnifhing Monimia with any little fancy pieces, which fhe may wifh._ On my return home, I made a difplay of my acquifition. Monimia _haftily and tremuloufly made fome round about inquiries, relative to the fair artificer— thefe I would not feem to underftand; I diflike every fymptom of fufpicion in ladies; fufpicion looks fo like jealoufy, and jealoufy looks fo like want of confidence, I remained filent; and affected a kind of what the ladies call, delicate embarraffment._ Perhaps I was wrong; but, had I been apprifed, that the impreffion made by fo _light_ a thing as a _watch paper,_ could have been fo ferious, I fhould certainly have endeavoured to have erafed it.

I have, Mr. Meddler, the honor— _the honor—no, that's wrong, I have not the honor_—I have _the condefcenfion_ to be, with honeft wifhes for your reformation, and little or no efteem, your conftant reader,

EUGENIO.

LETTER II.

To the GLEANER.

Candor Place, Dec. 18, 1794.

Mr. Vigellius,

AS you have given your examples under fictitious names, I am not furnifhed with a rational caufe of anger: and yet, fir, you have fo well pointed circumftances, that it is impoffible for the real claimant to avoid affuming habiliments, which can fit no one but himfelf.

Myftery

O Sir! Sir Save me! assist me!

Myftery is indeed the parent of conjecture, and concealment moft furely engenders fufpicion. Authors are doubtlefs juftifiable in procuring every warrantable illuftration of their fentiments, and of thofe inferences, which they wifh to deduce; and even a *defire* to inform, or to improve, is entitled to grateful refpect. If my Clariffa, or her favoured Altamont, can furnifh either amufement or inftruction to the Gleaner, and his numerous readers, any little anecdote relative to us, is extremely at their fervice. My Clariffa is more dear to my foul, than the life-blood which warms me to exiftence; fhe hath not, fhe never had, nor ever can have, a rival in my affections: She reigns fole miftrefs in my heart, and to her peerlefs virtues my every thought does homage. Yet, while I avow a fealty fo unreferved, I am bold enow to confefs my property in the beautifully gloffy lock of hair, a difcovery of which has been fo furreptitioufly obtained; that I have treafured up this lock of hair I alfo acknowledge; nor will I confent to part with it, until the laft breath fhall quiver upon my lips. Further, my own hands fevered the contefted lock from the head of a lovely female, who was dear to me as nature, as amity, or as my fondeft hopes of happinefs. All this is moft true; and it is likewife true, that this female was not Clariffa! Are you immeafurably aftonifhed? Step to the other fide of the piece, and it will affume another hue—I am not a native of America; I have lived only five years in this paradife of liberty. I had a fifter—good God, how unfortunate was that fifter! amiable as virtue, and indulgent as heaven; fhe merited every thing fhort of adoration, from that world which perfecuted her, almoft

from the firft hour of her exiftence. Execrable world! The virtues of a Clariffa were neceffary to reconcile me to an abode among thy deeply defigning, and treacheroufly murderous inhabitants! I have forborne to narrate to my Clariffa the ftory of my fifter's woes; her misfortunes were too ftrongly marked with anguifh, to be impofed upon the exquifitely tender feelings of that fufceptible bofom, which melts with foft regrets at the tale of woe; and which has a figh, even for the common ills of life. Thofe deplorable circumftances which hovered round the fteps of my ill-fated fifter, I have feduloufly fought to blot even from my own memory. I would remember only her virtues, her angel goodnefs, her beauteous image, and her faint-like fortitude; but, alas! thofe recollections are fo interwoven with the cruel events of her life, as to render a feparation impoffible. Orphanaged in her earlieft bud, the fport of caprice, malice, and duplicity, through the unfufpecting morn of life; and in her marriage choice, placing her virtuous confidence in a man, who, by a fpecious exterior, villainoufly deceived her, who wore the garb of integrity, honour, generofity, and a mild, and conceding difpofition of foul, on purpofe to betray her eafy faith; who no fooner exchanged the nuptial vow, than throwing off the mafk, and commencing tyrant, he became unweariedly ingenious in his devices to torment the victim of his power, who perfecuted her to the death, nor fufpended, for a fingle moment, his favage and detefted operations, until, with a broken heart, fhe yielded up her breath, falling the martyr of affumed prerogative, cruelty and defpotifm.— Angelic fufferer! mild and fubmiffive; thou uttered no complaint;

not a vindictive expreffion efcaped thee, and had thy murderer poffeff-ed but common prudence, the knowledge of thy unprecedented wrongs would have been configned to the grave with thee. Through all thy hard fortune I followed ftill an impotent fpectator of thy inju-ries ; but while appearances were preferved, cuftom forbid a brother's interference ! and an impeachment of thy hufband's character, would have been an incurable wound to thy delicacy. What fhall I further fay ? He who made her, regarded her with bland and facred pity, the pity of a God ; her emancipation was accelerated, and fhe drew her laft breath in my arms. I faw her lovely bofom furceafe the corroding figh ; I faw her heavenly form qui-etly difpofed upon the bed of death ; and, my Clariffa, it was in that ag-onized moment, that I fevered from its kindred treffes the fhining ringlet, which, ftraying from its in-clofure, fell unconfcious upon her fnowy forehead. I grieve, my love, that it hath been to you the fource of inquietude, but its value, at that diftreffing period, appeared to me immenfe, nor has reafon, or time, effentially depreciated its impor-tance ; I could never perfuade my-felf to part with it to an artift, who would have oftenfibly returned it to me, in the form of cherubs, urns, and infcriptions, for I have ftill pre-ferred contemplating its natural beauties, and I employed my firft fe-rene moments, in preparing thofe lines, in which to enfhrine it, that have been erroneoufly called poeti-cal. For the gratification of the curiofity of your readers, Mr. Gleaner, I take leave to fubjoin a copy of them :

AH then is the conflict no more !
    And hath fhe forgotten to weep !
Will nought the bleft vifion reftore !
    Hath pity no laurels to reap ?

How loud was that fhriek of defpair,
    The bloffoms of hope are all fhed,
No altars to friendfhip I rear,
    For friendfhip and honour are fled.

The ties are all broke which remain'd,
    The ftorm hath uprooted my peace,
Dark malice its purpofe hath gain'd,
    And love from my bofom fhall ceafe.

How bright was the morn of her days,
    How charming the bud of her years,
Her form, it tranfcended all praife,
    And her forrow was virtue in tears.

How foothing the words of her tongue,
    While harmony wafted the ftrain,
The chantrefs melodioufly fung,
    And gladden'd the liftening fwain.

Bright honour enlifted the fair,
    Maria her prieftefs fhe hail'd,
Ordained her paths to prepare,
    The virgin her altars unveil'd.

But envy, will ferpentine tread,
    And fcorn with its mercilefs fting,
The wiles of deftruction outfpread,
    How deadly the arrows they fling.

What glooms have pervaded the plain,
    The fhepherds are filent around,
Neglected each fweet flowing ftrain,
    So deep is the feftering wound.

And muft I her counfels refign,
    The guide and the ftar of my youth,
Muft friendfhip no longer be mine,
    Integrity, kindnefs, and truth !

Alas! no lov'd folace fuftains,
    How deep is the void in my breaft,
This ringlet is all that remains,
    Of what I fo largely poffefs'd !

Dear veftige of pleafures enjoy'd,
    By cruelty fnatch'd from my grafp,
By rancour infatiate deftroy'd,
    Though ftill the fweet fhadows I clafp.

Memento of friendfhip poffefs'd,
    On nature which bloffom'd and grew,
Which on my fond bofom imprefs'd,
    As innocence tender and true.

Athough you unconfcious entwine,
    Yet beauty your texture defign'd,
Sweet relic of charms that were mine,
    Of elegance bland and refin'd.

My

My penfive regrets you fhall aid,
Companion of every woe,
Of forrow the talifman made,
While my tears all unceafing fhall flow.

The reader will indulge his own reflections ; and I have chofen this method of making my communications to Clariffa, as the emotions which fwell my bofom, when I would attempt to retrace the misfortunes of my injured fifter, are too big for utterance.

I am, fir, with due refpect, and unfeigned wifhes, for your private felicity, and public celebrity, your moft obedient, humble fervant,

ALTAMONT.

LETTER III.
To the GLEANER.

Sententious Alley, No. 3, Dec. 21, 1794.

Courteous Gleaner,

IF Cordelia will take the trouble to order her fervant to make the proper inquiries at Mr. Lovegold, the jeweller's, in Middle-ftreet, fhe will find that her fleeve buttons are laid up there, for the purpofe of obtaining the neceffary repairs. As Cordelia and you feem to underftand one another, I thought beft to give her this information through the channel of your paper.

I am, moft profound, and fage fir, the inconfiderate, and timely admonifhed, HENRY.

" Malice doth merit, as its fhade, purfue."

I could very modeftly propofe myfelf as a new proof of the truth of this oft-cited fentiment, which, if I miftake not, time and obfervation hath elevated into an approved axiom. I could, I fay, leaving thofe who are offended to chew the cud of refentment, eafily confole myfelf, by fo convenient an appropriation ; but I freely confefs, that I fet a high value upon the opinion of the world; I mean the worthy part of the world, to

be fure ; and that ftimulated by this my ruling paffion, I feel myfelf impelled to make my defence, by producing a fhort fketch of my plan of operations.

When I was firft feized with the mania of fcribbling, I very wifely endeavoured to combat it by much deliberate confideration, and many a falutary antidote. Wifdom, attired in the alluring habiliments of tranquillity, and armed with the rhetoric of reafon, fagely advanced her plea, and with great perfpicuity, and energy of argument, fhe advocated that kind of ferenity, which is the accompaniment of the unambitious man; who, gliding down the ftream of time, inhaleth not the feverifh gale ; but wafted onward by the bland and equal breath of contentment, partakes its mildly influence, and lives but to blefs the gently undulating zephyr, that is thus filently impelling him athwart that ocean, upon which the adventurous voyager is fated to contend with hopes, and fears, and with all thofe tumultuous winds of paffion, which frequently involving him in a fearful hurricane, fail not to wreck his peace, whelming beneath their tremendous waves, the brighteft moments of his exiftence ! Wifdom pointed out the wretched ftate of inquietude, anxiety, nightly watchings, and daily fatigues, to which that unhappy and mifguided wight is condemned, who, betrayed by an ignis fatuus, is allured from the humble, vail of foft and filent repofe ; from the calm poffeffion of each focial and domeftic enjoyment, to encounter the various ills attendant upon a purfuit of artificial good. Wifdom enumerated a hoft of weary toils, of woe-begone regrets, of unrecompenfed deeds of worth, of thanklefs achievements, and of barbed difappointments ; and fhe painted

painted in glowing colours the ingratitude of that world to which I would madly devote thofe hours, which, zefted by the fweets of calm reflection, and entwining fubftantial pleafures, would otherwife revolve, marked by the moft refined, rational, and exquifite fatisfaction. Wifdom delineated the thorny circles which begird the hill of fame ; fhe bid me hafte from the magic of her voice, from the mad contagion of her votaries, and, fheltering in the fweet and flowery walks of my natal humility, fhe conjured me to embofom my afpiring views, in the deepeft receffes of that lowly grade, in which nature had indifputably defignated my walk ; and, that fhe might forever dafh my proud pretenfions, and invigorate that defpair, which, with icy grafp, and torpid influence, hovered round my fteps, fhe reprefented in forms tremendoufly terrific, thofe deadly fiends, that with ghaftly features, and unrelenting rigour, eternally guard the glittering domes of fame. Envy, with fnaky locks, empoifoned veins, and peftilential breath—Malice, with tongue envenomed, armed with ten thoufand fhafts of inftant death, and fmiling at deftruction—Pale difappointment, marked by forrow's train, with fad and folemn ftep, heaving corroding fighs, quaffing her copious tears, and in defpondence garbed—and, laft of all, deep Shame, with face averted, eyes withdrawn, and red confuming anguifh, confeffed thy power—Oh, heart appalling, fpirit damping, foul abafhing, Scorn—afflicting Ridicule—Satire's dread fting—the Critic's whip, which hiffed along the air—with every plague which a poor author ever knew ; thefe, wifdom fummoned, and, in fearful order the direful phalanx ftood. Yet, my afpiring mind, fteeled for the

conflict, all in armour clad, and fhielded by temerity—affuming refolution, and armed by perféverance, prefumed with hardy fteps, and enterprifing rafhnefs, to penetrate the embodied oppofition—*and, Reafon plead in vain!* Headlong Ambition, all precepts notwithftanding, continued inflexibly obftinate, and contumacious perverfenefs triumphed in the conflict. Ambition felected its ornaments, and it wore on its left breaft, clofe to the heart, a bouquet, whofe perfumed buds were, with intrepid daring, fnatched from the ftock of ever blooming hope ; in this it prided much, and foully fancied, that fome future day, bedecked with funny beams, would give the deathlefs flowrets to enwreath its time diftinguifhed, time adorned brow. Thus breathing mid fuch odoriferous airs ; incenfe fo fweet inhaling, no wonder that intoxicated Reafon, treading enchanted ground, by magic fpells enfolded, and wrapped in gay delufion, its firmnefs loft—Ambition feized the reins—the die was caft—and helter-fkelter round the world we drove. But, ferioufly, although thus rafhly embarked, judgment occafionally officiates, and while temerity fets at the helm, fhe often, matron like, interpofes her cautionary directions, and to be duly influenced by her counfels, is a prime object, even in the arrangements of ambition.

There is hardly any thing which I have fo much feared, as the fands of oblivion ; and that I might produce a ftream of fufficient depth, to fleet my little fkiff, my faculties pretty diligently exercifed, have been kept in almoft conftant circulation. Mankind have generally furnifhed my refervoir ; and I have fet in the circles which I frequent, induftrioufly improving a hint, marking

marking the fentiment of worth, catching every unwrought gem, and eagerly availing myfelf of thofe circumftances, which I conceived that I might *honeftly* appropriate. Names I have been careful to conceal ; and ftudioufly embellifhing events, and qualifying them to convey amufement, information, or even inftruction, I have produced them as candidates for the attention of a vacant moment. Thus occupied, it will ceafe to be matter of furprife, that I have treafured even the *whifpers* of converfation ; my ear is conftantly on duty, and it hath proved to me a truly faithful fcout. Collected in myfelf, I am often regarded as a mute in fociety ; but I am careful to hoard every remark, and bearing the multifarious burden to my working hive, it undergoeth a chymical procefs ; and after receiving in my pericranium the deftined form, it is with all due humility fubmitted to public obfervation.

Thus Eugenio, if he will give his candour full play, may perceive, that without being the favorite confidantee, " *of all the young handfome married women of my acquaintance,*" I may, *the loquacity of the fex confidered*, legally become poffeffed of *fecrets*, which are *whifpered to felect friends*, which are gathered from myfterious words, and which fometimes refult from thofe expreffive looks, in which the female world are fuch proficients, and which they fo well know when to affume. Upon the whole, while I have generally aimed at utility, I have ftudioufly endeavoured to avoid all occafion of offence ; but if my honeft intentions have not been crowned with fuccefs, as it is impoffible to recal the paft, I can only affure Eugenio, and every reader of his defcription, that I will be indefatigably induftrious to render my future numbers lefs exceptionable.

The CAPRICIOUS LOVERS.

FLORIO and Emelina had lived even from their infancy in the habits of friendfhip ; but at an age in which the fexes find a vacuity in their hearts, they fanned the embers of friendfhip to that height, which neither of them chofe to own under the title of love.

The ftronger the attachment of Emelina became, the more cautious fhe was of difcovering the predilection fhe had ; fhe wifhed for an *ecclairciffement*, but was refolved to fhun it.

Florio, either from pride, from too great delicacy, or from the fame principle by which Emelina was actuated, would often fupprefs his attentions, left they fhould difplay the feelings of his heart. Though

he was fenfible that the queftion could not come with any propriety from Emelina, he was almoft determined it fhould not come from him.

In thefe fluctuations of fufpenfe, they vifited each other for fome time ; and the reftraints with which they fhackled each other, at length made them fufpect, that the lamp of friendfhip began to grow dim, and that the flame was going to expire.

In thefe moments of fufpicion, they were each of them invited to a ball in the neighbourhood ; but before they fat out, both of them refolved to affume a mutual coolnefs, to prevent any difcovery of their attachment, or to afford the leaft fufpicion that they were in a train

which

which might poffibly terminate at the temple of Hymen.

Emelina was afked by the mafter of the ceremony, whether fhe would dance with Florio : fhe refufed with the frown of indignation, and confented to dance with another. A friend of Florio's had previoufly hinted to him, that he expected he would lead out Emelina ; but was anfwered with fo quick a reply in the negative, as convinced him that he was not well pleafed with the queftion.

The dance began, but the agonies of jealoufy embittered all its pleafure. While Emelina thought Florio too affiduous in his attentions to his partner, he, on his fide, thought fhe was more than merely complaifant. After an elegant refrefhment, in which they behaved with an extraordinary coolnefs, which was noticed by every one that was prefent, the company broke up. On which Florio was in fufpenfe whether he fhould offer his hand to Emelina or not : yet good-breeding getting the afcendency of refentment, he made her the proffer of his protection, which fhe accepted of with the greateft reluctance ; a reluctance that was vifible both in her countenance and in the manner in which fhe gave him her hand.

During the whole time they were on their way, no fyllable broke the ftillnefs of filence, and they parted with a very cold adieu on both fides.

On going to bed, Florio gave himfelf up to all the tortures of jealoufy, and imputed Emelina's flight of him to a predilection fhe had for her partner. Sleep did not clofe his eye-lids the whole night ; and when the morning beam darted through his curtains, he rofe in the fame tortures with which he went to bed.

The emotions of Emelina were fimilar, and her fufpicions were equally ftrong of his attachment.

Florio now longed for an ecclairciffement, and for that purpofe went to Emelina's houfe. In his way he fometimes thought of chiding her for her behaviour, at other times he was fearful that fuch a conduct might give her fome intimations, and that he might, by doing fo, convince her that his attachments were more ardent than he chofe to own, or could wifh to difcover. At laft he was determined to be guided by the reception he might receive from her.

On the opening of the door he was acquainted by the fervant, that her miftrefs did not ftand in need of his fervices any longer.

The meffage filled him with horror ; and in the heightof his furprife he formed a refolution to fhorten his exiftence. He walked about the fields, for fome time, like one who was frantic. A fervant of Emelina, who was paffing that way, noticed his behaviour, and on his return informed his miftrefs of what he had feen. Emelina now loft the reftraints of caution, and liftened only to the voice of love ; fhe rufhed out of the houfe in difhabille, with an intent to prevent an event which fhe prefaged.

Florio in the height of his paffion entered into a grove, flung himfelf on the ground, agitated with all the emotions of defpair. His feelings were too great for nature to fupport long ; and his want of reft operating with his paffions, he at laft fell into a kind of flumber.

In this condition Emelina found him, and fufpecting that he had fhortened his life, gave way to her love, accufing herfelf of cruelty, and profeffing that happinefs fhould never reaffume its throne in her breaft.

breaſt. Florio was waked with her lamentations; he roſe with tranſport on hearing her flattering expreſſions, owned a mutual flame, and preſſed her to name the day when he might have the happineſs of leading her te the altar. Emelina at firſt reſumed her former coyneſs, but finding love a more powerful principle than reſerve, ſhe conſented; and they now live in all that warmth of attachment, which muſt always render life deſirable, and matrimony happy.

An Account of MORNE GAROU, a Mountain in the Iſland of St. Vincent, with a Deſcription of the Volcano on its Summit.

[In a letter from Mr. James Anderſon, Surgeon, to Mr. Forſyth. From the Philoſophical Tranſactions, Vol. LXXV. Part I.]

THE many ridges of mountains which interſect this iſland in all directions, and riſe in gradations, one above the other, to a very great height, with the rivers tumbling from their ſides over very high precipices, render it exceeding difficult to explore its interior parts.

The moſt remarkable of theſe mountains is one that terminates the N. W. end of the iſland, and the higheſt in it, and has always been mentioned to have had volcanic eruptions from it. The traditions of the oldeſt inhabitants in the iſland, and the ravins at its bottom, ſeem to me to vindicate the aſſertion.—As I was determined, during my ſtay in the iſland, to ſee as much of it as I could; and as I knew, from the altitude of this mountain, there was a probability of meeting with plants on it I could find in no other part of the iſland; I ſhould have attempted going up if I had heard nothing of a volcano being on it. But viewing the mountain at a diſtance, the ſtructure of it was different from any in the iſland, or any I had ſeen in the Weſt-Indies. I could perceive it divided into many different ridges, ſeparated by very deep chaſms, and its ſummit appeared quite deſtitute of any vege-table production. On examining ſeveral ravins, that run from the bottom a great way up the mountain, I perceived they were quite deſtitute of water, and found pieces of pumice-ſtone, charcoal, ſeveral earths and minerals, that plainly indicated there muſt be ſome very ſingular place or other on ſome part of the mountain. I alſo recollected a ſtory told by ſome very old men in the iſland, that they had heard the captain of a ſhip ſay, that between this iſland and St. Lucia, he ſaw, towards night, flames and ſmoke iſſuing from the top of this mountain, and next morning his decks were covered with aſhes and ſmall ſtones. This, you may readily imagine, was excitement enough to examine it, if I poſſibly could; but I was much diſcouraged upon being told, it was impoſſible to gain the ſummit of it: nor could I get either white men, caribbee, or negro, that would undertake to conduct me up for any reward I could offer; nor could I get any information relative to it. But as difficulty to attain inhances the value of the object, ſo the more I was told of the impoſſibility of going up, the more was I determined to attempt it.

After I had examined the baſis of

of it, as far as I could for the sea and other mountains, to find the most probable place to commence my journey, I observed an opening of several large and dry ravins, that seemingly ran a great way up : but I was not sure if they were not interfected by some rocks or precipices I could not get over. I came to Mr. Maloune's, about a mile distant from the mountain, but the nighest house to it I could stay at all night. Here I met with a friendly reception and great hospitality. After communicating my intentions to him, he told me he would give me every affiftance he could, by fending some trufty negroes with me, and wifhed he was able to go with me himfelf. This was a kind offer to me in my then fituation, as negroes were what I only wanted, having only one boy belonging to Dr. Young with me. I knew, if I had great difficulties in the woods, he and I both fhould be inadequate to the tafk, as in a fhort time we fhould be fo wearied as to be unable to proceed : from what I had feen of the mountain, I knew I muft be under the neceffity of carrying water with me ; and from the great diftance to the top, and obftruftions we might naturally expeft, I fhould at leaft require two days to accomplifh it.

By examining the fide of the mountain towards me with a glafs, I imagined I faw two ridges I might get up. I perceived they were covered, great part of the way, with thick wood ; yet I hoped, with a little cutting, I fhould be able to fcramble through them. I appointed next morning to begin my route by one of thefe ridges.

February 26, 1784, I left Mr. Maloune's about funrife, with two ftout negroes, and Dr. Young's boy ; each of us having a good cut-

lafs, as well to clear our way through the woods, as to defend us in cafe we fhould be attacked by caribbees, or runaway negroes.— We arrived at the bottom of the mountain a little before feven in the morning. To get to either of the ridges, we found we had a rock to climb above forty feet high : it was with great difficulty we fcrambled up, affifting one another in the beft manner we could ; here we found it neceffary to contraft our baggage. After getting up this rock, I found myfelf in the bottom of a narrow and deep ravin. Having afcended this ravin a little way, I faw fome cleared ground on its fides, with tobacco growing. This I conjeftured was the habitation of fome caribbees ; but I was much furprifed when one of the negroes I had with me told me, it was the habitation of a Mr. Cafco, a Frenchman. What could induce a ftout healthy man in the prime of life, and a good mechanic, with feveral negroes, to take up his refidence among rocks and precipices, excluded from the whole world, is a myftery to me. Befides, by every torrent of rain that happens, he may expeft himfelf and all his habitation to be wafhed over the rocks into the ocean. Notwithftanding his fingular fituation, I found him an intelligent man, and I experienced every hofpitality his poor cottage could afford.

The difficulty of going through woods in the Weft Indies, where there are no roads or paths, is far beyond any thing an European can conceive. Befides tall trees and thick underwood, there are hundreds of different climbing plants twifted together like ropes, and running in all direftions to a great extent, and even to the tops of the higheft trees ; by pufhing on they
cannot

cannot be broke, and many of them with difficulty cut; besides a species of grass, the *Schoenus Lithospermos*, with serrated leaves, that cuts and tears the hands and face terribly. With such obstructions as these, it was above two hours before we got on the ridge, where I was in hopes our passage would have been easier; but I soon found my mistake, for I was surrounded with a thick forest, much more difficult to get through than before, on account of the large piles of trees broken down by the hurricanes, to pass which in many parts we were obliged to creep on our hands and feet to get below them, and in other places to climb a great height above the surface of the ground, to get over large trunks lying on one another, and these being frequently rotten, occasioned us to tumble headlong down to a great depth, among rotten wood and grass, so that it was with great difficulty I and the negroes could extricate ourselves. By constantly cutting to clear our way, I, as well as my companions, grew much fatigued, and they wished much to return back. About four in the afternoon I could not prevail upon them to proceed farther; if they did, they could not return before dark, and they would not sleep all night in the woods, but said if I stayed they would return to me next morning. I saw it was impossible to gain the summit of the mountain with the boy only by that route: I likewise saw the woods growing more difficult, my water also totally expended: From these considerations I intended to go down to the Frenchman's, and remain there all night, and try another route with my boy next morning, hoping I might be fortunate enough to find an easier passage. I

arrived at Mr. Gascoe's a little after sun-set, being much fatigued and thirsty, and never experienced more hospitality and kindness than from this man in his miserable cot; for we ought not to judge of the value of the things received, but of the disposition of the heart with which they are given. He parted with his hammock to me, and slept on a board himself. This I at first refused; but he insisted on it, telling me, from my hardships of the day I was much more tired than he. I took the hammock, but I found it was impossible to close my eyes during the night with cold. His hut was built of *roseaux* or large reeds, between each of which a dog might creep through, and the top was covered with dry grass. It is situated in the bottom of a deep gully, where the sun does not shine till nine in the morning, nor after four in the afternoon. It is surrounded by thick wood, and during the night the whole of the mountain is covered with thick clouds, from which it frequently rains; this makes the night air exceedingly cold. I got ready to renew my journey next morning, having only Dr. Young's boy with me, who continued very faithful to me during this excursion, being very active and hardy: I do not know if I could have gone through this fatigue had it not been for his assistance. I now determined to commence this day's route up the ravin, as it seemed to widen and apparently run a considerable way up in the direction I wished for; and if I could get out of it upon the other ridge, it would at least be two miles nearer than the way I had attempted yesterday, and probably, after getting out of it, I might find wood easier of access. In this ravin I got up about a mile

mile and a half, without meeting with any confiderable obftruction. Encouraged by getting fo far, although the ravin was narrowing faft, with numbers of rocks and precipices to climb over with vines and bufhes difficult to get through, I was refolved to perfift in this route and determined by every poffible means to get to the object of my wifhes, well knowing if I could not perform it this way, I might abandon it entirely. After climbing over a number of difficult paffes, the ravin terminated at the bottom of a very high precipice; how far it was to the fummit I did not know, being covered toward the top with thick wood: but from the bottom upwards it was loofe fand as far as I could fee, with ferns and tufts of grafs which, as foon as I took hold of them, came out at the roots. The precipice being fo very fteep, with no trees or bufhes on it to affift me in getting up, I plainly faw the attempting to climb it was at the rifk of my life: However, I was refolved to try it; and telling the boy to keep fome diftance behind me, in cafe I fhould tumble and drive him down along with me, I began to afcend, holding the tufts of grafs as lightly as poffible, and digging holes with my cutlafs to put my feet in; but I often loft my hold, and frequently flipped down a confiderable diftance; however, as it was nothing but loofe fand, I could eafily pufh my cutlafs into it to the handle, and by grafping it could recover myfelf again. Had I not taken the refolution, before I began to afcend, to diveft myfelf of fear, I could not poffibly have gone, for the terror of falling would have been the means of it every inftant. I got up to fome wild plantains, which I faw continued all the way to the place where the bufhes and

trees began to grow. I here refted myfelf, and. waited for the boy's getting to me, which he did much eafier than I, although he had the provifions and water, owing to the track I had made, and becaufe, being much lighter, he could better truft himfelf to the grafs and ferns. After fome labour we arrived at the top of the precipice. I found myfelf on a very narrow ridge, thickly covered with wood, and bounded by two ravins, the bottoms of which I could not fee; the defcent to them feemed to be nearly perpendicular, yet all the way covered with thick wood. After refrefhing ourfelves, we began our fatigue, the boy and I cutting, and carrying our water and provifions alternately. When we had got fome way, I found I was on an exceeding narrow ridge, in many parts not fix feet broad; on each fide a tremendous gulf, into one or other of which I was often in danger of falling, fo that with great caution I was obliged to lie down on my belly, to fee through the bufhes how the ridge tended. Here I began to fmell fulphur, or rather a fmell like gunpowder. As I knew this fmell muft come from the top of the mountain, being in the direction of the wind, I was in hopes we could not be far from it, as the fmell grew ftronger and ftronger as I afcended. I faw a rifing before me, and thought if I was once on it, if the top of the mountain was near I could have a view of it, but having got on this rifing I could only fee a high peak on the N. W. end of the mountain, and by appearance I thought myfelf very little nearer than when I was at the bottom. The woods now became very difficult to get through; great quantities of fallen trees lying buried under long grafs, and being
rotten,

rotten, when I thought myself walking on the ground, I was frequently buried a great depth among them. Being now about noon, and my turn to carry the baggage, and confequently my turn of reft, I was furprifed to hear a ruftling among the bufhes, and fomething like a human voice behind me. As we were now in a place where I had little reafon to fuppofe there had been a human foot before, and could not imagine there could be habitations of caribbees or run-away negroes, fince from the barrennefs of the mountain they could not poffibly find any provifions to fubfift on, I told the boy to ftand ftill, and let us wait their coming up; for if they were caribbees advancing with an intention to hurt us, there was no alternative but to defend ourfelves. You may imagine my furprife when I faw one of the negroes who had been with me the day before, with three others, which Mr. Maloune had fent to my affiftance, with plenty of provifions. After refrefhment, with this affiftance, I renewed my labours with frefh fpirits, and thought I was fure of reaching the top before night. Having proceeded a little, I had a fair view of the ravin on my left, which was of prodigious depth, and ran from near the top of the mountain to the fea; its bottom feemed to be a rock of a colour nearly refembling lava, and appeared as if there had been vaft torrents of fulphureous matter running in it fome time. I regretted much I knew not of this ravin before I commenced my excurfion, as by paffing a head-land in a canoe, and getting into the ravin, I might have gained the fummit of the mountain, without experiencing the delays and difficulties I here encountered. It was now about 4 P. M. and I had no profpect of the mountain's top; but from the afcent of the ravin below, I knew it was a great way off, I thought if I could get into the ravin before night, I could get eafily up next morning. After cutting a great way through wild plantains, the fun near fitting, I found myfelf almoft over the verge of a precipice; by catching hold of fome fhrubs, I prevented myfelf from falling. We were now about half way down; but all the way below us, as far as we could fee, was a perpendicular precipice of rock, feveral hundred feet high, to pafs which was impoffible. I had a view of fome part of the top of the mountain, which I faw was yet far from me; nor could I attempt any other way than the ridge I had left. Being now fun-fet, and the negroes very difcontented, becaufe they could not return that night, I found we muft take up our night's refidence in the place where we were. It was a very unfavourable one, there being nothing but plantains growing, which retaining the rain long in their leaves, and being frequently agitated by the wind, were conftantly dropping, and kept the ground always moift. Being almoft dark, we had time to make us no other habitation, than placing two or three fticks againft an old ftump of a tree, and flightly covering them with plantain leaves. After getting together fome little wood to make a fire to keep us comfortable, it began to blow and rain violently, which continued all night. We foon found our building afforded us no fhelter, and the wood would not burn, fo that we could not get any fire; and the ground on which we were fituated would not allow the leaft exercife to keep us warm. From fuch a miferable night I experienced no mitigation

mitigation for the fatigues of the day. I wifhed for the rifing fun, to renew my labours ; which I at laft beheld with inexpreffible joy.

As foon as we could fee, we returned to the ridge we left the night before, and began to work with alacrity, as we were almoft chilled with cold. I pufhed on as faft as poffible, and about ten o'clock found the woods began to grow thin. I could not fee the top of the mountain, but had a view of feveral ridges that joined it. From the wind falling, and the heat growing intenfe, I thought we muft then be under the cover of the fummit: I here found many new plants. About eleven A. M. I was overjoyed to have a full view of the fummit of the mountain, nearly a mile diftant from us, and that we were nearly out of the woody region. The top feemed to be compofed of fix or feven different ridges, very much broken in the fides, as if they had fuffered great convulfions of nature ; they were divided by amazing deep ravins, without any water in them. I obferved where the ridges met the edge of a large excavation, as it feemed to be, on the higheft part. I imagined this might be the mouth of the crater, and directed my courfe to a high peak which overlooked it. I found here a moft beautiful tree which compofed the laft wood. After that I entered into a thick long grafs, intermixed with fern, which branched and ran in every direction. To break it was impoffible, and with great difficulty I could cut it ; fo that in clearing our way through the grafs, eight or ten feet high, there was equal difficulty as in the woods, and it feemed to continue very near to the top of the mountain. Being now about noon, I and the negroes were fo fatigued

as hardly to be able to ftand ; our thirft very great, to allay which, as much as poffible, we chewed the leaves of the Begonia obliqua. Two of the negroes returned, and the others faid they would go no farther with me, as they muft perifh for want of water, and it would be impoffible to get to the bottom before night, and they muft all die in the woods. The propriety of their reafoning was evident to me ; yet I thought it hard, after the fatigues of three days and two nights, to be within half a mile of the top, and not to be able to get up, and to know little more about it than I did at the bottom. As the negroes had not the fame motive for going up as I, all my reafoning was to them ineffectual : I found I was obliged to return myfelf, as I could not perfift alone. At half paft twelve we began to defcend the fame way we came. As there was now a clear pafs all the way to the bottom, we got down to Mr. Cafco's by fun-fet. After fitting fome time here, I was hardly able to rife again I was fo tired, and my feet were fo fore I could hardly ftand on them ; for, my fhoes being torn to pieces, I came down the whole way barefooted. I continued my journey, however, to Mr. Maloune's, where I arrived between fix and feven at night.

March 4th, being the day I had fixed to finifh my excurfion, about four in the morning, I left the houfe of Mr. Frafer, who out of curiofity agreed to accompany me, of which I was very glad, as he was a fenfible young man ; and with the affiftance of two negroes we purfued our journey. We found very little obftruction in our way up, until we got to the place where I returned ; and there, for about a quarter of a mile, we had confiderable uble difficulty to clear our way through grafs and ferns. After we came within a quarter of a mile, from the top, we found ourfelves, in another climate all at once, the air very cold, and the vegetable productions changed; here was nothing but barrennefs over the whole fummit of the mountain. On the confines of the graffy region and the barren I found fome beautiful plants. Mofs grows here in fuch plenty, that I frequently funk up to my knees in it. This is the only place in the Weft-Indies that produced any mofs that I have feen. About noon we had gained the top of the peak I had directed my courfe to before; when, in an inftant, we were furprifed with one of the grandeft and moft awful fcenes I had ever beheld. I was ftruck with it amazingly, as I could not have conceived fuch a very large and fo fingularly formed an excavation. It is fituated on the center of the mountain, and where the various ridges unite. Its diameter is fomething more than a mile, and its circumference to appearance a perfect circle. Is depth from the furrounding margin is above a quarter of a mile, and it narrows a little, but very regularly to the bottom. Its fides are very fmooth, and for the moft part covered with fhort mofs, except towards the fouth, where there are a number of fmall holes and rents. This is the only place where it is poffible to go down to the bottom: It is exceedingly dangerous, owing to the number of fmall chafms. On the weft fide is a fection of red rock like granite, cut very fmooth, and of the fame declivity with the other parts. All the reft of the furrounding fides feems to be compofed of fand, that looks to have undergone the action of intenfe fire. It has a

cruft quite fmooth, of about an inch thick, and hard almoft as rock; after breaking through which, you find nothing but loofe fand. In the center of the bottom is a burning mountain of about a mile in circumference, of a conic form, but quite level. On the fummit, out of the center of the top, arifes another mount, eight or ten feet high, a perfect cone; from its apex iffues a column of fmoke. It is compofed of large maffes of red *granite-like* rock of various fizes and fhapes, which appear to have been fpilt into their prefent magnitudes by fome terrible convulfion of nature, and are piled up very regular. From moft parts of the mountain iffue great quantities of fmoke, efpecially on the north fide, which appears to be burning from top to bottom, and the heat is fo intenfe, that it is impoffible to go upon it. Going round the bafe is very dangerous, as large maffes of rock are conftantly fplitting with the heat, and tumbling to the bottom. At the bottom, on the north fide, is a very large rock fplit in two; each of thefe halves, which are feparated to a confiderable diftance from each other, is rent in all directions, and from the crevices iffue efflorefcences of a gloffy appearance, which tafte like vitriol, and alfo beautiful cryftallizations of fulphur. On all parts of the mountain are great quantities of fulphur in all ftates; alfo alum, vitriol, and other minerals. From the external appearance of this mountain, I amagine it has only began to burn lately, as on feveral parts of it I faw fmall fhrubs and grafs, which looked as if they had been lately fcorched and burnt. There are feveral holes on the fouth, from which iffues fmoke, feemingly broken out lately, as the bufhes round are but lately burnt.

burnt. On two oppofite fides of the burning mountain, eaft and weft, reaching from its bafe to that of the fide of the crater, are two lakes of water, about a ftone's throw in breadth ; they appear to be deep in the middle ; their bottom to be covered with a clay-like fubftance. The water feems pleafant to the tafte, and is of a chalybeate nature, I fuppofe thefe lakes receive great increafe, if they are not entirely fupported, by the rain that tumbles down the fide of the crater. I obferved on the north fide of the bottom traces of beds of rivers, that to appearance run great quantities of water at times to both thefe lakes. By the ftones at their edges, I could perceive that either abforption or evaporation, or perhaps both, go on faft. The greater part of the bottom of the crater, except the mountain and two lakes, is very level. On the fouth part are feveral fhrubs and fmall trees.

There are many ftones in it that feem to be impregnated with minerals : I faw feveral pieces of pumice-ftone. I alfo found many ftones about the fize of a man's fift, rough, on one fide blue, which appearance, I imagine, they have got from heat, and being in contact with fome mineral. Thefe ftones are fcattered over the whole mountain, one or two of which I have fent you, with fome others.

After I had got up from the bottom of the crater, I could not help viewing it with admiration, from its wonderful ftructure and regularity. Here I found an excavation cut through the mountain and rocks to an amazing depth, and with as much regularity and proportion of its conftituent parts, as if it had been planned by the hand of the moft fkilful mathematician. I wifhed

much to remain on the mountain all night, to examine its feveral ridges with more attention next day ; but I could not prevail on my companion to ftay, and therefore thought it advifable to accompany him. I obferved the motion of the clouds on this mountain to be very fingular. Although there are feveral parts on it higher than the mouth of the crater, yet I faw their attraction was always to it. After entering on its eaft or windward fide, and whirling round the northweft fide, they funk a confiderable way into it ; then, mounting the oppofite fide, they ran along a ridge, which tended nearly north-eaft, and afterwards funk into a deep ravin, which divided this ridge from another on the north-weft corner of the mountain, and the higheft on it, lying in a direction nearly fouth and north. They keep the courfe of this ridge to the fouth end, and then whirl off weft in their natural courfe.

I took my departure from the mountain with great reluctance. Although I encountered many difficulties to get up, yet it amply rewarded me for all my toil ; but I had not time to examine it with that attention I wifhed. When I got on the peak from which I had my firft view of it, and from which I could fee its different parts, I could not help reviewing it feveral times. After imprinting its ftructure on my mind, I took my final adieu of it, and returned down, and got to Mr. Frafer's houfe about feven at night, much fatigued.

I am forry I had no inftruments to take the ftate of the air, nor the exact dimenfions of the different parts of the mountain ; but, I believe, on meafurement, they will be more than I have mentioned.

From the fituation of thefe iflands to one another, and to the continent

nent of South-America, I imagine there are fub-marine communications between the burning mountains or volcanoes in each of them, and from them to the volcanoes on the high mountains of America.—The iflands which are fituated next the continent, feem to tend in the direction of thofe mountains ; and I have obferved, that the crater in this ifland lies nearly in a line with Soufriere, in St. Lucia and Morne Pelée in Martinique, and I dare fay from Morne Pelée to a place of the fame kind in Dominique, and from it to the others ; as it is certain there is fomething of this kind in each of thefe iflands, Barbadoes and Tobago excepted, which are quite out of the range of the reft.

There is no doubt but eruptions or different changes in fome of them, although at a great diftance, may be communicated to affect the others in various manners. It is obferved by the inhabitants round thefe burning mountains, that fhocks of earthquakes are frequent near them, and more fenfibly felt than in other parts of the ifland, and the fhocks always go in the direction of them.

I cannot omit mentioning the great affiftance I received in the above excurfion from Dr. Young, Mr. Maloune, and Mr. Frafer ; for, without the aid of their negroes, I I could not have poffibly gone through with it.

The SPECULATOR. No. V.

Non obtufa adeo geftamus pectora Pœni,
Nec tam averfus equos Tyria fol jungit ab urbe.——VIRG. Æn.

THE hiftory of the human mind, as exemplified in its progreffive paffage, from the depreffion of barbarifm to the elevation of refinement, is to the philofopher an object of refearch equally fafcinating and profitable. To follow the firft faint drawings of intellect, which, in the infancy of nations, burft by intervals through furrounding darknefs, to that blaze and energy with which the powers of mind expand in the maturity of more polifhed times, is a contemplation that foothes the pride of man, and fills the foul with elevated ideas of the dignity of its own nature. Nor are fuch inveftigations to be held as merely abftract or inapplicable to utility. To him who carefully examines and compares the various pictures of national advancement, the chain connecting caufes and effects is laid o-

pen, while he learns the influence of thefe powers, by which the progrefs of refinement had been hitherto haftened or retarded ; he gains a knowledge which may not be unprofitably applied to the future.

In the ftudy of a hiftory fo important as that of the mind, inquiries into the ftate of polite literature, as modified by various caufes in different countries, have ever made a principal part. The more delicate and loftier efforts of imagination, the keen tafte of beauty and elegance, tardily unfold themfelves in the foul. They mark the maturity of nations like that of individuals, and the progrefs of the finer arts, is the ftandard by which the real intellectual rank of a people is ufually beft eftimated.

The inquifitive and philofophic fpirit of the Englifh, has peculiarly prompted them to fuch refearches.
The

The plenteous field of foreign improvement has always excited the industry of innumerable labourers, and our eagernefs to inveftigate the caufes and conditions of refinement among the neighbouring nations has ufually kept pace with our own advancement. At a period when this tafte appears rather to be increafing than upon the wane and when the mutual intercourfe of nations becomes, from a thoufand caufes, every day more facilitated, it appears fingular, that one country alone, in which the fciences have been long and fuccefsfully cultivated, fhould experience a neglect as mortifying as it is undeferved. The polite literature of the Germans, has efcaped the general fpirit of inquiry, and by fome fatality feems hitherto to have repreffed learned curiofity, and damped the ardor of inveftigation. While the productions of the French, however uncongenial to the fpirit of our ifland exert, as foreign, a peculiar claim on our complacency ; this province, rich and inexhauftible as it promifes to be, has little excited the ambition of conqueft, or roufed the cupidity of literary induftry. A language inimical to the Germans, has been propagated among us by tradition, till it has nearly gained the authority of prefcription. Dullnefs is, by a kind of charm, affociated with their names, and the herefay farcafm detailed from hand to hand, has filled our minds with prejudices againft a people, whofe merits we have hitherto been little able to appreciate. The profeffed language of panegyric, and the blind ignorance of prepoffeffion, are equally unfriendly to the caufe of truth. Later years have witneffed in Germany the cultivation of many of the finer arts ; with what fuccefs, it is for candour and coolnefs only to determine. To attract fome fhare of attention to a fubject where curiofity is fo laudable, and, by giving an idea, faint as it may be, of the exertions of the Germans, in works of tafte and imagination, to enable others to judge a little better of the rank which literary juftice fhould affign them, will be attempted in a few fketches, interwoven with the plan of the prefent work. Of thefe the execution may claim much indulgence, but their intention can hardly be unfavourably confidered.

The introduction of German literature into England has taken place under circumftances the moft unfavourable to its adoption. Our firft acquaintance with the German Mufe was formed on the commencement only of her progrefs to that maturity fhe has fince attained. With this, other caufes concurring, curiofity was little roufed, indifference foon fucceeded, and the impreffions then received were tranfmitted to fucceeding times. Thefe continue to exert an influence in the prefent period, when the rapid progrefs of German improvement has rendered their application abfolutely unjuft. The French, from a variety of caufes, ever inimical to their lefs volatile neighbours, have formerly exerted, at their expenfe, the powers of ridicule, which, however applicable, when directed to the dark age of German genius, lofes all point, when the modern era is the object. The charge of tamenefs and want of fire has been made, till the ftigma becomes difficultly infeparable from the efforts of German imagination. The wide diffufion of the French tongue, and the little fphere to which the other language is confined, has on one fide given every advantage to propagate an accufation, and on the other rendered a public appeal almoft moſt impracticable. At a late period, however, the prepoſſeſſions even of the French are beginning to relax. The merits of thoſe, they once oppoſed with acrimony and contempt, are daily making more impreſſion; and the hoſtile obloquy they ſo long preſerved, is, atoned for by the eagernefs with which the German literature is received and transfuſed into their language.—Little as our nation is acquainted with the modern writers of Germany; ſome ſpecimens are familiar to us; which yield ſufficient proof, that whatever deficiency of ſtrength might mark the earlier compoſitions of that country, the ſpirit which pervades the later literary performances is of a character directly oppoſite.

The Sorrows of Werter, the beauties of which, glowing with all the fire of genius, and the enthuſiaſm of exquiſite paſſion, have furniſhed ſo many themes to the poet and the painter, has, as a compoſition; long excited our admiration, though apparently without awakening much curioſity for the other numerous productions of Goethe's bold and vivid pencil. In the ſiſter art of poetry, the Germans have long vindicated to themſelves a rank among the higheſt; the whole of Europe has recogniſed the merits of a ſtyle of muſic; as original and touching as it is incompatible with mere laborious tameneſs. A muſic, to whoſe excellence the heart of feeling will ever bear the trueſt teſtimony, while it vibrates to the fiery wildneſs of an Haydn, or melts to the ſoft and paſſionate ſtrains of the tender Pleyel.

To the common prepoſſeſſion of want of ſpirit and intereſt, in the productions of the Germans, another cauſe has contributed. A peculiar fate attended ſome of the firſt poems which appeared among us in an Engliſh dreſs. Stripped of the poetic beauties of the original; the tranſlations reduced the ſublimity and varied meaſure of Klopſtock's verſification; and the harmonious ſoftneſs of Geſner, to one ſtandard of monotonous proſe, which; from the peculiarity of ſtructure, has long attracted the ſarcaſms of criticiſm. Little would it be ſuſpected by the mere Engliſh reader, that Klopſtock, in his Meſſiah has taken the Greek hexameter as the model of his verſe; and has almoſt exhauſted the riches of a language the moſt copious, in the varieties of his modulation and cadence. A literary proceſs like this, few poems can ſuſtain without the loſs of half their beauties. Homer and Virgil themſelves; would probably; if ſubjected to it, but little attract wonder; or arreſt attention. An idea of difficulty almoſt inſuperable; annexed to the acquiſition of the language of the Germans, has tended to produce an indifference to their literature. That the language is not among thoſe moſt eaſy of acquiſitions will readily be allowed, though no ſmall portion of the impediments may perhaps appear to examination founded on prejudice.

The ſarcaſtic criticiſms of the French and other nations on the harſhneſs of our own tongue, will incline us not to ſit in judgment too ſevere on the want of harmony in the German. Wieland, in his Muſarion and Oberon. by ſhewing that the German language is not unſuſceptible of muſical ſoftneſs and elegance, has performed a ſervice to his native tongue, like that for which our own is indebted to Pope. The immediate connexion of the German language with the Engliſh, and the light which its direct relation is ſo able to throw

on

on many dark and ambiguous parts of the latter, is a claim to attention which it is singular to find has produced so little effect. The productions of a nation, near to us in point of situation and connexion, in a language from which so great a part of our own is evidently borrowed, have in some of our writers experienced a neglect, which would lead us to suppose the Germans were as remote and little interesting to us as the Chinese ; and that their tongue emulated the Egyptian hieroglyphics in obscurity. Fortunately for the extension of English letters, these opinions have not been mutual. The language of England makes in Germany a part of education, and is even regularly taught by the professor of an university. The Germans have received the productions of the English with a degree of cordiality and eagerness which marks congeniality of sentiment, and have translated into their own language, most of our works that are distinguished by celebrity.

The progress of Germany towards the refinement of the politer arts, has been complicated with circumstances not a little singular. At a period when the more important of the European nations, after shaking off the mental slavery of so many ages of ignorance and darkness, were rising high in the scale of intellect, it was difficult among the writers of that country to find a single vestige which marked the development of those faculties of mind, which have elegance and beauty for their object. The taste for the theology and logic of the schools, and the spirit of minute and laborious research, continued long after the revival of letters to keep possession of Germany, and effectually to repress the exertions of imagination, or the invention of ge-

nius. Even that great event in which Germany had so proud a share, which loosened the shackles from human reason, and vindicated the dignity of man, did not produce the effect of bringing forward the finer faculties of the mind, to which it seemed necessarily to lead. The efforts of Luther, Melancthon, Reuchlin, and Hutten, were able to break the bands of tyranny and superstition, but little to advance their cotemporaries in refinement.

A few exceptions to the general inactivity in which Germany appears so long to languish, are, however, to be made. The Minnesingern, a species of Troubadours, in the 13th, 14th, and 15th centuries, have vindicated their existence from oblivion, by some works which are said to possess peculiar merit, as those of Reynard der Zeter, and Walter der Vogelweide ; and in the later periods which were prior to the shining era of Haller, some names have reached posterity. Opitz, who preceded Haller by near a century, is even at present able to claim attention and admiration.

Various causes, the concurrence of which continued for so long a time to exert an influence unfriendly to the progress of the finer arts in Germany, are obvious to research. Among the first of these, is that severity of fate, which, from the earliest periods, has visited Germany with a series of destructive wars, of which the local situation has rendered it too opportune a theatre. When the darkness which had so long brooded thick and heavy over Europe, was beginning to disperse, and the exiled Muses once more claiming their naive seats, dared to vindicate their pristine honours, this country was visited by few and distant gleams of mental light, and could offer little shelter
or

or protection to returning fcience. The influence of the feudal fyftem continuing to operate from local caufes for fo great a length of time, the anarchy arifing from the difcordant principles of the Germanic conftitution, and the ravages of war raging in the very heart of the empire, rendered Germany no afylum for elegant literature, when juft efcaping from the long oppreffion of the dark ages. Caufes of this kind, particularly the laft, have continued to act, though with diminifhed powers, even to a late period. As the fcattered fovereignties that compofe the imperial body, inftead of multiplying the patrons of the arts, divided and weakened the power of protection; this circumftance contributed ftill farther to render the progrefs of the finer arts precarious, from the want of conftant foftering care, and the funfhine of power. To this was added, a contempt of literature, not difficult to be traced to its proper origin, which for a long time marked the character of the nobles of Germany. Thefe, impreffed with ideas of feudal dignity, looked down on the profeffors of literature as of a lower rank, and little entitled to refpect. or encouragement; while the man of fcience, excluded from courts and condemned to obfcurity, felt the elevation of learning degraded, and the motives of activity grow languid. At a time when, from obftacles like thefe, the progrefs of Belles Lettres had been weak and tardy among the Germans, they became acquainted with French literature, which had arrived at a ftate of high elegance and polifh. The little efforts they had made before this period became for a time ftill lefs; and dazzled with the fuperior fplendor of French letters, they feemed almoft to defert their own

language. The decided preference of the great Frederic for the French tongue, and the contempt he fo openly expreffed for his own, contributed at leaft partially to keep up a tafte fo uncongenial to the real fpirit of the Germans. Unable to contend in point of harmony and delicacy with the language of the French, the German writers felt their ardor damped, and the native literature was feverely checked by the introduction of the foreign riches of another tongue.

Thus, for a long and barren period, the Mufes of Germany flumbered in ufelefs inactivity, while the fpirit of patient inveftigation, or laborious induftry feemed effectually to have extinguifhed the efforts of imagination, and the enthufiafm of the fine arts. The few and fhort exertions of native genius, which at intervals blazed for a moment, only marked more forcibly the furrounding darknefs. But the opening of the prefent century, ufhered in the dawn of that fplendor which was at laft to difpel the graceful fhade that had fo long hovered over Germany. The venerable names of Haller, and his cotemporaries, ftand firft on that lift of fame which vindicates the Germans from the reproach of deficiency in inventive talents.— The call went forth which was to roufe the fleeping genius of the nation from the lethargy of ages.— An emulative fpirit feemed to pervade the fucceffion of writers that followed; and the creative wit of Wieland, the deep pathos of Leffing and Schiller, the tender fimplicity of Gefner, and the fiery enthufiafm of Goethe, began to difclofe themfelves. The brilliant era was eftablifhed in which the Germans faw the foundation of their literary glory fecured, and looked forward, in well-founded confidence, to the
speedy

ſpeedy approach of that time when they ſhould be enabled to conteſt the palm of fame with the proudeſt of thoſe nations, who would once have thought themſelves diſgraced by the very competition.

R E V I E W.

The Natural and Civil Hiſtory of Vermont.—By Samuel Williams, L. L. D. 8vo. price 12ſ.

THIS work we confidently pronounce a moſt valuable acquiſition to the republic of letters.

A wiſh to favour the moſt trifling literary effort in our country, or a more ſordid motive, has in too many inſtances proſtituted public commendation. The ſincere friends of genius and of ſcience, while, from the nature of the work, and the reputation of the author, they promiſed themſelves little amuſement or inſtruction, would not withhold their names from the liſt of ſubſcribers, much leſs would they withhold from the work ſo cheap a tribute as that of praiſe. But, we are confident, the talents and the exertions to which the public is indebted for the Hiſtory of Vermont, will find a recompenſe in a more intereſted motive. The philoſopher, the ſtateſman, and the naturaliſt, will find themſelves much amuſed and more inſtructed. Perhaps we ſhould not detract from the merits of the publications extant, ſhould we challenge their extenſive number for a work of this ſize, which diſplays a more general acquaintance with ſcience.

The ſtyle is not without its faults. Yet they are ſuch faults, as are always to be found in the writings of thoſe authors, who are more intent upon the matter of their narration, than upon the manner of framing their ſentences. Like the country which our author deſcribes, his ſtyle exhibits a native majeſty, not deprived of the charms of variety by the refinements of modern cultivation.

The work commences with the natural hiſtory of the ſtate. In this the reader will find an account of the ſituation, ſoil, mountains, rivers and lakes, climate, and vegetable productions of the country. In this account, many curious and philoſophic obſervations and remarks are made, which evince the author to be well qualified for this part of his undertaking.

The author then preſents us with a deſcription of the various quadrupeds, birds, fiſhes, &c. In this part of the work, the reader will find much amuſement, particularly in the hiſtory of the beaver.

To this ſucceeds a very intereſting account of the employments, government, education, manners, and cuſtoms of the original inhabitants of America. This part of the work is concluded with the following remarks upon the progreſs of ſociety among the Indians.

" The progreſs of ſociety among the Indians, would make a curious and the moſt uſeful part of their hiſtory. The rudeſt and moſt ſimple ſtate that took place among them, was that which I have been deſcribing. Whereſoever the ſavages continued to derive their ſupport from hunting, they continued from age to age in the ſame condition,

dition, and made no improvements. Where the means of fubfiftence were plentiful, and eafy to be procured, the Indians had advanced beyond the ftate of an hunter, and began to increafe their numbers, and their agriculture. In fuch places, fociety began to affume a different form, from what it bore in their rudeft and moft fimple ftate. And the tendency of it was every where to *monarchy.*—In the fouthern parts of Newengland, and Virginia, fome of the tribes were advancing faft to the form of hereditary monarchy. In the hotter climates it was already eftablifhed. This was the cafe in Florida, among the Natchez on the Miffifippi, in Cuba, Hifpaniola, and all the large iflands. In Bagotta, Mexico, and Peru, monarchy had acquired its perfect form, its full powers, and a complete eftablifhment. In each of thefe places, the progrefs of government had been from perfect freedom and independence, to almoft abfolute and unlimited monarchy. In the courfe of this progrefs, two remarkable phenomena appeared : In one part of America, an empire and a monarchy was eftablifhed, in moft refpects refembling thofe which had arifen in the other hemifphere. In another part of America, an empire and a monarchy was produced, far fuperior to thofe which were produced in the other parts of the globe.

"In the empire of Mexico, almoft every thing had taken the Afiatic, and European courfe. The great body of the people were reduced to a degraded and humiliating ftate ; and held their lives, and performed their labours, under various names and degrees of degradation and abafement. A body of nobility were poffeffed of ample territories, of great privileges, powers, and honours, under different names and degrees. Above and over all, was the monarch, enjoying fupreme power and dignity. After being elective during the reign of eleven of their fovereigns, the monarchy was become almoft abfolute and hereditary, in Montezuma. The fyftem of religion agreed perfectly well to the nature of the government : It was fevere, cruel, and barbarous ; and delighted in the fprinkling and fhedding of blood : Human facrifices of all others were efteemed the moft acceptable and availing ; and the priefts had the privilege, the honour and the profit, of announcing or removing the vengeance of the gods. This fyftem of monarchy had acquired a ftability, a regularity, and a vigour equal to any monarchy that was then upon the earth. Upon comparing the fpirit of monarchy, untempered by reprefentation, in America, in Afia, and in Europe; the fpirit and the principles of it, will be found every where to have operated alike. It degrades the body of the people below the condition and nature of man. It exalts the nobles and the fovereign above the condition and ftate, which nature defigns or admits. In one form or another it has always been attended with a perfecuting, cruel, and bloody religion, put into the hands of a wealthy and powerful priefthood. It has conftantly produced the fpirit of war and deftruction ; and generally derived to itfelf fecurity, wealth, and power, from the mifery, deftruction, and flaughter, it has entailed on the human race. By placing the rulers in a fituation altogether unnatural, that is, above all fenfe of accountability to their fellow men, it has produced that conftant, fteady, and univerfal abufe of power, which in every part of the globe, has been the diftinguifhing and

and certain effect of this form of government. Its spirit and principle have every where been the same; not the *honour* which the great Montesquieu wished to ascribe to it, and wanted to find in it, but that total want of regard and accountability to man, which with great accuracy and propriety, has been lately named *a contempt of the people.*

"The empire of Peru was formed and governed by a species of monarchy, different from what has ever taken place among any other people. Twelve successive monarchs, for a period of more than four hundred years, had been invested with hereditary and absolute power. They claimed this authority, not as derived to them in any manner or degree from the people, but as the absolute and exclusive donation of heaven. They announced themselves to be the children of the sun, and clothed with divine and unlimited power to direct all the civil and religious affairs of the people. The sovereign was named *Inca ;* and so sacred and pure were the family of the inca's, in the minds of the people, that they were universally esteemed incapable of committing a crime, or falling into an errour : No other family might marry or mingle with it, for fear of polluting the heavenly blood. The people looked up to them, as to beings of a superior and heavenly race : And all disobedience to them, was viewed not barely as a crime committed against men, but as an act of rebellion against God. The nobility of course was nothing more than families of office. Though a difference of rank had taken place throughout the empire, all but the children of the sun, were supposed to belong to the common race of men. The people were well clothed and fed ;

every where distinguished for their industry, economy, moderation, contentment, and happiness. Over this people, the incas, though absolute in power, established a government the most mild and gentle, that has ever taken place in any part of the earth. The morals of the people were so pure, that few crimes were ever committed : The genius of the government was so mild, that few punishments were ever executed : And when they were, they were viewed as the necessary acts of God, and not of men. Their government, the dominion of prosperity and virtue, was esteemed by the people the dominion of God and his inca.—Their system of religion, like their government, was mild, gentle, and pacific. The sun, the emblem of light, serenity, fertility, beneficence, joy, and life, was the object of their adoration. They offered to him a part of those productions, which they derived from cultivating the earth, enriched by his genial warmth. They presented to him specimens of those works of ingenuity, which they had performed by his light. And they brought to him some of those animals, which were nourished by his influence. But the inca never stained their altars with human blood ; or admitted the savage idea, that the source of beneficence could be pleased with the persecution, cruelty, and destruction of men.—Their system of war partook of the same spirit of mildness, and wisdom. They fought not to exterminate, but to conquer : They conquered not to enslave, but to improve, to civilize, and refine. No cruel torture awaited the captive ; no barbarous marks of degradation, disgrace, triumph, or slavery, were reserved for the prisoners. They were taught the same system of government and religion,

as

as the reft of the people ; they were admitted to the fame privileges, and treated with the fame lenity and mildnefs. Of all the triumphs of the inca, the nobleft and the greateft was to diffufe the manifold bleffings of peace and happinefs, to the people whom they had fubdued.

"Such was the genius, the fpirit, and the effect, of the fyftem of monarchy that was eftablifhed in Peru. We need not hefitate to pronounce it fuperior to any, that was then to be found upon the face of the earth. The genius and the fpirit of it were above all others, mild and gentle ; the object and the aim of it, were in fact, the improvement and the happinefs of the people. And if any government ever produced this effect, that government was the monarchy of Peru : Not the attainment of the moft polifhed nations of Afia, and Europe, of their arts, fcience, and improvements ; but of the greater wifdom and fimplicity of the Indians, and incas of America.

" We have here a phenomenon, new, and almoft incredible in the political world. Abfolute, unlimited, and hereditary monarchy, which has never failed before or fince to prove one of the heavieft curfes, which has fallen upon mankind ; in Peru became mild, gentle, and beneficent : And was conftantly employed during the reign of twelve fucceffive monarchs, to refine, civilize, and improve the people ; and to do the greateft good to mankind. And yet this was a fyftem not founded in truth, or in nature ; but in delufion and fuperftition. What could give it a direction fo fteady, uniform, and benevolent ? Not the form, but the principle of it. It contained the beft and the pureft principle, that can enter into the nature of human

government. Its origin, duration, and power, depended wholly upon *the public fentiment*. The inca claimed immediate defcent, and relation to the fun. The fun was the emblem of peace, and benevolence. Had the monarch ftained his character by enormity in crimes and vices, or by a conftant abufe of power, nature would have taught the Peruvians that monfters in corruption, vice, and cruelty, could not have been the favourite children of the Deity. If the inca had been viewed in this light, all his divinity, and his power would have ended. His power was founded altogether in the opinion the people had formed of his divine defcent, qualifications, character, and virtues. So folicitous had the incas been to preferve this opinion, that through the whole period of their fucceffions, they had taken the moft fcrupulous care not to endanger or oppofe it, by any bafe and unworthy conduct. And while they thus proved the conftant friends and benefactors of the people, the public efteem and veneration increafed.— In the benevolence and ufefulnefs of the inca, the people believed they faw the children of the fun : And in the affections and opinions of the people, the inca found an abfolute and unlimited power. But if his conduct had plainly difcovered, that inftead of being the child of the fun, he was the child of folly, of vice, and abominable iniquity, his divinity, his power, and his empire would have ceafed with the public opinion.

" Inftead then of being founded in a contempt of the people like the empire of Mexico, the monarchy of Peru had the fingular good fortune of being founded in the public fentiment. This rendered the inca accountable to the people for every part

part of his conduct: And this sense of accountability would keep a constant sense of duty and character upon his mind. Thus under the form of absolute hereditary monarchy, the government of Peru had the uncommon advantage of excluding nobility with all its odious distinctions and claims; and of embracing the best and purest principles, upon which civil government can ever be founded. The Indians seem to have been the only people, among whom, a regard to the public sentiment and benefit, did in fact constitute the spirit and principle of hereditary and absolute monarchy."

The civil history of the state is then introduced with an account of the first settlement of Vermont by the English: The opposition to the formation of Vermont into an independent state, and the consequent difficulties and disturbances; together with the political consequences of the controversies, respecting the admission of Vermont into the Union, are then stated with much apparent impartiality. After an account of the employments, customs, and manners of the people; their institution and laws; with many useful remarks on the means of acquiring subsistence; on the cause and effects of the American war, the history concludes with the following beautiful observations on the nature and preservation of freedom.

" No other cause but that which first produced the freedom of America, will prove sufficient to support and preserve it. It is in the state of society that civil freedom has its origin and support. The effect can never be more pure or perfect, than the causes from whence it arises; and all those causes terminate in the state and condition of the people. The form of government by which the public business is to be done, a bill of rights to ascertain the just claims of the people, a constitution to direct and restrain the legislature, a code of laws to guide and direct the executive authority, are matters of high importance to any people; and are justly esteemed among the wisest productions, of ancient or modern times. But no people ought to expect that any thing of this nature will avail to secure, or to perpetuate their liberties. Such things are consequences, not the causes; the evidences, not the origin of the liberties of the people. They derive their whole authority and force from the public sentiment; and are of no further avail to secure the liberties of the people; than as they tend to express, to form, and to preserve the public opinion. If this alters and changes, any bill of rights, any constitution or form of government, and law, may easily be set aside, be changed, or be made of none effect. For it will never be dangerous for the government of any people, to make any alterations or changes, which the public opinion will either allow, justify, or support. Nor ought any people to expect, that their legislators or governors will be able to preserve their liberties, for a long period of time. Any body of men who enjoy the powers and profits of public employments, will unavoidably wish to have those profits and powers increased. The difficulties they will meet with in the execution of their office, the unreasonable opposition that will be made by many to their wisest and best measures, and the constant attempts to displace them, by those whose only aim and wish is to succeed them; such things, joined with a natural love of power and

and profit, will not fail to convince all men in public employments, that it would be beft for the public to put more confidence and power in them. While they thus wifh and aim to increafe and add ftrength to their own powers and emoluments, thofe powers and emoluments will be called the powers and the dignity of government. It may be doubted whether men are much to blame, for wifhing and aiming at that, which their fituation and employment naturally leads to.— The effect feems to be univerfal. It has ever been the cafe that government has had an univerfal tendency, to increafe its own powers, revenues, and influence. No people ought to expect that things will have a different tendency among them : That men will ceafe to be men, or become a more pure and perfect order of beings, becaufe they have the powers of government committed to them.

" Upon what then can the people depend, for the fupport and prefervation of their rights and freedom ? Upon no beings or precautions under heaven, but themfelves. The fpirit of liberty is a living principle. It lives in the minds, principles, and fentiments of the people. It lives in their induftry, virtue, and public fentiment : Or rather it is produced, preferved, and kept alive, by the ftate of fociety. If the body of the people fhall lofe their property, their knowledge, and their virtue, their greateft and moft valuable bleffings are loft at the fame time.— With the lofs of thefe, public fentiment will be corrupted : With the corruption of the public fentiment, bills of rights, conftitutions written upon paper and all the volumes of written law, will lofe their force and utility. Their government will im-

mediately begin to change : And when the people have themfelves loft the caufe; the principle, and the fpirit of freedom, they will no longer be capable of a free government : They are better fuited for the reftraints of ariftocracy, or what is far better, for the regulations of monarchy. The confti tions and the laws of fuch a people, will no more preferve their freedom, than the tombs and the coffins of Montefquieu and Franklin, will retain their abilities and virtues.

" Ye people of the United States of America, behold here the precarious foundation upon which ye hold your liberties. They reft not upon things written upon paper, nor upon the virtues, the vices, or the defigns of other men, but they depend upon yourfelves ; upon your maintaining your property, your knowledge, and your virtue. Nature and fociety have joined to produce, and to eftablifh freedom in America. You are now in the full poffeffion of all your natural and civil rights ; under no reftraints in acquiring knowledge, property, or the higheft honours of your country ; in the moft rapid ftate of improvement, and population ; with perfect freedom to make further improvements in your own condition. In this ftate of fociety, every thing is adapted to promote the profperity, the importance, and the improvement of the body of the people.—But nothing is fo eftablifhed among men, but that it may change and vary. If you fhould lofe that fpirit of induftry, of economy, of knowledge, and of virtue, which led you to independence and to empire, then, but not until then will you lofe your freedom : Preferve your virtues, and your freedom will be perpetual !"

The

The WELL-BRED MAN.

THE character of a well-bred man cannot be drawn to perfection by any but dramatic writers; because they only have the power of placing him to advantage, in particular circumstances and relations.

Other writers must be content with general descriptions, it being too great a difficulty to desire *good breeding* in the abstract as moral virtue, which depends upon circumstances, and the relations in which one man stands to another; but like virtue too, it consists in a happy mediocrity between two extremes, of which bluntness is the one, and fawning servility the other.

A well-bred man hath, in his behaviour, an equal mixture of modesty and boldness, of loquacity and taciturnity, of freedom and reserve, and of every other quality, *that* degree which is useful or commendable, but whose extremes are either criminal or ridiculous. Such a man is always condescending without falling into the meanness of ad-

oration. He is not backward in professing, but more solicitous in doing acts of beneficence : He is not scrupulous of owning his regard for merit, and of giving it due praise, for fear of being thought a flatterer. nor of expressing a just dislike of vice, however dignified, to avoid the imputation of rigidness. In short, all his actions flow from a good heart, and are noble, generous, sincere, uniform, and graceful.

If these observations are true, good breeding is a social virtue : It is benevolence brought into actions with all the advantages and beauty of proportion and symmetry. Complaisance is indeed its resemblance, as a shadow is of a substance; but complaisance is only the varnish, good breeding is the real beauty of the soul, made visible and set in the fairest point of light. The only difference therefore, between the virtuous and well-bred man, is, that the latter seems to act his part in life with a superior grace.

ANECDOTE.

THE celebrated Voltaire, in his Treatise on Toleration, says, "Take a view of the Royal Exchange in London, a place more venerable than many courts of justice, where the representatives of all nations meet for the benefit of mankind : There the Jew, the Mahometan, and the Christian, transact business together, as though they were all of the same religion, and give the name of infidels to none but *bankrupts :* There the Presbyterian confides in the Anabaptist, and the Churchman depends on

the affirmation of the Quaker. At the breaking up of this free and pacific assembly, some withdraw to the synagogue, and others to the bottle ; this man goes and is baptised in a great tub ; that man has his son circumcised, and causes a set of Hebrew words, to the meaning of which he is an utter stranger, to be mumbled over the infant ; others retire to their churches, and there wait the inspiration of heaven, with their hats on ; and all are satisfied."

CABINET

CABINET OF APOLLO.

For the MASSACHUSETTS MAGAZINE.

The SONGS

of the five Bards, who sung by night : versified from the notes of M'Pherson's Offian, by
LINUS.

(Concluded from page 696.)

FIFTH BARD.

DREARY is night and calm are all the winds ;
Far in a cloud the weſtern moon deſcends.
Slow moves that beam along the ſhaded hill ;
The wave is heard ; the torrent murmurs ſtill.
In the lone booth the cock his clarion ſounds ;
The ſtars have travelled half their nightly rounds.
The houſe-wife, watchful of her little train,
Kindles with care her ſettled fire again.
The hunter thinks he ſees the early day ;
He calls his bounding dogs ; his dogs obey.
Whiſtling he goes and mounts the woody height :
The ſurly blaſt removes the clouds of night.
Along the north the ſtarry plough he ſees ;
And yet no day-ſtar tops the eaſtern trees.
Much of the night is yet to paſs, he finds ;
In ſleep he nods regardleſs of the winds.

Hark! a diſtant whirlwind ſeems to roar!
A murmuring flood ſeems thro' the vale to pour !
Lo! lo! the hoſt of mighty dead appear,
Returning from their manſions in the air.
The moon has ſunk behind the weſtern hill,
The farewel beam is on the tall rock ſtill.
From the high trees, the length'ned ſhadows fall,
A ſober melancholy gloom now ſaddens all.
Me, from the cheerleſs night, my friends, receive ;
And conſolation to the wretched give.

THE CHIEF.

Upon the mountain let the dark clouds reſt :
Let fear pervade the panting traveller's breaſt.
Let ſpirits fly ; and let the winds ariſe ;
Let ſounding ſtorms in thunder ſweep the ſkies ;
Let windows flap and mountain torrents roar ;
And green winged meteors in the dark air ſoar.
Let the pale moon her ſilver radiance ſhed,
So deep in ſky-born clouds encloſe her head.
Stormy or fair, alike to me is night ;
Dreary with clouds, or with the new moon bright.
Night flies away before the early beams,
When o'er the hill the golden morning gleams.
From the dark cloud young day returns again,
But man forever moulders on the plain.

Where are our chiefs of old, renowned in fame ?
And where our many kings of mighty name ?
Silent their battles on the crimſon plain,
And ſcarce, alas ! their maſſy tombs remain.
Theſe domes muſt fall and we muſt alſo die,
And undiſtinguiſhed in the duſt muſt lie.
Our ſons ſhall view the ruin of our halls,
And aſk the old, " where ſtood our father's walls ?"

Come, raiſe the ſong ; the harp of glory found ;
And ſend the feſtive ſhells of joy around.
An hundred tapers from the wall ſuſpend ;
Ye youths and maids, the ſportive dame attend.
Let ſome gray bard the ſong of honour raiſe,
And tell to me the deeds of other days ;

OF

Of kings and chiefs whofe glorious race is
o'er,
Illuftrious dead! whom we behold no
more.
Thus let the night in pleafure pafs away;
Till o'er the mountain peeps the dawn of
day :
Then roufe the dogs, and let our bows be
near,
Afcend the hill with day, and wake the
drowzy deer.

For the MASSACHUSETTS MAGAZINE.

An ELEGY.

DEAR fpotlefs fhade! receive thefe
lays,
Which flow from friendfhip moft fincere ;
If round this globe thy fpirit ftrays,
Or haunts the fcenes which once were
dear.

The mufe who knew thy tuneful powers,
Who oft admired thy flowing verfe,
Shall deck thy grave with early flowers,
And all thy matchlefs worth rehearfe.

When night his ebon throne refumes,
When Cynthia fheds her feebleft ray
When plants exhale their foft perfumes,
Around thy dewy grave I'll ftray.

Some friendly hand a tomb fhall raife,
Or fcience rear the fculptured ftone,
Which juftly fhall record thy praife,
And tell how bright thy virtues fhone.

The youths, whofe generous bofoms fwell
With rapture at thy rifing fame,
Shall all thy manly graces tell,
And hand to future time thy name.

For thee, on each revolving year,
Mary will heave the tender figh ;
For thee, fhall drop the briny tear,
And all her native numbers try.

Eliza, too, with plaintive ftrains,
Shall tell thy virtues o' er and o'er ;
Whilft mem'ry one fond trait retains,
In filence fhe'll thy lofs deplore.

Around yon kind, paternal dome,
Where oft thy early footfteps ftrayed,
Methinks there hangs a folemn gloom,
Which faddens all the diftant glade.

Like virtue's image fent on earth,
Thou charm'd'ft awhile our wondering
eyes ;
Then fought the climes that gave thee
birth,
And wing'd thy way to happier fkies.

If virtue can a crown receive ;
What dazzling glories deck thy head ?

No longer then let friendfhip grieve,
Since thou from care to blifs art fled.

But why did all-indulgent heaven
Form fuch a faultlefs piece of clay !
Why was the tranfient bleffing given,
Thus to be torn fo foon away!

LINUS.

To a MOUNTAIN DAISY.
On turning one down with the plough, in April,
1786.

WEE, modeft, crimfon-tipped flower,
Thou's met me in an evil hour ;
For I maun crufh amang the ftoure
Thy flender ftem,
To fpare thee now is paft my pow'r,
Thou bonie gem.

Alas ! its no thy neebot fweet,
The bonie lark, companion meet ;
Bending thee 'mang the dewy weet
Wi fpreckl'd breaft,
When upward-fpringing, blythe, to greet
The purpling eaft.

Cauld blew the bitter-biting north
Upon thy early, humble birth :
Yet chearfully thou glinted forth
Amid the ftorm,
Scarce rear'd above the parent earth
Thy tender form.

The flaunting flowers our gardens yield,
High fhelt'ring woods and wa's maun
fhield ;
But thou, beneath the random bield
O'clod or ftane,
Adorns the hiftie ftubble field,
Unfeen, alane.

There, in thy fcanty mantle clad,
Thy fnawie bofom fun-ward fpread,
Thou lifts thy unaffuming head
In humble guife ;
But now the fhare uptears thy bed,
And low thou lies !

Such is the fate of artlefs maid,
Sweet *flow'ret* of the rural fhade !
By love's fimplicity betray'd,
And guilelefs truft,
Till fhe, like thee, all foil'd, is laid
Low i'the duft.

Such is the fate of fimple bard,
On life's rough ocean lucklefs ftarr'd !
Unfkillful he to note the card
Of prudent lore,
Till billows rage and gales blow hard,
And whelm him o'er !

Such fate to *fuffering worth* is giv'n,
Who long with wants and woes has ftriv'n,
By human pride or cunning driv'n
To mis'ry's brink,
Till

Till wrench'd of every stay but Heav'n,
    He, ruin'd, sink!
Ev'n thou who mourn'ft the daify's fate,
That fate is thine—no diftant date;
Stern RUIN's *plough-fhare* drives, elate,
    Full on thy bloom,
Till crufh'd beneath the *furrows* weight,
    Shall be thy doom!

For the MASSACHUSETTS MAGAZINE.

LINES, to a Mourning DOVE.

SAY, why lovely mourner, that mufical
    fall;
That accent that fpeaks a difconfolate
    mind?
Does fome hidden tumult thy bofom appal,
Which leaves the fad fting of reflection
    behind?

The caufe of thy anguifh full well I dif-
    cern,
The feafons of beauty and pleafure are
    paft:
Yet filence, dear mourner, they foon fhall
    return,
And nature with beauties be frefh over-
    caft.

Though dark ftormy winter howls over
    the plain,
Though the brooks ceafe to murmur, the
    vallies to fing,
Yet earth fhall be cloth'd with her fra-
    grance again,
And creation revive in the fplendor of
    fpring.

Even now, deareft warbler, my fancy can
    fee,
The feafons of blifs in futurity roll;
The far-fpreading verdure, the white
    blooming tree,
And the funfhine of ecftacy burfts on my
    foul.

Ye fields which but lately were filver'd
    by flowers,
My mind into rapture was kindled by
    you,
Now fancy impatiently waits for the
    hours,
When May's fairy pencil your charms
    fhall renew.

How chang'd in a moment the furface of
    things,
The groves and the gardens are cover'd
    with fnow;
Soon zephyr fhall flutter your leaves with
    his wing,
And bathe his light limbs in the dews of
    the rofe.

Then faireft complainer forbear thy foft
    lays,
Nor grieve for thofe bleffings which fpring
    fhall reftore;
But mourn for the current of man's fleet-
    ing days,
That feafon which flies and revifits no
    more.

                THE HERMIT.

For the MASSACHUSETTS MAGAZINE.

LINES, addreffed to LINUS.

" Tu eris Mæcenas mihi."

WHILE others ftrive to ftamp an he-
    roe's name
On the tall pillars ef eternal fame;
I choofe a nobler theme—I fly to greet
Sequeftered merit in his dark retreat.

You firft enfnar'd me with poetic
    chime,
And taught my fimple mufe to lifp in
    rhyme;
You taught her firft to rife, and nobly dare
Her new fledg'd pinions thro' the depth
    of air.
To thee, as to her parent, now the mufe
Returns, and all her pleafures paft reviews.
O facred poefy, how oft thy lays
Have wandered in dark falfehoods dreary
    maze;
Forfook plain reafon, that illuftrious guide,
To whifper flatt'ry in the ear of pride;
Still may I ever fpurn the golden bait,
Or live in this retreat, obfcurely great.
Not thofe that in the round of affluence
    roll,
Direct, O Linus, thy afpiring foul.
While humble, unaffuming merit, fhines,
Wove in the texture of your polifh'd lines,
How oft have we in tranfport ftruck the
    lyre,
And felt our bofoms glow with mutual
    fire;
To notes of rapture wak'd the filver
    ftring,
And foar'd fublime on fancy's airy wing.
But when old Homer, with majeftic ftrains,
Sung the dire terror of the Trojan plains,
In quick fucceffion on our ravifh'd eyes,
The illuftrious fhade of laurell'd heroes
    rife.
What form is this that flits along the
    glades,
And fhiv'ring wanders in the midnight
    fhades,
Half wrapt in clouds the ghoftly form ap-
    pears,
His face bedew'd with vifionary tears,

                                    In

In fize a mountain, and in ſtrength an hoſt,
'Tis Ajax—obſtinately ſullen ghoſt.
But who is this that ſtalks of milder mein,
Calm is his aſpect, and his brow ſerene ?
Hail, mighty Hector, thy renown ſhall laſt,
And brave the rage of envy's blighting blaſt.
The ſtateſman's policy, and hero's power,
Shone forth refulgent in that gloomy hour ;
When rous'd to glory by the martial flame,
You ſtood the foremoſt of the Trojan name.
What ſullen ſpectre moves with graceful pride,
His beamy faulchion glitters at his ſide ;
His radiant veſture purer than the ſnows,
And on his cheek the richeſt crimſon glows ;
His ſhining helmet ſhoots a thouſand ways,
And to the moon in quiv'ring radiance plays ;
Illuſtrious ſhade, renown'd Achilles, hail,
Thy deathleſs deeds ſhall over time prevail.
Thus the full moon, when midnight damps ariſe,
And clouds of darkneſs hover round the ſkies,
Still ſhines ſerene a floating orb of light,
Breaks from the clouds and gilds the brow of night.
But when ſoft Virgil tunes the Roman ſhell,
And bids his lays in mild meanders ſwell,
So ſtrong, ſo muſically ſweet, they roll,
A tide of ſoft emotions o'er the ſoul ;
The waving trees the ſoftly murmuring gales,
That hum delightful thro' the ſcented vales,
With pleaſure bear the attentive mind along,
In the rich melody of Virgil's ſong.
There ſportive flocks, like mountain ſnows are ſeen,
And earth ſeems ſmiling in her livelieſt green.
But Oſſian, wild, irregularly wild,
The pride of genius—nature's darling child,
All blind and comfortleſs, would often go
Where the rude winds thro' dreary foreſts blow,
And ſtop to hear the mountain ſpirits rave,
In mild conjunction with the roaring wave.
Auſpicious fancy, hear my laſt requeſt,
Reviſit this fair empire of the weſt ;

On ſome young poet all thy powers beſtow,
Bid from his pen ſpontaneous numbers flow ;
Soar to the regions of immortal fame,
On time's ſwift wing, and Linus be his name.

THE HERMIT.

To the Editors of the Maſſachuſetts Magazine.

GENTLEMEN,

You expreſſed a wiſh that ſome of your Readers would furniſh you with lines upon the cloſe of the preſent year—if you are not better ſupplied, the following are much at your ſervice, and their publication will oblige a correſpondent.

L I N E S,

Written DECEMBER Thirty-firſt, 1794.

" AND dare a female touch thoſe hallow'd ſtrings ?
" Where ſtrains undying, Della Cruſca flings ?
" Whoſe ſolemn, mellow, grave, melodious notes,
" Swell in the gale, and on the zephyr float !"

Ah, let the critic ſpare the unequal line,
Below his art the numbers I entwine !
Shield me ſweet candour, thy mild pleas prepare,
And, bleſt good nature, thy rich phalanx rear ;
Nor let compariſon with blighting breath,
Prejudge, arraign, and follow to the death.
Some little niche the trembling victim give,
Permit her in the breezy vale to live :
For ſure, tho' heav'n-born genius cuts the ſkies,
Fathoms the depths, and new found ſtreams ſupplies,
Yet gratitude, implanted in the breaſt,
May ſtill in humble language be expreſt ;
The world's benignant prince but waits thoſe fruits,
Which ſuits the ſoil, and which the culture ſuits,
Nor, if the occupant improves his time,
Imputes the ſingle talent as a crime,
'Tis for the indolent and liſtleſs mind,
The righteous cenſure was by heaven deſign'd.

" But of this day, pray what remains unſaid ?
" Can Della Cruſcan laurels need thy aid ?"
Yet let me ſwell the tribute of a tear,
And humbly conſcious in the vaſe appear,
The lowly flower may round the margin creep,

And

And common forrows, common minds
may weep ;
The language of the peerlefs bard, I own,
From rich parnaffian founts hath copious
flown ;
And, with the painter, fam'd in days of old,
While art and nature all their charms un-
fold—
Abforb'd in wonder, with rapt tongue I
cry,
I too have written, and have fwell'd the
figh ;
Have mourn'd the lapfe of time, departed
joys,
Thofe death-wing'd hours, whofe torpid
flight deftroys ;
December oft hath mark'd my drowned
eyes,
And its return mementos fad fupplies!
Its gathering glooms, attir'd in fable veft !
With all their horrors on my mind im-
preft,
Hears, or creates the ftorm, howe'er ferene,
May's dewy zephyrs feem to intervene.

And, e'en fince laft its mantle fwept the
plain,
Drear harbinger of winter's fnow clad
reign,
Though oft before of many a good bereft,
And few to folace my torn heart were left !
Yet once again the miffive weapon fped,
To fwell the annals of the hallow'd dead,
With aim too fure the fatal mifchief flew,
And from my grafp its beauteous victim
drew !
Cherubic innocent, her lovely form,
Thus early fainted, 'fcap'd from every
ftorm,
Retention melancholy fhall retrace,
Fond to delineate her angel face,
Too foon, alas, the infant voyager crown'd,
Her ærial manfion, and her heav'n hath
found !
And tho' thro' paradife fhe wings her way,
Yet circling friends ftill tread the thorny
way ;
Regretting tears we o'er fweet Anna fhed,
And breathe new forrows round her clay
turf'd bed.

How fad the retrofpect, how many
throng !
What venerable fhadows pafs along.
Dear fhades belov'd, next to my God rever'd,
Full many a pang of heart for me ye
fhar'd ;
Peace to your fpirits, hovering feraphs
wait,
Years muft roll on, the hour ordain'd by
fate ;

My work perform'd, the tafk affign'd com-
plete,
Beyond this woe-fraught fcene my friends
I meet.
I hail this parting day, this clofing year,
Full charg'd to me the length'ning hours
appear,
This revolution tardy to my fight,
Delay'd too long its heavy, ling'ring flight,
Pregnant, and crowded with events it rofe,
And ftill replete with ills the vifion fhows !
My native rocks, my native hills refign'd,
To my lorn breaft new hopes and fears I
bind ;
Boldly adventuring o'er the untry'd way,
Neceffity my weary fteps obey ;
And what, tho' wintry time advancing on,
Loudly proclaims of life the waning fun.
Tho' o'er the glofly honours of my head,
Its fleeting influence is infidious fhed ;
What tho' the boifterous winds of heaven
defcend,
And to the narrow houfe I rapid bend,
Let me not mourn the univerfal doom,
Nor fhrink reluctant from the opening
tomb :
For fure thefe glooms which feem to fhroud
the grave,
Oblivion's wand o'er each career to wave,
Are but the prelude of returning fpring,
Which in its train immortal joys fhall
bring,
The perfum'd breeze—gay fummer's flow-
ery veft,
Prolific autumn in rich purple dreft ;
Thefe fhall perennial live, mid mildeft
fkies,
While funs eternal fhall unfading rife ;
No more fhall winter's ever ponderous
wing,   [fling,
Wide o'er the globe its ftormy horrors
But banifh'd to the dark abodes of
night,
Mankind fhall hail the gladfome beams of
light !
Through fpace interminable bend their
courfe,
Knowledge inhaling from its parent fource ;
Retracing funs and fyftems as they roll,
Amply dilating the expanfive foul.
Then fhall philanthropy—bleft fove-
reign reign,
And every fentiment her rule maintain,
Sincerity with fky rob'd peace entwine,
And order, born of heaven, the trio join,
Till happinefs eventual gathers round,
And truth confummate is with honour
crown'd,
Till the bright day with deathlefs fplendor
breaks,

To

To new born joys till every senfe awakes,
Till man, no more regretting Adam's fall,
" One vaft unbounded fpring encircles
all."

CONSTANTIA.

For the MASSACHUSETTS MAGAZINE.

The FUNERAL.

WITHIN an oak's diffufive fhade,
whofe top
Waved high in air, and kiffed each paff-
ing gale,
I gently laid me down; while naught was
heard,
Save the foft found that whifpering fancy
wrought.
Sudden the deep-toned death-bells aw-
ful found
Came like low thunder rolling on the
gale,
I turned, and lo! a melancholy train,
Moving in filence o'er the gloomy fields.
Juft o'er their heads the difmal urn was
feen,
Slowly majeftic waving; while the pall
Stretched its black fkirts and flapped with
every breeze.
Behind, the mournful, melancholy band,
Hung down their heads, and wet the
ground with tears.
Slow they approached to where yon fculp-
tured ftones
In length'ning folitary order ftand! there
ftopt,
And freed their fhoulders of the precious
load.
Then in the bofom of the yawning grave
They laid their much-loved friend; and
turning round,
Bade him a lingering, long and laft fare-
well.
Then quick departing from the mournful
fcene,
With heavy pace, they meafured back the
ground.
All but Salima, who remained there ftill,
To pay her laft fad tribute to her love,
And mourn the man fhe ever held moft
dear.
With pleafure once I view'd the fun's
broad beam;
But, now his joyful, foul-enlivening ray,
The clouds of forrow hide, alas! from me.
Once I, enraptured in the flow'ry fpring,
Beheld the trees in all their beauty bloom;
From them I now avert my weary eyes,
Sad emblems of the youth whofe lofs I
mourn.
Once I frequented yonder pleafing grove

And heard the nightingale's melodious laye
With pleafing rapture and devotive awe.
Ye tenants of the air, no more will I
Attend to your enchanting fongs, but
feek
Some fympathetic fhades to eafe my woe.
When gloomy midnight reigned, I often
ufed
To ramble o'er the fields and tafte delights,
Whofe every breeze brought pleafure,
health and love.
But, now far diftant all thofe pleafing
fcenes,
Thofe fprightly thoughts that revel in my
breaft.
Adieu, ye venerable plains, where oft
In mufing folitude I loved to ftray;
Ye dear retreats of innocence and mirth,
Receive my fad, my long, my laft adieu.
Soft fighs the grafs that on the green tomb
grows,
And fofter ftill the turtle coos her fong;
So fhall my numbers tell thy early fate.
With melancholy grief alone I'll feek
Yon dreary mountain's folitary cave,
And count my forrows all the live-long day:
For thee, dear youth, I'll tune my mourn-
ing harp,
And there fecurely fing down fummer
funs.

LINUS.

A DESCRIPTION of WINTER.

FROM mountains of eternal fnow,
And Zembla's dreary plains;
Where the bleak winds for ever blow,
And froft for ever reigns;

Lo! Winter comes in fogs array'd,
With ice, and fpangled dews;
To dews, and fogs, and ftorms be paid
The tribute of the mufe.

Each flowery carpet nature fpread,
Is vanifh'd from the eye;
Where'er unhappy lovers tread,
No Philomel is nigh.

No blufhing rofe unfolds its bloom,
No tender lilies blow,
To fcent the air with rich perfume,
Or grace my charmer's brow.

Hail! ev'ry pair whom love unites,
In Hymen's pleafing ties;
That endlefs fource of pure delights,
That blefling of the wife!

Tho' yon poor orb no warmth beftows,
And ftorms united meet,
The flame of love, and friendfhip glows
With unextinguifhed heat!

MONTHLY GAZETTE.

Summary of Foreign Intelligence.

GERMANY.
VIENNA, Sept. 23.

THE laſt official advices from Holland, received ſome days ago. ſtate, that their condition is altered vaſtly for the better. In the different actions lately near the capital, the Poles always attacked, and were uniformly victorious. On the nights of the 28th and 29th, 200 men from the camp of General Zapazezek ſurprized two Ruſſian batteries, cut the men to pieces, and carried off their artillery. The details of the particular actions which preceded the retreat of the King of Pruſſia, would be uninteresting, but all accounts concur in declaring, that the Pruſſians have entirely evacuated the territories of the republic.

The Auſtrians having continued to advance, though in an apparent friendly manner, were met by ſome Poliſh battalions, which defeated them, and took ſeventy of them priſoners with their arms and baggage.

The inſurgents in Great Poland, on the 21ſt, ſunk at Wrocklawck, fourteen veſſels laden with military ſtores for the ſiege of Warſaw.

The Poliſh troops took poſſeſſion of the Palatinate of Sandamin, and Cracow; and Koſciuſko hangs upon the rear of the Pruſſian army. Diſcontents are manifeſting themſelves ſo ſtrongly in Sileſia, as to cauſe apprehenſions for the ſafety of that province; and in Lithuania, the Poles have already poſſeſſed themſelves of the cities of Minſk and Niefwick.

The two Engliſh plenipotentiaries have had their audience leave, and will ſhortly quit this city; but whether they will go direct to London, or to any other place firſt, we do not know.

With regard to the treaty between Great-Britain and Auſtria, the following farther particulars have tranſpired:

1. Great-Britain will immediately pay the ſubſidies to be granted as ſoon as Auſtria ſhall requeſt them.

2. Great-Britain will moſt earneſtly co-operate in the re-conqueſt of the Netherlands, to be effected as ſoon as poſſible.

3. The Netherlands ſhall have a ſtanding militia ſufficient to cover them.

4. The convention entered into at the Hague ſhall be annulled

5. Auſtria is to receive of Great-Britain the ſum of 4,000,000 of florins per annum, for which it ſhall cover with troops, Maeſtricht, Breda, and all the frontier provinces.

BERLIN, Sept. 23. The king is arrived at Potſdam. The army of the Rhine will certainly be withdrawn, except ſeventeen thouſand men as the electoral contingent. According to the moſt recent advices from ſouth Pruſſia, the inſurrection is ſtill predominant. The inſurgents are ſaid to maſſacre all the ſmall detachments of Pruſſians they fall upon unawares, and to hang the officers. This misfortune lately occurred to a counſellor of war, and a young receiver of the exciſe. Propoſals of peace are generally talked of; and it is added that an officer of diſtinction will ſhortly be ſent to Warſaw for the purpoſe of negociating.

NETHERLANDS.

MANHEIM, Sept. 25. Every thing in our neighbourhood has been quiet ſince day before yeſterday. A ſtrong corps of French were ſaid to be ſeen yeſterday marching towards Ricſbeck. Field marſhal Mollendorff is again at Kreutznach. The report of Neuſtadt being taken by the Imperialiſts is not true; on the contrary, the enterprize of Gen. Wartenſleben has failed, and he has retreated with ſome loſs.

MUNSTER, Sept. 30. We have heard nothing here of the approach of a Pruſſian army ſo much talked of, for the relief of Holland: But it appears certain that Gen. Mollendorff is preparing to advance with 12 or 5000 men to ſuccour the Auſtrians near the lower Rhine

ENGLAND.

LONDON, Sept. 25. The following particulars, which have not yet appeared, are extracted from a variety of letters, which we have received from correſpondents in the Britiſh army.

General Pichegru was near being taken on the 12th inſt. when his adjutant gen. and another officer were taken by a party of the Huſſars of Choiſeuil.

The war of poſts that has lately been carried

carried on, has given room for inftances of cruelty unknown but in civil wars. The Huffars of Choifeuil, almoft all emigrants, attacked on the 12th inft. a party of the French called the Huffars de la liberte, and cut every man to pieces.—The French Huffars called out for mercy ; but the emigrants, recollecting the mercy their unfortunate brethren had received, did not fpare a fingle man.

A fquadron of fix fail of the line and 3 frigates, failed from Breft on the 12th of Sept. to intercept the Mediterranean convoy; twenty other frigates are faid to be cruifing in the bay of Bifcay. The port of Genoa is again open, and the Englifh Minifter is fhortly expected there.

The towns and villages in France, which have changed their names fince the Revolution, amount to 6000.

The contribution which the French levied on Ghent was 7,000,000 of florins.

The laft mail brought a letter from Laufanne, containing the following intelligence ; Lyons has refumed its name—It is rebuilding—The ariftocrats have been recalled to it, and trade begins to revive there.

Yefterday a courier arrived at the Spanifh Ambaffador's, with letters from the court of Madrid, by which we learn, that the courts of Spain and Naples are come to a determination to profecute the war with the utmoft vigor.

Sept. 29. It is with a degree of emotion which it is impoffible for us to defcribe, but in which we are certain that every loyal fubject, and good man, will ftrongly participate, that we communicate to the public the exiftence of a plot for the affaffination of our moft gracious king.

The particulars of this alarming and atrocious defign it would be improper at prefent fully to difclofe; but upon a point on which the public intereft will be fo much excited, the people have a right to expect fome fatisfactory information.

Yefterday the privy council fat in their chamber at Whitehall to examine two perfons, who where apprehended upon fufpicion of being materially concerned in this plot—The council met early in the afternoon and fat until 4 o'clock—The perfons examined were of the names of William Higgins and John Pierre-Lemaitre. A poifoned arrow was to be aimed at the breaft of the king——This was to be directed from the pit, through an air machine of particular conftruction, while a riot was to have been raifed, which would of courfe, have attracted the general attention of the audience. Who was to have been the immediate agent in this bufinefs, we do not know, but Higgins was to have fupplied the poifon.—The fufpicion of the bufinefs firft arofe from the mechanic employed to make the inftrument.

FRANCE.

Sept. 7. A letter was read from Cumell, adjutant general of the army in the Alps, informing the convention, that the Piedmontefe to the number of 8000 men, attacked the French on the 17th, at three o'clock in the morning; but the difpofitions which the French commander with 3000 men, had made to receive them, prevented any defire to return to the charge, and they left 30 prifoners in the hands of the French.

Sept. 17th. Report of the telegraphe.—The Republicans purfued, beat the enemy before Bois le Duc, the 28th Fructidor, to the evening ; 1500 prifoners, 8 cannon, a number of fufils, waggons and horfes are the fruits of the day.

DOMESTIC OCCURRENCES.

Extract of a letter from a gentleman in Europe, to his correfpondent in this town.

" THOUGH I often pay my refpects to Mr. Jay, when all prefent are in the American intereft, yet we, none of us, ever could get from him, any thing refpecting the ftage or forwardnefs of his bufinefs, and from the neceffity alone of the Britifh cabinet's granting all and even more than he at one time would have exacted, we have reafon to fuppofe that he will by and by return back, and be heartily welcomed by his fellow-citizens. It is rumoured, and not without fome truth, that the Britifh cabinet never had a harder or tougher hand to deal with than they find in Citizen Jay; this, with the critical fituation of Great Britain juft now, will infure him fuccefs ; and it has been mentioned in circles where I have been, who are not in the American intereft, that he, Mr. Jay, is embracing the prefent opportunity, and will obtain the privilege of the carrying trade to the Weft Indies,

Indies, fo far as that the United States fhall have accefs to all the iflands with free liberty to carry and bring any thing to and from them they pleafe : For inftance, a veffel not exceeding 120 tons burthen, may go from Bofton, with a cargo of any thing to the ifland of Jamaica ; there fell and purchafe a cargo of fugar, and carry it back to Bofton, land it, and then if you pleafe, refhip it, in any fize veffel, and carry it to any European market, except Great Britain and Ireland—

"This point gained, as the United States can carry, in times of peace, for about one half what Great Britain can, fhe will go near to make a monopoly of the whole carrying bufinefs. Altho' Mr. Jay, as before obferved, is clofe in the extreme, yet from this leaking out of the other party, I hardly doubt its truth, and as Great Britain muft be at peace with the United States, fhe will juft now grant almoft any thing Mr. Jay may demand, and I do not think he will be wanting or fparing in his exertions.

"To attempt to give you a particular account of the political world at this time, would be endlefs, and needlefs, as you will doubtlefs have things detailed in your own papers ; and give me leave to obferve, generally, That France is every where fuccefsful, and fuch extraordinary genius and energy does fhe poffefs, that if the executive of that country fhould declare they would build a bridge from Calais to Dover, I fhould think it accomplifhed. Going on for three months more as they have for the three paft, they will have all the cannon in Europe and half the merchant veffels of Great-Britain—Holland muft either make a feparate peace or be conquered in all the prefent month; and in either cafe, France will have the Dutch navy in her fcale, and then, by next fpring, fhe will be able to break the back of the Britifh navy ; of fuch importance does France conceive this object to be, that fhe will not make peace till it is accomplifhed."

————

Philad. Nov. 27.

By the Pigou, Loxley, arrived yefterday, papers are received only one day later than thofe before come to hand, but they contain intelligence of the firft importance. The fiege of Maeftricht, that key to part of Holland, may be confidered as the immediate confequence of the victory.

From the Courier of Sep. 26.

Yefterday a meffenger arrived from the continent, with intelligence of an event perhaps as calamitous as any that has occurred this war.

General Clairfayt has been defeated after an engagement of three days. His army confifted of between 60 and 70,000men, and was pofted between Maeftricht and Liege ; his right wing encamped in the neighbourhood of the former, and his left occupying the ftrong poft of La Chartruefe.

It was on the left wing the French made their principal attack. It commenced on the 17th inft. and it was not till the 19th, that the French fucceeded with a lofs on the fide of the Auftrians of from 12 to 13,000.

The Duke of York was defeated on the 17th, with the lofs of 500 men—From the morning herald of Sep. 27. Government, we are informed, are in poffeffion of intelligence of the moft melancholy nature from the army of General Clairfayt. This brave, but unfortunate officer, with about 70,000 men under his command, was attacked by the enemy, in immenfe force, on the 17th inftant, between Maeftricht and Liege. He fuftained the vigorous affault with his wonted courage and intrepidity, in a manner, which, although eventually overpowered by fuperiority of force, muft reflect on him immortal honor. The engagement, it appears, lafted near three days with very little intermiffion ; the two firft of which he had apparently the advantage ; but on the third the enemy unfortunately fucceeded in turning his left wing, and obliged him to make a precipitate retreat to Aix la Chapelle, with the lofs of upwards of 12,000 men.

This of courfe occafions a total change in the plan of operations in that quarter. Maeftricht is now, we fear, left entirely unprotected, and Gen. Clairfayt muft content himfelf with acting on the defenfive in the beft manner he can, and faving the fhattered remains of his defeated army. General Jourdan commanded the French troops in this affair, whofe lofs is not mentioned, but muft have been confiderably greater than that of the allies.

General Pichegru is purfuing the Duke of York with a force confifting of 80,000 men ; and as his Royal Highnefs cannot hope for any fuccour from the Auftrian army, his plan, doubtlefs will be, to affect a farther retreat from the dangers with which he appears to be threatened.

The accounts from Holland are moft alarming. The Duke of York is faid to have

have paff'd Nimeguen and to be evidently on his retreat across the Rhine; while by the laft moveme it of Clairfayt, he feems alfo to be on the route to crofs the fame river. What may be the compiete furrender of the field to the French, our intelligent readers will readily fee—The poffeflion of Holland which nothing could have given the French but the guilt and folly of our minifters, will add to the marein of our enemy fuch power as muft be tremendous, particularly when we confider the fituation and extent of the coaft and ports from which this additional force will enfue—If already they have committed fuch devaftations on the north feas, what muft be the havock on our trade, when, to fuch a length of coaft they add the fhipping, the fkill and the induftry of the Dutch—We may then be reduced to the melanchol, fituation, when even our ariftocrats will not object, in parliment, to the cutting of canals, as there will be other means of fupplying London with coals.

BULLION.

In one of the veffels juft arrived from France, near three tons of filver in ingots have been imported—This may be a valuable acquifition to the mint of the United States.

Dr. PRIESTLY

has been unanimoufly elected profeffor of Chymifty, of the univerfity of Pennfylvania—He has, however, declined the appointment, having purchafed a lot on the banks of the Sufquehannah, in the town of Northumberland, where he intends next fpring to build a houfe, and enjoy the pleafures of rural and domeftic life.

The troops which ware called out to act againft the Pennfylvania infurgents, have returned to their refpective homes; except thofe who have enlifted to ferve nine months in order to fecure the execution of the laws in the feat of infurrection.

TREATY,

lately concluded between the United States and the Indians of the fix nations. The United States to relinquifh all claims to the lands known by the name of the Oneida, Onondago and Cayuga refervations, and another tract of country lying partly upon the lakes Ontario and Erie; to pay the fix nations an annuity of 4500 dollars forever; and to deliver to them at the conclufion of the treaty, 10,000

dollars worth of goods. In confequence of which, the fix nations relinquifh their claims to all other lands within the United States, and alfo grant the privilege of a waggon road from Slufher to lake Erie, and the privilege of lading veffels in any of the creeks or harbors within their country.

IN A TEMPEST,

which took place on the coaft of England, about the 1ft of october, a great number of veffels were caft away—we fincerely hope that none of our American mariners, were among the unfortunate.

HARVARD COLLEGE LOTTERY.

On the 16th. the drawing of the firft clais of Harvard College Lottery ended—When lefs than an hundred remained in the wheels—No. 18547 drew 10,000 dollars. This is the property of the College.

MARRIAGES.

MASSACHUSETTS——Bofton, Mr. Matthias Crocker to Mifs Rebecca Vollentine. Mr. Jofeph Bond to Mifs Ruthy Chittenden.

Barre, Eleazer James, Efq. attorney at law, to Mifs Brooks.

Holden, Mr. Rufus Flagg to Mifs Rachel Dwella.

Worcefter, Capt. Jofeph Torrey to Mrs. Azubah Goulding.

Lancafter, Francis Blake, Efq. attorney at law, to Mifs Eliza Augufta Chandler.

Watertown, Mr. John Williams to Mifs Rhoda Willington.

DEATHS.

MASSACHUSETTS—Bofton, Mr. Jofeph Dolbeare, 30; Mr. Alexander Galloway, 32; Mrs. Ann Holden, 55; Mr. William Kennedy, 40; Mafter John Green, 12; Mrs. Martha Sniveron, of Newyork, 59; Mr. Ebenezer Weld, 37; Col. Jofiah Flagg; Mrs. Mary Woart, 57; Mr. Samuel Cooke.

Danvers, Mr. Nathaniel Goldthwait, 87; Northfield, Rev. John Hubbard, 69. Sutton, Rev. Grendall Rawfon of Doyer, 73.

Warwick, Mr. Jofiah Gale, 72.

Worcefter, Doct. Thomas Nichols, 82; Mr. David Johnfon, 24.

Ipfwich, Mr. Benjamin Fellows, 83.

Gorham.—Mrs. Elizabeth Gould, aged 26, daughter of the Rev. Paul Coffin, of Buxton.

I N D E X.

I N D E X.

INDEX to the POETRY.

I N D E X.

Directions to the Binders for placing the Plates.